LINCOLN
The Man

LINCOLN
The Man

By
EDGAR LEE MASTERS

With Illustrations

Originally Published 1931

Copyright © 1931
By Edgar Lee Masters

Copyright © Renewed 1959
By Ellen C. Masters

REPRINTED 1997
Permission by Hilary Masters

Introduction to this edition Copyright © 1997
by The Foundation for American Education

All Rights Reserved

Library of Congress Cataloging-in-Publication Data

Masters, Edgar Lee, 1868-1950.
   Lincoln the man / by Edgar Lee Masters.
     p.   cm.
   Originally published: New York : Dodd, Mead & Co., 1931.
   Includes index.
   ISBN 0-9623842-6-7
   1. Lincoln, Abraham, 1809-1865.
   2. Presidents—United States—Biography.
   I. Title.
E457.M41   1997
973.7'092-dc21
[B]   97-40670
                                        CIP

The Foundation for American Education
P.O. Box 11851 • Columbia, SC 29211

To the Memory of
THOMAS JEFFERSON

THE PREEMINENT PHILOSOPHER-STATESMAN
OF THE UNITED STATES,
AND THEIR GREATEST PRESIDENT;
WHOSE UNIVERSAL GENIUS THROUGH A LONG LIFE
WAS DEVOTED TO THE
PEACE, ENLIGHTENMENT AND LIBERTY OF THE UNION
CREATED BY THE CONSTITUTION OF 1787

CONTENTS

	INTRODUCTION xiii
I.	LINCOLN'S ANCESTRY 1
II.	LINCOLN'S BOYHOOD AND YOUNG MANHOOD. 15
III.	LINCOLN AT NEW SALEM AND IN THE LEGISLATURE 29
IV.	LINCOLN'S ROMANTIC ADVENTURES 45
V.	LINCOLN IN CONGRESS AND JUST BEFORE. 77
VI.	BACK IN SPRINGFIELD AND RIDING THE CIRCUIT 108
VII.	LINCOLN: THE MAN 138
VIII.	THE COMPROMISES OF 1820 AND 1850 157
IX.	THE KANSAS-NEBRASKA ACT 197
X.	LINCOLN GRADUALLY AWAKES................................ 213
XI.	THE DRED SCOTT DECISION.................................. 252
XII.	THE LINCOLN AND DOUGLAS DEBATES 277
XIII.	THE UNION OF THE CONSTITUTION BEFORE THE WAR........ 316
XIV.	LINCOLN'S NOMINATION AND ELECTION TO THE PRESIDENCY. . 345
XV.	LINCOLN AS PRESIDENT, AND THE WAR 378
XVI.	LINCOLN'S WAR MESSAGE AND THE WAR..................... 414
XVII.	LAST DAYS OF LINCOLN 451
XVIII.	THE ONE CAUSE WHICH WAS LOST........................... 478
APPENDIX:	REVIEWS OF *LINCOLN THE MAN*....................... 499

A section of photographs follows page 264

INTRODUCTION

Edgar Lee Masters is remembered principally for the American poetry classic *Spoon River Anthology*, a free verse best-seller that scandalized readers on both sides of the Atlantic when it was published in 1915. Masters also published fifty-two other books during his long life (from 1868 to 1950)—poetry, plays, novels, histories, essays, his autobiography, and an edited volume of Emerson's works. He was the author of five biographies—of writers Mark Twain, Walt Whitman, and Vachel Lindsay, and two Illinois lawyers, Chicagoan Levy Mayer and President Abraham Lincoln. The first four named biographies excited limited interest, and except for the life of Lindsay are today regarded as having little merit. But Masters' unfriendly biography *Lincoln: The Man* (1931) set off a public debate that rivaled that of *Spoon River Anthology* and is still causing ripples today.

Edgar Lee Masters came from a central Illinois family that had had personal dealings with Lincoln as well as with Lincoln's law partner and early biographer, William H. Herndon. Masters' Menard County hometown of Petersburg was only two miles from Lincoln's village of New Salem, the Sangamon River hamlet into which Lincoln drifted in 1831 and from which he left in 1837 with his mind on the law and politics. Between the time of Lincoln's arrival and the time Masters was born, Petersburg became the county seat and trading center for the region, and New Salem became a ghost town. Masters learned of New Salem's history from the ground up, literally, playing with his boyhood friends among the foundation stones of Lincoln's deserted village. Long before the State of Illinois turned New Salem into a shrine, Masters had wandered over the area where the Rutledge tavern and other buildings had stood and saw where Lincoln had paused to speak with Mentor Graham, pitch horseshoes, or watch a gander pull.[1]

Masters learned other information about Lincoln from his paternal grandfather, Squire Davis Masters. He was living on his grain and cattle farm a few miles north of Petersburg when he hired Lincoln as his lawyer in an 1847 case involving a promissory note. Lincoln and Squire Masters (his first name was "Squire") met a second time in a dispute which never came to trial, and once again after Masters' grandfather was elected justice of the peace in 1849:

> Lincoln tried a case before my grandfather under the maple trees in front of the Masters' homestead, for my grandfather was a Justice of the Peace for a time.[2]

Later, Squire Masters and Lincoln were pulled in different directions as the 1850s moved the nation toward Civil War. U.S. senators were still selected by the Illinois legislature at this time, and when Squire Masters was elected to the Illinois General Assembly, he shifted his allegiance away from Lincoln:

> In 1854 he was elected to the Illinois legislature, where he voted against Lincoln for United States senator because he thought Lincoln's policies would bring on war between the states.[3]

Squire Masters' son Hardin (the father of Edgar Lee) was for a time ambivalent about his Civil War leanings, being first for the North and then the South. Hardin Masters did not fight in the war, but was unambiguously pro-Southern by the time the war ended and his first son was born, as Masters remarked in an early draft of his autobiography:

> I came into the world early on Sunday morning, August 23, 1868, and was named for Gen. Robert E. Lee, for whom my father had the greatest admiration.

Masters the author would be known simply as "Lee" for much of his youth, an important matter symbolically, for like the general for whom he was named, "Lee" Masters would ultimately view Abraham Lincoln as his adversary.[4]

Political sympathies notwithstanding, Masters' lawyer-father soon after the Civil War began a business relation with Abraham Lincoln's former law partner, William Herndon. Herndon and Lincoln had occupied offices across from the state capitol in Springfield, but after Lincoln's death Herndon's law business fell off, and when he inherited a farm north of Springfield, he moved there and began to look to nearby Menard County and Petersburg to provide him clients. (He was already familiar with the area, having spent some time in Petersburg while associated with Lincoln.) He and Hardin Masters had met years before when Hardin was still a boy and Herndon had visited the farm of Hardin's father, Squire Davis Masters. Now Herndon and Hardin formed what Edgar Lee Masters called "a special legal partnership." It is unlikely that the two practiced much law during these years (beginning in 1872 and concluding in 1880), for Hardin Masters was serving as state's attorney while Herndon was battling alcoholism, but the two did become close friends, and Edgar Lee Masters was exposed to a bona fide authority on Abraham Lincoln.[5]

When Herndon subsequently collaborated with Jesse Weik on *Herndon's Lincoln: The True Story of a Great Life* (1889), he validated his knowledge of Lincoln and lent a lasting frame to the debate concerning Lincoln's supposed romance with Ann Rutledge. Herndon's book surprised some readers by remarking on Lincoln's shortcomings as well as his greatness, and this would later influence Masters' biography, although he had already been exposed to negative commentary on Lincoln, not only through his grandfather, but also through other natives of Petersburg, many of whom were unreconstructed Southerners who remembered Lincoln simply as a political opportunist.[6]

In addition to these people, Masters during his boyhood and later met other individuals permanently associated with Lincoln, including the schoolmaster Mentor Graham, members of the Armstrong clan (Lincoln's friends), and John McNamar, the man sometimes reputed to have been engaged to Ann Rutledge before her story became entwined with Lincoln's. There were stories, too, about Menard County old-timers such as Bowling Green, the New Salem justice of the peace before whom Lincoln practiced law, and Jack Kelso, the unambitious fisherman thought to have shared his knowledge of books with Lincoln during his New Salem years. So all of these influences helped form Edgar Lee Masters' early impressions of Lincoln.[7]

In 1892, after a year of college and passage of the Illinois bar, Masters left downstate Illinois for Chicago where he worked from 1903-11 as a lawyer with Clarence Darrow. He continued his readings in law, literature, and history during these years, and he also continued to recall the people and events of his youth. In 1914, when he began the poems of *Spoon River Anthology*, he naturally turned to the area he knew best and included Lincoln lore and facts, including poems about William Herndon and Ann Rutledge. The Herndon poem was somewhat cynical (for Lincoln was portrayed as only an "actor" playing a part), but Masters found nothing unpleasant to say about Ann (or Anne) Rutledge, who was buried in Petersburg's Oakland Cemetery:

> Out of me unworthy and unknown
> The vibrations of deathless music;
> "With malice toward none, with charity for all."
> Out of me the forgiveness of millions toward millions,
> And the beneficent face of a nation
> Shining with justice and truth.
> I am Anne Rutledge who sleep beneath these weeds,
> Beloved in life of Abraham Lincoln,
> Wedded to him, not through union,
> But through separation.
> Bloom forever, O Republic,
> From the dust of my bosom![8]

The Rutledge poem eventually became Masters' most frequently reprinted poem, and achieved the status of Americana in 1921 when Petersburg's town fathers and a local historian asked for and received permission to engrave it upon a large stone over Rutledge's grave. Masters was happy with such attentions through 1925 when he drafted a version of his autobiography and gave it the tentative title of "My Years in the Lincoln Country."[9]

But ongoing scholarship and emerging Lincoln myths would shortly disturb his tranquility. In 1926, Masters' poetry rival Carl Sandburg published his fictionalized and very flattering biography, *Abraham Lincoln: The Prairie Years*. Sandburg and Masters had been friends in Chicago while Masters was drafting his *Spoon River* pieces—but their writings were somewhat similar, and when literary critics and reviewers began to compare the two, Masters sensed that he and Sandburg were competitors. When Sandburg's *Lincoln* turned out to be very popular, Masters complained to friends that Sandburg had trespassed on "the Lincoln country" in an area Masters felt was his own:

> I found Sandburg's footprints in Petersburg, Illinois, among my intimates, and almost everywhere I had lived.... The truth is that he has no country; he is not attached to Galesburg, where he was born, while I have the Lincoln country as mine, by right of birth, because of the affection of the people, and because I have portrayed it.[10]

Masters was upset, too, with the nature of Sandburg's Lincoln biography: *Spoon River Anthology* had described the New Salem-Petersburg area in largely realistic terms, but Sandburg had stood this formula on its head, and never let the truth stand in the way. He had enlarged on Herndon's *Lincoln* and other lives as well as the Lincoln myths and stories, and presented a favorable view of the President that was distinctly at odds with some of the boyhood tales Masters had heard.[11]

During these same years, Lincoln scholar Albert J. Beveridge was at work on his landmark life of the President. Masters was well aware of Beveridge's study, not only because Beveridge had corresponded with Masters' father concerning the Lincoln-Herndon relation, but also because Beveridge and Masters had communicated. Unlike Sandburg, Beveridge was exceptionally careful as to the facts of Lincoln's life, but before he could complete his study, his own life was cut short. Beveridge's biography, *Abraham Lincoln (1809-1858)*, was published in 1928 and gathered the respect it deserved as the first factual (if incomplete) life of Lincoln.[12]

Beveridge's book "blew up" the earlier Lincoln stories (as Masters was fond of saying), and he began to think of writing his own biography. He had recently published his first full-length biographical study and saw how he could combine his family's relations with Herndon and Beveridge and their books along with the Lincoln stories he had heard in his youth. In other words, Masters would enlarge upon Beveridge's incomplete work and Herndon's biography and give the country what it needed—the first, full-length factual biography of Lincoln. No less important, such a book would correct the mythicizing done by Masters' poetry rival Carl Sandburg, and reclaim "the Lincoln country," which was Masters' "by right of birth."[13]

Masters was in the mood for such revisionism, in part because it was ingrained in his personality to be a nettle in the side of the establishment, in part because he felt that Republicans such as Lincoln had been responsible for some of the setbacks in his family's personal and professional lives. In 1880, the Masters family had moved from the predominantly Southern town of Petersburg to the more Northern-oriented county seat of Lewistown, Illinois. Masters remembered that his father had there felt the sting of Lincoln's party through the GAR—the Grand Army of the Republic—Northern army veterans who could make it hard on a former Southern sympathizer trying to make a living in a small Illinois town.[14]

Masters himself had chafed under the smug conservatism of Illinois villages (a trait which he associated with the Republican party), and like his father he had gravitated to the liberal wing of the Democrats. During his early years in Chicago, Masters was a tireless worker for the Democratic party: he formed the Jefferson Club to support liberal Democrats, and sat enthralled as William Jennings Bryan delivered his famous 1896 "Cross of Gold" speech at the Democratic National Convention in Chicago; Masters and Bryan later became friends, and Masters worked personally with Bryan in an effort to win the 1908 presidency.[15]

Unfortunately for Masters, the Democrats would place only one man in the White House between 1860 and 1912, and while this person (Grover Cleveland) would be elected twice (in 1884 and 1892), national policies enacted by Democrats between the Civil War and The Great War did not really amount to much. Masters regarded these years as a half-century of Republican misrule, citing the prolonged injustices of Reconstruction in the South, boodle politics and the Grant Administration, and the turn-of-the-century expansionism of the Spanish-American War. The latter was popular with the public at large, but it brought islands such as Puerto Rico and the Philippines under American control—and brought America into the role of an imperialistic power, or so Masters claimed in a monograph he self-published about 1900, *The Constitution and Our Insular Possessions*.[16]

The foundation for Masters' political catechism had been laid by his Southern-born grandfather, Squire Davis Masters, in whom Masters found all the desirable traits of Jeffersonian agrarianism. This had mixed with the populism of Masters' father (as manifested in the political career of William Jennings Bryan), and caused Masters to be suspicious of industrialism and big-city moneyed interests of the East. Instead, he found his ideal in early nineteenth century agricultural communities he associated with the South and the Midwest. As time went on Masters found himself fighting a losing battle over these issues—as is reflected in *The Constitution and Our Insular Possessions*, in parts of *Spoon River Anthology*, and in much of its successor, *The New Spoon River* (1924). One Masters' scholar phrased the phenomenon thus: Masters was "fighting, not the Civil War, but the greater war of the century that encompassed it— the immense struggle in which Northern factories and mines overcame Southern plantations, and substituted industrialism for agrarianism, and nationalism and imperialism for state sovereignty." If Lincoln was not personally responsible for all these things, the transformations had begun or been accelerated during his presidency, and that was enough.[17]

Later, when people would read Masters' life of Lincoln, they would infer from its rich array of details that the book must have taken him years to write, and he did draft anti-Lincoln statements prior to this time. But it was not until the Beveridge biography that Masters felt he had the scholarly encouragement to begin his study. When he finally sat down to write his book on April 29, 1930, he completed it in only forty-seven days. In other words, it was a task for which he had been preparing all his life.[18]

Lincoln: The Man did not become the controversial book it did because of the new facts that Masters assembled. Indeed, he made little use of his family's association with Lincoln, and relied chiefly on the works of Beveridge and Herndon. What made Masters' book different were the interpretations that he lent to virtually every aspect of Lincoln's life.

Masters' Lincoln did not simply have humble roots but came from "worthless" stock characterized by "callousness and dumbness" to the point of "semi-barbarism"—traits that explained why Lincoln was "mannerless, unkempt, and . . . unwashed," in addition to being an emotionally "cold" man who denied his mother a stone over her grave. Where others had seen Lincoln come alive intellectually at New Salem, Masters discovered that it was there that Lincoln learned (through wrestling) how to cheat at public orations of the type later made famous as the Lincoln-Douglas debates. It was grappling with the Armstrong clan and the Clary's Grove boys that taught Lincoln "to elude, to dodge under, to get away, to come to, to grip, to get the best hold short of a foul, and even to foul, when it can be safely done[;] all these tactics of wrestling entered into Lincoln's forensic performances."[19]

As to the possibility of romance with Ann Rutledge, Masters considered that highly unlikely: "Lincoln was an under sexed [sic] man," Masters explained—although the future President did take a voyeuristic delight in repeating "filthy" stories. Since the "homely" Lincoln could never have attracted a pretty woman, and since Ann Rutledge was apparently too simple-minded to have forecast Lincoln's greatness, neither of them had the proper incentives to begin a relation.[20]

Masters' Lincoln routinely trampled on the rights of the disabled and poor in order to aid the barons of industry and those favorably circumstanced—and he would have done even more harm had he not been such a poor lawyer. A man this inept and terrible would naturally gravitate to the newly formed Republican party along with other "imposters and hypocrites," and it was natural, too (Republicans being what they are), that these would elect him President.[21]

Once in the White House, it was a toss-up as to whether Lincoln's worst moment came when he provoked South Carolina into starting the Civil War, or whether it occurred during the Gettysburg Address when he lied about the American character. In any event, Lincoln's conquest of the South was a matter of "disastrous wickedness," and one for which there was no reason: "Travelers from New England went into the South and were surprised to find how mild the institution of slavery was on the plantations and in the cities." In short, "there was no irrepressible conflict."[22]

The bullet that ended Lincoln's life was "the last one fired for States' Rights," Masters concluded, thus dignifying Lincoln's assassin while showing that the President's death was merely an extension of the legalized killing on the battlefields. The book was dedicated to Thomas Jefferson, our "greatest president."[23]

Years later, midwestern scholar John T. Flanagan would claim that no other book of Masters, not even *Spoon River Anthology*, attracted "so much attention in reviews, editorials, news stories, and letters to the press." Such attentions came not only because Masters' book was one of the most virulent anti-Lincoln studies ever published, but also because Masters turned on those who had helped enshrine Lincoln:

> It is not for lack of facts that the myths have grown up about Lincoln. The facts have been disregarded in order that the portrait of him might be drawn which America wanted.

In other words, Masters' book attacked not only the President but also the American public, which reacted in a variety of ways.[24]

Professional historians were for the most part reserved in their judgment, saying that a re-evaluation of Lincoln's career was needed, but that Masters' point of view was so partisan as to nullify his efforts. Intellectuals associated with religious publications were less tolerant since Masters had made ugly attacks on Lincoln's religion as well as his politics. *(The Catholic World*, for example, wondered if Masters hated Lincoln more than he did God.) Mainstream publications tended to be more extreme: *Time* magazine invented the word "Lincolnoclast" to describe Masters' iconoclastic attacks; and the influential *New York Times Book Review* described the study as "a Copperhead life of Lincoln" that "might have been written by an Indiana Knight of the Golden Circle," a reference to Northern partisans who supported the South during the Civil War.[25]

The "Copperhead" reference is especially helpful in highlighting what many readers felt was Masters' chief sin: anyone could understand why a son of the Confederacy might write as Masters did; but in 1931 it was well nigh unthinkable that a son of the Lincoln country would do so.

The book was banned in Boston, and a large Philadelphia retailer refused to carry it. Schoolchildren sent denunciatory letters to Masters and his publisher, and a bill was introduced in Congress to bar *Lincoln: The Man* from the mails:

> The book entitled "Lincoln, The Man," edited by Edgar Lee Masters, is hereby declared to be obscene, lewd, lascivious, filthy, and indecent, and a scurrulous [sic] attack on a good man.

Back in Illinois, citizens spoke of going to Ann Rutledge's grave in Petersburg and chiseling Masters' epitaph from her tombstone![26]

The book also generated unfriendly cartoons: newspapers on both coasts showed Masters slinging mud at the Lincoln Memorial and sticking out his tongue at the statue of the Great Emancipator. Newspaper interviews vilified Masters:

> Sitting in the skyscraper offices of his publishers, his mouth a grim, austere slit, only his battered hat to show him a poet, Masters confessed he had little hope. A major poet of the Republic, he tilted his chair back and stared through shelled spectacles and blamed Lincoln for all of it.[27]

Nor had Masters helped his case by reminding the influential East of certain facts it would rather not have heard, namely that slavery had once been condoned throughout the East, and that the practice had not been abandoned for altruistic, ethical, or moral reasons but for economic ones. John Adams had so stated.[28]

Masters' book did, however, generate some support—from those who knew that much Lincoln commentary was so overblown as to be myth; from those who held states' rights views similar to Masters'; and from those who knew that images of the South were frequently distorted (a phenomenon that continues to this day). It is safe to say, too, that many people found Masters' book intriguing because it asked this ongoing question: how much power should the federal government have?[29]

Unfortunately for Masters, those who did the most to shape public opinion were decidedly against his interpretations, and *Lincoln: The Man* eventually hurt Masters with his public. Nothing he published after it sold particularly well, in part because none of these books were very well done, in part because the public had soured on Masters, though it had bought over 7,000 copies of his book.[30]

In the end, *Lincoln: The Man* (like the war it reflects) created both winners and losers. The big loser was Masters. It was his seeming good fortune to have dealings with the authors of three of the most influential Lincoln biographies ever written—those by Herndon, Beveridge, and Sandburg—but Masters failed to capitalize on the insights of the others, and produced a book more memorable for its quarrelsome parts than for any new understanding of Lincoln.

In fact, Lincoln's reputation was so staunchly defended by Masters' detractors that the President probably gained in stature, as did Carl Sandburg, whose cheerful half-truths in *Abraham Lincoln: The Prairie Years* gave the American people exactly the image of Lincoln they wanted. Later, when Sandburg published the more objectively written *Abraham Lincoln: The War Years*, profits from the two books helped make him reasonably well off, and increased his hold on the Lincoln country that Masters considered his "by right of birth."

But American historical scholarship benefited from *Lincoln: The Man*. Just as Masters' very frank poetry best-seller *Spoon River*

Anthology helped clear the way for the "new" poetry of the twentieth century, so too did his unfriendly biography of Lincoln anticipate a time (in the 1960s and later) when the nation would begin to see all its past heroes in a more critical light. Masters' biography will still strike many readers as severe—but his work marks a step in a process that is ongoing, the effort to capture and encapsule in words the spiritual and intellectual qualities of Abraham Lincoln the man.

Because it was Lincoln the man that Masters was seeking (as opposed to Lincoln the myth), he would no doubt have approved of the two reviews that the publishers have appended to this edition. Reviewer Andrew Nelson Lytle and Masters had much in common, for both belonged to the Southern agrarian tradition. And Masters had a long and lasting friendship with reviewer H. L. Mencken, whose iconoclastic views often matched Masters' own.

Herbert K. Russell
Carterville, Illinois

NOTES

1. Masters, *Across Spoon River: An Autobiography* (New York: Farrar & Rinehart, 1936), p. 23, early Petersburg and New Salem; Masters, "The Genesis of *Spoon River*," *The American Mercury*, 28 (January 1933), 41, played at New Salem.

2. Masters, "Days in the Lincoln Country," *Journal of the Illinois State Historical Society*, 18 (January 1926), 781-86, 1847 case, case that did not go to trial, "Lincoln tried a case."

3. *Across Spoon River*, p. 5, "In 1854."

4. "My Youth in the Spoon River Country," TS, pp. 21-22, Hardin and Civil War; *Across Spoon River* draft, TCCMS, dated November 4, 1927, p. 1, "I came into" — both at the Harry Ransom Humanities Research Center, University of Texas at Austin; *Spoon River Anthology*, an Annotated Edition, ed. John E. Hallwas (Urbana: University of Illinois Press, 1992), p. 5, called "Lee" as a boy.

5. Charles E. Burgess, "Masters and Some Mentors," *Papers on Language and Literature*, 10 (Spring 1974), 178n-179n, law partnership and likely year of beginning; Masters, *The Sangamon* (New York: Farrar & Rinehart, 1942), pp. 71, Herndon and Hardin meet, law partnership, 73, Herndon a family friend; *Across Spoon River*, p. 45, "special legal partnership," friendship; David Donald, *Lincoln's Herndon* (New York: Knopf, 1948), pp. 45, 246-47, 285, Herndon's personal habits, Petersburg, and law practice; Masters to Mr. Marner, February 7, 1927, Harry Ransom Humanities Research Center, University of Texas at Austin, 1872-1880.

6. *Across Spoon River*, pp. 24, Southerners, 172, negative view of Lincoln; *Spoon River Anthology*, An Annotated Edition, pp. 3-4, Southern views; "The Genesis of *Spoon River*," p. 41, Southern views.

7. *Across Spoon River*, pp. 25 and 45, Graham; *The Sangamon*, pp. 102, Bowling Green, 56, Kelso, 93, Armstrong family, 119, John McNamar; "The Genesis of *Spoon River*," pp. 41, Armstrong, 52, McNamar.

8. Herbert K. Russell, "Edgar Lee Masters," *Dictionary of Literary Biography, American Poets, 1880-1945*, Third Series, Part 1, ed. Peter Quartermain (Detroit: Gale Research Company, 1987), pp. 293-312, overview of Masters' life; *Spoon River Anthology* (New York: Macmillan's Collier Books, 1962), pp. 233, "actor," 229, "Out of me unworthy."

9. Charles E. Burgess, "Ancestral Lore in *Spoon River Anthology*: Fact and Fancy," *Papers on Language and Literature*, 20 (Spring 1984), 204, most anthologized poem; "The Genesis of *Spoon River*," p. 52, stone; "Ann Rutledge Monument," *The Petersburg Observer*, January 14, 1921, [p. 4]; Masters to Mr. [Henry] Rankin, July 31, 1920, Illinois College, permission; Masters to *The Saturday Evening Post* (Mr. Lorimer), November 7, 1925, Harry Ransom Humanities Research Center, University of Texas at Austin, "My Years in the Lincoln Country."

10. Masters to Agnes Lee Freer, September 17, 1924, Newberry Library, "I found Sandburg's footprints."

11. Masters to "George" [Stokes?], February 1, 1926, Harry Ransom Humanities Research Center, University of Texas at Austin, upset with Sandburg's *Lincoln*.

12. Albert J. Beveridge to Masters, March 1, 1926, Masters' father helps Beveridge with biography; Masters to Albert J. Beveridge, February 26, 1926, re Beveridge biography—both Harry Ransom Humanities Research Center, University of Texas at Austin; Masters to [Ferris] Greenslet, July 23, 1928, Harvard University, Beveridge and Masters corresponded.

13. Masters to H.L. Mencken, February 8, 1931, Harry Ransom Humanities Research Center, University of Texas at Austin, "blew up"; "The Genesis of *Spoon River*," p. 52, Beveridge exploded Lincoln myth.

14. *Across Spoon River*, p. 56, GAR.

15. *Across Spoon River*, pp. 209, "Cross of Gold," 211-12, works for Bryan, 277, Jefferson Club, 282, Jefferson Club and 1908 campaign.

16. Masters, *The Constitution and Our Insular Possessions* (Chicago?, 1900?).

17. Herbert E. Childs, "Agrarianism and Sex: Edgar Lee Masters and the Modern Spirit," *Sewanee Review*, 41 (1933), 336, "fighting, not the Civil War."

18. Masters' Diary for 1930, April 29-June 14, property of Hilary Masters, drafts in forty-seven days.

19. *Lincoln: The Man* (New York: Dodd, Mead, 1931), pp. 9, "worthless," 13, "callousness," "semi-barbarism," no gravestone, 142, "mannerless," "cold," 32-33, "to elude."

20. *Lincoln: The Man*, pp. 145, "Lincoln was," 87, "filthy," "homely"; "The Genesis of *Spoon River*," p. 53, Ann has a "simple" heart.

21. *Lincoln: The Man*, pp. 119, disabled, helps those well off, 124, poor, 109, inept lawyer, 116, "imposters and hypocrites."

22. *Lincoln: The Man*, pp. 122, 391, provoked South Carolina, 479, Gettysburg and the American character, 99, "disastrous wickedness," 161-62, "Travelers from New England," 235, "there was no."

23. *Lincoln: The Man*, p. 477, "the last one fired."

24. John T. Flanagan, *Edgar Lee Masters: The Spoon River Poet and His Critics* (Metuchen, N.J.: Scarecrow, 1974), p. 112, "so much attention"; *Lincoln: The Man*, p. 124, "It is not."

25. Flanagan, *Edgar Lee Masters: The Spoon River Poet and His Critics*, p. 114, reactions of professional historians; "Lincoln[:] The Man," *The Catholic World*, 133 (April 1931), 115; "Lincolnoclast," *Time*, 17 (February 16, 1931), p. 15; Charles W. Thompson, "A Belittling Life of Lincoln by Edgar Lee Masters," *New York Times Book Review*, February 8, 1931, p. 5, "a Copperhead."

26. Masters to Harry Hansen, n.d., banned in Boston; Masters to "Dear Kid" [Ellen Masters], March 8, 1931, barred from store; "Letters re *Lincoln: The Man*," children write letters; House Resolution 17036, Kimball Flaccus file for 1931, "The book entitled *Lincoln The Man*"—all at the Harry Ransom Humanities Research Center, University of Texas at Austin; the best collection of commentary is at the latter research center in "Letters re *Lincoln: The Man*"; "Deny Masters Picture of 'Unkempt' Lincoln," *New York Times*, February 9, 1931, p. 8, Illinoisans think of removing Rutledge epitaph.

27. "Letters re *Lincoln: The Man*," Harry Ransom Humanities Research Center, University of Texas at Austin, cartoons; "Lincoln Killed Our Freedom, Says Masters," *New York Telegram*, February 6, 1931, p. 6, "Sitting in the skyscraper."

28. *Lincoln: The Man*, pp. 38-39, slavery, John Adams.

29. See "Letters re *Lincoln: The Man*," Harry Ransom Humanities Research Center, University of Texas at Austin.

30. Kimball Flaccus conversation with publisher Frank Dodd, June 30, 1953, in Flaccus file for 1931, Harry Ransom Humanities Research Center, University of Texas at Austin, 7,100 copies.

LINCOLN
The Man

Chapter I *Lincoln's Ancestry*

THIS work is not in strictness a biography of Lincoln. It will deal, to be sure, with the events of his life, but rather as an examination of his mind and nature than as a year by year chronicle of his career. After Beveridge's searching and thorough work it would be useless to present a mere story of Lincoln's rise from failure and obscurity to world fame. But Beveridge carried his record only to the last debate which Lincoln had with Douglas, in the fall of 1858; while the present work treats of Lincoln through the War and to the time of his death. Even had Beveridge gone to the end, and written a history of the War between the States, with Lincoln as the central point of record, there would still be novelty in dealing with Lincoln and that frightful struggle by way of argument and interpretation. Beveridge did not argue or interpret; he did not write from any point of view. He merely gathered from every quarter, by the most tireless industry, whatever facts about Lincoln could be found. He set it all down in the true, fearless spirit of philosophical history. Neither trying to idealize Lincoln, nor to depreciate him, he had no regard for the Lincoln idolaters whom nearly all previous biographers of Lincoln consulted. But as Beveridge had no preconceptions to justify, his method did not comprise a specific inquiry into Lincoln's mind and nature. Now that inquiry may be made, just as an argument may be advanced in a court proceeding when all the evidence touching a given matter has been adduced. As no new fact of moment about Lincoln can now be brought to light, the time has arrived when his apotheosis can be touched with the hand of rational analysis. The many things in Herndon's work, which put Lincoln in no favorable light have been confirmed by Beveridge's thoroughly authentic biography; moreover Beveridge greatly added to the previously known facts of Lincoln's life. Also he stripped away the reticences respecting names and alliances in politics which Herndon out of tenderness for his revered friend maintained by the use of dashes and deletions. The result is that Herndon has been more than justified; and inevitably he will enjoy a credit and a respect which were denied him in 1888, and long after, when partisanship and myth making were at flood tide, repelling all reports that dimmed Lincoln's deification. While Beveridge's work is so factual and dispassionate that no judicious mind can refuse it credit. The present work uses Herndon's biography, and Beveridge's monumental assemblage of facts, as well as other lives of Lincoln, as the basis of analysis of Lincoln's mind and character. The facts are here set down completely and with care; and upon them the delineations and arguments are based. The purpose has been to bring together the testimony in full touching Lincoln's career, so that the reader will be enabled to judge for himself whether that testimony justifies the conclusions which are drawn by way of analytical portraiture.

War makes brutes of those who practice it, and cowards and sycophants of those who have to endure it against their will; and when thinking is cowed and judgment is shackled, great reputations can be built both by stifling criticism and by artificing the facts. When the means of life, not to say advancement in the world, depend upon accession to a certain acclaim, that acclaim is subjected to lessening challenge. Under such economic circumstances not only are political and social institutions founded, but the reputations of those men are made and magnified, who inaugurated the particular historical condition, and especially if their names can be used as words of magic with which to perpetuate and strengthen it. The materialist conception of history holds good in cases of this sort.

We should begin to regret the waste of the good and useful men by the tens of thousands in every county in America, from that fateful April of 1861 to very recent days, who were shut out of political life, out of their part in the management of their country by the standards and discriminations which were set up to enforce the view of the triumphant party of the War between the States, with the magnification of Lincoln as the concrete test. This rejection of human worth and intelligence has been beyond computation; and still there is left the corruption of the intellectual life of the country to be reckoned, as modern biography is beginning to reckon it, with its emancipated and realistic attitude toward records once touched so gingerly and with such regard to Lincoln as the colossal and sacred figure of a just war waged for liberty!

As late as 1858 Lincoln was denying with all his might that he was an abolitionist; and he was avoiding, as if they were contagion, the contact of fanatics like Garrison and Giddings and Phillips. In a few years he was at the head of an army which was singing hymns of praise to John Brown, who had robbed and murdered under the inspiration of that religious zealotry which claims to divine the purposes of God, and, under the warrant of heaven, proceeds to execute them. The Democratic Party, broken by the incredible radicalism of Southern leaders, fell down in 1860, and was walked over by the mongrel breeds who knew nothing and cared nothing about liberty and constitutional government; when, by compromise that affected no principle of moment, Douglas would have been elected president and the war averted, at that time, and perhaps for good. After that, with an army at the command of centralists and fanatics, with that army carrying on to victory, supported by great wealth, which saw its chances of fortune in military success, and in the despotisms of reconstruction, there was nothing of strength left in the country to oppose the sordid imperialism which arrived to rule.

For nearly twenty-five years the all-potent political argument against the Democrats was that they sympathized with the South, or that they had favored slavery; until at last they were compelled to accept the judgments which centralists reiterated touching the necessity and the justice of the war. But as to Lincoln there was much in the man that appealed to the hearts of those who most stoutly resented his politics, and his acts as president. Along the way before he became president he had spoken many words of great truth on the rights of labor, on the equality of men, on democracy and liberty, in a word; and in the weakness and confusion that follow a war there were few to think, and less to say, that, while he had remembered that part of the Declaration of Independence which announced that all men are created equal, he had ignored and trampled its principles that governments derive their just powers from the consent of the governed.

Meanwhile numberless writers were bent upon giving Lincoln apotheosis, and none that was heeded said anything of influence against him. Who in the North, for example, read Pollard's *The Lost Cause*, or Stephens' *Constitutional View of the War*, or the work of Jefferson Davis? Who read these but to jeer? These could call Lincoln a sophist and a usurper, only to be smiled at by the rich and populous North, the North of poets and historians, and great captains, and the statesmen of a new régime of political control, of a government made a nation from a confederacy of states by the glorious acts of an army headed by Lincoln! With monopoly and bureaucracy taking the country over as the result of the War and the Fourteenth Amendment, a phenomenal thing appeared in political appeal. Lincoln began to be quoted as authority by libertarians, even more than Jefferson. One can imagine what Calhoun and Douglas and Jackson would have thought of this, even though it was Populists who were Hamiltonians reversed, and war Democrats, and the motley forces who had joined the Republican Party, and had seceded from it, who by such appeal looked up to Lincoln as one who could save them and the country from oppression.

But gradually it has dawned upon the liberal mind in America that Lincoln's wise and eloquent utterances, on abstract matters of justice, racial equality, and the rights of labor, influence neither American statecraft nor jurisprudence; even while at the same time they redound to and even increase the sentimental fame with which he is clothed. The reason is that his acts were against liberty, and so much to the advantage of monopoly and privilege, from his first days in 1832 at New Salem, Illinois, to the end of his life. It was in vain, therefore, that the Democratic Party looked to Lincoln for help when a coterie of plunderers and centralists raped the Philippines. They understood better than the friends of Liberty what was the true significance of Lincoln's spirit. Well could they say that the Dred Scott case, with its principle that the Constitution goes hand in hand with the flag, was shot to death at Gettysburg. The abolitionists, the Charles Sumners and the Thaddeus Stevenses, who had no conception of liberty, and the conscious imperialists, who had no regard for it, were historically triumphant when McKinley, who was a major in Lincoln's army, by a military order, took over the entire Philippine Islands, and its execution resulted in the slaughter of three thousand Filipinos near the walls of Manila.

Those who denounced these atrocious acts in the campaign of 1900 were reminded that they were the sons of those who tried to destroy the Union in 1861, and of the spirit of those who wanted to keep the negro in slavery! History furnishes no more absurd

LINCOLN'S ANCESTRY AND YOUTH

irony than this. But in truth the Congressional imperialism of Lincoln was no whit different from that of McKinley. The first was used sentimentally by those who did not understand its nature and its tendencies to keep slavery out of the territories, and consciously by those who fully comprehended what it meant in the way of central power to monopoly; and the second was used almost entirely by those who wanted to embark America upon the ways of world adventure and conquest.

These things considered, is it wonderful that Lincoln's fame is so much greater than Jackson's whom he did not equal in character or in gifts, or in achievements as a soldier or a statesman; whom he only excelled in talent in the use of words? And since America has largely discarded the principles of Jefferson it is not remarkable that Lincoln overtops him, in spite of Jefferson's superior comprehensiveness of mind and interests, his vast learning, compared to which Lincoln was unlettered, the philosophy of his statesmanship and his profound understanding of liberty, as well as his unconfused career in protecting it. Finally the anomaly is presented of Lincoln standing side by side with Washington, with no other American statesmen to fellow them in equality. The obelisk to Washington and the memorial to Lincoln on the Mall of the capital of America express the judgment which has been worked out from the American culture to which so many inscrutable things have contributed in the last sixty-five years.

In 1859 Lincoln wrote a letter to J. W. Fell in which, among other things relating to himself and his family, he said: "I was born February 12, 1809, in Hardin County, Kentucky. My parents were both born in Virginia of undistinguished families—second families, perhaps I should say. My mother, who died in my tenth year, was of a family of the name of Hanks, some of whom now reside in Adams, and others in Macon County, Illinois." [1] He then proceeded to tell of his grandfather and to say that an effort to identify his grandfather with the New England Lincolns had ended in nothing more definite than discovering a similarity of Christian names between the two branches. This letter to Fell was written when Lincoln's fame was traveling beyond the boundaries of Illinois, and when biographical material concerning him was beginning to be

[1] Lincoln's Works, I, 596.

sought. It is to be noted that he wrote guardedly and briefly of his mother, Nancy Hanks, which imported a state of mind and feeling later to be more carefully considered; but in writing of the Lincolns he not only betrayed that ignorance of ancestry which was common to people in Illinois, who had arrived there after family wanderings from distant states, but he stated the case with full modesty respecting their standing. The Lincolns were a second family only if Washington's family was a second family; and as to distinction, Lincoln might have spoken of them with just pride if he had known about them.

The name Lincoln is an ancient one in England and of honorable associations. It is identified with the second largest county in England, and with one of the colleges of Oxford University where John Wesley and John Morley pursued their studies with distinction. Lincoln evidently knew nothing of the family of his name who originated in Norfolk County, England, at the village of Hingham which is near Norwich with its many venerable buildings, its Norman castle and Norman cathedral, built in the 11th century. It was from Hingham that Samuel Lincoln came to Hingham, Massachusetts, in 1637, during the persecutions of the detestable Archbishop Laud; and there with other dissenters, who had fled the evil days of religious bigotry, abode in Massachusetts Bay Colony, and submitted themselves to be governed by the common law of England and the Bible.

Samuel Lincoln had four sons, whose progeny in later generations took part in the Revolution. Samuel's great-great grandson, Levi, was a graduate of Harvard, and an attorney-general under Jefferson. Levi had a son named Levi, who was, as well, a graduate of Harvard, and distinguished his life by becoming governor of Massachusetts. The elder Levi had a son named Enoch who was governor of Maine in 1827. This line of descent gathered honors. Samuel's fourth son, named Mordecai, had a taste for money and worldly prosperity. As his father Samuel was a weaver's apprentice, Mordecai took to blacksmithing, and acquired iron works, saw mills and grist mills. Mordecai had a son named Mordecai who left Massachusetts for New Jersey and afterward for Pennsylvania. This second Mordecai had a son named John, who was the father of Abraham, the grandfather of the President, to whom Lincoln referred in the Fell letter just quoted from. The lineage, then, is: Samuel, the

LINCOLN'S ANCESTRY AND YOUTH 7

weaver; Mordecai, the blacksmith, or iron-worker; Mordecai, who wandered to New Jersey and to Pennsylvania, where he became prosperous; John, who inherited three hundred acres of land from his father; the second Mordecai; and Abraham, the son of John, who inherited a tract of land in Rockingham County, Virginia. Abraham had a son named Mordecai, and a son named Thomas; and Thomas was the father of the President.

What was done to the Lincoln strain of blood by intermarriage, what new traits and characteristics were introduced into its species by the infusion of other stocks is beyond all human solution. There was nothing to indicate a nervous instability in the circumstance of the second Mordecai, who left Massachusetts for New Jersey. But question arises somewhat as to Abraham, the President's grandfather. He had a large and excellent farm in Rockingham County; and when the Revolution needed him he sold it for £5000 and moved to Kentucky. This was February 18, 1780. But before that, in 1776, he had been to Kentucky and entered a thousand acres of land. There may be no explanation of this step, save that which occurs for the Illinoisians of the 1880's who abandoned their good farms in Illinois for the treacherous wheat lands of Kansas, and the no better corn lands of Iowa. When the Revolution broke out, this Abraham Lincoln of Virginia became a captain of militia; but there is no record of his taking any part in the struggle. For some reason, good or bad, he deserted his country's cause. If he tried to escape the stress of war, not to say its service, or to rid himself of oppressive taxation, he did not profit by the attempt. In the Fell letter referred to, Lincoln wrote that, a year or two subsequent to 1781 or 1782, his grandfather Abraham was "killed by the Indians, not in battle, but by stealth, when he was laboring to open a farm in the forest." The date is not important, except as it may throw some light on the character of the man.

Beveridge, by that indefatigable industry which distinguishes his work, gathered much curious material on this subject. He found the record of a suit, brought in 1797, in which Mordecai Lincoln, Abraham's son, stated in one of the papers in it that Abraham died without a will in May, 1786. He also got trace of a law suit which was pending in Nelson County, Kentucky, in November of 1787, and in which an alias summons was issued to another defendant in the suit, living in Jefferson County. By this time, but just when is not disclosed by Beveridge, the original summons had been served on Abraham Lincoln as a resident of Nelson County; so that he was living in Nelson County when the writ was impetrated. This suit was discontinued in the Nelson County Court in May, 1788; and on the same day another suit against Abraham Lincoln and his wife was discontinued in the Nelson County Court. The Beveridge note leads one to infer that these discontinuances were due to the death of Abraham Lincoln, but this is not explicitly stated. Judge L. S. Pence, of Lebanon, Kentucky, furnished these facts, derived from the examination of old records, to Beveridge in a letter dated May 24, 1924; and in this letter Pence went on to give it as his belief, based upon these records and others, which it would be tedious to recapitulate here, that Abraham Lincoln, the grandfather of the President, was wounded by an Indian in Jefferson County, Kentucky, and fled to Nelson County, where lived a brother-in-law, about which there is no doubt; and where Abraham survived until April, 1788, just a month before the suits referred to were discontinued.[1] If he ran away from the Revolution, he may have decamped from Jefferson County when he could use the excuse of being wounded and pursued to conceal something in his purposes which was more impelling than wounds or Indians. Be this as it may, and whenever he died and wherever he died, he left surviving him his son Thomas Lincoln, who became the father of the President, and whose date of birth in Rockingham County, Virginia, is most obscure.

In the Fell letter Lincoln wrote that his father was "but six years of age" when Abraham was killed by the Indians; and if that happened in 1781 or 1782, then Thomas was born in 1775 or 1776. In 1797 Thomas was listed in a tax book of Hardin County, Kentucky, as twenty-one or over—that is, for aught that such a record proves, he might then have been twenty-one, or thirty, or forty. In a family Bible, which, however, is mutilated, his birth date is given as January 6, 1778; and if this be true, then Thomas was three or four years old when Abraham was killed. Beveridge suggests that there may have been some reason why Thomas Lincoln concealed his age; but at any rate none of this sounds like the Massachusetts

[1] Beveridge, I, 11.

Lincolns, like Levi and his descendants, about whom to this day there are records and monuments in plenty.

There are pictures extant of the respectable dwellings and well-kept gardens of some of these Massachusetts, New Jersey, and Pennsylvania Lincolns. With the advent of Abraham, one gets the impression that a deterioration of the stock was setting in, or that possibly primitive conditions were overcoming and modifying natural strength. One would like to have some explanation of Abraham's taking no part in the Revolution, save as a judge advocate during its first three years, and why, since he was known as Captain Lincoln, he did not fight through with Virginia to the end. At all events he begot Thomas Lincoln, who proved to be one of the most worthless men who ever fathered a man of distinction, such as Abraham Lincoln, the President, who somehow, and from somewhere, came into being with a spark which weathered bad food, bad housing, and the communications of beggarly companions like Dennis Hanks, the vagrant, and others.

Thomas Lincoln had all the indicia of the Southern poor white. In himself he was less than of undistinguished blood, less than second grade. He behaved as if he was sprung from the lowest stratum of American life in the early part of the nineteenth century. He was unmoral, shiftless, bound down in poverty, in spite of the fact that he inherited enough from his father Abraham to have made him well circumstanced, if he had possessed ambition and prudence. He was described as a man five feet, ten and one-half inches in height, and of great strength, and in disposition rather good-natured and amiable. Though his brother Mordecai had a fair education, Thomas was utterly ignorant. In September of 1803, with £118 given him by his brother Mordecai, he bought 238 acres of land in Hardin County, Kentucky, some eight miles from the village of Elizabethtown; but there is no record that he ever worked that farm. In March of 1805 he was appointed a patroller of Hardin County, and by the duties of that office he became a slave catcher, empowered to catch and whip insubordinate negroes. In Elizabethtown lived Joseph Hanks the carpenter; and soon Thomas Lincoln was drifting about that village picking up what he could learn of the carpenter craft. On June 12, 1806, he married Nancy Hanks, a niece of Joseph Hanks, when he was 28 or 30 according as his age be computed from the various reputed dates of his birth; and when she was 25 or 26.

He took up his married life in Elizabethtown, where he and Nancy were the humblest persons of all the primitive people of that frontier village. In May of 1808 he bought 66⅔ acres of land in Hardin County; and this place has come down to us as the Sinking Spring Farm. In October of 1814 he moved to another place ten miles from the Sinking Spring Farm. In the autumn of 1816 he emigrated beyond the Ohio River into Indiana; and in December of the same year the Sinking Spring Farm was sold over his head, under a decree of court, for $61.50. In Indiana he landed at the farm of Francis Posey; but he was not long for there. By turns he lived on a brush farm; then on one near Knob Creek. He sold the Knob Creek farm for a quantity of whisky while the land was in litigation. He was living here and there by raising a little corn and vegetables. At one time he had a patent for 160 acres of land in Indiana; but finally he took up his abode on Pigeon Creek in Indiana. Here, in October of 1818, Nancy Hanks Lincoln died, leaving two children: Sarah, eleven years old, and Abraham, the future president, aged nine.

In the winter of 1819 Thomas journeyed from Indiana back to Elizabethtown, Kentucky, where he married Sarah Bush Johnston, a widow, to whom he had proposed marriage before he married Nancy Hanks. He brought her back to Pigeon Creek, where Lincoln and his sister Sarah were living in squalor with the happy-go-lucky Dennis Hanks. To finish his peregrinations, he moved to a farm near Decatur, Illinois, in the fall of 1829; in 1831 he went on to Buck Grove, Coles County, Illinois; from there to Muddy Point in the same county, after about a year at Buck Grove. Then in a few months he traveled on to Goose Nest Prairie in Coles County, where he lived until his death, which occurred in 1851, in poverty to the last, and accepting help from his son Abraham, who, by 1840, anyway, was making enough to spare him small doles.

Like most poor people of the time, Thomas Lincoln was a Jackson Democrat; but we shall see that his son Abraham was an ugly duckling, not understood of the father. The son from the first was nursing dreams and thinking thoughts far beyond the comprehension and sympathy of the father. The old man joined the Pigeon Creek Baptist Church in 1819, after a long period of utter religious indifference, the indifference really of the dull witted. But his conversion did not bring him to any tenderness toward his son. He had more affection for his stepson, John D. Johnston, than for his own. According to Dennis Hanks, Thomas Lincoln was used to whip Abraham with severity, and on occasions would deal the boy a blow that knocked him feet away. Abraham, by reason of his liveliness, and his inquisitiveness, was often in his father's way. Thus when the two would be standing in the fence corner when a neighbor passed by, the boy would be out with a question to the neighbor before the old man could open his mouth; and then the father would knock the boy down.[1] With his mother dead when Abraham was but nine years old, and with a father such as Thomas Lincoln was, it was natural for the boy to grow up with a detached mind, one who stood off and observed, and whose affections were so guarded, so controlled by the intellect.

One conspicuous thing to be noted about Lincoln is that he was profoundly ashamed of the poverty of his youth, and of the sordid surroundings in which he grew up; and much of the ambitious striving of his life was motivated by a fierce desire to rise above the life into which he was born. We do not find these feelings all in all stirring in the heart of Andrew Jackson; and we should not expect Walt Whitman to be ashamed that his mother was the product of a natural union, if such had been the case. When Lincoln was nominated for the presidency he was visited by J. L. Scripps, a correspondent for a Chicago paper, seeking biographical material. According to Scripps, Lincoln communicated to him some facts concerning his ancestry, which Lincoln did not wish to be published, and which Scripps kept in confidence to the day of his death. Political life in America is such that a candidate for the presidency would not care to have the fact that his mother was an illegitimate child sent forth to the country in a campaign text book. But on the other hand Lincoln was all his life secretive to the last degree about his mother. In 1850, however, when Lincoln had long been in intimate association with Herndon, he confided to Herndon that Nancy Hanks was the natural child of Lucy Hanks and a well-bred Virginia planter; and at the time of this confidence he told Herndon that it was from this Virginia planter that he inherited his logic,

[1] Beveridge, I, 66.

his mental activity, his ambition and all the qualities which distinguished him from the Hanks family. It is evident that Lincoln was reasoning by a process of exclusion. If he inherited no mental gifts from the Hankses, he must have got them from this Virginia planter. Though if he did not know who the Virginia planter was, it was impossible for him to say whether the Virginia planter had any mental gifts to transmit. Also evidently it did not occur to Lincoln that there might be something in the Lincoln blood which overleaped his father Thomas and entered into the being of himself. If he had known about the Massachusetts Lincolns, as we do, he might have credited them with what gifts had come to him; but one fancies that his thorough understanding and justified dislike for his father, Thomas Lincoln, made him turn to his mother's unknown father as the most satisfactory explanation of himself.

Nancy Hanks was the daughter of Lucy Hanks, a sister of Joseph, the carpenter. Late investigators have found that Lucy was indicted in the Mercer County, Kentucky, Court in November, 1789, for "unbecoming conduct." This is no great matter, considering the primitive society, and the irregular habits of a people living almost as Indians. She was married to Henry Sparrow in 1791, and in all likelihood made a good wife. But if Nancy Hanks in any wise followed in the steps of her mother, there is no record of it. She has come down to us as a good enough woman of the pioneer days. One would not be justified in classing her with Mary, the mother of Washington; but so much has been written in prose and verse of Nancy Hanks that Mary Washington is quite put in the shade by comparison. Nancy Hanks has been variously described as of low stature, but heavy and well set, as squatty even; as spare and of thin visage; as of light hair and blue eyes; as of dark hair and blue-green eyes; as of black hair and coarse features; as of pale complexion and sharp features; as a tall woman, not a squatty woman, who was five feet and seven inches in height, who was five feet eight inches in height, who weighed 120 pounds, or, according to others, 130 pounds. There is one record of her that her forehead was high. Remembering that few educated people are sharp enough in observation to describe the eyes, the hair, the height, the weight or any characteristics of persons, though sometimes knowing them intimately, it is not wonderful that such varying portraits of Nancy Hanks have been passed on by the Hankses and the Grigsbys, and other acquaintances of Nancy Hanks, who, indeed, had no occasion to make careful note of what she looked like.

When Lucy Hanks married Henry Sparrow, Nancy went to live with them; and with them also lived Dennis Hanks, the vagrant. In after life he made statements about Lincoln which did not tally with each other; and in 1865, after Abraham Lincoln was entombed in Springfield, and all possible curiosity was excited about the origin and early life of Dennis's celebrated nephew, the President, then recently assassinated, Dennis made a statement to Herndon touching Nancy Hanks, his maternal cousin, and grew eloquent over her virtues as he recounted them. "She was keen, shrewd, smart," he said. "I do say highly intellectual by nature. Her memory was strong, her judgment accurate. She was spiritually and ideally inclined." Nathaniel Grigsby belonged to the family of Aaron Grigsby, who married Sarah Lincoln, the sister of Abraham; and Nathaniel reported of Nancy Hanks that she was known for the extraordinary strength of her mind, that she was a brilliant woman, of great good sense and morality.[1] But Beveridge declares that Nathaniel Grigsby was not of an age to remember what Nancy Hanks was. This is the substance of what history has respecting Nancy Hanks. It is regrettable that Lincoln himself left no description of her; and indeed the omission is to be remarked. He was nine years old when she died; and her lonely burial had elements of vividness which one would think Lincoln never could have forgotten. Thomas Lincoln used his skill as a carpenter to make a coffin for her; her body was hauled on a sled to a sylvan knoll, and there she was buried, to lie with no stone or board to mark her grave during the whole life of her husband, and the whole life of her son Abraham, who died in the presidency at the age of 56 years, worth more than $100,000.

There was a callousness and dumbness about some of the pioneer people of the Middle West, which persist to this day, and have become the nourishment of a sort of semi-barbarism, sometimes becoming cruel bigotry, at others a sort of savage indifference to the refined interests of life; and of this quality, in some particulars, was Abraham Lincoln.

In 1865, J. B. Helm wrote an account of a camp meeting held at

[1] Beveridge, I, 16.

Elizabethtown, Kentucky, in 1806;[1] and, as that was the year in which Nancy Hanks married Thomas Lincoln, Herndon was of the opinion that it was Nancy Hanks who figured in the religious orgy which Helm described as having been witnessed by him. Helm wrote that the Hanks girls were great at camp meetings, and that their conduct furnished some explanation, and apology, too, for the superstition which was in Lincoln's character. The meeting had arrived at a point when a general shout was about to commence, when the religious ecstasy was seizing the celebrants of the rites. At this juncture of affairs a strong, athletic young man, about twenty-five years old (in 1806 Thomas Lincoln was 28 or 30, as before noted) was being prepared for the scene, soon to be enacted, by ridding himself of all clothing except his shirt and his trousers. At the same time a young woman was being divested of all her apparel, which would be in the way of the gyrations soon to be performed by her; and the combs of her hair were being loosened and her hair arranged so that when the religious dance, which she was entering upon, became furious enough to spill her combs, her hair would uncoil in graceful braids. Thus being in readiness, this man and this woman began to "work" themselves toward the center of the camp, while singing and shouting, while hugging and kissing persons of their own sex, and while gradually approaching each other. At last the two reached the altar and there closed, with their arms about each other, while the man was singing and shouting at the top of his voice:

> I have my Jesus in my arms,
> Sweet as honey, strong as bacon ham.

While Helm was watching this Corybantic ceremony, standing on a bench, a woman next to him whispered that these dancers were to be married the next month; and to that end they were here and by this sacrament imbibing the Holy Ghost, and the inspiration of true religion. We have seen that Thomas Lincoln did not join any church until 1819; and whether he could go through with this ceremony with Nancy Hanks without conversion is a question of Kentucky theology of the long ago. No less it is true that this sort of religion was a part of Lincoln's environment; and that the Hanks girls, whether Nancy or not, so performed, is certain enough.

[1] Herndon, I, 11–12.

Chapter II   Lincoln's Boyhood and Young Manhood

NOT longer than fifty years ago, log cabins exactly like the one in which Lincoln was born, on the Sinking Spring Farm, stood in Illinois and Indiana and other parts of the Middle West, as well as in Kentucky and Tennessee; and doubtless some may be there still or in the Ozarks. In Lincoln's day the windows were fitted with greased paper to admit light, in lieu of glass, which was not obtainable. The floor of these cabins was of earth; the doors were of broad slabs hinged with wood or hide; the fireplace was built of stones and sticks held together by clay. The spaces between the logs were daubed with clay. The bed was made of poles resting in notched sticks, and covered with rags. From the crude rafters hung bacon and ham, if the family happened to have any; also tobacco stalks and leaves. On the wall somewhere, resting in wooden forks, was the needful rifle. There might be the skins of animals here and there on the wall, undergoing the last stages of tanning. The kitchen utensils, pots, kettles, and the like, were scanty enough. The whole family, whether there were few or many children, slept in one room. In summer the heat was terrific in Kentucky and middle Indiana; in winter the cold was pitiless, and all the logs that could be cut and thrown on the rude hearth gave no more heat than would keep a human being in comfort when sitting close enough to it almost to be scorched, while affording no warmth when the shivering children stood back and encountered the bitter wind blowing between the chinks of the logs. Bathing was unknown, and washing was rather avoided than otherwise, especially in winter when the brook was frozen, or the well or spring afforded water stinging with ice.

Living was in every way indecent. The cabins were filthy, and rats and other vermin abounded. Men and women undressed before each other; and the children were cognizant of the most intimate relationships carried on within a few feet of where they slept, and where everyone slept, including the hired man or the stranger guests. The food was vile, consisting of pork or game, but much meat at any rate, and of corn and wheat bread which was made from meal ground in crude mortars. The cooking, too, was conducive to all stomach ailments, since nearly everything was fried and in over quantities of grease. People had bad colds in the winter, and fevers in the summer, and a strange scourge called milk-sickness, of which Nancy Hanks died. Much whisky was drunk; and all weird superstitions abounded concerning the moon, the flight of birds, the bringing of a shovel into a room, which meant a near death; and there were ghosts and witches about, whispering in dark corners, or flying over the roofs. In this sort of cabin was Abraham Lincoln born, in an obscure back settlement of Kentucky of cane brake society, in no wise fit to be called the home of a human being. This was the kind of home which Thomas Lincoln provided for Nancy Hanks, when he might have lived in some comfort in Elizabethtown, from which he moved, as it is supposed, because he could not stand the attitude of a better class of people toward him. Rather than labor to rise to their level, he preferred the woods and loathsome poverty, rats and cold and filth. Galton, in his work entitled *Inquiries into the Human Faculty,* made some observations on late and early marriages, based upon statistics, from which he deduced that mothers, married at the ages of 17, 22, 27 and 32 years respectively, were fertile in a ratio of 6, 5, 4, 3. From which it will be seen that Nancy Hanks might well have given birth to more than three children. One of her children died, and Sarah was of ordinary mentality; the son Abraham almost from the first showed something different in his make-up from the average run of boys.

When Lincoln was six or seven years of age, he attended school for a few weeks at the Knob Creek School. By this time, 1816, schools were being opened all about in Kentucky and Indiana and books were beginning to be plentiful. In Kentucky Lincoln went to school but briefly; and, according to his own word, he attended school less than a year in his whole life. In Indiana he learned to read, to write and to cipher to the rule of three. From his tenth to his fourteenth year he had no schooling whatever. But about 1822 he came under the instruction of a teacher named Azel W. Dorsey, where Webster's and Dilworth's spelling book, the Bible, Pike's arithmetic were the texts used. And under Dorsey he learned the fine and characteristic penmanship which is conspicuous in the earliest document which we have in his hand. He also excelled in spelling from the first. It is clear, therefore, that from the first Lincoln manifested the literary cast of mind. He was not expert in arithmetic; though his mind was more mathematical than intuitive; and very early, when about fourteen years of age, he began to write verses. At about seventeen years of age, when his sister Sarah married Aaron Grigsby, Lincoln composed a song in honor of the occasion, some of the stanzas of which may be set down here to show that satire was his first expression, and also what kind of satire it was.

> When Adam was created
> He dwelt in Eden's shade,
> As Moses has recorded,
> And soon a bride was made.
>
> Ten thousand times ten thousand
> Of creatures swarmed around
> Before a bride was formed,
> And yet no mate was found.

Dropping a stanza or two we have a faulty rhyme; but not much worse than some of Emerson's:

> And closed the flesh instead thereof,
> And then he took the same
> And of it made a woman,
> And brought her to the man.

And finally:

> The woman was not taken
> From Adam's head, we know,
> To show she must not rule him—
> 'Tis evidently so.
>
> The woman she was taken
> From under Adam's arm,
> So she must be protected
> From injuries and harm.

Before the time of these verses, and when Lincoln was about twelve years of age, he was writing rhymes at Dorsey's school. There is this in his boyish handwriting in a copy book which comes down from his first school days:

> Time what an empty vapor 'tis
> And days how swift they are
> Swift as an Indian arrow
> Fly on like a shooting star. Etc.

The man who was thus early practicing harmonious numbers and the condensation which belongs to verse did not suddenly emerge to the command of an oratorical style in the debates with Douglas at forty-nine years of age. By that time he had for quite forty years been weighing and testing words, arranging and balancing clauses, searching out exactness in expression. And some of his early reading in law books had greatly helped him to those ends. Before the matter of poetry be left, it should be said that when Lincoln was thirty-seven he journeyed to Indiana and went over the ground of his boyhood there, with the result that he wrote some verses in reminiscence of the past which he sent to a friend named Johnston. In the letter he referred to Poe's "Raven," which he had not then seen; and he alluded to some poem, denying his authorship of it, as one infers, because Johnston had attributed it to Lincoln. The poem alluded to was probably, "Oh, Why Should the Spirit of Mortal Be Proud?" which had fastened itself upon Lincoln's imagination some years before. Lincoln in this letter wrote: "I would give all that I am worth and go in debt, to be able to write so fine a piece as I think this is." It must be said that Lincoln's taste in poetry had not advanced to any extent, nor at any time did he take an interest in the work of Tennyson and Browning in England, or in the American poets beyond Holmes' "Last Leaf." But to the poem:

> My childhood's home I see again,
> And sadden with the view;
> And still as memory crowds my brain,
> There's pleasure in it too.
>
> * * *
>
> I hear the loved survivors tell
> How naught from death could save,
> Till every sound appears a knell,
> And every spot a grave.

BOYHOOD AND YOUNG MANHOOD 19

There is no great originality here, and true to his self-contained nature there is no fire; but the wonder is that he should have written this at all. Six months after this letter he wrote again to Johnston and sent him some more verses. These celebrate the fate of one Matthew Gentry who went to school with Lincoln in Indiana, the son of the rich man of a very poor neighborhood, who had become furiously mad at nineteen years of age, and who by 1844, when Lincoln visited his old home, had settled down into harmless insanity. So Lincoln wrote in a somewhat Wordsworthian manner:

> But here's an object of more dread
> Than aught the grave contains—
> A human form with reason fled,
> While wretched life remains.
>
> When terror spread, and neighbors ran
> Your dangerous strength to bind,
> And soon a howling crazy man
> Your limbs were fast confined.
>
> * * *
>
> And when at length the drear and long
> Time smoothed thy fiercer woes,
> How plaintively thy mournful song
> Upon the still night rose!
>
> * * *
>
> But this is past, and naught remains
> That raised thee o'er the brute;
> Thy piercing shrieks and soothing strain
> Are like forever mute.
>
> Now fare thee well. More thou the cause
> Than subject now of woe.
> All mental pangs by time's kind laws
> Hast lost the power to know.[1]

Lincoln had as well used the plural of strain so as to make the rhyme; and this last stanza betrays the material that escaped his control; but there is feeling and a certain poetical atmosphere to this production. This sufficiently covers Lincoln's experiments with

[1] Lincoln's Works, II, 85–88.

versification, if indeed it does not take note of all that he wrote in verse that is extant.

"He was always at school early," wrote Nathaniel Grigsby of Lincoln, "and attended to his studies. He was always at the head of his class, and passed us rapidly in his studies. He lost no time at home, and when he was not at work was at his books. He kept up his studies on Sundays, and carried his books with him to work, so that he might read when he rested from labor." This characterization should be kept in mind when we come to Lincoln's habits after he was settled in the practice of law at Springfield, where he seemed to sink into a kind of torpidity, as if biologically he was living through a stage of life which repeated the nature of his father, the lazy Thomas Lincoln. But from the first Lincoln was physically inactive; he disliked labor; it was impossible to make a carpenter of him, though he had dreams of becoming a blacksmith, which sounds as if he were carrying on from Mordecai the Massachusetts iron-worker. He did not care for fishing and hunting, the common sports of the rural people of Indiana. He loved everyone, so the report of him is, and his cheerful friendliness won all hearts. His homely face broke into merriment that rescued his small gray eyes from their sunken haziness; he was an innocent tease, a boy capable of wonderful mimicries, and he was full of all sorts of pranks. Where everyone drank, he did not drink; and where everyone had some sneaking kindness for a girl, Lincoln stood back shy and awkward and afraid. His attitude toward women to the last day of his life was but a continuation of this boyhood diffidence. What was the cause of it, beyond a lack of real passional nature, and a consciousness of his own homely and ungainly appearance, remains for conjecture. In these days he was always reading; and at times he mounted a stump in the forest and made a speech. Was it wonderful that he was so practiced a talent even at twenty-four, when he was in the legislature of Illinois?

When Sarah Bush Johnston married Thomas Lincoln and came back to Indiana with him, she brought with her to the log cabin where the ten-year-old Abraham Lincoln was abiding with Dennis Hanks and the sister Sarah Lincoln, a copy of *Robinson Crusoe*, and one of *Sinbad the Sailor*, and also *Æsop's Fables*. Thomas Lincoln had inherited a copy of the Bible from his father Abraham;

BOYHOOD AND YOUNG MANHOOD 21

so that Lincoln had had access to that from the time he could read. But if Dennis Hanks is to be believed, Lincoln did not read the Bible much, though he was aways reading something. In a community where the religious revival swept the inhabitants as if with flame which drove them to repentance, Lincoln stood aloof, not joining any church; and according to his stepmother Lincoln as a boy had no religion, and never talked about religion, and, so far as she could observe, did not even think about religion. This is a phase of that imperviousness of Lincoln's nature which enabled him to stand against innovation and clamor, but which also kept him strange to new ideas, and which, coupled with his torpidity, made him indifferent to the great books that were being produced in England and America between 1832 and 1860. He acted all his life much as if there was no use in much of the reading that others did, Herndon, in chief, to whom he once said that history was unreliable and biography but a panegyric of the subject, not to be trusted. It is clear now that he would have been better fitted for the presidency, and for the tasks legal and other that confronted him, if he had spent the long Springfield years, when he did little but travel the circuit, in advancing his self-culture. He might have become as learned as Franklin if he had done this.

At eleven years of age Lincoln began to shoot up to the great height which afterward made him conspicuous. And with this sudden and phenomenal growth a soberness took hold of him not before noticeable. He became more thoughtful, and his timidity was greater, especially in the presence of men and women. With his former companions he manifested a disposition to keep away from them. At fifteen or sixteen he was over six feet tall and still growing, and at seventeen he reached his full height of six feet four inches. He now weighed about one hundred sixty pounds, with large hands and feet, long arms and legs, and a small head; but he was wiry and strong and vigorous. The poor food of the log cabin had evidently agreed with him.

In addition to the books already mentioned, Lincoln had the use of a most valuable volume when he was as young as fourteen years of age. This was Bailey's *Etymological Dictionary*, which came to him through his uncle Mordecai. It was the dictionary which Samuel Johnson had used for the preparation of his lexicon. There was enough here for all the intellectual industry of which he was capable; and as Herndon wrote that Lincoln had an insatiable passion for knowledge of the exact meaning of words, he was able through this dictionary to gratify it to the full at the very early years of his intellectual formation. Another book which he read at about sixteen years of age was Grimshaw's *History of the United States,* which it will be noted could not have brought a report of the country beyond 1825. The closing words of this history by no fanciful speculation may be said to have made an indelible impression upon his mind. "Let us not only declare," it reads "by words, but demonstrate by our actions that all men are created equal; that they are endowed by their creator with the same inalienable rights: that among these are life, liberty and the pursuit of happiness."

At this period of his life Lincoln pored over Weems' *Life of Washington* and Weems' *Life of Franklin;* and for discipline in the finest art of expression he had Scott's *Lessons in Elocution, or Selections of Pieces in Prose and Verse for the Improvement of Youth in Reading and Speaking.* This contained quotations from the speeches of Chatham, Mansfield, Cicero and Desmothenes; also portions of *Hamlet, Julius Cæsar* and other Shakespearean plays. The *Kentucky Preceptor* now came to his attention with its essays on "Liberty," "Industry" and the like, and one on the general subject of "Slavery"; also Jefferson's First Inaugural; and the speech of Gouverneur Morris at the funeral of Alexander Hamilton. But it may reasonably be said that Lincoln derived as much benefit, if not more, from the reading of the *Revised Laws of Indiana* as from any of the single books already mentioned. This volume contained 500 pages; and it was not that it did him any good to know, if he did in fact learn, what those laws were, that he read it through and through again. Old law books of this sort were written in the style of the English treatises with their quaint but succinct phrasing; and quite likely Lincoln's power of condensation was increased by a study of these laws. From the earliest of Lincoln's spoken and written speeches there is to be observed the flavor of a traditional eloquence and simplicity which he may well have drawn from these laws, and which was so suited to the pioneer culture which surrounded him. Lincoln was about seventeen when he wrote an essay on the American Government, in which he stressed what was then

BOYHOOD AND YOUNG MANHOOD

being talked and had been talked for forty years, namely, the necessity of preserving the Constitution, and perpetuating the Union. Well was the soil prepared for the reply of Webster to Hayne, so much so that its bombast and its historical inaccuracies did not count against it in the popular mind.

Between these studies and these literary efforts, Lincoln was spending much time at the country store at Gentryville, whose proprietor took a great liking to the tall, odd youth. Here Lincoln regaled the crowd with stories and witticisms, and with political speeches, much to the amusement of Baldwin, the village blacksmith, and Dennis Hanks, the vagrant, who followed Lincoln with admiring servitude. Before the justice of the peace at Gentryville cases of drama and color and human nature were tried; and Lincoln attended these. He also wandered off to Rockport and Boonville, not so far away, where he heard issues of more moment debated in the Court of Record, where Lawyer Pitcher was a conspicuous practitioner, who, having seen Lincoln's compositions on the American Government and one on temperance, declared that the world could not beat them.

What attracted attention to Lincoln at this period, even as much as his stories, his witticisms, his speeches and his essays, was his phenomenal strength. The strong man is always the famous man all down through the poetry and the chronicles of men, from Achilles to Folker the Fiddler, and to Lincoln of Pigeon Creek, Indiana. With all his strength there is no record of Lincoln having played the bully. He had a tenderness for animals, and wrote in these youthful days a composition denouncing cruelty to dumb beasts. And once when one of the Grigsbys was being worsted in a fist fight, Lincoln intervened, threw the contestants apart and, waving a whisky bottle above his head, declared that he could whip both of them.

This is the education of Lincoln up to this time, and it is one not to be despised. It had richness and variety; it was carried on in a picturesque country of hills, and it was diversified by walks and talks and happy trips to the mill, where Lincoln took grain to be ground. Just now an educational opportunity of great influence came to him.

In April of 1828 Lincoln was hired by James Gentry to take a flatboat of produce to New Orleans. This was hard work, but it was also great adventure for a land youth like Lincoln; and when political appeal was made on the basis of Lincoln's humble work as a flatboat man, it was not enough taken into account that Lincoln was at the time but nineteen years of age and that he derived great excitement and pleasure from the experience. Up to this time he had never seen a city; and now he looked upon the wharves of the southern metropolis. He saw in the markets the products of tropical lands; and he gazed upon the ships fresh from distant ports, or making ready to depart thither. He saw colorful populations of all breeds here and there about the city: French, Spanish, Mexicans, Creoles and Indians. James Gentry's son Allen was along. The only contact that Lincoln made with slavery on this trip that has come down to us is comprised in an event that occurred not far from New Orleans, when a band of negroes armed with clubs boarded the flatboat intent on robbery. Lincoln seized a club and beat the desperadoes off. He doubtless saw the slave markets and the auction blocks, but if so he regarded them with that detachment which so marked his character. The pleasant story that he made up his mind at this time if he ever had a chance he would hit slavery a blow perhaps originated with Dennis Hanks. It has no other place in the Lincoln annals. Having seen New Orleans with its French balconies, its picturesque dwellings, its old cathedral, its old-world, narrow streets, and the majesty of the Mississippi crowded with sails Lincoln returned to Indiana in June of 1828.

Considering that Lincoln was surrounded everywhere in his youth by Jeffersonian adherents, and in Indiana by Jackson followers, and that the Hankses were all Democrats, one wonders what it was in all that that made Lincoln at an early age turn from his political nurture and become a worshipper of Henry Clay. It could not have been very profound conviction that at first thus set him apart from his people and his community; it must have been largely something of distaste for the specimens of Democracy about him, and a desire like Shelley expressed to be as different as possible from his father, that first spread through his emotions until they hardened into matters of principle. Running all through Lincoln's life was a desire to lift himself, to arrive at a higher state of association and respectability than was the portion of his youth. For to admire the Declaration and Jefferson, as he did, entailed in the circumstances an adherence to Jefferson's principles of administration, and to his Constitutional interpretations. We shall find in Lincoln's mind all through a division in his thinking, which sometimes involved him in contradictory statements, and at others in plain solecisms of argument. From the time of Washington's administration there had been the Hamiltonians who were latitudinarians, who based the right of the Federal government to charter corporations upon the implied powers of the Constitution, when the convention that framed it had expressly voted down that power. The Hamiltonians by the same sort of twisted reasoning had stood for the protective tariff, as a possible policy under the general welfare clause of the Constitution, when the instrument itself warrants only the imposition of duties for the purposes of revenue.

This strict construction on the one hand and liberal construction on the other engaged the debates regarding internal improvements and other policies. The Hamiltonians were opposed from the beginning by Jefferson, who submitted to Washington an able state paper when Hamilton brought forward his reports respecting the funding of the state debts in the Revolution, and the one on the bank and the tariff. Madison and Monroe for the most part followed in the steps of Jefferson; and Jackson was their descendant and of the full blood. In 1824 the presidential contest was between Henry Clay of Kentucky, John Quincy Adams of Massachusetts and Andrew Jackson of Tennessee; and Lincoln was fifteen years of age. Jackson carried the full five electoral votes of Indiana, and all around Lincoln was the roaring enthusiasm which all over America made the hero of New Orleans the most arresting figure of his day. When the returns were in, Jackson had carried the country by a considerable popular majority; he had 99 electoral votes in the College to Adams' 84, and to Clay's 37. As no candidate had received a majority of the votes of the College, the election was thrown into the House of Representatives, where Adams was made president. This produced great bitterness. As Henry Clay was made secretary of state by Adams, a bargain and corruption was charged by Jackson and his friends as having occurred. Jackson called Clay "the Judas of the West," and asserted that the result was due to "a combination between the Puritan and the blackleg."

Why did not Lincoln attach his fortunes to Jackson, who led one of the great popular movements which have distinguished American politics? It was natural for the East, with its commerce and its banks, its financial power, its cities of life established in wealth and luxury, to oppose Jackson. But why would a carpenter's son in Indiana, living in direst poverty, line up with the forces of privilege? Why, indeed, except to advance his own fortunes in life? Lawyers and bankers and traders and merchants were in plenty all over the land, who hoped to get drippings from the privilege of the tariff, and from the overflow of the bank. But so great was the power and the appeal of Jackson that by 1830 there were only four anti-Jackson legislatures in the Union, namely, Vermont, Massachusetts, Connecticut and Delaware. In the six years from 1830 to 1835, when Lincoln was from twenty-one to twenty-six years of age, twenty-seven states held one hundred sixty-two sessions of their legislatures, and of these, one hundred eighteen had Jackson majorities, and only forty had anti-Jackson, with four for Calhoun.

The vast popularity of Jackson with the people was phenomenal, but entirely justified on his part and creditable to them. He had said, with reference to his own measures, "I'll take the responsibility," and that utterance went like a current of fire through the hearts of the masses who rejoice when a strong man is in charge of their affairs, and on guard against their robbery. It is something requiring explanation that Lincoln, who is held up as an apostle of liberty, who himself along the way said so much of the Declaration of Independence and Jefferson, turned in his youth to the rhetorician Henry Clay and clung to him into maturity, and followed his lead essentially to the end. On the supposition that Lincoln was a man of the people who understood the business of preserving the liberties of his country, one views with wonder the failure of Lincoln to stand by the rugged warrior of the Hermitage, who, whatever his mistakes were, kept warm a rough and honest devotion to the rights of the common man, and who vetoed the bank bill because it created a monopoly, and because it would increase the distinction between the rich and the poor.

On the other hand Clay was the champion of that political system which doles favors to the strong in order to win and to keep their adherence to the government. His system offered shelter to devious schemes and corrupt enterprises. He was the founder of that political faith in America which, in the language of John Randolph, is of seven principles: five loaves and two fishes. He was the beloved son of Alexander Hamilton with his corrupt funding schemes, his superstitions concerning the advantage of a public debt, and a people taxed to make profits for enterprises that cannot stand alone. His example and his doctrines led to the creation of a party that had no platform to announce, because its principles were plunder and nothing else, and which chose as its candidates nonentities like Harrison and Taylor, log-cabin men who loved hard cider and eschewed champagne, who were rough and ready, plain and ingenuous, to lead the army of loose constructionists, of miners and sappers and looters. Thus these Whigs adopted the tricks of the pickpocket who dresses himself like a farmer in order to move through a rural crowd unidentified while he gathers purses and watches.

In 1860 who was the better candidate for the Republican Party brought together from all the lanes and by-ways and alleys and cellars of the country—Seward who was graduated from Union College, who was a New York lawyer and governor and senator, and who believed in the bank, in the tariff; or Lincoln, the rail splitter, the self-educated flatboat man, whose boyhood was spent in the wilds of Pigeon Creek, Indiana, but who at Pigeon Creek had become a convert to the bank and the tariff and had been a consistent devotee of those faiths from that time forth? Mainfestly Lincoln was the better candidate; and assuredly this is politics as human beings play the game. But let us beware of shedding tears when the name of Lincoln is linked with that of Emerson, with that of Jefferson.

In spite of anything that can be said, there is still something incongruous in the tall youth of Pigeon Creek taking up with Henry Clay and Whiggery, that deceiving appellation for the discredited Hamiltonians who were put down by Jefferson in 1800, but who were rising again in 1824 and 1830 under the pretense that Jackson's policies were Tory in character and that there was need of a Whig party to resist them.

So it was that over Indiana and Illinois walked Lincoln to Macon County in the latter state, in February of 1830, reading the *Louis-*

ville Journal as he ambled along. This contained the reply of Webster to Hayne, which had been delivered in the Senate on January 26. The Lincoln caravan on this journey consisted of two oxen, and a wagon with three women in it, and the entire household effects of the Hankses, the Johnstons and the Lincolns. Lincoln was one of five men who conducted the trek, and he was driving the oxen, with a dog following at his side. He walked and read, as was now his habit for some time, listening to the empty thunder of Webster in which there was sheet lightning, but no bolt. Thirty-one years later this speech became the inspiration and the logic-structure of Lincoln's First Inaugural. But during those thirty-one years Calhoun had driven Webster to cover and to capitulation on the propositions of the reply to Hayne; and Webster in his speech of March 7, 1850, had recanted from his position of 1830. But fate has nothing to do with such things. Lincoln's apt and plastic mind received an impression in 1830 which matured to the hard convictions that made him a war president in 1861, sternly to execute the principles which his teacher had abandoned long before.

In March of 1830 Thomas Lincoln and his family reached a spot near Decatur, Illinois, where they abode. Soon Lincoln was off to New Orleans again, for his fame as a flatboat man had come with him to Illinois. This time he was in the service of Denton Offutt of New Salem, twenty miles from Springfield, on the Sangamon River. On his return from New Orleans, and after a farewell visit to his family near Decatur, Lincoln came to New Salem to live for the next six years.

Chapter III   Lincoln at New Salem and in the Legislature

OFFUTT conceived a great liking for young Lincoln, as indeed everyone did at New Salem. When, therefore, Lincoln came to New Salem as his permanent home in July, 1831, Offutt hired him to clerk in the store. He did odd manual work at intervals at New Salem, but for the most part he was clerking, or running a store himself, or surveying, but in chief he was in politics and running for office. In less than a year Offutt's store failed, and in 1832 the Black Hawk War broke out and Lincoln gathered up a company, and was elected captain of it. His rival for the captaincy was a man who had overreached Lincoln in a contract for the handling of some logs, and the reactive sympathy for Lincoln won him the honor. He was thus beginning to have a taste of the advantage of seeming to be wronged and being humble. Lincoln had great physical strength and could do kinds of work which young men of lesser muscle cannot undertake, such as rail splitting and lifting heavy objects. But for actual days spent in labor up to this time, and all his life, he did no more than many boys of his time did, though in better walks of life than he was; nor did he do more days of labor than boys of the country and the villages over the country do at this present time. It satisfies the imagination and helps to build the myth to put Lincoln in the rôle of the rail splitter. In June of 1860 Lincoln wrote a short biography of himself to be used for the campaign of that year; and in it he thus speaks of rail splitting: "Here they (meaning himself and his father and the Hankses and Johnstons, and at Decatur) built a log cabin . . . and made sufficient rails to fence ten acres of ground. These are, or are supposed to be, the rails about which so much is being said just now, though these are far from being the first or only rails ever made by Abraham." [1] Lincoln was in various mercantile ventures in New Salem, but none prospered. Indeed some of them put him in debt which he did not discharge for years thereafter. In one of the debates with Douglas, the one at Ottawa on August 28, 1858, Lincoln denied that he ever was

[1] Lincoln's Works, Vol. I. 640.

a grocery keeper. "The Judge is wofully at fault about his early friend Lincoln being a 'grocery keeper.' I don't know as it would be a great sin, if I had been, but he is mistaken. It is true that Lincoln did work the latter part of one winter in a little still house, up at the end of a hollow." [1]

What Lincoln meant by this denial it is impossible exactly to say. For Herndon, in writing of Lincoln's mercantile venture with Berry, said: "While Lincoln at one end of the store was dispensing political information, Berry at the other was disposing of the firm's liquors, being the best customer for that article of merchandise himself." [2] And on March 6, 1833, such proceedings were had in the Commissioners Court of Sangamon County, in which New Salem was then located, that "William F. Berry in the name of Berry and Lincoln have license to keep a tavern in New Salem to continue twelve months from this date, and that they pay one dollar in addition to six dollars heretofore paid as per treasury receipt. And that they be allowed the following rates, viz: French brandy per pint 25"; and so on, fixing the rates for whisky, gin, wine, rum and other spirits; besides rates for lodging and food. It is true that Lincoln was not in partnership with Berry for many months, but that he dissolved with him because of moral scruples against the sale of drink is not a maintainable position. Beveridge, in fact, in notes relating to this subject quoted many persons and books all of which went to the point that these stores, such as the store of Berry and Lincoln was, sold tea, coffee, sugar, salt, whisky, calico, brown muslin, hats and the like; [3] and that they sold whisky by the drink. That was the custom of the time, and no turpitude attached to the transaction. The wonder remains, however, as to what Lincoln meant when he denied that he ever kept a grocery store.

When Lincoln arrived in New Salem in July of 1831, everyone was for Jackson; but in less than a year from this time Lincoln presented himself for the Illinois Legislature, and as a Whig. On March 9, 1832, he issued an address to the people of Sangamon County announcing his candidacy and stating his platform and his program. He was for internal improvements, a specifically Clay

---

[1] "Lincoln and Douglas Debates," 180. Scott, Foresman.
[2] Herndon, I, 99.
[3] Beveridge, I, 127.

proposal; but he was against the practices of usury, and he was for better advantages for the education of everyone. He favored the chance for a moderate education of the humblest members of society, in order that they might be enabled to read "the Scriptures" and other works of moral instruction; and he stood for morality, sobriety, enterprise and industry. It was probable that for one of his youth he had spoken in a manner "more presuming" than became him; but no less he had spoken as he thought.[1] And finally: "I am young and unknown to many of you. I was born and have ever remained in the most humble walks of life. I have no wealthy or popular relations or friends to recommend me." Considering that at that time men of Lincoln's then age were given to bombast in their political speeches, this first address of Lincoln must be noted as having remarkable restraint. It proceeds with a sort of impersonal flow, aside from the passages where he is seeking to enlist the feelings of the people, using therefore the art of the orator; but its plain, sensible, continuity reminds one of Cæsar's *Gallic War*, in which he told of the taking of Avaricum, as if it had been the account of a walk to the Forum. Usury was bad enough to be sure; but what were the bank and its branches doing with reference to a money monopoly? Was there nothing to be said about the tariff? Nothing about popular rights to be kept against the encroachment of implied powers? There was nothing on these subjects for Lincoln to say. His mind did not run in these channels. He was for Henry Clay.

His service in the Black Hawk War kept him from making a canvass of any moment; but the fact that he was so serving was of advantage to him. He arrived back in New Salem in time to make speeches at Pappsville and at Island Grove. He now went about dressed in a mixed jeans coat, cut clawhammer style, whose sleeves were too short, whose tail was not long enough to sit on. His trousers were of linen; his hat of straw. At Pappsville he mounted a rude platform, and began by saying: "Fellow citizens, I presume you all know who I am. I am humble Abraham Lincoln." He then went on to say that he had been solicited by many friends to become a candidate for the legislature. "My politics are short and sweet like the old woman's dance," he continued. "I am in favor of a national bank . . . and a high protective tariff. These are my

[1] Lincoln's Works, I, 3–4.

sentiments and political principles." At Island Grove the Jackson men made fun of him. But he told stories and made grimaces. The stories, according to A. Y. Ellis, who heard them, were of the bar-room order, which Ellis, from modesty and out of veneration for Lincoln, refused to report to posterity.[1] With these stories he managed to weather the Jackson opposition which confronted him as an audience. That fall Lincoln voted for Henry Clay for president; who lost Illinois by a vote of about three to one in favor of Jackson. Jackson won the country at large by a popular vote of 687,502 against Clay's vote of 530,189. In the Electoral College Jackson had 219 votes to Clay's 49. Lincoln was defeated for the legislature; but he received a flattering vote in compliment to his personal popularity. Of the entire 208 votes in his precinct, he received 205.

And now whatever he was doing, whether as surveyor, or as postmaster, which office he received because the place was so insignificant that his politics in no way mattered, he was again reading, indeed reading much of the time, while lying under the oak trees of the New Salem Hill, while lounging on the counters of the stores, while rocking the cradles of the village infants, or walking to the Rutledge Mill below the hill. As of old he disliked manual labor, and kept out of it as much as possible, but he did odd jobs at times to eke out a subsistence. His mind was all absorbed in politics; and while other men of New Salem were making money in land, as even the man John McNamar, who was betrothed to Ann Rutledge, grew very prosperous in business at New Salem, Lincoln remained poor because he did nothing. There was a good deal of his father Thomas in him; and there was much in his nature to make him seek out and associate with the fisherman, Jack Kelso, and to stand about the village stores telling stories, or to take part in the horse races, and the foot races, the wrestling matches and contests at pitching horseshoes in front of the Rutledge Tavern, though in these things he acted in the rôle of judge, rather than as a participant. He did, however, wrestle with Jack Armstrong, a much smaller man than himself, whom he had great difficulty in throwing; and he wrestled with Lorenzo D. Thompson, whom he did not throw. What he learned in wrestling undoubtedly had its influence upon his debating mind. To elude, to dodge under, to get away, to come to, to grip,

[1] Herndon, I, 95.

to get the best hold short of a foul, and even to foul, when it can be safely done, all these tactics of wrestling entered into Lincoln's forensic performances, just as athletics unquestionably have great influence on the intellectual activities.

What he learned of surveying was but little, and so he confessed in the biographical sketch of 1860, referred to. He had no aptitude for mathematics; but for grammar he showed a sufficient talent, and under the tutelage of Mentor Graham, the village school teacher, he did well, if not to the point of mastery of Kirkham's *Grammar*. But politics was the subject that fascinated him. Accordingly he was poring day by day over the *Sangamon Journal*, the *National Intelligencer*, the *Missouri Republican*, the *Louisville Journal*, and other newspapers. At New Salem he read Gibbon's *Decline and Fall of the Roman Empire*, Rollin's *Ancient History*, Burns's *Poems*, Shakespeare, Mrs. Lee Heintz's novels, one or two, a book on American military biography, Byron, something again about Washington; but as Herndon wrote that Lincoln never read any book through, the chances are that he did not go through the great volumes of Gibbon's masterful work. He did not so much as look into Scott, Sir Thomas More, Plutarch, Spenser, Bacon, Locke, Sir Thomas Browne, Bentham, Hume, Adam Smith, or Rousseau. He read no Vattell, no Burlamaqui, no *Chitty on the Law of Nations*. When he began to read Blackstone's *Commentaries* he found them exceedingly difficult; but one fancies that he took into his mental equipment a good deal of *Chitty on Pleading*, which is a treatise of great excellence for the training of the mind to handle logical issues. It is a book, indeed, full of intellectual cunning, with its rules which lay down how much should ever be stated, and no more; how much should be denied and no more; how to admit the adversary's statement of his case by demurrer and to worst him no less; how to set up matters of puis darrein continuance, and so to avoid what has happened before in the way of discomfiture, how, in a word, on the whole to make it difficult for an adversary in law, and to get on the defensive side most of the time, where, according to the rules, the adversary will have the burden of proof by being the holder of the affirmative. At New Salem Lincoln also read Volney, that book of skeptical and archaic eloquence; and Paine and Voltaire. How much of Voltaire is not known. Lincoln at this time and place was regarded as a skeptic; but to call him such then, and especially within a few years of this time, is to take a superficial view of the man. He was immersed in Hebraic-Christianity from his earliest years, which is something deeper than belonging to a church or professing a creed. He was really a Jehovah man all his life; and he early realized the advantage of using the Bible for his appeals to the people.

At New Salem Lincoln has come down to us as an affectionate friend of children, showing great tenderness for them. But, as he behaved at Gentryville, so did he continue at New Salem to stand back with bashful fears in the presence of women. In another place all that is known of him respecting his relations with women, his courtships and his marriage, will be brought together; and so for the time, though chronologically speaking his attention to Ann Rutledge belongs to his life at New Salem before the year 1835, the subject is passed.

In 1834 Lincoln again accepted the nomination for the legislature; this time, strange to say, from the Democratic Party. In this campaign he was discreetly silent about his Whig idol, Henry Clay, and in consequence of this, and because of his personal popularity, he was elected. He now held three offices at once: postmaster of New Salem, surveyor under appointment of the county surveyor, Calhoun, and member of the legislature, and he was twenty-five years old. Borrowing money to buy suitable clothes, he set off for Vandalia, the state capital.

Lincoln's career in this session of the legislature is a maze of contradiction; though in the main he held to his convictions about the United States Bank, and to his opposition to Andrew Jackson. Very early in the session, and on January 5, 1835, a resolution was offered against the Bank, commending Jackson's course in trying to overthrow it. A motion was made to lay the resolution on the table. Lincoln voted against this. Then he voted for an amendment to the resolution which declared that the Bank was a useful and expedient institution. Then he voted against the Democratic preamble to the resolution that the Bank was an evil thing and that Jackson was right in waging war upon it. Then he voted in favor of condemning the Senate for refusing to enter upon its journal Jackson's protest. Finally the resolutions were amended and Lincoln

LINCOLN AT NEW SALEM

voted for them. But, to show the state of mind of the Illinois legislature, the Bank was condemned at last by a vote of 37 to 14; Jackson's course in removing the deposits from the Bank was approved by a vote of 35 to 15; Illinois congressmen who were supporting Jackson were approved by a vote of 44 to 7. Jackson was on the whole triumphant in Illinois; but Lincoln wound his way by a strange path through all this tangled politics. Lincoln, however, heard much economic and other debate on all the phases of the United States Bank controversy. The legislature adjourned sine die February 13, 1835.

On December 7, 1835, the legislature was called by the governor into special session. At once, almost, a resolution was offered to reapportion the state. When Lincoln delivered his Cooper Institute Speech, William Cullen Bryant made an opening address. He said, among other things, that Lincoln would have won the senatorship over Douglas in 1859 but for the unjust apportionment of Illinois. This is frequently a complaint of defeated politicians. But now, in 1835, when an effort was made to create fairer districts in Illinois, Lincoln moved to lay the resolution on the table. Proposals to amend the charter of the state bank at Springfield were made. Lincoln voted to reserve to the state the right to repeal the law; he then voted to strike this out, and to give the state power to require specific reports from the bank touching its financial transactions to be made to every session of the legislature. The house voted Lincoln's striking out proposal; then Lincoln voted against an amendment for a penalty against the bank for extending time for the redemption of its notes. He was unquestionably for the bank.

At the next election for members of the legislature in Illinois, Lincoln was a candidate to succeed himself. On June 13, 1836, he issued a manifesto at New Salem responding to a request of the *Sangamon Journal* for candidates to show their hands. "I go for all sharing the privileges of the government who assist in bearing its burdens," he said. "Consequently I go for admitting all whites to the right of suffrage who pay taxes or bear arms (by no means excluding females)." [1] At this time, and for long before, negroes had voted in some of the Northern states; but Lincoln did not include negroes in this advocated enlargement of the suffrage. He went on

[1] Herndon, I, 157.

in this letter to the *Journal* to say that he was in favor of distributing the proceeds of the public lands among the several states for the building of canals and railroads, a Democratic policy; and finally he announced that if alive on the first Monday in November, 1836, he would vote for Hugh L. White. Hugh L. White gets no footnote after these years. He was one of the Whig nonentities who tried to defeat the Democratic Party in the days before the capitalistic way was learned of doing it. He had been a district attorney, a judge of the Supreme Court of Tennessee, which was his state, a state senator and a senator of the United States from 1825 to 1835. Coming from Tennessee there was symbolical and political reason for bringing him forward. If he were elected, the rebuke to Jackson's policies would be the more pat. Webster was also put forward, but for some reason Lincoln's admiration of the reply to Hayne had failed of its power to win him to Webster's candidacy. The Democratic candidate was Van Buren, who had been a secretary of state in Jackson's administration, a United States senator, and who was otherwise distinguished in political life. Much was said against Van Buren on the score of his evil astuteness, and the like, to drive from him the honest yeoman. But when the vote was counted he had 762,678 votes to the 735,651 combined votes of White, Harrison, and Webster. In the Electoral College Van Buren had 170 votes, Harrison 73, White 26 and Webster 14. Evidently something else was required in order to defeat the Democratic Party, something no doubt in the way of a great moral issue in which Jehovah could be made to take an interest. This was the election in which the young Douglas, but three years in Illinois from Vermont, carried the state for Van Buren. He also had introduced into Illinois politics the convention system for nominating candidates, which was so bitterly assailed at first by the Whigs, but was soon embraced by that irresolute and wavering body of office seekers. So it was that Lincoln and Douglas were members of the same legislative body when Lincoln was 28 and Douglas 24, and henceforth they continued to face each other in Illinois politics.

Douglas was well born. His mother was an Arnold of Rhode Island, a descendant of that Governor Arnold who was associated with Roger Williams, who was driven out of Massachusetts Bay Colony where Samuel Lincoln settled in 1637. Douglas's father was

LINCOLN AT NEW SALEM 37

a physician, whose sudden death, when Douglas was three months old, threw the mother and the boy upon their own resources. Douglas, by the marriage of an uncle, who thereby assumed other obligations, lost the chance of a promised education, with the result that the self-reliant boy trudged off fourteen miles to Middlebury, Vermont, where he learned the trade of cabinet making, at which he worked two years. He then attended for a year an academy at Brandon, Vermont, the place of his birth, and afterward finished what schooling he ever had at Canandaigua Academy, New York. Meanwhile he read law, and showed great precocity for the science, as well as for the classics. He was just twenty years old when he arrived at Jacksonville, Illinois, with thirty-seven cents in his pocket, after a severe illness on the way, at Cleveland. He found no work at Jacksonville and tramped sixteen miles to Winchester, where he picked up a job as an auctioneer's clerk. Within a week he was teaching a school. He borrowed law books from a lawyer at Winchester and read at night in Blackstone and the like. Before he was twenty-one he was admitted to the bar. When he was twenty-two he was elected district attorney for the district in which Jacksonville was located. And thus, by such rapid rises, he was in the legislature of Illinois, where Lincoln came to serve his second term. Douglas from the first was a forthright man, outspoken and courageous. Though of very small stature, he had an enormous head; and his energies were exhaustless. Where Lincoln was slow and fumbling, Douglas was swift and to the point; where Lincoln was cautious, watchful like the wrestler, uninformed and without early conviction, Douglas was bold, well versed in what he undertook to manage, and firmly grounded in the Jeffersonian faith. On scores such as this Lincoln was at a disadvantage, because he had taken Henry Clay for his exemplar, who had no fundamental principles on anything. This is enough to say of Douglas now for the purposes of contrasting the activities of him and Lincoln in the legislature.

Lincoln did much log rolling in the legislature with reference to the location of the capital at Springfield. Largely he subordinated everything to the success of this enterprise. He was also working to prosper the State Bank at Springfield; and on one occasion he crawled out of a window of the capitol and escaped so that no quorum could be counted. This was done to save the charter of the bank. Lincoln championed internal improvements by a vast omnibus bill which included provision for railroads, for canals, for dredging shallow rivers. Douglas opposed the omnibus bill, but presented a separate plan for the construction of a railroad through the whole length of Illinois. The omnibus bill referred to involved the state in frightful debt. Governor Ford, who wrote an interesting history of Illinois, declared that the whole state was bought and bribed on the matter of the removal of the capital to approve the most disastrous policy which ever crippled the energies of a growing country. Lincoln was never a financier or an economist, as indeed few of these law makers of these legislatures were. Douglas, even, finally voted for the omnibus bill, but only because his county gave him special instructions to do so. "Thus," wrote Governor Ford, "it was made to cost the state about six million dollars to remove the seat of government from Vandalia to Springfield, half which sum would have purchased all the real estate in that town at three prices." Later Lincoln was denounced by General Ewing for corruption in the management of the capital's removal. Lincoln replied with great heat; whereupon Ewing said, "Gentlemen, have you no other champion than this coarse vulgar fellow to bring into the lists against me? Do you suppose that I will condescend to break a lance with your low and obscure colleague?"

The next day after Lincoln's victory for Springfield, March 1, 1837, he was licensed to practice law. Soon he left New Salem for Springfield, there to make his future home. He served in the legislature until 1842, being elected from Springfield in 1838, and 1840. His legislative career may be done with here by saying that Illinois suffered for years on account of the improvident legislation connected with the removal of the capital and that the Springfield Bank, which Lincoln fought for with such devotion, failed in 1842. There remains to note the position that Lincoln took on slavery in the days of his career as a legislator.

It should be remembered that in 1776, when the Declaration was adopted, every one of the colonies, which by that instrument assumed sovereignty, had slavery. When the Constitution was framed in 1787 all but one of the thirteen states had slavery. New England grew rich on the slave trade; but by 1780 Massachusetts, by its constitution, abolished the system in that state. Gradually other Northern states put it away; but John Adams gave a worldly reason for this course. It was that negro slavery was not adaptable to the climate and the economic conditions of the North. New England and the other states which became free of the system took care not to lose by the change. They took their slaves South and sold them, thus preserving their fortunes while they rose to the morality of giving liberty to an oppressed people. At last the institution was confined to the Southern states where cotton raising made slavery profitable, at least according to the political thinking of the time in the South. Helper's *Impending Crisis of the South* showed a different side of the ledger but that book was not published until 1857, written by a poor white like Thomas Lincoln.

It seems clear now that slavery was doomed by economic laws, and that there was only need to let the peaceful processes of time work out the problem. But there is a dangerous kind of mind which raises moral issues where they were better kept out; and this mind, possessed of emotional states and communicating them to others by a sort of mob psychology, makes reasonable adjustments impossible by furiously urging forward, in the name of God, or morality, immediate changes. For the word "moral" is akin to the word "sacred," and has the same effects on thinking. This is another way of describing the fanatic; and by these words William Lloyd Garrison of Massachusetts was a fanatic. The Northern states were not economically affected by the institution of slavery in the South; that is, as the Southern people had to invest their money in slaves, and then had to feed and clothe and house and take care of the slaves, and even support them in their old age, there was as much expenditure in these outlays as in wages paid in the North to free labor. But if this was not true, the disadvantage of the North was a feature of trade competition which the North in other matters insisted was an inevitable consequence of business. All this being so, the matter of slavery was a moral question but one that founded itself on that false theory of social rights, like prohibition, that it is the absolute social right of every individual to compel every other individual to act in every way exactly as he ought; and that whatsoever fails in that regard violates the social right of the complaining moralist. This is a monstrous principle which justifies any interference with liberty. And thus, about the first third of the nineteenth century, a morality which flowed from the thinking of the motley dissenters who first peopled Massachusetts began to agitate what was called the temperance question, and the slavery question and later polygamy in Utah, all to the end that there might be a Christian republic in America consecrated wholly to the laws of God. It is not a question of the goodness or the badness of these things. As John Stuart Mill pointed out in his essay on "Liberty," one might be opposed to loathing to polygamy, or to intemperance, but it is tyranny to prevent people, who are harming no one else in any logical sense, from having plural wives or having drink. So it was that the South, when its nose was wrung until blood came, by the agitators concerning slavery, began to strike back; and so it was that Lincoln at the entrance of his political life was pitched into the midst of the fierce agitation which ensued and progressed till the War between the States arose. How did Lincoln first meet this question?

On January 1, 1831, Garrison founded his *Liberator* at Boston, declaring that he would be heard, he would not equivocate, and he would not retreat. Soon the country was flooded with abolition pamphlets; and abolition societies scattered over the country the vituperation and violence of Garrison, which, being everywhere disseminated, stirred up the ugliest feelings. No fire eater, so-called, of the South, when aroused by these attacks, equaled Garrison in bitter invective and in denunciation. Virginia was contemplating emancipation of her negroes to go into effect in 1832. This warfare inaugurated by Garrison changed Virginia's course. That state settled itself down to slavery in resentment of this interference with her own domestic policy. In the session of the Illinois legislature of 1837, a committee was appointed to consider the resolutions of the Southern states made in protest of Northern agitation against slavery. On this committee was a man named McClernand and another named Dan Stone, both colleagues of Lincoln.

This committee reported that they appreciated the anxiety and alarm which had been caused in the slave states by the misguided and incendiary movements of the abolitionists; that abolition activities had been and would continue to be disastrous to the interests of the slaves; that before the organization of abolition societies public opinion had been rapidly changing for the amelioration of the slave; that the slave had already been elevated in morality and intelligence far above the low estate of his father and his kindred, and that he had been lifted out of pagan darkness; that abolition societies had forged new irons for the black man, and added thereby to the rigors of slavery; that such societies had scattered firebrands of discord and disunion, and that they had excited the turbulent passions of the monster mob, whose actions were marked by every deed of atrocity; and that finally the abolitionists were clinging to doctrines which would deluge the country in blood, and rend the Union. Discussion of this report followed; and thus Lincoln, at twenty-eight years of age, had brought before him all the questions, saving perhaps the constitutional ones, which related to slavery and its abolition. Resolutions based on this report were adopted by a vote of 77 to 6, Lincoln quietly voting no. The resolutions set forth that the general assembly of Illinois disapproved of the formation of abolition societies, and of the doctrines promulgated by them; that the right of property in slaves is sacred to the slave-holding states by the Federal Constitution, and that they cannot be deprived of that right without their consent; that the General Government cannot abolish slavery in the District of Columbia against the consent of the citizens of that district without a manifest breach of good faith; and that the governor of Illinois be requested to transmit to the states of Virginia, Mississippi, New York and Connecticut copies of the report and the resolutions. Be it explained here that Connecticut and New York had taken a similar course to that of Illinois before this time, both condemning abolition societies.

Five days after the Illinois legislature had so acted, and when the removal of the capital from Vandalia to Springfield had been secured by Lincoln's colleagues, but largely by himself, Lincoln and his friend Dan Stone, already mentioned, emerged and took a more definite stand. It was March 3, 1837, that they put on the records of the legislature certain resolutions of their own. First reciting that resolutions respecting the subject of domestic slavery had passed both houses of the General Assembly, they protested against their passage, believing that the institution of slavery "is founded on both injustice and bad policy, but that the promulgation of abolition doctrines tends rather to increase its evils." In other words, slavery was an evil thing, but it was unwise to attack the evil. "They believe that the Congress of the United States has no power under the Constitution to interfere with the institution of slavery in the different states." Then how was this evil institution to be destroyed? "They believe that the Congress of the United States has the power under the Constitution to abolish slavery in the District of Columbia, but that the power ought not to be exercised unless at the request of the District." Why not? Congress was given power by the Constitution "to exercise exclusive legislation on all cases whatever" over that District; and if slavery was based upon injustice and bad policy why not stand for its abolition, whether the District requested it or not?[1] For long complaint had been made of the slave mart and the slave catcher plying their work under the very dome of the capitol of the Republic. Herndon wrote that twenty years after these Lincoln-Stone protests, when Lincoln was being charged with being an abolitionist, a careful reading of them furnished a complete refutation of the characterization, so perilous to Lincoln's ambitious progress in politics. But if he was not an abolitionist what was he but a wrestler whose tactics were cunning enough to make it difficult for an adversary to know where he stood, and where he was to be found and grappled? There is not here any of the courage which inspired Luther when he said "Here I stand." Nor of the idealism of Shelley who at twenty years of age imperiled his life to make speeches for the freedom of Ireland and in that land; nor of the intellectual integrity of Jefferson who at thirty-three years of age tried to write into the Declaration a clause against slavery; nor of Franklin's philanthropy, who in 1790 headed a petition addressed to Congress to abolish slavery in the states; nor of Emerson who left the church and went out he knew not where rather than administer the so-called Lord's Supper, against which he had arrived at conscientious scruples. All here in the Stone-Lincoln resolutions is prudent, cautious political dissembling and equivocation, as it was regarded by such radicals as Wendell Phillips, who later called Lincoln a "slave hound," all so worded that no one could by the terms of the record call Lincoln an abolitionist; while unalert moralists might be tricked into believing that Lincoln must be sound

---

[1] Herndon, I, 170. In 1860, Lincoln in an autobiographical sketch referred to these resolutions and said that they still expressed his position. Lincoln's Works, I, 642.

on the slavery matter, since he had denounced slavery as founded on injustice and bad policy. These Lincoln words meant: If the wind come my way I have set my sail for it; and if it does not come my way it is not much of a sail that I have flung forth, and not dangerously noticeable.

Of the same quality of paltering, if it be not called duplicity, were the votes of Lincoln in the legislature on other subjects. For example he presented a temperance petition from Sangamon County. On consideration of it a bill was reported regulating the granting of tavern licenses. Before the House could act, the Senate passed a bill of like import. On a roll call of the House bill, Lincoln voted no. Then the Senate bill was amended by the House where it passed by a vote of 43 to 27, Lincoln voting no. Not long after he made a temperance speech in Springfield, in which he adverted to church people in words rather critical, on account of which he lost favor. Indeed he reversed his vote frequently in the legislature; he blundered enough to have wrecked many political careers, if the balance had been sensitive with which he was dealing; but in the gross of things he went on. By 1838 he was the leader of the Whig Party in the Illinois legislature; and because of the popularity he had achieved at the new capital for the work which he had done in winning the distinction for Springfield, he took up his residence there after the adjournment of the 1837 legislature, and was hailed and fêted as one of the idols of that village, then of 1500 people. He was by now, too, the intimate friend of Ninian W. Edwards, who was in the legislature with Lincoln. Edwards was one of the aristocrats of the frontier capital, in whose brick mansion, with its conservatory, its handsomely shuttered windows, its hospitable porches, Lincoln four years hence was to take in marriage the sister of Mrs. Edwards, Mary Todd. There was also at Springfield John T. Stuart, who bore the sobriquet of "Sly Jerry," and he was one of Lincoln's friends and his first law partner. Stuart had been with Lincoln in the Black Hawk War. And now in Springfield did he ally himself with the common people? Rather did he make all the patrician alliances that were available to him, so much so that he was soon accused of belonging to the aristocracy; and on the stump he was compelled to defend himself against the ridicule of swashbucklers like Col. Dick Taylor, whom to discomfit, Lincoln pulled down his vest rudely, while Taylor was addressing the multitude, exposing to the gaping rustics Taylor's frilled shirt, and great watch seal. As Lincoln went about unkempt and badly dressed, in trousers too short, and coat too tight or too bobbed, there was nothing to expose about him except his principles; and that required something more intellectual than pulling down his vest. To all appearances he was still humble Abraham Lincoln, out of reverence for whose poverty a friend furnished him meals for nothing for several years to come; and as he slept in the law office there was no expense on that score. It was not strictly necessary therefore to thrive in the law at once. Other expenditures were kept down. He did not drink, nor use tobacco, nor play at cards. His diversion was talk at the store of his friend Speed where the men gathered, and where soon Douglas was to come; for the rest he debated with all comers, and told stories, and indulged in anonymous journalism, matters to be more fully told later.

He was licensed to practice law March 1, 1837, at about the time that he went to Springfield to live, but as his legislative career did not end until 1842 there were eight years in all in which to make a record for the good of his state, but we find Lincoln to have been an average assemblyman so far as achievement of note was concerned. He became a practiced leader in the House of his party; but he did nothing against usury, which seemed to him a worthy work of reform at the start; and what he did for education during these eight years or at any time does not measure up to the importance of Douglas's founding the Chicago University. Before going any further with his life as a lawyer and politician at Springfield, the story of his love affairs must now be told, in order to form a judgment of his mind and nature in one of the chief departments of human behavior.

Chapter IV   *Lincoln's Romantic Adventures*

A VAST literature has grown up about Ann Rutledge and Lincoln, and yet when its source is examined there is very little to be found to justify it. When a man rises to distinction it does a family proud to say that he would have married one of its members except for the accident of death, or something else; or that he wanted to marry into the family and was not found acceptable at the time, which was such a misjudgment as things have turned out. Such stories grow by the imagination that they feed upon. Industrious biographers search far and wide for old men and old women who are solicited to remember something about the woman in the case, and about the man and what he did and said. If there are letters they are printed, if any are found. Letters lead to analysis and elaboration. And so the books grow. It is poetically possible, when Lincoln was in Springfield waiting to go on to Washington to take up the great burden of the presidency, that his memory ran back to the happy days of New Salem, when on that hill grown with oaks, with the sunlit prairie beyond, with the songs of the birds about, and the winding Sangamon below, and the pastoral hills and woodlands beyond the river, that he thought of Ann Rutledge, and spoke of her to Isaac Cogsdale, an old New Salem friend who called upon him. Shadows were falling at this time about Lincoln. He had said not long before that he was not fitted to be president. Now that he was elected he may have had grave misgivings of his ability to fill the office, in view of the stormy days so evidently ahead. He was a superstitious man, as we shall see later; and he had presentiments that he would die a violent death; and his friends had fears for him and showed it too plainly in their eyes when bidding him farewell. Also youth was gone. It had fled so quickly. Now he considered himself an old man; and his youth days naturally came before him clothed in ideal lights. Under such circumstances he may have spoken to Isaac Cogsdale of Ann Rutledge. But did he say: "I have loved the name of Rutledge to this day. I have kept my mind on their movements ever since. I loved her deeply. She was a handsome girl, would have made a good, loving wife; she was natural and quite intellectual, though not highly educated. I did honestly and truly love the girl, and think often of her now"? [1] Herndon wrote that Isaac Cogsdale told him that Lincoln so spoke. Is it true? Does it sound like the Lincoln whom we have studied thus far? Granting that the memories of youth were passing through his heart during these days, and that the recollection of a woman who died in youth and whom he had daily seen about the joyous ways of New Salem village, in some mystical transmutation of spirituality affected the rhythm of his best words, yet did he so talk to Isaac Cogsdale; or shall we believe that Ann Rutledge really paid very little attention to him, being betrothed to the prosperous John McNamar, and courted by the equally affluent Samuel Hill, one of the merchants of New Salem? On this score shall we believe the written report of Henry C. Whitney, one of the lawyers of the Circuit which Lincoln rode, in which he said that Lincoln said in his presence that a certain Mrs. Hillis, a member of the Newhall Singers, itinerant performers about the country of the 1850's, was the only woman who had ever seemed to exhibit any liking for him? It should be explained that Lincoln had no relation to Mrs. Hillis, that is known, saving to run across her here and there in the offices of the country hotels in the Circuit, when she would manifest delight in seeing him again, and come forward warmly to greet him.

Did Lincoln go out of his mind when Ann Rutledge died? It is possible that he did. The spectacle of death befalling one so young, whom he had seen so much, may have overwhelmed his mind. But was it because he loved Ann Rutledge with such tender love that his mental faculties could not support the shock of her death? Did he hide away at the log cabin of Bowling Green, and there did Mrs. Green comfort him, and guide him back to normality? Bowling Green died in 1841, leaving no written record of this travail. The whole story rests on neighborhood talk, which augmented itself after Lincoln's rise to national fame. Did Lincoln shake with emotion and weep bitterly for thinking that the rain was falling on Ann's grave, as some of the traditional stories are? The best way to answer these questions is to set down all the known facts.

James Rutledge was descended from that Edward Rutledge of

[1] Herndon, II, 192.

ROMANTIC ADVENTURES 47

South Carolina who was one of the signers of the Declaration of Independence. He had come to the New Salem Hill about 1829, and in company with Rev. John Cameron had built a mill on the shore of the Sangamon River, and founded the village of New Salem on the hill just above the mill, and he had built a tavern also, where Lincoln later boarded, but not until Rutledge had given up the management of the tavern and had moved to the Concord neighborhood about seven miles north of New Salem. Ann Rutledge was the daughter of James, and was born January 17, 1813, and died August 25, 1835. There is a family Bible record of these dates. When Lincoln came to board at the Rutledge Tavern in 1833, James Rutledge with his family, all but Ann, had already moved to Concord, leaving Ann to run the Tavern. Before Lincoln arrived at New Salem in July, 1831, Ann was betrothed to John McNamar. The next summer, that is, of 1832, John McNamar went back to his boyhood home in New York, so that so far as his presence was concerned the romantic field was free for Lincoln. It may be true that McNamar did not write Ann very frequently, as the story has come down to us; and that Lincoln as postmaster of New Salem was often importuned by the anxious Ann for a letter from her affianced afar in New York. But McNamar in 1866 made a statement to Herndon in which he said that he never knew that Lincoln paid any attention to Ann, and further that Ann was not impressed with Lincoln, but rather leaned toward himself, McNamar, who had prospered in life, and after himself toward Samuel Hill, who was a prosperous merchant of New Salem. One would have to know a good deal about John McNamar before being able to let belief take hold of him fully as to the truth of these observations; but their truth is not of controlling importance. Nor is it of much matter whether Ann had light hair or red hair, blue or gray eyes, or whether she was fair of face, as she has been reported by some of the mythmakers, unless we knew what Lincoln's preferences were about these things. The writer knew as a boy, and for many years saw at intervals, both Magrady Rutledge and Jasper Rutledge, who were cousins of Ann; and today a daughter of Magrady Rutledge lives in Petersburg (two miles from the New Salem Hill). The Rutledges were always respectable and esteemed farmer people of the Concord neighborhood; but what Lincoln did to keep track of them is not preserved for history. I find no reference in all of Lincoln's works to any Rutledge except to John Rutledge, who was one of the framers from South Carolina of the Constitution; and was barely mentioned by Lincoln in the Cooper Institute address of February, 1860.

Was there an engagement to marry between Ann and Lincoln, tentative on Ann's honorable release from McNamar; or was there any sort of engagement to marry between them? James Short was one of the Concord residents; and it was he who bid in Lincoln's surveying instruments at execution sale when Lincoln was about to lose them on a judgment against him. Short was Lincoln's devoted friend in politics and otherwise. In 1844, when Lincoln was trying to be a congressman, and his own county of Sangamon had instructed for one Baker, Lincoln, in an attempt to circumvent Baker in Menard County, wrote a letter to Martin Morris of that county, who was a delegate to the Congressional Convention, in which he said: "If yourself and James Short were appointed from your county all would be safe; but whether Jim's affair of a year ago might not be in the way of his appointment is a question. . . . I know him to be as honorable a man as there is in the world. Show this letter to Short but to no one else, unless it be to a very particular friend, who you know will not speak of it." [1] Parenthetically, Lincoln was at the time of the writing of this letter a delegate to the convention from Sangamon County, instructed for Baker; yet he was trying to undermine the chosen candidate of Sangamon County; and that was to be done by enlisting James Short, "as honorable a man as there is in the world." So much then for Short's standing; and what did he say about Lincoln and Ann Rutledge? It was that Lincoln frequently visited him at his Concord home, which was a half mile from the Rutledge home there; and that he never knew of any love making between Ann and Lincoln. That is, if Lincoln ever used the Short home as a stopping place from which to walk one-half mile in order to pay court to Ann Rutledge, he knew nothing about it. It is fair to say that Lincoln never courted Ann Rutledge when visiting the home of James Short, and probably at no time.

No letter has been found that Lincoln wrote Ann Rutledge, and none that she wrote him. As late as 1929 the *Atlantic Monthly* had

[1] Lincoln's Works, I, 81.

palmed off upon it some love letters which were pretended to have been written by Ann to Lincoln. But it was soon shown that they were spurious and obviously so, and the magazine had to retreat with the best grace that it could command under the embarrassing circumstances. Yet if there was an engagement between Lincoln and Ann Rutledge, why did he not write her letters in the winter of 1835, when he was absent from New Salem in attendance upon the Illinois Legislature at Vandalia more than a hundred miles distant from New Salem? And why did she not write him there? Lovers in separation do not so act. According to one story, when Ann was dying, in August of 1835, she sent for her brother David and for Lincoln, who went to her. Some sort of a solemn and tender parting is said to have occurred at that time; but Lincoln told no one what it was. But when she was dead she was buried in a lonely country graveyard, and Lincoln did not attend the funeral, nor ever visit her grave, nor ever give her a memorial stone. A rude small stone with her name on it was all that Ann Rutledge ever had at her grave until 1921 when a large square granite block was erected to her memory in Oakland Cemetery at Petersburg by descendants of the Old Settlers of Menard County, her remains having been removed from the country burying ground in 1890. But there is much more to come touching the fact that Lincoln had no lasting love, if any love, for Ann Rutledge.

In 1833 Lincoln was boarding at the Rutledge Tavern, in charge of Ann, or but recently in charge of Ann. There lived then in New Salem Mrs. Bennett Abell who had a sister in Kentucky named Mary Owens, and both were cousins of Mentor Graham, the New Salem schoolmaster, under whom Lincoln studied grammar and surveying. In the summer of 1833 Mary Owens came to New Salem from Kentucky to visit her sister Mrs. Abell; and Lincoln frequently called on her at the Abell cabin. There had been some trifling talk on the part of Mrs. Abell that her sister was coming to New Salem, and that she would come if Lincoln would take her for a wife. There is evidence that Lincoln took this badinage seriously, but, whether so or not, he was soon involved in a sort of romantic adventure with Mary Owens. There is a picture of Mary Owens preserved, and she is shown in it to have been more than personable. At the time of her visit to New Salem she was an intellectual, well-educated woman of twenty-five years, of a handsome face showing character; and she was born of an excellent family, of means. Later, in 1841, she married Jesse Vineyard, and to the last spoke disparagingly of Lincoln, particularly with reference to his manners and his political career, something later to be more fully noticed. What happened between Lincoln and Mary Owens is capable of being shown by Lincoln's own letters; first saying that after Mary Owens' visit to New Salem in 1833 she returned thither in 1836, when she was twenty-eight years of age. It was in the fall of the year; and on an election day that Lincoln met her about the ways of the village. We shall have the history of the romance later from a letter written by Lincoln to Mrs. O. H. Browning. But first there is Lincoln's letter of December 13, 1836, when Ann Rutledge had been dead one year and four months.

He commenced this letter "Mary," and it was sent to New Salem. He wrote that he had been sick, and that he was experiencing mortification in "looking in the post office for your letter, and not finding it. You see I am mad about that old letter yet. I don't like very well to risk you again. I'll try you once more anyhow." After giving what news there was at the capital about internal improvements, prospective canals and the like, he continued: "I really cannot endure the thought of staying here ten weeks. Write back as soon as you get this, and say, if possible, something that will please me, for really I have not been pleased since I left you." He signed the letter, "Your friend, Lincoln." [1] The next letter of Lincoln to Mary Owens is dated Springfield, May 7, 1837. He began it by saying that he had written two letters to send her before this one, but both displeased him and so he tore them up. "The first I thought was not serious enough, and the second was on the other extreme. I shall send this, turn out as it may. This thing of living in Springfield is rather a dull business, after all; at least it is so with me. I am quite as lonesome here as I ever was anywhere in my life. I have been spoken to by but one woman since I have been here, and should not have been by her if she could have avoided it. I've never been to church yet, and probably shall not be soon. I stay away because I am conscious I should not know how to behave myself. . . . I am often thinking about what we said about your coming to live at

[1] Lincoln's Works, I, 8.

Springfield. I am afraid you would not be satisfied. There is a great deal of flourishing about in carriages here, which would be your doom to see without sharing it. You would have to be poor without the means of hiding your poverty. Do you believe you could bear that patiently? Whatever woman may cast her lot with mine, should any ever do so, it is my intention to do all in my power to make her happy and contented; and there is nothing that I can imagine that would make me more unhappy than to fail in the effort." If these words be contrasted with what Lincoln wrote in history of the whole affair, it will be seen that they were offensively presuming; because, according to his own version, Mary Owens took no real stock in him at any time. And in this letter he added here: "what you have said to me may have been in the way of a jest, or I may have misunderstood it. If so then let it be forgotten; if otherwise, I much wish you would think seriously before you decide. What I have said I will most positively abide by, provided you wish it. My opinion is that you had better not do it. You have not been accustomed to hardship, and it may be more severe than you now imagine. I know you are capable of thinking correctly on any subject, and if you deliberate maturely upon this before you decide, then I am willing to abide by your decision. . . . You must write me a good long letter after you get this. You have nothing else to do. Tell your sister I don't want to hear any more about selling out and moving. That gives me the 'hypo' whenever I think of it. Yours, etc., Lincoln." [1]

The next and last letter of Lincoln to Mary Owens is like the two just quoted from, without a particle of passion, without a single tenderness. It was not memory of Ann Rutledge that stayed his hand from terms of endearment, for, with or without words of love sent to Mary Owens, he was unquestionably seeking a marriage with her. This last letter is dated Springfield, August 17, 1837. The tone is slightly changed from the first in the address. It begins, "Friend Mary." "You will no doubt think it rather strange that I should write you a letter on the same day on which we parted, and I can only account for it by supposing that seeing you lately makes me think of you more than usual. You must know that I cannot see or think of you with entire indifference; and yet it may be that you

[1] Lincoln's Works, I, 15–16.

are mistaken in regard to what my real feelings toward you are. If I knew you were not I should not trouble you with this letter. Perhaps any other man would know enough without further information; but I consider it my peculiar right to plead ignorance, and your bounden duty to allow the plea." This was *Chitty on Pleading* applied to romantic correspondence. "I want in all cases to do right, and particularly so in all cases with women. I want at this particular time, more than anything else, to do right with you; and if I knew it would be doing right, as I rather suspect it would, to let you alone, I would do it. And for the purpose of making the matter as plain as possible, I now say that you can now drop the subject, dismiss your thoughts (if you ever had any) from me forever, and leave this letter unanswered." Considering that there was never any bond between them, sensible Mary Owens must have thought that Lincoln was cracked to write her such presumptuous stuff as this, in which he put himself in the rôle of a just man who would not further urge her into a doubtful alliance, if she wished him to desist his attentions to her. She was told that she could leave this letter unanswered "without calling forth one accusing murmur from me. And I will even go further and say that if it will add anything to your comfort or peace of mind to do so, it is my sincere wish that you should. Do not understand by this that I wish to cut your acquaintance. I mean no such thing. What I wish is that our further acquaintance shall depend upon yourself. . . . Nothing would make me more miserable than to believe you miserable—nothing more happy than to know you were so. If it suits you best not to answer this, farewell. A long life and a merry one attend you. But if you conclude to write back speak as plainly as I do. My respects to your sister. Your friend, Lincoln." [1]

So wrote the well-seasoned Illinois legislator to the Kentucky woman Mary Owens, using the feints of the wrestler and the skill of *Chitty on Pleading* to get the right hold on the lady; and in this correspondence he already shows the disposition to place himself on a high moral ground as a matter of good tactics. One cannot say from these letters what Mary Owens' actual attitude toward Lincoln was. If all was lost but these letters, it might be inferred that Lincoln had engaged himself to her, that he was experiencing doubt about

[1] Lincoln's Works, I, 16–17.

the wisdom of going on to marriage; but that he would act in every way in honor and give her the opportunity to decide what to do as she might please. But it happens that Lincoln wrote Mrs. O. H. Browning, the wife of his political friend, with the result that we have the whole story from Lincoln's pen. The letter to Mrs. Browning is dated Springfield, April 1, 1838. He begins it "Dear Madam." He will not apologize for being egotistical, but he will make the history of his life since he saw Mrs. Browning the subject of his letter; and to make that intelligible he will have to go back to the year 1836. He then recounted that in the autumn of 1836 a married lady of his acquaintance, and a great friend, was about to pay a visit to her father in Kentucky, and proposed that on her return she would bring a sister of hers on condition that he would engage to marry her. "I, of course accepted the proposal, for you know I could not have done otherwise had I really been averse to it; but privately, between you and me I was most confoundedly well pleased with the project. I had seen the said sister some three years before, thought her intelligent and agreeable and saw no good objection to plodding life through hand in hand with her." So, he proceeded to write, the lady took the journey to Kentucky and brought the sister back with her to New Salem, "sure enough." "This astonished me not a little, for it appeared to me that her coming so readily showed that she was a trifle too willing; but on reflection it occurred to me that she might have been prevailed on by her married sister to come without anything concerning me ever having been mentioned to her." Had she not come to New Salem three years before without knowing that Lincoln was in existence; and had not Lincoln then called on her repeatedly of his own interest and will? But he was willing to waive her willingness to hurry back to New Salem and marry him—let it go. So he was thinking when she arrived at New Salem. "In a few days we had an interview, and although I had seen her before, she did not look as my imagination had pictured her. I knew she was oversize, but she now appeared a fair match for Falstaff. I knew she was called an 'old maid,' and I felt no doubt of the truth of at least half of the appellation"—old but not a maid, perhaps. "But now as I beheld her I could not for my life avoid thinking of my mother; and this not from withered features—for her skin was too full of fat to permit of its contracting into wrinkles

—but from her want of teeth, weather-beaten appearance in general, and from a kind of notion that ran in my head that nothing could have commenced at the size of infancy and reached her present bulk in less than thirty-five or forty years; and in short I was not at all pleased with her. But what could I do? I had told her sister that I would take her for better or for worse, and I made a point of honor and conscience in all things to stick to my word, especially if others had been induced to act on it, which in this case I had no doubt they had, for I was now fairly convinced that no other man on earth would have her, and hence they were bent on holding me to my bargain." Let it be observed here that Lincoln at this time as a judge of wrestling, racing and sport at New Salem, and in the relation of lawyer and client, very largely at all times deserved to be called "Honest Abe"; but as a member of the Illinois legislature, and in his relations with Mary Owens, the designation is of more than doubtful accuracy. " 'Well,' thought I, 'I have said it, and be the consequences what they may, it shall not be my fault if I fail to do it.' At once I determined to consider her my wife, and this done, all my powers of discovery were put to work in search of perfections in her which might be fairly set off against her defects. I tried to imagine her handsome, which but for her unfortunate corpulency was actually true. I also tried to convince myself that the mind was much more to be valued than the person, and in this she was not inferior, as I could discover, to any with whom I had been acquainted." Lincoln then referred to his departure for Vandalia from where the letters already quoted from were written to Mary Owens; adding that he there had letters from her. Meanwhile, though he was as fixed in his resolve to do the right thing as the "surge repelling rock" he was continually repenting the rashness which had involved him in the bond. "Through life I have been in no bondage, either real or imaginary, from the thralldom of which I so much desired to be free." After he returned to New Salem he saw nothing in the woman to win him to her, and so he was devising means, "how I might procrastinate the evil day for a time, which I really dreaded as much, perhaps more than an Irishman does a halter." Truly indecision and delay and doubt followed Lincoln all the days of his life, in peace and in war.

But now he was writing Mrs. Browning that he was out of the "scrape." "After I had delayed the matter as long as I thought I could in honor do (which by the way had brought me around into the last fall) I concluded I might as well bring it to a consummation without further delay, and so I mustered my resolution and made the proposal direct." So now we have it from Lincoln himself that when he wrote Mary Owens the patronizing and presumptuous letter of May 7, 1837, he had not proposed marriage to her, there was nothing between them requiring the observance of good faith, there was no word from which to release her, there was no point of honor at stake for scrupulous regard on his part, which he was so carefully protesting. And what now? In this Lincoln letter to Mrs. Browning he related that when he did propose to Mary Owens she promptly rejected him. "Shocking to relate, she answered No," are his very words. But this was not enough. "At first I supposed she did it through an affection of modesty, which I thought but ill became her under the peculiar circumstances of her case; but on my renewal of the charge I found she repelled it with greater firmness than before. I tried it again and again, but with the same success, or rather with the same want of success. I was finally forced to give it up, at which I found myself mortified beyond endurance. I was mortified, it seemed to me, in a hundred different ways. My vanity was deeply wounded by the reflection that I had so long been too stupid to discover her intentions, and at the same time never doubting that I understood them perfectly; and also that she, whom I had taught myself to believe nobody else would have, had actually rejected me with all my fancied greatness." Humble Abraham Lincoln! "And to cap the whole I then for the first time began to suspect that I was really a little in love with her. . . . I most emphatically in this instance made a fool of myself. I have come now to the conclusion never again to think of marrying, and for this reason—I can never be satisfied with anyone who would be blockhead enough to have me." [1] In this letter we have an explanation, a key to the unlocking of the secret of Lincoln's melancholy: it was not that he was grieving for the injustices of the world, for man's inhumanity to man, but because he could not endure defeat, he could not stand the pangs of obscurity

[1] Lincoln's Works, Vol. I, 17, 18, 19.

and rejection; and these feelings were made the more bitter by the envy that makes inequity of honors bestowed on others and not on one's self.

There is much in this letter to throw light upon Lincoln's character, and it is not a favorable light. Lamon inserted the letter in his biography of Lincoln; and Herndon put it in his, which was published by 1888, copying what Lamon had written in comment upon it. Lamon was friendly enough to Lincoln's memory; indeed he expressed the wish that the conscience of a biographer could be reconciled with its omission, its complete loss from the Lincoln annals, which shows how idealism and idealization may possibly play their part in drawing the portraits of men whom destiny has selected for fair report. But Lamon did not stay his hand, having inserted the letter in his book. He called its humor coarse, its exaggeration untruth in caricaturing the person of a woman whom Lincoln pursued to marry, and who, instead of being toothless and wrinkled, was young and handsome. He wrote of Lincoln's indelicacy, his unchivalrous satire which lent themselves to detraction and mockery of a late inamorata, and expressed to another woman. Herndon passed the matter off, after quoting Lamon's reproof, by saying that Lincoln was not gifted with a ready perception of the propriety of things in all cases; and that nothing with Lincoln was intuitive.[1] But in fact the letter is thoroughly dishonest in its tangled inconsistencies. He was a little in love with her, but not quite in love with her, and yet enough in love with her to pursue her and to incur her rejection of him over and over again. She was fair enough to view until she rejected him; and then he would have his correspondent believe that he was disillusioned when he first met her after her return to New Salem in 1836. He would make it out that the whole matter began in a jest, which the woman's sister took too seriously; but that when that happened there was nothing for him to do but to stand up morally and go through with it. He was a man of his word! Mary Owens was too willing when not in fact, not really sought; but then she was firm in her denial of him when he pressed his suit with all the will that he could command to win her. "There is a politeness of the heart," said Goethe, "and it is allied to love. It produces the most agreeable politeness of outward demeanor."

[1] Herndon, I, 148.

Lincoln had neither love nor anything allied to love in his heart for Mary Owens. He had arrived at a time of life when to be married was one of the human things to do; and Mary Owens had enough of worldly place and family to make him regard her as desirable. In his matter of fact way, animated by his realistic nature, he set out to marry Mary Owens and when she would not have him he was enraged and he then proceeded to degrade her by a vulgarity of words which were as well untrue. The letter proves the truth of what Mary Todd Lincoln said of Lincoln, namely, that he could not penetrate into the motives and thoughts of people. He was in these particulars "stupid" to use his own expression. He was blinded moreover to what Mary Owens' feelings were by an egotism which could not conceive that she did not see his greatness as he himself fancied it to be; and thus he was unprepared for the valuation which she put upon him when forced to decide what she would do with him. Now that he was a well-known member of the Illinois legislature, and a lawyer of the state capital, he was like men sometimes are who imagine that honorable ladies are languishing for them. This letter does not fit in with that portrait of Lincoln which makes him the humble, honest, ingenuous, kindly, truthful man of the soil—our first American of new fresh earth!

But on Mary Owens' part what was there in Lincoln to make her want to marry him? He was most certainly not handsome to behold, nor graceful, nor gallant, nor charming, nor devoted, nor gifted with those winning arts which come easily to those who are in love. He was not prosperous but incredibly poor; he was not started in life; he was the flatboat man who had but a few years before landed by chance at New Salem. Why would Mary Owens journey from Kentucky in a kind of mad fascination in order to take him up on a casual word spoken to Mrs. Abell? These questions can be partly answered by reading what Mary Owens wrote about the affair in 1866, to Herndon, who gathered most of the materials and thus laid the foundation for all future appraisals of Lincoln.

Mary Owens, or Mrs. Jesse Vineyard as she was in 1866, did not want at first to comply with Herndon's request for information of the New Salem days of twenty-nine years before. Perhaps she was suspicious of Herndon's intentions in reviving those old days, knowing no doubt what Herndon's relations had been to Lincoln.

In fact Herndon had relatives who had run stores at New Salem, and Mary Owens may have known them. She may have seen Herndon himself as a boy running about the river's shore and over the New Salem Hill. But all life had changed with her. She had two sons who had served in the Confederate army, and there is a tone in her first letter to Herndon which is dated Weston, Mo., May 1, 1866, from which one might infer that she shared the not uncommon hatred of Lincoln for inaugurating and prosecuting the War. "My associations with your lamented friend," she phrased it; not with our beloved and martyred president. "My associations with your lamented friend were in Menard County while visiting a sister who then resided near Petersburg." Petersburg was the town which succeeded to the place that New Salem was making for itself, when about 1837 New Salem was beginning to be abandoned; and when Menard County was formed by slicing off the northern portion of Sangamon County, leaving the New Salem Hill in the former, two miles away. Petersburg became the county seat, and by 1866 was a town of 1500 people or so and of considerable business enterprise. Hence Mary Owens' identification of the place, where she knew Lincoln, as being near Petersburg. "After quite a struggle with my feelings I have at last decided to send you the letters in my possession written by Mr. Lincoln, believing that you are a gentleman of honor and will faithfully abide by all you have said." She accordingly sent some of Lincoln's letters to Herndon; but they were not sufficiently revealing. So Herndon wrote to her for more information. On May 22, 1866, Mary Owens Vineyard wrote Herndon again, jesting good-naturedly about the manner in which he catechized her. "You say you have heard why our acquaintance terminated as it did. I too have heard the same bit of gossip; but I never used the remarks which Dame Rumor says I did to Mr. Lincoln. I think I did on one occasion say to my sister, who was very anxious for us to be married, that I thought Mr. Lincoln was deficient in those little links which make up the chain of a woman's happiness—at least it was so in my case. Not that I believed that it proceeded from a lack of goodness of heart; but his training had been different from mine; hence there was not that congeniality which would otherwise have existed. From his own showing you perceive that his heart and hand were at my disposal; and I suppose that my feelings were not sufficiently enlisted to have the matter consummated. About the beginning of the year 1838 I left Illinois, at which time our acquaintance and correspondence ceased, without ever again being renewed. My father, who resided in Green County, Kentucky, was a gentleman of considerable means; and I am persuaded that few persons placed a higher estimate on education than he did." [1]

Again she wrote Herndon on July 22, 1866. In this letter she mentioned an occasion when Lincoln, who was her escort going to "Uncle Billy Green's," let her get across a brook the best way she could, offering her no assistance. With this she contrasted what Lincoln had told her about seeing a hog mired down, and going to its rescue, though he was dressed up at the time. "In many things he was sensitive to a fault,"—some of which were helping mired hogs, so Mary Owens still thought after nearly thirty years. She went on: "In many things we saw eye to eye, though since then we differed as widely as the South is from the North." "The last message I ever received from him was about a year after we parted in Illinois. Mrs. Abell visited Kentucky, and he said to her in Springfield, 'Tell your sister that I think she was a great fool because she did not stay here and marry me.' Characteristic of the man!"

The secret is now out. Lincoln's presumptuous letters, his egotistical manner with her killed any chances he ever had with her. But on her part she had had advantages in life, for in those days there were seminaries and colleges about everywhere in the West much beyond what is supposed, by those who have not looked into the matter, to have existed then. And she was a well-educated woman for her day. Her father was a man of wealth; and it is possible that the ambitious Lincoln conceived that her father's means would be a help to his ambition. It is possible and probable too. The inconsistency of character shown by Lincoln in his relations with Mary Owens, the cautious advancing, the covering up, the attempting to get her to declare herself, and to do it first, the change about, the delaying, all of these things are evident in everything of his whole

[1] Herndon, I, 139.

career; and naturally so because his character remained the same and continued to react to circumstances according to its inherent nature.

Within ten years of the time that Lincoln was walking from Indiana to Illinois driving the oxen, and reading Webster's reply to Hayne, he had been three times a member of the Illinois legislature, he had become a lawyer, he had formed aristocratic friendships like that with Ninian W. Edwards, he had, by standing for the high protective tariff, by his championship of the United States Bank, by his services to the State Bank at Springfield, by his labors for internal improvements, which involved centralization and the disbursement of vast public moneys—by all these things he had made himself admired and looked up to by the Whigs of Sangamon County who were growing very numerous, and by the higher classes of the frontier capital. In a word he had made great strides; and at twenty-eight years of age he was well started; and few men in a city or anywhere in the country were better circumstanced than he —all saving the matter of money. When a man is ambitious in a field in which there is no money for a living, he must marry it. If he does not do this he must neglect his ambition and make it for himself in some other field. Lawyers make money through politics; but Lincoln could not do this. He did not know how. He was not too honest, he simply lacked the skill by which money making in the law is made to follow political activity and the friends that brings. He learned everything slowly. If he had lived through the presidency and come to Chicago to practice law, he might have made much money on the prestige of having been president; even as his son Robert became a millionaire in the law and in corporation dealings through the chances which came to him as the son of Lincoln. But Lincoln's standing, from having been in the legislature, and later from having served in Congress, did him little good in his advancement as a lawyer on the score of money. He had been practicing law for nearly a quarter of a century when he was elected president, and yet his total accumulation were a house in Springfield worth about $1500, and some land in Iowa which the government had given him for his services in the Black Hawk War; and his yearly income from the law was then not above $3000. But all this worked to his advantage. He had been a rail splitter, and he was a poor man, and he was "Honest Old Abe." There was nothing lacking to the hands of the mythmakers to draw the portrait of him that has come down to the present day.

Herndon wrote: "Conscious, therefore, of his humble rank in the social scale, how natural that he should seek by marriage in an influential family to establish strong connections, and at the same time foster his political fortunes." [1] It may have been natural for Lincoln; it was not natural for Andrew Jackson, who married his landlady's daughter; nor is it natural for any man who consults his heart and his taste before he allows ambition for money or social position to dictate his course in a matter so delicate, but of such profound effect upon all the days of one's life. Lincoln paid a thousand fold in suffering and in torture of mind, in humiliation of soul and in bitter self-reproach for any benefit that he ever derived from his marriage with Mary Todd.

In Springfield when Lincoln came there to live there were gaiety and social functions; there were literary interests and debating clubs. At the High School, Greek, Latin, French and Spanish were taught. True the streets in summer fogged with dust; in winter the wagons mired in front of the capitol; hogs wandered about the streets; at night the town was in darkness due to the lack of street lamps; and the night air was redolent of the effluvia of the ubiquitous privy. But it was the capital; and when Lincoln rode into it from New Salem on a borrowed horse, woe struck and poverty struck, he felt depressed, and shamed by the life about him which was superior to what his purse could afford him. He went to Joshua F. Speed, who was running a store there, from whom he obtained a room without rent, and thus his life began in the capital. We shall hear much more of this Joshua F. Speed. He was a man of some worth, handsome to look at, and capable of being a good friend. Then there was the mansion of Ninian W. Edwards, already referred to; and soon Mary Todd was to come to it from Lexington, Kentucky, and the threads of Lincoln's fate were to be badly woven. She arrived for the first time in 1837, remaining for three months on a visit to her sister Mrs. Edwards. She returned in 1839 and stayed for good.

Mary Todd was nine years younger than Lincoln, and well de-

[1] Herndon, Vol. I, 191.

scended from Revolutionary stock. She had one great-uncle who was a governor of Michigan; another who was secretary of the navy in the administration of President Tyler; another who was a governor of Pennsylvania. Her father, Robert S. Todd, had served in both houses of the Kentucky legislature; he had been for twenty years the president of the bank of Lexington, Kentucky; he was well to do and a slave owner. The cause of her coming to live with Mrs. Edwards in 1839 was a stepmother with whom she could not get along. For Mary Todd herself was of a quick temper, and of a strong and impulsive nature. She had a sharp tongue and she wrote with a certain wit and satiric force. Herndon, who knew her, described her as she appeared in 1839 at twenty-one years of age, as of the average height for women, weighing about one hundred thirty pounds, compactly built, with rounded face, dark brown hair, and bluish gray eyes. "In her bearing she was proud, but handsome and vivacious." [1] She had been well educated for the times, and spoke French with some fluency. "Ordinarily she was affable, and even charming in her manners; but when offended or antagonized, her agreeable qualities disappeared beneath a wave of stinging satire or sarcastic bitterness, and her entire better nature was submerged. In her figure and physical proportions, in education, bearing, temperament, history—in everything she was the exact reverse of Lincoln." [2] Being this when she was twenty-one, what was she to become as the wife of the unkempt and disorderly product of Pigeon Creek?

Indeed these two persons were not made for each other. She was quick, he was slow; she was passionate, he was cold; she was intuitive, he was reason; she had a taste for well-bred living, he had none; she was impulsive, he was deliberate. Yet with all this confessed, there may have been biological urges to the union arising out of these disparities, at least that may have been the case on her part. One cannot escape the conclusion that Lincoln did not want to marry her. He vacillated as he did with Mary Owens; but it was worse finally than vacillation: he ran away to avoid marrying her. If there was no biological urge on Mary Todd's part that made her marry Lincoln, then it was ambition, because she was intuitive

[1] Herndon, I, 194.
[2] Id., 194.

enough to divine that the man who, before twenty-eight years of age, from such unpromising origins had risen to a political position and to a lawyership, and to a certain notability, would go farther.

He might go to Congress, or to the Senate, or become a judge. But it must be remembered that Mary Todd was not too happily circumstanced at her sister's house. There was dependence in it, and the lack of a life being lived and made. Above all she was not rushed to death by suitors. There has been an attempt to show that the young and brilliant Douglas contested with Lincoln for her hand; but that is now known to be one of the Lincoln myths. Douglas was too worldly wise, too discerning of character to want to ally himself with the shrewish young lady from Lexington, Kentucky. His subsequent marriages to brilliant and beautiful women proved what his taste was and what he could win. Still Mary Todd at once became one of the belles of Springfield, the village capital, and she was a figure in all the social events from the start of her residence there. Soon Joshua F. Speed took Lincoln to call on her.

Here now is love psychology. Speed was contemplating marriage at this time, and he was passing through periods of exaltation and depression, of confidence and doubt. The masculine principle, even in the rudest heart, senses the love death ahead; and this was what terrified Speed, it all seems clear enough. Soon we shall find Lincoln in the rôle of the confidential friend, who explained to the bewildered male in the toils what the woman meant by this or the other word or glance, or sudden coldness, or penitent yielding; and then we shall find Speed sustaining the wavering interest of Lincoln, though at the last Lincoln plunged into matrimony, evidently persuaded by the already married Speed that all was well with the state and that he need not fear.

Lincoln, being introduced by Speed to Mary Todd, began to make frequent calls upon her. Soon he was captivated by her facility in conversation, her aptitude in French. He would sit by her side and listen to her as if in a trance, saying scarcely a word. So Mrs. Edwards described the courtship. To Mrs. Edwards, Lincoln seemed "attached" to Mary, yet she soon began to doubt that the two would be congenial. She expressed this opinion to Mary, saying that Mary and Lincoln were not intended for each other.[1] Herndon wrote that

[1] Herndon, I, 196.

all was going smoothly, however, until Douglas came along as a rival for Mary's hand. He even went so far as to quote the word of a woman who lived with the Lincolns for two years after they were married, who reported Mrs. Lincoln as saying that "she loved Douglas, and but for her promise to marry Lincoln would have accepted him." [1] At once it occurs to one to ask why she did not marry Douglas when Lincoln ran away from her; but there are many facts to overcome the claim of the Douglas suitorship. Beveridge completely disposed of this myth, in an analysis of Mrs. Edwards' contradictory statements. It fitted in well with the fables growing up around the martyred president to have Mary Todd reject Douglas on account of his shocking morals, his drinking bouts and the like, and to marry the upright temperance lecturer, the honest and steady Lincoln. But it is true that Mary Todd flirted outrageously with Douglas to draw on her slow and awkward catch, Lincoln; and Lincoln, who hated Douglas from the first days of 1836, had risen to hate him the more for this coquetry of his beloved. Lincoln was driven half mad when Mary paraded the streets of Springfield with Douglas, laughing and talking; and he was compelled to pass them by and witness their delight. Finally Lincoln could endure no more. By this time there seems to have been an engagement to marry between Mary and Lincoln. But at any rate, according to Speed, Lincoln came into the store one evening wrapped in the deepest gloom. He had written a letter to Mary Todd which he wanted to show Speed and to get his advice upon it. "The letter," said Speed, "made a plain statement of his feelings, telling her that he had thought the matter over calmly and with great deliberation, and now felt that he did not love her sufficiently to warrant her in marrying him. This letter he desired me to deliver. Upon my declining to do so he threatened to entrust it to some other person's hand." [2] Speed counseled Lincoln to have the courage of manhood, and to go to see Mary and tell her that he did not love her and would not go on. So Lincoln buttoned up his coat and started out in the darkness for the Edwards mansion, with Speed waiting for him to return, and report what had happened. Finally Lincoln came back; it was after eleven o'clock. Lincoln brought the

[1] Herndon, I, 197.
[2] Herndon, I, 198.

word that, when he told Mary that he did not love her, she burst into tears, wrung her hands in agony, and called him a deceiver, adding that the deceiver might be himself deceived. It was too much for Lincoln. He caught Mary in his arms. "I found the tears trickling down my own cheeks," Lincoln told Speed. And that was the way the engagement was not broken—if there was one then. Often have such scenes been enacted over the world from the beginning of time.

But Lincoln did not find any peace in this decision. He sank into melancholy. The wedding was finally fixed to take place on January 1, 1841, at the Edwards mansion, and great preparations were made for the event. The rooms were decorated, the cakes baked. By the time the hour arrived Mary Todd was dressed in her bridal gown and veil, with flowers in her hair, waiting for Lincoln. But he did not come. An hour slipped by, and messengers were sent forth into the town to find him. They returned with the word that he could not be found. Finally Mary Todd gave up and went weeping to her room. The guests departed. The lights in the mansion were blown out, and all was in darkness. Lincoln's mind was in darkness too. He had gone mad under the strain.

Three weeks after this night, January 23, 1841, Lincoln wrote to his law partner Stuart, saying, "Yours of the 3d instant is received, and I proceed to answer it as well as I can, though from the deplorable state of my mind at this time, I fear I shall give you but little satisfaction." He then proceeded to write of politics and business. The letter concluded with these words: "I am now the most miserable man living. If what I feel were distributed to the whole human family there would not be one cheerful face on the earth. Whether I shall ever be better, I cannot tell; I awfully forebode I shall not. To remain as I am is impossible; I must die or be better, it appears to me."[1] At the time of this letter he was trying to attend to his duties in the legislature; but he could do nothing. He rarely attended its sessions. His friend Ninian W. Edwards made a statement on September 22, 1866, in which he said that "Lincoln went as crazy as a loon," at this time. The shame that he had caused Mary Todd tortured him to madness; and to cure himself he doubtless yielded and married her two years later. On her part there was

[1] Lincoln's Works, 44–45.

nothing to do better to wipe away her humiliation than to marry him. But wounds had been inflicted which never healed; nor did Lincoln's forebodings as to the fitness of the match prove to be unfounded, but rather underestimated.

What was the exact nature of Lincoln's mental malady? Doctors do not agree about it, nor are they clear, even with all the known facts before them for diagnosis. Lincoln wrote to a distant physician at the time for medical aid; but the physician would not prescribe for him without seeing him. Some doctors call Lincoln's state one of mere depression due to dwelling upon the suffering of Mary Todd whom he rightly believed he had so deeply wronged. All have spoken of Lincoln as a sensitive man, even Mary Owens remarked him in that particular. One doctor said that Lincoln's emotional reactions were strong rather than complicated, simple rather than intricate; and as Lincoln had no fantasies at the time of this trouble, he believed Lincoln not to be in the strict sense insane. But in such matters lay observers are trusted, even in the courts; and Lincoln's friends held the opinion that he was crazy for a week or so after the night that he ran away. This was the belief of many of the Springfield people of the time.

The state of his thinking day by day is not hard to divine. He had given his word, but the prospective marriage was unwelcome to him, he was afraid to go on with it. He had broken his word and the consciousness of such bad faith wracked all his nature. He was torn between feelings that he should have kept his word, and the conviction that he was wise to keep away from the final step. Hostile devils had thus entered into him and were tearing him apart. He understood that his breeding did not fit him for association with a woman like Mary Todd, who had been raised with regard to the proprieties and the decencies of life. He may have given himself up to thoughts of his mother Nancy Hanks, whose illegitimacy always stung his pride, and while doing so speculated on just what was in his own blood to be transmitted to his children to be. He also had penetration enough to see that Mary Todd had grave faults of temper, which married life would sharpen rather than smooth away. Her sarcastic tongue may have terrified him with a forecast of its increasing edge. And he may have foreseen, being already familiar with her whims and her changing moods, that these were not just the expression of a harmless idiosyncrasy, but rather the premonitive symptoms of some mental condition deeply seated in her brain, to end in mental trouble such as finally overtook her.

And now Lincoln did one of the most unaccountable things of his whole life. His friend Speed on January 1, 1841, sold his Springfield store and went to Louisville, Kentucky, to live, begging Lincoln to come there soon on a visit as a way to be relieved from Springfield and the talk there, and his own troubled thoughts. Lincoln, thus being deprived of the room over Speed's store, where he had been sleeping since 1837, went to a room at the house of William Butler in Springfield where he had all along been taking his meals. Mrs. Butler had a sister named Sarah Rickard, sixteen years of age, whom Lincoln had known day by day since she was twelve years of age. And now that Lincoln had broken his engagement with Mary Todd, and had run away from her, he sought healing by proposing marriage to Sarah Rickard. The general trend of the evidence is that it was at this time that Lincoln made this proposal of marriage. Sarah Rickard, nearly fifty years after the time of Lincoln's flight from Mary Todd, wrote Herndon that it was in the summer or later of 1840 that Lincoln made the proposal of marriage to her. If it in fact occurred before the appointed night for the wedding, then Lincoln, while giving Mary Todd no hint that he was not satisfied with his engagement to her, was trying to engage himself to another woman. Any way the matter be taken, it shows Lincoln in no admirable light. Sarah Rickard wrote that Lincoln brought to her attention the accounts in the Bible of the patriarch Abraham's marriage to Sarah, and used that historical union as an argument in his own behalf. "My reason for declining his proposal was the wide difference in our ages. I was then only sixteen, and had given the subject of matrimony but very little, if any, thought. I entertained the highest regard for Mr. Lincoln. He seemed almost like an older brother, being, as it were, one of my sister's family." [1]

That Lincoln had an urge to marry someone, is clear enough. The tragedy is that he did not find his mate—not in Mary Todd. For the purposes of this study of Lincoln, and to be done with his romantic adventures, his friendship and correspondence with Speed, and last experiences in anonymous journalism will finish the story. By

[1] Herndon, I, 216.

writing to Speed and receiving letters from Speed he was living in a vicarious way the romantic phases through which Speed was passing, and by this correspondence he was analyzing and testing and assaying his own heart; and through the anonymous journalism which he had been practicing since coming to Springfield he was brought again in contact with Mary Todd upon a basis of mutual effort in that kind of literary work, which, as it happened, served to join their hours in an association of raillery and satire against one James Shields, a sensitive Irishman who had been elected state auditor in 1839. Shields was a Democrat, and that was one reason to attack him; he was a friend of Douglas, and that was another reason. When Lincoln first went to Springfield he got into the good graces of the editor of the *Sangamon Journal* and in that way began to contribute articles to its columns, and to have his speeches published in it; and later Herndon used this newspaper to advance the fame of Lincoln. It was an extremely useful adjunct to Lincoln's political plans and ambitions. Lincoln might be walking about the square in poor and badly fitting clothes, and an obvious victim of poverty, but the printing press was kept running around the corner. The editor of the *Sangamon Journal* was Simeon Francis who was wholly devoted to Lincoln, and it was his wife who set about to bring Lincoln and Mary Todd into reconcilement with each other. To do this she surreptitiously contrived for their meeting at her house; and there, while Mary Todd and Lincoln composed articles and absurd satires against James Shields, the courtship was renewed. It is only necessary here to say that Shields grew furious, discovered the authorship of the articles published in the *Journal* and challenged Lincoln to a duel. This will be dwelt upon somewhat when it will not interrupt the romantic history now in hand.

We retrace here in time a little to say that in the summer of 1841 Lincoln went to Kentucky to visit his friend Speed, and while there enjoyed himself hugely, and took great delight in Speed's relatives, the young girls who were about the house; and also lay for long in bed of mornings, being served with coffee by a slave, before arising, and thus saw what slavery was in its more agreeable aspects in the homes of planters. Once when he and Speed were returning together to Illinois they saw some negroes who were chained together and being transported on the steamboat. This aroused Lincoln's pity and resentment; and yet he had to remark that the negroes so manacled sang and played the banjo and seemed happier than any of the passengers. But slavery in the homes of planters was a different thing.

While Lincoln was on this visit to Speed, Speed became engaged to the woman he afterward married. And Speed wrote Herndon in 1866 that something of the same feeling which he had regarded as so foolish in Lincoln respecting Mary Todd took possession of himself with reference to his prospective wife. "If I had not been married and happy—far more happy than I ever expected to be—he (Lincoln) would not have been married." [1] It is interesting to see how these men influenced each other. Lincoln's letters to Speed and to Miss Mary Speed must have brief reference, just because they breathe a sort of sweet serenity which had come over Lincoln in the late summer of 1841, and because they have as much tenderness and charm as anything that he ever wrote. In a letter to Mary Speed, a niece of Joshua's, Lincoln told of the trip back to St. Louis on the way to Springfield and described graphically the negroes chained on the boat. "Having resolved to write to some of your mother's family, and not having the express permission of any one of them to do so . . . I remembered that you and I were something of cronies while I was at Farmington, and that while I was there I was under the necessity of shutting you up in a room to prevent your committing an assault and battery upon me. . . . I am literally 'subsisting on savory memories'—that is, being unable to eat, I am living upon the remembrance of the delicious dishes of peaches and cream we used to have at your house. When we left Miss Fanny Henning was owing you a visit. Has she paid it yet? If she has are you not convinced that she is one of the sweetest girls in the world?" He then observed that there was only one thing about her that he would have otherwise, and that was her melancholy, a misfortune, not a fault. There is no other Lincoln letter written to a woman so full of a certain grace and charm as this one. It is so in contrast with the Mary Owens letters and with all that he wrote to Mary Todd. But we find now in letters to Joshua Speed something of the same quality.

There is one preserved, dated in January of 1842. Lincoln, having

[1] Herndon, I, 204.

gone through varying emotions concerning Mary Todd, was expert in dissecting the same feelings in another; and he assumed to act as spiritual physician to his friend. "I know what the painful point with you is at all times; it is an apprehension that you do not love her as you should. What nonsense! How came you to court her? Was it because you thought she deserved it, and that you had given her reason to expect it? Did you court her for her wealth? Why, you knew she had none. . . . Say candidly, were not those heavenly black eyes the whole basis of all your early reasoning on the subject? After you and I had once been at the residence did you not go and take me all the way to Lexington and back for no other purpose but to get to see her again? . . . What earthly consideration would you take to find her scouting and despising you and giving herself up to another?"

In a letter of February 3, 1842, Lincoln wrote thus to Speed: "Your letter of the 25th, January came to hand today. You well know that I do not feel my own sorrows much more keenly than I do yours, when I know of them. I hope and believe that your present anxiety and distress about her health and her life must and will forever banish these horrid doubts which I know you sometimes feel as to the truth of your affection for her. If they can once and for ever be removed (and I almost feel a presentiment that the Almighty has sent your present affliction expressly for that object) surely nothing can come in their stead to fill their immeasurable measure of misery. The death scenes of those we love are surely painful enough; but these we are prepared for and expect to see; they happen to all, and all know they must happen." Two side reflections obtrude themselves here: it is to be noted that Lincoln at this time held to a belief in a punishing Almighty who sends afflictions for the good of mortals, something he expressed in his Second Inaugural in similar words, which justifies the judgment already passed that Lincoln was a Jehovah man from the first of his life. The second thing is that one almost expects Lincoln in speaking of death scenes to name Ann Rutledge; and yet she does not come forth from the oblivion to which Lincoln consigned her.

On February 25, 1842, Lincoln wrote Speed acknowledging receipt of the news that Speed had been married. "I have no way of telling you how much happiness I wish you both. I feel somewhat jealous of you both now." In March Lincoln wrote to Speed, "The sweet violet you enclosed came safely to hand." Speed had a farm and had written Lincoln about the delights of rural life, and had sent the flower. He did not write again until July. Evidently Speed had written Lincoln to return to Mary Todd; for now Lincoln wrote: "I acknowledge the correctness of your advice too; but before I resolve to do the one thing or the other I must gain my confidence in my own ability to keep my resolves when they are made. In that ability you know I once prided myself as the only or chief gem of my character; that gem I lost—how and where you know too well. I have not regained it; and until I do I cannot trust myself in any matter of much importance. I believe now that had you understood my case at the time as well as I understood yours afterward, by the aid you would have given me I should have sailed through clear, but that does not afford me sufficient confidence to begin that or the like again. . . . You make a kind of acknowledgement of your obligation to me for your present happiness. The truth is I am not sure that there was any merit with me in the part I took in your difficulty. . . . I always was superstitious; I believe God made me one of the instruments of bringing your Fanny and you together, which union I have no doubt he had foreordained. What he designs he will do for me yet. 'Stand still, and see the salvation of the Lord' is my text just now." [1]

In August of 1842 Lincoln and Mary Todd were collaborating on the attacks on James Shields. In October of 1842 he wrote Speed: "But I have your word for it, too, and the returning elasticity of your spirits which is manifested in your letters." That is, that Speed was happier than before his marriage. "But I want to ask you a close question, 'are you now in feeling as well as judgment glad that you are married as you are?' From anybody but me this would be an impudent question, not to be tolerated; but I know you will pardon it in me. Please answer it quickly, as I am impatient to know." [2] Lincoln was trying to get a fact basis for his own action. It must be not a matter of feeling, but of judgment—"cold reason." And here is a strange break in the correspondence. Lincoln was married to Mary Todd November 4, 1842. He did not write Speed

[1] Lincoln's Works, I, 65, 66, 67.
[2] Lincoln's Works, I, 71.

again until March 24, 1843, that is, he did not until then write after the letter of October, 1842; and in this March letter he said nothing of his marriage four months before. The letter related to the convention which nominated Baker for Congress, in which Lincoln was a delegate, under instruction for Baker, though he had tried to get the Menard County delegation for himself by writing Morris to see James Short, a man as honest as there was in the world, which has already been noticed in another connection. Why did Lincoln write nothing to Speed, even if it were but formal words, concerning his marriage to Mary Todd four months before? It seems that such shame and regret had come over him that he could not trust himself to write about it; and that as he had nothing joyous to say, nothing that showed satisfaction with what he had done, he could do nothing but preserve silence. Either this is the case or else he wrote something to Speed too intimate and unpleasant to be printed. There are marks indicating that something has been deleted from the beginning of this letter of March.[1]

Springfield in 1842 was scarcely larger than Elizabethtown, Kentucky, was where Thomas Lincoln married Nancy Hanks in 1806, nor were ceremony and style more fitting to it than they would have been to the Southern town in that time. But someone, doubtless the bride and her relatives the Edwardses, decided that the wedding should have all the ritualistic solemnity of ring and Book, and this although the union had been suddenly resolved. Early on the morning of November 4, Lincoln aroused his friend Matheny from bed to tell him that he was to be married that night and to ask him to act as best man for him. The same morning Mary Todd hurried to the house of a woman friend and secured her attendance as maid of honor. Meanwhile the Episcopal rector, Rev. Charles N. Dresser, was asked to come to the Edwards mansion and perform the ceremony according to the rites of the Episcopal Church. While Lincoln was dressing for the wedding, at the Butler boarding house where lived the sixteen-year-old Sarah Rickard, to whom he had proposed marriage, one of Butler's little boys asked Lincoln where he was going. Lincoln replied, "To hell I reckon."

The wedding was painfully ludicrous. Lincoln was pale and trembling as if being driven to slaughter, as Herndon described

[1] Lincoln's Works, I, 79.

him. One is reminded of the wedding of Lord Byron to Miss Millbanke, where Byron, too, was blanched and in fright. The rector stood forth in his canonical robes, and at the proper point handed the ring to Lincoln, repeating the words of the ritual that the groom was thereby endowing Mary Todd with all his worldly goods. One of the judges of the Supreme Court was present, a most plain and blunt man whose mind was disturbed by the absurdity of the penniless Lincoln endowing the bride, and by the needless pledge that he was so endowing her when the state statute provided for all that. "God Almighty, Lincoln," he bawled, "the statute fixes all that." This convulsed the rector, who was scarcely able to proceed with the reading of the ritual. One has to imagine what Lincoln felt, and how he looked. But the wrath of Mary Todd is not hard to imagine. With the union solemnized, the bride and groom went to the Globe Tavern in Springfield where the couple took board and room at $4 a week. A picture of this hostelry was taken in 1886, which showed it as it was in 1842. It was a two-story, frame structure with four windows in the second story, and two windows and two doors in the ground story. At one side of it was a shed half hidden by a blind fence. It was altogether less than a commonplace house; it was the ugly, almost shabby sort of building that succeeded the picturesque log structures. And here the daughter of the Kentucky banker abode for some time to come with Lincoln, her husband, whose mind was now more divided and complexed than it had been before.

Soon after Byron was married he wrote a woman friend: "I am married at last, and mean no disrespect to Lady B., who though she may be a seraph to her friends, and really is, I believe, a good woman, is a devil to me. We have nothing in common except disquiet, and heaven knows how much ennui." Lincoln, with some changes in words, might have expressed much the same ideas to his friend Speed, or to someone. But strange quiet had now come over him. He did not have ennui, one believes; because he was immediately at work in the plots and plans of politics. In a letter to Martin M. Morris, of Menard County, the one already quoted from, he made the first mention of his wife. "It would astonish, if not amuse the older citizens to learn that I (a stranger, friendless, uneducated, penniless boy, working on a flatboat at ten dollars per month) have been put down here as the candidate of pride, wealth and aristocratic distinction." Lincoln was beginning to feel the gossip, and the Springfield laughter about the Episcopal service, and the Edwards alliance. He was trying to be nominated for Congress, and to that end to undermine Baker who was the selection of Sangamon County, with Lincoln as an instructed delegate for Baker to the convention. Lincoln went on in the Morris letter to say that there was "the strangest combination of church influence against me. Baker is a Campbellite; and therefore, as I suppose, with few exceptions got all that church. My wife has some relations in the Presbyterian churches, and some with the Episcopal churches; and therefore, wherever it would tell, I was set down as either the one or the other, while it was everywhere contended that no Christian ought to go for me, because I belonged to no church, was suspected of being a deist, and had talked about fighting a duel."

This is Lincoln's first written reference to his wife. On May 18, 1843, he broke the silence which he had interposed between Speed and himself since March 24. "By the way," he wrote, "how do 'events' of the same sort come off in your family? Are you possessing houses and lands, and oxen and asses, and men-servants, and maid servants and begetting sons and daughters? We are not keeping house, but boarding at the Globe Tavern, which is very well kept now by a widow lady of the name of Beck. Our room (the same that Dr. Wallace occupied here) and boarding only costs us four dollars a week." [1]

There is not a sentiment of any sort expressed in this letter.[1]

One can search all through the records of Lincoln to the last without finding any passion in them, any tenderness of moment expressed to Mary Todd or any other woman, who occupied any intimate relationship toward him. During the War he was used to telegraph Mrs. Lincoln, who was away at times in Philadelphia or in New England. He addressed her as "Mrs. A. Lincoln," and signed himself "A. Lincoln," without sending her a word of love. He seemed to think that she wanted news of the progress of battles; more likely she wanted some word of love from him. Sometimes he telegraphed her that there was no news; sometimes he made references to the state of the weather; sometimes he said that he would be "glad for

[1] Lincoln's Works, I, 81–82.

you to come"—that is to come home to Washington; sometimes he said "I wish you to stay or to come just as most agreeable to yourself"; sometimes it was a curt message, "All going well"; or "all doing well" or "all very well"; or "we are all well and have not been otherwise." On April 2, 1865, a few days before he was assassinated, he sent her a dispatch of some length telling her that Grant had taken Petersburg with 12,000 prisoners and fifty guns; and that Tad and himself were both well and "will be glad to see you and your party here at the time you name." These communications can be found in his works by whosoever wants to look into them further. They are entirely colorless, saving perhaps one of August 8, 1863, in which he addressed her, as "My dear Wife," and signed himself "affectionately." [1]

The search for new Lincoln material has gone on steadily since the ponderous work of Hay and Nicolay; but apparently there is now little that is new to find. As late as 1930 *New Letters and Papers of Lincoln* was published by Paul M. Angle. The uncritical state of book reviewing in America is shown by one review of this volume which appeared in a leading New York review. Lincoln's tenderness was supposed to be proved by referring to a letter which he wrote Mrs. Lincoln when he was in Congress in 1848, in which he wrote: "I hate to stay in this old room by myself." These alleged new letters do contain affectionate mention of his boys; they send kisses to the "dear rascals," they relate that Lincoln had hunted for "plaid stockings to fit Eddy's dear little feet." In one he wrote Mrs. Lincoln not to do without a domestic. "Get another as soon as you can to take care of the dear codgers." To lift the burden from Mrs. Lincoln? No, but to take care of the boys. There is no question that Lincoln loved children from the time of his boyhood days in Indiana. He was noted for this characteristic when he lived at New Salem. And he loved his own children with a boyish delight. He played and romped and rolled on the floor with them; and in his desolate days in Springfield he was often along the streets followed by one or more of them. They gave him comfort. Herndon related that often Lincoln would be at the office very early in the morning, and behind drawn curtains would be breakfasting on cheese and crackers with his son Robert for a companion. He had been driven forth by the

[1] Lincoln's Works, II, 382.

irate wife. For animals in distress, mired down or wounded, for a crippled man, for negroes in manacles, he had pity, which was his own indifference obverted: he would not want to be so treated himself, or to be in such state. A sense of justice, that fear of being unfair, of doing less than the right and honorable thing, as he expressed himself to Mary Owens, made his emotions active when animals or abused human beings were the objects of his contemplation. Children, as helpless creatures, thus awoke his liveliest affections, not to mention a certain æsthetic appreciation of their beauty. But tenderness for women is another matter. It is clear that he might have been deeply attached to some woman. The tragedy is that he never was. He married Mary Todd out of fear for his own conscience, out of torturing pity for her that he had so shamefully humiliated and wounded; and in consequence we have no letter from him to her in which he wrote as a man does who loved a woman as Jackson loved his Rachel. If he had ever loved Ann Rutledge there was enough of remembrance of the windswept and tree-grown New Salem Hill, enough to stir the imagination in thinking back to those happy days of study and joyous association in the beginning of life, even as he felt and expressed lively gratitude for the fast friendships there formed, to have stirred him to verse about the fated woman who died in the hot summer of 1835 amid the silence of Sandridge. First and passionate love is never eradicated from the memory even when the heart has become realistic under the pitiless beat of time and change, and be the woman what she may have been, whether of real beauty and worth or not. But there is no line of Lincoln's about Ann Rutledge—not a word. We are not dealing with a man who was inarticulate; but with one whose whole study was words from the days of Bailey's *Etymological Dictionary* at Pigeon Creek, who did not have the genius of Burns, to be sure, but who knew how to express himself, even at fourteen years of age. And yet Ann Rutledge would have gone into utter oblivion except for the people of Menard County and Herndon.

Chapter V   *Lincoln in Congress and Just Before*

AARON BURR brought himself into such infamy by killing Hamilton in a duel that the practice was under increasing condemnation over America after 1804, though duels were fought on occasion by Jackson and others after that time. The sentiment in Illinois was so much against the monomachy that when the new constitution of 1848 was adopted a provision was inserted in the instrument: "Any person who shall after the adoption of this constitution fight a duel shall be deprived of the right of holding any office of honor or profit in this state, and shall be punished otherwise in such manner as is or may be prescribed by law." Lincoln, who was about to fight a duel with James Shields in the autumn of 1842, would not have incurred this stricture, though his political career might have been damaged if he had killed or wounded Shields, considering that Shields was provoked to calling Lincoln to account by the anonymous attacks on him in the *Sangamon Journal* written by Lincoln and Mary Todd. This might have happened if the marks of buffoonery on the affair had not set it down as pure nonsense. There is one serious thing to note, and that is that Lincoln's reply to Shields' request for an explanation and for a declaration or denial of the authorship of the satirical articles and verses against Shields, had a flavor of the wording of Hamilton's reply to Burr when asked to say whether he was the author of the attacks upon Burr. Hamilton had risen up in his dignity and by much cloudy evasion had demanded by what authority he was to be catechized. We shall find that many of Lincoln's ideas and attitudes were derived from other sources than his own originality. Shields, in fact, had gone to Francis the editor of the *Journal* and learned from him that Lincoln was the author of the attacks upon him; and this information he communicated to Lincoln when asking for an explanation. Lincoln when replying to Shields wrote that the latter "without stopping to enquire whether I am really the author, or to point out what is offensive in them," had acted on Francis' word; "and then you proceed to hint at consequences. Now, sir, there is in this so much assumption of facts, and so much of menace as to consequences, that I cannot submit to answer that note any further than I have, and to add, that the consequences to which I suppose you allude would be matter of as great regret to me as it possibly could be to you." This is the rhetorical language of the Hamilton-Burr days, and of pompous sound for Illinois in the mouth of the youth who was running a flatboat ten years before, and alluding to that fact as late as 1843 when protesting against the charge of aristocracy. Lincoln was evidently dramatizing himself after the manner of Hamilton whom he admired so greatly. He might have simply written to Shields that he was or was not the author of the *Sangamon Journal* articles; that would have sounded like the revered Lincoln of this day. But there is further resemblance to the Hamilton-Burr correspondence: Lincoln refused to receive further communications from Shields until Shields withdrew his first note, the one asking for an explanation. However, it was finally delivered to Lincoln, who said that "it was not consistent with his honor to negotiate for peace with Shields unless Mr. Shields would withdraw his former abusive letter."[1] It should be said that Shields with a man named Merryman, who is characterized as Shields' second, went to Tremont, Illinois, where Lincoln was, and where these first notes were passed through the medium of one Whiteside who was acting for Lincoln. Shields and Merryman returned to Springfield at this juncture of affairs, where the noise of the impending duel was shaking the capital. And finally after a good deal of orotund quibbling on the part of Lincoln, he acknowledged that he wrote the articles in question, but for political effect, and without any intention of injuring the personal or private character of Shields—and this in spite of the fact that in one of the articles, Shields' position as a Whig or Democrat being first questioned, language was used to place him among "the present hypocritical set" who disgraced the places they filled in the public service.[2] Shields at the time was state auditor, and he was pictured ludicrously in the articles as performing the duties of his office in a half bewildered and disorderly way. Shields was an unquestioned Democrat and more than that a Douglas Democrat, and his friendship for Douglas was possibly, in part, the cause of Lincoln's satiric assault

[1] Statement of Shields' second, Sangamon Journal, Oct. 4, 1842.
[2] Herndon, I, 225.

IN CONGRESS AND JUST BEFORE 79

upon him. After disavowing any intention to injure Shields as a man, or a gentleman, and adding that Shields' conduct toward him had always been gentlemanly, and that he had no personal pique against Shields, Lincoln said if Shields was not satisfied with this *amende honorable*, then the preliminaries of the fight were to be that cavalry broadswords were to be used in a duel, and the contestants should meet three miles from Alton, Illinois, on the Missouri side of the river on Thursday evening at five o'clock. Lincoln's second stipulation made the whole thing a farce.

This was, that a plank ten feet long, and from nine to twelve inches broad, should be firmly fixed on edge, on the ground, as the line between the duelists, which neither was to pass his foot over upon forfeit of his life. Next a line was to be drawn on the ground on either side of the plank and parallel with it, each at the distance of the whole length of the sword, and three feet additional from the plank. If that line was passed by either party during the fight, it should be deemed a surrender of the fight. By these terms it is impossible to see how Lincoln, even with the great length of his arms, could reach Shields; but unquestionably Shields could not reach Lincoln, who also had an advantage over Shields because of his superior strength with which to handle heavy cavalry swords. Independent of a constitutional clause, dueling in Illinois at the time fell under the general ban of homicide; and it is to be remarked that Lincoln now was willing to disregard his preachment of law observance, which by this time had filled so many essays and speeches and homilies. Shields refused to accept terms laid down by Lincoln, or to make any until they arrived in Missouri. Broadswords were procured at Jacksonville, however, by Shields' second; and when Lincoln arrived at Alton, Shields and his party were there. They all crossed to the Missouri side, where Shields' second withdrew Shields' first note to Lincoln, but without Shields' knowledge. An apology of Lincoln to Shields was read to Shields, and the duel was called off.

This encounter with Shields ended Lincoln's anonymous journalism. Light is thrown on the quarrel and upon Lincoln's justice in it by considering that Shields has come down to us as a man of courage and honor. He showed both qualities in this contact with Lincoln, and won for himself a vindication by his fortitude and his respect for himself. Herndon wrote of him that he was a gallant and hot headed bachelor who had made himself somewhat ridiculous by assuming the airs of a beau; and that he became a target for the bitterness and mockery of the village capital by his devoted support of the Democratic Party. He was not of the Edwards set, nor of the Whig coteries; and thus, on the score both of politics and social climbing and possibilities, he was a fair target for the verses of Mary Todd and the satire of Lincoln. But what is most to be noted, he was as auditor struggling with the tangled finances of the state which Lincoln had helped to create by his legislation for internal improvements. Keeping in mind Lincoln's talent for mimicry, his histrionic gift on the stump, his tendency to pattern himself after men like Hamilton and Webster, his thirst for distinction, for publicity, and his literary borrowings, the origin and the conduct of this duel are clear enough. Finally of Shields it may be said that he saw brave service in the Mexican war, being wounded both at Cerro Gordo and at Chapultepec; that he was United States Senator from Illinois from 1849 to 1855, and from Minnesota from 1858 to 1859; and finally, when the War between the States came on, he served on the Northern side and performed distinguished service at Winchester, on March 23, 1862. Between 1837, when Lincoln came to Springfield to live, and the time of his meeting with Mary Todd in 1839, Lincoln had happy days; they were days indeed of leisurely diversions, of much loafing at Speed's store, of hand to hand debates with Douglas, and others by the fireplace, and at the churches and halls of the village with Douglas and with others. Lincoln was doing no reading of moment in these very precious years. No man ever had an easier time of it in his early days than Lincoln, according to Herndon. Lincoln had influential friends, who almost fought each other for the privilege of serving him. He was the town's pet; and Herndon said that he deserved to be. He was full of gay spirits and good humor and stories. The time had not quite arrived when he could see what it meant to have Douglas surpassing him in every way and in every field.

Douglas had that prime indicium of genius, energy. He was always doing something; while Lincoln, though ceaselessly playing at politics, seemed to confine his industry to letter writing and to scheming. By the time that Douglas was thirty-four he was elected

United States Senator from Illinois; and before this he had been successively in the state legislature, register of the land office in Illinois, secretary of state for Illinois, a judge of the Supreme Court of Illinois, and a member of Congress from Illinois. With all these achievements he had become a lawyer of standing, and he was making money—something that Lincoln never could do. Stuart, Lincoln's law partner, defeated Douglas for Congress in 1838 by 36 votes in a total vote of 36,000. Lincoln, having from the time of their meeting in the legislature in 1836 regarded Douglas as an intellectual rival, did all he could to compass Douglas's rejection; and when Douglas half planned to have a recount of the votes, Lincoln busied himself greatly in Stuart's behalf, writing many letters and sending word here and there to be on the lookout for moves on the part of Douglas. Douglas finally abandoned the contest and Lincoln derived great happiness from the fact. It was Douglas who at last made Lincoln. At first depressed to intellectual impotence by Douglas's success, Lincoln rose to energy and activity when the chance came to overcome Douglas. Envy of Douglas all along is the key to much of Lincoln.

Between December 14 and December 20, 1839, Lincoln and Douglas debated the sub-treasury question in the court house at Springfield, Lincoln standing for the Whigs as against Jackson's plan for the sub-treasury, while Douglas supported the cause of Jackson. Lincoln's Hamiltonian principles were thus all along avowed. He was at this time an apostle of the so-called implied powers of the Constitution, which were so casuistically expounded by Hamilton and so fairly refuted by Jefferson, and which were afterward elaborated judicially by Chief Justice Marshall in holding the charter of the United States Bank to be constitutional, and in arrogating to the Supreme Court the power to decide upon the constitutionality of laws, a power that the Court at the start disclaimed to possess. All of these usurpations Jefferson characterized as the "twistifications" of John Marshall. Always from the beginning of the government the statesmen and moral leaders who were calling loudest for the observance of the laws were themselves rending it out of shape and violating it, as if their moral purposes were a law above the law, even indeed as Seward said that there "is a higher law than the Constitution." And regretfully we shall see more and more that

Lincoln was of this political association and faith, and that the War gave him the chance to express his will as being above the law, because allied with the purpose of God in measures which trampled the Constitution and the law.

When Lincoln debated, or wrote an essay, or made a speech, or delivered a lecture, he took it over to the *Sangamon Journal* where it was published; and thus he kept his name constantly before the people. In 1844 he lost the nomination to Congress to the man Baker, before referred to, in spite of the wily arts which he practiced to win over to himself the Menard County delegation. But in the campaign which followed, this being the one in which William Henry Harrison the Whig was elected president, Lincoln was very active and came out in speeches for the protective tariff, which he had espoused in his Pappsville address when but twenty-three years of age. There is no justification for considering him at any time as a disciple of Jefferson in matters of fundamental principle, or as having any Jeffersonian blood in his veins, saving on the sole tenet of the equality of men; and as to that we shall see what that meant to him when he tried to state its application to the negro. He was a Hamiltonian always, though his awkwardness and poverty, and somewhat gregarious nature and democratic words seemed to mark him as the son of Jefferson. His protective colorations were marvelous for verisimilitude and for deceptive changes. In the history of liberty he has arisen to great proportions in virtue of his Emancipation Proclamation; but when the story of that is told his claim to stand with Milton, and again with Jefferson falls away; while his many very orphic utterances on freedom of speech and freedom in general seem like the words of a spirit that had taken possession of a body that was acting contrary to the voice that was speaking. He was a house divided against itself; he did not fall. Many of his contemporaries saw him as an intellectual contradiction. To Judge David Davis of Bloomington, Illinois, whom Lincoln as president placed on the Supreme Bench, Lincoln was a mystery; and to Herndon he was the source of endless speculation and analyses, which ended at last in the best portrait we have in words of Lincoln; but when we get to it the reader will be prepared to judge of it for himself. Perhaps he will say that there is a Lincoln who has been made out of strange mixtures of clay, and passed through the fires of many kilns the better to come forth a colossus in statuary to bestride America; and that critical assault upon this Lincoln is unavailing, because the real Lincoln with whom we are dealing is dead and quite forgotten.

Lincoln's law partner Stuart having defeated Douglas for Congress in 1838, and Stuart having gone to Washington to take up his work as a congressman, Lincoln severed his relationship with Stuart as a law partner and soon thereafter formed a partnership with Stephen T. Logan, an orderly, methodical, able lawyer five years older than Lincoln, who made money in the practice of law and who saved it. He was studious in the law and Lincoln was a desultory reader of law; he was industrious, Lincoln was lazy; he was thrifty, Lincoln was improvident; he was formal in his relations with clients, Lincoln was familiar even to vulgarity, never neglecting an opportunity to perpetrate a bit of humor. The positions of the two partners should have been reversed. Lincoln, the younger man, should have been the one to have kept the office in order, to have done the studying, to have prepared the cases; and Logan should have been the reception committee, the man at ease to whom the briefs on the law and the statements of the witnesses were handed, all in readiness, by the younger man Lincoln. But one feels that Lincoln was spoiled already by the adulation that had been poured out upon him since he came to Springfield as the conquering hero of the state capital contest. All along the years, until this day of wider education and standardized information, there came out of the rural districts many a young man who, having read Paine, or some other controversial work, assumed to set himself intellectually apart from the common run of folk, and to imagine himself specially gifted. Lincoln had read Paine, and he had reason to believe that in many ways he was superior to the average man; but there is no egotist so great as the poor boy of some gifts who acquires some education, particularly if he be endowed with language and argumentative talents.

In this association with Logan, Lincoln became conscious of his own lack of intellectual system, and he tried to mend his ways, but to little purpose. Then political rivalry entered between the partners to disturb their business relationship. Lincoln was already sneering at Douglas as the "Little Giant," but it was with a depressed beat of the heart, for Douglas had been elected to Congress in 1843. So Lincoln wanted to go to Congress, but so did Logan. Herndon believed that many quarrels ensued between Lincoln and Logan because of this conflicting aspiration for the same honor. One day quite suddenly Lincoln rushed in upon Herndon, who was a beginning lawyer, and said that he was going to sever his partnership with Logan, and asked Herndon to be his partner. Herndon was delighted, and the partnership between them came to pass at once. Lincoln was now thirty-five and Herndon twenty-six years of age; and Lincoln found in Herndon just what he wanted, namely, the younger partner who was the studious and self-effacing member of the firm, while, he, the older partner, could follow his natural bent of loafing, and talking and being the orator and jury man of the firm, which he was well equipped to be. Lincoln never made a more fortunate move in his life. Johnson had his Boswell, who followed him about and set down his sayings; and so did Herndon do this for Lincoln. But while Johnson was the well-read man, and Boswell the student who sat at the feet of his great tutor, Herndon was the tutor and Lincoln was the student; and for eighteen years thereafter Herndon bought and read the great books as they were published. He worked on Lincoln to get him to read them; and when he wouldn't Herndon told Lincoln what they contained. Herndon was a radical and an abolitionist; and he kept pushing Lincoln along toward a more definite stand politically, while Lincoln kept resisting and sticking by the Whigs. All along Herndon was writing and publishing editorials in the *Sangamon Journal* in praise of Lincoln. He armed Lincoln with authorities with which to fight Douglas; and when Lincoln began to loom as a presidential possibility after the debates, Herndon was indefatigable in Lincoln's behalf in writing letters over the country to keep the political fires burning bright and warm for the man he almost worshipped.

At last Lincoln had his desire. On May 1, 1846, he was nominated for Congress by the Whigs in convention assembled at Petersburg, where the faithful Herndon was secretary of the convention. Ten days later, May 11, 1846, the United States declared war against Mexico. Illinois took fire with martial spirit, with cries of "Avenge the Alamo." Congressman Baker wanted to resign from Congress and raise a regiment. He was finally allowed to lead troops to the war without giving up his seat; and soon he was off to battle. Jeffer-

IN CONGRESS AND JUST BEFORE 85

son Davis would not run for office while the war was on; and so he played an active and distinguished part for his country in several engagements. U. S. Grant also saw service; and Robert E. Lee, neither of them politicians then or afterward. And John J. Hardin, who won the nomination for Congress over Lincoln and Baker, too, in 1844, and was elected that fall, put himself at the head of a regiment and was killed in battle. But Lincoln did not enlist. His Democratic opponent was Rev. Peter Cartwright, who had defeated Lincoln for the legislature in 1832.

Both Cartwright and Lincoln in the campaign played the rôle of patriots in the usual perfervid style. In June Lincoln spoke to a great war meeting at the State House, and, according to the *Sangamon Journal*, his and the other speeches were "warm, thrilling and effective." There was great opposition to the war over the country; but at that time an American was permitted to speak out against a war if he chose to do so. Lowell was pouring forth the satire of the "Biglow Papers" upon the war; and much was said concerning its purpose, which was, according to lofty-minded men, but a scheme of the slavocracy to get more territories for slaves. But the slavocracy had not learned, or did not care to exercise the war powers of the government, to shackle the press and to gag the mouths of those who wanted to say and did say that the war was criminal and without justification. It was in the war that Lincoln prosecuted, and in the World War that Wilson led against Germany, that these constitutional rights, so precious to liberty and to wisdom, not to say to the intelligent action of the people, were despised and broken. If either Lincoln or Cartwright had made any speech against the war, or so much as hinted that he did not wholly believe in it, he would have been overwhelmed by the Illinois electorate. All the while it seems certain that Lincoln was against the war. His course in Congress, to be noticed, was not one dictated by anything that happened after the campaign to change his opinion on the propriety of the war. He was not Debs who went to prison for what judges extracted from an attack upon the mine owners, making it a violation of the espionage act; for to say that the mine owners were profiteering, and were interested in making American boys fodder for cannon in order to increase profits in coal was to bring the holiness of the war into contempt. Lincoln was not Debs; he was not the brave, truthful, earnest, spiritual, highly moral colossus that now belongs to poetry and myth. He was the cautious, astute, special pleader educated in the cunning of *Chitty on Pleading*.

Nor did the slavery question come up at all. Cartwright did not believe that slavery was a sin. The Bible did not say so; but it said much, on the contrary, in favor of slavery. At this time the abolitionist societies had been running for fifteen years. But Lincoln was not of them or with them. Indeed not much about this need be said now; for Lincoln scarcely changed his views on slavery from the days of the Stone-Lincoln resolutions, even as he said he had not in his autobiographical notes of 1860. But if Lincoln was against more territory in the southwest, he was not against it in the northwest. The matter of Oregon was then depending, and Lincoln on that took the position of the Democrats which by this time was so eloquently championed by Douglas with his dream of an ocean-bound republic from which Great Britain should be completely excluded. It is to be remarked that the tariff interests were against the annexation of Texas; but Lincoln, though always a tariff man, did not find himself forced by that token to oppose the Mexican War. So it was that Lincoln defeated Cartwright, and thus at thirty-nine years of age he was a member of Congress. He took the oath of office December 6, 1847.

In the interval he was writing poetry and riding the circuit. When Lincoln was doing this he was thoroughly in his element. It was the Eighth Judicial Circuit, and it included fifteen Illinois counties, and large they were. The whole territory was about 150 miles long and about 100 broad. He traveled from Springfield to Petersburg, from there to Havana, then to Pekin, or perhaps Tremont also, to Peoria, to Matamora, to Bloomington, to Danville, to Charleston, to Taylorville. He made this route for years before 1858, the year of the debates with Douglas; and it was thus that he became acquainted with such hosts of traders and farmers, merchants, innkeepers and the like throughout this extended country. There were no railroads when he began these travels; the stages were not numerous or very dependable. And at first Lincoln had no horse, so he borrowed one; or else he joined a company of lawyers also going to court; and thus they fared around much as the Chaucer pilgrims going to Canterbury. When Lincoln got more prosperous

IN CONGRESS AND JUST BEFORE 87

he owned an old buggy which rattled, and a horse that fell asleep along the way. When a county seat was reached the lawyers repaired to the inn, where also the judge was stopping, and perhaps the grand jury, and those summoned for service on the petit jury. Then the raillery, the story telling commenced. In the office of the hotel where suitors lingered, where jurymen paused on their way to dinner at noon, and to supper at night; or in the judge's room at night when a select company of wits were gathered, Lincoln told his stories. No one listened with more fascinated interest than Judge David Davis, the huge jurist from Bloomington, nor laughed louder at the inimitable drollery of the lank, homely Lincoln. All the while Davis was studying Lincoln, and could not make him out; he confessed that he never understood him. What tales were told, what wit was struck at the Mermaid Tavern! But what roaring jokes were cracked, what apt fables woven, what choice obscenity was perpetrated at the Menard House at Petersburg and at the other inns in the circuit! The memory of all this persisted until thirty years ago all over that part of Illinois; and lately it was a frequent matter to meet with some old man who had heard Lincoln tell the story which he proceeded to tell himself. Some were sex stories justified by their really witty points, others were of the filthy variety for which no point is good enough to make them permissible. One about Lincoln was current in Illinois when I was so much there around the Petersburg country. It was to the effect that when Lincoln was trying a case against an able but very dignified attorney, and felt that the speech which this adversary was making was winning the jury, he resorted to the expedient of picking up a newspaper from the trial table and rushing out of the court room as if an emergency had suddenly come upon him. The court room rocked with laughter; even the judge joined the spectators; and the jury roared, with the result that the oratorical effect was dispelled. This was riding the circuit. A poet some day will make a book of Lincoln going from county seat to county seat, staying at the inns and entertaining the attendants at court and the villagers with the Æsopian stories which he invented, or borrowed and improved. Such a book would stand side by side with Chaucer's *Canterbury Tales*, if it were well done. And it was a beautiful country of gentle hills and rolling or level grasslands, with rich forestry here and there, and a profuseness of wild flowers, and many meadow larks, robins, orioles which sang joyously in the spring days and in the more temperate days of summer. June and often July are beautiful months in Illinois; and the autumns are a complete delight. This is the country which Bryant visited in 1833, and which inspired him to write his poem "The Prairies."

Henry C. Whitney became a lawyer at Danville in this circuit in 1854, and soon formed a warm attachment for Lincoln. We are dealing now with the late forties, after Lincoln was elected to Congress; but Whitney's description of Lincoln when he first saw him cannot be far from one which might have been faithfully made of him at the very time of which we are now writing. "He was six feet four inches in height," wrote Whitney. "His legs and arms were disproportionately long, his feet and hands were abnormally large, he was awkward in his gait and actions. His skin was a dark, sallow color, his features were coarse; his expression kind and amiable. His eyes were indicative of deep reflection, and in times of repose of deep sorrow as well. His head was high, but not large; his forehead was broad at the base but retreated. His ears were large, his hair coarse, black and bushy, which stood all over his head, with no appearance of ever having been combed."[1] Whitney said that Lincoln wore a seven and one eighth hat; but Beveridge went to the rooms of the Chicago Historical Society in Chicago on March 30, 1927, and measured one of the hats of Lincoln there preserved, finding it to be six and seven eighths and barely seven by stretching.[2] But there are things which have more bearing on Lincoln's intellectual and moral nature than hat measurements. One of the most significant of such things may now be taken into account.

The Ordinance for the Government of the Old Northwest is often spoken of as having kept slavery out of the states which were formed out of it, Illinois included, of course. In point of fact it did not altogether do this; but what is certain, it did not give the negro any civil rights, and Illinois did not until after the War between the States give him any civil rights. Under the Illinois constitution of 1818, which was in force until 1848, a negro could not vote; he was therefore taxed without representation. He could not belong to the

---

[1] Beveridge, I, 503-4.
[2] Id., 504.

militia, and therefore he could not defend the state or himself. He could not serve on a jury, nor intermarry with a white woman, nor have equal rights with whites to the service of inns, restaurants, stage coaches, railroads, nor did he have equal rights of admission to places of amusement. He might be indentured, if twenty-one years of age, provided that while in a state of freedom he contracted so to be for a consideration *bona fide*, not necessarily valuable. The men who framed that instrument and the abolitionists as well labored under the economic delusion that to work and receive wages was liberty; to work and be supported was slavery; and that if a man could sell his labor freely he was a free man even though he had not a single civil right. We shall see that Lincoln expounded that absurdity in the Douglas debates. But the constitution of 1818 went further. It permitted the bringing in of slaves to work at the salt mines near Shawneetown, provided that was to be for not longer than one year; and it was not to be at all after the year 1825, which bears upon the matter soon now in hand. And also this constitution took care of the negroes who were indentured while Illinois was a territory, and held them to a specific performance of their contracts to serve out their contractual time, which might be for years or for life. Lincoln never lifted his hand to change any of these regulations, except to demand that negroes be permitted to earn their own bread and to eat it, which differs little from earning bread as a slave, or as an indentured servant, and eating it. In neither case are there civil rights.

Lincoln took no part in the constitutional convention of 1847, which on August 31 adopted a new constitution for Illinois. This was ratified at the polls on March 6, 1848. It carried forward many of the provisions of the constitution of 1818. This later constitution permitted only white men to vote, and to serve in the militia; and yet under a declaration of rights the framers of this instrument announced that "all men are born equally free and independent and have certain inherent and indefeasible rights among which are those of enjoying and defending life and liberty, and of acquiring, possessing and protecting property and reputation, and of pursuing their own happiness." The only escape from this contradiction is to say that a negro is not a man. In all the annals of the world no thinking was more irrational than that which was common on the subject of negro slavery and freedom, in which Lincoln fully participated. We are now prepared for one of Lincoln's strangest moves.

In Coles County, Illinois, where Thomas Lincoln was residing, and of which Charleston was the county seat, there lived, in 1847, and before, one Robert Matson, of Bourbon County, Kentucky, who was accustomed for years before to bring his slaves to his farm in Coles County for the working season, and after it was over to take them back to Kentucky. In the fall of 1847, while Lincoln was a congressman elect, but before he had taken the oath of office, Matson got into difficulty with his slaves in Coles County. One of these was Jane Bryant, a mulatto, a reputed child of Matson's brother. This Jane Bryant was the wife of another slave of Matson's named Anthony Bryant. Matson's housekeeper had a frightful quarrel with the mulatto woman, Jane Bryant, and threatened to have her and her husband Anthony, and her children sent back immediately to Kentucky, and from thence sold into the far south. Anthony in terror then rushed off to a near-by village in Coles County, and laid his troubles before a man named Ashmore who kept the village inn, and a doctor named Rutherford. The latter told Anthony to go back to the Matson farm, get his wife Jane, and the children, and bring them to the village inn. Anthony did this; the anti-slavery men of the community were notified of the exciting difficulty and soon there were much anger and loud talk. Matson arrived on the scene eventually and tried to get these slaves to return to him at the farm. They refused, and Matson then swore out a warrant for the slaves and had them lodged in jail. A trial was had before a justice of the peace, in which Orlando B. Ficklin represented the negroes. We shall see this Orlando B. Ficklin on the platform during one of the Lincoln-Douglas debates, and there vouching for Lincoln on a disputed point when Douglas was driving Lincoln into a bad corner. He had also been in the legislature with Lincoln. There was a statute of Illinois at the time which provided for the sale of recalcitrant negroes; and now the justice of the peace, deciding that he had no jurisdiction in the instant proceeding, recurred to a statute which empowered him to turn these negroes over to the sheriff to be kept until they could be advertised for sale and sold for the cost of their jail fare. This the justice did; and the

IN CONGRESS AND JUST BEFORE 91

negroes were in jail for two months. A good deal of legal campaigning ensued: proceedings in habeas corpus, a suit by the sheriff against Matson the owner of the slaves for their keep in jail, and the like. But at last Watson sued Rutherford for damages for enticing his slaves, charging that he was injured to the amount of $2500. And now Lincoln, traveling the circuit, and a member elect of Congress on the Whig ticket, and one of the authors of the Stone-Lincoln resolutions which denounced slavery as founded in injustice and bad policy—this Lincoln came to Charleston, and there allied himself with Matson the slave owner to help him with legal ability and eloquence to win back his slaves. Rutherford, not knowing that Lincoln had already assumed to act for Matson, approached Lincoln on the subject of representing him in all this tangled litigation. Lincoln heard Rutherford's story, meanwhile looking troubled out of his eyes, with his gaze in the distance, and with his head shaking as he communed with himself. Lincoln then told Rutherford that he was under professional obligation to serve Matson the slave owner, unless he could be released. Rutherford had heard of Lincoln; he believed him to be an honorable lawyer, a high-minded man, who detested slavery as founded in injustice and bad policy; and when Lincoln told him that he had agreed to represent Matson, the slave owner, Rutherford's anger knew no bounds. Lincoln, now realizing what he had done, tried to free himself from the Matson employment; and he finally was about to be released by Matson. He communicated this fact to Rutherford with the announcement that he could serve Rutherford now if wanted. Rutherford would have none of Lincoln now; and so Lincoln went into the litigation for the slave owner, Matson. But the heart was out of him. The argument was directed to the habeas corpus proceeding; and Lincoln, in feebleness, without wit, stories, humor, invective or logic, got through a miserable performance. A lawyer named Constable, who was in the case against Lincoln, quoted from Curran's speech: "I speak in the spirit of the British law, which makes liberty commensurate, and inseparable from the British soil." Under these words Lincoln writhed, he twisted and winced, according to Ficklin who was watching Lincoln narrowly at this point of the debate. Lincoln lost the case, and, throwing his saddle bags over his horse, went on to the next county seat.¹ In a few weeks he was in Washington. Mrs. Lincoln and the children were with him.

Lincoln's record in Congress is a tracing of his wavering mind, his incoherent thinking, though it is not quite so contradictory as his votes and actions in the Illinois legislature were. He was a young man yet, and the novelty of Washington life afforded him great enjoyment. He attended the band concerts in front of the Capitol, and played at bowling with new-found friends. In the House he became acquainted with Robert C. Winthrop, and with David Wilmot, and with the greatly gifted Alexander H. Stephens, whose marvelous oratory on one occasion moved Lincoln to tears, so he wrote Herndon back in Springfield. He looked in at the Senate Chamber and there saw Webster, Clay, Cass, Benton, Crittenden, Cameron, Bell and Hale, some of whom were to play a part in his life as president. But there was a sight in the Senate which annoyed him. Stephen A. Douglas was there. He had been sent to the Senate by the Illinois legislature in 1846, and had taken his seat March 4, 1847. In April of 1847 Douglas had married, and very happily, Martha Martin of Rockingham, North Carolina; and he was grieving not at all for Mary Todd Lincoln. Martha Martin was a beautiful woman of fine breeding, out of a family of wealth; and Douglas was already at the top of the wave in Washington life, and moving in circles to which Lincoln as a congressman did not belong.

Soon in the House the Mexican war was to be a subject of debate. Lincoln had come to Congress after the time when the supplies for the war were voted, even if he had dared to vote against them, though given the chance. But there was something else which arose; and Lincoln in speaking of it and in dealing with it proved that his war speeches when running for Congress were not made in good faith; or if made in good faith that he had greatly changed his mind. In order to understand this matter some preliminary reference must be made to the general subject of Texas.

Mexico had been governed by a Spanish viceroy and council from 1519, when, about 1821, after many revolutions, riots, and insurrections, Spain was driven out. She had treated the Mexicans as she treated the Filipinos, using their land for the enrichment of the Catholic Church and taxing the people into poverty and famine.

¹ Beveridge, I, 392–7.

In 1821, after prolonged revolutionary activity, Mexico won her independence, and Augustin de Iturbide was made emperor. Soon he was forced to abdicate. He tried to regain his power and was shot. In 1824 Mexico was proclaimed a republic, a constitution was adopted similar to that of the United States, under which the various states of Mexico, of which Texas was one, enjoyed local self-government. Liberal laws were passed by the Mexican republic, which attracted immigration; and very soon Americans began to pour into Texas. The United States had acquired from France in 1804 the Louisiana territory; and by consulting a map it will be seen what it meant when John Quincy Adams, never to be suspected of having been in the service of the so-called slavocracy, advocated the purchase for the United States of the territory to the Rio Grande. In other words, he wanted to buy the Texas realm, just as it stands and looks on the map today. He advocated this in 1819, and 1827, and in 1832. He said in 1832, "the increasing settlements in Texas were all from this country (the United States), and that the inhabitants would prefer to belong to the United States." So much is now said to show that the wild charge later made, and which inflamed the country and influenced Lincoln, to the effect that Texas was maneuvered into the United States by the ever-scheming Southern Statesmen, who were thereby getting more land for slaves—that all this was pure senseless agitation on the part of intermeddlers who had no business except to interfere in the business of other people. To catch up again the thread of affairs in Mexico, it should be said that, after Mexico became independent of Spain, revolutions occurred at intervals. During one of these, slavery was abolished, but peonage was retained, which was slavery by another name. By this time there were many American settlers in Texas, who had taken their slaves thither; and they protested against the abolition of slavery; whereupon the Central Mexican government excepted Texas from the general abolition. Then came Santa Anna, a dictator over Mexico. He abolished the constitution modeled after that of the United States. He crushed resistance to his arbitrary will with ruthless, military severity. There was no issue about slavery at all. But there was an issue. The Texans were deprived by Santa Anna of the means by which they could defend themselves against hostile Indians; and the Americans in Texas rebelled against Santa Anna;

and these were Americans from the Northern States as well as the Southern. And so in 1836 Santa Anna swept into Texas to settle matters according to his will. Then followed the butchery of 180 Texans and Americans in the Alamo. The Alamo was a Franciscan Mission, which had become a fort by the end of the 18th century, located in what is now the city of San Antonio, Texas. Santa Anna and his forces assaulted the Alamo, while the Texans and Americans stood their ground as the Greeks did at the pass of Thermopylæ. Finally all were killed but five, and, the garrison being reduced, these were cruelly put to death.

About 1835 a mendacious reformer named Benjamin Lundy went into Texas to get land. He had been there twice about six years before that, and for the same purpose. And now he began to circulate in a contemptible little paper that he was editing, called the *Genius of Universal Emancipation,* the inflammatory calumny that the struggle for Texas independence was a plot of the Southern so-called slavocracy. He went further to play upon the prejudices and the wraths of Americans by asserting that the Texans were just nullifiers, as South Carolina was in 1832, and that all their acts were inspired by treasonable purposes against the rightful sovereignty of Mexico. If he had been before a Senate committee and there questioned and cross-examined as to what he really knew, it would have appeared that what he knew was little, and what he invented was much. But being an editor his wild talk went undisproved though not without challenge. The New York papers quoted him, and other newspapers, and in a measure the country was set afire, though not to the same extent as it was in 1854 when Chase flung a similar firebrand, as we shall see. The editors who work for universal emancipation are not concerned with emancipating the mind of man from prejudice, hatred, and untruth.

After becoming an independent nation, Texas wanted to join the Union of the United States; and in 1844, when the Democratic nominee was James K. Polk, the platform declared for the annexation of Texas, as well as for the reoccupation of Oregon at the "earliest practicable period," as "great American measures." The Whig nominee was Henry Clay, who ran upon a platform which said nothing about Texas, but a great deal about Henry Clay as a man actuated by the great principles of the Whig Party, a principles "inseparable from the public honor and prosperity." It also advocated the protective tariff. Polk was called by Roosevelt a man of monumental littleness; but in fact he was a man of education; and he was neither without character, nor judgment, and what he did for the territorial enlargement of the United States may to remotest history stand him in as good stead as the Panama Canal will ensure memory to Roosevelt. These were the most notable acts of the two men, and they are of the same quality of statesmanship. In the election which followed, Polk carried large states like New York and Pennsylvania; he even carried Maine and New Hampshire; he carried Illinois and Indiana; but he lost Massachusetts and Vermont. His popular vote over Clay was not very considerable, but he had 170 votes in the Electoral College to Clay's 105. Polk took up the presidency on March 4, 1845; and on July 4, following, Texas was annexed to the United States. The war with Mexico followed, and during its progress, as before shown, Lincoln was running for Congress and was making war speeches.

When Lincoln took his seat in Congress in December, 1847, the Mexican war had been in progress for twenty months, and the country was tired. The public mind was confused as to the real posture of affairs, as to the real *casus belli*, or whether there was any; as to what exactly the ever scheming slavocracy was up to, having been belied into believing that it always sought its own. There was bitterness in the Whig heart, too, because Henry Clay had been defeated, and a disciple of Jackson, now happily two years in the grave, had been chosen for president. Polk was called "Young Hickory," in compliment to his supposed resemblance to "Old Hickory"; and he was from Tennessee, too, though he had lost that state to Clay by 113 votes. It is evident that there was material here for infinite misunderstanding and quarrels, and congressmen and senators acted in that petty and ignorant and self-serving way, and to the distraction of the country, which seems to be inseparable from human nature where offices, honors, promotions, distinction are at stake. The Whigs, ever truculent in their impotence, saw a chance to strike back, both at Polk and at the Democrats, and to do this, and to mask their intentions they took moral ground. When men begin to talk righteousness they have run out of logic, if not out of honesty; and they are getting ready to sneak up to undeserved victory. Hence when Polk asked for $2,000,000 with which to settle up with Mexico respecting Texas, David Wilmot, from the tariff state of Pennsylvania, came forward with a rider to the bill that, in any territory acquired from Mexico, slavery should be excluded. We shall see a little further on, when considering the Missouri Compromise, so-called, of 1820, that Texas, being wholly South of 36° 30′, and extending as far west as the middle of Colorado, was controlled in spirit by the compromise; and gave Texas to slavery, just as Canada west of the Mississippi, if it had been annexed, would in spirit have been given to freedom, being north of 36° 30′. Indeed Oregon, which was far west of the end of the Missouri Compromise line, which terminated at the western boundary of the Louisiana Purchase, somewhat west of the middle of Colorado, was dealt with on the principle that climate determined whether slave labor could be used in a given country, and upon the clear conviction that Oregon had no use for slave labor. There was no cotton to be raised there. God or economic laws controlled the matter, according as one happened to be a theologian or a Douglas. The Wilmot Proviso, in the circumstances, appealed to the Lincoln mind. It satisfied his Whig resentment, and furnished him with a moral basis of attack on the Democrats. It was an addendum to the Stone-Lincoln resolution of 1837, in that it applied the doctrine that slavery was founded in injustice and bad policy to the territories, where they had applied it only to the District of Columbia, and that guardedly. Lincoln afterward in the debates with Douglas declared that he voted for the Wilmot Proviso, or rider, forty times. He did not do quite that; but he voted for it many times during its stormy course through the Congress.

Here should be interpolated what Lincoln wrote Williamson Durley on October 3, 1845. "I never was much interested in the Texas question. I never could see much good to come of annexation, inasmuch as they were already a free republican people on our own model. On the other hand I never could very clearly see how the annexation would augment the evil of slavery. It always seemed to me that slaves would be taken there in about equal numbers, with or without annexation. And if more were taken because of annexation, still there would be just so many the fewer left where they were taken from. It is possibly true to some extent, that, with annexation, some slaves may be sent to Texas and continued in slavery that otherwise might have been liberated. To whatever extent this may be true, I think annexation an evil. I hold it to be the paramount duty of us in the free states, due to the Union of the States, and perhaps to liberty itself (paradox though it may seem) to let the slavery of the other states alone; while on the other hand, I hold it to be equally clear that we should never knowingly lend ourselves, directly or indirectly, to prevent that slavery from dying a natural death—to find new places for it to live in when it can not longer exist in the old. . . . I understand the Liberty men to have viewed annexation as a much greater evil than ever I did."

This letter shows that as Lincoln was slow to think, so also was his conscience slow to be touched; and that he could not make up his mind, as radical men do. And further that he seemed to be deluded with the idea that to keep slavery from the new soil, and to preserve its purity, as soil, in that way, was more important than the consequences of such a course on the negroes themselves, who under such a policy would eventually be crowded in such populous districts that they could not live. The strangulation of slavery by such a remedy was the strangulation of human beings themselves; and the purity of soil which ensued from no slave's physical foot touching it was a consummation economically ludicrous. Yet Lincoln advocated this in the Douglas debates.

With so much of the background sketched, we are prepared to consider Lincoln's speech in Congress. It was January 12, 1848. It raised the question whether the Mexican war had been constitutionally commenced; where the boundary was between Texas and Mexico, and, by that determination, whether the United States had invaded Mexico or Mexico had invaded the United States. He proceeded with due regard to the rules of *Chitty on Pleading*, arguing boundary and other questions relating to them. He attacked Polk with bitterness. The speech did not make any stir in Congress; but Herndon in Illinois was concerned over it and wrote Lincoln in remonstrance of some of its arguments. Lincoln had said that Polk had invaded Mexico, and had thereby usurped power. Herndon claimed that the United States to repel possible invasion might invade the territory of another country first. To this Lincoln replied in argument to Herndon: "Allow the president to invade a neighboring nation whenever he shall deem it necessary to repel invasion, and you allow him to do so whenever he may choose to say he deems it necessary for such purpose, and you allow him to make war at pleasure. Study to see if you can any limit to his power in this respect, after having given him so much as you propose. If today he should choose to say he thinks it necessary to invade Canada to prevent the British from invading us, how could you stop him? You may say to him, 'I see no probability of the British invading us'; but he will say to you, 'Be silent, I see it, if you don't.' . . . The provision of the Constitution giving the war-making power to Congress was dictated, as I understand it, by the following reasons: Kings had always been involving and impoverishing their people in wars, pretending generally, if not always, that the good of the people was the object. This our convention understood to be the most oppressive of all kingly oppressions, and they resolved to so frame the Constitution that no one man should hold the power of bringing this oppression upon us. But your view destroys the whole matter, and places our presidents where kings have always stood." [1] These words must not be forgotten. They must be kept steadily in mind when we come to deal with Lincoln as the president, who did invade the Southern States, and on his own motion entirely; and without any Congressional warrant whatever, if that had sufficed to justify that crime against the law and humanity. This sound doctrine uttered in Congress when Lincoln was thirty-nine years old, if observed by him when he became president, would have saved billions of treasure and the lives of myriads of men, and all the fouling of the life of America in the days of Reconstruction, and all the loss of liberty which at the present time is evidenced by daily decisions of the Federal Courts, and by presidential usurpations. It would have saved the weakening of the American spirit, the falling off of intellectual and moral courage everywhere noticeable among the people. It would have prevented the reduplification of all those corruptions of public and private life, in business and in politics, in thinking and in writing and in newspapers and journals, which followed upon the Sicilian expedition, and the ruin of Athens. And if these consequences, when balanced

[1] Lincoln's Works, I, 111–12.

against the preservation of the Union by force, do not prove the Union not to have been worth saving at such a cost, then nothing of a historical nature is susceptible of proof.

But Lincoln in this speech in Congress uttered still other words of great fundamental truth; and they are such as condemn him out of his own mouth, and affix to his greatly celebrated conquest of the Southern States the stigma of disastrous wickedness. "Any people anywhere," he said, "being inclined and having the power have the right to rise up and shake off the existing government, and form a new one that suits them better. This is a most valuable, a most sacred right—a right which we hope and believe is to liberate the world. Nor is the right confined to cases in which the whole people of an existing government may choose to exercise it. Any portion of such people that can may revolutionize and make their own of so much of the territory as they inhabit. More than this, a majority of any such portion may revolutionize, putting down a minority, intermingled with or near about them, who may oppose this movement. Such minority was precisely the case of the Tories of our own Revolution. It is a quality of revolutions not to go by old lines or old laws; but to break up both and make new ones."

In other words, the secession of Texas from Mexico was accomplished by the assertion of a "most valuable, a most sacred right"; protest as Mexico might against the step; and though at the time of the secession Texas had less than 200,000 people, both whites and negroes, they or any portion of them had the right to revolutionize and to get free of Mexico. The question then arises what happened between 1848 and 1860 to make it wrong for 11,000,000 people, with an organized national government in every particular, to go their own way as the Confederate States of America, and under a constitution more liberal than that of the United States in that it forbade the protective tariff, the evils of which had by 1860 so distressed the people of the United States? "Nor shall any duties or taxes on importations from foreign nations be laid to promote or foster any branch of industry," is the language of the Constitution of the Confederate States. The men who framed that instrument had learned from experience and from Adam Smith that there were other things, besides slavery, embodied in the mercantile theory of economics, which make for inequality before the law, and for injustice and spoliation.

Lincoln's votes in Congress were nearly as contradictory as they were when he was in the legislature of Illinois. A petition was brought in by eighteen citizens to abolish slave trade in the District of Columbia. A motion was made to table the petition, and Lincoln voted against this. In a few days he voted with the pro-slavery members on a resolution relating to the same subject. A bill was offered to repeal all laws for establishing or maintaining slavery or the slave trade in the District of Columbia. Lincoln voted against it. Giddings made a fiery attack on slavery; and finally Lincoln offered a bill of his own. It provided that slavery in the District should be confined to the slaves then existing in the District; except that government officials who owned slaves might bring them in as servants for themselves and families while attending on public business in Washington; that children of the District born of slave mothers after 1850 should be free; and that negroes now slaves in the District should continue to be so; that if any owner wanted to free his slave he should be paid out of the national treasury for such slave. He added to this scheme a provision for catching and returning fugitive slaves found in the District. Later another bill was reported by another member which prohibited the slave trade in the District. A motion was made to table it. Lincoln voted no. There was great and hot debate on this bill but Lincoln took no part.

He voted consistently through both sessions of this Congress for the protective tariff and for internal improvements. The matter which vexed Congress and the courts in 1898, and just later, as to whether the Constitution follows the flag, came up. Should the Constitution be extended over California and New Mexico? Lincoln voted no on this. In the debates with Douglas he could not sufficiently denounce Douglas's so-called squatter sovereignty. Yet in Congress, and on July 27, 1848, he said, "I am in favor of leaving the people of any territory which may be hereafter acquired the right to regulate it [slavery] themselves, under the general principles of the Constitution." If so, why did he vote for the Wilmot Proviso five times, that being the exact number of times that he did vote for it?

Lincoln left Congress a failure and discredited. In June of 1848 he attended the Whig Convention at Philadelphia. The candidates were Zachary Taylor, a slave owner of Louisiana, and Henry Clay and Daniel Webster. There were others, but they have no place in this part of the history of Lincoln's mind and behavior. There were alternate delegates from Illinois who were for Henry Clay, who were trying to be seated in the convention. Lincoln opposed seating them; he was now determined to win for the Whigs, and Clay had not shown winning power in previous elections. Perhaps Zachary Taylor, the warrior in the struggle with Mexico, could beat the Democrats. Taylor received but six votes in the convention from New England, all the rest going to Clay or Webster. On the final ballot he had 171 votes to Clay's 32 and to Webster's 14. This gave him the nomination. According to the Whig practice no platform was adopted. But there was a party announcement, largely in praise of Taylor, who won the battles of Resaca de la Palma and of Palo Alto! Taylor was held forth to the American people as a man who would bring peace, prosperity and union. There was vague language like this: that "the Whigs are cherished in the affections because protective of the interests of the people." That might mean the tariff; but it was not explicit. The people were assured that Taylor would "make Washington's administration the model of his own." This was to gull the well meaning. "We ask our Whig friends throughout the nation to unite . . . in behalf of our candidate, whom calumny cannot reach, and with respectful demeanor to our adversaries, whose candidates have yet to prove their claims on the gratitude of the nation."

In this campaign the Native Americans recommended but did not nominate Taylor; the Liberty or Abolition party nominated John P. Hale of New Hampshire. The Democrats were torn by party strife, with Barn Burners and Hunkers emerging as names of dissentient delegations. The Barn Burners were opposed to slavery in the territories. The Free Soilers held a convention at Buffalo and nominated Martin Van Buren, a Democrat. The Democrats finally nominated Lewis Cass of Michigan. Taylor in the election polled 1,360,099 votes; Cass 1,220,544 votes; Van Buren 291,263. But Lewis Cass carried Illinois. A little later we shall see Lincoln's part in the campaign in his state. But before that, when he was in Worcester, Massachusetts, he wrote Herndon under date of June 22, 1848, to organize "Rough and Ready Clubs"; to take in everybody; to gather up all the shrewd, wild boys about town, whether just of age or a little under. "Let everyone play the part he can play best—some speak, some sing, all 'holler.'"

Lincoln made his last speech in the House on July 27, 1848, and it was a speech intended for circulation during the campaign, for the benefit of the Whigs. It was a poor performance of the demagogue variety. Referring to internal improvements, he confessed himself incompetent to discuss the constitutional aspects of the question. When he spoke of Zachary Taylor's principles, in answer to the Democrats who said, and truly enough, that he had none, Lincoln exclaimed that Taylor's principles were of the very essence of principle, for behold they were bound up with the policy of "allowing the people to do as they please with their own business." To the mock that Taylor was but a military coat-tail, to which the Whigs were holding, he retorted that the Democrats had lived for years under the coat-tails of Andrew Jackson. Defending the Whigs, and himself, as well, for having turned Henry Clay out like an old horse to die, he recriminated that the Democrats had done the same thing with Martin Van Buren. If Taylor were elected he did not know what Taylor would do with the Wilmot Proviso. He might veto it. Just the same he would vote for Taylor. Why? In order to defeat the Democrat Cass. "The people say to General Taylor, 'If you are elected shall we have a national bank?' He answers, 'Your will, gentlemen, not mine.' What about the tariff? 'Say yourselves.'" What was the tariff anyway? Lincoln had said in a Whig circular in 1843 that "by the tariff system the whole revenue is paid by the consumer of foreign goods, and those chiefly the luxuries, not the necessities of life."[1] "You Democrats, and your candidate, in the main are in favor of laying down in advance a platform—a set of party positions—as a unit, and then forcing the people, by every sort of appliance, to ratify them, however unpalatable some of them may be. We and our candidates are in

[1] Lincoln's Works, I, 74.

favor of making presidential elections, and the legislation of the country distinct matters; so that the people can elect whom they please, and afterward legislate just as they please without any hindrance, save only so much as may guard against infractions of the Constitution, undue haste, and want of consideration." [1] As a part of the Lincoln myth, Lincoln's voice has come down to us as a deep, good-natured drawl; and some of his words sound so when taken in by the inner or the outer ear. But he spoke in a treble, thin and high; and this language just quoted in logic and manner belongs to the falsetto voice. Consider, too, what he said about the war: "General Taylor himself, the noblest Roman of them all, has declared that as a citizen, and particularly as a soldier, it is sufficient for him to know that his country is at war with a foreign nation, to do all in his power to bring it to a speedy and honorable termination by the most vigorous and energetic operations, without inquiry about its justice, or anything else connected with it." This is a kind of intellectualization of things which permits attack upon a war as being not constitutionally commenced, then a support of the war because it has been commenced, even though the war be unjust when prosecuted. It enables the sponsor of such doctrines to be first a dutiful observer of his oath to support the Constitution, then a patriot when the Constitution has been overridden, then a loyal man in an unjust cause; and to be all at once. There is no better manifest of the Lincoln mind than these words. By the same sort of inconsistency it was possible to be for the Wilmot Proviso, yet to favor the rule of the people of a territory regulating for themselves the matter of slavery in it—subject to the Constitution.

The Free Soil party had been formed by radical Democrats of New York in 1848; and as we have seen it nominated Van Buren that year. It received the accession of the so-called "Barn Burners" who derived their name from the story of a Dutchman who burned his barn to be rid of rats. So these would destroy the Democratic party if necessary to destroy slavery. In Massachusetts the Free Soilers were quickly joined by Whittier, Longfellow and Lowell. Sumner had been fooled into the belief that the Mexican War was a mere plot of the slavocracy; and he had become a Free Soiler too. On June 28, 1848, he made a speech at Worcester, Massa-

[1] Lincoln's Works, I, 139.

chusetts, in which he denounced all wars, a position which he abandoned when a war came on to abolish slavery, as he conceived it to be waged. This type of idealistic radical goes where his emotions go. He was committed to a style of Christian oratory which has gone on in America to the corruption of the art as well as to the confusion of thinking about all important questions of state, and nearly everything else. "But it is said," he exclaimed, "that we shall throw away our votes, and that our opposition will fail. Fail, sir! No honest, earnest effort in a good cause can fail. It may not be crowned with the applause of men . . . But it is not lost; it helps . . . to animate all with devotion to duty which in the end conquers all. Fail! Did the martyrs fail when with their precious blood they sowed the seed of the church? . . . But where is it written that slavery finally prevailed?" This is the old doctrine that righteousness has some inherent strength which finally carries a cause to triumph, when nothing can be made a success except by men. And what are men? Are there more good men than evil men in the world? Are the good more active, more able than the evil? Slavery in some form has always had the victory. Sumner unconsciously was laying the foundations of a slavery over America more widespread and more intricately rooted than any slavery in the Southern states, however luridly exaggerated; and he was doing this by fanatical idealism which was used, nay linked in his own mind to principles of economic monopoly. To this faith Lincoln had not yet come. He could not now see that the Whig Party was worthless and doomed, and that it was futile to stick to it; and he had not at this time been sufficiently worked upon by the radical and persistent Herndon back in Illinois.

So it was that Lincoln, in September of 1848, was sent by the campaign committee of the Whigs at Washington to Massachusetts to spy out what the Free Soilers were doing, and to undermine them. Beveridge pointed out that Lincoln received no invitation from the Whigs to make speeches during this campaign. He was *persona non grata* because of his record in Congress. Winthrop, the Speaker of the House, was not pleased with what Lincoln had done in Congress. And so when Lincoln arrived in Massachusetts, by what authority did he make any speech? He came into town unheralded, and his presence was unknown until word leaked out that he was registered at a hotel. Then he was sought out to make a speech at the Town Hall on the evening of September 12, 1848. The Whig Convention was to be held the next day. Worcester was in a district which was being hard pressed by the Free Soilers, and the Whigs were badly in need of speakers to sustain their failing cause. Lincoln's Works contain no report of what he said at Worcester, and none of his New England tour which followed. We must depend upon the word of Edward L. Price of Milton, Massachusetts, who wrote to Herndon about Lincoln's visit to Worcester, and upon the newspaper accounts of his speeches elsewhere, at Boston and Cambridge.[1]

In the Town Hall Lincoln spoke nearly two hours. He defended General Taylor against the charge of having no political principles, saying that Taylor stood on the true Whig principle that the will of the people should prevail against executive influence and the veto power. In other words none of the Toryism of Jackson. He justified the Whigs in having no platform. He spoke against the Free Soilers, saying that their position on the exclusion of slavery from the territories was a Whig position, and that the Free Soilers had but one idea while the Whigs had many ideas. He condemned the Free Soilers for their activities, arguing that they were really trying to elect Cass. The Sumner idealism which advocated a devotion to duty, leaving the rest to God, he excoriated as follows: "When divine or human law does not clearly point out what is our duty, it must be found out by an intelligent judgment, which takes in the results of actions." He referred to the anti-slavery agitators with the remark that they were better treated in Massachusetts than in the West, and in Illinois, where recently one of them had been killed. This was a cold reference to Lovejoy, which infuriated the Free Soilers of Worcester. The speech as a whole was praised by the Whigs, but the Free Soilers called it a tedious affair. The next day the convention met. Rufus Choate was there, as were Winthrop and other celebrities. Choate made a brilliant speech. Lincoln was in the convention but was not invited to address it.

Lincoln then went on to Boston, where on the fifteenth of September he addressed a meeting at Washington Hall. He spoke at

[1] Herndon, I, 281 et seq.

Lowell on the sixteenth, at Dorchester on the eighteenth, at Chelsea on the nineteenth, where the night before Sumner had defended the Free Soil cause. On the twentieth, in the daytime, he addressed an audience at Temperance Hall. Two Whig conventions were being held there that day. At Dorchester he was described as a "capital specimen of a Sucker Whig, six feet at least in his stockings." His speech was characterized by the local press as plain, direct and to the point, powerful and convincing, and of capital effect upon the immense audience. His last speech was at Tremont Temple, where he followed William H. Seward. The Whig newspaper, the *Atlas*, gave more than a column to Seward's speech, but stated that it had no room for the notes which had been taken of Lincoln's, but that it was powerful and convincing, and was cheered to the echo. The Tremont Temple meeting was presided over by George Lunt, a lawyer of ability, later an author of several books of verse and prose. We shall hear later what he thought of Lincoln, and what he thought of slavery and abolitionism. He turned a Democrat when the Whig Party died, and to his death in 1885 led an active, useful, public spirited life, high minded in all his ways. Seward had uttered resistance to slavery at Tremont Temple. He said that the Democratic Party had its foundations in South Carolina, and the Whig Party on Plymouth Rock, not realizing evidently the full meaning of that figure when worked out to all conclusions. If the Free Soilers drew away all the advocates of Liberty there would be but Whigs and Democrats left compelled to bow to the will of the Southern aristocracy. Lincoln listening to these words was impressed with their Ciceronian dignity. The next day, according to Seward, Lincoln approached him and said, "I have been thinking about what you said in your speech. I reckon you are right. We have got to deal with this slavery question, and got to give much more attention to it hereafter than we have been doing."[1]

But many years passed from this day before Lincoln took a stand on slavery other than he had already taken. He did not know what to do about it. He could think out no program about it. He had none when he debated with Douglas in 1858. He did not see it in such a way that he was fired to attack it; and meanwhile there was

[1] "Memoirs of Seward," 79–80.

his own career to consider always with reference to what he did about it; and there was no time when he was not thinking of his career. He loved the Whig Party with a strange infatuation; and he held it in his arms until it gasped its last breath, this false, unprincipled aggregation of men who wanted to run the country, and who were bent on the tariff and the banks as consummations above all others, saving getting into office.

So Lincoln started back to Illinois in late September of 1848. Arriving in Chicago he made a speech in which he recapitulated what he had said in Massachusetts. He reached Springfield, but no notice was taken of his presence. During the campaign he made one speech at a small town in Sangamon County, where the audience proved to be unfriendly, and where a Democratic orator treated him to rude and disrespectful attack. His former law partner, Logan, was running for Congress. Lincoln gave him no aid; and Logan was defeated, not because of Lincoln's failure to help him, because Lincoln's help would have hurt him more than it would have done him good. And thus his district, the only Whig district in Illinois, went Democratic. In Menard County a whole ticket made up of patriots who had served in the Mexican war went to victory on a war wave. Worse yet, Illinois went Democratic. The cup was not yet full, but it soon spilled over. Shields, with whom Lincoln had almost fought the duel, was soon sent to the United States Senate. Yes, and Douglas was already there, and in rising fame. It seemed that Lincoln's career was ended, and that it had been ended by his own conduct—that was the bitterest reflection. With all these things on his mind, Lincoln sank into melancholy. He may have had a lazy colon, but it was made lazy by his physical habits and his brooding; and then the colon turned about and deepened his dejection. It is art to write pathos on his face in bronze or stone; but the secret of the pathos is what is here set down. He was doubtless wondering what was now to be done; how to lift himself out of the life of Springfield, how to create himself into something of significance; how as a human being to widen the horizon, to escape the corner of Fate, to breathe a clearer air and more freely, to rise above the dreary and meaningless days. They were now to be many and long.

Chapter VI   *Back in Springfield and Riding the Circuit*

SPRINGFIELD was now a town of 4553 inhabitants, slovenly and smoky and dull. Let us suppose that Lincoln had a constitution too robust, and nerves too strong, and an æsthetic too untrained to realize all its offending qualities. No less he had been in Washington, where he had heard the band concerts, and where as a congressman he had received a certain attention. He had been in New England and in Boston, and he had had a taste of the great world there and at the Capital. And now here was the Springfield which he had left for a career; the career was ended and he was farther down than when he started to rise. What was to be done? Political currents change, and he might be swept along again to some success; but when was that to be and just how? There was the practice of law; but he liked politics so much better by comparison. And then there was the problem of getting something to do at the law. He needed fees, for he was poor, perhaps poorer than any of his contemporaries at the bar. Many of them by this time had the foundations of fortune already laid, men like David Davis and O. H. Browning, perhaps Judd. In Fulton County near by there was Lewis W. Ross, a strong lawyer growing rich by this time, and about Lincoln's age; and also W. C. Goudy in the same county, younger than Lincoln but who was making money in land litigation and in that way preparing to go to Chicago later as the general solicitor of one of the railroads there. And there was Hugh Fullerton in Mason county, who was to be Lincoln's adversary in the Armstrong murder case of 1858; he was prospering. The list might be added to much more; but Lincoln's poverty was plain enough without more comparisons. It was not his honesty that kept him in straitened circumstances. Many lawyers remain in small prosperity because they have scruples about engaging in profitable branches of practice, such as corporation work in this day, and in that kind of litigation where popular interests are exploited by financiers. The Matson case already mentioned shows that Lincoln

RIDING THE CIRCUIT

was not over sensitive on the kinds of cases he took; though it should be said that he generally represented the defense, which was as much due to a sort of intercessor spirit as it was to the nature of his mind which made him more effective at resisting than in attacking. What kept Lincoln poor was his failure to see the chances about him, his lack of enterprise in taking advantage of the chances he did see, his habits as a lawyer, which sent him into court badly prepared, and his faculty for losing cases that should have been won; and finally his reputation as a lawyer with a jury, which dimmed his talents as a court lawyer to public understanding, rather to the clear understanding of men with important property interests at stake, who do not think that a jury lawyer is a good man to trust with questions which belong to the court itself for decision.

But now there were to be long days in Springfield, and about the circuit. It is a part of Illinois where the summers are unspeakably hot with all vitality gone out of the air; and of winters where the cold is bitter, down to zero and below for days at a time, with great snow and piercing winds. At that time the town, with no paved streets, was fogged with dust in the long summer days; and in winter the mud was fathomless, into which the farmers' wagons mired to the hubs about the square of the capitol. Let us take a summer day: Lincoln is in the law office on the second story of one of the small buildings on the square. What is he doing? He is reading newspapers, or else he is lying on the old sofa, or else he is talking to some man from the country, or a near-by town about some matter of law; or else he and Herndon are discussing politics, or Herndon is telling Lincoln what some book that he has read says about this or the other thing. Outside there is almost complete silence on the square. Some man may be calling to another on the street, or boys may be playing, with an occasional shout. A farmer's wagon goes by with the wheels chuckling. A dray passes rapidly making a rattle for a time, and sending up clouds of dust. Grocerymen and butchers are standing in their doorways; there is no trade for the moment. Well dressed clerks in the dry goods stores have come to the front door for air; they are looking about, and up at the sky. Perhaps it is going to rain. The air is very close. Perhaps there are clouds and the far rumble of melancholy thunder. Or a bell may be tolling, already the hearse is going by. The banker is bent over his ledger; one can see him through the front window. Once in a while one may hear the click of a billiard ball. Some of the entrances breathe forth a cool air weighted with the odor of lager; and a man may be staggering from some saloon, or reeling on his way to his horses, hitched to the rack of the square, where he may untie the halter and go home to the farm. Idle walkers pace the streets with nothing to do. It is too hot to work, or there may be no work. In the clerk's office of the court house scriveners are making entries in the books of record; while a farmer may be asking the clerk about some deed or document. Outside again a temperance lecturer is talking to someone on the corner, and making prophecies of what will come to pass. Some day there will be no saloons, no pool rooms, no men staggering about. All will be order, thrift, happiness at home. On another corner the ubiquitous savior of his country is telling someone whom he has buttonholed what is necessary to be done, and how it was that Lincoln fell down in Congress, why he is now upstairs in his office on this hot day, back again in the practice of law. Farther on an old fiddler, such as used to go to the country fairs, is playing old Celtic tunes on a squeaky fiddle, tunes which remind one of far-away Munster, or of Kentucky or Tennessee. And how strange the people look in their hats and trousers, long ago vanished out of memory, to us who are here now in life. And meanwhile far and near over this town of 4553 people housewives are cooking and washing and hanging out sheets and shirts on the line. Black coal smoke pours from chimneys; or it may be here and there the fragrant mist of burning hickory or maple. Whatever is going on, there is much futility here. One feels it to the point of melancholy. And if it be the end of the summer and the exhausted leaves are drifting down in the silence of the sunshine one thinks of far places, and is sure that somewhere something is going on that is worth while; and that there are life and happiness in lands of better circumstanced people.

Or if it be a winter day the wind is blowing, making all the lawyers' signs swing and creak. The snow is blown into the doorways and the stairways, and into the faces of people pressing their course against the blast. The butcher is now inside; but to keep his meat fresh he has but little fire, and his breath may be seen to wreathe from his mouth as one looks in while passing. The groceryman has a fire, and about it are gathered the farmers and their wives, pausing a time after having made their purchases, before braving the cold on the way home. The children may be romping from school, throwing snowballs and scuffling. But if politics is now talked, and there is no doubt that this is the case, the discussion goes on by the fire of the druggist, or possibly in the saloon; while the click of the billiard balls is kept from the ears of the moralist by the closed door.

On such a day Lincoln is upstairs in his office, if not away attending court in Charleston, or somewhere in the circuit. But the roads are now all but impassable. Around the square great ruts, frozen hard as stone, make the wagons rattle, and pitch and sway. But if Lincoln is in town he is at the old pastime of talking to Herndon; or else he is lying on the couch reading newspapers, the *Intelligencer*, perhaps the *New York Tribune*. Or else a client has come in and by the fire his clothing and boots reek as they thaw out and the air is redolent of the barnyard. The conference may be long, too; but besides Lincoln may be telling him a story, or else listening to one from the client, which he will later re-shape and by doing so give it a more telling point.

Then there is Mrs. Lincoln at home. She did not go with Lincoln to New England, to Boston, she did not get to see Niagara Falls on the way home. She may be in wrath for this at the very time of one of these pictured days of winter or summer; but if she has forgotten this offense, there is no day that Lincoln does not do something to arouse her distaste, her indignation. He has forgotten to do something that she asked him to do; or else he has been lying about on the floor reading newspapers, and when there was a knock at the door he has gone to answer the summons, and has presented himself in his stocking feet to the well dressed lady caller; and he has stood before her, with his coat off, and his one suspender barely holding up his trousers. To the inquiry whether Mrs. Lincoln is in he has said, "I reckon she is," and he has admitted the fashionable lady about the time that Mrs. Lincoln appears to witness the unceremonious and shocking conduct of her husband. Her eyes have told him what is to come when the lady is out of the way, and he has gone uptown to escape for as long as possible the wrath that is surely to descend.

Amid all the tedious routine of the days and the weeks in Springfield where nothing happens he is probably asking himself if life is worth living. Is it of any earthly moment to be living in such a town, or in any town with nothing to do with which to employ his energies to some end that solves the meaning of life, and to be consorting with such a wife? Is this marriage? Is there nothing more ahead than the petty law cases, or even the harder and more important law cases; and is there nowhere to go but around the circuit again to Havana, to Pekin, to Charleston and Beardstown, stopping at the same inns, meeting mostly the same lawyers and going through the same processes of picking juries, examining witnesses and making arguments to juries? But after all, these are the most interesting happenings of his life; and when he is away he does not have to face the gathering brows of Mary, his wife; and to submit to the sharp words that she rains upon him like quick hail. All things considered, is there enough here to make Lincoln self-absorbed, woe struck in appearance, dripping with melancholy as Herndon expressed it? Might this not be a good time for reading and self-culture, and getting ready for a new office? One may be in store for him.

The one unhappy man, to paraphrase Goethe, is he who is possessed of an idea which he cannot carry into action, and vainly tries to do so. This was Lincoln at this time when he was forty years of age. He wanted to be esteemed of the people, and to be worthy of that esteem. But for him to be esteemed was to hold office, and to do work in office for which he was praised and rewarded. That was his forte in life; his only way to reach the respect and reverence of his fellows, which he craved so earnestly, if not passionately. And now he was denied what he most wanted, with the likelihood that he was never to have it. If he had only seen at this time that he was at the parting of the ways, all history would have been different. It was the time now to get away from Whiggery with its vicious protective principle, with which the young Republic had been inoculated by the Mephistophelean Hamilton; and to learn that if Jefferson and Madison in the Kentucky and Virginia Resolutions stood for the rights of the states, it was not to oppose any Union, but only to prevent monopolists and centralists from crawling into the Union as into a wooden horse, wherefrom they might leap when the horse was hauled within the walls of the city, and capture its wealth. It was time to get away from the shifty Henry Clay, not merely by supporting the nondescript Taylor, but by casting over for good and for all the unprincipled influence of that man. It was time to search out Webster in all his resounding hollowness, and to do this by testing him by profounder and truer thinkers like Jefferson. In that way the lamentable hold of his reply to Hayne would have been shaken loose, particularly as Webster himself abandoned his ground in 1850.

Lincoln read Milton's poetry in these years; but not Milton's great prose. The essay on Government and Liberty, and what Milton wrote of Cromwell would have been good for Lincoln. He would there have found words of apt application to the impostors and the robbers who got hold of the government under Lincoln and afterward engineered the abhorrent era known as Reconstruction. He might have read in the twelve years to ensue in Springfield the essays of Mill, and particularly Adam Smith, where he would have seen that negro slavery is only one form of labor service, only one phase of the labor problem, and that masters are everywhere and always in a conspiracy against the workers to use them and to rob them by taxes, by banks, by privileges, and by superstitions like the balance of trade. He might have read Montesquieu, and there seen the idea which the framers of the Constitution used in dividing the sovereign powers granted the general government by the states into legislative, executive and judicial functions; and how by a subtle device the general government became a nation in powers while remaining a confederation in system. He did not read Montesquieu. Lincoln more or less knew Story's *Commentaries on the Constitution*, which was unfortunate, as Story was a better lawyer than he was a historian; and there were more reliable studies of the Constitution than those that Story made. Besides there were the original documents and notes, Madison's and the like, which he might have investigated with care. He did not have the intellectual inclination to do this; or else he was satisfied with the daily life of reading newspapers. There was Hallam's *Constitutional History of England.* Lincoln did not read it. There was Grote's *History of Greece* with its historical deductions as to the institutions of Athens as an ideal state, all published between 1846 and 1856. Lincoln never looked into it. There was De Tocqueville's *Democratie en Amerique*, translated into English between 1835 and 1840 more than once. He did not read it. Hildreth's *History of the United States* appeared between 1849 and 1856; Lincoln never turned a page of it that anyone knows of. The first volume of Bancroft's *History of the United States* was published in 1834. It passed Lincoln by. Spencer's *Social Statics* was given to the public in 1850. This may have been one of the books that Herndon told Lincoln about, as he spoke to him of Darwin's *Origin of Species* in 1859. But Lincoln read neither of these works. Mill's *Political Economy* came out in 1848. It might never have been published for aught that Lincoln cared for it for his own reading. His mind had a certain philosophical turn, but he read no Bacon, no Butler's *Analogy*, not to say no Aristotle, no Plato, no Berkeley, no Descartes, no Spinoza, no Locke. His mode of self-expression was in oratory, but he did not study Fox, nor Pitt, nor Burke; though he admired the style of Calhoun, and read some of his speeches. He loved the homely wisdom of Æsop. One would have expected Lincoln to have progressed to Montaigne, Epictetus, perhaps Carlyle. He did not do so. He was not interested in the past, in the rise and fall of other empires or democracies. It might have been of profit to his countrymen if he had known something of this history as written by Herodotus and by Thucydides. He did not learn the story of England as reported by Hume. Macaulay's first two volumes of the *History of England* were published by 1848, but Lincoln was oblivious to its existence. He read no Grotius, no Pufendorf, no Hobbes, no Sir Thomas More. He made no exploration into international law. When he was in Congress the Congressional Library had about 45,000 volumes. Many men of limited chances in youth and of hungry minds would have spent long hours in study in that library. He did not do so. He knew little or nothing of the history of liberty, as the debates with Douglas showed.

Here were twelve years ahead of him before he would be president, in the quiet of Springfield, and with what Herndon called an energetic mind; and yet during this time he read only parts of

Shakespeare, Burns, Byron's *Childe Harold* and *Bride of Abydos*, some of Milton's poetry; and for the rest newspapers. The course was well enough if there was nothing in life for him to do but to learn the use of words, by which to write the First Inaugural's close better than Seward could do it, and to turn the rhythms of the Gettysburg address. But he was to be clothed with the power of deciding whether there should be war upon the South, and it was fatefully unfortunate that he did not know the nature of the government, that he did not know what sovereignty was, nor where it resided in the American system. He was to have great decisions to make involving international right; but in the idiocy of Time it made no difference, as what he did, wrongly, was supported by armies and expunged by the processes of victory. The question then is, however, was he now making himself according to a predestined pattern, or did everything happen as it would? If there is anything of worth in civilization, and if man be responsible to its calls, Lincoln is censurable for wasting these years, just as men at the time of their neglects may be properly reproved for idling and playing. It did not matter that he did not read Tennyson as he was being published, or Browning; or that he had no taste for Keats or Shelley, for Homer or for Virgil. He had the capacity to enjoy these books, and one feels that if he had roused himself to read them he would have spent many happy hours in Springfield which were otherwise heavy on his hands. But such works were not in his line of life. As he liked Petroleum V. Naseby and Artemus Ward at a later time, it is clear enough that his fondness for humor was an arrested inclination, considering that he read no Smollett, no Sterne, no Fielding, no Dickens. Lincoln has done as much as any prominent figure in America to instruct the youth of limited advantages and outlook to loaf and to trust God. The intellectual eagerness of Emerson, the passion for culture which was Jefferson's, the industry which was Franklin's, were not in his nature. He was a lazy mind.

Again if he was to be a lawyer, and nothing else, there was much to study, as he found out at the near close of his career as a lawyer when he went to Cincinnati, as an associate of Stanton in a patent case. We shall see this later. Beginning to ride the circuit again he took up the study of Euclid and carried the volume with him, reading it at odd times. Sometimes he would be found early in the morning by the fire of the inn poring over Euclid. This was akin to *Chitty on Pleading*. His resort to this book leads one to believe that he distrusted the legitimacy of his logical faculties, and wanted to strengthen and straighten them. "He was naturally indisposed to undertake anything that savored of exertion," wrote Herndon of Lincoln; and so he read at Shakespeare, at the Bible, books that he had read in part and desultorily all along from the New Salem days. What one has once read one can read again in a listless way, in an idle mood. But he did not know Shakespeare. In 1863 he wrote Hackett, the actor, "some of Shakespeare's plays I have never read; while others I have gone over as frequently as any unprofessional reader. Among the latter are Lear, Richard III, Henry VIII, Hamlet, and especially Macbeth. I think that nothing equals Macbeth." [1] There is no Julius Cæsar here, no Othello, no Tempest, no Antony and Cleopatra, no Troilus and Cressida, and no Romeo and Juliet; none of the comedies, none of the historical plays, save the two which he mentioned. "He never in his life sat down and read a book through, and yet he could readily quote any number of passages from the few volumes whose pages he had hastily scanned," wrote Herndon. Many others spoke of Lincoln's astonishing memory, particularly his memory of stories which were humorous. It has already been shown that his first verses were satirical; and so it was that he cared most for Burns's "Holy Willie's Prayer." How did he escape visiting his own sense of satire on the vulnerable Whigs? They were made up of Holy Willies, impostors and hypocrites—and they begot the Republican Party which elected him president.

When Lincoln arrived in Springfield in the fall of 1848, he had a few months yet to serve as a Congressman, as a lame duck. He tried, therefore, to use his position to get office for some of his constituents, but without success. He tried in his own behalf to be appointed land commissioner of Illinois, the place that the successful Douglas had occupied. He failed in this after using devious and censurable methods to win the office. He played both ends against the middle, and split hairs north by northwest side to this end. He repeated the exact psychology which he showed when trying to take

[1] Lincoln's Works, II, 393.

RIDING THE CIRCUIT

Menard County away from Baker in 1844. He had promised to support Cyrus Edwards, brother of Ninian, for the registership. But when Lincoln looked upon the office with desiring eyes he conceived a compromise with the circumstances, and wrote that he would take it provided it could be secured for Illinois only by himself taking it. Otherwise he would not take it. He must not only be chaste but above suspicion, were his words. Finally both Lincoln and Edwards were passed by, and a man named Butterfield got the place. The Whig mechanics of Springfield had filed with the Department of the Interior a protest against the appointment of Lincoln, basing their objections to him upon his record in Congress. So was Lincoln reduced in his own town. Someone suggested to Lincoln that he might be appointed governor of the territory of Oregon. Lincoln did not want the place, and Mrs. Lincoln rose in her wrath against the idea. She would not leave Illinois. But in truth the office was never offered to him. Finally out of all this Lincoln was appointed Secretary of Oregon, and so the Whig measurement of Lincoln was taken. Lincoln promptly and with spirit declined the appointment.

There was much to do in Springfield now of a public nature, and in Illinois. The school system was in bad condition. Movements were started to better the educational facilities. Lincoln took no part. The reader will remember his address to the people of Sangamon County in 1832. He was not carrying on to give everyone the advantages of enough education to read the Scriptures and books of moral instruction. He was not Franklin. Soon Douglas was to found the Chicago University, and to that end give it a large amount of land. Yet Douglas has been put aside, by hosts of scribblers, and by writers of rank as well, as a man inferior to Lincoln in depth of spirituality, in moral integrity. There was never anything falser written. In the debates and to the last Douglas showed himself to be franker, more forthright, more honest of mind than Lincoln. His drawback with the sentimentalist has been that he was an intellectual who refused to mix morals, so-called, and statecraft.

A great deal has been written of Lincoln as a lawyer. When I was a youth in central Illinois the law was practiced and the courts were run exactly as they were in Lincoln's time. The court house at Lewistown, Illinois, where my father practiced for twenty-five years, was built in 1837, and in it Lincoln appeared on a few occasions. It was a brick building with great limestone columns in front; and between these and the front wall was a right and left stairway leading to the landing where the door was that led into the court room. Between these columns Lincoln stood and spoke in the summer of 1858 when he was running for the Senate against Douglas. In these days of my youth, and in Lincoln's life to the end, the jury was supreme. The right of trial by jury was revered with the whole Bill of Rights as the gospel of the law. No cases were taken from the jury. That expedient by which the judge, elective or otherwise, has grown to usurp the whole function of the law's adjudications was one of the inventions of the Federal Judiciary. There was always the matter of law to be raised after verdict, that the verdict was against the weight of the evidence, and on that ground to seek to have the verdict set aside. But the practice in this particular was jealously circumscribed by rules and precedents. Hence in Lincoln's day the great objective was to win the jury, and Lincoln knew how to do this. What would Lincoln say now of the jurisprudence which has grown up as the fruit of the War for Liberty and Union, by which the jury has been turned into dummies, and by which corporations are called citizens, so that if one is organized by New York men, but under the laws of New Jersey, it is a citizen of New Jersey, and if sued in New York's state courts may fly to the Federal Courts as to a city of refuge to escape the laws of the state, and under the constitutional clause which gives the Federal Courts jurisdiction over "controversies between citizens of different states"? The work of moralists against the Fugitive Slave Law became the head of the corner for fugitive corporations. In such court rooms as that one at Lewistown, Lincoln now was trying cases. The farmer and village audience gathers; and sits in benches outside the railing which bars the privileged space for lawyers, the jury and the judge. The jury has rattan chairs, or benches for its use; the judge is throned somewhat above the jury. A long trial table is at the right or left of the judge's seat where the lawyers sit with their clients back of them, and the witness chair is at one side or the other of the judge, sometimes a little above the level of the trial table, sometimes not;

but in any case the witness is facing the lawyers, and the judge can look down upon him, frowning or doubting, or admonishing him to speak louder, or commanding him to repeat what he has said or not to do so.

Lincoln wrote a letter to a young man who wanted to become a lawyer, telling him to read Blackstone and *Chitty on Pleading*, and to work and work, that the whole secret of success in the law was work. Lincoln did not follow his own advice. The man who becomes the learned, the good lawyer is he who, in the intervals of courts, and when there is no business, reads the books of the law. When Lincoln started to practice law there were not many volumes of the reports of the Supreme Court of the United States. He could have read every one of them. One young lawyer in Chicago, having nothing to do, read all the reports of the state Supreme Court, and in that way became the most learned lawyer of his day, and very rich at last into the bargain. Lincoln would not do this. In the office he told stories, talked politics with farmers and townsmen, read poetry aloud to Herndon, lay sprawled upon the old sofa reading the newspapers. Or else he was in fits of abstraction, apparently seeing nothing before him, but still staring into space. If he was not occupied in any of these ways he was writing letters. He wrote letters by the score, mostly on political situations, and what to do about them. In these years he was trying to get law business, and he was not averse to writing letters to get it. In this way he secured the lucrative employment in the tax case in which the Illinois Central Railroad was involved, later to be noticed. He did not have moral scruples about the kind of cases he took, as witness the Matson case already mentioned. When a railroad was sued by a man with a leg off, or by an injured passenger, or by a farmer struck on the highway, or encroached upon by the tracks and highways of the corporation, Lincoln was quite willing to defend the railroad before the jury. He did this sort of work for years under the lawyer who had the legal business for the Illinois Central Railroad for the district between Iroquois County and Effingham County.

The stuff that has been written about Lincoln as the just, conscientious lawyer who would take no bad case is pure unctuous twaddle. It is in a measure supported by a habit of business on Lincoln's part, of which there is evidence. As he went about the circuit he was used to meet with farmers or townsmen who had small matters upon which they consulted him on the street or in the court room. They related to a crib of corn, or to a boundary fence, or to the title to a hog, or a cow, or a horse. Lincoln advised such people freely, and charged them nothing for it on many occasions. Indeed he was glad to help such trivial suitors to escape the expense of litigation, which he knew beforehand, and which they did not so well know; as they did not appreciate the real worth of success even if Lincoln won for them in the courts. Many lawyers do such things; all lawyers do who have any regard for their own standing at the bar. In the New Salem Museum there are today letters which Lincoln wrote to men who had consulted him on such little disputes, in which Lincoln expressed satisfaction that the matter, whatever it was, had been adjusted without a suit, and in which he wrote that he had no fee to ask. In such experiences in a lawyer's life there would be no fee to ask of any moment anyway; and any lawyer worthy the name is glad to help distressed humanity here and there, especially when it costs him nothing but a word spoken in advice on the street corner out of his wisdom and experience. Lincoln was also a fair lawyer, an honest lawyer. By this is meant that his stipulations were reliable; he did not try to deceive the court, and he did not do so. He did not overcharge his clients. He did not take advantage of them. He did not commit maintenance, or champerty, though he may have helped poor clients with their costs of suit, and he took cases, no doubt on a contingent basis of reward. That is done now and was done then with perfect propriety. But this is not to say that he never over-argued the facts, or used his logic to play with the facts and the law, or resorted to dramatics to win the jury, or made appeals that moved them to tears and washed away what reason they had. He did all of these things. And as his cunning and his skill became famous over the circuit he was suspected of tricks which he did not do, and of which stories grew up about him as much against his integrity as the myths which have persisted in favor of his great morality as a practitioner.

He was an honest lawyer, just as Browning, and Judd, and Herndon, and many of his contemporaries were honest lawyers; and as men are honest lawyers to this day. A lawyer dare not be anything else, who does not want to sink to the dregs of the profession. But honesty as a lawyer has nothing to do, necessarily, with the kind of cases that a lawyer will manage for a fee. The judges are elevated out of this school of complaisant morality, and they are supposed to hold the scales evenly balanced between the rich and the poor. They do not do so. The abolitionists screeched against the Supreme Court, because many of the judges were appointed from the South, and, bred in the principles of states' rights, ruled for slavery as an institution to be controlled by local law. Today the judges are appointed out of the offices of corporations and they actually weave a jurisprudence which gives privilege all it asks for. The wrong of slavery was as nothing to the wrongs of imperial business, which has effectuated a deeper and more cruel slavery of both whites and negroes. But are the Supreme Court Judges dishonest? On the contrary they are honest, honest as lawyers are; but they are following their masters' wishes, as a lawyer obeys the instructions of his client, and tries to serve him fully. So it was that Lincoln would defend a saloon keeper for selling without a license where the fine was $10; and he would do his best to bring about the acquittal of a killer, or to win a divorce case, or to prevent a brakeman from recovering damages for the loss of a leg. When the matter is refined to the last degree, or perhaps short of that, such championships are immoral; and in similar situations of ethical choice an Emerson would stand strictly for what is just and true. But by the standards which are applied to the conduct of lawyers, Lincoln was honest. It was not his honesty that kept him from making money, however. He had no head for speculation, and indeed none for investing his money profitably; and though he was busy a good deal of the time in the courts, he gathered no great fees. He couldn't pay his own debts, and judgments were rendered against him which remain unsatisfied of record to this day in the Circuit Court of Sangamon County.

Lincoln was an advocate, a barrister, or he was nothing. He disliked the work of the office; he loved the action, the freedom of the court room where he could employ his powers of mimicry and acting, his story telling, his invective, and his oratory. He drafted few legal papers. He had no order, no method about the law. He did not prepare his cases. He would go into court and lose a case that anyone should have won; and Whitney reported that Lincoln in a single year was beaten in every case he had in the whole circuit. In spite of all this he acquired great fame as a jury lawyer. Some called him the best of his day in Illinois. But this is an appraisement that can have no facts to support it. One would have to know all the jury lawyers of Illinois, and to know what their performances were, and under what circumstances, to be able to pass a judgment like this upon which anyone could rely. There were many able jury lawyers in Illinois at the time, and one of these was Leonard Swett, who was Lincoln's friend. Swett was a great lawyer as well as a great advocate. And he handled jury cases of much greater difficulty than any Lincoln ever did. An aspect of psychology emerges in the consideration of Lincoln as a lawyer, and that is that he was for the most part on the defendant's side. He was resisting. He was saying, "you must prove the case against me. I have nothing to do but to prevent you from doing this. I can defeat you if I can keep you from laying a good wrestling hold upon me. I can discomfit you by driving holes in your testimony, in your plan of campaign." One will find this method of dialectic in his debates with Douglas, in his inaugurals, and in his maneuverings to make the South fire the first shot.

John T. Richards, an industrious lawyer of Chicago, went through all the reports of the Supreme Court of Illinois, and made a tabulation of the cases in which Lincoln appeared in that tribunal. He also searched through the reports of the Supreme Court of the United States with the same object in view. He found that Lincoln appeared in the state court in 175 appeals between 1837 and 1861, though several of these were split appeals, that is, the same case appealed on different issues or questions. By another tabulation he found that Lincoln was assisted by other lawyers in 110 of these cases, out of which he lost 43 and won 67. In appeals which he conducted alone he won 38 and lost 63. Another story is told by considering the matters involved in these appeals. They were about promissory notes, trespass, false imprisonment, mechanics' liens, trover for hogs, suits against innkeepers for money stolen from a guest, breaches of contract, constructions of municipal charters, to enforce bets on elections, *quo warrantos*, malpractice of physicians, foreclosures, actions of debt on bonds of officials, slander, condemnation, divorce; one case where the assignment of a patent was involved; one where a fire insurance question was the issue. And there was the Illinois Central litigation which Lincoln conducted by himself, and in which he got a fee of $4750, or $5000, counting his retainer. This case will be noticed in the final words on Lincoln as a lawyer. It is apparent that none of this litigation is of the most important kind.

In the Supreme Court of the United States, Lincoln appeared in the case of William Lewis for the use of Nicholas Longworth against Thomas Lewis, administrator of Broadwell. He was assisted in this case by another lawyer. It was first heard in the Federal Circuit Court, and because of a division of opinion it was certified to the Supreme Court. Lincoln and his associate lost the case, the opinion being written by Taney, with McLean dissenting. The other case was Forsyth against Reynolds, which involved land in Peoria. Lincoln and his associates won this case, with Salmon P. Chase and a well-known lawyer of Illinois, N. H. Purple, opposing him. This was in 1853.

These are the appeals. Lincoln tried many cases where there was no appeal. A few words may be said concerning the Illinois Central case where Lincoln received the handsome fee mentioned before. The Illinois Central Railroad by its charter was to pay a certain per cent of its earnings into the public treasury, which was to be in lieu of all taxation. But it was questioned that the charter meant quite this; and some of the counties through which the road ran were bent on taxing the railroad, and to have the question tested whether they could do so. Lincoln was interviewing county officials with a view of representing the counties, and finally, according to words in one of Lincoln's letters, some kind of tentative employment of him had been made to force the railroad to pay more taxes than a percentage of its earnings. "I am somewhat trammeled by what has passed between you and me," he wrote the clerk of the court of Champaign County, on September 12, 1853, "feeling that you have the first right to my services, if you choose to secure me a fee something near as much as I can get from the railroad. 'The question' is the largest that now can be got up in this state and therefore in justice to myself, I cannot afford, if I can help it, to miss a fee altogether. If you choose to release me, say so by return mail, and there an end. If you wish to retain me, you had better get authority from your court, come directly over to Bloomington, in the stage and make common cause with this county," that is, McLean. This letter is not in Lincoln's Works. It will be found in Townsend's *Litigant*, pages 22-3. The end of this matter was that the counties did not bestir themselves, and so Lincoln wrote to Mason Brayman, the local attorney of the Illinois Central, on October 3, 1853. He said: "Neither the County of McLean nor anyone on its behalf has yet made any engagement with me in relation to its suit with the Illinois Central on the subject of taxation. I am now free to make an engagement for the road, and if you think of it you may 'count me in.'" Brayman did so and paid Lincoln $250 by way of retainer. When the work was done Lincoln made his fee $5000, which was considered rather much by the railroad, and besides it was not very affluent at the time; but after some delay, and a friendly suit, Lincoln had his fee allowed and it was paid by the railroad which had come out of the creative brain of Douglas. In this whole transaction Lincoln did not show a very high sense of professional ethics, of professional propriety, though there was nothing dishonest about it. He was willing to be on either side, just as he was in the Matson case. From the time of this tax case he was attorney for the railroad until he was nominated for the presidency.

It is quite clear altogether that as a lawyer Lincoln did not champion the poor and the downtrodden; he was doing his best to make money, and to that end he took the side of the strong. In this day in Chicago or New York City he would have graduated into corporation practice, as far as he could have done so. There was a time when he had an inclination to follow his profession in Chicago; but as he believed he had a disposition toward consumption he was afraid of the cold and the lake winds. If he had done so he would likely have become what his son became, a corporation director, and a counsel for gas and street railways. It is not for lack of facts that the myths have grown up about Lincoln. The facts have been disregarded in order that the portrait of him might be drawn which America wanted. This of itself is a spiritual fact. It is a struggle on the part of the people to become that which they love. That is well if they do not at the same time pardon or even admire what they would hide in Lincoln, by which intellectual dis-

RIDING THE CIRCUIT

honesty they have him for high minded moralities for private example, and for wars and political oppressions where his course has made a precedent for them.

Two other cases may be detailed briefly before Lincoln as a lawyer is shown in his more effective rôle, that of a barrister. The first is the McCormick reaper litigation, which passed through the courts in 1854–55. McCormick sued John H. Manny, who had a factory at Rockford, Illinois, and some others, for infringement of the McCormick patents. At once the two ablest patent lawyers of the land were arrayed against each other in this contest. They were Edward M. Dickerson of New York for McCormick, and George Harding of Philadelphia for Manny. Harding afterward, in 1876, wrote a full account of what happened, so far, at least, as Lincoln was concerned. The case was before Judge Drummond at Chicago; and Harding wanted some local lawyer to assist in the defense, one who knew the judge and was respected by the judge. After some inquiry, and some tentative consideration of a Chicago lawyer, someone suggested the name of A. Lincoln, or Abe Lincoln at Springfield. So Harding sent a man named Watson, who afterward became the president of the Erie Railroad, to Springfield to call upon Lincoln, with a view to employing him in his discretion. Watson when he arrived in Springfield found Lincoln's office closed; so he went to Lincoln's house. It was still a one-story affair; the second story such as it is today, where there is now a Lincoln Museum, was not put on the house until 1857; and that was done on an occasion when Lincoln was away on the circuit and unable to interfere with Mrs. Lincoln's ambition for a better house. As there was neither bell nor knocker, Watson rapped with his knuckles. Finally a woman stuck her head from a window and inquired who was there. It must have been Mrs. Lincoln, for the voice which spoke demanded whether the caller had come upon politics or business. Being told by Watson that the matter was business, Lincoln came forth with neither coat nor vest, and conducted Watson into a room, poorly furnished, where the talk commenced, and where Watson began to study the man whom he had been sent to employ in this important litigation. Watson was anything but impressed with Lincoln. However, as the talk proceeded he decided that he would better employ him for what he might be worth, as a lawyer of the community who knew Judge Drummond. Having gone so far, not to employ Lincoln was to risk Lincoln's possible hostility. Lincoln was greatly surprised when in addition to being retained he was paid a good fee with promise of considerable more when the litigation was finished. Lincoln was left with the impression that he was to make an argument in the case, and that he would have a prominent part in its management. One can imagine the happiness, the satisfaction that came to Lincoln and to Mrs. Lincoln in that little house on that afternoon when their work of setting up a bed was interrupted by this fortunate visitation from afar.

But when Watson told Harding what Lincoln looked like and acted like and the circumstances of the call, and why it was that he had employed Lincoln, despite the unprepossessing appearance of Lincoln, Harding approved it no less, believing that Watson was wise to keep Lincoln from taking the other side of the case, particularly as arrangements had gone forward to retain Edwin M. Stanton, a brilliant, aggressive lawyer from Pennsylvania, on the side of the defense with Harding. These arrangements were soon perfected and thus there were Harding, Stanton and Lincoln for the defense arrayed against Dickerson and his associate Johnson for the complainant McCormick. Lincoln set to work with hopeful industry to prepare himself. He wrote out pages of notes, and gave his most studious thought to the case. It was removed to Cincinnati for trial, and Justice McLean of the Supreme Court was called in to sit with Judge Drummond on the hearing.

In September, 1855, the case was called, and Lincoln was present to take part in the most important employment of his life. But Harding and Stanton had decided to shut Lincoln out of the case. They didn't want him, and particularly was this true when they saw him standing on the steps of the Cincinnati Hotel in his provincial clothes, with his trousers hitched up between his knees and his ankles, and with his habitual umbrella of rusty cotton. When Lincoln, Harding and Stanton were introduced to each other, the eastern lawyers barely spoke to the uncouth Lincoln. And when Harding proposed to Stanton that they go now together to the court house, Lincoln, not yet fully snubbed into an understanding of the attitude of Stanton and Harding, interposed in the vernacular of New Salem, "Let's go up in a gang." Stanton mumbled to

Harding, "Let that fellow go up with his gang," and with this they walked away, leaving Lincoln standing alone on the steps of the hotel. The lawyer mind is capable of all possible insult and contempt when occasion seems to require them and these two lawyers did all in their power to humiliate the tall barrister who had in his pocket a huge bundle of carefully written notes, over which he had worked with such pride and expectation. So Lincoln strode to the court room alone.

When the case was called for hearing the question arose as to the number of arguments which should be allowed each side. The McCormick lawyers, seeing Harding, Stanton and Lincoln all against them, protested that if there were to be three arguments on the part of the defense, then Dickerson for the complainant should be permitted to speak twice. Stanton and Harding were afraid of Dickerson; he was too able. And so Stanton, shaking his fists and showing the fiery bellicosity which always distinguished him, told Dickerson in effect to mind his own business, and that there was no intention to have more than two arguments on his side. Stanton then took Lincoln in hand and, in connection with what had just happened at the bar, made it clear to Lincoln that he was not needed. Lincoln then offered to withdraw, and Stanton snapped at the chance to get rid of him. So Lincoln sat in the court room, treated by Stanton and Harding as having nothing to do with the case. At the hotel he was not conferred with, nor asked to sit at table with Stanton and Harding. He sat alone, munching his food abstractedly as usual. Justice McLean gave a dinner for the lawyers in the case, but Lincoln was not invited. The arguments came on and Lincoln listened with rapt attention. The cold, hard, compact lawyer logic of Stanton fascinated him. During the progress of the case there was talk of compromising the disputed matters. Stanton exclaimed with anger, "Compromise! I know of but one way to compromise with an enemy, and that is with a sword in your hand, and to smite and keep smiting." We have these words from one Emerson who was interested as a party on the defense side of the litigation.[1] So Stanton, by degrading Lincoln and by his bitter pugnacity, fastened himself in Lincoln's memory. Would he not be a good man to deal with heartless firmness with treason and

[1] "Personal Recollections of Mr. and Mrs. Emerson," 1909.

rebellion? He would be, and Lincoln gave him the chance in 1861. Esoteric forces may then have been pranking, flashing intimations of what they knew would come to pass. The Harvester machine was one of the great factors in the victory of the North, and so was the work of Stanton. For the McCormicks went on, even though they lost this suit. The defendants were not substantially infringing the McCormick patents.

Lincoln returned home saddened, but braced to become a lawyer. He was now forty-six; and if he left off newspapers and could rouse himself against the Springfield climate, and his own predisposition to lounging and dreaming, he might yet be able to make an argument like Stanton's and Harding's. To Emerson, after the case was over, he said again and again, as if half to himself, "I am going home to study law. I am going home to study law." Again was come to him the supervising will which he wrote about to Speed in July of 1842, where however only the matter of Mary Todd was the influential subject. "I must gain my confidence in my own ability to keep my resolves when they are made. In that ability you know I once prided myself as the only or chief gem of my character." At this very time he was deep in politics. He had been elected to the legislature of Illinois in the fall of 1854; and soon, instead of studying law, he was to be trailing Douglas over the state, and working toward the debates. By the time the Harvester case was decided, in 1856, Lincoln was making speeches about the Missouri Compromise and related subjects. He didn't study law; but some have observed that his style of oratory changed after his contact with Harding and Stanton at Cincinnati, and that it became more dignified, more polished.

In September of 1857, Lincoln, with his friend Norman B. Judd, represented the Rock Island Bridge Company which had been sued by the owners of the steamer *Effie Afton* for damages. The steamer had been thrown by the currents of the Mississippi river against the piers of the bridge; the stoves were upset, the boat took fire and, with its cargo, was burned. The question was should there be commerce on the river, or should there be bridges across it, or both; and finally did the bridge company do wrong in having the piers in the river, or at the place where they had been built; or was the injury *damnum absque injuria?* Much evidence was taken, and the trial produced widespread interest. The newspapers gave full reports to the proceedings; for the rivalry of cities raged in the court and out of it. St. Louis was larger than Chicago at the time, but being crowded for supremacy while trying to hold to it. Lincoln's speech to the jury was praised by a Chicago newspaper as successful, "so far as clear statement and close logic was concerned." Evidently he abandoned for the occasion the colloquial and familiar style of address which he had been used to employ before juries; and perhaps under the influence of Stanton. The jury stood nine to three, and, being unable to agree, were discharged. Then the fight was taken to Congress, where it dragged its slow length. When the War came on in 1861, the river interests gave up the fight. The railroad had proved that the steamboat was antiquated, and Chicago by reason of that fact was soon to tower over St. Louis. All this was symbolical of Lincoln's career. As a young man he had striven to have the Sangamon River made navigable; at forty-eight he helped the railroads against the navigability of the Mississippi; and as a war president the capitalism of railroads and manufacturers began to establish its supremacy.

Let us now have a picture of Lincoln in his best rôle, where his talents shone the brightest, where he had his most notable successes. It will be remembered that at New Salem Lincoln knew Jack Armstrong and his wife Hannah, who lived at Clary's Grove some four miles or so from the village on the hill. Afterward they moved to the Sandridge neighborhood, not a great distance from where James Short and the Rutledges lived. Not far north from Sandridge the Sangamon River flowed toward the Illinois; and across the Sangamon was Mason County. From 1913 until the time of his death, in January, 1925, this writer knew John Armstrong intimately. He lived during those years and for long before at Oakford, a village in Menard County, and at the edge of Sandridge. John Armstrong was a brother of Duff Armstrong, and both were sons of Jack and Hannah Armstrong. In August of 1857 Duff Armstrong attended a camp meeting in Mason County where many fist fights took place, and where finally a man named James Preston Metzger was assaulted by someone, and three days after was dead. James H. Norris and Duff Armstrong were indicted at the October term of the Mason Circuit Court for having murdered Metzger. Norris was immediately tried, convicted and sentenced to eight years in the penitentiary for manslaughter. The mitigating circumstance may have been that Metzger himself was drunk and fighting at the time that he was assaulted by Armstrong and Norris. There was a kind of free for all battle. John Armstrong at this time was a boy of about eight years of age, but he went with his mother Hannah to see Duff in jail at Beardstown after the venue had been changed to Cass County in Duff's behalf. More than that, he grew up with the case; he heard his mother talk it over and over; and the fact that Lincoln, who became president, defended Duff added romance to all the circumstances. If anyone would know exactly how John Armstrong told about the part that Lincoln played in the case, and about John's visit to Duff in jail at Beardstown, let him read *Mitch Miller*. There he will find John's words, vernacular, profanity and all, just as John told the story in his cottage at Oakford in 1913, and all along until his death. It will be seen that he followed factually all that has been written by historians of this fascinating struggle in the court of Cass County.

As John said, so do historians say, that near the camp there was a place to get whisky. The two intoxicants of religion and spirits go together; and, as John said, roughs and rowdies would sit in the camp a while and then they would repair to the wagon where the whisky was. And then there would be fights. It was an emotional occasion all around. The indictment charged that Norris struck Metzger with a neck yoke three feet long, and that Duff Armstrong hit him in the eye with a sling shot. But no less Metzger, after all this, got on his horse and rode some miles to his home near Mason City, and on the way fell off his horse two or three times. This was the evidence. Did Metzger receive his death blows from Duff and Norris, or did he die from injuries received in these falls? The case against Duff and Norris, one would think, was greatly weakened by the fact of these falls from the horse. The case was one not hard to win. The sentence of Norris seems of debatable justice. There was prejudice against the defendants in Mason County, arising from the fact, no doubt, that at a religious revival they had been drinking and carousing. In that day and since, in this country, prosecutions and cases of other kinds were decided on

RIDING THE CIRCUIT 131

the lack of morality of the parties, rather than on the issues raised. It was on account of the prejudice of the inhabitants of Mason County against Duff Armstrong that the indictment against him was sent by the judge of Mason County to Cass County for trial.

Somehow Lincoln took no part in the proceedings upon which the venue was changed. Sometimes to have that done requires the best skill of a practiced lawyer, especially where there is prejudice which operates at the beginning to keep the prisoner where he can surely be dealt with as the community desires him to be. But at any rate Hannah Armstrong procured Lincoln to defend her son Duff. She had little to pay him for his services, and in fact she paid him nothing for them. One concludes that Lincoln was animated to take the case in part by gratitude for what Hannah Armstrong had done for him in the New Salem days, when she often cooked him meals and mended his clothes; but surely he was influenced to give his services by the consideration that in such a case he was in his element, and he did give them, after his resolutions made at Cincinnati that he would become a lawyer, and after the notable bridge case. There is a reputed letter of Lincoln's dated Springfield, Ohio, September 18, 1857, in which Lincoln offered his aid to Hannah Armstrong because of favors he had received from her and her husband in the old days.[1] The original of this letter has not been found. Another chronicler wrote that Hannah Armstrong drove to Springfield and there engaged Lincoln to defend her son. Could we be surer about these things we could know better how to judge what Lincoln's motives were in leaving what he should have done, in the pursuit of his resolution to become a better lawyer, to take a case of this sort. He was not a man of the liveliest gratitude, though moved by regard for his own feelings, which tortured him when he did what he thought was an unjust thing; and he was not an emotional man, but for the most part a cold man, as we shall see later from the words of his friends. At all events, Lincoln was at the November term of the Cass County Circuit Court, but really, as far as could be observed, for the purpose of assisting a local lawyer in a divorce case into which he had been invited by letter from the latter. The divorce case was tried by Lincoln and his as-

[1] Beveridge, I, 562–74.

sociate, and they lost the case; but the matter of the alimony to be allowed the woman whom they were opposing was continued to the May term, 1858, of the Court.

Directly after the end of the divorce proceedings Lincoln made a motion to the Court that Duff Armstrong be admitted to bail. No one up to this time had dreamed that Lincoln was in the Armstrong case. He had behaved until he made this motion with that secretiveness which marked his course as a lawyer, as a politician and as president later; and it was justifiable enough in this defense. One wonders if the prosecuting attorney from Mason County was present to represent the state on this application, or whether it was attended to entirely by his representative, or just what happened in this regard. But Lincoln did not succeed in having Duff Armstrong admitted to bail. In May, 1858, at the next term of the court, Lincoln was again on hand. The matter of the alimony in the divorce case was to come up; and there was still another case that Lincoln had an interest in, while he said nothing to anyone about an intention to defend Armstrong. There was no occasion for secrecy now, since in November he had argued the matter of bail for Armstrong. But when the murder case was called, Lincoln stood forth as the defending attorney. This was the so-called almanac case, the case in which Lincoln produced an almanac on the point as to where the moon stood on the night of August 27, 1857, when Metzger was in the fight with Norris and Duff Armstrong. Affidavits, statements have been made without end on the subject of Lincoln's use of the almanac; and John Armstrong in telling about it said what is still said after the most thorough research, namely, that after a witness for the state had testified that he saw Duff strike Metzger with a sling shot, and that the blow was clear to his vision because the moon was about where the sun would be at ten o'clock, or near the meridian, Lincoln brought forth the almanac to confute him, and to show that the moon set that night at 12:05. The time of the altercation was fixed at about 11 P. M. Also in this gathering of material to make manifest exactly what Lincoln did, and whether the almanac was manufactured for the occasion or not, astronomical surveys were taken by the astronomer of the University of Illinois, and by the astronomer of Harvard University; and both these surveys showed that the moon on the night in question was not at the meridian or near it, but that it was setting at 12:05 A. M. And this was done to quiet the story which spread through Illinois that Lincoln had gone to St. Louis or elsewhere and had a new page inserted in an almanac for the year and month of August of 1857, which showed what he wanted to prove in the case against the witness named.

Lincoln's reputation here and there was that of a cunning lawyer, and surely after the Matson case he could not have been believed to be above reproach as a practitioner. But nothing more absurd was ever said to the discredit of Lincoln. He could not have gone to St. Louis, or Chicago or anywhere, or sent anyone upon the mission of having an almanac changed by the printing of a whole new page to prove that the moon was setting, and not at the meridian, without some leak of what he had done or procured to be done. The peril of attempting such a thing was momentous. If the forgery had been discovered, if when the almanac had been passed to the judge to enable him to consider its admissibility, if when the jury had seen it, suspicion had been aroused and the falsity of the almanac discovered, Lincoln would have been ruined in reputation beyond the hope of recovery. The story of the forged almanac which persisted in Illinois for years was preposterous to the last degree. But the question remains, how did Lincoln know that he was going to need an almanac? That he had one with him is certain. He handed it to the sheriff with the request that it should be delivered by the sheriff to him when he asked for it. Lincoln had the notes of the trial of Norris at the Mason County Circuit Court; but there the witness Allen, the one who was confuted by Lincoln with the almanac, had not testified about the moon at all, as he was not asked anything about it. How did Lincoln foresee that he would need an almanac? Or did he consult an almanac and, after seeing that the moon set that night at 12:05 A. M., did he, in some meticulous forecast of what might happen and with care to be ready for anything, have the almanac? Any practitioner of criminal law who knew his business would investigate all the circumstances attending the homicide: what the place was, who were present, and where they stood. He knew that the time of the altercation was about 11 P. M. And if certain people saw it, including Allen, where were they standing, what was the nature of the light around in order to see with what Metzger was struck, with a neck yoke or with a sling shot, or with both; and just where were the blows given on the person of Metzger? Lincoln as a capable lawyer in such cases must have thought of all these things; and thus he may have taken the almanac to court with him to be ready for any emergency.

John Armstrong when telling about the use of the almanac, and all he could have told about it was what his mother or Duff told him, gave the impression that Lincoln maneuvered Allen into testifying about the moon, and got Allen to repeat more than once the statement that the moon was where the sun would be at about ten o'clock in the morning. And having done this he brought forth the almanac to show that Allen was testifying falsely. For Allen, in chief, had made a strong impression upon the jury. In the first place he was an unwilling witness for the state, whose attendance was procured by a bench warrant after he had disobeyed a subpœna to come to court. But when he was brought in by force of law he told a clear story, testifying that he saw Norris hit Metzger on the back of the head with a neck yoke, and that he saw Duff Armstrong hit Metzger in the right eye with what appeared to be a sling shot. The jury was fully satisfied with Allen's testimony and believed him; until Lincoln's use of the almanac threw possible doubt upon his credibility. The trial judge thought that the almanac cut slight figure in the case, and that it was rather the testimony of Dr. Parker which freed Duff Armstrong, and this was to the point that the blow with the neck yoke, confessedly administered by Norris on the back of Metzger's head, accounted for the fracture of the skull near the right eye. He gave his professional word that it was the fracture of the skull near the right eye that killed Metzger, demonstrating his expert opinion with a human skull, which he held while testifying. And all the while it was true that Metzger had fallen off his horse several times while on the way home. With so much said, we come to Lincoln as the lawyer, at forty-nine years of age, and in the part that he best played in court, with all the dramatics he could command for the purpose of swaying a jury. Lincoln was profoundly an actor.

It was a May day and very warm. Lincoln arose to address the jury. He took off his coat and vest and began calmly to speak in a measured, distinct voice, without emotion. Very soon he discarded the stock from his neck. He started now to work himself into feeling. He was wearing suspenders knitted of wool. One of them fell from his shoulder, and he let it hang as he picked the evidence to pieces, as he shouted and declaimed. He appealed to the sympathies of the jury, telling of the day when he arrived in New Salem without a penny in his pocket, and how Hannah Armstrong, and Jack Armstrong, the latter now in his grave, had succored him in those hard days. He pictured the plight of Hannah if her son were taken from her and sent to prison, of the poverty that was now hers, and of the disgrace that would be hers with her son convicted of murder. Now tears poured down his homely, wrinkled face, they dripped from the cheeks of Honest Abe Lincoln; and the jury wept, sobbed to think of the sorrow of the lawyer, utterly moved by his earnestness, and grieving for Hannah Armstrong, if they should do what they were now resolving not to do, not to punish Duff Armstrong. Meanwhile Hannah was in the back part of the court room. She was a comely pioneer woman, a genuinely good woman; and there with her face hidden by a large sunbonnet, such as women of her class wore at the time, she was sobbing piteously, as Lincoln hypnotized the jury with his eloquence and his tears. The jury retired and after one ballot brought in a verdict of not guilty. Lincoln at the door of the court house handed Duff Armstrong's sling shot to a man named Shaw, as a keepsake to remember him by. As to the almanac, Shaw thought, and said, that Lincoln had two almanacs, and that by a sort of sleight of hand Lincoln shifted them; but as the truth about the matter cannot be known it is futile to pursue the subject. It is only important to observe that many people of Lincoln's time thought that there was something wrong about the use of the almanac, and so reported themselves with various explanations; and it is a matter to be noted that tales could grow up about it until an astronomical survey was taken to prove that the moon set as Lincoln claimed it did when impeaching the witness Allen.[1]

Such cases as this have been tried over and over again and won, and even much harder cases to win have been won, by lawyers in rural Illinois, in Lincoln's day and since. Many such were the object of absorbed interest on the part of myself in the old court house at Lewistown and Petersburg. These defenses require a lawyer of just

[1] See Beveridge, Vol. I, 571.

Lincoln's mode of appeal; but to be won they do not need the learning and the skill of a man well read in the law, and studiously grounded in its principles. Could anyone in that court room in Beardstown on that day in May, 1858, who listened to Lincoln harangue the Armstrong jury, imagine that within three years he would be the president of the United States? Harrison the Indian fighter had won the honor, and so had Taylor the "rough and ready" soldier of the Mexican War. But in 1852 Pierce, the friend of Hawthorne and his college mate at Bowdoin, had restored the Democratic Party to power; and this had been followed by the election in 1856 of James Buchanan, but recently before ambassador to England. The likelihood of the "log cabin and hard cider" decoy being repeated in any mode was remote. Besides there was Douglas, easily the strongest man now in the Senate, and at the head of his party. In the convention which nominated Buchanan he received on the sixteenth ballot 121 votes to Buchanan's 168, and lost the nomination on the seventeenth ballot. But everyone looked forward to his winning the nomination in 1860, which he did at the hand of one of the Democratic conventions. By contrast, Lincoln, in 1856, in the Republican convention which nominated Frémont for president, rose to 110 votes for the nomination for vice-president. That was on the first ballot when William L. Dayton received 259 votes and was thereby declared the nominee. That was the difference between Lincoln and Douglas in 1856, and it furnished the basis of forecasting what the difference between them would continue to be. It is to be remembered, too, that the Democratic Party in 1856 was an old organization with many distinguished and tried men among its adherents, who were rivals for its honors, and that a nomination at its hands was not the easy thing that it was at the hands of the Republican Party, which was only organized in 1854 and had few men of great note in it, and none who had achieved in public life what Douglas had by this time achieved. No one in America, not to say in the Beardstown court room, could have conceived of the triumph of Lincoln in 1860. He had not yet had the debates with Douglas, and even after those occurred his fame was mostly confined to Illinois; while the more radical and more famous Seward, a senator from New York, was the man commonly talked of as the most fit to pit against the Democrats, who had

RIDING THE CIRCUIT

gathered party strength under Pierce and Buchanan after the futile Whig victories of 1844 and 1848, led by Harrison and Taylor respectively.

After so much said of Lincoln the circuit rider, is there more to add in order that the full picture may be had of that Lincoln who debated with Douglas and who was nominated for the presidency at Chicago in 1860? For after we see him, all in all, as well as we possibly can, then we shall take up the history of the questions with which he dealt so that we may understand as fully as possible how he rose to them, and what he meant when he took this or the other course, or made arguments for or against various things that stirred the public between 1850 and 1860. Before this is done there are other observations to make on Lincoln the man. Remembering that Lincoln was an enigma to his associates, that he was secretive, reticent of his plans, "uneven" as Whitney said of him, the task now in hand requires the best use that can be made of the literature on Lincoln, including his own words, and not forgetting to analyze what he did.

Chapter VII Lincoln: The Man

HENRY CLAY WHITNEY was a lawyer and a friend of Lincoln, and one of his great admirers. He published in 1892 a book entitled *Life on the Circuit with Lincoln;* in 1908 a *Life of Lincoln.* In one place he wrote as follows: "I repeat that his was one of the most uneven, eccentric and heterogeneous characters. One of the most obvious of Mr. Lincoln's peculiarities was his dissimilitude of qualities, or inequality of conduct, his dignity of deportment and action, interspersed with freaks of frivolity and inanity; his high aspirations and achievement, and his descent into the most primitive vales of listlessness, and the most ridiculous buffoonery." Herndon said of him: "This terribly reticent, secretive, shut-mouth man never talked much about his history, plans, designs, purposes, intents; and when a man tells you this or that about what Lincoln said, believe what you must and no more." Judge David Davis wrote of Lincoln: "I knew the man so well; he was the most reticent, secretive man I ever knew or expect to see." Whence came this lack of forthrightness—from the unknown father of Nancy Hanks, from the Hanks blood, or did it stream down through two centuries from the Hingham Lincolns, whither it came from the obscurities of Norfolk County, England? But in any case a man who acts so, who keeps everything to himself, is acting in fear, he is planning to take his enemies by surprise, he is behaving so that antagonists cannot know where to lay hold upon him. These are not qualities to be admired in the highest sense. Herndon wrote that Lincoln could be vindictive to the point of cruelty, and he related a circumstance of 1840. A man named Thomas had made some humorous references to Lincoln when speaking at the court house in Springfield. As soon as Lincoln heard about this he hurried to the room, and just as Thomas stepped from the platform Lincoln mounted it, and proceeded to mimic Thomas in gesture, in voice, in talk, and to take off all his peculiarities. The rude crowd roared with laughter, while Thomas, caught and unable to leave the audience, writhed with embarrassment, and finally broke into tears. No sooner had Lincoln inflicted this unusual punishment on a harmless man who had only made a humorous reference to him, than he was stricken with remorse. He had been vindictive, but he was also magnanimous, and soon sought out Thomas and apologized to him.[1]

By remembering this episode much can be read into Lincoln's words here and there in the debates, when for example he said, "this is the perfect liberty they sigh for," referring to Douglas's plan to leave the territories free to have slavery or not as they chose; or where he questioned the integrity of the Supreme Court or Buchanan. If one will read such passages and visualize to himself Lincoln's facial grimaces, the mocking intonation of his voice, he will get some of the effect of the whole malediction that Lincoln poured forth on those occasions; and if it be remembered how powerful Lincoln was in body, and how though quick enough to wrath, even as the sea can be easily kicked into waves, he was not stirred to the depths nor did he become stormy until all his resources were delivered into his hands for use. Here is another passage from Herndon respecting Lincoln's power of mimicry: "His countenance and all his features seemed to take part in the performance. As he neared the pith or point of the joke or story every vestige of seriousness disappeared from his face. His little gray eyes sparkled; a smile seemed to gather up, curtain like, at the corners of his mouth, his frame quivered with suppressed excitement; and when the point, or 'nub' of the story as he called it, came, no one's laugh was heartier than his."

Lincoln was a cold man. There was no one besides Herndon whom he called by his first name. He adressed his friends as Gillespie, Whitney, Judd, or what not. And on the other hand no one called him Abe, not even Herndon, who was in the office with him for seventeen years, day by day. This sort of behavior results from indifference of the heart. To call a man by his given name is to express affection. It may be too honorific to address men as Mr., but there is something harsh, unconcerned, matter of fact, and regardless alike of affection and respect in addressing everyone by his surname. Herndon wrote, "What in the first place do we mean by a warm-hearted man? Is it one who goes out of himself and reaches for others spontaneously, seeking to correct some abuse to

[1] Herndon, I, 188–9.

mankind because of a deep love for humanity, apart from equity and truth, and who does what he does for love's sake? If so, Mr. Lincoln was a cold man." [1] Does this not sound like Robespierre? And indeed Lincoln had some of the makings of a fanatic. It was his sense of humor, his intellectual and critical faculties, coupled at last with a sort of sluggishness and indifference, that kept him from being one. His obstinacy, his capacity of hatred, his Calvinistic theology fitted him to be a fanatic. He was not an abolitionist, and never became one until the time of the Emancipation Proclamation, just because there were rooted in him vast conservative forces which stubbornly refused to yield to drastic innovation.

He had good reason to have no love and no respect for his father. The memory of the times when he was knocked down by his father undoubtedly rankled in Lincoln's heart as long as he lived. But when such a father is old and is in poverty, a tender heart will not carry resentment. It will leap over on the other side, and do generous things. Herndon further wrote, "If a man, woman or child approached him, and the prayer of such an one was granted, that itself was not evidence of his love. . . . When he freed the slaves there was no heart in the act." On this score Herndon analyzed Lincoln as moving through a sense of justice. So it was that he treated his father with justice. He sent him money from time to time; but to that father Lincoln never gave his heart. Down at Goose Nest Prairie in Coles County, in the winter of 1850–51, Thomas Lincoln became ill, and showed signs of soon dying, as he did. Lincoln's stepbrother wrote him touching the aged man's condition. Lincoln did not answer. Then another letter was written Lincoln, this time by Harriet Hanks. Now in the extremity of death the old man wanted to see the son who had been in the legislature, who had won the capital for Springfield, who had become notable locally as a lawyer, and who had gone to Congress. How natural to desire to take the hand of such a son, to bid him farewell, perhaps to look or express contrition for the past, for the poverty which he kept that son in at Pigeon Creek, and for the regretted blows. Lincoln had imagination of a sort, but it was limited, it concerned itself with rhetoric and materialized as oratorical figures. Shelley

[1] Herndon, Vol. I, 310.

disliked his father too, and kept away from him; but would Shelley have gone to him, if summoned to his death bed? Lincoln did not penetrate with imagination into the heart of his father, who was lying on his death bed in Coles County. But on the other hand at this time Mrs. Lincoln was confined. So when Lincoln did write, and to his stepbrother at that, he said, "My business is such that I could hardly leave home now, if it was not as it is, that my own wife is sick a-bed. (It is a case of baby sickness, and I suppose is not dangerous.)" So that he could not leave on account of business; and if it were not business then Mrs. Lincoln's illness might keep him at home. But the rest of the letter shows the making of the Lincoln mind. "I sincerely hope father may recover his health, but at all events, tell him to remember to call upon and confide in our great and good and Merciful Maker who will not turn away from him in any extremity." And here our "Merciful Maker," was now turning away from him in the circumstance that he was not inspiring this son to hasten to Goose Nest Prairie. Lincoln went on with his sermonizing: "He notes the fall of a sparrow, and numbers the hairs of our heads, and He will not forget the dying man who puts his trust in Him. Say to him that if we could meet now it is doubtful whether it would not be more painful than pleasant; but that if it be his lot to go now, he will soon have a joyous meeting with many loved ones gone before, and where the rest of us, through the help of God, hope ere long to join him." [1] There is grave question that Lincoln believed these words when he wrote them, or that at any time of his life he had such a faith, as we shall make clearer when we come to Lincoln's religion. But when he expressed the doubt that a meeting would be pleasant he was thinking of the old days at Pigeon Creek; he was not imagining how he could take his father's hand and give him consolation by evidence that he had forgiven, if not forgotten the blows and the poverty. All witnesses testify that Lincoln could not forget the meanness of his origin, and that the memory of it galled him always. This may be natural enough; but sons do, out of filial tenderness in the days of sickness and death of an improvident and unaffectionate father, pour out their hearts remembering that "our frame is dust," and that we all

[1] Lincoln's Works, I, 165.

wander about, scarcely knowing where and not knowing at all why. This is the imagination of the heart; and out of it come all beautiful words and deeds, forgivenesses and tendernesses.

Lincoln was a cold man. He went about grotesquely dressed, carrying a faded umbrella, wearing a ludicrous plug hat. He was mannerless, unkempt, and one wonders if he was not unwashed, in those days of the weekly bath in the foot tub, if a bath was taken at all. For these reasons the myth has grown up of the easy, good-hearted Lincoln, the democratic Lincoln, who loved everyone, and whom people everywhere hailed as Abe, or Uncle Abe. This was not the case. He allowed no one to be familiar with him. No one slapped him on the back with a hearty hello. Always he was addressed as Mr. Lincoln. In the debates Douglas called him Lincoln being his superior in achievement at the time; and when Lincoln spoke more ceremoniously of Douglas, calling him Judge Douglas, there was hidden satire in it. Douglas had been judge of the Supreme Court of Illinois for a brief time in his late twenties; but he had been senator for eleven years at the time of the debates. We shall see in many instances where Lincoln subtly and covertly put poison in his words when referring to Douglas, and with a truculence that penetrates the sensibilities of the comprehending reader to this day.

On the other hand there was his sense of humor, perhaps the only æsthetic gift that he had; and by this he drew people to him and held them. He passed through days, as we have seen, when popular feeling was against him, and indeed he experienced this after he became president. But all the while he kept at his side devoted friends, like Davis, Judd, Whitney, Herndon and others. The story-telling gift is an irresistible endowment for a man in any walk of life. His sense of humor rose from his comprehension of the incongruous, the illogical, the ridiculous, and it was related to his mimicry, and expressed itself through mimicry. Thus he could be a satirist, he could command terrible invective, and he was forever gathering stories and making them up with which to illustrate logical absurdities, or with which to burlesque preposterous phases of human behavior. In the realm of æsthetics he was deficient in an appreciation of harmony. He told Herndon that he did not know what the harmony of sound was;[1] and he could not carry a tune

---

[1] Herndon, I, 47.

LINCOLN: THE MAN

to save his life. He sometimes attempted to sing "The Missouri Harmony," but it was a sad attempt. Yet side by side with this failure was his memory, which was remarkably tenacious. He could remember the words, and indeed anything that he heard or read he kept forever in his mind. He had no interest of moment in beautiful things. When he saw Niagara Falls he wrote some notes about it, indulging in geological speculations, though he never studied geology. He was impressed with the antiquity of the Falls: they had been there when Moses led the Jews out of Egypt, and when Adam "first came from the hand of his Maker"![1] He meant to prepare a lecture on the subject; but in his notes there is no word of appreciation of their beauty, there is nothing but mechanistic questioning as to how they came there, where the water came from and the like. He had nothing beautiful about him, in his house or in his office. He perhaps did not realize that on a higher level he was repeating the habits of his father, Thomas Lincoln. He had but a single tree in his yard, no apple trees, no cherry or pear or peach trees in his garden. There were no flowers set out—only once did he plant a rose bush. Some of his neighbors blamed Mrs. Lincoln more than Lincoln for these neglects, but unjustly. Others said that neither of them loved the beautiful in the slightest degree. He made a vegetable garden but once, while he needed just that sort of physical exertion to prevent the downward displacement of his viscera which resulted from lounging and loafing, and contributed to his melancholy. He didn't hunt or indulge in sports of any kind, which would have been good both for his mind and his body.

Let us consider his black despondency. It came on him slightly during the Mary Owens affair, more terribly when he ran away from Mary Todd, and latterly during those years when his political career was seemingly ended. He brightened with an intellectual renascence when about 1854 he saw a chance to undo Douglas because of the Kansas-Nebraska Act. These hours of depression were intermingled with fits of boisterous humor, with laughing and telling stories. It is just so with those affected with melancholia. Melancholia is not exactly mania, though it may become that. It is a state of depression greater than is warranted by the circumstances. Sometimes persons afflicted with melancholia grow defective in at-

[1] Lincoln's Works, I, 162.

tention. Lincoln was so affected: he ate without observing what he ate; he sat in trances, so to speak. In melancholia, memory may fail more or less; Lincoln's memory held its own. In melancholia there may be disorientation, and Lincoln sometimes seemed to forget where he was and what he was. Herndon wrote that on an occasion when Lincoln was attending an elocutionary recital he broke into a loud guffaw when nothing humorous was being spoken by the performer. The audience turned about and saw that it was Lincoln who had thus forgotten where he was. Lincoln was greatly mortified by what he had done. His mind had wandered off and had picked up some humorous story, and in his concentration on that and his obliviousness of where he was he had burst forth with sudden laughter. In melancholia the victim is full of gloomy thoughts, he is apprehensive of the future, he overemphasizes his wrongdoings; and Lincoln showed all these symptoms. He seemed to think a good deal of a tragic and sudden end to his life, and this is out of melancholia, if it be not also a recognition that one is moving in a path that leads to disaster. Lincoln had anxiety neuroses, with fears and dreads and doubts. "Anxiety," wrote McDougall, the psychologist, "is the name by which the means we are taking towards the desired end begin to seem inadequate, when we cast about for possible alternatives, and begin to anticipate the pain of failure." This surely describes Lincoln. Turn to his little talk in 1855 when only two persons were in the audience, Herndon and the janitor of the hall. Herndon had hired a band, posted the town with bills; but Lincoln was in disrepute with the Whigs now, and not in much standing with the Republicans. We shall say more of this particular time and occasion later. Now Lincoln says: "These are bad times, and seem out of joint. All seems dead, dead, dead." Then his understanding of oratory and his obedience to its rules correct this gloomy speech; and he adds: "But the age is not dead yet; it liveth as sure as our Maker liveth." His brighter mood came on him, just as it did when he would break from darkest clouds into the telling of a story.

What produces melancholia? Intestinal toxæmia may do it, and that is caused by a sluggish liver, by sedentary habits which crowd and displace the intestines and weaken the abdominal wall. Lincoln had had an outdoor youth, and considerable physical exercise, but from twenty-three years of age he was not careful of his bodily life. Then anxiety leads to intestinal atony; and finally there may be an oversecretion of adrenalin, and that is a mystery yet to be solved. Lincoln also had illusions or hallucinations, as one may choose to express the matter under the circumstances. When he saw himself and a pale shadow of himself in the mirror at Springfield just before he started for Washington to take the oath as president, that was an illusion if there was something in the light or in objects in the room to make his perception false; or it was a hallucination if there was nothing of sensation to give him realization of the apparition. Or shall we be mystical and say that Lincoln saw himself in that divided personality which was his: the bright self which could say, "With malice toward none," and the pale insensible self which could devastate the South? There may be demigorgons who flash by human beings at times, brushing their coats with astral lightness, but no less, with half mischievous purpose, giving a second's evidence that they have been called or sent to show man what he is, or what is to come, yet to show it from an angle of reflection so vast and so profound that the human being can only glimpse something which is sudden and gone, and understand its source and its meaning not at all.

Lincoln was an under sexed man. That is the simplest way to express it. He liked to be with men when he liked to be with anyone; and to that extent, with all his reticence and dignity, he was gregarious. He was one of those manly men, whose mind made him seek masculine minds. Marriage with him had the slightest sexual aim. It was rather taken for social reasons, or other self-regarding motives, all apart from romantic impulses. If the story of Ann Rutledge, and Mary Owens and Mary Todd do not prove this, nothing could. Lincoln's social sense was the origin of his moral sense. It was his response to the call of the herd to regulate his conduct according to the herd law. His desire for esteem, and his shaping his course to popular feeling, his sticking to the Whigs was his social sense become his moral sense.

The moral sense has regard for the conventions of society, not speaking now of manners at table, or in a drawing room, for Lincoln did not have these, and he scorned them, but in the interest of a larger social rightness, so to speak. The moral sense concerns itself with the right and the wrong, and with religion, or rather with the precepts of religion. Yet his heart, according to Herndon's careful word, was the lowest organ of his nature. His conscience ruled his heart; but after all what were the instances where that took place? Was it with reference to the negroes, especially in Illinois? Before coming to that, and to Lincoln's religion, let us gather more delineation from Herndon, who knew Lincoln better than anyone, and whose remarkable book proves that he had more imagination, penetration, psychology, power of analysis than Davis, Whitney, Swett or anyone else, with which to know him and to appraise him. "Mr. Lincoln's perceptions were slow, cold, clear, exact. Everything came to him in its precise shape and color. He was not impulsive, fanciful, or imaginative; but cold, calm and precise. . . . His fault if any was that he saw things less than they really were; less beautiful and more frigid. He saw what no man could dispute; but he failed to see what might have been seen." He lacked the capacity to decide "on the fitness, the harmony, or if you will, the beauty and appropriateness of things." If by common sense be meant that a man can judge in the whirl of things as wisely as if he had much time to do so, then Lincoln "had no great stock of common sense." "But give him time and he could show judgment." "He could form no just construction of the motives of the particular individual." He had love in his heart; "but the object must first come in the guise of a principle, next it must be right and true—then it was lovely in his sight." "He loved humanity when it was oppressed—an abstract love as against the concrete love centered in an individual." "He loved the true first, the right second, the good last." "Generally he took no interest in town affairs or local elections." So it was that he did not grieve for the scorned, the rejected, "the men hemmed in with spears," the negroes of Springfield or elsewhere in Illinois. These were practical matters for his philanthropy when he was aroused by slavery going into Kansas and Nebraska, where it would not have gone, or where if it had it would not have stayed. Even men of the interlocking directorate which Lincoln had in his mental equipment, with reason and coldness and calmness to aid, may stir themselves, like ordinary radicals, by things afar, when there are wrongs to be righted at home.

Above both Lincoln and the radical, there is the Milton who hungered for the right, who grieved for the world's wrongs, for men defeated and disinherited, who through illness and poverty, dishonor and blindness, fought tyranny and privilege, and advocated tyrannicide and the freedom of the press and divorce where hearts were no longer married; who knew what liberty meant, and what its historical stresses were. This was not Lincoln, the champion of Whiggery, of tariffs and banks, and loose construction of the Constitution, which he at last trampled; this was not Lincoln the politician of all the expedients and vacillations which we have already recorded, and of which more are to come. But this is the Lincoln who was equipped to be president scarcely better than Harrison and Taylor, though with more mind than either, and with more power of expression than any president but Jefferson; who was to have a task as great as Washington to carry; who by usurpation self-justified by the sophistical mind which these pages have attempted to portray, was to take command of one of the greatest armies of subjugation that the world has known. Altogether this is one of the most anomalous pages of all time.

Let us recall Lincoln's letter to Speed in those days when the two men were consoling and advising each other with respect to their love affairs; and in particular to Lincoln's reference to the chained negroes on the steamboat going to St. Louis. On August 24, 1855, Lincoln wrote to Speed as follows: "You may remember as well as I do that from Louisville to the mouth of the Ohio there were on board ten or a dozen slaves shackled together with irons. That sight was a continued torment to me, and I see something like it every time I touch the Ohio or any other slave border. . . . I confess I hate to see the poor creatures hunted down and caught and carried back to their stripes and unrequited toil; but I bite my lips and keep quiet." But did Lincoln ever advocate the repeal of the fugitive slave clause of the Constitution, which applied as well to the New England white apprentices? He never did. In the debates with Douglas he stood for the Fugitive Slave Law. Did he have any remedy for the ills of the slaves? He never had. Other men proposed remedies. He had none, other than keeping slavery out of the territories. All of this will be fully dealt with in its place. Meanwhile there were phases of slavery in Illinois. And besides, the state of the negro in Illinois was truly pitiable. He had not a civil right until after the War; the state constitution of 1848, to which we have referred already, was not displaced by a new one until 1870. Social liberty is at least as precious as political liberty; and of social liberty the negro had none in Illinois. Compared to the negro slaves in the South his state was wretched beyond words. The former were fed and clothed and housed, but the Illinois negro had to earn what he had and under economic conditions that made the work difficult at every step. As late as 1858 Lincoln said all over Illinois in speeches made to win the United States senatorship for himself, that he was not in favor of giving the negro the vote, or of allowing him to sit on juries, or of intermarrying, or of associating with white people. He called the negro an inferior being, and he said that there was a physical difference between the white and the black race, which would forever forbid the two races living together upon terms of social equality, and that he was in favor of the superior position being assigned to the white man. Yet all men were created equal. But that equality was fulfilled when the negro was permitted to work for wages! It was this idea of social inferiority that dictated and perpetuated Southern slavery. It was a social system, a way of handling the inescapable fact, that the negro was amidst the whites and had to be treated in some way, either as an equal and as free, or as an inferior and under social and political regimentation.

Allied to Lincoln's religion was his superstition. He was not, as Cæsar, "superstitious grown of late," but in his Pigeon Creek days and later he imbibed beliefs in dreams and wonders which influenced his mind to the last. Herndon wrote that his early Baptist training made him a fatalist up to the day of his death. He saw apparitions from time to time during his life; and thus he presented the contradiction of a mind which examined everything in the cold light of reason, and as Herndon expressed it, had to touch, to put his hand in the wound in order to believe, yet who brooded with freakish credulity over the meaning of what he had dreamed. He believed in the mad stone; and one of his sisters-in-law related that Lincoln took one of his boys to Terre Haute, Indiana, to have the stone applied to a wound inflicted by a dog on the boy. Equally with Cæsar he believed in his destiny, that he had been marked by esoteric forces for some notable part in the world; but not as Cæsar is drawn by Shakespeare did he say the valiant never taste of death but once. The prospect of a disastrous and sudden end to his life darkened his thoughts from time to time, and especially when he left Springfield for Washington, in February, 1861, was he depressed by evil intimations. Herndon became convinced that Lincoln had been chosen by Fate or God for some great work in the world, and this was due not to anything that Lincoln said to Herndon, but because Herndon by close study of the man day by day saw in him traits and endowments which set him apart from all other persons. There was no contradiction, as some seemed to think at the time, between his fatalism and orthodox religion. To believe that the means are foreordained, as well as the end, is Calvinism. But if this interpretation of life be rationalized it is nothing but estimating the trend of the world and the men who are in it as causes of certain results.

Thirty-five years ago Ingersoll claimed Lincoln as one of his own, as a free thinker, or infidel. Lincoln is not as easy as that to classify. Already many letters and some speeches of Lincoln have been quoted in which he spoke of God, or of his Maker; and there are others to come which related to the most solemn occasions evocative of the deepest feelings and the sincerest expressions. He was running for office now and again and he knew that it was bad policy to speak of his doubts, his unfaith. One does not know whether to believe or not that in his New Salem days Lincoln wrote an essay against the Bible, in which he attacked its inspiration as God's revelation, and in which he strove to prove that Jesus was not the son of God. Herndon affirmed in his book that Lincoln did this. But Herndon knew at first hand about Lincoln's state of mind after he came to Springfield; and he wrote from the report of a friend of Lincoln's who claimed to hear what Lincoln said, that at the clerk's office on several occasions Lincoln had a Bible with him and proceeded to read a chapter and then skeptically to dissect it. John T. Stuart, Lincoln's first law partner, said of him that he was an open infidel; and others called him an avowed atheist. This was in the early Springfield days before he developed caution. Stuart further asserted that Lincoln always denied the divinity of Jesus. On the other hand the sober David Davis scouted the idea that Lincoln talked about his religion, especially to any stranger. He added, however, that Lincoln had no faith in the Christian sense, but that he had faith in laws, principles, causes and effects. Another man, a friend of Lincoln's, gave the opinion that Lincoln believed in a Creator; and that, as to the Christian theory that Christ is God, Lincoln stated to him that it had better be taken for granted; and while the divinity of Jesus came to man in doubtful shape, yet the system of Christianity was an ingenuous one, and perhaps was calculated to do good. We find other witnesses saying that Lincoln was utterly incapable of insincerity on this subject, as on all others.

The reader is almost as well equipped to pass upon Lincoln's sincerity as Lincoln's associates were. One man stated that Lincoln repelled the idea of the innate depravity of man, the possibility of miracles, the nature and design of future rewards and punishments, and other orthodox tenets of the churches. He believed that Lincoln coincided with Channing and Theodore Parker in his faith. In May, 1865, John G. Nicolay, one of Lincoln's secretaries, wrote Herndon that Lincoln did not change his religious opinions in any way from the time he left Springfield to the time of his death. And Mrs. Lincoln, who came on to Springfield to meet Herndon and talk to him about Lincoln for the purposes of Herndon's contemplated biography, said: "Mr. Lincoln had no faith and no hope in the usual acceptation of those words. He never joined a church; but still, as I believe, he was a religious man by nature. He first seemed to think about the subject when our boy Willie died, and then, more than ever, about the time he went to Gettysburg; but it was a kind of poetry, and he was never a technical Christian." [1] In these words Mrs. Lincoln unquestionably touched verifiable points of psychology.

As the horror and the vastness of the war increased and spread their mystical shadows about him, he naturally reflected on the littleness of man and the greatness of natural and historical forces. But it will be seen that sometimes he invested destiny with the spirit and will of the Hebraic Jehovah, and sometimes with the more compassionate and reasonable God of the new dispensation. Leonard Swett wrote in 1866, "As he became involved in matters of the

[1] Herndon, II, 149 et seq.

greatest importance, full of great responsibility and great doubt, a feeling of religious reverence, a belief in God and his justice and overruling power increased with him. He was always full of natural religion; he believed in God as much as the most approved church member, yet he judged of Him by the same system of generalization as he judged everything else." [1] In August, 1863, after the battle of Gettysburg, to fully date the letter, Lincoln wrote James C. Conkling, and ended as follows: "Let us be quite sober. Let us diligently apply the means, never doubting that a just God, in his own good time, will give us the rightful result." It was this belief that God was in the war, and was watching its battles, even as Zeus sat in judgment over the strife of the Greeks and the Trojans, and more than this, it was Lincoln's belief that God was on the side of the North, and that, after sufficiently chastising the North as well as the South for the sin of slavery, God would give the victory to the righteous North, that made Lincoln of such perdurable strength and patience through bloody defeat and amid carping and distracting factions. Of such stuff are conquerors and warriors made, whereof the radical has his portion. The first vice in such reasoning is that there is a Mind who would directly interest himself in the debates and wars of men respecting such a thing as slavery, or anything else, after giving them intellects whose best use could not solve the question; and the second is that he would let them come to war in their blindness and futility, and butcher each other, both to abolish the sin, and to suffer for its past effects. Vengeance is mine, saith the Lord, is at the core of this sort of thinking; and it interpenetrated all of Lincoln's. It is quite another belief to see all human events as unfolding fatefully, the nature of men being first premised. All else is of that Hebraic and Christian anthropomorphism which has done so much to curse the world. Lincoln believed in this, and because he did he became one of the world's greatest benefactors or scourges, just as one may think that he was carrying out the designs of God, or as one who was seized with madness, and wrought woes which time may never undo.

Before dispensing with witnesses on the subject of Lincoln's religion, Newton Bateman should be heard. In 1860 he was a man of thirty-eight years of age, residing in Springfield as the Super-

[1] Herndon, II, 248.

intendent of Public Instruction to which office he was elected in 1858 as a Republican. He had been educated at Illinois College under the presidency of Rev. Edward Beecher, a son of Lyman. Afterward he had studied theology at Lane Theological Seminary; and later still he became president of Knox College, at Galesburg, Illinois, and died as president emeritus of this school in 1897. Bateman had an office in the State House next the executive chamber, where he was frequently visited by Lincoln in the fall of 1860. Lincoln was then greatly disturbed by the attitude of the Springfield clergymen toward his candidacy for president. The account of the interview about to be given will be found in Holland's *Life of Abraham Lincoln*. Lincoln came in to see Bateman, and locked the door. He then produced a book of voters, and turning page by page he reflected sadly that this minister, or this Sunday School superintendent, or this elder or member of a church was against him. "Here are twenty-three ministers, of different denominations, and all of them are against me but three; and here are a great many members of the churches, a very large majority of whom are against me. Mr. Bateman, I am not a Christian—God knows I would be one—but I have carefully read the Bible, and I do not so understand this book." He then drew forth a New Testament, and according to Bateman, as set down by Holland, proceeded. "These men well know that I am for freedom in the Territories, freedom everywhere as far as the Constitution and laws will permit, and that my opponents are for slavery." Lincoln then grew very serious. His voice trembled, his cheeks were wet with tears, as he said: "I know there is a God, and that He hates injustice and slavery. I see the storm coming, and I know that His hand is in it. If He has a place and work for me, and I think He has, I believe I am ready. I am nothing, but truth is everything; I know I am right, because I know that liberty is right, for Christ teaches it, and Christ is God. . . . It seems as if God had borne with this thing (slavery) until the very teachers of religion have come to defend it from the Bible, and to claim for it a divine character and sanction; and now the cup of iniquity is full and the vials of wrath will be poured out." If infidels have not ceased to claim Lincoln as an authority of their cult they might consider this language. "Christ is God," and "the vials of wrath will be poured out." This was histrionic, almost hysterical. Such words do not sound honest, sensible, coming from the Lincoln that we know. If he spoke so he was acting; he was dramatizing himself for effect. It matters nothing that Lincoln did not go to church in Springfield, nor in Washington; but the reasons for not going to church are various. Many people keep out of the church because they do not believe in the creed; they cannot subscribe to election, to predestination, to the virgin birth, to Christ as God. Or they detest Jehovah, and have little more respect for the Christian God. Lincoln, however, would not join the church, though believing in Jehovah and in God, and in Calvinistic teleology such as war being inflicted upon the people to purge them of their sins. As in everything else, he was both in and out, both part way and not altogether, against abolition, but against the slavery which it would abolish, for the Fugitive Slave Law, but biting his lips in insupportable wrath when he saw that law enforced. More profoundly searched, his negative psychology, his analytical defensiveness, his constant attitude which demanded proof from the affirmative side, his coldness, his realism, his intellectual detachment, his separateness from the mob, which made him indifferent to local interests and politics, and no doubt a certain intellectual pride which came to him in the New Salem days and gave him belief that he was different from other men, as he was,—all these things operated to keep Lincoln out of the church. Nor did he weakly yield to public opinion and join a church, even when it would have been of advantage to him in politics to have done so.

But just as his emotions were stirred and the war hysteria entered his being, after having been created by him, other moods came to him. Out of these came writings like the Bixby letter with its pious words: "I pray that our heavenly Father may assuage the anguish of your bereavement, and leave you only the cherished memory of the loved and lost," the five sons who "have died gloriously on the field of battle." [1] This letter was dated November 21, 1864. Many would pray, if they believed prayer availing to any god, for something better for the world than the consolation of a mother. We may fight again, we may have many wars in the future, but may they be waged with pagan honesty, and with open declaration

[1] Lincoln's Works, II, 600.

that their battles are fought for gold and spoils, not for God. That will be a spiritual prophylaxis which will prevent the infections of hypocrisy.

Fear also operated to modify Lincoln's religious reflections; and if this be taken into account the words which Bateman put into his mouth increase in credibility. He was constantly haunted by the probability of assassination, it was scarcely ever out of his mind. When Herndon saw Mrs. Lincoln in August of 1866 she told him much of Lincoln's words and moods through the days of the presidency; and she also gave Herndon a written statement of Lincoln's life in Washington. "I often told Mr. Lincoln that God would not let any harm come to him," she wrote. "We had passed through four long years—terrible and bloody years—unscathed, and I believed we would be released from all danger. He gradually grew into that belief himself, and the old gloomy notion of his taking-off was becoming dimmer as time passed away." [1] In the emotional orgy of the war, religion played its full part, and Lincoln with his half mystical nature could not well avoid yielding to it by gradual degrees. His nerves were strained to the tension of breaking. There were around him the cries of widows and orphans; there were scenes of blood before him in the hospitals, and the reports from the battlefields were written red with slaughter. In such case where can the human heart turn? There was enough in his first faith, in that faith which believed himself to be an instrument of God in the adjustment of Speed's love affair, to furnish the basis of the religious feelings which he expressed in his Inaugurals and in the Gettysburg Address. Fear and pity, doubt and self-torture did their work. How otherwise on March 30, 1863, did he publish the Proclamation appointing a National fast day? Grant had not at this time captured Vicksburg. Congress had given Lincoln the control of the purse and the sword at the session which opened December 1, 1862, influenced by the terrible defeat which Burnside had suffered at the hand of Lee at Fredericksburg in November, in which the Union loss was 12,653 to the Confederates' 5309. Sumner wrote to his friend about now: "These are dark hours. There are senators who are full of despair—not I. But I fear that our army is everywhere in a bad way." Under these circumstances

[1] Herndon, II, 224.

Lincoln issued the proclamation referred to: "Whereas the Senate of the United States, devoutly recognizing the supreme authority and just government of Almighty God in all the affairs of men and of nations, has by a resolution requested the president to designate and set apart a day for national prayer and humiliation. And whereas it is the duty of nations as well as of men to own their dependence upon the overruling power of God; to confess their sins and transgressions in humble sorrow, yet with assured hope that genuine repentance will lead to mercy and pardon; and to recognize the sublime truth announced in the Holy Scriptures and proven by all history, that those nations only are blessed whose God is the Lord. And insomuch as we know that by his divine law nations, like individuals, are subjected to punishments and chastisements in this world, may we not justly fear that the awful calamity of civil war which now desolates the land may be but punishment inflicted upon us for our presumptuous sins, to the needful end of our national reformation as a whole people? . . . We have forgotten the gracious hand which preserved us in peace and multiplied and enriched and strengthened us; and we have vainly imagined, in the deceitfulness of our hearts, that all these blessings were produced by some superior wisdom and virtue of our own. Intoxicated with unbroken success, we have become too self-sufficient to feel the necessity of redeeming and preserving grace, too proud to pray to the God that made us: It behooves us then, to humble ourselves before the offended Power, to confess our national sins, and to pray for clemency and forgiveness." [1]

This proclamation was sufficiently pious to have satisfied the Springfield clergymen. But if Nicolay was right in saying that Lincoln did not change his religious beliefs from the time he left Springfield to the time of his death, what explanation is there of certain portions of this obsequious appeal, so out of tone too with the firmer prose of Lincoln? If Lincoln in the words of Mrs. Lincoln had no faith and no hope in the usual acceptance of those words, with what sincerity did Lincoln put forth the orthodox theological doctrines of this proclamation? The most reasonable conclusion that can be arrived at is that his nervous organization was exhausted, and that as in other things he had capitulated to the war

[1] Lincoln's Works, II, 319.

party and to the churches who were asking for vengeance on the South and looking upon themselves as in sin, and as not sufficiently placating Jehovah to win battles and crush the Confederacy. Strange is it that it was Lincoln who was the first president to introduce the cant and the hypocrisy of Christianity into American politics.

There remain, in further portraiture of Lincoln, his movements and words before he rose out of political retirement and reëntered the field as a candidate for office. His procrastination with respect to joining the Republican Party is of immense importance in judging the man. What has already been written concerning his intellectual and other ways, and his religion has been in preparation for an understanding of the man who after years of lethargy awoke to assert for himself a career. In order to appreciate the circumstances of his renascence, and particularly in order to follow intelligently his first speeches after the Kansas-Nebraska Law of 1854, and his debates with Douglas in 1858, it will be necessary to give a history of the Missouri Compromise, the Compromises of 1850, and the legislation concerning Kansas and Nebraska under the leadership of Douglas, who was chairman of the Committee on Territories in 1854.

Chapter VIII   The Compromises of 1820 and 1850

WHEN the war of the Revolution ended there was the vast territory west of Pennsylvania and of Virginia, which afterward became the states of Ohio, Indiana, Illinois, Michigan and Wisconsin, which was called the Northwest Territory, or the territory north of the Ohio River; and which was later called the Old Northwest in contradistinction to the Northwest of Idaho, Washington and Oregon. This Old Northwest came to the original thirteen states as the fruits of the Revolution, in addition to their independence; and by 1784 question arose in the Congress under the Confederation as to its control and administration. Thomas Jefferson tried to have slavery excluded from it at this time, but he was overruled, as he was when he wanted to put words in the Declaration of Independence denouncing the slave trade which the King of England had forced upon the colonies. Later, 1787, but still in the Continental Congress, the question arose again, and the Ordinance of 1787, as it is called, which was for the government of the territory, was passed. Before more is said of this ordinance some survey of negro slavery should be made, so that the nature of the controversy may be better understood relating to slavery going into the territory, and in later territories like those west of the Mississippi River, and with which Lincoln was concerned.

In the course of history there have been many kinds of slavery, brutal and mild, military and social. There was that slavery described by Thucydides to which the Athenians were subjected by the Syracusans, where the slaves were crowded into the quarries and worked to death under the heat of a pitiless sun and in a stifling air which tormented them night and day. Columbus on his second voyage sent back to Spain in lieu of gold which he did not find, a cargo of Indians to be kept in slavery. Negro slavery in America dates from 1502. The Spanish governors were prohibited from bringing into Haiti and Cuba, and the other West Indies, captive Jews and Moors, but they were permitted to import negroes who had been in the power of Christians. They needed labor to work the mines, and the native Indians could not stand the severity of the toil. In 1510, fifty negroes were brought over, taken out of the wilds of Africa. In 1517, four thousand negroes were brought to the New World. Spain and Portugal went into the business of slave catching and marketing on a systematic basis. Spain farmed out the wholesale business to Portugal, and, under a form of contract called an *asiento*, the Portuguese undertook to furnish negroes to Spain. The yearly average importation of slaves up to 1750 was 3000. Besides these there were the illicit forced importations of the English and the French. Sir John Hawkins, who was one of the commanders of Elizabeth's fleet which overcame the Spanish armada, was accustomed to market kidnapped negroes with guns trained on reluctant customers. By 1808, according to an estimate of Humboldt, the negro population of Spanish America was 776,000. It was not long in coming to the mainland, to South Carolina of rice and indigo; because when England wrested America from France she joined in the traffic, which Jefferson wanted to denounce in the Declaration.

Morality and the pocketbook go hand in hand; and South Carolina and Georgia would not hear to Jefferson's idealism. "The clause, too, reprobating the enslaving the inhabitants of Africa was struck out in complaisance to South Carolina and Georgia, who had never attempted to restrain the importation of slaves and who on the contrary still wished to continue it," were the words of Jefferson who made a report of the proceedings of the Congress of the Colonies on June 7, 1776.[1] Should the words be retained to the loss of Georgia and South Carolina in the Revolution; or should they be stricken out, with those colonies kept in line to fight George III?

Moral choices frequently have such mixed alternatives. Rarely may men choose between two goods. There is a kind of malice in the affairs of men which stands by to involve them in present and future woes, in stultifications and in wars to come. Massachusetts came out of these deliberations with pure hands. But the economic factor must be kept in mind. Massachusetts abolished slavery in 1780, nearly ten years before the United States government under the Constitution went into operation. But John Adams wrote: "Argument might have had some weight in the abolition of slavery in Massachuetts, but the real cause was the multiplication of laboring white people, who would not suffer the rich to employ these sable rivals so much to

[1] Jefferson's Writings, I, 18–29.

their injury." Later, in the Congress of 1776, he said that it made no difference whether people were called freemen or slaves when considering a basis for taxation, and the wealth of a state. "What matters it whether a landlord employing ten laborers on his farm gives them annually as much as will buy the necessaries of life, or gives them those necessaries at first hand?" [1] This bears upon the constitutional clause of representation and direct taxes, later to be considered in connection with observations of Lincoln.

When the Constitutional Convention met in the summer of 1787, every state except Massachusetts had negro slavery. Now after so long a time the scene has become clear. The great men there were not all burning with liberty; they were thinking of business, and they had come into convention because business was hobbled and lamed by the loose regulations of the Articles of Confederation adopted by the states during the Revolution. Taxes were hard to gather, commerce was enervated, money was not on the right basis. The movement for the new Constitution originated in money, public securities, manufactures, trade and shipping. And the fathers were interested in these things, and they were bent on deriving an advantage from a stronger system of government which would ensure them. The South had many men who were rich in other things besides slaves; and the story that grew up through the agitation of abolitionists that the free and moral North had to bend to the demands of the Southern slavocracy is a myth now dispelled. The truth was that the financiers of South Carolina and New York made common cause on all economic questions, and the nationalism achieved by the Constitution, such at it was, came about through a fusion of economic interests which cut across state lines, as much as interstate commerce does today between Pennsylvania and California. Slavery being one of the economic matters to resolve, the most practical considerations determined its solution. The institution of slavery was in America by this time thoroughly imbedded in the economic life of the people. Originally forced upon the colonists the question was what was to be done with it. Slavery could not be abolished. Abolition had to come by State action, and the sovereignty of the states at that time was as unquestioned as the law of gravitation. It resulted that by the 3d clause of the 2nd section of the 4th article it was pro-

[1] "The Lost Principles of Sectional Equilibrium," 39.

vided that "no persons held to service or labor in one state by the law thereof, escaping into another, shall in consequence of any law or regulation therein be discharged from such service or labor, but shall be delivered up on claim of the party to whom such service or labor may be due." This is the provision on which the Fugitive Slave Laws were based, and which the abolitionists refused to obey, as Seward did when he was governor of New York.

Lincoln, as will be seen, made much of the fact that the word "slave" was not written in the Constitution, but always the word, "person" where he was referred to. This is the way the Lincoln mind so artfully worked. But there were apprentices to be "delivered up" and they were persons held to service, and there were slaves who were persons held to labor, and they were likewise to be surrendered. Both slaves and apprentices were factors in the labor scheme of the time. The 4th section of the 4th article provided that Congress should protect each state, "on application of the Legislature (or of the executive when the Legislature cannot be convened against domestic violence)." The 15th clause of the 8th section made it the duty of Congress "to provide for the calling forth the militia to execute the laws of the union, suppress insurrections and repel invasions." The men who wrote the Constitution knew the meaning of words, and when they used the word "insurrections" they had in mind a specific kind of disobedience to law. It was the opposition to the law of a city or state, and within its confines. The South was apprehensive of negro insurrections, just as capitalists today stand in dread of strikes, and do all they can to forestall and defeat them by resort to the courts, and to policemen and soldiers. Madison in the XLIIIrd number of the *Federalist* discussed this clause, with concealed reference to Shays' Rebellion, which happened in Massachusetts just before, in 1787. That rebellion, be it observed, was waged to prevent the collection of debts and taxes. The seaside had overreached the western hills and the rebellion followed.

Mr. Beard, in his *Economic Interpretation of the Constitution*, wrote: "The southern planter was also as much concerned in maintaining order against slave revolts as the creditor in Massachusetts was concerned in putting down Shays' desperate creditors. And the possibilities of such servile insurrections were by no means remote. Every slave owner must have felt more secure in 1789 when

COMPROMISES OF 1820 AND 1850

he knew that the governor of his state could call in the strong arm of the federal administration in case a domestic disturbance got beyond the local militia and police." Beard further observed that the North might, with its tariff, make discriminatory commercial regulations; but that it was better to ship products under adverse legislation than to have no products to ship.

Finally the Constitution provided, "the migrations or importation of such persons as any of the states now existing shall think proper to admit, shall not be prohibited by the Congress prior to the year 1808, but a duty may be imposed on such importation, not exceeding ten dollars for each person." To make this secure it was provided that this clause could not be struck out by amendment to the Constitution before 1808. In his Cooper Institute speech in 1860 Lincoln denied that the right of property in a slave was distinctly and expressly affirmed in the Constitution, as Taney had declared it to be in the Dred Scott case; and he resorted to definitions: " 'distinctly,' that is not mingled with anything else; 'expressly,' that is in words meaning just that without the aid of any inference, and susceptible of no other meaning." This was characteristic of Lincoln's dialectic. He seized upon a possible misuse of words whereby to overthrow the otherwise impregnable basis of the argument in which the words were used. It cannot be doubted at all that the Constitution protected slavery and that its framers intended it to do so to the full.

Then what was slavery, what did it grow to be in America after the days of Hawkins, what was it at the time of the Ordinance of 1787, and in Lincoln's day? Harriet Martineau, an English woman who was critical enough of the South when she traveled through America in 1833, was greatly delighted with Charleston. In New Orleans she found the slave quarters pleasing to the eye. "The cottages of the negroes were embowered in green." Mobile was to her a dream of loveliness. She saw other negro quarters where "the little children are basking in the sun." Lady Emmeline Stuart-Wortley was another traveler in the South from England, and she wrote a book in 1849. She visited the plantation house of President Taylor's son near Natchez. She was pleased with the cleanliness and the good health of the slave children. Travelers from New England went into the South and were surprised to find how mild the institution of slavery was on the plantations and in the cities. Field work of course was hard; but so is digging coal in Pennsylvania, or running spinning machines in Massachuetts. There was brutality to the negroes without doubt. But in strikes men were shot down after being overworked and underpaid. Child and woman labor in New England in the North had brutality enough about it. The eight hour day in America, and before it the ten hour day, were won only after jails and bloodshed could do their worst to cow the laborers.

But it requires only one work of imagination properly conceived with reference to stirring emotion, and published at the right time to overcome all the facts and all the reasoning based upon them, wherever the subject is one about which a morality can be raised. Hence Mrs. Stowe's description of the death of Uncle Tom at the hand of the slave driver Legree put all the South into speechless rage. Of what use was it to show against such melodrama what the position of the Southern people was with reference to the presence of the negroes for which they were not primarily at fault, or to offer in mitigation of the system an explanation of the difficulties they were in with reference to the numerous negroes about them, or to prove that slavery was a social regimentation necessary to prevent negro domination?

None of the Northern people who were inveighing against the crimes of the South growing out of slavery would have been willing to have lived in a community where negroes far outnumbered the whites, and if given civil, not to say political rights, would have been master of every social and civil situation. In the Senate in 1839 Henry Clay said: "In the slave states the alternative is, that the white man must govern the black, or the black govern the white." Alexander H. Stephens called slavery a social regulation, and said that it was not really slavery. This might have been as true as he said it was; yet slavery always had the concrete disadvantage of visible traffic in which human beings were bought and sold, and manacled for transportation. What can be seen with the eye is so much more exciting than what can be truly visioned with the mind. Calhoun declared that slavery was the most safe and stable basis for free institutions in the world, perhaps with prophetic reference to what has come to pass in America under the wage system with its corruption of politics and its degradation of jurisprudence. There is not as much liberty in America today, with slavery abolished, as there was in America with slavery all over the Southern states. Men differed about the institution; churches differed about it. For long in the North even, before the abolitionists had stirred the country with dissension, presidents of colleges, like Wilbur Fisk, president of Wesleyan University, Connecticut, and Rev. Nathan Lord, president of Dartmouth College, and many others, bishops and theologians and scholars, stood for slavery and justified themselves out of the Bible as well as by reason. Robert Toombs went to Boston in January of 1856 to tell the people of the North what slavery was, in an attempt to quiet the rage that had been stirred up by agitators. Among other things he said:

"The question was not presented for our decision whether it was just or beneficial to the African to tear him away by force or fraud from bondage in his own country and place him in a like condition in ours. England and the Christian world had long before settled that question for us. At the final overthrow of British authority in these States our ancestors found 700,000 Africans among them, already in bondage, and concentrated from our climate and productions chiefly in the present slave holding states. It became the duty to establish governments for themselves and these people. . . . They sought that system which would secure the greatest and most enduring happiness to the whole society. They incorporated no Utopian theories into their system. They did not so much concern themselves about what right he ought to have in a state of nature, as what rights he ought to have in a state of society; they dealt with political rights as things of compact, not birthright, in the concrete not in the abstract. They held and maintained . . . that it was the duty and right of the state to define and fix as well as to protect and defend the individual rights of each member of the social compact, and to treat all individual rights as subordinate to the great interests of the whole society. Therefore they denied 'natural equality,' repudiated mere governments of men necessarily resulting therefrom, and established governments of laws—thirteen free sovereign, and independent republics. A very slight examination of our state constitutions will show how little they regarded vague notions of abstract liberty or natural equality in fixing the rights of the white race as well as the black. The elective franchise, the cardinal feature of our system, I have already shown, was granted, withheld, limited, according to their ideals of public policy and the interest of the State. . . . The slave holding states acting upon these principles, finding the African race among them in slavery, unfit to be trusted with political power, incapable as freemen of securing their own happiness, or promoting the public prosperity, recognized their condition as slaves, and subjected it to legal control. There are abundant means of obtaining evidence of the effects of this policy on the slave and on society, accessible to all who seek the truth. We may say its wisdom is vindicated. . . . Upon the theory of the anti-slavery men, the most favorable condition in which you can view the African ought to be in the non-slaveholding states of this Union. There we ought to find him displaying all the capabilities of his race for improvement and progress—in a temperate climate, with the road of progress open before him, among an active, industrious, ingenious and educated people, surrounded by sympathizing friends, and mild, just, and equal institutions, if he fails here, surely it can be charged to nothing but himself. He has had seventy years in which to cleanse himself and his race from the leprosy of slavery; but he finds it is truly a 'heritage of woe.' After the seventy years of education and probation among themselves, his inferiority stands as fully a confessed fact in the non-slaveholding as in the slaveholding states. By them he is adjudged unfit to enjoy the rights and perform the duties of citizenship—denied social equality by an irreversible law of nature and political rights, by municipal law, incapable of maintaining the unequal struggle with the superior race; the melancholy history of his career of freedom is here most usually found in the records of the criminal courts, jails, poor-houses, and penitentiaries. These facts have had themselves recognized in the most decisive manner throughout the Northern States. No town, no city, or State encourages their immigration; many of them discourage it by legislation; some of the non-slaveholding states have prohibited their entry into their borders under any circumstances whatever. Thus it seems this great fact of 'inferiority' of the race is equally admitted everywhere in our country. The Northern states admit it, and, to rid themselves of the burden, inflict the most injuries upon an unhappy race; they expel them from their borders and drive them out of their boundaries, as wanderers and out-casts. . . . Our political system

COMPROMISES OF 1820 AND 1850

gives the slave great and valuable rights. His life is equally protected with that of his master; his person is secure from assault against all others but his master, and his master's power in this respect is placed under salutary legal restraints. He is entitled by law to a home, to ample food and clothing, and exempted from excessive labor; and when no longer capable of labor in old age and disease, he is a legal charge upon his master. His family, old and young, whether capable of labor or not, from the cradle to the grave, have the same legal rights; and in these legal provisions, they enjoy as large a proportion of the products of their labor as any class of unskilled hired laborers in the world. We know that these rights are in the main faithfully secured to them; but I rely not on our knowledge, but submit our institutions to the same tests by which we try those of all other countries. These are supplied by our public statistics. They show that our slaves are larger consumers of animal food than any population in Europe, and larger than any other labor population in the United States. . . . The immoralities of the slaves, and of those connected with slavery are constant themes of abolition denunciation. They are lamentably great; but it remains to be shown that they are greater than with the laboring poor of England, or any other country. And it is shown that our slaves are without the additional stimulant of want to drive them to crime, we have at least removed from them the temptation and excuse of hunger. . . . Lord Ashley's report to the British Parliament shows that in the capital of that empire, perhaps within hearing of Stafford House and Exeter Hall, hunger alone daily drives thousands of men and women into the abyss of crime."

With so much said as to what slavery was, and with some more to say, it will be seen what was a part of the motivation of the restriction of slavery when the Northwest Territory was taken under the control of Congress, and what bearing that act had on liberty whether abstractly or concretely considered. If the negro was so much in the just consideration of the North, his wretched plight in the North raises many questions. Why was he an alien, an outcast, in the North? Why in Illinois was he denied civil rights as we have seen? Why in August of 1834 did a race riot break forth in Philadelphia in which thirty negro houses were sacked or destroyed, a negro church demolished and many people killed? This was followed by negro mobbing at Trenton, and other towns in New Jersey. A decade ago there was a riot in Chicago arising out of hatred of the negroes, in which several negroes lost their lives, and to this day discriminations are made against negroes all over the North as contradictory of their social equality as are the jim crow cars of the South. The right or wrong of these things is not the present matter; the fact of the social and political state of the negroes is the point of discussion. Forty years after the Revolution Lafayette was surprised to find, when making a tour of the country, that the feeling against the negro had increased since he knew the country in 1780. All along the Southern statesmen were trying to convince the North that the South was the negro's best friend, and begging the North to mind its business. The abolitionists would not heed this advice. And *Uncle Tom's Cabin* awoke the mob. It was published nine months after the Compromise of 1850.

The Ordinance of 1787 did not contain the clause forbidding slavery in it in order to induce negroes to migrate thither and settle there. By no means was that the case. At the end of the Revolution many soldiers had gone there to live and to advance their worldly interests. They no more wanted the negro immigrant than any other part of the North wanted him. It was known that if the negro did not come there as a slave, he would not come to any extent at all. This is said making full acknowledgment of the philanthropic feelings of Jefferson and other advanced men of the time. There is an imaginative impulse involved, too, which regards the earth and would see a free people on a free soil. What we are considering now and about to investigate are instances of slavery restriction in the territories, so that Lincoln's argumentations both on the stump and in debate with Douglas can be intelligently followed. It must be borne in mind, if the reader would clearly see Lincoln's positions and Douglas's, that until the Missouri Compromise of 1820 no act was passed by Congress which asserted the primary constitutional power to prevent any citizen of the United States owning slaves from removing them into the territories, and there receiving a legal protection for his property; and until that time such persons did remove them into all the territories owned or acquired by the United States, except the Northwest Territory. Even in the Northwest Territory there were slaves, both negro and Indian, at Cahokia, Kaskaskia and Vincennes, at the French settlements on the Wabash and the Illinois, and at Detroit, before the Ordinance of 1787, and afterward, as the Ordinance did not of itself set such slaves free. Slavery never flourished in most of this Territory, because the climate was not suited to the growth of the products for which slave labor was used; or in other words the law of God did not encourage the owning of slaves in this territory, something that Douglas pointed out again and again as to the territory west of the Mississippi and north of 36° 30'.

The Ordinance of 1787 was adopted on the 13th day of July, 1787, by the Congress of the Articles of Confederation, and before the Constitution was even reported out of Convention, which happened on September 17, 1787. This Ordinance purported on its face to be a perpetual compact between the state of Virginia, which had owned and ceded most of the Territory, the people of the Territory, and the then government of the United States. It contained a bill of rights, and it guaranteed the habeas corpus, right of trial by jury, compensation for property seized, religious freedom, free schools, all as " articles of compact" forever "unalterable unless by common consent," which meant the consent of Virginia, the people of the Territory and the United States; and to come to the matter in hand now, it pledged the abolition of slavery. There should be no slavery in the Territory. This was the compact, what might be called the consideration of Virginia's cession.

Not until June, 1788, had as many as nine states ratified the Constitution; and the government under it did not go into operation until March, 1789. On August 7 of that year the Congress, under the Constitution, passed an act making the offices of governor and secretary conform to the Constitution; and it did nothing more. There was then a government in full operation under the Ordinance; and there was no occasion to do anything, especially as to things which were established or those provided for by "compacts," unalterable except by "common consent." Similarly it would have been beyond what was necessary to reëstablish the writ of habeas corpus, or the right of free worship, or any other rights already fixed. That would have been but rhetoric. When we come to Lincoln's Cooper Institute speech we shall see with what disregard of these historic facts he proceeded to treat the Northwest, as if the United States Congress under the Constitution had excluded slavery from it. Whether the old United States had the power to do so, need not be inquired into, and for the reason that there was nothing in the Articles of Confederation which forbade the acceptance of territory upon covenants and compacts made a part of the deed of cession.

But there was territory south of the Ohio as well as north; and already at this early time one may perceive that territory was dealt with not on the basis of morality but upon that of economics. The South territory was adapted to slave labor. On the 2nd of April, 1790, Congress accepted the cession of North Carolina of her western lands, which became afterward the state of Tennessee, with a clause in the deed of cession that "no regulations made, or to be made by Congress, shall tend to emancipate slaves." On the 26th of May, 1790, Congress passed a territorial bill for the government of all the territory south of the Ohio River. This included what was to become Tennessee, and much more. This act put the whole territory south of the Ohio under the pro-slavery clause of the North Carolina deed. The whole legislation of the first Congress may be thus summarized: it acquiesced in a government of the Northwest Territory, based upon a preëxisting anti-slavery ordinance; it established a government for the country ceded by North Carolina in harmony with a pro-slavery clause in its deed of cession; and it then extended this pro-slavery clause to the rest of the territory then claimed by the United States south of the Ohio River. In 1802 Georgia ceded her western lands, covenanting for slavery in her grant, and the United States government honored the stipulation. In 1803 the United States acquired the Louisiana Territory. While there was no reference to slavery in the grant, it was protected under the general classification of property. The government of the Louisiana Territory was by act of Congress vested in a governor and thirteen persons of the territory acting as a council whose legislative powers should extend to "all the rightful subjects of legislation; but no law shall be valid which is inconsistent with the constitution and laws of the United States." The Louisiana Territory was soon after divided into the territories of Orleans and Louisiana; and slavery was protected in both, with the exception that Congress prohibited the foreign and domestic slave trade; but gave the express protection of slave owners emigrating thither with their slaves. Upon the ad-

COMPROMISES OF 1820 AND 1850

mission of Louisiana into the Union on April 30, 1812, a new government was established over the rest of the territory under the name of the Missouri Territory, as to which no slave exclusion was attempted. Slave holders entered it with their slaves and were protected by the government. In 1819, Florida, which had slavery and enjoyed legal protection of it, was acquired by purchase. The United States extended recognition and protection to it. It will be found that in all our acquisitions, even that of the Philippines, the local law and customs were recognized where possible, because it is in the interest of peace and progress for a new governmental owner not to disturb too much a régime under which the inhabitants have previously lived.

To recur now to the Constitution. It was drawn with the eyes of the convention looking directly at the Northwest Territory; and just as Jefferson, in 1784, had planned that it should be carved into states, and had even chosen names for the states, like Michigiana, Polypotamia, Sylviana and the like, so did the convention with the same idea in mind put in the Constitution the clause: "New States may be admitted by the Congress into this Union." And by the third section of the Fourth Article it was provided: "The Congress shall have power to dispose of and make all needful rules and regulations respecting the Territory and other property of the United States." There is no other word in the Constitution on the subject of territory; no naming of any specific territory, as the Articles of Confederation did, which provided for the admission of Canada as a state; not a word, be it observed, empowering Congress to make laws for the territory—but only regulations. The men who phrased the Constitution were among the best intellects of the time in America. They were such men as Alexander Hamilton of New York; Benjamin Franklin and James Wilson, the latter a famous lawyer, of Pennsylvania; James Madison of Virginia, who has been called the Father of the Constitution; James Rutledge and Charles Cotesworth Pinckney of South Carolina; while George Washington was a deputy from Virginia in the Convention and its presiding officer. Surely these men knew better than to use the word "regulations," when they meant "laws." Taney when deciding the Dred Scott case had this to say: "It does not speak of any Territory, not of Territories, but uses language which according to its legitimate meaning points to a particular thing. The power is given in relation only to the territory of the United States, that is to a territory then in existence and then known or claimed as territory of the United States. It begins its enumeration of powers by that of disposing, in other words making sale of lands, or raising money from them, which as we have already said was the main object of the cession, and which is accordingly the first thing provided for in the article. It then gives the power which was necessarily associated with the disposition and sale of lands—that is the power of making needful rules and regulations respecting the territory. . . . And the same power of making needful rules respecting the territory is, in precisely the same language applied to the other property belonging to the United States, associating the power over the territory in this respect with the power over movable or personal property—that is the ships, arms and munitions of war, which then belonged in common to the state sovereignties." [1]

But what a spider for spinning is human reason! Webster contended that the clause now being considered empowered Congress to exclude slavery from a territory; Lincoln followed Webster, though with guarded language. It was the "right" and "duty" of Congress to keep slavery out of Kansas and Nebraska. While Calhoun belonged to Taney's school, holding that the clause related solely to the Northwest Territory, and that as to any other some other power in Congress constitutionally derived had to be invoked for the exclusion. Since their day "dispose of" has been advanced to mean "acquire," and the treaty-making power has been pointed to as warranting the acquisition of the Philippines. Also if the power to make needful rules and regulations is an empty one, if the United States cannot acquire territory, upon what may the needful rules and regulations be exercised? This is the Constitutional march, or gavotte. With so much prefaced, the Missouri Compromise of 1820 may now be considered.

The Louisiana Purchase of 1803–4 was a vast tract of land. It included first all of the present state of Louisiana. Its western line, running along the western boundary of that state, began at the Gulf of Mexico and extended north for a hundred miles along the western line of the state of Arkansas as it now is; it then turned west meandering somewhat along the Red River for more than 300 miles; it

[1] Scott vs. Sanford, 19 Howard 393.

COMPROMISES OF 1820 AND 1850

then turned straight north to a point in what is now Kansas, more than 50 miles from its southern boundary and about 100 miles from its western boundary; it then meandered west through the lower part of Colorado to a point more than 50 miles west of what is now Denver; it then turned due north proceeding to a point in Wyoming about 50 miles north of that state's present southern boundary, and about 100 miles west of its eastern boundary; it then slanted and looped to the western side of the Yellowstone Park; and on up west of Helena to the Canadian line. All of this was the Louisiana Purchase, as also determined by the Spanish Treaty of 1819.

In the Senate, in February, 1820, a bill originated for the admission of Maine into the Union. An amendment was made there to tack on to this bill a provision for the admission of Missouri which had before applied for admission in 1818. To this Senator Thomas of Illinois moved an amendment that in all that territory ceded by France, under the name of Louisiana, which lay north of 36° 30′ north latitude, except only that part included in the territory of Missouri itself, slavery and involuntary servitude should be prohibited; but also providing for the reclamation of fugitive slaves. This bill, with all the amendments, passed the Senate by a vote of 34 to 10. All the negative votes but two were from the South. They had regard for the Constitution. The other two were from Indiana. The bill and its amendments went to the House and were taken up on February 19, 1820. There the Thomas amendment was beaten by a vote of 159 to 18, on February 22nd. The Senate then sent a message to the House that it insisted upon the Thomas amendment. Then the House voted down the Thomas amendment by a vote of 160 to 14. The Senate now requested that a committee be appointed by the House to confer with one from the Senate on the impasse which had arisen. The House appointed a committee, every member of which was from Northern states, except Lowndes of South Carolina. Two were from Massachusetts, one from New York, and one from New Jersey. But with the committee so appointed the House without delay proceeded to deal with the Missouri Bill, which by this time contained a restriction of slavery in Missouri through an amendment offered by a congressman from New York, named Taylor. This bill passed the House by a vote of 91 to 82, and was sent to the Senate. On March second, Holmes, the Massachuetts member of the House Committee, made a report on the Maine Bill, which recommended that the Senate should recede from its amendment to the Maine Bill, both Houses should pass the Missouri Bill by striking out the House amendment which prohibited slavery within the state of Missouri, and substituting for that the Thomas amendment of restriction of slavery without the state of Missouri and north of 36° 30′. A similar report was made to the Senate on March 3 and adopted without a count of votes. Then the House took up the striking out of the restrictions on the state itself, and this passed by a vote of 90 to 87; only 14 of the 90 were from slave-holding states. Then the House concurred with the Senate on the Thomas amendment which divided the whole territory outside of Missouri itself between what was south of 36° 30′ and what was north of it; and this passed by a vote of 130 to 42 on March 2, 1820. By this division of the public domain which belonged in common to the states as a whole, the North got 308,052 square miles and the South 59,268 square miles of territory. We shall see now what Jefferson thought of dividing by a sectional line the land which belonged to all the states alike.

"The Missouri question is a mere party trick," he wrote in a letter to a friend. "The leaders of Federalism defeated in their scheme of obtaining power by rallying partisans to the principles of monarchism, a principle of personal, not of local division, have changed their tack, and thrown out another barrel to the whale. They are taking advantage of the virtuous feelings of the people to effect a division of parties by geographical line; they expect that this will ensure them, on local principles the majority they never could obtain on principles of Federalism; but they are still putting their shoulder to the wrong wheel; they are wasting jeremiads on the miseries of slavery, as if we were advocates of it." [1] It may be added that they were doing exactly what Lincoln did when he made his "House divided against itself" speech, and when he assumed to stand for what was morally right against Douglas, who was standing for what was morally wrong.

In another letter Jefferson wrote, "But this momentous question, like a fire bell in the night, awakened me and filled me with terror. I considered it at once as the knell of the Union. . . . A geographical line, coinciding with a marked principle, once conceived and held

---

[1] Jefferson's Works, Vol. VII, 159.

COMPROMISES OF 1820 AND 1850

up to the angry passions of men, will never be obliterated; and every new irritation will mark it deeper and deeper. . . . Of one thing I am certain, that as the passage of slaves from one state to another would not make a slave of a single human being who would not be so without one, so their diffusion over a greater surface would make them individually happier, and proportionately facilitate the accomplishment of their emancipation by dividing the burthen on a greater number of coadjutors. I regret that I am now to die in the belief that the useless sacrifice of themselves by the generation of 1776, to acquire self-government and happiness to the country, is to be thrown away by the unwise and unworthy passions of their sons, and that my only consolation is to be that I live not to weep over it." In a letter to Madison he wrote, "The Missouri question, by geographical line of division is the most portentous one I ever contemplated."

Indeed the Missouri Compromise was one of the causes of the War which Lincoln led. There were many causes remote and proximate, but this was one of them. The Bible was one cause, with its Jewish concepts of divine wrath, and its arsenal of prophetical denunciation. Such a war could not have happened under the rational culture of the Athenians, nor carried on under the lofty poetry of Æschylus. It needed for its inspiration the Jewish culture of Job and Isaiah, and the barbarism of the Pentateuch. Within forty years of the time that Jefferson wrote these letters, armies dealing death upon each other were tramping not so far from where his body lay in its grave at Monticello; and the Missouri Compromise was bearing its fruit.

To show that these men who engineered the Missouri Compromise were bent upon the old Federalistic plot of centralizing the government, and that they were a dishonest lot, let us proceed to consider the rest of the story. At the very next session of this Congress, that is, the 16th, Missouri was denied representation in the Senate and in the House, as a state in the Union, under the bill which had been thus passed admitting Missouri. In addition to this, Missouri's vote, which had been cast for president and vice president at the fall election of 1820, was not allowed to be counted. On the 13th of December a resolution was offered in the House recognizing Missouri as a state in the Union in pursuance of the law passed at the previous session; and the vote was 79 in favor of the recognition, and 93 against it. Of these 93, 72 were of those who had tried to prohibit slavery within the confines of Missouri, and were beaten on that. At this juncture of affairs Henry Clay came forward. On the 2nd of February, 1821, he moved that a committee of 13 be appointed to report proper action to be taken with the difficulty. Clay as the chairman of the committee reported on February 10 to the effect that Missouri should be recognized as a state within the Union on condition that its legislature should pass no law in violation of the rights of citizens of other states. The rights of citizens depended upon the Federal Constitution; so that Clay's resolution meant nothing more than that Missouri as a state of the Union should be bound by the Constitution. Yet this resolution was defeated in the House by a vote of 85 to 83; and meanwhile Missouri was out in the cold.

There was much strife and bitterness, and accusations of bad faith and tricky politics. Clay went on, however, to further effort. On the 22nd of February he moved for the appointment of joint committees of the House and Senate; the committee of the House to consist of 23 members. The Senate concurred. Clay was made chairman again and another report was submitted on February 26. There was no difference between it substantially and the other report. It provided that no law should be passed by Missouri under its constitution "by which any citizen of either of the States of this Union shall be excluded from the enjoyment of any of the privileges and immunities to which such citizen is entitled under the Constitution of the United States." This resolution passed the House by a vote of 87 to 81. In the Senate it passed by a vote of 26 to 15. It was approved by the president March 2, 1821; and Missouri was in the Union. But what became of the Compromise by which slavery was excluded north of 36° 30'? Missouri did not enter the Union under any such condition. She entered it under a condition superfluously imposed, that she should be subject to the Constitution. These facts should be kept in mind when we come to Lincoln's denunciations and moralizings touching the iniquitous repeal of the Missouri Compromise by the labors of the satanic Stephen A. Douglas.

But upon the supposition that the Missouri Compromise was enacted, even though the consideration of its enactment was withdrawn by keeping Missouri out of the Union to await other tests

COMPROMISES OF 1820 AND 1850

of statehood, however absurd, how did the party of centralization treat it? By 1836 the Jeffersonian party was strong in Congress, for Jackson was president; and on June 13, 1836, a bill was offered for the admission of Arkansas as a state of the Union. John Quincy Adams, of many great virtues, and of noted ability, was at this time a member of the House. For years he had been presenting in the House abolition petitions, at the instance of Massachusetts and pharisaical bodies, and by doing so keeping the House in a constant state of irritation and uproar. War was surely impending about this matter of slavery; but men can never know the truth at the time. If they had known what slavery was, if they had minded their own business, there would have been no war, no treading of grapes of wrath, no triumphant Jehovah of the Jews. Adams was a Whig, as Lincoln was; and Whigs cared for the law when it was on their side. When the law was against them they appealed to revealed morals, to God. If compromises like that supposed to have been made about Missouri violate God's law, then it is right to violate one's oath in its disobedience. This Adams proceeded to do with reference to Arkansas. To the bill for its admission he offered an amendment as follows: "And nothing in this act shall be construed as an assent by Congress to the article in the constitution of said state in relation to slavery, or the emancipation of slaves." [1] The North having gotten the best of the bargain in territory, but at that where slavery would not in the nature of things come or thrive if it did come, the South was to be denied all benefit under the Compromise as to its lesser lands, and where slavery could be used for the raising of cotton. It happened however that Adams was beaten on his resolution.

In the histories that have been written of the acquisitions of the United States, the impression has been given in many of them that there was a spirited race between the free North and the slave South to get more land for liberty on the one hand and for slavery on the other. The truth is that the Southern states were by far the more reasonable and pacific, and that the North worsted the South at every turn. Back of the cry of free soil was the ambition to get more Northern states from which Senators and Congressmen could be recruited for the strengthening of the tariff and other economic plans of the North, and for party spoils and all that goes with a

[1] Congressional Globe, 24th Congress, 1st Session, 434–42.

political supremacy. It was futile for the South to contest for Northern territory, where slavery could not flourish because of the climate; but if the North could keep slavery out of Southern territory and restrict it in states admitted therefrom, there was that much more political power gained for its economic rulerships. The strife that tore the country, and divided Congress, from the time of Missouri until the War, was not one between human rights and human bondage, but between those who fought so valiantly to preserve the Federal system on the one side and those on the other who worked with the principle of implied powers, following the instructions of Hamilton, to centralize, to imperialize the government. There was vastly more land where negro labor could not be used than there was land where cotton made it profitable to employ it. Florida was acquired in 1819 as slave territory. It contained 59,268 square miles. In the same year the Oregon territory was settled by treaty, and this contained 308,052 square miles, and it was free territory.

Texas came into the Union in 1845, as a slave state, the South agreeing that north of 36° 30′ slavery might forever be excluded. But, that stipulation obtained, the North proceeded to encroach upon what the South had hardly kept for its own, namely, the right of states south of 36° 30′ to come into the Union with slavery or without it as they chose.

The Mexican war and the territorial acquisitions which followed it brought fresh troubles. On August 8, 1846, David Wilmot offered his proviso for the exclusion of slavery from the public domain, which might come to the United States in the settlement with Mexico. Nearly all of New Mexico and Arizona and one half of California were south of 36° 30′; and this was to be taken away from the South in the teeth of the provision which had passed with reference to Texas. Wilmot's Proviso received a large vote in the House, but failed in the Senate. Wilmot had before this voted with those who were against restricting slavery; he had been with those who favored the policy of leaving the problem with the states under the control of state sovereignty. On January 15, 1847, the bill for the organization of a territorial government for Oregon came up in the House; and for the purpose of weighing the good faith of the North, Mr. Burt, a representative from South Carolina, moved an amendment to the Oregon bill which excluded slavery from the Territory, and pointed it with these words: "inasmuch as the whole of said territory lies north of 36° 30′ latitude, known as the line of the Missouri Compromise." The Burt amendment was lost by a vote of 82 to 113, every one of the 113 being Northern representatives; while every Southern representative voted for it. Of those who thus voted to adhere to the Missouri Compromise there were but six representatives from the North. One of these was Stephen A. Douglas from Illinois. The Northern men knew that they did not need any restriction on slavery in Oregon; and they did not want to do anything confirmatory of the Missouri Compromise principle and thereby ensure to the South what benefit it derived from that settlement.

On February 19, 1847, Calhoun offered a series of resolutions in the Senate. The first one was, "Resolved, That the territories of the United States belong to the several states composing this Union, and are held by them as their joint and common property." The second one was, "Resolved, That Congress, as the joint agent and representative of the states of this Union, has no right to make any law, or do any act whatever, that shall directly, or by its effects, make any discrimination between the states of this Union, by which any of them shall be deprived of its full and equal right in any territory of the United States, acquired or to be acquired." The last one was, "Resolved, That it is a fundamental principle in our political creed, that a people in forming a constitution have the unconditional right to form and adopt the Government which they think best calculated to secure their liberty, prosperity, and happiness; and that, in conformity thereto, no other condition is imposed by the Federal Constitution on a state, in order to be admitted into this Union, except that its constitution shall be republican; and that the imposition of any other by Congress would be not only in violation of the Constitution, but in direct conflict with the principle on which our political system rests."

Against the inexorable logic of this announcement there was not anything to be said except on the score of the immorality of slavery; or something about the higher law, which leads to the inquiry whether the higher law could have a source higher than the Constitution itself. When the bill appropriating $3,000,000, to enable the president to carry out the treaty with Mexico, came before the Senate, on March 1, 1847, Mr. Upham, a senator from Vermont, moved to amend the bill by inserting the Wilmot Proviso in it. The amendment was agreed to by a vote of 21 to 31; and every one of the 31 was from the non-slaveholding states; that is, they repudiated the principle of the Missouri Compromise; while every one of the votes in the negative was from the slaveholding states, except seven, one of these being Sidney Breese from Illinois, and another Lewis Cass of Michigan. A further analysis showed that there were only five votes, five senators, out of the entire North, who were in favor of the principle of the Missouri Compromise. These with Southern votes succeeded at last in defeating the amendment, so that the appropriation bill went to the House without any provision of slavery restriction in it. When the bill came to the House, Wilmot moved to insert his proviso in it; and Graham of North Carolina moved a substitute as follows: "Provided, That if any territory be acquired by the United States from Mexico, the Missouri Compromise line of 36° 30' shall be extended direct to the Pacific Ocean; that is, slavery shall be prohibited north of that Line and allowed south of it." Graham's substitute was rejected, and the Wilmot Proviso inserted by a vote of 90 to 80 while the House was in committee of the whole. But when the bill was reported to the House from the Committee the Wilmot Proviso was lost by a vote of 97 to 102. Every one of the aye votes was from the North, except one from Delaware; and of those who voted against it every one was from the Southern states, except thirteen, among whom was Stephen A. Douglas from Illinois. As Lincoln voted five times for the Wilmot Proviso, he repudiated the Missouri Compromise; and his bitter attacks on Douglas for causing its supposed repeal by the Kansas-Nebraska Act are among the inconsistent positions which he took in the debates with Douglas. In New England Lowell was writing about the Mexican War:

> Ez fer war, I call it murder,—
> There you hev it plain and flat;
> I don't want to go no furder
> Than my testament fer that.

COMPROMISES OF 1820 AND 1850

The profounder and more powerful mind of Calhoun opposed the policy which led to the Mexican War on better grounds than those of sentiment. He saw the territory which dropped into the lap of America as the forbidden fruit which would work the country irremediable woe. In this forecast Toombs also shared. This war and its complications, and the bitterness growing out of them was another cause of the War between the South and the North. But what was murder in the Mexican War became, in the Hebraic-Puritan mind of Lowell, that heroic death for the right which brings purifications to the world.

> Many loved Truth, and lavished life's best oil
> Amid the dust of books to find her,
>
> * * *
>
> But these, our brothers fought for her,
> At life's dear peril wrought for her,
> So loved her that they died for her.

In the debates between Lincoln and Douglas the Hebraic-Puritan culture which dominated clergymen and moralists and to a large extent the hypocrisy of the press of Illinois made furious assault upon Douglas's declaration that he cared not whether slavery was voted down or up in a territory, and that he cared more for the principles of local self-government and the rights of the states than he did for all the negroes in Christendom. On the other hand Lincoln was lifted up for praise for his brave moral stand for the right, for his strong stand against the selfish and criminal slavocracy. Lincoln, with an ingenuity which might have been better employed, affixed upon Douglas the stigma of having repealed the Missouri Compromise by the Kansas-Nebraska Act. The facts utterly demolish this accusation. The remainder of the history bearing upon it will make this clear.

On August 2, 1848, a bill was offered in the House for the organization of Oregon as a territory. This was after the treaty of peace with Mexico, by which the United States had acquired what is now one half of New Mexico (the other half was acquired from Texas in 1850), all of Arizona, Utah, California, and a part of Wyoming and Colorado. The Louisiana Purchase included a part of Colorado, though that part was north of 36° 30'; which means that the Missouri Compromise line would have run along the southern boundary of Colorado if the grant of France had been a hundred miles further south, instead of turning straight west from a point about a hundred miles north of the southern boundary of Kansas. The point is that the geography was sufficient to rest a principle upon, of extending the line to cover, to the Pacific, the accessions of the Mexican grants. In the bill for organizing Oregon, there was a general restriction of slavery, but without any reference to the Missouri Compromise. A motion was made to strike out the restriction, which was lost; and the bill went to the Senate with the restriction on slavery in it. Douglas was now a senator. Having regard to the principle that this new territory belonged to the states in common, and had been won by their united efforts in war, he moved to strike out the restriction and to insert in its stead: "That the line of thirty-six degrees, thirty minutes of north latitude, known as the Missouri Compromise Line, as defined by the eighth section of an act entitled 'An Act to authorize the people of the Missouri Territory to form a constitution and state government, and for the admission of such state into the Union on an equal footing with the original states, and to prohibit slavery in certain territories,' approved March 6, 1820, be and the same is hereby declared to extend to the Pacific Ocean; and the said eighth section, together with the Compromise therein effected, is hereby revived and declared to be in full force and binding for the future organization of the territories of the United States, in the same sense and with the same understanding with which it was originally adopted."

Suppose this had passed, what would the South have derived from it? It would have secured New Mexico and Arizona, for the most part; a small triangular part of Nevada and about one third of California; while the North would have taken all of Utah, nearly all of Nevada, two thirds of California, all of Idaho and all of Oregon and Washington. The Douglas amendment was carried in the Senate by a vote of 33 to 21. But in the House it was lost by a vote of 82 to 121; and Oregon was organized under congressional restriction of slavery. An analysis of the vote shows that the North arrayed itself against the South in this contest. The North, which

COMPROMISES OF 1820 AND 1850

had originated the Missouri Compromise, refused to extend it. It was not abandoned by the South, but by the North. It was not struck down by Douglas, but by every Northern state both in the Senate and in the House.

Though the war against Mexico had been waged by a Democratic administration, the party strangely enough lost the election of 1848. Both the House and the presidency fell to the hands of the Whigs. And soon in the organization of the house tumultuous scenes were enacted. Howell Cobb, of Georgia, was elected speaker finally; but by a plurality of votes only. Storms were blowing, and there were much worse days to come. Clay, having been defeated by Polk for the presidency in 1844, was now back in the Senate. Webster and Calhoun were also there. As to Clay, he had been against restricting slavery in Missouri, though, like Jefferson and many others who clung to the principle of states' rights, he was distressed by negro slavery and opposed to it. Calhoun, of course, had never changed his mind about the principles embodied in his resolutions of February 19, 1847. Webster was modifying his opinions of the Constitution as expressed in his reply to Hayne, of January 26, 1830. These were the men about to deal with the perplexing questions involved in the Mexican grants. As we have seen, Lincoln by this time was in party disfavor, and was soon to go to Massachusetts to see what the Free Soil Party was doing; and from thence by way of Niagara Falls, back to Springfield and enforced retirement.

In the summer of 1849 General Riley, by military proclamation, without any authority from Congress, called a constitutional convention, which met and framed a constitution for California, which excluded slavery. California was now applying for admission to the Union. On the 29th of January, 1850, Clay proposed a compromise, which was intended to solve all the questions which were dividing the country. He proposed that California be admitted under the irregular constitution which it had adopted. This was believed to have been done at the instigation of President Taylor, who conceived that autonomy on this subject, freed of Congressional regulation, would relieve the national government of vexation, while it would awake in the people themselves a sense of responsibility. It might be called a soldier's idea of local self-government. Clay further proposed that territorial governments be organized for New Mexico and Utah, without any restriction as to slavery. There were other matters in his resolutions which need not detain us. Some Southern Whigs were against the admission of California at all under the military constitution of General Riley; others were willing to waive the illegal constitution, provided there was no restriction as to slavery in New Mexico and Utah. While these Clay proposals were depending in the Senate, a congressman from Wisconsin offered in the house a resolution instructing the committee on territories to report a bill for the admission of California under the Riley Constitution, and called for the previous question. Filibustering ensued, because the Southern Whigs wanted all the questions settled at once. The votes were sectional. Parliamentary tactics moved every way in a maze. Finally John A. McClernand, Lincoln's friend, Lincoln's colleague in the Illinois legislature, approached Toombs and others of the House and suggested an adjustment. Stephens in conversation told McClernand that he did not object to the admission of California if the whole territorial question could be settled, meaning by that that he wanted the territorial governments distinctly empowered to do as they pleased about slavery, and to come as states into the Union with or without slavery as they chose. All of these men were in the House at this time. An informal committee was appointed, which met at the house of the speaker, where it was agreed that California should be admitted, and that the territories should have autonomy as to slavery. There were bills soon prepared by Douglas of the Senate and McClernand of the House. The Wisconsin congressman was still at work in an independent way, it seems; and he introduced into the House on February 27, a bill for the admission of California. At this juncture of affairs, with all these parliamentary moves complicating the subjects, Toombs spoke to the House, covering all that was involved in all the bills and all the proceedings. Because this speech so clearly and forcibly presents the case of the North and the South, some of it may be quoted here; for Lincoln's speeches and his debates with Douglas cannot be thoroughly weighed without knowing this background touching the Missouri Compromise and the Compromise of 1850.

Lincoln, who read the *Intelligencer* diligently, probably pon-

COMPROMISES OF 1820 AND 1850

dered this speech of Toombs in February of 1850. Turning to the North, he said: "We had our institutions when you sought our alliance. We were content with them, and we are content with them now. We have not sought to thrust them upon you, nor to interfere with yours. If you believe what you say, that yours are so much the best to promote the happiness and good of society, why do you fear our equal competition with you in the territories? We only ask that our common government shall protect us both, equally, until the territories shall be ready to be admitted as states into the Union, then to leave the citizens free to adopt any domestic policy in reference to this subject which in their judgment may best promote their interests and their happiness. The demand is just. . . . The fact cannot longer be concealed—the declaration of members here proves it, the action of the House is daily demonstrating it—that we are in the midst of a legislative revolution, the object of which is to trample under foot the Constitution and the laws, and to make the will of the majority the supreme law of the land. In this emergency our duty is clear—it is to stand by the Constitution and laws, to observe in good faith all its requirements, until the wrong is consummated, until the act of exclusion is put upon the statute book. . . . It will then be demonstrated that the Constitution is powerless for our protection."

In the Senate the sick and dying Calhoun had his remarks read. "What was once a Constitutional Federal Republic, is now converted in reality into one as absolute as that of the autocrat of Russia, and as despotic in its tendency as any absolute government that ever existed." The Union "cannot be saved then by eulogies on the Union, however splendid or numerous. The cry of 'Union, Union, the glorious Union' can no more prevent disunion than the cry of 'health, health, glorious health' on the part of the physician, can save a patient lying dangerously ill. . . . But how stands the profession of devotion to the Union by our assailants, when brought to this test? Have they abstained from violating the Constitution? Let the many acts passed by the Northern states to set aside and annul the clause of the Constitution providing for the delivery up of fugitive slaves answer. . . . Again have they stood forth faithfully to repel violations of the Constitution? Let their course in reference to the agitation of the slavery question, which was commenced and has been carried on for fifteen years, avowedly for the purpose of abolishing slavery in the states—an object all acknowledged to be unconstitutional, answer."

On March 7, 1850, Webster addressed the Senate on the troublous questions pending. He was now sixty-eight years of age. This is the speech which caused the poet Whittier to write "Ichabod," in which he put quotable infamy on Webster for time to come, but without any justice whatever. Whittier wrote "Barbara Frietchie" upon the false report of a clergyman touching what happened, what did not happen rather, when Lee was taking his army north into Pennsylvania. And in the instance of Webster's speech of March 7, he was as badly advised. Between the time that Webster debated with Hayne and 1850, Webster had met the abler Calhoun in discussion in the Senate. The result was that, in 1839, Webster advanced constitutional theories at variance with those that he gave expression to in 1830; and these will be considered in another connection. He was forced to abandon his ground by the inexorable logic of Calhoun. It is to be observed that Herndon wrote that when Lincoln was preparing his First Inaugural he called for Henry Clay's speech of 1850, Jackson's proclamation against Nullification, a copy of the Constitution, and Webster's reply to Hayne, which he had read in that long ago as a young man when walking from Indiana to Illinois. He did not call for Webster's speech of 1839, or 1850.

The March 7th speech was the one that Lincoln evidently followed in his Cooper Institute address. The historical and argumentative points follow, with parallel similarity. It also contains some Lincoln doctrine on other questions; and some which Douglas made use of by re-phrasing. It is quoted from now for its bearing upon the compromises of 1850, and to prove in general what was running through the minds of the people of the country and what the great senator from Massachusetts thought about them. Speaking of territory where slavery would not go for climatic reasons, he said: "For myself I will say that we hear much of the annexation of Canada; and if there be any man, any of the Northern democracy or any one of the Free Soil Party who supposes it necessary to insert a Wilmot Proviso in a territorial government for New Mexico, that man will of course be of opinion that it is necessary to protect the everlasting snows of Canada from the foot of slavery, by the same overpowering wing of an act of Congress. Sir, wherever there is a particular good to be done—wherever there is a foot of land to be staid back from becoming slave territory—I am ready to assert the principle of the exclusion of slavery . . . but I will not do a thing unnecessary that wounds the feelings of others, or that does disgrace to my own understanding."

Then he turned to the complaints of the South: "But I will state these complaints, especially one complaint of the South, which has in my opinion just foundation; and that is that there has been found at the North, among individuals and among legislatures of the North, a disinclination to perform fully their constitutional duties, in regard to the return of persons bound to service, who have escaped into free states." This language was doubtless partly the inspiration of Whittier's "Ichabod." Webster should have sided with the abolitionists and upheld the escape of slaves. If he had met the complaints of the South as to the tariff and acknowledged their merit, Whittier might not have been so much disturbed, though the tariff had almost brought the country to war in 1832. Webster then proceeded to elaborate the idea of the just complaint of the South as to fugitive slaves. "And I desire to call the attention of all sober minded men," he said, "who are not carried away by any fanatical idea, or by any false idea whatever, to their constitutional obligations. I put it to all the sober and sound minds at the North, as a question of morals, and a question of conscience. What right have they, in all their legislative capacity, or any other, to endeavor to get around this Constitution, to embarrass the free exercise of the rights secured by the Constitution, to the persons whose slaves escape from them? None at all, none at all! . . . Therefore I repeat, sir, that here is ground for complaint against the North, well founded, which ought to be removed—which it is now in the power of the different departments of this government to remove—which calls for the enactment of proper laws, authorizing the judicature of this government, in the several states, to do all that is necessary for the capture of fugitive slaves." In regard to petitions and resolutions sent to the Congress for action for the abolition of slavery, he used this language: "Complaint has been made against certain resolutions that emanate from legislatures at the North, and are sent here to us, not only on the subject of slavery in this district, but sometimes recommending Congress to consider the means of abolishing slavery in the states. I should be sorry to be called upon to present any resolutions here which would not be referable to any committee or any power in Congress, and therefore I should be unwilling to receive from the legislature of Massachusetts any instructions to present resolutions, expressive of any opinion whatever on the subject of slavery, as it exists at the present moment in the states, for two reasons; because first I do not consider that the legislature of Massachusetts has anything to do with it."

As to abolitionists: "Then, sir, there are those abolition societies, of which I am unwilling to speak, but in regard to which I have very clear notions and opinions. I do not think them useful. I think their operations for the last twenty years have produced nothing good or valuable. . . . As has been said by the honorable member from South Carolina, these abolition societies commenced their course of action in 1835. It is said—I do not know how true it is—that they sent incendiary publications into the slave states; at any event they attempted to arouse, and did arouse, a very strong feeling; in other words they created great agitation at the North against Southern slavery. Well, what was the result? The bonds of the slaves were bound more firmly than before. . . . Public opinion, which in Virginia had begun to be exhibited against slavery, and was opening out for the discussion of the question, drew back and shut itself up in a castle."

As to the press: "Again, sir, the violence of the press is complained of. The press violent! Why, sir, the press is violent everywhere. There are outrageous reproaches in the North against the South, and there are reproaches in not much better taste in the South against the North." He then proceeded to discuss possible disunion as the result of these wrongs and these inflamed feelings. "I will not state what might produce the disruption of the states but, sir, I see it as plainly as I see the sun in the heavens—I see that disruption must produce such a war as I will not describe in its twofold character." "Never did there devolve on any generation of men higher trust than now devolves upon us for the preserva-

COMPROMISES OF 1820 AND 1850

tion of this Constitution, and the harmony and peace of all who are destined to live under it."

These words give a picture of the state of mind at the time, out of the mouth of a man noted for strength of intellect, and who, as a senator from Massachusetts, spoke not as a Southern man, but as he said at the opening of his address, as an American. He had come to the position where he was unwilling to vote for laws restricting slavery in a territory where slavery could not exist by natural laws "more irrepealable" than the law that "attaches to the right of holding slaves in Texas." "And I would put in no Wilmot Proviso for the purpose of a taunt and a reproach." In addition to this he had made full allowance of the wrongs of the South, the whole being intended to adjust the vexed state of affairs growing out of the Mexican acquisitions. All the old leaders spoke, Benton and Cass, in addition to Webster, and Clay and Calhoun whose remarks were read; and no one addressed the Senate with greater power and eloquence than Douglas, now 37 years of age, to whose tireless energy and skill was due the credit of effecting this compromise of 1850, though the plan and the idea were Clay's.

There were those who wished to preserve the principle of the Missouri Compromise. The bill offered by the Wisconsin congressman for the admission of California without settling the status of Utah and New Mexico, on which he had asked the previous question, was being considered from day to day. A congressman from Missouri moved as an amendment to this bill that the Missouri Compromise be extended through all the new territory. The motion was rejected by a large majority of the House. The Missouri Compromise, having been hawked and torn in the previous years by the North, was now being rejected, only to be acclaimed as something holy with respect to Kansas and Nebraska when Douglas struggled in Illinois for the senatorship in 1858, and was opposed by Lincoln. A congressman from Tennessee moved that it should be no objection to the admission of a state lying south of 36° 30′ that its constitution authorized slavery. This was rejected by a sectional vote. Toombs took the floor to repudiate the accusation that the opposition to the admission of California was based upon its free constitution. He insisted that the position of the South and its statesmen always had been that a state should form its own constitution and should be permitted to come in free or slave as it chose; and he said that this doctrine had been asserted by the South with reference to Missouri in 1820 and denied by the North. "But how stands the case with the North?" he asked. "She denied the truth of this great principle of constitutional right in 1820, acquiesced in the Compromise then made, as long as it was to her interest, and then repudiated the Compromise and reasserted her right to dictate constitutions to territories, seeking admission into the Union. . . . We do not oppose California on account of the antislavery clause in her constitution. It was her right, and I am not even prepared to say that she acted unwisely in its exercise—that is her business; but I stand upon the great principle that the South has right to an equal participation in the Territories of the United States."

Toombs was the man who for hours fought the mob congressmen in the House upon the organization of that body in 1849, already touched upon. He had great forensic power and courage and he was a true hearted man; but one of those who, being selected for disfavor and oblivion, has been calumniated with all the malice that interest could invent. He was charged with having said that he would call the roll of the slaves on Bunker Hill, something he never said, and was fully proved not to have said; but as his opponents could not stand against him in debate they struck him down by attacks of this kind in the rear.

The result at last was that the South, being unable to preserve the Missouri Compromise, which should never have been introduced into the territorial question and the consequences whereof were so accurately forecast by Jefferson, fell back into solid position for no slavery restriction whatever on territory either north or south of 36° 30′. They took up the constitutional position that Congress had no power to impose terms of admission on new states, and that the constitutional requirements for admission were fulfilled when a state applied which had a republican form of government. It was now that Senator Soulé of Louisiana offered an amendment to the Clay Compromise Bill which read: "And when the said territory, or any portion of the same, shall be admitted as a state, it shall be received into the Union with or without slavery, as their constitution may prescribe at the time of their admission."

Webster took stand for this amendment. "Sir, my object is peace," he said. "My object is reconciliation. My purpose is not to make up a case for the North, or to make up a case for the South. My object is not to continue useless and irritating controversies. I am against agitators, North and South; I am against local ideas North and South, and against all narrow and local tests. I am an American, and I know no locality in America. This is my country. My heart, my sentiments, my judgment, demand of me that I should pursue such a course as shall promote the good, and the harmony of the Union of the whole country. This I shall do, God willing, to the end of the chapter." As in the case of Toombs his glory should depart if he did not follow the Hebraic-Puritan fanaticism of the abolitionists.

The proceedings which followed the introduction of the Soulé amendment were noisy and tangled beyond description, and for days. There were previous questions, motions to reconsider, protests, queries as to whether the Wilmot Proviso was in the bill, points of order, calls for the yeas and the nays, motions to adjourn. Adjournments were taken, and upon re-convening the same tactics ensued. The North and the South had each other now in a death grip. The sectional line drawn by the Missouri Compromise had become the boundary between duelists who were marching up to it and thrusting to kill. Finally weariness seemed to overcome the contestants. In the weakness of fatigue they seemed to wonder what it was all about. And thus the bill went to engrossment. In strict accuracy it is due to say that the Clay Bill had gone to pieces, but that it had been joined together at last, largely through the energy and skill of Douglas. Thus it was that California came in as a free state, Utah and New Mexico were organized as territories without any restriction as to slavery, and the slave trade was prohibited in the District of Columbia. This was the Compromise of 1850, under which the Southern states contented themselves to stay in the Union. They demanded and secured a repudiation of the principle that the public domain should be divided on sectional lines; and they won a recognition that the territory belonged in common under the Constitution to all the states alike.

With this history come to pass, what had become of the Missouri Compromise of 1820? Repeals by implications are not favored; and in consequence it was legally possible for the Missouri Compromise to be in force to the western boundary of the Louisiana Purchase, that is to a point about three quarters of the way west in Kansas; and from there on for the Compromise of 1850 to be in force. These two things did not hopelessly conflict. But even as to Kansas there were about 5000 square miles in its southwest corner to which the Missouri Compromise could not apply, because it was territory not included in the Louisiana Purchase but was ceded to the United States by Texas in 1850. Also the Utah settlement under the Compromise embraced within its boundaries a part of the Louisiana cession. The New Mexico settlement embraced a degree and a half of the territory north of 36° 30′, where slavery had been restricted by the law under which Texas was admitted to the Union. In these particulars the Missouri Compromise was repealed by implication, because it was in conflict with the Compromise of 1850. Considering the vote of the House by states, New Hampshire, Pennsylvania, Illinois, Iowa, Delaware, Maryland, Virginia, North Carolina, Georgia, Florida, Tennessee, Kentucky, Missouri, Texas, Indiana were in favor of doing this; and Massachusetts, Connecticut, Vermont, New York, New Jersey, Ohio, Michigan, Wisconsin, South Carolina, Alabama, Mississippi, Arkansas and Louisiana were against, or fifteen states for and thirteen against.

If, however, instead of testing the matter by legalism solely, the whole history of the discussion and the settlement be considered there was not enough left of the sacred Missouri Compromise to furnish material for Lincoln's denunciation of Douglas in the debates, respecting the Kansas-Nebraska Law, for which Douglas was the responsible sponsor. Douglas did not by that law undo the Missouri Compromise. Neither did he frame it with regard to the wishes of the so-called slavocracy. Those were the calumnies of moralists, to which Lincoln yielded himself after a long period of intellectual imperviousness.

By the time 1854 arrived, the year of the Kansas-Nebraska Act, Lincoln had long been out in the cold. The Whig Party was all but dead. Lincoln had nothing to lose by deserting it. If there was nothing to gain by joining the fanatics, the abolitionists and the Republicans, it was better than inaction, better than restless torture in the limbo of detachment. What Webster had done, or Clay, or Cass or Benton in the denting of the Missouri Compromise furnished Lincoln with no opportunity to emerge from political retirement. They were too far off; and there were other reasons for remaining silent. The Whig Party was still alive and it was soon to approve in its platform the Compromise of 1850. The case was different with the Kansas-Nebraska Law. There the man to be attacked, if any, was in Illinois. It was Douglas then, Lincoln's rival from 1836, who all these years had distanced him, whom he had envied all these years, according to Herndon. It is true that Illinois was greatly wrought up by the Compromise of 1850, and that Douglas encountered great unfriendliness upon his return to Chicago. The city Council voted to release officials from all obligation to enforce the Fugitive Slave Law. This is accountable upon the basis of the population, made up as it was so much from accessions from New England and New York. Excited by the action of the city council, a mass meeting was about to pass resolutions approving what the city council had resolved, when Douglas appeared, and asked them to wait action until he could address them, and show what had been done by the Compromise and what caused it to be done. His forensic courage never was surpassed. The next night he spoke before an immense audience in Chicago, stood his ground while he was questioned from every angle of the matter; and at the end of his address he proposed resolutions which pledged the meeting to stand by the Constitution and the laws. The resolutions were carried. Further the meeting voted to repudiate the action of the city council, with but ten nays. The next night the council met and repealed its resolutions. Such was the power of Douglas.

The Compromise of 1850 was confirmed by both the Whig and the Democratic parties in their platforms of 1852, which leads one to ask was everyone wrong except the abolitionists, and Lincoln after he deemed it wise to come forth and take a hand in the struggle? In that year the Democrats met at Baltimore on June 1. "Resolved," they declared, "That Congress has no power under the Constitution to interfere with or control the domestic institutions of the several states, and that such states are the sole and proper judges of everything appertaining to their own affairs, not prohibited by the Constitution; that all efforts of the abolitionists, or others, made to induce Congress to interfere with questions of slavery, or to take incipient steps in relation thereto, are calculated to lead to the most alarming and dangerous consequences; and that all such efforts have an inevitable tendency to diminish the happiness of the people, and endanger the stability and permanency of the Union, and ought not to be countenanced by any friend of our political institutions. . . . Therefore the Democratic Party of the Union, standing on this national platform will abide by, and adhere to a faithful execution of the acts known as the Compromise measures of the last congress."

The Whig Party met in convention at Baltimore on June 16, 1852, and adopted a platform of which it is sufficient to quote this: "That the series of acts of the 31st Congress, known as the Compromise Measures of 1850 . . . are received and acquiesced in by the Whig Party of the United States as a settlement in principle and substance of the dangerous and exciting questions which they embrace; and so far as they are concerned, we will maintain them, and insist on their strict enforcement, until time and experience shall demonstrate the necessity of further legislation to guard against evasion of the laws on the one hand, and the abuse of their powers on the other."

Notwithstanding all the history of the 1850 Compromise, and the part in it played by Webster and by Clay, the absurd claim was set up that this platform was forced upon the convention by the slavocracy, by the Southern Whigs. In truth the platform was submitted to Webster, who was the leading candidate for the Whig nomination, and it was approved by him. Stephens gave it as his opinion that the platform was drawn by Northern men. He stated as a fact that Rufus Choate and Webster called at his living quarters in Washington a few days before the meeting of the convention in Baltimore and submitted to him a draft of resolutions which were substantially the resolutions adopted by the convention.[1]

Webster lost the nomination to General Winfield Scott, who was at the head of the army which invaded Mexico in 1847 and captured Vera Cruz. The Whigs invented the insignia of the "bloody

[1] "Constitutional View of the War," Vol. II, 238.

COMPROMISES OF 1820 AND 1850

shirt," and in its name the great Webster was thrust aside. True to the characteristic reticence of the Whigs, their covert politics, Scott refused to approve the platform by any direct expression. The wily Seward had him under control. Pierce on the other hand came out frankly for the Democratic platform, which also included a resolution in recognition of the political validity of the Kentucky and Virginia Resolutions of 1798–99. The result at the polls was emphatic in its meaning. Pierce carried every state but Vermont, Tennessee, Kentucky, and the stronghold of Puritanism, Massachusetts. In the Electoral College he had 254 votes to Scott's 42. John P. Hale, of New Hampshire, who ran upon a Free Soil platform received but 155,825 votes in the whole country.

The attitude of Lincoln toward the Whig platform of 1852 is shown by a speech which he made before the Scott Club of Springfield on August 25, 1852. He was during this campaign the Illinois member of the National Whig Committee, and was in management of the party's affairs in that state. The reliable word of Beveridge is to the effect that none of Lincoln's letters or other writings during this year, in which he was the Whig committeeman for Illinois, have come to light. There is a quiet about Lincoln now as if he were hiding; while he seemed to have been practicing a mimesis which prevents his location accurately. Douglas was campaigning the state for Pierce; and Lincoln's Scott Club speech was an answer to Douglas. Lincoln had now begun to trail Douglas. He was also still pursuing his old enemy Shields, of the duel fiasco of 1842. The Scott Club speech was in Lincoln's most riotous vein as a mimic, buffoon and coarse satirist. It has not been included in Lincoln's Works, but was resurrected from the files of the Illinois *Daily Journal* by Beveridge.[1] As a whole it was a laudation of Scott and a mocking depreciation of Pierce. A sample may be given. He took up the Democratic hatred of Seward, saying that it was due to the fear that Seward as the Whig leader might carry New York for Scott. He contrasted the military records of Scott and Pierce to the ludicrous degradation of Pierce. He declared that the Free Soil Party was now broken and that its votes were in contest and "are the stakes for which the game in New York is being played. If Scott can get nine thousand of them he carries the state and is

[1] Beveridge, II, 161.

elected . . . while Pierce must get nearly all to win. Standing in the way of this, Seward is thought to be the greatest obstacle—hence their insane malice against him," that is, the Democrats'. . . . "Why, Pierce's only chance for the presidency is to be born into it as a cross between New York old hunkerism, and free soilism, the latter predominating in the offspring. Marryat, in some one of his books, describes the sailors weighing anchor, and singing:

> Sally is a bright mulatter,
> Oh, Sally Brown—
> Pretty gal, but can't get at her,
> Oh, Sally Brown.

Now should Pierce ever be president, he will politically speaking, not only be a mulatto; but he will be a good deal darker one than Sally Brown." The meeting then adjourned with "three deafening cheers for Scott and Graham," according to the *Illinois Daily Journal*. Lincoln was asked to prepare a copy of his speech for publication.

Thus Lincoln was speaking for Scott, who was running on a platform which approved the Compromise of 1850. On July 16, 1852, more than a month before the date of the speech before the Scott Club, Lincoln delivered a eulogy on Henry Clay in the State House at Springfield, Clay having recently died. This was an effort of some dignity, in which he spoke with propriety of Clay's achievements. After touching upon what Clay had done in the settlement of the Missouri question, he said: "Accordingly in the days of nullification, and more recently in the reappearance of the slavery question connected with our territory newly acquired of Mexico, the task of devising a mode of adjustment seems to have been cast upon Mr. Clay by common consent—and his performance of the task in each case was little else than a literal fulfillment of the public expectation. . . . Those who would shiver into fragments the Union of these States, tear to tatters its now venerated Constitution, and even burn the last copy of the Bible, rather than slavery should continue a single hour, together with all their more halting sympathizers, have received, and are receiving, their just execration; and the name and opinions and influence of Mr. Clay are fully, and as I trust effectually and enduringly arrayed against

COMPROMISES OF 1820 AND 1850

them." [1] Clay's Compromises were so to overwhelm them, is the implication.

When Lincoln pronounced this eulogy on Clay, and thus approved the Compromise of 1850, he was not ignorant of what was being said over the country by the Hebraic-Puritans, the agitators and the abolitionists in condemnation of the law. He was reading the *Intelligencer* as usual, and mentioned it in his Scott Club speech as a publication "which is not often misled and is not misleading." And thus he knew how the Compromise was attacked in whole, and especially for its change of the Fugitive Slave Law of 1793. For now the return of fugitive slaves was in the hands of the Federal Government. It was like turning state prohibition into national prohibition. The execution of the Fugitive Slave Law was now under the Compromise in the hands of Federal officers. What were Wendell Phillips and Beecher and Parker and Chase now to do? Parker said, immediately after the Compromise went into effect: "The natural duty to keep the law of God overrides the obligation to observe any human statute. . . . The law was not morally binding on officers of the United States. Obedience to law 'lies at the base of every despot's throne.'" Beecher declared that "whenever the Union comes between a Christian people and their Christianity, it becomes a snare. . . . There are many evils greater than dissolution of our Union. . . . Religion and humanity are a price too dear to pay even for the Union." Phillips counseled insurrection. "You will say this is bloody doctrine—anarchical doctrine; it will prejudice people against the cause. I know it will . . . we will ourselves trample this accursed Fugitive Slave Law under foot." And there was Chase who condemned slavery by the law "of sublimer origin and more awful sanction than any human code" which enjoined every person "to do unto others as we would that others should do unto us." Seward's "higher law" had also been promulgated. But Lincoln in the Scott Club speech expressly dissented from it. He had not yet arrived at the point when these wild vaporings out of the Hebrew Bible had clouded his judgment, as it had maddened the shallow intellects of these reformers, and as it had refined the sophistry of Chase. He was to become a devotee of the "irrepressible conflict" under a slogan of his own invention,

[1] Lincoln's Works, I, 174.

namely, the "house divided against itself" doctrine; and he was to raise the moral cry against the Kansas-Nebraska Act. The Compromise of 1850 did not keep the storms down. There were people who wanted offices and honors, and to get them proceeded to call the nation to repentance. Other causes of the War were now to arise.

Chapter IX   The Kansas-Nebraska Act

THE political history of America has been written for the most part by those who were unfriendly to the theory of a confederated republic, or who did not understand it. It has been written by devotees of the protective principle, by centralists, and to a large degree by New England. Where foreigners have examined our system of government and appraised our leading statesmen they have leaned, like Von Holst, to the Hamiltonian-Marshall theories; and in virtue of that they have magnified those men over Jefferson and Taney. Webster has been lifted above Calhoun, and Douglas placed below Lincoln in moral character and in intellectual power. Lincoln, who had little confidence in history, would be not the least surprised of all men to know how he has been set beside Washington and above all other American statesmen. Rhodes and others have severely impugned the motives of Douglas in framing the Kansas-Nebraska bill, charging him with doing so in selfish ambition for the presidency. Nothing could be further from the truth. The attempt of Von Holst to make Douglas infamous, by calling upon his second name, Arnold, to bring it into association with Benedict Arnold, should be resented by every fair American. It is calumny of the most malicious sort.

The history has been plain since 1850 that the Southern extremists, like Jefferson Davis, disapproved the Compromise of 1850, because they wanted the doctrine sustained that slavery went into the territories by its own force and that nothing could keep it out. On such a platform did Davis run for governor of Mississippi in the year 1851. He was defeated because the Compromise was sustained by the people of that state. Since, then, Davis and his followers conceived that principle at the start and developed it, what had Douglas to gain from them by carrying forward the rule of the 1850 Compromise into the Kansas-Nebraska Act? It was what he did in that regard, and what he said in support of that principle that turned Davis against him at Baltimore in 1860, resulting in the division of the Democratic convention, with Douglas finally nominated by only a part of the old convention. His defeat at the hands of Lincoln followed in the demoralization of a split Democracy. If Douglas had entertained no other idea than to be president, he would have courted the South; and in the campaign of 1860 he would not have said to a Virginia audience that he would, if elected, suppress secession. There was never a man in our history who figured in politics who spoke more openly and with less reservation on all occasions when he was required to state what he believed and would do than Douglas. In these particulars Lincoln offers a contrast that makes Douglas's intellectual honesty all the more striking. If we have not already seen how Lincoln kept his own counsel and hid his convictions, or failed to express them, there will be other revelations to carry conviction that he was a secretive, cautious politician, making no man his confidant, saying no more than he had to say, and refusing to speak when the legal issue did not compel him to speak.

Now that Douglas is long dead and the historians of the tariff and of centralism have said everything that they could against him, or invent to his discredit, the truth has come out. Douglas was not a statesman of the slavocracy at all. He was a railroad statesman, belonging to the new age which he heralded, and laying the foundation of what America is today in domain and in commerce. He did more than any other man to make Chicago the railroad center of the Middle West. In 1850 he carried through the land grant for the building of the Illinois Central Railroad. As chairman of the Committee on Territories in the Senate, he reported bills by which Utah, New Mexico, Washington, Kansas, Nebraska, Oregon and Minnesota became territories; and by which Texas, Iowa, Florida, California, Wisconsin, Oregon and Minnesota became states. He proposed the bill by which the United States Circuit Court of Appeals was formed for the relief of the Supreme Court. He founded the Chicago University, as before mentioned. He was in genius a builder, with a mind full of plans for the increase and for the honor of his country. And to say that his great powers were enslaved to the mere purpose to win over the South, that he might be president, disregards all the history about him so plainly written for those who will read it.

In 1845 Asa Whitney began the agitation for a transcontinental railroad, which aroused interest in the need of a railroad to the Pacific. But there were difficulties in the way. Disputes arose as to where such a road should start from. Naturally different sections of the country wanted the advantage of the eastern terminus. Eastern capital, which controlled navigation on the Great Lakes, wanted the road to run west from Chicago through Iowa and by way of South Pass. When Minnesota and Oregon began to be developed, it was proposed to build the road so as to connect Lake Superior and Columbia. St. Louis in 1845–50 was the largest city in the Middle West. St. Louis demanded that the road should run from there through Missouri and across the mountains. The South wanted the railroad, that is, it wanted one built so that Charleston would be connected with the West. Memphis planned to connect with the Charleston road and to go on to Albuquerque, and thence to California. Vicksburg hoped to connect with Charleston, and then to get west by way of El Paso to San Diego. Louisiana and Texas wanted an outlet at the Gulf and objected to the road passing north of them. Thus the North and the West were against the South; the South had several competing plans, and so had the North. It was a big project in that day to build such a road. One railroad to the Pacific was the height of the dream of the day. If there was to be but one, who was to get it? There were other things besides slavery to influence the location of the road. There was another factor. The Pacific Steamship Company, owned by New York capital, had a line of ships to Panama, and in 1849 incorporated a company to build a railroad across the Isthmus of Panama. At this time New Orleans was trying to build a railroad across the Isthmus of Tehuantepec. So it was that the steamship and isthmus railroad interests were opposed to any Pacific railroad whatever. Here was a puzzle for Douglas to work; but it was the solution of such complexities that delighted his restless energies.

As it was after 1845 that the United States acquired the Mexican territory, so before that time the northern route to the Pacific had the lead, because there was no other place to build it. In 1849 Benton introduced a bill into the Senate for a great central railroad from St. Louis to San Francisco, which was to run between the parallels of 38° and 39°, that is, in line with Omaha and Cheyenne, Salt Lake City, Carson City to the Pacific. In 1849 and in 1850, conventions were held in different parts of the country in the interests of various terminals which were being discussed. Douglas presided over the convention at St. Louis. A resolution was passed that logically required an Iowa or a Chicago terminal. By this time Douglas had large interests in Chicago, where he was growing rich, and besides he was truly devoted to the development of his city and his state. No man was ever more so. On the other hand he was the senator from Illinois, and from a little below the northern tier of counties to the southern part of the state were the Kentuckians and Virginians and Tennesseeans, who, as Democrats, were most loyal to him. It may be said here that about 1850 the German immigration to Illinois began to be very great, and so continued until 1854; and we shall see Lincoln making very adroit appeals to this foreign vote in the debates with Douglas. If the American party which became a part of the Republican Party had succeeded in its plans to discriminate against foreigners in America, Lincoln's career might have been all different. These Germans had gone to Alton, to Vandalia, to Peoria, to Springfield, and to Quincy, in that part of Illinois tributary to St. Louis which wanted the Pacific railroad terminal. In sum, if Douglas chose St. Louis, he sacrificed Chicago and his own interests; if he chose Chicago he might be accused of consulting his own interests.

It is obvious that after 1850, when New Mexico was organized as a territory, the southern route to the Pacific had a great advantage. To build any road required the sale of land, and land could not be sold in Kansas-Nebraska until those places were territorially organized. Neither could such a road have protection against Indians and marauders while being built, nor get business after it was built, unless the area through which it ran was an organized one. In Iowa, which was admitted into the Union in 1846, and in Missouri, a demand arose, and grew stronger rapidly, that Nebraska should be organized as a territory in order that the Pacific railroad might have a northern terminal. Benton had been senator from Missouri since 1821, and by 1849 Missouri wanted to be rid of him. In 1847 Benton influenced the state legislature to pass resolutions affirming the Missouri Compromise. But in 1849 the legislature passed resolutions denouncing the Compromise, and Benton ran for the Senate, making those resolutions the issue. He was defeated by the Whigs and the general combination against him. He was then at once elected to the House. In 1853 he ran for the Senate again, upon a platform of a Pacific railroad with a St. Louis terminal. Simultaneously with these events in Missouri, Iowa, under the leadership of Senators Dodge and Jones, was holding meetings requesting the immediate organization of Nebraska for the purposes of the railroad. The Wyandot Indians were a factor in this railroad enterprise. In 1843 they had come from Ohio and settled on the west bank of the Missouri River near the mouth of the Kansas River. They were part white and of considerable intelligence. They sent a delegate to Congress in 1852. In 1853 the Wyandots held a convention which passed resolutions favoring the Pacific railroad with a central terminal, and asking for the organization of Nebraska. They wanted to sell their lands to the best advantage, seeing that they would soon be crowded again by the advancing white man.

To return to Douglas: he was in the House from 1843 to 1847, where he was in 1845 made chairman of the committee on territories. In that year he proposed a grant of land to the states of Ohio, Indiana, Illinois and Iowa for a railroad from Lake Erie by way of Chicago and Rock Island to the Missouri River, and he prepared a bill for the organization of the territories of Nebraska and Oregon; and a land grant to those territories for a railroad from the Missouri River to the Pacific. The title to Oregon was at the time in dispute, and California had not been acquired, so that the plan fell through. When Douglas went to the Senate in 1847, he was elected chairman of the committee on territories in that body. From the first, therefore, his statesmanship was employed with the territories, with railroads as a necessary parallel interest. He had opportunity thus, fortunate and fitting to carry out his dream of an "ocean bound republic," his own phrase; and to reduce his stature to the subserviency of a so-called slavocracy belies him, and contradicts the history of the times.

In 1848 Douglas introduced into the Senate bills for the organization of Nebraska. But nothing came of it. Gold by this time had been discovered in California, and the vast stream of emigration to California made the organization of Nebraska a necessity, and the building of a railroad more and more emergent. But in 1850 the preoccupation with the Compromise of that year precluded the consideration of anything else. In 1852, however, Senator Dodge of Iowa, with Senator Jones of the same state, introduced a bill for the grant of land to Iowa for the construction of two railroads: one running from Dubuque to Keokuk; the other running west from Davenport to the Missouri River. In April of 1852, a month after the Jones-Dodge bill, Douglas introduced a bill for the protection of the emigrant route, and for a telegraph line from the Missouri River to California and Oregon. The Douglas bill was referred to a committee, which reported a substitute bill for the construction of a Pacific railroad, providing that the president should have power to designate the route and the terminus. This was February 1, 1853. As a result of this, Jefferson Davis, secretary of war under Pierce, ordered surveys; and they were being made when Davis and Pierce visited New York in July of 1853. Davis, on the way to Philadelphia, made a speech in favor of the railroad project which won the greatest praise from the press.

On February 2, 1853, Richardson of the House reported a bill for the organization of Nebraska without any mention of slavery, and the bill passed, February 10, by a vote of 98 to 43. Nearly all the votes against it came from the South; and the charge was freely made that these votes were thrown against a northern route. Slavery or no slavery a northern route was against the commercial interests of the South. "Everybody is talking about a railroad," he said. "In the name of God how is a railroad to be made, if you will never let people live on the lands through which it passes?" This House bill would have come before the Senate for full consideration if Douglas could have brought this about. He tried in vain to do so. As already said, this bill made no mention of slavery whatever. Finally, on March 3, 1853, the bill was laid on the table in the Senate by a vote of 27 to 17. So ended the second session of the Thirty-second Congress.

On the first day of the first session of the Thirty-third Congress, December 5, 1853, Senator Dodge of Iowa gave notice of his intention to introduce a bill for the organization of Nebraska; and on the fourteenth he introduced one, which was identical in form with the Richardson bill of February 2, 1853, in the House. The bill was referred to the committee on territories, of which Douglas

THE KANSAS-NEBRASKA ACT

was chairman, who on January 4, 1854, returned it to the Senate with the amendments, and accompanied by his report, which have been the basis of the libelous charges made against him that in this tangled railroad and territorial situation, he was serving the slavocracy and advancing his own selfish interests for the presidency. These charges have been repelled by Beveridge,[1] by Paxson, and by Frank Heywood Hodder, professor of history in the University of Kansas, from whose brochure entitled "Genesis of the Kansas-Nebraska Act," many of the details of this history of the Act have been taken.[2] To quote the words of Beveridge is to make the point clear: "Whatever may be thought of Douglas' purposes at this time, it is only common fairness to admit that there is not a shred of evidence that desire for the presidency, or any personal political advancement had anything to do with any phase of his connection with or management of the Kansas-Nebraska bill. He could have dropped it without discredit or serious continued criticism, at least twice after the attacks began upon it. If the motives attributed to him by the Appeal really inspired Douglas in the desperate fight we are now to witness, he was one of the most stupid politicians of whom history makes any mention."[3] To make all clear here, the Appeal mentioned by Beveridge is a reference to Chase's Appeal, to be taken up in its place, and which was one of the causes of the War.

To return now to Douglas's report of January 4, 1854, upon Dodge's bill, with its reasons for changing the phraseology of it. Douglas said: "We were aware that from 1820 to 1850, the abolition doctrine of Congressional interference with slavery in the territories and new states had so far prevailed as to keep up an incessant slavery agitation in Congress, and throughout the country, whenever any new territory was to be acquired or organized. We were also aware that in 1850 the right of the people to decide this question for themselves, subject only to the Constitution, was substituted for the doctrine of Congressional intervention. The first question, therefore, which the committee were called upon to decide, and indeed, the only question of material importance in framing this bill, was this: Shall we adhere to and carry out the principle

[1] Beveridge, II, 171.
[2] "History of American Frontier," 434.
[3] Beveridge, II, 187.

recognized by the Compromise Measures of 1850, or shall we go back to the old exploded doctrine of Congressional interference, as established in 1820, in a large portion of the country, and which it was the object of the Wilmot Proviso to give a universal application, not only to all the territory we then possessed, but all which we might hereafter acquire? There were no other alternatives. We were compelled to frame the bill upon the one or the other of the two principles. The doctrine of 1820, or the doctrine of 1850 must prevail. In the discharge of the duty imposed upon us by the Senate, the committee could not hesitate upon this point, whether we consulted our own individual opinions and principles, or those which were known to be entertained and boldly avowed by a large majority of the Senate. The two great political parties of the country stood solemnly pledged before the world, to adhere to the Compromise Measures of 1850, 'in principle and in substance.' A large majority of the Senate, indeed every member of the body, I believe, except the two avowed abolitionists [Mr. Chase and Mr. Sumner] profess to belong to the one or the other of these parties, and hence was supposed to be under high obligation to carry out the 'principle and substance' of those measures in all new territorial organizations." [1]

Douglas then read from the report: "In the judgment of your committee, those measures [Compromise of 1850] were intended to have a far more comprehensive and enduring effect than the mere adjustment of the difficulties arising out of the recent acquisitions of Mexican Territory. They were designed to establish certain great principles, which would not only furnish adequate remedies for existing evils, but in all time to come avoid the perils of a similar agitation, by withdrawing the question of slavery from the halls of Congress and the political arena, and committing it to the arbitrament of those who were immediately responsible for its consequences. . . . The substitute for the bill which your committee have prepared, and which is commended to the favorable action of the Senate, proposes to carry these propositions and principles into practical operation, in the precise language of the Compromise Measures of 1850."

At this time there was nothing in the bill which by express words

[1] Appendix to Cong. Globe, 33d Congress, 1st Session, p. 326.

THE KANSAS-NEBRASKA ACT

repealed the Missouri Compromise. But the principles of the Compromise of 1850 and the language in which they were expressed could not be applied to Nebraska without superseding, if not repealing, the Missouri Compromise. Therefore the cry was already raised against Douglas by the fanatics. As to this he said: "But my accusers attempt to raise up a false issue, and hereby divert public attention from the real one, by the cry that the Missouri Compromise is to be repealed or violated by the passage of this bill. Well, if the eighth section of the Missouri Act, which attempted to fix the destinies of future generations in those territories for all time to come, in utter disregard of the rights and wishes of the people when they should be received into the Union as states, be inconsistent with the great principle of self-government and the Constitution of the United States, it ought to be abrogated. The legislation of 1850 abrogated the Missouri Compromise, so far as the country embraced within the limits of Utah and New Mexico was covered by the slavery restriction. It is true that those acts did not in terms, and by name, repeal the act of 1820, as originally adopted, or as extended by the resolutions annexing Texas in 1845, any more than the report of the committee on territories proposes to repeal the same acts this session. But the acts of 1850 did authorize the people of those territories to exercise 'all rightful powers of legislation consistent with the constitution,' not excepting the question of slavery; and it provided that when those territories should be received into the Union, they should be received with or without slavery as the people thereof might determine at their date of admission. These provisions were in direct conflict with a clause in any former enactment, declaring that slavery should be forever prohibited in any portion of said territories, and hence rendered such clause inoperative and void to the extent of such conflict. This was an inevitable consequence, resulting from the provisions in those acts which gave the people the right to decide the slavery question for themselves, in conformity with the Constitution. It was not necessary to go further and declare that certain previous enactments, which were incompatible with the exercise of powers confirmed in the bills 'are hereby repealed.' The very act of granting those powers and rights has the legal effect of removing all obstructions to the exercise of them, by the people as prescribed in those territorial bills. . . . We were content to organize Nebraska in the precise language of the Utah and New Mexico bills. Our object was to leave the people entirely free to form and regulate their domestic and internal concerns in their own way, under the Constitution; and we deemed it wise to accomplish that object in the exact terms in which the same thing had been done in Utah and New Mexico, by the acts of 1850."

The South was cold toward this bill. Already the germ of the idea that the Constitution carried slavery into a territory against the will of the people thereof had come into being; and the organization of Nebraska meant a northern terminal for the Pacific railroad. On the precise subject, why should the people of a territory control the matter of slavery when the Constitution, which was over every foot of American soil, by its own force carried slavery into every territory acquired? While affairs stood thus, a move was made from the side, which changed the whole complexion of the controversy. Archibald Dixon, a Whig senator from Kentucky, without consulting Douglas, offered an amendment to Douglas's bill which expressly repealed the Missouri Compromise. This was on January 16. Douglas tried in vain to get Dixon to withdraw his amendment. On the next day, the 17th, Sumner, the abolitionist, introduced in the Senate a memorial against slavery generally, and gave notice that when the Nebraska bill should come up he would offer an amendment reaffirming the congressional restriction of 1820—the Missouri Compromise, in a word. His amendment was at this time informally presented and ordered to be printed. So the storm was let loose. It was out of a hard, stubborn, Hebraic-Puritan spirit that Sumner did this. He was full of hate and pride. He cared nothing about a railroad, nothing about the country's peace, nothing about a war to come. God's will must be done, and he was there to do it!

Then if the Compromise of 1850 did not repeal the Compromise of 1820, the Senate had the right to repeal it by the act of 1854 relating to Nebraska. It was all puerile, the fight which was provoked and which raged; for it was about territory where slavery would not enter, if Congress had provided that slaves could be taken there. It was fixed for freedom to use Webster's expression; and if Sumner had been a man of respectable calibre and vision, he

THE KANSAS-NEBRASKA ACT

would have said with Webster, "I will not do a thing unnecessary that wounds the feelings of others, or that does disgrace to my own understanding." Sumner's sadistic psychology rejoiced in injuring the feelings of others, especially those of the South. There is a large world justice, a wise oversoul that consigns such men to oblivion, and, before that, to ill fortune in men's eyes. Under Grant, Sumner sank from view, and died deserted and miserable.

What was now to be done? Dixon wrote in a letter to Foot, of date October 1, 1858, that Douglas took him for a ride and proposed to engraft upon his bill the Dixon amendment. There were only two courses: either to make the bill more express on the matter of the repeal of the Missouri Compromise, and hold the favor of the South, or refuse to do so and let the bill be defeated; let Nebraska stay out, and the railroad die. Dixon and Douglas conferred then with President Pierce, who drew the amendment embodying the Dixon idea; and on January 23, 1854, Douglas reported the new Nebraska bill which declared that the Missouri Compromise had been superseded by the principles of the Compromise of 1850. Two weeks later Douglas moved to strike out "superseded by" and "inoperative," and to insert in their stead "inconsistent with" and "null and void." Dixon now said to Douglas that he only wanted to have the bill conform to the principles of the Compromise of 1850. To this Douglas replied that he was glad to hear it; that he had thought Dixon intended to legislate slavery affirmatively into the territory.

All along we find causes of the war, which befell the country in 1861. One of the most influential of all the various causes was set in motion at this juncture of affairs. At this time the Whig Party was moribund; the Free Soil Party had shown its impotence. The fact that New Hampshire had Hale in the Senate, and that Massachusetts had Sumner, and that New York had Seward did not suffice. How were honors, offices, fames, money, power, to be won at large, for an organization, for a party with patronage to dispense, with commands to be given which could be enforced, for everything that goes with control of the government politically? That was to be done by the organization of a new party in the name of God and Liberty. But also the Democratic Party had to be destroyed, its President Pierce had to be put away, and its great leader Douglas discredited and set upon by the mob fury of the country, to be hunted to his death. This was what was in the mind of Chase and Seward and Sumner, concealed under their talk of higher laws and golden rules.

Chase with the golden rule in one hand, carried in the other a firebrand, intended to burn Douglas to death, and to do that by setting the country afire so that he could not escape the flames. Chase had been raised by an uncle, an Episcopal Bishop in Ohio, and he had been graduated from Dartmouth in 1826. Originally a Whig, he joined the anti-slavery movement in 1836; but be it said to his credit he opposed the abolitionism of Garrison. He left the Whig Party in 1841 and joined the Liberty Party. In 1848 he drafted the Free Soil platform which Lincoln, it will be remembered, tried to undermine in Massachusetts. In 1849 he was elected to the Senate as a result of a coalition between Democrats and Free Soilers. He was against the Compromise of 1850. He was the first Republican governor of Ohio, and he lost the Republican nomination for the presidency in 1860 because he was tainted with free trade theories, while Lincoln was for protection. Chase, Sumner and Seward wanted Douglas out of the way. He had wounded their egotism beyond measure, solely by the exhibition of superior ability. He filled them all with consuming envy, just as he did Lincoln. The whole verdict of the times is that in keen mindedness, in readiness, in vigor, in knowledge of legislation and the history relating to it, in the give and take of debate, in repartee, in poise that could not be unbalanced, and in alertness that could not be surprised by flank attacks, Douglas towered above the Puritan Sumner, the crafty Seward and the legalistic Chase. He had undone them over and over again. How could they go on with their holy program without making it appear to the country that Douglas was a man without principles, without moral integrity? It could not be done by their arguments against his; it might be done by proving that they were good men and that he was a bad one. They, that is Chase and Sumner, therefore struck Douglas in the back. They sowed against him falsehoods which have thriven to this day in the shallows, in the places of dead waters, in the backwashes; while only in the deeps where the sunlight has full sway, and where the waves keep life fresh, is the truth about Douglas known. They crippled Douglas's career, though but for the War he would have risen over their malice; but they helped greatly to bring on the War which unhappily ended his great and useful life, useful no more in the great change which had come to pass.

With so much said, the thread of the narrative respecting the Nebraska bill may be taken up, which at last emerged as a bill for the organization of Kansas and Nebraska. On January 24, Douglas asked that his bill might be taken up. Chase and Sumner requested delay that they might further examine it. Douglas, not knowing that they were deceiving him, consented to the delay. They had already punctured Douglas with a poisoned dirk; they wanted the poison to be fully working before engaging in conflict with him. They had in fact, on January 19, sent forth a violent attack on Douglas's bill in a screed entitled "Appeal of the Independent Democrats in Congress to the People of the United States." On this 24th day of January, 1854, this Appeal was published in the *New York Times*, and was making its mob-creating way over the country. It was composed by Chase, not a Democrat; and by Joshua R. Giddings, who had been a Whig and then a Free Soiler, a member of Congress. It was signed by these two, and by Sumner, not a Democrat, and by three abolitionist members of Congress. It was the beginning of the storm of calumny which troubled Douglas to the end, and which led to the War.

A few of the incendiary announcements of this Appeal may be noticed. "We arraign this bill as a gross violation of a sacred pledge; as a criminal betrayal of precious rights; as a part and parcel of an atrocious plot to exclude from a vast unoccupied region immigrants from the Old World [the Germans perhaps] and free laborers from our own states, and convert it into a dreary region of despotism, inhabited by masters and slaves." It was impossible for human mendacity to sink lower than by the use of such words. It was blared that the Pacific railroad could not be built by the Central or Northern route, because "inducements to the immigration of free laborers will be almost destroyed," and "the blight of slavery will cover the land." The German and other foreign press was urged to expose Douglas's satanic plot. "It is a bold scheme against American liberty, worthy of an accomplished architect of ruin." The plan was to "subjugate the whole country to the yoke of slaveholding despotism. We implore Christians and Christian ministers to interpose. Their divine religion requires them to behold in every man a brother, and to labor for the advancement and regeneration of the human race." This was to be done by bearing false witness, and by arousing hate over the land! The Appeal then declared that Douglas was the guilty man in chief of this "enormous crime"; that to get support for the presidency from the South he had undertaken to repeal the Missouri Compromise. We shall find Lincoln in the debates recapitulating this atrocious falsehood against Douglas—to get the senatorship of Illinois!

In consequence of this Appeal, hatred and slander ran like prairie fires over the whole land. It was the most perfect piece of mob excitement that America has known. Three thousand New England clergymen, speaking for God, for what God wanted, and what God hated, and what God would do to the slavocracy, joined in the hue and cry; while Chase and Sumner sat back in hiding and watched the fury grow and spread.

On March 3, Douglas rose in the Senate to speak for his bill. When he had finished, the mangled remains of Seward, Sumner and Chase lay about the Senate chamber. To Sumner he said; "I must be permitted to remind him of what he certainly can never forget, that when he arrived here to take his seat for the first time, so firmly were senators impressed with the conviction that he had been elected by dishonorable and corrupt means, there were very few who for a long time could deem it consistent with personal honor to hold private intercourse with him. So general was that impression, that for a long time he was avoided and shunned as a person unworthy of the association of gentlemen. . . . Sir, you will remember that when you came into the Senate and sought an opportunity to put forth your abolition incendiarism, you appealed to our sense of justice by the sentiment 'Strike, but hear me first.' But when Mr. Webster went back in 1850 to speak to his constituents in his own self-defense, to tell the truth and to expose his slanderers, you would not hear him, but you struck him first." One by one, Douglas in this manner of attack disposed of his detractors.

Of the tenor of the bill as a whole he declared that it did not legislate slavery into the territory nor out of it, but left the people to do as they pleased about it, as the Clay-Webster Compromise of 1850 did with respect to the Mexican accessions. The tornado had been raised by abolitionists. Lines of settlement had to be provided for from the Mississippi Valley to the Pacific. The bill would destroy all sectional parties and agitations. "Northern rights and Southern rights! I know of no such divisions or distinctions under the Constitution." In the morning of March 4, Douglas brought his powerful speech to a close. Sumner had said that he would reply. He thought better of trying to do so. Chase held his peace, and so did Seward. The vote was then taken, and the bill passed by 37 to 14. The yeas were from New Hampshire, New Jersey, Pennsylvania, Illinois, Indiana, Michigan, Iowa, Delaware, Maryland, Virginia, North Carolina, South Carolina, Georgia, Florida, Mississippi, Missouri, Arkansas, Kentucky, Alabama, Louisiana, and California. The nays were from Maine, Massachusetts, Rhode Island, Vermont, New York, Ohio and Wisconsin. Connecticut, Tennessee and Texas were divided. In the House the bill passed on May 20 by 113 to 100. But Douglas and the country had to face the mob spirit which Chase and Sumner had aroused.

This is the sum of the repeal of the Missouri Compromise, through the evil machinations of Douglas! The stormy quarrel that arose over it was factitious, and out of the heated vaporings of fanatical malcontents, urged on by conspirators like Chase and Sumner. There was not enough of reality involved to engage the interest of an honest mind, sincerely concerned with the welfare of his country, and with appreciation of what ruin can be wrought by turning loose the Hebraic-Puritan madness so peculiar to America. All the way to Chicago, as Douglas journeyed thither, returning to his home, his figure was burned in effigy. He was assailed in the furious press as "Benedict Arnold" Douglas. He had betrayed his country! When he got to Chicago he tried to address a mass meeting, in order to make clear to his constituents just what had been done and why it was done. In the name of Liberty he was denied the liberty to speak. Chicago in its capacity as a mob, and to its capacity as such, hooted him down, drowned out his great voice, overcame his attempts to speak with vile insults, with cat calls and epithets. Real-estate swindlers, pious confidence men, rogues and pharisees of every description assuming to themselves virtues over the so-called dishonest Douglas assailed him vilely as he tried to speak. But he did not quail. He fought with the mob until past midnight. Then at the risk of being struck with bricks or fists he marched through the insane crowd to his carriage and drove away. Chase and Sumner, who could not meet him in debate in the Senate and hold their own, thus could worst him by making him detestable to the mob, by setting the hue and cry of traitor after him, by clamping the censorship of ochlocrats upon his utterance. The Chase Appeal had begun to create a Christian Republic! The Negro was to be treated upon the basis of the golden rule; Douglas deserved Jehoviac vengeance, to be administered by faithful priests of the Hebrew cults, by Chase and by Sumner and the mobs which they could evoke.

In Springfield Lincoln was waiting for Douglas. In his slow way he was beginning to see that the ducks were flying toward his blind. The greatest statesman, the most famous and useful in America, belonged to Illinois. Perhaps there was something of great advantage in having that statesman right at home, right within striking distance, not afar and out of reach, as he would have been if he had belonged to Ohio, where to engage him Lincoln would have to travel thither, and meet him upon an alien soil and before strange audiences. It was better to have Douglas at hand, and coming to Springfield, and to Peoria where Lincoln could follow him and speak before familiar crowds.

Chapter X   Lincoln Gradually Awakes

LINCOLN, as we have seen, supported Scott in 1852, who was running upon a platform which affirmed the Compromise of 1850. It had declared "That the series of acts of the 31st Congress, the act known as the Fugitive Slave Law, included, are received and acquiesced in by the Whig Party of the United States as a settlement in principle and substance, of the dangerous and exciting question which they embrace; and so far as they are concerned we will maintain them, and insist upon their strict enforcement, etc." This Lincoln had adopted as his own creed by supporting Scott; he had confirmed its political truth by pronouncing an oration upon Clay, who was the father of the Compromise of 1850. Since the Compromise of 1850 did not awake him from slumber in a useless world where all "seems dead," and where he was mired in the foul days, and could not pluck his legs from the muck into which they had been sunk while walking in darkness not of his making, and by a way that was not of his choice, what was it in the Kansas-Nebraska Act that began to make him turn and yawn and come out of slumber? Was it Douglas? Should Douglas longer be famous and preeminent? Should he go on living in Washington, and traveling to Russia and England, and growing richer out of well-advised land investments? If he was to continue to be a lion, should it not be now as a dead lion, with whom a live dog might have a chance? As Douglas had run into evil days, and was now being jeered at as Benedict Arnold Douglas, he was more vulnerable than formerly, he was easier to hit and to hurt.

The history of these days of Lincoln's coming out of his trance, out of lounging and reading newspapers, out of deepest gloom, out of the dull tedium of traveling the circuit, must be narrowly scrutinized to get at Lincoln's psychology. For if it be granted that the Compromises of 1850 did not repeal the Missouri Compromise, they did let slavery into Utah north of 36° 30', and open it up to New Mexico which was far west of Kansas. That is, the evil of soiling the purity of fresh territory by letting slavery into it had been done in 1850. It was sticking in the bark, therefore, to attack the Kansas-Nebraska Act for its repeal of the Missouri Compromise. It was applying *Chitty on Pleading*, and Euclid, where a broader logic only could adequately deal with the good or the evil that had been done, and measure up the whole result in terms of statesmanship. Nobody pretends now that the great evil of slavery suddenly came to Lincoln's consciousness, and that he was stricken from death into a new life by the flash of a great revelation. Nothing of the kind happened. In proof whereof let us consider what was going on in that summer of 1854, when Douglas was in Illinois buffeting the storm which Chase had stirred up against him.

At Jackson, Michigan, on July 6, 1854, a great concourse of people, called together by a petition of ten thousand signatures, met in a grove of trees and organized a new political party called the Republican Party. They adopted a platform and nominated a state ticket. Before this, at Ripon, Wisconsin, in February, and while the Kansas-Nebraska bill was pending in the Senate, there was an assemblage of people, who resolved that if the bill passed they would discard both the Whig and the Democratic parties, all parties in a word, and form a new party, and make its sole end of being the resistance of the further extension of slavery. Soon there in Wisconsin the Whig and Free Soil committees were dissolved, and a fusion committee of three Whigs and one Free Soiler and one Democrat was formed, and the name Republican was proposed for the new party. During the summer of 1854, so-called Republican organizations sprang up in New England, in Ohio, and over Wisconsin. In Illinois in county after county, Whig conventions, people's conventions, fusion conventions were held in the excitement of the times, and the name Republican was adopted. None of these deserved to call themselves Republicans, any more than the centralist party of Hamilton could honestly call itself the Federal Party. It was as much of a misnomer as the name Whig was for that organization of protective tariff and bank economists. We shall see that despite the motley and mongrel elements which went to the organization of the Republican Party, it was in brains and in character the legitimate offspring of Hamilton and Webster, by a straight line of descent. The radicals, the fanatics who were its infantrymen were soon set down in their place in the administration of Lincoln. The newspapers of Illinois knew at first hand of what stuff the new party was made. The Joliet, Illinois, *Signal* reported that the Republican Party of the Joliet district was made up of Whigs, Abolitionists, dissatisfied Democrats; another local paper called one of the Republican meetings an assemblage of Whigs, Abolitionists, Know-Nothings, Sore-heads, and fag ends. And so went the word up and down Illinois. The most active organizer of the new party in Illinois was Ichabod Codding, a temperance lecturer; and it was charged that he was in the pay of the Chicago coterie bent upon fusion in the name of a great morality.

Nothing more need be said of the Whigs to have a clear understanding of what they were. The other strains of blood of the new party may well have genealogical tracing. There was the Anti-Masonic party which came into being as the result of the mysterious death of William Morgan in 1826. He had revealed the secrets of Free Masonry, and then had suddenly disappeared. It was claimed that he had been done to death. Opposition to Masonry was then taken up by the churches as a religious crusade, and a political issue was made of Masonry in New York in 1827. At this time the National Republicans, another false name for the Centralists, were weak in New York, due to the unpopularity of John Quincy Adams, the chief National Republican. Shrewd political impostors determined to utilize the inflamed feelings against Masonry with which to create a new political party, to oppose the rising power of Andrew Jackson, the Democrat. In 1828 it practically destroyed the National Republicans in New York. In 1829 it showed its hand by espousing internal improvements and the protective tariff. From New York the movement spread into New England, and it became strong in Vermont and Pennsylvania. In 1831 the party in national convention at Philadelphia nominated William Wirt for president; and in the election of 1832 he carried the state of Vermont against Jackson. Seward was first a National Republican, but after 1828 he joined the Anti-Masonics, and attended its national convention of 1830 and 1831. He served until 1834 as a member of its national committee. When in 1833 the party had run its course, he became a Whig, that is, in effect a National Republican again. The Anti-Masonics, changed over into

Whigs, thus became a component part of the new Republican Party of 1854.

Another element was the Know-Nothings, or American Party. They were organized to oppose Roman Catholicism and the foreign immigrant. It was a secret organization formed in 1852. In 1854 this party carried the state elections in Massachusetts and Delaware; in 1855 it elected governors and legislators in New York and four New England states. In 1856 eight states had so-called native American governors. Finally the so-called slavery question operated to absorb this erratic group into the Republican Party. Then there were Free-soilers, abolitionists of various bloods, Barn Burners, the radicals of every hue, the dreamers, the bankrupts in purse and character, the hungry seekers for office, every strange sect and group in which America has been prolific since the Puritans started the American Hebraic culture; these went to the making of the Republican Party. But its brains from the first lay with the Whigs of Henry Clay and Daniel Webster. In this summer of 1854 Lincoln was not ready to join such an organization as this, even though it was formed specifically for the purpose of resisting the extension of slavery, and in Illinois to undo Douglas. He meant to follow Douglas around Illinois, but he was going to do it as a Whig. It did not matter that the Liberty Party, formed in 1840, was ready to join the Republicans. Perhaps he disliked these men because they had split the Whig vote in New York in 1844, thereby compassing the defeat of Clay. Nor was his love greater for the Free Soil party, which was soon to amalgamate with the Republicans. He had taken his stand against them in Massachusetts in his speech at Worcester, already detailed.

It must be remembered that Lincoln, though he was in an occultation, was easy to recognize as the leading Whig of Illinois. He had been the Whig leader in the legislature. When he was in Congress he had the honor of being the only Whig representative from Illinois. Any way it is viewed, it would have been a great catch if Codding could have drawn Lincoln into his net. He was unable to do so. On October 5, 1854, Codding was in Springfield for the purpose of organizing the state Republican Party. The watchful Herndon, though always pushing Lincoln into deeper radicalism, yet had regard for the political fortunes of his idol. Herndon knew

LINCOLN GRADUALLY AWAKES

that Codding and his coterie would try to get Lincoln to address this new Republican organization; and that would not do now. For who could tell what was to come? The Whig Party might inhale more vital breath and come back into vigor. If so where would Lincoln be if he were present where a Republican platform was adopted, as indeed one was adopted at this Codding meeting? Lincoln was soon to be suspect, and it was in vain to hide. We shall see how Douglas tried to fasten the Springfield platform of this occasion on Lincoln, in the first debate, and how Lincoln glided away from the blow, but after all only by a quibble which Douglas exposed. Yet Lincoln did disappear from Springfield, and stayed away until Codding and his crowd had left the town. Herndon sent Lincoln to Tazewell County upon the pretense of business there; and so Lincoln could, with *Chitty on Pleading* accuracy, reply to Douglas in the debates that he had nothing to do with the Springfield resolutions and knew nothing about them. Though Lincoln was not at the Codding meeting, Codding assumed to place Lincoln on the state central committee of the new party. Lincoln seems not to have noticed this impertinence. But when Codding wrote him on November 13, 1854, to come to Chicago on the 17th to attend a meeting of the state central committee as its member from the Springfield district, Lincoln replied as follows, after ignoring the invitation: "While I have my pen in hand allow me to say I have been perplexed some to understand why my name was placed on that committee. I was not consulted on the subject, nor was I apprised of the appointment until I discovered it by accident two or three weeks afterward." Is it possible that Herndon, who was watching the Codding meeting, did not tell Lincoln at once on his return from Tazewell County, a day or two after Codding and his crowd had gone away, that Lincoln had been placed on this committee? It seems incredible that Herndon did not tell him this. In this town of about 5000 people how could such a thing happen without talk about it going all about the square and in every store and office and place where men met? To resume quotation from the letter to Codding: "I suppose my opposition to the principle of slavery is as strong as that of any member of the Republican Party; but I have also supposed that the extent to which I feel authorized to carry that opposition, practically, was not at all satisfactory to that party. The leading men who organized that party were present on the 4th of October at the discussion between Douglas and myself at Springfield, and had full opportunity to not misunderstand my position. Do I misunderstand them? Please write and inform me."

Did he resign from the Committee? He did not. This letter is out of the psychology which wrote the Stone-Lincoln resolutions of 1837. Was Lincoln walking in the van of Liberty? He was to take no definite stand until the Whig Party was dead, and there was no place to go but to the house of the Republicans. As to the resolutions of the Codding convention, Lincoln was already in agreement with some of them, though at variance with others of them. The resolutions declared that Kansas and Nebraska should be restored to the position of free territories; that the Fugitive Slave Law should be repealed; that slavery should be restricted to those states in which it existed; that slavery in the District of Columbia should be abolished; that slavery should be abolished wherever Congress had jurisdiction; that no more slave states should be admitted; that no further territory should be acquired unless slavery should have been therein forever prohibited.[1] Lincoln's letter to Codding shows plainly enough that he did not want to offend the Republicans, he was anxious to know what they thought of his position as against Douglas on October 4th, and he referred to it to invite comparison between it and the resolutions. Their tenor must have been known all over Springfield, so that, when Lincoln in the debates said that he knew nothing about them, the least that can be said of that is that it is incredibly strange. Herndon joined the Republican Party at the Codding convention. Is it believable that Herndon did not recount to Lincoln everything that happened at that meeting?

In the summer and fall of 1854, Illinois was about the political business of selecting a legislature, which would elect a United States senator; and so far as the Whigs were concerned they were trying to defeat Shields, of duel fame, who was a candidate to succeed himself. This was the more desirable to the Whig heart because Shields was a devoted follower of Douglas. To reprobate the Kansas-Nebraska Act was the moral aspect of the Whig endeavor. If

[1] Nicolay and Hay, I, 386 n.

LINCOLN GRADUALLY AWAKES 219

there were no better reason for it, Lincoln was aloof from the Republicans because he was running for the legislature himself on the Whig ticket. It is asserted that he did not want to make this race; but he did not positively decline the nomination. He abided by it, and allowed his name to be voted upon, and he was elected. In campaigning for the office, he had the opportunity to trail Douglas and to attach his name to that of the great Democratic senator, but much in the guise of "humble Abraham Lincoln." Wherever he went there was talk of his lowly origin, his rise from obscurity by the hardest efforts, talk that was industriously multiplied by his political friends. All this was in key with the American folk-making lore of the times; and it became the basis of the myth that Lincoln was a man of the people springing out of the very soil, autochthonous, and natural, a man of cordial amenities and simple fraternities, and democratic in principle and in practice.

In the afternoon of October 16, 1854, Douglas addressed a great audience at Peoria, with Lincoln present. Douglas announced to the audience that Lincoln would answer him; and that evening Lincoln did so. Lincoln began by saying that he would discuss the repeal of the Missouri Compromise. He began by referring to the Ordinance of 1787, leading the audience to believe that it was Jefferson who had brought about the exclusion of slavery from the Northwest Territory. He then took up the Missouri Compromise, lending the impression that Missouri had come into the Union under it. He took up the Compromise of 1850, showing what he considered the North and the South had gotten as the result of mutual concessions; and he admitted that the Whigs and the Democrats adopted platforms in 1852 approving the Compromise; and that the Illinois legislature in 1851 had endorsed it.

Coming to the Kansas-Nebraska Act, he alleged that on "the Judge's own motion," it was amended so as to make the Missouri Compromise "inoperative and void." This was said with mildness; but then he launched out: "I think, I shall try to show that it is wrong, wrong in its direct effect, letting slavery into Kansas and Nebraska; and wrong in its prospective principle, allowing it to spread to every other part of the wide world, where men can be found inclined to take it. This declared indifference, but as I must think covert real zeal for the spread of slavery, I cannot but hate."

But what was he going to do about slavery? Was he an abolitionist? Let us hear. "When Southern people tell us they are no more responsible for the origin of slavery than we are, I acknowledge the fact. When it is said that the institution exists, and that it is very difficult to get rid of it in any satisfactory way, I can understand and appreciate the saying." If so, why discuss the embroiling subject; and as to territory where it would not go, though the law let it go? "If all earthly power were given me," he went on, "I should not know what to do, as to the existing institution. My first impulse would be to free all the slaves and send them to Liberia—to their own native land. . . . If they all landed there in a day, they would all perish in the next ten days. . . . What then? Free them all, and keep them among us as underlings? Is it quite certain that this betters their condition?" Nay, in Illinois at this very time the negroes were worse off than they were in the South, and Lincoln knew this. But it is strange that Lincoln had no more affection for the negroes than these words show that he had. There were many men in his day who were fond of them, as there are today; and who were not averse to accepting them as human beings in the general scheme of life. He would not hold any in slavery. "What next? Free them, and make them politically and socially our equals? My own feelings will not admit of this. . . . We cannot make them equals." Yet he had just referred to the author of the Declaration of Independence, which in "the pure, fresh breath of the Revolution" forbade slavery in the Northwest. Upon what basis did he make that reference except that of the equality of the negro as being included in the designation that "all men are created equal"?

To the argument that slavery would not go into Nebraska because of its climate, he observed: "As to climate, a glance at the map shows that there are five slave states—Delaware, Maryland, Virginia, Kentucky and Missouri—and also the District of Columbia, all north of the Missouri Compromise line." But all of these had both climate and soil suitable for cotton and tobacco; they were all states where slavery had long been, not where it was to go if conditions favored its reception. "What I do say is that no man is good enough to govern another man without that other's consent." If this was true, then the negro was entitled to the ballot, in order that he might help make the laws; he was entitled to serve

LINCOLN GRADUALLY AWAKES 221

on juries and in the militia in order that he might assist in administering and enforcing the laws. Yet Lincoln had just said that he would not make negroes equal with white men, either socially or politically. Then he contradicted himself by these words: "Allow all the governed an equal voice in the government; and that and that only is self-government."

"But you say this question should be left to the people of Nebraska, because they are more particularly interested. If this be the rule, you must leave it to each individual to say for himself whether he will have slaves." That is, without any law for it, a man might seize another and put him in slavery as rightfully as he could do so with a law made by the sovereign power. "What better moral right have thirty-one citizens of Nebraska to say that the thirty-second shall not hold slaves, than the people of thirty-one states have to say that slavery shall not go into the thirty-second state at all?" Much depends on how this question is to be answered. "In the course of his reply, Senator Douglas remarked, in substance, that he had always considered this government was made for the white people, and not for negroes. Why, in point of fact, I think so too." If so who was to rule, the whites or the negroes? If so, was not slavery as a social regimentation perfectly justifiable? But then "in our greedy chase to make profit of the negro, let us beware lest we cancel and tear to pieces even the white man's charter of freedom." There was no chance of this disaster from negro slavery; there was great probability of it by exciting men to war, and by destroying the white man's charter on the score of the consent of the governed to be ruled, and by the privilege which might be built up on the ruins of that principle.

We come now to a portion of Lincoln's speech which was the source of great controversy at the time, and which created angry discord whenever opponents on the issue met. Considering that the times were badly enough inflamed, it cannot be regarded otherwise than with regret that hatred and envy of the South should be exacerbated on the matter of the three-fifths principle of direct taxation and of representation embodied in the Constitution. Let us present what Lincoln said about it, and then contrast that with what the Southern statesmen contended as to its meaning and effect. The Second Section of the First Article of the Constitution reads: "Representatives and direct taxes shall be apportioned among the several states which may be included within this Union, according to their respective numbers, which shall be determined by adding to the whole number of free persons, including those bound to service for a term of years, and excluding Indians not taxed, three fifths of all other persons."

This is what Lincoln said: "In regard to what I have said of the advantage the slave states have over the free, in the matter of representation, the Judge replied that we, in the free states, count five negroes as five white persons, while in the slave states they count five slaves as three whites only; and that the advantage at last was on the side of the free states. Now, in the slave states they count free negroes just as we do; and so it happens that, besides their slaves, they have as many free negroes as we have and thirty-three thousand over. Thus their free negroes more than balance ours; and their advantage over us, in consequence of their slaves, still remains as I have stated." What was the purpose in Lincoln's mind in stirring up this source of discord? If he did not know what to do with slavery, what was he going to do with this principle of representation and taxation that had been settled in the Constitutional Convention, after the most thorough consideration? It made no difference if free negroes in the South were counted the same as free negroes in the North, the fact remained that the South had representation for its slaves not for five fifths of a man but only for three fifths of one.

As this issue arose again in the debates between Lincoln and Douglas, it will serve the reader to make the history of this constitutional clause clear at this time. Under the Articles of Union and Confederation of July 12, 1776, Article XI, all charges of war and all other expenses were provided to be defrayed out of a common treasury, which should be supplied by the several colonies "in proportion to the number of inhabitants of every age, sex, and quality, except Indians not paying taxes." This principle of levying taxes rested upon the theory that population was the best and most reliable standard for estimating the ability of a people to raise money for public purposes by taxation. Numbers, or the relative population of the states, was made the criterion of just contribution for the common defense.

Under the Articles of Confederation which were adopted July 9, 1778, and by Article VIII, taxes were provided to be supplied "by the several states in proportion to the value of the land within each state." This method was found to be unworkable; and on April 18, 1783, a proposition was made in Congress to amend the articles and to return to population as a basis of taxation. Negroes were considered as wealth-producing factors, and the inquiry was how much of a man he was when compared to a white man. Mr. Walcott of Connecticut thought that he was three fourths of a white man; two members from Massachusetts agreed to this. A South Carolina member contended that slaves were an incumbrance to society, and lessened its ability to pay taxes. A vote was taken on a motion to rate three negroes to two white men. Mr. Madison then proposed that slaves be rated as five to three, and this was adopted. It had no reference to representation at all. At that time, that is, under the Articles of Confederation, each state had one vote, as provided by Clause 4 of Article V. When the Constitutional Convention met, Rufus King of Massachusetts raised the question that the states should not have an equal vote in Congress, as they had had under the Articles of Confederation, and without regard to population; but that representation should have some equitable basis for its estimation. Then Mr. Wilson from Pennsylvania offered this plan: that representation should be in proportion to the whole number of white and other free citizens, including those bound to servitude for a term of years, "and three fifths of all other persons." Every state, north and south, voted for this except New Jersey and Delaware; for be it observed one third of all the slaves at the time were in the Northern states.[1] In the LIVth number of the *Federalist*, written by Hamilton or Madison, and published in the *New York Packet* for February 12, 1788, the author brought together the arguments for and against the three-fifths clause; and, citing what the South was saying about it, this language was used: "It is agreed on all sides that numbers are the best scale of wealth and taxation, as they are the only proper scale of representation. Would the convention have been impartial or consistent, if they had rejected the slaves from the lists of inhabitants when the shares of representation were calculated, and inserted them on the lists

[1] Elliot's Debates, V, 79; 194.

when the tariff of contributions was to be adjusted? Could it be reasonably expected that the Southern States would concur in a system which considered their slaves in some degree as men when burdens were to be imposed, but refused to consider them in the same light when advantages were to be conferred? Might not some surprise be also expressed that those who reproach the Southern States with the barbarous policy of considering as property a part of their human brethren, should themselves contend that the government, to which all the states are to be parties, ought to consider this unfortunate race more completely in the unnatural light of property than the very laws of which they complain? ... After all, may not another ground be taken on which this article of the Constitution will admit of a still more ready defence? We have hitherto proceeded on the ideas that representation related to persons only, and not at all to property. But is it just? Government is instituted no less for protection of the property than of the persons of individuals. The one as well as the other, therefore, may be considered as represented by those who are charged with the government."

Clearly this was no subject to discuss safely in a political speech addressed to a popular audience; still less was it one to present in such a way that the audience gathered that the South had over-reached the North on the basis of representation, and for more than half a century had been enjoying the unjust benefits of that wrongful advantage. In the first place the South had not procured this clause to be adopted, it had not bullied or coerced the North into acquiescing in it. It was one of the adjustments of the Constitution. What was more illuminating than all else was the history of the working of this clause. For when the North settled down to the policy of protection, there were no direct taxes to be proportioned to population, while the South had representation for only three fifths of her slaves. Black men as well as white men consumed products and paid duties on them; but the black men, and through them the masters, had only a three-fifths voice in saying what the tariff duties should be, and on what imports imposed. It was calculated, too, that by the time the Missouri Compromise arose, the South was unrepresented to the extent of six votes in the House by the working of this clause, enough to have defeated the drawing of the sectional line which shook the soul of Jefferson.

Lincoln, who was sensitive and of a brooding imagination, saw the days drift by without anything happening to give any meaning to his life. At forty-five a man is near the climacteric of his powers, but of what use is that if there be no place or work in the world for him, and if his life does not ensphere itself and revolve on to some significant destiny? Locked up powers, obstructed energies and baffled dreams are daily death to a strong man; and Lincoln had been now for years a thwarted will. Running for the legislature could not have been other than galling to his pride, when he reflected that Douglas had been in the Senate for nearly two terms now, and that Shields, whom he ridiculed more than a decade before, had passed him in the race for distinction. Lincoln did not have the consolation either of a heart given to a good cause, which may reconcile a man, worthy of a higher service, to doing whatever comes to hand for the sake of a principle, an enthusiasm. He was running for the legislature on the Whig ticket. He was seeking an honor which young men at the beginning of political life capture when they can as the first rung to the ascent to power and fame. But if he could be sent to the Senate, life would be changed for him into something honorable to his powers. He would there be facing Douglas, and dividing with his rival of more than twenty years the attention of the people of Illinois, perhaps of the country; and he would there be in command of patronage, and with votes for freedom in the territories, perhaps, or for other great measures to come. How much longer could he endure the daily walk from his house to the little law office, and the old round of the circuit, now a shopworn experience, with some of the first faces already gone, either to death or to other fields? Life was passing rapidly. He was forty-five and had done nothing. There was chance now that he might go to the Senate; and to this end he resigned the place in the legislature to which he had been elected. If he could hold the Whigs in line, if he could capture the so-called Anti-Nebraska Democrats, he might win the coveted place. Lyman Trumbull, who had come to Illinois from Connecticut, who had been practicing law in Illinois for years now, who was a Democrat, had turned against Douglas on the Nebraska issue, for thus had the

Chase appeal affected reasoning minds. Shields was writing now that Trumbull and his associates did not care "two pins about Nebraska," but their passions were centered upon electing a senator who would help to "break down Douglas; for Douglas they have sworn to destroy. When they fail to find a man to aid them against Douglas they will vote for me." They did find one; but it was not Lincoln.

Lincoln began now to write letters here and there endeavoring to summon support for his ambition for the senatorship. One letter will illustrate the manner of his appeal. It was written from Clinton on November 11, 1854. "I have suspicion that a Whig has been elected to the legislature from Edgar. If this is not so, why then *nix cum arous;* but if it is so then could you not make a mark with him for me for U. S. Senator? I really have some chance."

Indeed in the division of the Democratic Party, in the blind wrath of men striking where they knew not, he did have a very considerable chance. The candidates were Shields, Trumbull, and Lincoln when the legislature met; but according to Lincoln, Governor Matteson was a secret candidate all the time. So Lincoln wrote to E. B. Washburne after the contest was over. There were men who were Democrats, and men who were Whigs, and those who were Douglas men refusing to surrender, and others, who for this or the other reason, for principle or for none, were against Douglas and everything that he desired. There were those who believed in slavery, and those who deplored its existence, but who like Lincoln did not know what to do with the institution. There were men who thought the Compromise of 1850 and the Kansas-Nebraska Act were wise adjustments of a vexed question, and that the further agitation of slavery, and of those measures would lead to war. My grandfather was in this legislature of 1855, as a Democrat, though he was never a strict party follower. He was a man of simple piety whose name to this day is spoken in the Petersburg-New Salem community with affection and reverence, and in recognition of his just and honorable life. He was against Lincoln and voted against him, as others of like conviction did. When I was growing up, and was imbibing the Lincoln myths, I was puzzled and shocked to know that my grandfather, whom I saw invested with all nobilities, had voted against Lincoln. I had heard as a boy at his knee of his youth in

Tennessee, of the negroes there, whom he liked as a class, and always spoke of with a certain tenderness, and of his father, who had emancipated his one slave, believing that it was wrong to hold her in bondage. How then could my grandfather vote against Lincoln, who afterward emancipated the slaves? When I asked him to explain his vote to me, he replied that he disliked Lincoln's politics, and disapproved of his career as a politician, and that he feared Lincoln's preachments would bring war.

When the balloting began in the legislature, Mrs. Lincoln was in the gallery expectant and hopeful. Perhaps she, too, was tired of the life in Springfield, the pocket into which Fate had thrust her. Lincoln began with 44 votes, Shields with 41 and Trumbull with 5. In Lincoln's letter to Washburne he wrote, "How came my 47 to yield to Trumbull's 5? It was Governor Matteson's work." Touching upon the phases of the balloting he said: "I became satisfied that if we could prevent Matteson's election, one or two ballots more, we could not possibly do so a single ballot after my friends should begin to return to me from Trumbull. So I determined to strike at once, and accordingly advised my remaining friends to go for him, which they did and elected him on the tenth ballot." A very usual thing had happened: in the use of political bowies someone must be cut, and the lot fell to Lincoln. Trumbull, an Anti-Nebraska Democrat, went to the Senate where he made all the trouble for Douglas that he could, being a man of ability and of inveterate hatreds.

The young and devoted Whitney immediately hurried to Lincoln's office with proffers of consolation and encouragement. There he found Lincoln sunk in a blackness of melancholy never before so completely in possession of him, often as Whitney had seen him wrapped in sombre reflections. Lincoln was now utterly dejected. Was there anything to be done? What office could he win? If none, was life to be nothing but Springfield and traveling the circuit? In three years, to be sure, Douglas's seat would be up again for contest. Could he defeat the great Douglas, having failed to defeat to his own advantage the lesser Shields?

After this time Lincoln's course was marked by listlessness, by eclectic choices, by a lack of choices, which evinced a slackened will. His fits of melancholy deepened and became more frequent, his bursts of humor more violent and more grotesque. He was not entirely idle, of course, because he was practicing law; he had the attorneyship of the Illinois Central Railroad, he had the cases to manage which have been already recounted. Despite, too, his hypochondria, and his unnerved purposes, something of life and determination remained in him. He began now to subscribe for newspapers here and there. Perhaps a way to political success lay along the path of favorable editors who became so by patronage of this sort. To one editor he sent ten dollars as compensation for a paper received for several years, and for which he had not hitherto paid. Soon Lincoln sent this editor an article for publication. The editor refused to publish it. Lincoln was not so fortunate as he had been with the *Sangamon Journal*. The so-called temperance question was raging in Illinois. In 1854 Herndon was mayor of Springfield, whose city council had prohibited the sale of liquor within the city. Herndon was known for his fondness for drink, but he enforced the ordinance of the city council. Lincoln did not drink, because, as he himself said, he did not like the taste of liquor; but he took no part in this moral crusade against the saloons. There were Know-nothing riots over the country. Lincoln took no notice of them. Sumner was beaten into insensibility by Brooks as retaliation for Sumner's execrable attack on South Carolina. Detestable words never deserve blows, and Sumner was from Massachusetts and for Freedom! Hence the country as a mob rang with the loud refrain "Bully Brooks." Lincoln's lethargy was not disturbed. There were race riots in Kansas, and Lincoln knew all about these; but he kept his peace. He knew much that was going on in Kansas, for he had a special informant there who was writing him about the developments in that fanatic-ridden territory. This was Mark W. Delahay, a dissolute lawyer who had married a fifth cousin of Nancy Hanks, Lincoln's mother. Lincoln had been frequently associated with Delahay at Petersburg in the conduct of cases. In the Spring of 1855 Delahay bought a pro-slavery paper at Leavenworth, Kansas, and changed its name to the *Territorial Register*. He was afterward chosen a Free State representative in Congress. Let us for now consider what was going on in Kansas and what brought strife and bloodshed there.

This was the War between the States in miniature. It was what

Clay foresaw in 1839. He predicted that the fanatics would unite the North against the South, and that the collision of opinion would be followed by a resort to arms. Wiser men saw that the growth of ages would require ages for its peaceful removal. The fanatic would not have this. Slavery must be destroyed now, or God would be mocked for the failure. Five weeks before Kansas and Nebraska were open to settlers, one Eli Thayer, of Worcester, Massachusetts, organized the Emigrant Aid Society, a corporation with a capital stock of $5,000,000. This was on April 26, 1854. Thayer meant to carry out his plans by force, to send settlers to Kansas and to Nebraska, and then similarly to colonize Missouri, Arkansas, Kentucky and Texas. There was enough program here for blood letting; and Phillips, Garrison and the old abolitionists drew back. Thayer did not succeed in getting subscriptions to the capital stock of his corporation, with the result that he and his fellow promoters organized the New England Emigrant Aid Company. And for this Edward Everett Hale, then a young clergyman, wrote a book entitled, *Kansas and Nebraska: an Account of the Emigrant Aid Companies*. One cannot miss the hand of Massachusetts all along this history. It began with Samuel Lincoln settling at Hingham; it was climaxed with the Sixth Massachusetts Regiment being the first to respond to Lincoln's call for troops to subjugate the South.

A citizen of Boston, evidently of penetration and who was against the schemes of the Emigrant Society, wrote a letter to the London *Times* in December of 1854, in which he said "They anticipate . . . that the philanthropic bread cast upon the waters will return in the shape of comfortable dividends." There was land to be gained, and business, and contracts and franchises, and charters, and all things by which men get power and money, and by which they devour their fellow men. All this was to be done in the name of free soil! As settlers arrived and the strife waxed fiercer, the real contest being for the government of Kansas, rifles were shipped to Kansas by friends of the cause of liberty, though not in the open name of the Aid Societies. These rifles were packed in boxes and barrels marked "crockery," "books" "Bibles." These rifles came to be known as Beecher Bibles. They were such in the very real sense that it was the Bible which inspired to a large degree these mad proceedings. This is not a history of the War, and therefore only enough of this chapter in that tragedy need be incorporated here for the purpose of our study of Lincoln. He was not prominent enough now, nor was anyone powerful enough to stay the storm which Chase had let loose by untying the bag of suspicion and hate when he issued his Appeal. We shall see something more of the war in Kansas when we come to the debates in which Douglas tried to make clear to a people, from whom reason was flying, what he had done with reference to helping Kansas to a constitution such as she might have by a free count and a fair ballot.

It remains, perhaps, to refer to the most notable, as he was the most notorious, character of the Kansas imbroglio. This was John Brown, who had settled at Lawrence, Kansas, and who was a fanatic to whom robbery and murder were the justifiable means for whatever plans entered his mind.

On the night of May 24, 1856, with his three sons to aid him, he went to the cabin of a settler who had come from Tennessee, and was living near Lawrence. The man's name was Doyle. Brown called him and his two sons forth into the night, where the murderers shot and stabbed one, split open the head of another, also cutting off his arms and legs. The third was mangled, and had his fingers chopped off. Then Brown took the horses of the dead Doyles and decamped. This is a sample of Brown's raids and crimes. The Doyle murder was brought to the attention of the Congressional Committee by the motion of a Democratic member very soon after it happened. This committee was taking evidence in Kansas at the time, touching the situation. It was proposed to the Committee that evidence be adduced with reference to Brown's murders. Sherman of Ohio, and Howard of Michigan, who were the majority of the Committee, refused to summon witnesses on this subject; and when the report of the Committee was made to Congress it contained no mention of Brown's infamous atrocity. This was the beginning of the deification of Brown, until at last his name was sung by the Northern troops carrying flame and sword through Georgia and around to the capital of South Carolina.

These bloody and riotous events in Kansas, and there were many of them, did not always end in success for the Beecher Bibles. On one occasion three hundred so-called pro-slavery men attacked

LINCOLN GRADUALLY AWAKES

Brown, who had thirty or more brigands under his command, and overcame them. In all such conflicts there will be partisans for either side, and there will be much said of the wrong and the right, of who started the fight, and who was animated by the purest motives in its prosecution. As this anarchical condition grew worse and worse in Kansas, the press proportionately increased its publication of inflammatory news matter, and in the utterance of mordant editorial comment. Newspapers accused each other of being responsible for these depredations and crimes, as the New York *Express,* a Whig paper, laid at the door of Greeley's *Tribune* responsibility for "all that is bitter and atrocious in the modern school of politics." This charge was made with good foundation; for no man in American history did more to stir evil passions by a peculiar journalistic malevolence and misrepresentation than Horace Greeley. His exit from this world was, in its loneliness and its rejection, at the hands of men whom he had led so deviously, fitting to the last degree. Some gods are just.

The months went by with these cyclones roaring around Lincoln's ears. Evidently, however, he was thinking. In August of 1855 he wrote to his friend Speed as follows: "I think I am a Whig; but others say there are no Whigs and that I am an abolitionist. When I was in Washington I voted for the Wilmot Proviso as good as forty times; and I never heard of anyone attempting to unwhig me for that. I now do no more than oppose the extension of slavery. I am not a Know-nothing; that is certain. How could I be? How can anyone who abhors the oppression of the negroes be in favor of degrading classes of white people? Our progress in degeneracy appears to me to be pretty rapid. As a nation we began by declaring that 'all men are created equal.' We now practically read it 'all men are created equal except negroes.' When the Know-nothings get control, it will read 'all men are created equal, except negroes, foreigners and Catholics.' When it comes I shall prefer emigrating to some country where they make no pretence of loving liberty—to Russia, for instance, where despotism can be taken pure, and without the alloy of hypocrisy." In another place he wrote, "the slave breeders and slave traders are a small, odious, and detested class among you; and yet in politics they dictate the course of all of you, and are as completely your masters as you are the master of your negroes." If Lincoln could only have seen that every engine of the mercantile system of economics—banks of issue, tariffs, national debts, a currency controllable by political cliques, and colonial possessions were also the masters of the producers, who were enslaved and always had been in England enslaved by these surreptitious manipulators of a country's wealth, it would have been all different with our history. He would then have been the Jefferson of his day. For in truth, though slavery was also a part of the mercantile theory and practice, it was as nothing in its power compared to the other machineries named, and in virtue of the fact that these other contrivances were not visible to the eye, while slavery was. Slavery of the negro as it existed in the South was wiped away; the other slaveries are more powerful in America than ever, and largely as the result of the War. The whole history of the South was that it asked little at the hands of the Federal Government. It was, to a degree, corrupted at times by the tariff; but being an agricultural country it did not request many favors. While the North, pursuing manufacture, demanded more and more tariff as protection for its industries, which the South, with its limited representation, could not resist.

On February 22, 1856, the Republican Party was organized on a national basis at Pittsburgh, which called a nominating convention to meet in Philadelphia on June 17. Its emergence into American political life was viewed with profound concern by many of the Whigs. Rufus Choate declared, "The first duty then, of Whigs, not merely as patriots and as citizens, but as Whigs, is to defeat and dissolve the new geographical party, calling itself Republican. By what vote can I do most to prevent the madness of the times from working its maddest act—the permanent formation and the actual present triumph of a party which knows one half of America only to hate and dread it; from whose unconsecrated and revolutionary banner fifteen stars are erased or have fallen; in whose national anthem the old and endeared airs of the Eutaw Springs, and the King's Mountain, and Yorktown, and those later of New Orleans, and Buena Vista and Chapultepec, breathe no more?" Webster's son, Fletcher, attacked the "sectional or black Republican Party," and became a Democrat. James B. Clay, the son of Henry, joined the Democrats, saying that the success of the Republican

Party would be "the dissolution of the Union." And in Springfield Lincoln's old time Whig friends denounced the Republican movement, and declared that the Whigs should not be sold out to black Republicanism. Where was Lincoln to take his stand?

If Lincoln be taken for just what he was at the time, it is easy to see why he procrastinated. If what he did and did not do be tested by the proportions of the colossal figure which he has become in the American imagination, then he seems to have been at the time under the spell of a negative influence, which may not with correctness be called conservatism, but is rather akin to weakness and poor spiritedness, and even cowardice. If he was as great in mind and in heart as he has been made by the processes of time, he was drugged in these days and could not effect his will and his thinking. The truth is that he was the man that this study up to this point shows him to have been. He did not know what to do; and there was no fire in him to burn up and light the way. Neither he nor anyone, for that matter, proposed a constitutional amendment by which slavery might have been abolished in 1910, fifty years after these days. It is true that there were 33 states then, of which 15 were Southern, so that such an amendment could not have passed if the South had stood against it. But slavery was an anachronism, and its life was waning. If there had been sensible discussion of such a plan, with provision for compensation to the slave owners for their slaves, the feelings of the Southern people would have been touched. Instead there was nothing done but to wring the nose of the South, and about an institution for which everyone admitted the South was not primarily responsible. It was not a very good show of magnanimity to talk of the sin of slavery when you had nothing to lose monetarily whatever happened to it. It was natural to defend it with religion and without religion when your fortune was bound up with it, particularly to defend it against those who were in equal fault with reference to something else. On the one hand the South wanted the Constitution observed, and the rights of the states respected. She was keeping to herself as much as possible. What she gained in the new territories was substantially nothing beyond the recognition of a principle upon which she insisted. She might have gone to New Mexico and to Kansas and Nebraska even with her states' rights doctrine; but she could not have taken slavery there. On the other hand there were Sumner and his kind whose lofty ideas were so intimately related to cruelty, and which needed the bayonet and the torch, which they afterward won, for their realization.

There was no supremely great man in the country to speak out. The American poets had dedicated themselves to Hebraic-Puritanism. Emerson was not so bound up with the fate of the multitude that he could not see the claims of philosophy and behold wider horizons than tariffs and slavery. Douglas in 1856 was only 43 years old, and gave promise of growing yet. But like the statesmen of the time, and as statesmen usually are, he was frankly unincumbered by any idealism, unless that be called such which bound him to adhere with eloquence to the principle of popular sovereignty as against central supremacy. His mind was vigorous and capable of expansion from these years forward. He had courage and clearness of mind above all his contemporaries. He had a coherent set of ideas, which no one else had, especially Lincoln. By his outspokenness, his intellectual courage, his readiness in debate in the Senate, and his imaginative conception of a great Republic, which spanned the continent, but in which local power was jealously preserved, his figure stands more distinctly limned than any of the men of the hour. If both he and Lincoln had died in 1856, or 1858, after the debates, it would be Douglas, not Lincoln who would be the more visible figure today; and as it is, with Douglas almost lost to the interest of biographers, he yet remains a book put aside on the shelf which some day history will take down in wonder that it should so long have been left unread.

If one can ever predicate a happier issue in the world's affairs upon the basis of some course having been taken than that which was taken, there is safety in saying that had the ideas of Webster and Clay and Douglas been followed through, with respect to allowing the territories to control slavery for themselves, by which the survival of the institution would have been committed to the gravitational workings of Nature, there would have been a peaceful solution of the whole problem. It was a plan worth every serious consideration, when the alternative was war, so clearly forecast by men like Choate, and by Webster in his speech of March 7, 1850, and by other competent minds of the time, from the days of Jefferson's troubled anxiety over the Missouri Compromise. As no one would listen to the approach of the storm, except to cower, to run, to stand inert, to defy its power, the America of that day moved along an oblivious way which led to disaster. There was no irrepressible conflict except that of men's own making, and that was not one to be invested with a mystical will which led men, and was beyond their control. It was a conflict capable of having been quieted by regard for the line which divided the business of the South from the business of the North. The South was not trying to invade the free states with her institution, nor attempting to persuade the North to adopt it. But the North was shooting across the line with pamphlets and incitements, and with menaces. In this sense only was the conflict irrepressible. The antagonism of moralities cannot in the light of the facts thrill the heart. If the poems on slavery of Whittier and Longfellow did not make the best use of the material, which better poets might have made of it, they expressed the level of the ethical passion of the time, and rose to all that any American prophet could extract from a warfare of ideas, involved with matters of liberty not greatly affected by negro subjection.

In Lincoln's case there is no point where his once-made and undeveloping conscience underwent a sudden transformation, and awoke to a new life, definitely and at once, new clothed with power and vision. Men have found another mind and life when religious disquietude has driven them forth from the tombs. The sight of suffering and oppressed workers has changed the philosophy of some men. Keats in poetry found himself through Spenser and Homer, and Shaw confessed that Socialism made a man of him. This conversion did not come to Lincoln. We find Lincoln in 1856 just where he was in 1837; and when he delivered the "house divided against itself" speech, to be noticed, he posed the moral problem which had raged in his own heart. His own heart was divided against itself. On the one side was his allegiance to the law, not so deeply rooted as he believed it to be, however; and on the other side was the problem of slavery which puzzled his intellectual equipment. He did not know what to do about it. Yet his own career required that he should do something about it. What should that be which would not utterly destroy his own ambition, or better still might advance it? The manner and the spirit of Lincoln's political change will demonstrate all this analysis.

On the same day that the Republicans met at Pittsburgh, February 22, 1856, the Illinois Anti-Nebraska editors convened at Decatur, where both Lincoln and Herndon were present. A platform was adopted, which merely opposed the extension of slavery into the territories. All references to prohibition, even then one of the stirring agitations of the Hebraic-Puritans, were studiously omitted. George Schneider, a German editor, offered a plank against the Know-nothings, which was adopted. A committee was appointed to call a state convention, of just those opposed to the Kansas-Nebraska act, it is to be inferred; for the name Republican was conspicuously absent from the call. On the committee appointed were Herndon, an abolitionist-Whig, Gillespie, a friend of Lincoln's, who was a Know-nothing, and Koerner, a German Democrat. In this way cautious politics was played, for the German vote had become one worth winning in Illinois. These men acted as if they were afraid, as if they were sneaking up upon the enemy in the darkness. They did not stand forth as vigorous radicals are wont to do. An exception to this criticism must be made in favor of Herndon, for he had joined the Republicans on October 5, 1854, in the Codding convention which Lincoln avoided by stealing away to Tazewell County, thereby confusing, if not wholly denying his identification with the abolitionist principles of that hybrid gathering. If the movement should prove prosperous there was something to be claimed of advantage to himself in the fact that his law partner and intimate, Herndon, was in the Codding consultation; if the movement came to nothing, then he could say with truth that he was in Tazewell County, and, as he did say in the debates, that he had nothing to do with it and knew nothing of its platform. But further, in Decatur, Lincoln was offered the nomination for governor at the hands of this group; but he passed the proffered honor with the self-deprecatory remark that it would not do for an old line Whig like himself to be at the head of the ticket; that it would be better to choose an out-and-out Anti-Nebraska Democrat. Lincoln did, however, make a speech to these delegates at the Decatur hotel in the evening of this day. It is evident from all this that Lincoln flirted with this gathering; and that he was wooed but not won.

LINCOLN GRADUALLY AWAKES

On May 24, 1856, Herndon convoked a meeting in Sangamon County of all those who favored "the policy of Washington and Jefferson," whatever that was, to select delegates to the Bloomington state convention where these incoherent elements, afraid to name themselves, were to convene the latter part of May. Perhaps Herndon was now tired of Lincoln's dilatory ways and ventured to take the chance of pushing Lincoln into the movement; perhaps he and Lincoln had had some understanding, something indicated in the way of an exchange of looks or nod of heads. At any rate Herndon signed Lincoln's name at the head of those making this call. As soon as the call became public, Herndon was beset by shocked and terrified men who asked if Lincoln had authorized him to put Lincoln's name at the head of this list. When Herndon replied that he had no authorization from Lincoln so to use his name, the indignation against Herndon was outspoken. "You have ruined him," said the cautious Stuart, who had been elected to the legislature with Lincoln in the fall of 1854. Herndon then sent off a letter to Lincoln in Tazewell County apprising him of what he had done. The spirit of Lincoln's reply seemed to indicate that a load had been taken off his mind; if not that, then that it made little difference one way or the other. There was a touch of abandon in Lincoln's words, of careless humor. There was no tone in them expressing moral satisfaction, nothing that signified that in a cause so just the use of his name was permissible and that the worthiness of the movement exacted the decision of all conscientious men. Lincoln merely said, "All right; go ahead. Will meet you radicals and all." Radicals and all! Even he could stand radicals in these days when the world spirit was concealing its purposes, when the currents of life drifted here and there deceiving the eye as to their direction. Something might come to pass to give definiteness to the days; if not, what was lost? Could he be more wedged in and weather bound than he now was? The Whig Party, that object of his long devotion, was dissolving. His old friends, like Browning, were abandoning the Whig position of the platform of 1852. Where would he be left if all, if many, of the strong Whigs broke the old ranks and hastened forward to form a new line with an advance guard made up of radicals, and already standing forth facing whatever fate was to come?

Hence it was that Lincoln suffered himself to be chosen as a delegate to the Bloomington convention. But Lincoln stood by his old form in demanding that the platform should be conservative, and that it should be written by men like himself, and like Browning. One does not, to join a political party, sign some roster, or make some party pledge, of necessity. It only happened that, as at Bloomington on May 29, 1856, the Whig Party died, and the Republican Party, its heir, was born, Lincoln may be said to have joined the Republican Party on this date. From thenceforth in Illinois the Republican Party was rising and waging war upon Douglas as the head of the Democratic Party, and with Lincoln as the antagonist sent forth to destroy the author of the Kansas-Nebraska Act.

The task before Lincoln and his associates was to abolitionize the Whigs, and to join with the Anti-Nebraska Democrats in the formation of an army to overcome Douglas. Douglas characterized their policy in this way, and the facts fully justified him in doing so. And already Lincoln, who was following the circuit as the date for the Bloomington convention approached, was sometimes in high spirits, and at other times sunk in his characteristic melancholy. He had fears, at intervals, that corrupt Whigs, as he expressed himself, in the stress of this new alignment, would join the Democrats; in more hopeful moments he believed that both the Democratic and Whig parties were reliable at heart and would prove themselves to be so upon test.

Lincoln found gathered at Bloomington many of the strong and leading Whigs; but also some former Democrats of prominence, one of whom was John M. Palmer, who was a renegade to the Democratic Party and was imbued with all the rancour of an apostate. This was the man who was governor of Illinois when President Grant sent troops to Chicago to handle the disorder which followed upon the great fire there in 1871. He resented the action of Grant on the basis of states' rights. Afterward he was sent to the Senate by the Democrats of Illinois. Still later he led a bolters' ticket against Bryan in 1896. He was a man not animated by independence of thinking, but by the willfulness which marks the truculence of the dissenter. Altogether the Bloomington assemblage was made up of incoherent elements, all jealous and all watchful of each other,

LINCOLN GRADUALLY AWAKES 239

without a basis of unity except hatred of Douglas. The task devolved upon the Whigs, Lincoln, Browning, and Lincoln's other Whig friends, to mold this mob of sharked-up resolutes into working form, to keep them sane, to force them to subordinate their angers and their plotted revenges to the main purpose of organizing a party capable of winning the people. If they came forth from their deliberations divided, how could they expect the electorate to be harmonious?

The times were very tumultuous and growing worse. Into Bloomington poured the Chicago papers, heralding riot and murder in Kansas; while all around was news of the daily flouting on the part of the North of the Fugitive Slave Act of 1850, and the consequent rising wrath of the South. How did Lincoln deal with this spirit of ruin, with these couriers of fanaticism which were hastening the country into war? Browning drew the platform as Lincoln sat by in collaboration. Its preamble was false, from its declaration that those assembled meant to forego all former differences of opinion, to the announcement that the intention of this new party was to bring the government back to the "principles and practices of Jefferson." There was not a delegate present worth noting who believed in Jefferson's principles, since the whole purpose of the assemblage was to carry to more dangerous extremity the policy which Jefferson had denounced in the Missouri Compromise. Could Lincoln have been oblivious to this historic truth? There was an attempt in the platform to placate the Germans without offending the Knownothings. Hence it was promulgated that liberty of conscience as well as political freedom were written in the Constitution; and we will "proscribe no one on account of religious opinions, or in consequence of his place of birth." As to Douglas it contained this language: He "has given the lie to his past history, proved himself recreant to the free principles of his Government, violated the confidence of the people." With the mob turned loose upon America, the bitterness of the times was aggravated by a plank which excoriated the repeal of the Missouri Compromise, as an "open and aggravated violation of the plighted faith of the states," and to "force slavery into Kansas against the known wishes of the legal voters of that territory"; was a tyrannous denial of the right of self-government. Could mendacity be better calculated to whip the mob into deeper fury? The platform went so far as to declare that Congress had the power to prohibit slavery in the territories. We shall see that Lincoln was more cautious in making a constitutional interpretation on this subject. In the Freeport debate with Douglas he declared it was the right and duty of Congress to prohibit slavery in the territories; for in the Lincoln dialectic there was a right and duty where the power could not be deduced from the Constitution. If not there was no point in using the words "right and duty," instead of the word "power." To finish with the convention work, a state central committee was appointed, Lincoln was sent as a delegate to the National Convention to be held at Philadelphia on June 17, 1856; but the name Republican was not adopted by the convention as a designation of the new party. With these things settled, Lincoln was called on for a speech.

That Lincoln did not expect to address the convention is proven by the fact that he had not, according to his custom, written out beforehand the remarks which he made. Undoubtedly he meant to let the circumstances determine whether he spoke or not. Perhaps it would be wise to remain silent. Again the hour might require an utterance which could not be decided upon in advance. If he had been of the crusader spirit he would have gone to Bloomington with something prepared out of his convictions to impress upon these men, and with which to win them to his vision. That was not the case. The result was that he spoke extemporaneously, and what he said has come down to us as the Lost Speech. But Herndon, who had now intrigued his idol into the present commitment, such as it was, sat in the room in an ecstacy as Lincoln worked himself into oratorical fervor. Soon he lost track of what Lincoln was saying and could not proceed with taking notes. But the devoted Whitney recorded Lincoln's words. Joseph Medill, at the time a reporter on the venomous *Chicago Tribune*, and present when Lincoln spoke, afterward verified Whitney's notes. But there are other means of verification. Much that Whitney reported parallels Lincoln's other speeches, so that on the whole it may be said that the speech was measurably preserved. There is internal evidence also that Whitney's version is sufficiently accurate. Who but Lincoln could have said, "We must not promise what we ought not, lest we be called upon to perform what we cannot"? In antitheses of this platitudinous character, very deceiving to an audience, and very valuable as mottoes to those who will not declare their full minds, Lincoln's genius was fecund. He observed that in the peaceable and orderly fashion of the present convention was public opinion to be emphasized. For if this were not done, "blood will flow,"—perhaps other blood than that shed by John Brown, and by the machinations of the Emigrant Aid Societies! The Missouri Compromise had to be restored; that is, the quarrels of 1850 must be reopened. "Men who will march up to the mouth of the loaded cannon without shrinking will run from the terrible name of Abolitionist." Lincoln was here speaking for himself for he had run to Tazewell County. He referred to the assault on Sumner in the Senate. "The fearless Sumner was beaten into insensibility, and is now slowly dying; while senators who claim to be gentlemen and Christians stood by, countenancing the act, and even applauding it afterward in their places in the Senate. Even Douglas, our man, saw it all and was within helping distance, yet let the murderous blows fall unopposed. Then at the other end of the line, at the very time Sumner the man was being murdered, the city of Lawrence was being destroyed for the crime of Freedom." This incendiary talk to the "peaceable and orderly" convention which was to register calm public opinion! The present troubles were caused by "this man Douglas" and he will be carried in triumph through the state, which shows where the times tend. But the South was entitled to a Fugitive Slave Law, because that was the constitutional bargain. But why denounce Brooks, who assaulted Sumner, when he and his kind "are the cat's paws, and did what only the Kansas-Nebraska Act made necessary? This man Douglas and his supporters in Congress were more guilty than a thousand Joneses and Stringfellows with all their murderous practices." But calmness and moderation would make converts for the Republicans. "Be patient." "As sure as God reigns and school children read, that black foul lie can never be consecrated into God's hallowed truth," which was what he said about slavery, though willing to give the South the Fugitive Slave Law, and to let the institution alone in the states.

Let all unite in harmony and appeal to the good sense and conscience of the people. But the repeal of the Missouri Compromise had furnished the death dealing rifle, the bristling cannon, the smoking embers of the herald of Freedom, the stake on freedom's soil. "We see it in Christian statesmen, and Christian newspapers, and Christian pulpits applauding the cowardly act of a low bully, who crawled upon his victim behind his back and dealt him the deadly blow." Yet retaliation in kind was not justified. "Let the legions of slavery use bullets, but let us wait patiently till November and fire ballots at them in return." The Fugitive Slave Law he had already approved; but while when a horse was stolen everybody turned out to hang the thief, if a man was stolen, "a shade or two darker than I am," the same crowd would hang the persons who helped him to liberty. "The next thing you will see is shiploads of negroes from Africa at the wharf at Charleston; for one thing is as truly lawful as the other; and these are bastard notions we have got to stamp out, else they will stamp us out. Those who deny freedom to others, deserve it not for themselves, and under the rule of a just God cannot long retain it." He should have used the word Jehovah. "If this thing is allowed to continue, it will be but one step further to impress the same rule in Illinois." There was not the remotest chance of this becoming true. "We must make an appeal to battle and to the God of hosts; but calm and reasonable appeals would probably make a resort to force unnecessary." Where and how and upon whom was this force to be used?

What was the effect of this speech? Although 30 southern counties in Illinois had failed to send delegates to the Bloomington Convention, the northern counties, where New England was more numerously represented, took fire after Lincoln's speech. When he finished and was being congratulated, when some told him that he was now in line for the presidency, observers remarked that his eyes confessed the possibility of that achievement, and that an ambition to strive for it had entered his thinking. On May 1, a great meeting was held in Chicago in the court house square, where fifteen thousand dollars were subscribed for Kansas, while revolvers, balls, cans of powder, rifles, and shotguns were donated for the calm and deliberate settlement of the great question of the hour. The *New York Tribune* reported that "The prairies are all ablaze." It was true, but the fire was to be hotter and more extended in about five years, in 1861.

That these wild and whirling words came out of no philosophy,

LINCOLN GRADUALLY AWAKES

no reasoned survey of the questions discussed, that, in a plain word, Lincoln did not know what he was talking about, is shown by the inconsistency between different portions of this speech; but this is best proven by something which he said, which has been reserved for final comment. He contended that the time would come when "only local law," not the Constitution, would "shelter a slave holder." This meant that the Constitution might recognize slavery and by Congressional action or inaction let it into a territory, but that the local law of the territory would determine whether it could stay there. This was the very doctrine that Webster had announced in his speech of March 7, 1850; it was the constant argumentation of Douglas during the pendency of the Kansas-Nebraska Act, and it was reiterated time and again by Douglas in the debates. How did this stand with the Lincoln announcement that it was the "right and duty" of Congress to keep slavery out of the territories? How did it harmonize with menaces of force, with God's just law, with all the rest that Lincoln said in this incoherent philippic?

Thus the sectional Republican Party was born in Illinois. It was conceived in hatred and mothered in hatred, and went forth from a diseased womb without a name, because a name would have been a mark by which men could know it, and take arms against it. Its mission was to bruise and break, to blow rams' horns that the walls of iniquity might fall, to walk with David and his army to the walls of faithless Jerusalem, and there to shout, "Lift up your heads, O ye gates, and the king of glory shall come in." "Who is this King of glory?" Springfield was to ask. And Herndon, who had prepared for a great ovation to Lincoln, as we have already seen, would have had Springfield believe that the King of Glory was the rail splitter of New Salem who had risen to seal the doom of heathenism. But Springfield, in its blindness, in the coldness of its uninspired intellect, would have none of the man who had thrilled the Bloomington malcontents. Yet before Herndon and the janitor of the hall, named John Paine, Lincoln could say with unctuous resignation, "the age is not dead; it liveth as sure as our Maker liveth." God is not mocked, nor now was he to be mocked when there were men like Wendell Phillips in Massachusetts to rejoice that the vials of apocalyptic wrath had been opened, and the smoke of the pit released, that there was now a sectional party, that the line had been drawn between the North and the South with the chosen of God on the one side and the sons of Belial on the other. The Union was divided when this hatred stood forth definitely as the creed of a new party in the North; the secession of states against which that hate was directed was like the departure of a wife from a house where the marriage has already been dissolved by the loathing of her husband. The union between two of anything, whether in the material or the spiritual world, where hate has arisen between them, may be maintained by artificial cohesion of some kind; but it is not union, it is not atomic and internal. It is effected by external clamps, by rivets and bolts. The professed love of Hebraic-Puritanism is and was inverted hate, which has read the will of God and means to carry it out, though the whole land be made one tomb. In the spirit of this detestable philosophy Lincoln at Bloomington shouted, "We must make an appeal to battle and to the God of hosts. . . . We will say to the Southern disunionists we won't go out of the Union, and you shan't." The Union of amity and coöperation and respect for the rights of the states being destroyed at this time, there was nothing left but the sword to determine whether the North should raise imperial power over the South, or whether the South might win its independence as the colonies won theirs in 1776 from England and against her like assertion of the right to rule.

Meantime, in the balancing of all arguments, in the performance of the duty to see comprehendingly everything in issue, one must not forget the Southern planter, the coarse, opulent tyrant with his bloodhounds and his whip, with his chains and his blasphemous contempt for God's law, moreover with his perverse reading of the Bible whereby slavery was justified! One must not overlook what was said about this planter's long domination of the Congress, and how he had done it by the inequitable three-fifths clause. The infamous packing of the Supreme Court by the slavocracy was also an item to be industriously circulated in order that Jerusalem might be reclaimed, for the glorious entry of the King of Glory, shouting the pæans of the God of battles. These lurid and melodramatic pictures, drawn from Oriental hate hiding itself behind palms of peace and good will were not to be kept away from the eyes of a deceived people; but rather shown the more day by day, until the sword was drawn. All speeches and pamphlets, and lectures in back halls, and New England poems, and editorials of abolitionist scribblers were henceforth to be saturated with that moral hypocrisy to which the American ear lends itself so willingly, in the unctuous self-dramatization of self-righteousness, but which in practice it neglects save as it redounds to political or business advantage.

Four days after the Bloomington meeting, which we have just considered, the Democratic Party met in convention at Cincinnati. In order that we may see what choices were presented to the electorate at the time, it will be well to examine the pronouncements of its platform as well as those of the Whig Party, which was soon now to surrender for good, but was still battling to hold its historic forces in line. In this Democratic convention Douglas would have been nominated, except that the New York delegation, which was for him, was seated only in part; and thus for the time he passes from our chronicle. The Democratic platform contained these words in its first resolution: "We will contrast [the Democratic creed] with the creed and practice of Federalism, under whatever name or form, which seeks to palsy the will of the constituent, and which conceives no imposture too monstrous for the popular credulity." As to the tariff, it said: "That justice and sound policy forbid the Federal government to foster one branch of industry to the detriment of any other, or to cherish the interests of one portion to the injury of another portion of our common country." Of the bank, which was dormant, but was still waiting its chance to come back to power, it said: "That the Congress has no power to charter a national bank; that we believe such an institution one of deadly hostility to the best interests of the country, dangerous to our republican institutions and the liberties of the people, and calculated to place the business of the country within the control of a concentrated money power." It approved the presidential veto power, "which has saved the American people from the corrupt and tyrannical domination of the Bank of the United States, and from a corrupting system of general internal improvements." It declared that Congress had no power under the Constitution to interfere with or control the domestic institutions of the states; and that the Democratic Party would resist all attempts at renewing in or out of Congress the agitation of the slavery question. The platform recognized the right of Kansas and Nebraska to form a constitution with or without slavery, as they might choose to do. It pledged itself to sustain and advance constitutional liberty, and to that end it would resist all monopolies, and exclusive legislation for the benefit of a few. "The time has come," it announced, "for the people of the United States to declare themselves in favor of free seas and progressive free trade." It gave strong support to the Monroe Doctrine. There was nothing lacking which made it a manifesto of national destiny, scarcely inadequate to the needs of the present time.

Though the Whig Party did not meet until after the Republicans, or People's Party as it still called itself, or was called by Greeley and others, it will be better for a perspective upon the whole field to notice it first. It met at Baltimore on September 17, 1856. The third resolution of its platform was as follows: "That the government of these United States was formed by the conjunction in political unity of widespread geographical sections, materially differing not only in climate and products, but in their social and domestic institutions, and that any cause that shall permanently array these sections in political hostility and organized parties, founded only on geographical distinctions, must inevitably prove fatal to the continuance of the National Union." For authority for this appeal, the name and example of Washington were invoked. It further declared: "That all who revere the Constitution and Union, must look with alarm at the parties in the field in the present presidential campaign—one claiming only to represent sixteen Northern states, and the other appealing to the passions and prejudices of the Southern states." This animadversion against the Democrats may have been justified by taking into account what the Democratic stump was saying, but the Democratic platform made no such appeal to the Southern states.

The delegates to the People's or Republican convention were not chosen by any settled rule, nor was much regard paid to the number of votes to which a state was entitled. All the Northern states, however, were represented, and a scattering representation from Delaware, Kentucky and Maryland. Many preachers were present as participants, for Hebraic-Puritanism had at last found a political instrument. Giddings, of the Chase Appeal, was there, and the temperance lecturer Codding, from whom Lincoln had run away to Tazewell County in 1854. There was no lack of decorum, meaning by that that there were no assaults and batteries, but the spirit of the occasion was bellicose, it was hard and resolute. Whigs, Know-nothings, malcontents, men hungry for office and power, minds whose fanatical thinking had split great questions into small issues and made these the test of righteousness, composed the assembly. The first resolution of the platform appealed to the Declaration of Independence, whose author the Whigs had despised and maligned for thirty years, following up the hatred of the Federal Party, the father of the Whig. Lincoln was to use the Declaration to the full hereafter; but now he disliked the name Republican. It savored too much of the Democratic taint, despite the sanitative spirit of Jefferson. In the second resolution there was a deceitful weaving of material. One might be led to believe from reading it that the Fathers of the Constitution had abolished slavery from the Northwest Territory, and that, having done so, they proceeded to ordain that "no person shall be deprived of life, liberty, or property without due process of law," and hence "it becomes our duty to maintain this provision of the Constitution against all attempts to violate it for the purpose of establishing slavery in the territories." The third resolution declared: "That the Constitution confers upon Congress sovereign powers over the territories," and that "it is both the right and the imperative duty of Congress to prohibit those twin relics of barbarism—Polygamy and Slavery." It referred to Kansas as a place where the freedom of the press had been abridged, and where murder and robberies and arsons "have been instigated and encouraged, and the offenders have been permitted to go unpunished; that all these things have been done with the knowledge, sanction and procurement of the present national administration; and that, for this high crime against the Constitution, the Union, and humanity, we arraign that administration, the president, his advisers, agents, supporters, apologists and accessories, either before or after the fact, before the country and before the world; and that it is our fixed purpose to bring the actual perpetrators of these atrocious outrages and their accomplices to a sure and condign punishment hereafter." These were damnatory accusations. It was another thing to sustain them. But that was not important now. The objective was to embroil the country. The proof of these scurrilities lay in war yet to be waged, in which their falsity or truth were swept away in the storm of mightier ambitions. But finally this so-called convention, largely made up of centralists and the agents of monopolists, said no word favoring a tariff. The time had not come to unmask with reference to that partiality, nor with reference to the bank. As for freedom of the seas, the Monroe Doctrine, with constitutional liberty, with liberty rightly so called in any sense, what interest had this assemblage of preachers, moralists, and radicals in questions so far below the holy need of taking Jerusalem and ushering in the King of Glory?

This platform was read by David Wilmot amid shouts and amens, Wilmot of Proviso fame; and the adventurer Frémont was nominated for president. Lincoln wanted McLean, then a judge of the Supreme Court, to receive the nomination. It mattered not to Lincoln now that Phillips had denounced McLean for having made "more pro-slavery law than all the pro-slavery judges put together." There were nineteen delegates from Illinois, Whigs and Know-nothings, who agreed with Lincoln in preferring McLean to Frémont; but the radicals would have nothing to do with McLean. It happened then that one of the Illinois delegates, by way of reprisal, sought to capture the nomination for the vice presidency for Lincoln; but this failed. Meantime Lincoln wrote a letter to Trumbull, saying that nine tenths of the Anti-Nebraska men had come from the Whigs, and that the new party could not win if the Whigs were not placated. As for himself, he would stand by the new party, although none too strong for it. "I am in, and shall go for anyone nominated, unless he be platformed expressly or impliedly, on some ground which I may think wrong."[1] In this chaotic state of affairs, where success was not determined by a little here or a little there, it was not courage but caution that made Lincoln resolve matters in this fashion. The new party might wither away after one campaign. The Whig Party might, by some conceivable possibility, come back; and then those who had not gone too far from Whiggery would not be unforgivable apostates.

So the campaign of 1856 came on, with Fillmore running on

[1] Tracy, 66–68.

the Whig platform, Frémont on the People's and Buchanan on the Democrats'. Raging lies upon lies were blown over the country, pamphlets describing Brooks's assault upon Sumner, Sumner's speeches, and the like, and in Illinois Herndon was one of the prime distributors of these unbalancing anathemas. Lincoln had the delicate and careful task of persuading as many Whigs as possible to desert to Frémont; he was abolitionizing the Whigs, as Douglas phrased it afterward, and so he let Kansas severely alone, departing from the course of his inflammatory Bloomington castigation. He contented himself in an unreported speech, unreported save for the account in the *Illinois Daily State Journal,* with giving a historical survey of Kansas up to the time that the disturber Douglas had brought about the passage of the Kansas-Nebraska Act. Lincoln was appointed on a Kansas relief committee, but declined to act on the ground that he was too busy with other affairs. As he went about making speeches for Frémont, he took occasion to cultivate the Germans. Seward and others were brought to Illinois to campaign for Frémont. Greeley's *Tribune* circulated freely, with its combustible incantations, so well worded to excite the most dangerous passions of human nature. But the Whigs did not give up. They started a newspaper at Springfield, and labored to show the people that disunion was near if sectional animosity was thus fomented and sent upon its deadly mission.

Lincoln addressed the people at Galena, Illinois. Reversing his former position, he declared that the only thing that endangered the Union was the restoration of the Missouri Compromise. Thus what he had before denounced Douglas for doing must be left where it was, lest the Union be dissolved. If the Republicans had the power to restore the Missouri Compromise, they had no desire to dissolve the Union. Therefore, let the Missouri Compromise alone. Besides, it was said, he went on, it would be unconstitutional to repass the Compromise. Whether such a law would be unconstitutional or not was a question for the Supreme Court, "and we will submit to its decisions; and if you do also, there will be an end of the matter." These words should not be forgotten when reading Lincoln's attacks upon the Supreme Court for the Dred Scott decision, made in the debates with Douglas, two years from the time we are now reviewing. It may be a vain task to try to follow the inconstant mind of Lincoln, but at least its vacillations can be recorded. Would the Democrats, he asked, stand by the Supreme Court? "If not, who are the disunionists—you or we?" The answer is that he was, because he hawked at the Supreme Court and undertook to undermine respect for its decision.

For the first time in the history of America women took part in a political campaign. In Illinois they were distributing pamphlets for the Kansas relief organizations. And the clergymen, saving the Catholic and Episcopal priests, were acting for the Republican cause. In spite of all this mob activity, Kansas was becoming composed as the campaign approached its end. The Democrats were swarming over Illinois, listening to Douglas, who drew tens of thousands to ponder his appeals for the Union, for peace, and for sanity. Meanwhile Lincoln was referring to Douglas contemptuously as "that man Douglas." At Belleville Lincoln made one of his ablest efforts. His peroration was that of Webster in the latter's reply to Hayne in 1830; but Lincoln spoke it as if it were his own. We shall find along the way that Lincoln nearly always drew upon someone else for his ideas. Sometimes he did, however, improve upon their former expression. Forgetting the tenor and meaning of much that he had said for the Union and against disunionists, he declared that the nation could not endure half slave and half free—yet the Missouri Compromise was not to be restored! He had not yet come to "the house divided against itself" phrasing of this sophistical preachment. That belonged later, when he saw the advantage of enlisting the support of religionists by founding himself upon the Bible, which had so largely made the culture of Illinois suburbanism. He threw money hostility into an already tangled discussion by saying at Belleville that the slaves were worth a "thousand million dollars," whose market value would be doubled if slavery were extended. For this money reason were the Southern people united to slavery extension. Opposed to this was the North, acting entirely upon "moral principle," where there was no bond of "pecuniary interest." There were no bank and no tariff at stake, be it interpolated!

So the campaign ended in dust, abuse, falsehoods, mob appeals, dodging and turning, twisting and evading. It was a scene unworthy of civilized men, with these new Republicans playing by far the most unprincipled part. Thousands of Whigs in more or less honest spirit voted the Democratic ticket, and thereby compassed the loss of Illinois to Frémont. Yet he had over 96,000 votes to Buchanan's 105,000 and more; while Millard Fillmore, the straight Whig, received some 37,000 odd votes.

There is another drop that belongs to the *mise en scène* of Lincoln's intellectual operations, and without which his speeches hereafter, and especially his debates with Douglas cannot be satisfactorily followed and understood. This is the Dred Scott case, which had been argued in the Supreme court on February 11, 12, 13 and 14 of 1856, months before Lincoln's speech at Galena. The question raised there was whether Dred Scott, who was a negro, was a citizen of the United States, and admissible as a suitor in the Federal Courts. Whether Lincoln's remarks at Galena were made with reference to an understanding what the issue in the case was, and whether its determination might not also involve a constitutional construction of the Missouri Compromise, it is yet true that Lincoln said that he would abide by the ruling of the Supreme Court, and that Democrats who would not do so were the "disunionists." What the Dred Scott case was and what the decision of the court was require attention for an understanding of Lincoln.

Chapter XI The Dred Scott Decision

WE shall see that Lincoln argued that the Dred Scott decision was the result of a conspiracy on the part of the slavocracy to nationalize slavery. He contended that much of it was *obiter dicta*, that is, rulings by the way, having no necessary connection with the precise issue, and therefore not binding. With all the rest that he said he laid down a good principle, which was that the decision of the Supreme Court should not be a rule of political action which Congresses were bound not to depart from, in that particular making himself a disciple of Jefferson and Jackson. This principle is safest applied where the Supreme Court has ruled a law to be constitutional, but where the Congress is not obligated for that reason to pass such a law, or the president obligated not to veto it if the Congress does pass it. In the case of the Bank, Marshall held its charter to be within the constitutional power of Congress to grant. But that did not impose any duty upon Jackson to sign a bill for the charter of a new bank. He could veto it with perfect constitutional right. For not only was he sworn to support the Constitution as he understood it, and not as someone else understood it; but as a matter of economic necessity, and of political policy his presidential duty as well imposed the exercise of the veto power. Lincoln's twisting dialectic must be narrowly watched when he practices legerdemain with these subtleties. What the Kansas-Nebraska Act had done with the Missouri Compromise we have seen. If there be anything of force in that law which regards contemporaneous construction of law as making or repealing it; and if the action of an electorate passing upon a party platform may be taken as confirming an act of Congress, then the election of Buchanan on a platform which approved the Kansas-Nebraska Act cannot be disregarded in its bearing upon the status of the Missouri Compromise as it was before the Supreme Court annulled it. The history of the Dred Scott case may now be given.

In 1834 Dr. John Emerson, a surgeon in the United States Army, went from St. Louis, Missouri, to Rock Island, Illinois, tak-

THE DRED SCOTT DECISION 253

ing with him Dred Scott, a negro body servant and slave. Dr. Emerson stayed two years at Rock Island, then he was ordered to Fort Snelling, in Minnesota, where he went, again taking Dred Scott. Here the negro married, with the consent of his owner. Soon after Dr. Emerson was ordered back to St. Louis, and he went, taking with him Dred Scott and his wife. The wife of Dred Scott gave birth to two children, and these, with Dred Scott and his wife, were the slaves of Dr. Emerson. In 1844, Dr. Emerson died, and all these slaves were inherited by Mrs. Emerson, the doctor's widow, who was made administratrix of his estate. In 1846 Dred Scott brought a suit against Mrs. Emerson in one of the Missouri state courts at St. Louis, demanding his liberty. Dred Scott based his right to liberty upon the ground that while he was living with Dr. Emerson at Rock Island he had been made free by the Constitution of Illinois, which forbade slavery; and that while he was in Minnesota, or Wisconsin Territory, to speak strictly, he had been emancipated by virtue of the Missouri Compromise. The trial court in Missouri, a slave state be it noted, awarded Dred Scott his freedom. Mrs. Emerson appealed the case to the Supreme Court of Missouri, which held that, as Dred Scott had returned to Missouri with Dr. Emerson, his status as a slave was resumed. This decision was made in March of 1852.

We come now to the statement of facts which show that if there was any conspiracy to procure the Supreme Court of the United States to rule upon the Missouri Compromise, it was not on the part of any slavocracy, but that it was entered into by abolitionists. In 1850, while the Supreme Court of Missouri had Dred Scott's case under advisement, Mrs. Emerson, the widow, married Dr. Calvin Clifford Chaffee, of Springfield, Massachusetts, who was a Know-nothing and an abolitionist, and who was elected to Congress as such, and remained a member of the House while this litigation was proceeding. As the husband of Mrs. Emerson, he had a property interest in Dred Scott, his wife and children; and in conjunction with his wife, he continued to exercise ownership over the four negroes, though, as an abolitionist, he could have emancipated them at any time. Mrs. Emerson's brother, John F. A. Sanford, lived in New York and was a citizen of that state. With the purpose of creating a controversy between citizens of different states, in order to give a Federal Court jurisdiction, Mrs. Emerson Chaffee made a fictitious bill of sale of Dred Scott to her brother John F. A. Sanford; and then Dred Scott, claiming to be a citizen of Missouri, brought a suit in the Federal Court at St. Louis against Sanford, claiming his freedom under the same state of facts which he had alleged in the litigation in the Missouri state court. Sanford, having his residence in New York, was beyond the process of the Federal Court at St. Louis. To overcome this obstacle Sanford went to St. Louis and there submitted to the service of summons upon him. The suit was brought November 2, 1853, by a lawyer named Field, acting for Scott. Sanford was represented as counsel by an anti-slavery lawyer named Garland, who filed a plea to the jurisdiction of the court in Sanford's behalf, which denied that Dred Scott was a citizen, and raised the right of Dred Scott to sue in the Federal Courts. Dred Scott, alleged the plea, "is a negro of African descent; his ancestors were of pure African blood, and were brought, into this country and sold as negro slaves." To this plea Dred Scott filed a demurrer; and as the court took judicial notice of the Missouri Compromise Act, all the facts were before the court; and the court thereupon held with Dred Scott, and he was free. But this state of affairs did not suffice. The respective attorneys made up an agreed case of the facts as they have been given here; and upon their submission to a jury the same Federal judge reversed his former ruling and instructed the jury that Sanford still owned Dred Scott. So Dred Scott was again a slave. The point was to get the case to the Supreme Court. It was a prearranged plan from the first. Dred Scott, therefore, appealed to the Supreme Court and for his appeal a bond was signed by a son of the man who had sold Dred Scott to Dr. Emerson years before. This was a moot case through and through; and if the Supreme Court had known that it was such there would not have been any Dred Scott decision to trouble the Lincoln and Douglas debates. A moot case is a sort of conspiracy prosecuted for the purpose of getting the opinion of a court where there is no actual controversy, but where the parties, for the sake of their own ulterior interests, or out of curiosity, educe the judgment of the court.

As part of the same propaganda that was being engineered by the abolitionists, a pamphlet was issued at St. Louis on July 1,

THE DRED SCOTT DECISION 255

1854, and circulated over the United States, in which Dred Scott was dramatized as appealing to the people for funds with which to carry his case through the Supreme Court. Dred Scott was made to say, "I am now in the hands of the sheriff of this county, who hires me out and receives my wages. I have no money to pay anybody at Washington to speak for me." A few months before, in May of 1854, while the Kansas-Nebraska Act was stirring the country, and Chase's Appeal had sown suspicion and hatred everywhere, Scott's lawyer, the anti-slavery Field, wrote a letter in which he said that it would be desirable to have all the questions, the Missouri Compromise and everything at issue in Congress, decided by the court. In other words did the "needful rules and regulations" clause of the Constitution warrant Congress in drawing the sectional line of 36° 30'? If that clause did not warrant its enactment, was it the treaty-making power, or in a word where was the power to Congress granted?

When the Supreme Court met in December of 1854, the Dred Scott case was on its docket, placed there in due course by the filing of the records and the action of the clerk. It was precisely like any other case, and no one knew the plot by which the court was about to be used. If Douglas or the Democrats had been in any conspiracy to bring and to prosecute this suit and this appeal, would they have hastened its decision? If they had been back of the institution of this suit on the day that it was started in the Federal Court of St. Louis, November 2, 1853, would they have gone on in January of 1854 to the enactment of the Kansas-Nebraska law, and run the chance of incurring a collision between the theory of territorial sovereignty over slavery and constitutional control over it in the territories? The question answers itself. The Kansas-Nebraska Act was passed and two years elapsed before the Dred Scot case was reached on the docket of the Supreme Court. It abided its regular course, and no one has pretended to the contrary. Neither Field, the anti-slavery lawyer for Scott, nor Garland, the anti-slavery lawyer for Sanford, made any attempt to advance the case for hearing. It was reached in its order on February 11, 1856, and on being called, Montgomery Blair, who was to become Lincoln's postmaster-general in 1861, and who worked for Lincoln's election in 1860, argued the case for Dred Scott. For Sanford appeared

Reverdy Johnson of Maryland, a lawyer of great ability, who had volunteered his professional services because of a firm conviction, long entertained, that the Missouri Compromise was unconstitutional. So the case was argued on February 11, 1856.

In April of 1856 the court held two consultations on the case. It should be remembered that long before this Chief Justice Marshall, in Marbury against Madison, had decided that the Supreme Court possessed the power to annul a law of Congress. This was after that court had disavowed the power. Marshall in that case held that the court had no jurisdiction; and in solving the jurisdictional question it is sometimes necessary to decide the issue, for upon it the jurisdictional right may depend. Hence after the argument the press, in particular Greeley's *Tribune*, began to speak in a captious way about the imagined attitude of the justices. Would they let the case go off on a mere technicality? Would they decide the case on its merits? It was asserted with a sort of menace that, if the court decided against Scott, Justice McLean would overwhelm the whole court with a great dissent; and that Justice Curtis would neglect nothing to give a thorough ruling from his standpoint, of the entire controversy. McLean was a political judge who had long coquetted with the presidency. Before the Republican convention at Philadelphia, June 17, 1856, he had written a long letter to a political supporter in which he said that the Dred Scott case had been continued until December, 1856, and that he was glad that his correspondent liked "my views already publicly avowed as to the constitutional power of the general government over the subject of slavery in the territories." This letter was written in confidence, but a confession so precious could scarcely remain a secret; and it is likely that when Lincoln, in Illinois, in the campaign of 1856, from the stump was proclaiming the duty of everyone to obey and respect the decisions of the Supreme Court, he was the beneficiary of a leak, and that these words of the Judge whom he had known since the days of the McCormick case at Cincinnati in September of 1855, had come to him.

When the Dred Scott case was reached for re-argument, on December 15, 1856, there followed for four days one of the ablest legal contests that the court had ever known. As it was argued for four days in February of 1856, the court had now given days to the patient consideration of the case. In this second argument George Ticknor Curtis, a brother of Justice Curtis sitting in judgment upon the issues, appeared for the specific purpose of arguing the constitutionality of the Missouri Compromise. Curtis faced the whole situation with complete frankness. In regard to the territories he declared that if he had the whole legislative power in his hands, "I would prohibit the relation of master and slave, or permit and sanction it, according to the nature of the soil and climate, the character of the present, or the probable character of the future settlers." This was pragmatism worthy of Douglas himself. He then said that, as to the strict legal question, he believed that Congress had full power to prohibit slavery in the territories, though as a citizen and not as a jurist he was bound to hold that it would be unjust to a portion of the Union to exercise that power, "and in which I never would exercise it." Though Curtis despised the new Republican Party he gave them aid and comfort in his argument by predicating Congressional control of slavery in the territories upon the "needful rules and regulations" clause. When the arguments were concluded, on December 18, 1856, there was rife speculation as to what the court would do. The radicals made threats if the case were not decided their way. If Dred Scott was still held in slavery, they would make trouble for the court; and Stanton went so far as to plant himself upon the Virginia resolutions, saying that, when any law was a plain, deliberate violation of the Constitution, the states have a right to disregard it, and to refuse to obey it; the application being that the same principle governed political attitude toward a decision of the Supreme Court. It is now wonderful to contemplate the constitutional theories of this Republican Party at its inception, and with these to contrast its bitter repudiation of all of them in the War, in the name of Law and Liberty.

On February 15, referred to, the court resolved to ignore the Missouri Compromise entirely, and to base the decision on the ground that Dred Scott's return to Missouri with Dr. Emerson had brought him into slavery again; and that, being a slave, and not a citizen in consequence, he could not have standing as a suitor in the Federal Courts. Justice Nelson of New York was directed to write the opinion of the court accordingly. And so it would have been done except for McLean and Curtis. They announced their purpose now to file separate opinions emphatically affirming the constitutionality of the Missouri Compromise. If this had happened, the court would have presented itself to the country in the position of an absurd division: two Northern justices frankly meeting the Missouri Compromise issue and holding the law valid, and the other seven dodging the question and passing the whole controversy off on a technicality: Scott's mere lack of citizenship for having been returned to Missouri.

History is indebted to a letter of Justice Catron, written to Buchanan, for the full disclosure of what passed in conference among the judges, and what the circumstances and motives were which impelled the final decision of the court. Instead of there being a conspiracy between the justices, if such a thing could be, or a conspiracy between them and Buchanan, or Pierce or Douglas or anyone outside the court, there was on the contrary that difference of opinion, and that spirit in asserting it which belonged to legitimate counsels concerned with arriving at some solution of the case, and the tangles in which contrariety of legal judgment and discussion had involved it. The result of all this was that the Chief Justice, Taney, was directed to write the opinion of the court. On March 7, 1857, before an audience of distinguished lawyers and visitors, Taney, an old man, but of crystalline clarity of mind, and with undiminished vigor of thought, read the opinion of the court, which was that of himself and six other justices, with McLean and Curtis dissenting. Taney's opinion was written in a style of limpid harmony, as if he had set down his reasonings with a "pencil of light." Its logic was massive, it had structural symmetry, it was rich in historical and juridical learning, it was illuminated by a bright but mellow intellectuality. Taney was a man who had been highly trained in the law, he was of profound general studies, and he was of devout mind; while his concurring associates were all men of thorough education, in fact all the justices of the court were college bred except McLean and Catron. The legal reasoning of Taney was far beyond the capacity of Lincoln's mind, and indeed beyond his understanding, as we shall see. Taney considered the history of the Northwest Territory, showing that it had come to the United States under the Articles of Confederation, impressed with the provisions of the compact between Virginia, the people of the Territory, and the United States. He pointed out that when the Constitution was adopted there was no territory belonging to the United States except the Northwest Territory, and that therefore the clause "needful rules and regulations" could speak with no reference to any territory saving this; that "needful rules and regulations" sufficed as a grant of power to Congress to administer the Territory, since the Ordinance of 1787 with its bill of rights, organically provided for legislation by the Territory, while the Ordinance itself was superseded by the adoption of the Constitution, except with reference to its compact, or treaty provisions. As to the Louisiana Purchase he said: "As we have before said, it was acquired by the general government as the representative and trustee of the people of the United States, and it must, therefore, be held in that character for their common and equal benefit; for it was the people of the several states, acting through the agent and representative, the Federal Government, who in fact acquired the territory in question, and the government holds it for their common use until it shall be associated with the other states as a member of the Union. . . . The territory being a part of the United States, the government and the citizens both enter it under the authority of the Constitution with their respective rights defined and marked out." There was much elaborate and detailed discussion of the terms citizen and citizenship, in which reference was made to the laws of many of the states with respect to the status of the negro in them, in which it was shown, that, as in Illinois, which we have already noticed, the negro was not regarded as a citizen. But this phase of the decision need not detain us. There was one pronouncement which so profoundly stated the underlying principle of the American system that there is an ironic paradox in the circumstance that it was called forth by a ruling which made the negro slave property in Kansas and Nebraska. That was the holding that Congress can exercise nothing but authority granted by the Constitution over a territory of the United States. "There is certainly no power," said Taney, "given by the Constitution to establish or maintain colonies bordering on the United States or at a distance, to be ruled and governed at its own pleasure; nor to enlarge its territorial limits in any way except by the admission of new states.

That power is plainly given; and if a new state is admitted it needs no further legislation by Congress, because the Constitution itself defines the relative rights and powers and duties of the state, and the citizens of the state and the Federal Government. But no power is given to acquire territory to be held and governed permanently in that character."

If this rule had been followed, there would have been no Alaska, which was negotiated for by the lofty-minded Sumner; no Porto Rico, Guam, Hawaii and the Philippines. The paradox changed to the other side when the party which warred upon the South for negro freedom turned about in 1899 and entered upon colonial adventure, and did it in the name of Lincoln, the emancipator. That was right enough, however, and only a paradox superficially, for congressional control of the territories, against the Constitution, was congressional control over the Philippines, merely advanced under the specious claims of what a sovereign nation had the right to do. Well did Taney say: "A power therefore in the general government to obtain and hold colonies and dependent territories, over which they might legislate without restrictions would be inconsistent with its own existence in its present form."

Coming then to slavery, Taney said: "The right to traffic in it, [slave property] like an ordinary article of merchandise and property, was guaranteed to the citizens of the United States in every state that might desire it for twenty years. And the government in express terms is pledged to protect it in all future time, if the slave escapes from his owner. This is done in plain words, too plain to be misunderstood. And no word can be found in the Constitution which gives Congress a greater power over slave property, or which entitles property of that kind to less protection than property of any other description. . . . Taking this rule to guide us, it may be safely assumed that citizens of the United States who migrate to a territory belonging to the people of the United States cannot be ruled as mere colonists, dependent upon the will of the general government, and to be governed by any laws it may think fit to impose."

This was essentially the whole of the case so far as the unconstitutionality of the Missouri Compromise was concerned. This deliberate production of the best thought and the most careful reasoning that could be given the case was met by jeers and slanderous words from the radicals, and by charges of conspiracy against the court as having been entered into with the so-called slavocracy. Day by day Greeley denounced the decision of his *Tribune*. It was a part of a plot, of which the Kansas-Nebraska Act was another, to make slavery national. Greeley urged disobedience to the court, then the arming of the North to annul it; then the reconstitution of the court to reverse it. The *Chicago Tribune*, with inflammatory untruthfulness, charged a conspiracy. Another Illinois paper said that Taney was a brother of slave owners, forgetting that the father of Lincoln's wife was a slave owner; and that Taney was the abject tool of the slave oligarchy. The people were advised by other Illinois newspapers to take the government into their own hands, or, as Lincoln phrased the same thing, to overthrow those who had perverted the Constitution. Some journals of Illinois counseled the passing of laws by every republican state defining United States marshals as kidnappers who executed the Fugitive Slave Law, and to back such criminal enforcement by the whole police and military force of the states. The clergy took a hand. The pastor of the Church of the Puritans in New York declared that statesmanship and conscience went together, and that when sin and Satan usurped power everyone was in duty bound to disobey them. Submission to the court was sin. And if there was to be revolution, well and good; for virtue is required for revolution. Taney to all this wild abuse made no reply. He contented himself with saying that the opinion must speak for itself. And finally the safe and conservative press took the ground that there was nothing to be excited about, that slavery never could go into the free states. Slavery would finally be decided by the laws that govern labor and production, declared the *Harper's Weekly* for March 28, 1858. That the states would become all slave or all free was a forecast that entered the mind of no man of judgment. It was confined to the vaporings of radicals; and to Lincoln's speech of "the house divided against itself." But contemporaneous with Lincoln's foolish suspicions were Seward's too.

In the Senate Seward charged chicane in special pleading; he accused Buchanan of having approached the Supreme Court for the purpose of leaving nothing undone that would ensure success to the plans of the slave power. He asserted that Dred Scott's lawyers had acted for him gratuitously, while Sanford's lawyers were paid by the slaveholder. He insisted that the argument to the court was all a mock, a pretense, since the judges had already made up their minds to decide the case as Buchanan wanted it decided. He pictured a coalition between the executive and the judiciary for the purposes of the case, whereby the liberties of the people were intended to be undermined. "On the day of Buchanan's inaugural," exclaimed Seward, "the judges, without even exchanging their silken robes for courtiers' gowns, paid their salutations to the president in the executive palace." This was Charles I receiving the magistrates "who had at his instance subverted the statutes of Engglish liberty." It does not matter now what Seward said, as it does what Lincoln said. Before we come to that, Dred Scott and his family deserve a parting glance. Two months after the case was decided, Chaffee, the abolitionist, and his wife sold the whole Scott family to Taylor Blow of St. Louis, who had signed Dred Scott's appeal bond, for the purpose of their emancipation, it was expressed in the bill of sale. Blow delayed about their manumission, however. They were not freed until 1857.

On June 16, 1858, Lincoln was nominated for the Illinois senatorship by the Republican state convention, which met at Springfield. When the convention ended its work Lincoln was called upon for a speech, and, together with a discussion of some other things, he spoke of the Dred Scott decision. He was already taking all possible advantage of whatever contradiction could be erected between the right of a territory to admit or to forbid slavery, the Webster-Clay-Douglas doctrine, and the principle of the Dred Scott decision that the Constitution carried slavery into the territories by its own force. This was just the sort of a Euclidian antithesis that his meticulous logic delighted in. Speaking of the Kansas-Nebraska doctrine on this occasion he said: "The people were to be left perfectly free, subject only to the Constitution. What the Constitution had to do with it ousiders cannot see. Plainly enough now, it was an exactly fitted niche for the Dred Scott decision to afterward come in, and declare the perfect freedom of the people to be just no freedom at all. . . . Why was the court decision held up? Why, even a senator's individual opinion

THE DRED SCOTT DECISION 263

withheld, till after the presidential election? Plainly enough now: the speaking out then would have damaged the 'perfectly free' argument upon which the election was to be carried. Why the outgoing president's felicitations on the endorsement? Why the delay for re-argument? Why the incoming president's advance exhortation in favor of the decision? These things look like the cautious patting and petting of a spirited horse preparatory to mounting him, when it is dreaded that he may give the rider a fall. And why the hasty after-endorsement of the decision by the president and others? We cannot absolutely know that all these exact adaptations are the result of preconcert. But when we see a lot of framed timbers, different portions of which we know have been gotten out at different times and places by different workmen—Stephen, Franklin, Roger, and James, for instance—and when we see these timbers joined together, and see they exactly make the frame of a house or a mill, all the tenons and mortices exactly fitting, and all the lengths and proportions of the different pieces exactly adapted to their respective places, and not a piece too many or too few—not omitting even scaffolding—or if a single piece be lacking, we see the place in the frame exactly fitted and prepared yet to bring such piece in—in such a case, we find it impossible not to believe that Stephen and Franklin and Roger and James all understood one another from the beginning, and all worked upon a common plan or draft drawn up before the first blow was struck." In other words that there was that preconcert which he refrained at the beginning from charging.

No language could have been uttered better calculated to create contempt for the court than this of Lincoln's. For had it been true that the Dred Scott case was concocted and framed, as these words imply, impeachment of Taney and his associates would have been light punishment. To give utterance to such language to a popular assembly, in the circumstances when the honor of the court was in no wise impugned, except by the suspicions and the slanders of malicious demagogues, and ignorant radicals, proved Lincoln to be unfitted for the Senate of the United States. Again in Lincoln's speech at Chicago on July 10, 1858, he renewed his attack upon the court. "It is based upon falsehood in the main as to the facts; allegations of facts upon which it stands are not facts at all in many instances." Carried headlong by his own appeal to the mob spirit, he attacked Douglas, charging that Douglas was a co-conspirator in the procurement of the Dred Scott decision. At Springfield on July 17, 1858, with Douglas not present, however, he used this bitter language: "One more point on this Springfield speech which Judge Douglas says he has read so carefully. I expressed my belief in the existence of a conspiracy to perpetuate and nationalize slavery. I did not profess to know it, nor do I now. I showed the part Judge Douglas had played in the string of facts constituting to my mind the proof of that conspiracy. I showed the parts played by others. I charged that the people had been deceived into carrying the last presidential election, by the impression that the people of the territories might exclude slavery if they chose, when it was known in advance by the conspirators that the court was to decide that neither Congress nor the people could so exclude slavery." This mixture of false assertion with falser argument is one of the most amazing emanations of Lincoln's distorted mind.

There were no conspirators; and the fact that he did not know that, yet said that there were conspirators, would have put him in great jeopardy if he had taken his oath that there were conspirators. For what is sworn to as a fact, which is not known to be such by the person so swearing, is perjury, as much as if the matter is known to the witness to be false. Further, no one knew in advance how the case was to be decided, neither conspirators nor others, though the newspapers had correspondents haunting the capitol on purpose to pick up some inkling of what the court would decide. Finally Lincoln flung this poison at Douglas: "Judge Douglas has carefully read and re-read that speech. He has not so far as I know contradicted those charges. In the two speeches which I heard he certainly did not. On his own tacit admission, I renew that charge. I charge him with having been a party to that conspiracy and to that deception for the sole purpose of nationalizing slavery." Is it wonderful that the South wanted to get out of a government presided over by Lincoln? His protestations that he entertained no purpose to interfere with their rights could not quiet apprehensions which words such as these had solidified. No one could tell what he would do. And as we shall see he did what no one could have

MARY S. OWENS

EDWARDS MANSION WHERE LINCOLN WAS MARRIED

THE GLOBE TAVERN AT SPRINGFIELD

PETERSBURG, MENARD COUNTY COURT HOUSE. ERECTED IN 1843

Courtesy of Mrs. E. S. Cheney, Petersburg, Ill.

MENARD HOUSE

Where Lincoln stayed when attending court at Petersburg, Illinois. Built 1845; wrecked 1919

State of Illinois
Menard County & Circuit } Of the May term of the
                          Circuit Court for the county
                          aforesaid in the year A.D. 1847

Masters & Goodpasture
      ads   On Case & &c
Hill —   And the sd Defendants by
              their attorneys, come & defend the
force & injury when &c. & say
That the sd Plaintiff ought not to have or
maintain his aforesd action thereof against
the sd Defendants because they say — that at
the time the sd Defendants executed their note
to Thos Amos for which has been assigned as
collateral security to sd Plaintiff & on which
suit is brought, the sd Thomas Amos executed
his note to Saml D. Masters, one of the sd Defendts
                    which is herewith to the Court shown
being of same date & due same day as the one
declared on for nearly the same sum, & after
the date of the assignment as aforsd is in few days
previous to the notes becoming due & payable, yet
at the date of exhibiting his suit & long before
& even before he received sd note as collateral
security, to wit on the day & year   at
                        the sd Plaintiff
the County & county aforsd, will know. that sd
Amos was indebted to sd Defendt Masters in the
above sum, to wit equal if not greater than
the note aforesd — which sd sum of money
so alledged to be due & owing from sd Defendts
to sd Plaintiff as in sd Declaration mentioned &
out of which sd Defendts are ready & willing
& hereby offers to sett off & allow to the sd Plaintiff
the full amount of sd supposed debt, according
                                           to wages
to the form of the statute in such case made
& provided & this the sd Defendants are ready to
verify &c. Wherefore   Lincoln & Robbins p.D.

PLEA FILED BY LINCOLN AND ROBBINS IN THE SUIT OF SAMUEL HILL
AGAINST SQUIRE D. MASTERS

LINCOLN DURING THE DEBATES WITH DOUGLAS, OCTOBER 1, 1858

STEPHEN A. DOUGLAS

LINCOLN IN THE SUMMER OF 1860

LINCOLN ON NOVEMBER 15, 1863
ABOUT THE TIME OF THE GETTYSBURG ADDRESS

LINCOLN OCCUPYING CONFEDERATE WHITE HOUSE APRIL 4, 1865

LINCOLN ON APRIL 10, 1865
5 DAYS BEFORE HIS DEATH

LINCOLN ASSASSINATED BY JOHN WILKES BOOTH, APRIL 14, 1865

THE DRED SCOTT DECISION 265

conceived that he would do when he was clothed with power. The withering vehemence with which Douglas met these charges both upon the court and upon himself belong to our review of the debates. When we come to that recital, the imagination of the reader will be stirred to picture how Lincoln acted under the indignant fire of Douglas's powerful invective.

Having followed this indecent and flagitious charge of conspiracy into the mouth of Lincoln himself, and there will be more of it still, we must retrace here to note the steps by which Lincoln was drawing closer to Douglas for the purpose of grappling with him as the chief and highest head to be struck for a realization of the ambitions of the new Republican Party. Without Douglas there would not have been at this time, and so far as men can tell, at any time, just the critical fight which was made on the Democrats in the holy name of negro liberty. Douglas was the giant to be slain. For long he had been the object of consuming envy, having for so many years distanced men of middling ability like Trumbull, Judd, Palmer, Browning in Illinois; while in the Senate he was the dread and the scourge of visionaries like Seward, pharisees like Sumner, and conspirators like Chase. In Illinois, Lincoln, having risen to a visible stature by his ability to hold a crowd, was becoming the predestined man to destroy Douglas. Lincoln by this time was a name to conjure with about the Eighth Circuit, where for so many years he had entertained jurors and witnesses, judges and lawyers with his stories, and where his angular skill with a jury had given him local notability. If then the Sublime Irony, which is here, is there, is gone in the affairs of men, could not work its will save by the destruction of Douglas, there should be remembrance for him that he was in the world to be destroyed in order that the great purging of the War and the blotting of slavery from America might come to pass!

On June 12, 1857, Douglas came to Springfield, the session of Congress being ended. At the invitation of the Federal Grand Jury, Douglas made a speech in the hall of representatives of the state capitol, in which he took up, for elucidation to that body and to the great audience which had assembled, the Kansas-Nebraska Act and the recent Dred Scott decision. This speech was one of the few that Douglas wrote out for publication; and it became the Democratic platform in next year's senatorial contest. As the Dred Scott decision had been brought before the people for their approval or their reversal at the hands of town meetings and other political gatherings, by Lincoln and his school of politicians, Douglas defended the court from the attacks which temperance lecturers like Codding, and newspapers like the *Chicago Tribune* had made against it. In this speech he developed the doctrine of local control of slavery, contending that though the Dred Scott decision permitted the taking of slaves into a territory, it depended upon local legislation, which must be friendly to it, for it to exist where it was so brought. Lincoln's mathematical conundrum, propounded during the debates, in which he juxtaposed territorial sovereignty and the Dred Scott case supremacy, was no surprise to Douglas; and, whatever the press and the people made out of the supposed discomfiture which it caused Douglas, it was in fact a harmless shot against Douglas's position, as well as without decisive bearing upon the dialectics of the two debaters. It is evident that under the Dred Scott case slaves might have been taken into Kansas; but there were almost infinite laws which could have been passed entirely consonant to the Constitution which would have made the owning of slaves in Kansas intolerable. Many years after this time, when prohibition had become the law in Iowa, the question arose in the Supreme Court as to the shipment of liquor into Iowa.[1] Under the commerce clause of the Constitution, the court held that liquor could be carried and delivered into Iowa, and that the regulation of interstate commerce included the power to effect the delivery of the liquor into the hands of the consignee. When that happened the state law took control. The consignee could not sell it. Therefore what was the use to buy it? He could not give it away. Therefore why have it? Indeed he might be prohibited from drinking it. For what purpose then should he have it shipped to him? Anticipating this ruling by nearly forty years, Douglas reconciled the Dred Scott decision with the Kansas-Nebraska Act.

Douglas then took up negro equality, which Taney had handled in such masterly fashion, showing that the authors of the Declaration were themselves slave owners, and that it was to impugn their integrity and their intelligence to insist that they meant to in-

[1] Leisy vs. Hardin, 135, U. S., 100.

clude negroes when declaring that all men were created equal. With perfect logic he showed that Republicans were self-convicted of base inconsistency in shouting for negro equality while doing nothing to bring it about. Why not do so in Illinois where the negro could not vote, serve on juries or in the militia, and where they had no social equality at all? If the Declaration meant that negroes were equal to white men, then "as conscientious and just men" we should "repeal all laws making any distinction whatever on account of race and color, and authorize negroes to marry white people." Taney had shown in the Dred Scott case, by citing the laws of Connecticut and even Massachusetts, that the social equality of negroes was denied in those states by the severest penalties. Where was the boasted sincerity of the Republicans who were demanding mere economic freedom for the negro, and who were yet willing to keep him in social and political slavery? But he adverted to the activities of the more radical abolitionists who were already at work to wipe out all distinctions between the white man and the negro, in the name of divine right; saying that if this plan was successful there would be intermarriage and every other right given to the negro and exercised by him, which belonged to perfect equality.

On the 26th of June, 1857, Lincoln answered Douglas's speech just considered. He did not on this occasion charge the Supreme Court with being in a conspiracy in the rendition of the Dred Scott decision. He attacked it because it was not a unanimous decision, and because it was out of partisan bias, a *petitio principii*, since that was the very thing to be proven if it could be done. But partisan bias after all is only a way of saying that the court is with some group economic or political. It always had been and it has been since that day. He further required, for the decision's complete respectability, that it should have been one in line with previous decisions, one which affirmed others previously made. All these things being given it "might be, perhaps would be factious, nay even revolutionary not to acquiesce in it as a precedent." [1] As to the social equality of the negro, Lincoln said: "There is a natural disgust in the minds of nearly all white people at the idea of an indiscriminate amalgamation of the white and black races." He descended to this demagoguery: He [Douglas] "proceeds to argue

[1] Lincoln's Works, I, 228.

gravely that all who contend it does [that the Declaration meant the negro] do so only because they want to eat and sleep and marry with negroes. He will have it that they cannot be consistent else. Now I protest against the counterfeit logic which concludes that because I do not want a black woman for a slave I must necessarily want her for wife. I need not have her for either. I can just leave her alone."

Lincoln showed his profound ignorance of the social philosophy that had been written by this time in Europe and elsewhere, touching the distinctions in point of rights which had been raised on the circumstance of color. The radicals around him who were reading advanced books knew and were saying that the peace of the world would be ensured by racial amalgamation, and if he had given the matter intelligent thought he would have known that Douglas's arguments were founded upon a clear intuition into the heart of racial antagonism; and that Douglas had rightly divined that there were only two alternatives, one was the subjection of the negro and the other his complete political and social equality. That Douglas was the wiser of the two men is proven by the fact that, wherever the conditions have permitted, the negro in America has achieved the right of social equality, including the right of intermarriage with white persons.

As we have seen, the Republican Party came to birth in Illinois, on October 5, 1854, under the ministrations of Codding. It is now time to report what its platform was, because in the debates, soon now to be reviewed, Douglas, knowing Lincoln's reluctance to be identified with abolitionism, saw the tactical advantage of fastening the "black Republican creed" upon him. The Codding platform declared that they, those there assembled, where Herndon was, too, it will be remembered, will "hereafter coöperate as the Republican Party pledged to the accomplishment of the following purposes: to restore Kansas and Nebraska to the position of free territories; that as the Constitution of the United States vests in the states, and not in Congress, the power to legislate for the extradition of fugitives from labor, to repeal and entirely abrogate the Fugitive Slave Law; to restrict slavery to those states in which it exists; to prohibit the admission of any more slave states into the Union; to abolish slavery in the District of Columbia; to exclude slavery

THE DRED SCOTT DECISION

from all the territories, and to resist the acquirement of any more territories, unless the practice of slavery therein shall have been prohibited." And finally there was this resolution, which bore so heavily upon the fitness of Lincoln, as a Republican, to stand for the Senatorship against Douglas: "we will support no man for office under the general or state government, who is not positively and fully committed to the support of these principles, and whose personal character and conduct is not a guarantee that he is reliable, and who shall not have abjured old party ties."

Did Lincoln stand for these principles, was the crucial question that Douglas first put to Lincoln in the first debate which was held at Ottawa. If he did not, was he worthy the support of the Abolitionist Republicans who were so numerous in northern Illinois, where this platform had been adopted over and over again by county Republican conventions after the time of the Codding convention in 1854 and up to the time that Lincoln was nominated for the Senate by the Republican Party on June 16, 1858? On this date the Republicans adopted a platform for Lincoln to run upon; but it was greatly toned down from the Codding platform. By the platform of June 16, 1858, states' rights must be upheld; and where slavery existed it must be left alone. The general government was instituted for free men—therefore the public domain must be wrested from speculators and "greedy corporations." The rights of free labor must be maintained—in consequence, rivers and harbors must be improved and the Pacific railroad built—Douglas's plan! "We now compete in the markets of the country against the products of unpaid labor"—that is, the slave costs the owner nothing to feed, to clothe, to house, to nurse, and to support in his old age. Hence it was "eminently unjust" that slavery should be extended into the territories, there to further compete with the white free labor. The Dred Scott decision was a "political heresy," for Congress had sovereign power over the territories to root out the "curse of slavery" so that the domain might be kept pure for "free men and free labor." But the Know-nothing vote was needed—so nothing was said against their strictures on Catholics and foreigners. The Germans had been won anyway by the nomination of Germans to office. There was no better evidence, surely, of racial tolerance than by giving foreigners political office.

The night of June 16, 1858, Lincoln, as the nominee for the Senate by the Republicans, delivered his speech concerning "the house divided against itself." Lincoln's purpose was to put emotion into the campaign, to take some moral stand that would identify his political course with religion. Illinois was full of hard and soft-shell Baptists, Methodists, free and Wesleyan, Presbyterians of the old school and of the Cumberland division, Campbellites, Calvinists of every hue; and these were material which by some skill might be molded into a political army inflamed with holy zeal. If Lincoln could identify his cause with that of Jesus, his strength would be great with the churches. So he went to Jesus for a text. But others had chosen the same text before him, and made the same application of it. In 1806, John Parrish had published remarks on the slavery of the black people, and had used these words: "A house divided against itself cannot stand: neither can a government or constitution. This is coincident with the present Chief Magistrate's [Jefferson's] opinion in his notes on the state of Virginia." We shall see more and more that Lincoln originated nothing, and that he only wrote over, and said over, what someone else had said before; and that his arguments followed those of Webster or those of whoever came convenient to his eclectic talent. When an issue is declared to be a moral one, an emotional state is excited which renders reasonable considerations of it impossible, and adjustment and compromise are made execrable. To call a question a moral one is to call it a sacred one too, and thinking is similarly raised to the point of hysteria.

The "house divided against itself" doctrine was no other than Seward's "irrepressible conflict." But how mathematical and cold was Seward's formula compared to Lincoln's! In the mouth of Jesus these words were a sophism, and in the mouth of Lincoln they were as much so. Jesus believed in demoniac possession, and after he had gone about casting out blind and dumb devils, and devils of lunacy, the Jews challenged his thaumaturgy, saying that he worked by the power of Satan. Jesus had sent word to Herod, "Go ye and tell that fox, Behold I cast out devils, and I do cures today and tomorrow." Lincoln knew his Illinois audiences; he relied upon their belief in Jesus' miracles, and in their complete faith in his divinity; and therefore to identify himself with the words, if not the ministry, of Jesus was to cast a spell over the moral forces of the electorate. In spite of the fact that the Jews had held the superstition of demoniac possession since their contact with Persian modes of thought, out of which had arisen their dualistic system of God opposed by Satan as adversary and ruler over the kingdom of evil, in spite of this Jesus answered the Jews with the sophism: "A house divided against itself cannot stand." The belief which existed before the days of the Persian contact, that there were witches, and sorcerers who could work cures, and which persisted in Jesus' day, did not embarrass his swift answer to the Jews; nor was he stayed by the accepted doctrine among the Jews that devils could work miracles. Lincoln's audiences did not stop to think that a devil had entered into Judas to destroy the house of God; that Jesus himself went about accusing people of devil possession for not accepting his ministry. The holy ministry of Jesus was not proven by his casting out of devils, for witches and sorcerers could do the same thing. No house was left undivided either when, after Jesus had cast out the devil, the cured man could take "with himself seven other spirits more wicked than himself, and they enter in and dwell there."

There was much that Douglas could have said in reply to the use of this text, but all the while it was fragile and treacherous ground on which to walk, considering the religious convictions of the audiences the two were addressing, convictions built up by the Bible as marplot, and as an influence of re-barbarization. Douglas, if free to handle the whole text with searching power, might have said that Jesus had caused vastly more evil by spreading the belief of demoniac possession, than he had done good by the few devils that he did exorcise, if he did do it at all. It would have been disastrous to have proven, as he could have proven, that the crisis then impending over the country was embittered by this Jesus division into the good and the bad, with the South placed on the evil side by Northern clergymen of the Beecher type; and that this was the most crucial division of the house which existed.

It was not slavery on the one side and freedom on the other that was dividing the house, but it was the inner hostility of men's minds, who had thrown balance, the golden mean, to the winds, and who were now saying: "Who is this King of glory? The Lord strong and mighty, the Lord mighty in battle." This was the Hebraic-Puritan spirit of madness which was driving the North into war against the South. After running away from the Codding convention in 1854, Lincoln had become a convert to this fanatical Zionism, against which his sanest friends had warned him. Into his slow veins the virus had at last found an entrance. He was a divided house himself, for in other moods and for other persuasions he recognized slavery as a legal question, one of political policy.

Douglas might have shown that the Bible was standing, though it was surely divided against itself on the subject of slavery. If it counseled the golden rule, it also admonished slaves to be worthy of their masters through St. Paul's epistle to Timothy. Jesus did not forbid slavery; on the contrary he found no faith in Israel equal to that of the slave-owning centurion. St. Paul was a slave catcher when he returned the slave Onesimus back to his master Philemon; and Jesus, who had much to say about usurers, false witnesses, liars and hypocrites, said nothing against slavery. Plainly the Bible was no safe guide for America, when used by Lincoln in this manner to win the gathering mob. Other answers to Lincoln's moralism were plentiful enough if the delicate balance of an audience's psychology had permitted them to be made. The Christian churches had been divided since the days of Luther, and the platform on which Lincoln was running for senator carefully handled Catholics lest a breach in the churches should make division in his political following. Webster in his speech of the 7th of March, 1850, had referred to the division of the Methodist Episcopal church. "That separation," he said, "was brought about by differences of opinion upon this peculiar subject of slavery." So other churches had divided or were dividing, and yet all were standing, too much indeed for the good of the country. In the instant matter, the United States had stood for nearly seventy years divided into free and slave states. Lincoln's argument assumed as a fact beforehand what could become fact only by the exertions of himself and others like himself who assumed it. There was a wish that fathered the thought, covertly looking to the continuance of the division until a crisis ended the division. Under the dove words of Jesus was the serpent to be carried. From behind these words Lincoln was able to shoot arrows of fire against the South, protest-

THE DRED SCOTT DECISION 273

ing the while he meant peace. If there was to be any quarrel with what he had said it was not with himself that it should be raised, but with the Savior! The North and the South could not live together as free and slave states, because Jesus, who was God, had said so. Above all other things, Lincoln's mind was divided, as it always had been; and yet, such as it was, it was standing. But the witchcraft which seized Salem, Massachusetts, some few miles from Hingham where Lincoln's ancestor settled, was now but the influence of Lincoln to take the whole country. His power of exorcism if it cast out any devil whatever was to be one which would take "with himself seven other spirits more wicked than himself and they enter in and dwell there," bringing war and making the diabolical decade of reconstruction, and these days of our generation. After shooting his arrow of fire, what did Lincoln say as he watched it fall upon combustible roofs? "I do not expect it will cease to be divided. It will become all one thing or the other. Either the opponents of slavery will arrest the further spread of it, and place it where the public mind shall rest in the belief that it is in the course of ultimate extinction—" that is, in states too where Lincoln was protesting over and over again that neither he nor his party had any right to control slavery or do anything about it. Then if it could not be arrested— "its advocates will push it forward till it shall become alike lawful in all the states, old as well as new, North as well as South."

One of two things is true respecting this utterance: either Lincoln did not know what he was saying, or else he was dishonest in saying it. For there was not a chance within the scope of human possibility that slavery would return to the Northern states, where it had ceased to exist. The climate was against it; the economic laws were against it; the firm rooted principles of the state constitutions were against it; the South was not trying to force the North to it, or to force it upon the North. All the armed power of Europe could not have compelled the North to have accepted it. Douglas, as we shall see, later pointed out the inevitability of war if this hateful doctrine of the house divided against itself were allowed to go its way unrebuked. Whereupon Lincoln grew frightfully angry, and denied with vehemence that any such consequences would follow.

The Lincoln mind puzzles the best student at every step. It cannot be understood on any other basis than that he was a demagogue, and as dangerous as Douglas knew him to be. In his heart of hearts Lincoln had doubts of this doctrine of the house divided against itself. Two years before he uttered it he had prepared to announce it at the Bloomington convention in June of 1856, but was dissuaded from doing so by an old and trusted friend. This was Judge Dickey, who said to Lincoln that the idea "would make abolitionists of all the North, and slavery propagandists of all the South, and thereby precipitate a struggle which might end in disunion." [1] "Upon my soul," replied Lincoln to Dickey, "I think it is true." Then, after some reflection, Lincoln promised Dickey not to use the doctrine any more during the campaign, that of 1856. In 1858, the situation was such that Lincoln was emboldened to broadcast it to the country. Frémont had polled 1,341,264 Republican votes in 1856; there was a panic on for which the Buchanan administration was blamed; Douglas had come to rupture with Buchanan, and the Federal office holders in Illinois, under Buchanan, had been sent forth as Danites to destroy Douglas. There was the Kansas-Nebraska quarrel which Chase's Appeal had started; and there was the Dred Scott decision which demagogues could denounce to town meetings, where the mob spirit could be stirred from the dregs of ignorant men. In addition to these advantages in Lincoln's behalf, there were the churches and the Bible rejoicing that the forces of sin were now divided.

So we shall soon see Lincoln, the attorney of the Illinois Central Railroad, riding about on special trains furnished him, and posing again as "humble Abraham Lincoln." His long years of professional mediocrity, his poverty, when contrasted with the wealth of Douglas, the darling of the slavocracy, his failure to be senator in 1855, his melancholy, the pathos of his homely face, the stories about his hard youth, his reputation as "Honest Abe," which the bank and tariff Whigs had made into current coin over Illinois—all these things stood Lincoln in good stead. And he made the best use of them. His inveterate hatred of Douglas, from the days of their association in the legislature of 1837, from the time when they wrangled hand to hand in Speed's store, and debated publicly against each other in the halls of Springfield, now was offered the chance to sate itself. He was the nominee of the Republicans for

[1] Herndon, II, 67–8.

THE DRED SCOTT DECISION 275

senator. Douglas was nominated by the Democrats for a third term as senator. Douglas was of worldwide fame, as Lincoln phrased it. If Lincoln could engage Douglas in public debate instead of trailing him about where he could speak only as chance offered, there could be nothing but advantage in it. It was like the unknown fighter who seeks a chance with the champion. If Douglas defeated him in debate, he had no reputation to lose. If he held his own with Douglas, there was honor in it. If he overcame Douglas in the discussion, he might be elected to the Senate. If he won the senatorship, after routing Douglas on the stump, he was in power and in command of patronage; and he was in line for the presidency. For then he would be a senator; and Seward, whom everyone looked to to carry the Republican banner in 1860, was only a senator after all, and to be equaled by Lincoln becoming one. Therefore Lincoln challenged Douglas to debate. On the prairies of Illinois in the hot summer of 1858, up and down from the north of the state to the south went Lincoln and Douglas, where Hebraic-Puritanism gathered itself and scattered its seeds to the four quarters of America. Out of the days of Washington, Jefferson, Madison, even the hard intellectuality of Hamilton; out of the less classic days of Webster and Clay, and the manly democracy of Jackson emerged in more concrete form than ever before the Americanism of this hour: the half idiocy that is shrewd about business, and has a certain touch of genius, whose product and whose satisfaction are the comic strip, the moving picture that falsifies life and will not face it; the fiction that portrays half-honest amenities; the business men who become the great monopolists, the impostors in politics, the reformers and the religionists, and all who make lying and swindling in every sphere a study and a profession. Douglas understood what had been conjured out of the purlieus of the country against him. He could not foresee that these influences would exalt his opponent in debate to the first place among all Americans. He could not calculate to what lengths hypocrisy could go, nor how the forces of its historic strength would lend themselves to making the country forget what Lincoln was, nor how Lincoln's words floating up from the weed-grown shallows would become the Lincoln that nearly everyone knows today to the exclusion of every other Lincoln. Lincoln had something of the poet in him. Douglas was not a poet. He understood that a natural with a touch of genius can throw hesitation into the speech of a logician, particularly when the logician is going at full speed. He had stood on the floor of the Senate and met hecklers and disconcerting interpolators at every turn. That was different from attending to an awkward blow coming from an unanticipated quarter, from a left-handed jolt, where the right hand seemed to lack a sense of direction, as well as speed. But Lincoln was not a natural, though resembling one; and he had a touch of genius. He had an undisciplined analysis, and a gift for sophistry; and Douglas was to try whether he could hold him to the straightaway discussion, or whether, like a wrestler, Lincoln would dodge away, and then come in to gouge and to bite.

Chapter XII *The Lincoln and Douglas Debates*

THE setting of the debates is not complete without lowering upon the stage some other drops. The chief one, perhaps, was the warfare that President Buchanan was making in Illinois upon Douglas, which came about because Douglas would not support Buchanan's program to admit Kansas as a state, the people there not being given a chance to vote upon their constitution, but only upon the issue of slavery or no slavery. This was called the Lecompton Constitution. In Kansas the pro-slavery men had become Democrats in name and by party designation; the freedom men had become Republicans. The Lecompton Constitution was the work of the pro-slavery men, but they were greatly outnumbered by the Republicans. In the convention in Kansas which framed the Lecompton Constitution was John Calhoun, once the surveyor of Sangamon County, and under whom Lincoln worked as a surveyor when he lived at New Salem. Calhoun had also been in the legislature with Lincoln. He was a pro-slavery man, and always had been. But now in Kansas he was an appointee as surveyor general of the territory, by the grace of Douglas. Though he favored slavery, he believed with Douglas that the people should say for themselves whether they would have it. In consequence he made a valiant fight in the Lecompton convention to have the whole constitution then framed submitted to a vote of the people. He lost by one vote. Then a compromise proposal was offered, which was that the constitution as a whole was not to be submitted to the people, but only that part of it which was to effect slavery or freedom in the territory. Calhoun disliked this plan, but he finally accepted it; and the constitution thus drawn, and thus to be submitted, was sent on to Washington, to President Buchanan, by Calhoun, as president of the Kansas convention.

Douglas fought and defeated this constitution, saying with forthright courage that he cared not whether slavery was voted up or down, but that he did care above all things for the principle of popular sovereignty, and for the right of the people to say what they wanted in their constitutions. For this breach of what Buchanan considered to be party discipline, Buchanan undertook to defeat Douglas in the senatorial contest in Illinois. The special agent of the Post Office department in Illinois was one James who owed his office to Douglas, and who was devoted to him. Buchanan removed James and appointed in his stead Dr. Charles Lieb, who had been a clerk in the Illinois legislature. Lieb immediately upon receiving his appointment wired the Illinois Republican Secretary of State that he was now in authority, meaning that he was ready to coöperate with the Republicans against Douglas. He had passes on the railroads, and he started forth up and down Illinois making removals in the Post Office service of those who refused to desert Douglas, and appointing in their place the enemies of Douglas. Trumbull, calling himself an Anti-Nebraska Democrat, was helping Lincoln to the extent of his power; and Lieb was reporting to Trumbull what he was doing. In this way the Republicans had constant information of his movements. Lincoln protested all along that he had nothing to do with this guerilla warfare on Douglas. But there is this fact: Delahay, who had married a fifth cousin of Nancy Hanks Lincoln, as already mentioned, was in Illinois, having returned from his newspaper work in Kansas. He appeared on the stump in Edwardsville where Lincoln also spoke, and in a letter to Trumbull Delahay wrote: "My speech did not please the Republicans, [but] by Brown and Lincoln it was understood what I should say beforehand; my policy is to back up Douglas until after the Buchanan convention nominate their state ticket, then I am for Lincoln." [1] Also, "last night with Lieb I spent several hours. Lieb is drilling the faithful Lincoln." Lincoln was too secretive and politic to disclose any part that he had in this shabby coalition with his disreputable relative, if he had any express relation to it. But it is not credible that he did not know what was going on, and what Delahay was doing. Light is thrown upon Lincoln's knowledge of the campaign against Douglas by Buchanan, through a letter written by Herndon to Trumbull on July 8, 1858. "Mr. Lincoln was here a moment or so since," wrote Herndon, "and he told me that he had just seen Col. Daugherty [this was the Buchanan candidate for state treasurer] and had a

[1] Beveridge, II, 588.

conversation with him. He told Lincoln that the National Democracy intended 'to run in every county and district a national Democrat for each and every office.' Lincoln replied to this by saying, 'If you do this the thing is settled, the battle is fought.' This you may depend upon."

Without questioning the morality of this kind of political tactics, nor discussing it, the reserved criticism might be compensated by acknowledging that Douglas showed great principle of character in fighting Buchanan; for neither then nor now can anyone see what political advantage he was to gain anywhere—in Illinois where the Republicans were wholly bitter against him, in the South where Jefferson Davis was beginning to draw away from him—by coming to such sharp issue with President Buchanan. At the very inception of his parting of the ways, Buchanan in a conference at the White House had warned Douglas of the consequences of recusancy. Douglas had bowed himself from the White House with the remark that Andrew Jackson was dead, meaning to imply that there was not in the White House that imperial will which could override the judgment of a senator.

Another matter to be noted for an understanding of the debates is that portion of the platform on which Lincoln was nominated for the Senate, which declared that Lincoln was the first, last and only choice of the Republicans. If this was true, then did Lincoln stand squarely upon the principles of the Republican Party? Would he dare to come forth and say that he did? Douglas knew that Lincoln would not relish a commitment so extreme in Illinois where there were thousands of voters who believed that the radical pronouncements of the Republicans meant disunion and war. Was Lincoln, in a word, running for the Senate upon the Codding platform of 1854? Douglas was misled into believing that he was. One of Douglas's friends had sent Douglas the Codding platform informing Douglas that it was the one which Lincoln helped to draw, having been, as stated, in the convention which reported it. We shall now see how this confusion about the exact platform worked to take up much time between Douglas and Lincoln before the mistake was cleared; while at last it came out that the Codding platform had been adopted in many northern counties of Illinois, and constituted the political faith of thousands where Lincoln had to get votes in order to be elected, in order, more accurately, to carry the Illinois legislature in his behalf, which then had the office of electing United States senators.

The debates were scheduled by agreement between Douglas and Lincoln to take place in Ottawa in the heart of Codding devotion; in Freeport where the abolitionists were equally strong; in Jonesboro where the Democracy was strong; in Charleston, Coles County, where Thomas Lincoln had lived and died, which was a Democratic community; in Galesburg where Calvinisim and Abolitionism were both strong; in Quincy on the Mississippi River, in the lower central part of the state; and at Alton, still farther south on the river, where there were many Germans, but also a strong Democracy.

It was August 21, 1858, that the debaters met at Ottawa. It was such a sultry day as only Illinois of the Great Valley ever suffers from. The roads had grown dry as powder, and dust befogged the town, stirred up by wagons and carriages of the farmers who had driven in to hear what was to be said about Dred Scott and Kansas and Nebraska, slavery and freedom. A special train of fourteen cars brought Lincoln and he stepped from the car amid a thunder of applause and was driven away in a decorated carriage, preceded and followed by bands and music to which marched throngs of shouting partisans. He was taken to the residence of the mayor. Douglas, driving over from the near-by town of Peru, in a carriage drawn by four horses, was met four miles from Ottawa by a committee of hundreds of horsemen, who were fluttering banners and flags. When he came into Ottawa the guns thundered, the people shouted until he disappeared behind the doors of the local hotel. On a platform built in the square, where thousands stood jammed in the hot air, in the suffocating dust, the two debaters came at two o'clock. And there reporters from eastern newspapers, and stenographers pushing and squeezing to get a place where they could take notes, finally accommodated themselves for their work.

In these debates there is much that is without interest save to the curious investigator, and much that we have already considered when spoken before this time by one or the other of these antagonists; and also there were side issues, having only a local bearing. For example, there was Trumbull to be attended to; and the plot which Douglas charged Lincoln with having entered into to deliver the Whigs into the camp of abolitionism, together with Lincoln's denial that this was so, and his statement that Douglas could not know that it was so, while he, Lincoln, was in a position to know that the charge was false. Some of these contentious matters may thread their way into what must be examined in this study of the Lincoln mind. For the rest, the purpose will be to follow affirmation and denial about specific questions from the beginning until they evaporated or wore themselves out, or were settled by one or the other of these thoroughly angry men being thrown to the floor and pinned down. By this time Lincoln had too often referred to Douglas as "that man," and otherwise insulted him, and followed him, for Douglas not to be in thorough fighting spirit. He had had enough of Lincoln's following him about Illinois, enough of Lincoln's sitting behind the curtains of windows opening upon balconies where Douglas spoke, or gazing at him from the floor of audiences, or turning up, wherever Douglas had addressed the people, to answer him.

At Ottawa Douglas had the opening, and after calmly reciting that before 1854 there had been two political parties, the Whig and the Democratic, which were national in their scope, though differing about the tariff and the bank, he said that in 1854 Lincoln and Trumbull entered into an arrangement to dissolve the Whig Party on the one hand and the Democratic Party on the other, and to amalgamate their elements into an abolition party under the deceiving name of the Republican Party. Then he set himself to rush upon Lincoln. In pursuance of this arrangement, the conspirators met at Springfield, and adopted a platform to bring in Giddings, Chase, Fred Douglass the negro, and parson Lovejoy. This was the first mass convention of the Republicans, he said, that had ever met in Illinois. Then, gathering more strength, he read the Codding platform. When he had finished doing so the Republicans cheered lustily. To which Douglas swiftly retorted: "Now, gentlemen, your black Republicans have cheered every one of those propositions, and yet I venture to say that you cannot get Mr. Lincoln to come out and say that he is in favor of each one of them . . . when you were not aware for what purpose I was reading them, your black Republicans cheered them as good Republican doctrines. My object in reading these resolutions was to put the question to Abraham

Lincoln this day, whether he now stands and will stand by each article in that creed and carry it out." Is he pledged in favor of the unconditional repeal of the Fugitive Slave Law; is he pledged against the admission of any more slave states if the people want them; is he pledged against the admission of a state with such a constitution as the people want; is he pledged to the abolition of slavery in the District of Columbia; is he pledged to prohibit slavery in all the territories of the United States, north as well as south of the Missouri Compromise line; is he opposed to the acquisition of any more territory unless slavery is prohibited therein? These were the questions that Douglas flung at Lincoln in the terrific onslaught of his strength and his wrath.

Lincoln had thought of nothing else for years, except about these questions. He had read nothing to speak of since the days at New Salem, other than documents and laws and legislative proceedings, reported in the *Intelligencer;* he had read little besides the speeches of Seward, Sumner and others, all of which in every way and from every angle went over and over these problems of law and of policy. But though he knew all of this, he did not know his own mind; not in a hand-to-hand conflict with Douglas. This was Lincoln's answer therefore: "As to those resolutions that he took such a length of time to read, as being the platform of the Republican Party in 1854, I say I never had anything to do with them, and I think Trumbull never had. I believe this is true about those resolutions: there was a call for a convention to form a Republican Party, and I think my friend Lovejoy, who is here upon this stand, had a hand in it. I think this is true, and I think if he will remember accurately, he will be able to recollect that he tried to get me into it, and I would not go in. I believe it is also true that I went away from Springfield when the convention was in session, to attend court at Tazewell County. It is true they did place my name, though without authority, upon the committee, and afterward wrote me to attend the meeting of the committee; but I refused to do so, and I never had anything to do with that organization. This is the plain truth about all the matter of the resolutions." It was time now for the cock to crow!

Let us hear Douglas reply to this evasion. "But my friends," he said, "this denial of his, that he did not act on the committee is a miserable quibble to avoid the main issue, which is that this Republican platform declares in favor of the unconditional repeal of the Fugitive Slave Law. Has Lincoln answered whether he endorsed that or not? I called his attention to it when I first addressed you, and asked him for an answer, and then I predicted that he would not answer. How does he answer? Why, that he was not on the committee that wrote the resolutions. I then repeated the next proposition contained in the resolutions, which was to restrict slavery in those states in which it exists, and asked him whether he endorsed it. Does he answer yes, or no? He says in reply, 'I was not on the committee at the time, I was up in Tazewell.' The next question I put to him was, whether he was in favor of prohibiting the admission of any more slave states into the Union. . . . He is a candidate for the United States Senate, and it is possible, if he should be elected, that he would have to vote directly on that question. I asked him to answer me and you, whether he would vote to admit a state into the Union, with slavery or without, as its own people might choose. He did not answer that question. He dodges that question also, under the cover that he was not on the committee at the time, that he was not present when the platform was made. . . . I want to know whether he is the first, last and only choice of a party with whom he does not agree in principle. He does not deny but that that principle was unanimously adopted by the Republican Party; he does not deny that the whole Republican Party is pledged to it; he does not deny that a man who is not faithful to it is faithless to the Republican Party; and now I want to know whether that party is unanimously in favor of a man who does not adopt that creed and agree with them in their principles; I want to know whether the man who does not agree with them, and who is afraid to avow his differences, and who dodges the issue, is the first, last and only choice of the Republican Party?"

Six days elapsed between the Ottawa debate and the next one, which was held at Freeport. In this interval Lincoln had thought over Douglas's questions, and he came prepared to answer them. It must not be forgotten that Lincoln did not at Ottawa question the resolutions, or impugn their genuineness. If Douglas did not know but what they were the resolutions upon which Lincoln was running for the Senate, Lincoln was equally in ignorance about them; but Douglas was not wrong in saying that they constituted the creed of the Republicans in many counties of Illinois. Let us see Lincoln's answers at Freeport to Douglas's questions. "I do not now, nor ever did stand in favor of the unconditional repeal of the Fugitive Slave Law. I do not now, nor ever did stand pledged against the admission of any more slave states into the Union. . . . I do not stand pledged against the admission of a new state into the Union, with such a constitution as the people of that state may see fit to make. . . . I do not stand pledged to the abolition of slavery in the District of Columbia. . . . I do not stand pledged to the prohibition of the slave trade between the different states. . . . I am impliedly, if not expressly, pledged to a belief in the right and duty of Congress to prohibit slavery in all the United States territories." Let us note that he did not say that Congress had the Constitutional power to do this, but that it was its right and duty to do it. "I am not generally opposed to the honest acquisition of territory; and in any given case I would or would not oppose such acquisition, according as I might think such acquisition would or would not aggravate the slavery question among ourselves."

Lincoln then observed that he had answered Douglas's questions categorically as they had been asked by Douglas, that he had said that he was not "pledged"; and having done this he proceeded to amplify his answers. In the first place he believed that the Southern states were entitled to a Fugitive Slave Law; secondly, he would be sorry to be put in the position where he would have to pass upon the admission of any more slave states into the Union; but if the territory was kept free of slavery during its territorial state, and then applied for admission with slavery in its constitution, then he saw no alternative but to admit it into the Union; fourthly (his answer to the third being covered by previous answers) he would be exceedingly glad to see slavery abolished in the District of Columbia, and that Congress "possesses the constitutional power to abolish it," but it should be gradual abolition and upon a vote of the people of the District; fifthly, that whether he favored or was pledged to the abolition of the slave trade between the states, that he was pledged to nothing about it. "It is a subject to which I have not given that mature consideration that would make me feel authorized to state a position so as to hold myself entirely bound by it."

He then took up the resolutions, saying that he had as much to do with the Kane County resolutions as with the Springfield-Codding resolutions which Douglas had quoted against him. He charged that Douglas had so far forgotten his position "as to venture upon the assertion of that which the slightest investigation would have shown him to be wholly false." He then gave Douglas the following Hebraic-Puritan thrust: "I can only account for his having done so upon the supposition that that evil genius which has attended him through life, giving him an apparent prosperity, such as to lead very many good men to doubt of there being any advantage in virtue over vice, has 'decided' to forsake him."

In reply to Lincoln's affirmations as to what he was pledged, and to the resolutions, Douglas said, after recapitulating what his questions were, "He refused to answer; and his followers say, in excuse, that the resolutions upon which I based my interrogatories were not adopted at the right spot. Lincoln and his political friends are great on spots. In Congress as the representative of this state he declared the Mexican war to be unjust and infamous, and would not support it, or acknowledge his country to be right in the contest, because he said that American blood was not shed on American soil in the 'right spot.'" Douglas in extenuation of his mistake said that his friend Lanphier had sent him the *State Register*, which contained the resolutions, and which also had reported that Lincoln addressed the Codding convention, after which the resolutions in question were adopted. He then quoted at length the resolutions of the Rockford convention of the Republicans held in late August of 1854, in which the Codding resolutions were repeated, and upon which platform a Republican congressman was elected in that fall. He showed that the same platform was adopted in various counties in 1854, and that he intended to nail the responsibility of them upon the Republican Party and Lincoln. At this point one of the moderators of the debate, named Turner, interrupted Douglas to say that he had drawn the Rockford resolutions, and that they were the creed exactly of the Republican Party. Douglas rejoined quickly, "And yet Lincoln denies that he stands upon them." Douglas followed up then by reading the resolutions of the Republican Party in 1855, when Lincoln tried to be named senator. They were in substance the Codding resolutions. The second one was to the effect that Republican senators and representatives be instructed to vote against the admission of any more slave states. Douglas showed that everyone who voted for the resolutions, but two, voted the next day for Lincoln for senator. "Thus you see every member from your congressional district voted for Mr. Lincoln, and they were pledged not to vote for him unless he was committed to the doctrine of no more slave states, the prohibition of slavery in the territories, and the repeal of the Fugitive Slave Law. Mr. Lincoln tells you today that he is not pledged to any such doctrine. . . . Either Lincoln was pledged to each one of those propositions, or else every black Republican representative from this congressional district violated his pledge of honor by voting for him."

It looked now as though this issue was settled. Douglas had been deceived as to Lincoln's participation in the Codding resolutions; but he had shown that they were the exact resolutions upon which Republican congressmen had been elected, and the same largely as those upon which Lincoln was supported for the senate in 1855. On October 8, at Galesburg, in the heart of Hebraic-Puritanism, Lincoln felt a renewed bravery, and by way of impeaching Douglas, who was asserting what was perfectly true, that there was an alliance between the Buchanan democrats, Trumbull and Lincoln, for the purpose of defeating Douglas, he revived the discussion about the Codding resolutions. Speaking of them Lincoln said that "a fraud, and absolute forgery was committed and the perpetration of it was traced to the three, Lanphier, Harris and Douglas."

This was Douglas's reply: "He has used hard names; has dared to talk about fraud and forgery and has insinuated that there was a conspiracy between Mr. Lanphier, Mr. Harris and myself to perpetrate a forgery. Now, bear in mind that he does not deny that these resolutions were adopted in a majority of all the Republican counties of this state in that year; he does not deny that they were declared to be the platform of this Republican Party in the first congressional district, in the second, in the third, and in many counties of the fourth, and that they thus became the platform of his party in a majority of the counties upon which he now relies for support; he does not deny the truthfulness of the resolutions, but takes exception to the spot on which they were adopted. . . . In the first place the moment it was intimated to me that they had been adopted at Aurora instead of Springfield, I did not wait for him to call my attention to the fact, but led off, and explained in my first meeting after the Ottawa debate what the mistake was and how it was made. . . I will say now that I do not believe that there is an honest man on the face of the globe who will not regard with abhorrence and disgust Mr. Lincoln's insinuations of my complicity in that forgery, if it was a forgery. Does Mr. Lincoln wish to push these things to the point of personal difficulties here? I commenced this contest by treating him courteously and kindly; I always spoke of him in words of respect; and in return he has sought, and is now seeking, to divert public attention from the enormity of his revolutionary principles by impeaching men's sincerity and integrity, and inviting personal quarrels."

Lincoln himself was responsible in part for Douglas's mistake. For, as shown, the *State Register* in reporting the Codding convention had published that Lincoln participated in it. This Lincoln did not deny upon his return from Tazewell County or at any time before the debates in any public way, if at all. He was thus in a position toward that platform as he had been in many other episodes of escape already studied. It might prove disadvantageous to deny his part in the convention and the resolutions. If he kept silence he could take such stand, when any stand at all was made necessary, as the circumstances made wise. But Douglas went on at Galesburg thus: "One cardinal point in that platform which he shrinks from is this: that there shall be no more slave states admitted into the Union, even if the people want them." Here cheers arose, and Douglas hurled himself at the crowd: "Now you Republicans all hurrah for him, and for the doctrine of 'no more slave states,' and yet Lincoln tells you that his conscience will not permit him to sanction that doctrine and complains because the resolutions I read at Ottawa made him, as a member of the party, responsible for sanctioning the doctrine of no more slave states. If it be true, as I have shown it is, that the whole Republican Party in the northern part of the state stands committed to the doctrine of no more slave states, and that this same doctrine is repudiated by the Republicans in the other part of the state, I wonder whether Mr. Lincoln and his party do not present the case which he cited from the Scriptures, of a house divided against itself which cannot stand. . . . Whenever I allude to the abolition doctrines, which he considers a slander to be charged with being in favor of, you all endorse them, and hurrah for them, not knowing that your candidate is ashamed to acknowledge them."

Not only were Trumbull, Washburne, a candidate for congress, Douglass the negro, and hundreds of lesser pack hounds after Douglas, but the Hebraic-Puritan press, led by the violent *Chicago Tribune*, kept up the charge of "forger" against Douglas, dinning it into the ears of a people growing madder every hour, when all the while the resolutions which Douglas quoted against Lincoln were in fact fastened upon him in virtue of the fact that they were largely the principles of the Republican Party. Theodore Parker, the man of God, was watching the struggle from afar. His observation on Lincoln's behavior with respect to these resolutions may give us light on the moral aspect of affairs. "Mr. Lincoln did not meet the issue," he wrote Herndon; "he made a technical evasion." "Even if Lincoln had nothing to do with the resolutions, even if they were forged, they involved the vital issues, and stated them, and Lincoln dodged them," wrote Parker. "That is not the way to fight the battle of freedom." [1] But here and now had begun the American pharasaism which is satisfied with a cheap moralization, and will take it, not knowing and refusing to be shown that it baits a politician's hook, a banker's scheme. Lincoln had spoken of the evil genius which had prospered Douglas through life. He had sold himself to the devil, and therefore humble rail splitters had great difficulty in meeting his cunning arguments. From that day to this the story has grown, the myth has taken on the music of verse and the edge of satire that Douglas was a devil's disciple who worked spurious wonders, not that Lincoln dodged and evaded the real questions.

We shall now see how Lincoln pettifogged with the Dred Scott decision, and how he renewed his arguments that it was the product of a conspiracy. Seward had been making the same harangues in the East, so much so that the venerable Taney declared that, if by any chance Seward should be elected president, he would not as chief justice administer the oath of office to him. Lincoln was yet but a

[1] Newton, 208.

LINCOLN AND DOUGLAS DEBATES 289

stump speaker on the prairies of Illinois, but at that no less a candidate for the Senate, and he was now telling the hustings that the Supreme Court of the United States had conspired with politicians to make a false decision, untrue historically, and unsound in point of law, and for the purpose of nationalizing slavery. In the old days Jefferson had accused Marshall of twistifying the Constitution in order to favor the bank; but never before had the Supreme Court been arraigned before popular assemblies.

By way of method in handling the Dred Scott question, Lincoln fell back upon *Chitty on Pleading*. He insisted at Ottawa that he had several times made the charge of conspiracy and that Douglas had put in no plea of denial, and that in consequence he had taken what is called a default against him, in the phrase of lawyers. But finally Douglas had pleaded, but that the plea was demurrable, because Douglas said, claimed Lincoln, that no talk between Douglas and Taney had ever been held with regard to the Dred Scott decision before it was rendered. Therefore Lincoln would demur to such a plea, which admitted its truth. But "what if Judge Douglas never did talk with Chief Justice Taney and the president before the Dred Scott decision was made, does it follow that he could not have had as perfect an understanding without talking as with it?" And so if Douglas never talked to the judge nor to the president, "if the evidence proves the existence of the conspiracy, does his broad answer, denying all knowledge, information, or belief, disturb the fact? It can only show that he was used by conspirators, and was not a leader of them." Then Lincoln went on to insist that the only thing lacking for the nationalization of slavery was a decision that the states could not exclude slavery, just as the court had already decided in Dred Scott that the territories could not exclude it. If such a thing was to happen, it would have Marshall, Lincoln's political preceptor, for it. For Marshall had so enlarged by judicial construction the interstate commerce clause of the Constitution that the right to sell slaves and transport them from one state to another as subjects of commerce inevitably followed, if the question had been raised. But there was enough in the debates already that a popular audience could follow only with difficulty without a question of such subtle legalism being brought into it.

Here is Douglas's answer to Lincoln's charge of conspiracy, made at once in his rejoinder at Ottawa, and not after six days in which to think about what he should say. "In relation to Mr. Lincoln's charge of conspiracy against me, I have a word to say. In his speech today he quotes a playful part of his speech at Springfield, about Stephen, and James, and Franklin, and Roger, and says that I did not take exception to it. I did not answer it, and he repeats it again. He has a right to be as playful as he pleases . . . but I did take objection to his second Springfield speech, in which he stated that he intended his first speech as a charge of corruption or conspiracy against the Supreme Court of the United States, President Pierce, President Buchanan, and myself. . . . He then said that when he made it he did not know whether it was true or not; but inasmuch as Judge Douglas had not denied it, although he had replied to the other parts of his speech three times, he repeated it as a charge of conspiracy against me, thus charging me with moral turpitude. When he put it in that form I did say that . . . I would deprive him of the opportunity of ever repeating it again, by declaring that it was in all its bearings an infamous lie. He says he will repeat it until I answer the folly and nonsense about Stephen and Franklin and Roger and Bob and James. He studied that out, prepared that one sentence with the greatest care, committed it to memory . . . and now he carries that speech around, and reads that sentence to show how pretty it is. His vanity is wounded because I will not go into that beautiful figure of his about the building of a house. . . . I am not green enough to let him make a charge which he acknowledges he does not know to be true, and then take up my time in answering it, when I know it to be false and nobody else knows it to be true . . . I have not brought a charge of moral turpitude against him. When he or any other man brings one against me, instead of disproving it, I will say that it is a lie, and let him prove it if he can. I have lived twenty-five years in Illinois, I have served you with all the fidelity and ability which I possess, and Mr. Lincoln is at liberty to attack my public action, my votes, and my conduct; but when he dares to attack my moral integrity by a charge of conspiracy between myself, Chief Justice Taney and the Supreme Court and two presidents of the United States, I will repel it. Mr. Lincoln has not character enough for integrity and truth merely on his own *ipse dixit* to arraign President Buchanan, President Pierce and nine judges of

LINCOLN AND DOUGLAS DEBATES 291

the Supreme Court, not one of whom would be complimented by being put on an equality with him. There is an unpardonable presumption in a man putting himself up before thousands of people and pretending that his *ipse dixit* without proof, without fact, and without truth, is enough to bring down and destroy the purest and best of living men."

At Freeport Lincoln made the following reply upon this point: "I must be allowed to say that Judge Douglas recurs again, as he did upon one or two other occasions to the enormity of Lincoln—an insignificant individual like Lincoln—upon his *ipse dixit* charging a conspiracy upon a large number of members of Congress, the Supreme Court and two presidents, to nationalize slavery. I want to say that I have made no charge of this sort upon my *ipse dixit*. I have only arrayed the evidence tending to prove it, and presented it to the understanding of others, saying what I think it proves, but giving you the means of judging whether it proves it or not. This is precisely what I have done. I have not placed it upon my *ipse dixit* at all." This furnishes a good example of the Hebraic-Puritan integrity of mind, which has become so much the American political mind at large.

Douglas now at some length analyzed the conspiracy charge when he came to his answer to Lincoln. The sum of it was: "I say the history of the country proves it to be false, and that it could not have been possible at the time." He had referred to Buchanan's absence as minister to the Court of St. James's while the Dred Scott case was brought to the Supreme Court; and to the conclusive consideration that at the time the Kansas-Nebraska bill was passed the Dred Scott case was not on the docket of the Supreme Court. As we have seen, the Kansas-Nebraska Act was passed in the early winter of 1854, while the Dred Scott case was not on the docket of the Supreme Court until the following December, placed there by the abolitionist Chaffee, and as a moot controversy.

At the debate at Quincy, October 13, 1858, Douglas brought all the facts to light. After recapitulating what he had said before by way of deductive proof that there was not, and could not have been a conspiracy to bring about the Dred Scott decision, Douglas said: "Instead of coming out like an honest man and doing so (retracting his charge) he reiterated the charge, and said that if the case had not gone up to the Supreme Court from the courts of Missouri at the time he charged that the judges of the Supreme Court entered into the conspiracy, yet, that there was an understanding with the Democratic owners of Dred Scott that they would take it up. I have since asked him who the Democratic owners of Dred Scott were, but he could not tell, and why? Because there were no such Democratic owners in existence. Dred Scott at the time was owned by the Rev. Dr. Chaffee, an abolition member of Congress, of Springfield, Massachusetts, in right of his wife. He was owned by one of Lincoln's friends, and not by Democrats at all; his case was conducted in court by abolition lawyers, so that both the prosecution and the defense were in the hands of the abolition political friends of Lincoln. . . . Yet I could never get Mr. Lincoln to take back his false charge, although I have called upon him over and over again. He refuses to do it, and either remains silent, or resorts to other tricks to try and palm his slander off on the country." But it did not matter now whether Lincoln retracted the charge or not; the issue had thus gone heavily against him, and was ended.

At the second debate, at Freeport on August 27, 1858, Lincoln conceived that it would be good tactics to retaliate upon Douglas in kind by asking him questions, since Douglas had interrogated him at Ottawa with such critical sharpness with reference to the various similar resolutions of the Republican Party. Douglas contended at the start that Lincoln's questions to him were not justified, because they had no basis in any Democratic platform; but he waived this consideration, and answered them at once at Ottawa on rising to reply to Lincoln. Lincoln's first question was: "If the people of Kansas shall, by means entirely unobjectionable in all other respects, adopt a state constitution, and ask admission into the Union under it, before they have the requisite number of inhabitants according to the English bill—some ninety-three thousand—will you vote to admit them?" This was Douglas's answer:

"I regret exceedingly that he did not answer that interrogatory himself before he put it to me, in order that we might understand, and not be left to infer, on which side he is. Mr. Trumbull, during the last session of Congress, voted from the beginning to the end against the admission of Oregon, although a free state, because she had not the requisite population for a member of Congress. Mr.

Trumbull would not consent under any circumstances to let a state, free or slave, come into the Union until it had the requisite population. As Mr. Trumbull is in the field, fighting for Mr. Lincoln, I would like to have Mr. Lincoln answer his own question. . . . But I will answer his question. In reference to Kansas, it is my opinion that as she has population enough to constitute a slave state, she has people enough for a free state. I will not make Kansas an exceptional case to the other states of the Union. I hold it to be a rule of universal application to require a territory to contain the requisite population for a member of Congress before it is admitted as a state into the Union. . . . And now I would like to get his answer to his own interrogatory—whether or not he will vote to admit Kansas before she has the requisite population. I want to know whether he will vote to admit Oregon before that territory has the requisite population. Mr. Trumbull will not. . . . If there is any sincerity, any truth in the argument of Mr. Trumbull in the Senate against the admission of Oregon, because she had not 93,420 people, although her population was larger than that of Kansas, he stands pledged against the admission of both Oregon and Kansas until they have 93,420 inhabitants." Lincoln did not answer this question of Douglas's, not at Freeport. At Jonesboro, nearly a month later, he claimed that Douglas had not answered him categorically, when in point of fact Douglas had fully done so. He then declared that until Douglas came forward with complete definiteness, "I shall from this time forward assume that he will vote for the admission of Kansas in disregard of the English bill." Douglas had said the very opposite of this. At Galesburg on October 7, Douglas, with untiring energy, elaborated his position on the policy raised by Lincoln's question. "Now the question arises," he said, "what was that English bill which certain men are now attempting to make a test of political orthodoxy in this country? It provided, in substance, that the Lecompton Constitution should be sent back to the people of Kansas for their adoption or rejection, at an election which was held in August last, and in case they refused admission under it, that Kansas should be kept out of the Union until she had 93,420 inhabitants. I was in favor of sending the constitution back in order to enable the people to say whether or not it was their act and deed, and embodied their will; but the other proposition, that if they refused to come into the Union under it, they should be kept out until they had double or treble the population they then had, I never would sanction by my vote. The reason why I could not sanction it is to be found in the fact that by the English bill, if the people of Kansas had only agreed to become a slaveholding state under the Lecompton Constitution, they could have done so with 35,000 people, but if they insisted on being a free state, as they had a right to do, then they were to be punished by being kept out of the Union until they had nearly three times that popluation. I thus said in my place in the Senate, as I now say to you, that whenever Kansas has population enough for a slave state, she has population enough for a free state." Such intellectual honesty as this, such unmoral indifference, if one wants to phrase it so, based upon a large and not a capricious policy, fell upon ears growing deaf to common sense in Galesburg. At that moment the need of an antiseptic like Nietzsche occurred to arrest the spread of the hypocrisy which was breaking into ulcers in Illinois, and destined to spread to the whole country. But in this fashion Douglas settled Lincoln's first interrogatory.

Lincoln's second interrogatory raised a Euclidian crisis against the formal legal repugnance between the Kansas-Nebraska Act and the Dred Scott decision. At once the reflection is inevitable that if Douglas was in a conspiracy to bring about the Dred Scot decision he was raising up a supreme jurisprudence against his own creation, the Kansas-Nebraska Act. The word has come down to us that Lincoln asked the instant question with far sighted purpose to destroy Douglas, to end his chances for the presidency, and that the question and Douglas's answer to it effected that disaster. But manifestly Lincoln could not foresee in 1858 that Jefferson Davis in the winter of 1860, in the Senate, would present resolutions for discussion and adoption which would impugn the Kansas-Nebraska principle of territorial control of slavery, and insist upon a deduction from the principle of the Dred Scott decision, by whose force slavery would be thrust upon a territory. That was but the imperialistic doctrine of Congressional sovereignty which the Republicans had raised up under the leadership of men like Seward, and in Illinois by Lincoln, but for the opposite purpose of keeping slavery out of a territory. Nor could Lincoln foresee that the Democratic convention of 1860, at Charleston, on April 23, would under the injudicious policy of

Buchanan insist upon a new article in the Democratic creed in these words: "That the government of a territory, organized by an act of Congress, is provisional and temporary; and during its existence, all citizens of the United States have an equal right to settle with their property in the territory, without their rights, either of person or property, being destroyed or impaired by congressional or territorial legislation." These things could not have been foreseen by Lincoln, because there was no practical repugnance between the Kansas-Nebraska Act, and the Dred Scott decision; it was only a mathematical inconsistency, such as Lincoln with his studies in Euclid and as a village logician loved to mock with syllogisms framed out of an amateur's delight.

Lincoln's second interrogatory then was: "Can the people of a United States territory, in any lawful way, against the wish of any citizen of the United States, exclude slavery from its limits prior to the formation of a state constitution?" This was Douglas's answer: "I answer emphatically, as Mr. Lincoln has heard me answer a hundred times from every stump in Illinois, that in my opinion the people of a territory can by lawful means exclude slavery from their limits prior to the formation of a state constitution. . . . It matters not what way the Supreme Court may hereafter decide as to the abstract question whether slavery may or may not go into a territory under the Constitution, the people have the lawful means to introduce it or to exclude it as they please, for the reason that slavery cannot exist a day or an hour anywhere unless it is supported by local police regulations. Those police regulations can only be established by the local legislature; and if the people are opposed to slavery, they will elect representatives to that body who will by unfriendly legislation effectually prevent the introduction of it into their midst. . . . Hence no matter what the decision of the Supreme Court may be on that abstract question, still the right of the people to make a slave territory or a free territory is perfect and complete under the Nebraska bill." That the Dred Scott decision was academic and abstract with reference to territorial right was a matter of common comment by Republican statesmen then, who were opposed to the decision.

Lincoln's question was confined to a legal way on the part of a territory to exclude slavery and Douglas answered as though a legal way meant legislation by the territorial legislature; whereas there was very much more to be done, and as effectually done, by the people of a territory to exclude slavery, in the way of social opposition to the institution. People with slaves, surrounded by a hostile public feeling against it, expressed in the incalculable ways in which that could be done, and done with entire lawfulness would have made slave owning intolerable to the owners in Kansas. How far this social opposition might have been carried into laws consonant with the Dred Scott decision, and with the Constitution as interpreted by that decision, would be a speculative inquiry. But it seems probable that legal ingenuity would have invented constitutional legislation bearing upon some phase of the presence of unwanted slavery which would have made it impossible. This, undoubtedly was what Douglas had in mind when he spoke of "unfriendly legislation." He did not develop the precise instances in which such legislation could be created. Lincoln in his rejoinder at Freeport did not attack Douglas's answer to this question. He had to have time to think about it; for in fact Lincoln's friends had tried to dissuade him from asking Douglas this question. They warned him that Douglas would answer it, at least satisfactorily to the audience.

At Jonesboro on September 15, nearly a month after the troublous question was asked, Lincoln had prepared himself to dissect Douglas's answer to it. After showing what the Dred Scott case held, he launched into an elaborate attack upon Douglas's position. "I hold," he said, "that the proposition that slavery cannot enter a new country without police regulations, is historically false." This in face of the fact that it required force to introduce it in the American colonies, and the constant power of England to keep it imposed upon them, as shown by the resolution of Jefferson, which was stricken from the Declaration of Independence. "I hold that the history of this country shows that the institution of slavery was originally planted upon this continent without these police regulations which the judge now thinks necessary for the actual establishment of it." Yet whatever sentiment there was among the colonies against slavery, there was superior police power which overcame it. Was that situation to be repeated as between Congress and the people of a territory? Was this to be under the American system, as a practical policy? Lincoln then asked Douglas if he would pretend that Dred

LINCOLN AND DOUGLAS DEBATES 297

Scott was held in Minnesota Territory without police regulations. But in truth there was no question raised as to how he was held.

The Minnesota Territory was north of 36° 30'; but Dred Scott did not test the police regulations there one way or the other. At that time he was apparently contented as the slave of Dr. Emerson. If Douglas had known about the Matson case in which Lincoln represented the slave owner who was keeping and working his slaves in Illinois, he might have asked Lincoln whether it was the police power of Illinois, or the passive attitude of the people that allowed Matson to bring his slaves into Illinois and work them for the season as slaves. When the police power is invoked it is possible to tell what it is; when it is not invoked slavery may be allowed to exist without knowing what bearing the police power has upon it.

Lincoln in these analyses was in his rightful field. His mind worked better when he was exposing what he considered a fallacy than when he was constructing an original thesis. His faculty for sophistry was most active in forensics of this character. He then went on: "I will ask you, my friends, if you were elected members of the legislature, what would be the first thing you would have to do before entering upon your duties? Swear to support the Constitution of the United States. Suppose you believe, as Judge Douglas does, that the Constitution of the United States guarantees to your neighbor the right to hold slaves in that Territory; that they are his property: how can you clear your oaths unless you give him such legislation as is necessary to enable him to enjoy that property?" The sophism here is the same as Lincoln's argument about a United States bank: It was held to be a constitutional institution, but did that mere fact require congressmen to charter a bank for men who wanted to own one? He went on: How could you "assist in legislation intended to defeat that right?" "Is not Congress itself bound to give legislative support to any right that is established in the United States Constitution?" Is it required, it might be asked, to levy direct taxes, being given the right to do so, instead of raising revenue by the tariff? He then passed for illustration to the Fugitive Slave clause of the Constitution; but there we find express words that no person held to labor or service in one state, and escaping into another, be discharged in consequence of any law or regulation of the latter state, "but shall be delivered up on claim of the party to whom such labor or service is due." This is "powerless without specific legislation to support it," he said. But specific legislation is by this clause imposed on Congress; whereas specific legislation with reference to slaves held in a territory is not imposed.

For a moment let us come back to the precise question which was decided in the Dred Scott case. It was that Congress was without power to draw a line across the country north of which slavery was not lawful, and south of which it was. This being so, Dred Scott was not made free by being in the Wisconsin Territory north of 36° 30′. This meant that Dr. Emerson could take him into that territory and not forfeit title to him as a slave. It follows from this that a thousand men may take their slaves into a free territory without incurring their emancipation by such a congressional enactment. But to hold them there in slavery and to profit by them as such, as an institution, is something not decided by the Dred Scott case at all. At Galesburg Douglas fully developed this idea. In the case of liquor he said: "When you get it there, the merchant who is possessed of the liquors is met by the Maine liquor law, which prohibits the sale or use of his property, and the owner of the slaves is met by equally unfriendly legislation, which makes his property worthless after he gets it there." Lincoln came back with a syllogism in which the major premise was: "Nothing in the constitution or laws of any state can destroy a right distinctly and expressly affirmed in the Constitution of the United States." This premise is not true, for the right to real property, to its title, can be taken away under the law of eminent domain; and so far as slaves were concerned, no one contended that the right to own them could be abolished by a territorial legislature, but only that their use as such could be made intolerable.

There are many distinctions in the law as finely drawn as this, which were known to Lincoln to be daily recognized in the courts in which he practiced. To show the adroitness with which his dialectic could turn questions around, his language at Alton deserves to be cited. He said: "And the man who argues that by unfriendly legislation in spite of that constitutional right, slavery may be driven from the territories, cannot avoid furnishing an argument by which abolitionists may deny the obligation to return fugitives, and claim the power to pass laws unfriendly to the right of the slave-

LINCOLN AND DOUGLAS DEBATES 299

holder to reclaim his fugitive." That was just what the Northern states by state laws had been doing. It would have required time far beyond the limits of any tolerable debate for Douglas to have followed Lincoln in all these sinuous plausibilities. When Lincoln finally compared territorial sovereignty to soup made from the shadow of a starved pigeon, he became the inimitable stump satirist that he could be on occasion. When he called it a do-nothing sovereignty he gave the cue to the crowd to mock the principle. But that was only his own way of stating what Douglas had admitted it was. The practical question remained after all this: Was not Douglas's theory perfectly workable? That it was better than agitation to overthrow it, and war because of its overthrow, no one can doubt who is not inflamed by moral zealotry. Douglas said many times that he was speaking all the time "of rights under the Constitution, not of moral or religious rights." He knew that once legislation is made to depend upon religion, the next step would inevitably be to have law made to conform to a religious creed; and that when that was done the union of church and state was achieved. Lincoln was more and more taking moral ground as he saw the advantage in the orator's appeal to the religious feelings of an audience. But at the last we shall see how far his own morality went when he gave his solution of the negro problem and when he tested it by the Declaration of Independence. For now let us consider his ethical preachments at Alton, in the last debate.

Saying that Douglas contended that slaves, like other property, should be allowed to go into a territory, he declared: "This is strictly logical if there is no difference between it [slave property] and other property. If it and other property are equal, his argument is entirely logical. But if you insist that one is wrong and the other right, there is no use to institute a comparison between right and wrong. . . . This is the real issue. That is the issue that will continue when these poor tongues of Judge Douglas and myself shall be silent." There were many in the audience who instantly upon hearing these moving words remembered, perhaps with tears, the melancholy lines of Cowper's tragic hymn:

> When this poor lisping stammering tongue
> Lies silent in the grave,

which they had sung, and had heard sung in the humble churches of the Mississippi Valley. And it is such pathos as this which has filled a vast commonalty with a deep reverence for Lincoln; for that reverence could be supported by thinking, by asserting that Lincoln finally issued the Emancipation Proclamation. There also he went on with argument penetrated with economic doctrine: "It is the eternal struggle between these two principles—right and wrong—throughout the world. They are the two principles that have stood face to face from the beginning of time, and will ever continue to struggle." Well could the Germans, here but recently from the despotism of the Fatherland, put meaning into such appeals as these. To them he said specifically that he was in favor of such territories, that the white man might find a home. He was in favor of them "for our own people who are born amongst us, but as an outlet for free white people everywhere the world over—in which Hans and Baptiste, and Patrick, and all other men from over the world, may find new homes and better their condition in life." Words could not have been better used to win the hearts of struggling men. Speaking again of the right which is always opposed by the wrong he said: "The one is the common right of humanity, and the other the divine right of kings. It is the same in principle in whatever shape it develops itself. It is the same spirit which says, 'You work and toil and earn bread, and I'll eat it.' No matter in what shape it comes, whether from the mouth of a king who seeks to bestride the people of his own nation and live by the fruit of their labor, or from one race of men as an apology for enslaving another race, it is the same tyrannical principle."

In Douglas's heart there stirred a feeling for men, and a championship for their rights more fundamental and democratic than in Lincoln's; and he was aware of other issues too. He was deeply concerned for the peace of the country. He saw that agitation of this race question would lead to war, and that in war the democratic principle would go down, engulfing the white man of the country, and for the sake of the negro whose state had chances of amelioration without agitation and without war. War was sure to come if the divided house, so called, was to be made a united house in conformity to the Lincoln formula. What Douglas said about this seems now prophetical. Douglas had attacked the "house divided against

LINCOLN AND DOUGLAS DEBATES 301

itself" doctrine with great spirit at Chicago on July 9; now at Ottawa, in the first debate, he returned to the subject, as he did throughout the debates, with the evident purpose of driving it utterly from the minds of the people, to eradicate it as a source of discord in the nation. When he read Lincoln's words, "this government cannot endure permanently half slave and half free," there were cries of "good," and wild cheers from the audience. Douglas struck back with great quickness: "I am delighted to hear you black Republicans say 'good.' I have no doubt that doctrine expresses your sentiments, and I will prove to you, if you will listen to me, that it is revolutionary, and destructive of the existence of this government. . . . Why cannot it now exist divided into free and slave states? Washington, Jefferson, Franklin, Madison, Hamilton, Jay and the great men of that day, made this government divided into free and slave states, and left each state perfectly free to do as it pleased on the subject of slavery. Why cannot it now exist on the same principles on which our fathers made it?"

Lincoln answered: "In the first place, I insist that our fathers did not make this nation half slave and half free. . . . I insist that they found the institution of slavery existing here. They did not make it so, but they left it so, because they knew no way to get rid of it at that time." The difference between making it so, and leaving it so, was just the difference between getting rid of the institution when they were forming the government, and not trying to do so. To this Douglas rejoined: "It is true that they did not establish slavery in any of the states, or abolish it in any of them; but finding thirteen states, twelve of which were slave and one free, they agreed to form a government uniting them together as they stood, divided into free and slave states, and to guarantee forever to each state the right to do as it pleased on the slavery question. . . . I care more for the great principle of self-government, the right of the people to rule, than I do for all the negroes in Christendom." And what was Lincoln going to do with his doctrine? Did he intend to introduce a bill for the abolition of slavery in Kentucky or Virginia? He would do no such thing, and he would not say that such would be his course if elected to the Senate. "Suppose the doctrine advocated by Mr. Lincoln and the abolitionists of this day had prevailed when the constitution was made, what would have been the result? Imagine for a moment that Mr. Lincoln had been a member of the convention . . . and that when its members were about to sign that wonderful document, he had arisen in that convention as he did in Springfield this summer . . . and said, 'A house divided against itself cannot stand; this government divided into free and slave states cannot endure, they must all be free or all be slave, they must all be one thing or the other—otherwise it is a violation of the law of God, and cannot exist' . . . do you think the one free state would have outvoted the twelve slaveholding states, and thus have secured the abolition of slavery? On the other hand would not the twelve slaveholding states have outvoted the one free, and thus have fastened slavery, by a constitutional provision, on every foot of the American republic forever?"

At Chicago, on July 9, Douglas had shown what would result in the American system from enforcing uniformity upon the states. "There is but one mode in which it could be obtained, and that must be by abolishing the state legislatures, blotting out state sovereignty, merging the rights and sovereignty of the states in one consolidated empire, and vesting Congress with the plenary power to make all the police regulations, domestic and local laws throughout the limits of the republic. Then the states will be all slave or all be free; then negroes will vote everywhere or nowhere; then you will have a Maine liquor law in every state or none; then you will have uniformity in all things local and domestic, by the authority of the Federal government. But when you attain that uniformity you will have converted these thirty-two sovereign, independent states into one consolidated empire, with the uniformity of despotism reigning throughout the length and breadth of the land." This is exactly what the plutocratic interests of the time wished, and they were deploying the abolitionists, who knew nothing about the nature of the union and cared less, to bring this consolidation about. A moral question with which to do it was a possible means; it could not have been done openly for the principle of economic monopoly.

Lincoln, driven to flight by Douglas's logic, took wing in the moral empyrean, and perched high. He insisted that Douglas's quarrel was with the Savior rather than with himself. At Alton, in the last debate he said that Douglas "has warred upon them [the sentiments of the "house divided against itself" speech] as Satan wars upon the Bible." But Douglas was speaking more and more earnestly for peace, and with profound realization of the consequences of sectional agitation. "Why should we thus allow a sectional party to agitate this country, to array the North against the South, and convert them into enemies instead of friends, merely that a few ambitious men may ride into power on a sectional hobby?" It was true that the Democrats wanted the offices and were striving for them, but this new Republican Party had no other reason for existence except to get offices. Its pretensions to morality were specious. Only the Hebraic-Puritans were disinterested, if they were entirely so, but that was with the self-abnegation of madness. "How long is it," asked Douglas "since these ambitious Northern men wished for a sectional organization? Did any of them dream of a sectional party as long as the North was the weaker section and the South the stronger? Then all were opposed to sectional parties; but the moment the North obtained the majority in the House and Senate, by the admission of California, and could elect a president without the aid of Southern votes, that moment ambitious Northern men formed a scheme to excite the North against the South, and make the people be governed in their votes by geographical lines, thinking that the North, being the stronger section, would outvote the South, and consequently they, the leaders, would ride into office on a sectional hobby."

After all these years of thought upon slavery, after this contest with Douglas in many speeches before the debates, and in the debates, what would Lincoln do with slavery? If all earthly power were given him, he said, he would not know what to do about it. For what specific purpose, then, was he to be sent to the Senate by the people of Illinois? Having in the days of his young manhood in the legislature of Illinois come to the conclusion that slavery should not be allowed to spread into the territories, he had reached no other solution of the problem after years of thinking and reading political speeches and newspapers, nor after this dialectic contact with the ablest man of the country, in which his analyses should have been sharpened to more critical meanings. The negroes were in America. Should they be sent to Liberia? That could not be done. That being out of the case, the negroes must be kept where they were, and the states which had slavery should be permitted to keep it. Nothing could have been more visionary. At Alton, Douglas exposed Lincoln's divided mind, and he proved that Lincoln's program of keeping the slaves hemmed in was thoroughly impracticable. "He," said Douglas, "says that he will prohibit it in all the territories, and the inference is, then, that unless they make free states out of them he will keep them out of the Union; for mark you, he did not say whether or not he would vote to admit Kansas with slavery or not, as her people might apply (he forgot that as usual, etc.); he did not say whether or not he was in favor of bringing the territories now in existence into the Union on the principle of Clay's Compromise measure on the slavery question. I told you that he would not. His idea is that he will prohibit slavery in all the territories, and thus force them all to become free states, surrounding the slave states with a cordon of free states, and hemming them in, keeping the slaves confined to their present limits whilst they go on multiplying, until the soil on which they live will no longer feed them, and he will thus be able to put slavery in a course of ultimate extinction by starvation. He will extinguish slavery in the Southern states as the French general exterminated the Algerines when he smoked them out. He is going to extinguish slavery by surrounding the slave states, hemming in the slaves, and starving them out of existence. He intends to do that in the name of Christianity, in order that we may get rid of the terrible crime and sin entailed upon our fathers of holding slaves. Mr. Lincoln makes out that line of policy, and appeals to the moral sense of justice and to the Christian feeling of the community to sustain him. He says that any man who holds to the contrary doctrine is in the position of the king who claimed to govern by divine right. . . . Mr. Lincoln proposes to govern the territories without giving them a representation, and calls on Congress to pass laws controlling their property and domestic concerns without their consent and against their will. Thus he asserts for his party the identical principle asserted by George III and the Tories of the Revolution." All the while Douglas knew that under Lincoln's doctrine of the "house divided against itself" there was menace of complete abolition everywhere. The South well understood this. Lincoln himself would not come forth and avow its full meaning, he would not completely face the issue concealed in his figure of speech; though

Douglas dragged him forth to the light, where many audiences were aware of his hiding place and what his concealment meant.

The debates thus proceeded with Lincoln wrestling, running, dodging under, coming close when there was chance for a tight grip upon Douglas. Lincoln inflicted a wound by his second interrogatory, propounded at Freeport, opened it up whenever he had a chance. His long debating arms fouled Douglas when Douglas was too short armed to come back; and in close quarters he dug his sharp elbows into Douglas's face. Douglas quoted Lincoln's friend Matheny to prove that Lincoln and Trumbull had entered into a conspiracy to abolitionize the Whig Party and the Anti-Nebraska Democrats. Lincoln retorted his charge of conspiracy against Douglas and the Supreme Court and President Buchanan to bring about the Dred Scott decision. At Alton, in the very last debate, Lincoln exclaimed: "Then he wants to know why I won't withdraw the charge in regard to conspiracy to make slavery national, as he has withdrawn the one he made. May it please his worship, I will withdraw it when it is proven false on me as that was proven false on him." Herndon called Lincoln a weak man in many particulars; and he showed himself weak and indecisive when he was first in office as president. His stubbornness in sticking to a position was an evidence of weakness. It proved fear to withdraw from a false position, and a lack of strength to take a new one.

There were many places in the debates where Lincoln was tripped. He asserted that nothing had ever disturbed the nation but the slavery question. Douglas replied that the tariff had almost brought it to dissolution in 1832, when South Carolina resorted to nullification and Jackson was about to use the military power against that state. Lincoln referred often to the Declaration of Independence and accused the Democrats of hawking at it. Douglas, as Taney had done, showed that the Declaration did not, and could not have referred to the negroes when it declared that all men "are created equal." Over and over again Lincoln refused to avow what his principles were with reference to imminent issues like that of Kansas, which he should have spoken clearly upon, as a candidate for the Senate soon to be called upon to settle the legislation required for the admission of Kansas and other new states as well.

It is impossible to make out what Lincoln really meant when he spoke of liberty for the negro, when he invoked the Declaration in behalf of negro amelioration. He would not hold the negro in slavery; yet the point was not clear enough to denounce people upon. He would not free them and make them the social and political equals of the whites. But nevertheless the negro should have life, liberty and the right to pursue his happiness. If Douglas's library was "never clear of dust," Lincoln had no library to keep in order. The tariff question puzzled Douglas's kritique, while Lincoln had done little or nothing in the study of economics. The Marxian upheaval in Europe meant nothing to either one of them. Marx had long been a contributor to Greeley's *Tribune*. One wonders if Lincoln ever read a word of Marx. Outside of Jefferson, the philosophers of liberty were unknown to Lincoln. But if the negro was not to be made the social and political equal of the white man, how was he to have life, liberty, and the pursuit of happiness, which Lincoln was demanding for him? Slavery could be abolished, yet the negro could still be denied liberty and those rights which belonged to his happiness. But if he was given liberty, he would be freed from slavery, and with that liberty would come social and political equality. If he was to have liberty, was it to be civil liberty? If he was to have civil liberty, then he would have the rights and immunities which are protected by the state as the whole sum of civil rights. If he was to have political liberty, he would share effectually in framing and conducting the government. If he was to have individual liberty, he would be freed from external restraint to appear in the courts, he would have the security of property, and the right to believe and speak as he chose. In sum, if he was to have life, liberty, and the pursuit of happiness, as one of the human beings born equal with all other human beings, and by grace of the Declaration, then he would be invested with all political, civil and social liberties on even terms with the white man. When Lincoln was denouncing Douglas and others for hawking at the Declaration, he was scoring points with the abolitionists; but when he tried to expound what the Declaration meant, and to affix a precise stigma upon those who hawked at it, he found himself beyond his depth, with the result that he contradicted himself to the letter and in spirit.

Douglas made the best use of Lincoln's self-stultification. He accused Lincoln of shading his utterances according to the audience, and with preaching abolitionism at Ottawa and at Chicago in the northern part of Illinois, while reversing his doctrines in the southern part of the state, where the old-line Whigs, and especially the Democrats clove to the Taney interpretation of the Declaration, that it meant white men only, and not negroes when it announced that all men were created equal. Leaving motives out of consideration, Douglas speared Lincoln between the horns of his own dilemma before the Calvinistic audience at Galesburg. This seemed to make no difference with them; and in the roar of the incoming tide of destiny the absurdities of Lincoln's philosophizations have been drowned; but for study of Lincoln's mind nothing better shows its incoherence. This is the parallel that Douglas drew on Lincoln, first quoting against him what Lincoln had said at Chicago in July of 1858: "I should like to know, if taking this old Declaration of Independence, which declares that all men are created equal upon principle, and making exceptions to it, where it will stop? If one man says it does not mean a negro, why may not another man say it does not mean another man? If the Declaration is not the truth, let us get the statute book and tear it out. Let us discard all this quibbling about this man and the other man, this race and that race, and the other race being inferior, and therefore they must be placed in an inferior position, discarding our standard that we have left us. Let us discard all these things and unite as one people throughout this land, until we shall stand up declaring that all men are created equal."

Then at Charleston on September 18, 1858, two months after this Chicago declaration, Lincoln said this: "I am not, nor ever have been in favor of bringing about in any way the social and political equality of the white and black races; that I am not nor ever have been in favor of making voters of the free negroes, or jurors, or qualifying them to hold office, or having them marry with white people. I will say in addition that there is a physical difference between the white and black races which, I suppose, will forever forbid the two races living together upon terms of social and political equality; and inasmuch as they cannot so live, that while they do remain together, there must be the position of the superiors and the inferiors; and that I as much as any other man, am in favor of the superior position being assigned to the white man."

The Galesburg audience had applauded both of these pronouncements when Douglas brought them into sharp contrast by reading them side by side. "Fellow citizens," roared Douglas, "here you find men hurrahing for Lincoln, and saying that he did right, when in one part of the state he stood up for negro equality; and in another part, for political effect, discarded the doctrine, and declared that there always must be a superior and inferior race. . . . Now how can you reconcile these two positions of Mr. Lincoln? . . . Up here he thinks it is all nonsense to talk about a difference between the two races . . . down South he makes 'this quibbling' about this race and the other race being inferior as the creed of his party . . . you find that his political meetings are called by different names in different counties . . . here they are called Republican meetings, but in old Tazewell, where Lincoln made a speech last Tuesday, he did not address a Republican meeting, but a 'grand rally of the Lincoln men.' There are very few Republicans there, because Tazewell County is filled with old Virginians, and Kentuckians, all of whom are Whigs or Democrats; and if Mr. Lincoln had called an abolition or Republican meeting there, he would not get many votes. . . . When I was down in Monroe County a few weeks ago, addressing the people, I saw handbills posted announcing that Trumbull was going to speak in behalf of Lincoln; and what do you think the name of his party was there? Why the 'Free Democracy.' . . . Come up to Springfield, where Lincoln now lives, and you find that the convention of his party which assembled to nominate candidates for the legislature, who are expected to vote for him if elected, dare not adopt the name Republican, but assembled under the title of 'all opposed to the Democracy.' Thus you find that Mr. Lincoln's creed cannot travel through even one half of the counties of this state, but that it changes its hues and becomes lighter and lighter as it travels from the extreme north, until it is nearly white when it reaches the southern end of the state. I ask you, my friends, why cannot Republicans avow their principles alike everywhere? I would despise myself if I thought that I was procuring your votes by concealing my opinions, and by avowing one set of principles in one part of the state, and a different set in another part. . . . I will tell you that this Chicago doctrine of Lincoln's—declaring that the negro and the white man are made equal by the Declaration of Independence and by Divine Providence—is a monstrous heresy. . . . I see a gentleman there in the crowd shaking his head. Let me remind him that when Thomas Jefferson wrote that document, he was the owner, and so continued until his death, of a large number of slaves. Did he intend to say in that Declaration that his negro slaves, which he held and treated as his property, were created his equals by divine law, and that he was violating the law of God every day of his life by holding slaves? It must be borne in mind that when that Declaration was put forth every one of the thirteen colonies were slaveholding colonies, and every man who signed that instrument represented a slaveholding constituency. Recollect also that no one of them emancipated his slaves, much less put them upon an equality with himself, after he signed the Declaration. On the contrary, they all continued to hold their negroes as slaves during the Revolutionary War. . . . Now do you believe, are you willing to have it said, that every man who signed the Declaration of Independence declared the negro his equal, and then was hypocrite enough to continue to hold him as a slave in violation of what he believed to be the divine law? And yet when you say that the Declaration of Independence includes the negro, you charge the signers of it with hypocrisy."

Lincoln's reply to the parallel which had been drawn upon him was cloudy and wavering, and at last intellectually impotent. He made the observation first that the two speeches had been published, and that if there was any inconsistency between them the public had the opportunity to detect it. He knew all the while that the two speeches would be put in print, and therefore why do the foolish thing of exposing himself in an inconsistency? And finally "I have not supposed and do not now suppose, that there is any conflict whatever between them." That further irrationality could be swallowed with what he had said at Chicago and at Charleston by those who believed in the simultaneous existence of divine grace and predestination, but by no one else.

It is not to be denied that the negro question was perplexing to the best thought; but we are concerned with considering how Lincoln met it at this period of his life and what solutions he had to propose. It was an epigram of oratorical ingenuity to say that "if any one man chooses to enslave another, no third man shall be allowed to object," and thus with one gesture to dispose of the Kansas-Nebraska bill, which in fact did not leave it to one man to object or to agree to the admission of slavery, but which left it to a majority of the people. So was it magnanimous in sound to talk of negro equality; but Lincoln for years had practiced law and he had been in politics in Illinois, and he did not, when brought to actualities, favor the repeal of the clause of the Illinois constitution which forbade negroes from coming into the state. The migration which he favored was that of negroes as free men into the territories. He talked much of making the fight upon principle, without hope of reward, for "nobody has ever expected me to be president. In my poor, lean, lanky face, nobody has ever seen that any cabbages were sprouting." Yet on many points it was impossible to get him to declare his principles, though "we have to fight this battle upon principle alone." He could say in a tone of apology, for the "house divided against itself" war cry, that "it never occurred to me that I was doing anything, or favoring anything to reduce to a dead uniformity all the local institutions of the states," and he said this in the teeth of all that Jefferson and other philosopher statesmen had written about state sovereignty, and in particular with such remarks he ran against the grain of Jefferson's strictures upon the Missouri Compromise. In regard to Douglas's charge that he was stirring up bad blood by drawing upon the Bible to improve on Seward's "irrepressible conflict," he could say in extenuation of his course that he did not know that he was speaking words which would lead to "bad results," though he was thoroughly familiar with the course of events since Sumner and Chase had sent forth their Appeal to inflame passion with its forged processes. He could appeal to Henry Clay as authority for supporting the Declaration of Independence lest evil men "blow out the moral lights around us," and he could justify the right of that appeal by saying that Henry Clay was his beau ideal, "the man for whom I fought all my humble life"; but he had to meet the keen memory of Douglas who told an audience that Lincoln had opposed Clay for president in 1848. To show that there had been regression since the days of Washington, he went so far as to affirm that the negro had had an actual part as a voter in electing the delegates who ratified the Federal

LINCOLN AND DOUGLAS DEBATES 311

Constitution, without mentioning the fact that no one then voted unburdened of property qualifications; and that few negroes had anything to say about the adoption of that instrument under the laws which disfranchised thousands of white men.

There had been disunionists all along: Hale of New Hampshire who, in 1850, presented a petition from Pennsylvania and Delaware for a dissolution of the Union; and men like Phillips who openly declared that they were for disunion; and men like Garrison who denounced the Constitution as a covenant with hell. But the real disunionists were those who hated the Federal system, and who, after the Lincoln and Douglas debates, saw their chance to destroy it. To these men it mattered nothing that Clay had said that the people of a territory had the right to decide for themselves whether they would have slavery or no. Their warfare against Douglas was legitimate though he was standing upon the Clay doctrine. Calhoun's noble emphasis upon the "Chords" of the Union, which Lincoln himself used in his First Inaugural, deflected in no degree the course of men bound to rule or to ruin. Nor was anyone attentive to the historical facts that the whole trouble had been stirred up, not by Douglas, with his Kansas-Nebraska bill, but by those who perverted its meaning, and who denied or obscured its historical genesis in Webster and Clay. Lincoln was now coming into national influence; and Douglas, though defeating Lincoln for the Senate, was to be more and more borne down by irresponsible minds like Seward, Chase and their fanatical following. The cloud of war had now begun to mist the sky.

The Buchanan disloyalty had taken away over 5000 votes from the Douglas ticket, which if added to the votes that Douglas swept with him would have given his ticket a popular majority in Illinois. The state senators and state assemblymen were elected under an apportionment of the state which gave Douglas a slight advantage. Speaking of this Herndon remarked "ideal perfection is never attained in such matters." We shall hear Bryant at Cooper Institute, when introducing Lincoln, speak of this Illinois apportionment as one of the many instances in which the power of evil circumvented the will of heaven. Yet Lincoln was not counted out as Jackson and Tilden were. The rule of righteousness and of men's equality did not raise its standards of perfect conduct politically in their behalf. All that could be said in explanation of Lincoln's defeat was that the votes for him were not grouped effectively to give him their advantage in particular districts. In other words, if he could have added to the votes he received in the fifth district a few votes which he could well spare from the fourth, he would have carried both the fourth and fifth. This was the substance of the unjust apportionment of which Lincoln's friends made post-election complaint; just as in 1896 the Democrats showed that if Bryan had received 50,000 more votes, and these had been properly distributed in close states, he would have defeated McKinley for the presidency. To have the votes rightly placed, and to win enough of them are always objectives in elections, where the Sublime Gambler who has fixed the percentages of the game has also made it fascinating for men to divine them in advance if they possibly can do so. Douglas had made a heroic fight against all the odds that a tireless enemy could bring against him. This enemy had money, it had newspapers, like the *Chicago Tribune* which constantly throughout the campaign published reports of the debates which Douglas and his friends called willfully incorrect and unfair. The enemy had the great assistance of Buchanan and his office holders riding about the state on passes to cajole or coerce the friends of Douglas from standing by him. It had to some extent the clergymen, strabismic and violent as usual; it had the assistance of the Germans, who owed more to Jefferson and his disciples than to Hamilton and to Webster, but were unaware of the direction in which their gratitude should have walked. Douglas overcame all this; and he did it while announcing his principles on all the issues at stake and against Lincoln who kept dodging and evading, as a wrestler does who tires his antagonist by keeping out of the way. Financially the campaign was disastrous to the purse of both Douglas and Lincoln. Douglas was very well off, but his pride was aroused by the prospect of defeat at the hands of such adventurers and hypocrites; his courage and his will were set to overcome them at any cost. Hence he went heavily into his own pocket; while Lincoln, after the campaign, wrote to a friend: "I am absolutely without money now even for household expenses." And he was in debt to the campaign committee besides. He was trying to discharge the obligation by borrowing money.

Douglas had discovered, if he did not know it before, that the cause of the people is a devil's cause, a Promethean sacrifice. In

LINCOLN AND DOUGLAS DEBATES 313

essence his battle was waged for the principle that all governments derive their just powers from the consent of the governed. That was well enough, nearly everyone admitted, at least with mouth worship; but how could he assert that doctrine in a case and in a way which made a slave of the negro? On the other hand Lincoln's many speeches reduce themselves more or less to the support of the thesis that all men are created equal. But in reality he was maintaining this thesis actually for the tariff and the bank, for centralists and for the monarchic principle. All men are born equal to work for wages; but not born equal to govern themselves in order to command their wages.

A tree is known by its fruit—somewhat; when the tree is pruned and sprayed, and when its roots are given breathing room. What came of Lincoln's tree is well known. What would have come from Douglas's belongs to imagination, to historic speculation. Man's mind can discover political principles, and point out the good that ensues from their observance. But the Sublime Gambler has other perspectives, whose incidence upon the human scene comes in to human perception with obliquity—but possibly on a straight line when the distance is considered from which it is drawn. The human mind can demonstrate in the passing hours that a given cause is from hell itself, and that all its sponsors are impostors and scoundrels. But the human mind collapses when it attempts to show that the world would have been better in the long run if the evil cause had been defeated. Even a few hundred years of bitter fruit from the tree of the bad cause may be clearly seen and accorded with all proofs of their disastrous consequences; yet there is so much time ahead to which the phantasmagoria is moving, for which it is rightly fitted, and for an end which has reckoned all along with the success of the race, or has not considered it, because it was not worth taking into account.

In less than three years from the day of the last debate, the body of Douglas was to be lying entombed in Chicago by Lake Michigan, on a spot of ground which he had bought in the days of his youthful power and happiness, ground that he intended for his home in the honorable and mellow years of retirement from labor. It was now the camp of Federal soldiers, and of war prisoners. For the house divided against itself had brought the war which he had so clearly foreseen. The Missouri Compromise, so to speak, had, like an animistic thorn, shot itself from the Mississippi eastward to the Atlantic, fulfilling the corrupt blood of its heredity, just as Jefferson foretold that it would forty years before. Back of Douglas's tomb, about a mile away, was the Chicago University which Douglas had founded. It was soon to pass into decay, and be taken over by the ill-gotten wealth of one of the giants spawned by Lincoln's politics, and by their sequelæ, reconstruction crimes. We shall hear a little more of Douglas when the man who had always hated him became president. We shall see him briefly in the noblest and most self-subordinating activities and generosities; and then he must be left in the defeat of his genius where the trains of the Illinois Central Railroad were roaring past, and where the gulls just beyond the piers were crying their idiot hungers over the silted waters of Lake Michigan.

Now Lincoln had to go back to the practice of law. He tried lecturing, but without success. His subject, "Inventions," did not capture applause. No less after his failure he had invitations to deliver it, but he declined on the ground that he must "stick to the courts for a while." Before the debates closed he went to Columbus, Ohio, and delivered a political speech. As the lecture field failed him, for he was not happy in it, he returned to the stump, despite the necessity for making money in the practice of law. Hence in September of 1859 he was in Cincinnati where he addressed the people to great applause. In December he was in Kansas, speaking at Atchison, Troy and Leavenworth, and other places. Meanwhile he was writing many letters on political subjects to a large number of correspondents. He was maneuvering to have the Republican national convention held in Illinois in 1860. His name was beginning to be mentioned in connection with the presidency; but he wrote a friend, "I beg that you will not give it further mention. Seriously, I do not think I am fit for the presidency." He never self-appraised himself better. He was desirous of addressing the people of New York; and after some correspondence he received the invitation to come to Cooper Institute. For an understanding of that speech we must devote some time now to a consideration of what the Union was, and what the Constitution was that created it. We cannot critically weigh his Inaugurals, or his acts as president without this survey.

LINCOLN AND DOUGLAS DEBATES

The Lincoln mind cannot be laid out for dissection without seeing what the material was upon which his thinking and speaking exercised themselves at the maturity of his intellectual powers and in the gravest of circumstances.

Chapter XIII   *The Union of the Constitution Before the War*

ALEXANDER H. STEPHENS wrote of Lincoln: "I do not think that he intended to overthrow the institutions of the country. I do not think that he understood them or the tendencies of his acts upon them. The Union with him in sentiment rose to the sublimity of a religious mysticism, while his ideas of its structure and formation in logic rested upon the subtleties of a sophism." [1] Stephens and Lincoln had been in Congress together; they had exchanged friendly letters after the election of 1860 touching the secession of Georgia, then pending, which was a step that Stephens opposed on policy, but believed in thoroughly as a right. Stephens' characterization, therefore, did not issue out of unfriendliness. His critical eye saw Lincoln fed upon the fallacious doctrines of Webster, which induced giantism in this tall, long armed and long legged lawyer of central Illinois, who having freed his body from the creative muck in which it had been submerged, had lifted his small head to the level of the tree tops in order to breathe the élan vital of power. Having risen so, he had stalked across the country like Typhon, and with ignorant ideas of his rights as president had grasped the war powers of the Constitution with which he accomplished a *coup d'état*. In his imagination the Union was a mystical paraclete which had hovered in mid air before it descended into the lifeless bodies of the states, and gave them breath. The Union was an entity. It was once a noun, like beauty, goodness, justice. But it had achieved an existence all its own, as tangible as that of the flag. It was a soul, a body, a Messiah for whom men should fight and die, regardless of everything else. It was a precious and sacred reality to be saved even at the cost of the continuance of negro slavery. If some slaves could be freed to save the Union, that should be done. If the Union could be saved by not freeing any slave, that should be the course. What he would do about the colored race, he would do because it helped to save the Union; and what he forbore to do would be for the same purpose.

[1] "Constitutional View of the War Between the States," II, 448.

UNION OF THE CONSTITUTION 317

In this epigrammatic manner he wrote to the complaining Greeley in 1862. All this furnishes material for an analysis of Lincoln's complex and irrational thinking. It is evident that Lincoln, with his desultory intellectual habits, was not fitted to make a careful and profound study of the Constitution, and of the history which preceded its formation. So far as he did study it, nothing came into his mind except odd scraps of material of which his imagination made strange comments, and irrelevant conclusions. This was one operation of his so-called originality of mind, which, as a whole, many of his friends observed in him; but it was not a normal, a legitimate originality.

In his youth, as we have seen, he had pored over Webster's reply to Hayne. If he ever read Webster's retractions of those arguments it did not remove the impression of Webster's first utterance. Lincoln knew Story's *Commentaries on the Constitution,* without following up those thinkers who overthrew all that Story had erected into a fabric of national sovereignty and national supremacy, and the nature of the Union and the states. When one looks at the list of books which Lincoln read, a list now made complete by the research of biographers, by Beveridge the most thorough of them all, it is clear that Lincoln had no better than a country lawyer's understanding of the Constitution and the Union, and that this was confined to the doctrines put forth by the Hamilton-Marshall-Webster school. What he read of Calhoun, though Lincoln had great admiration for Calhoun's style, was not likely to penetrate deeply into his thinking. For while Lincoln had analytical ability if let to go his own so-called original way, he was not equipped in mind to follow with patience and with care the compact and thoroughly woven reasonings of Calhoun. Thus it was a man unschooled in the very learning which was most necessary for Lincoln to know, who went to Washington in March, 1861, and there was sworn to preserve, protect and defend the Constitution, and faithfully to execute the office of president. He took no oath to preserve the Union, save as he could do that by preserving and protecting the Constitution. To destroy the Constitution in order to protect the Union was something like saving the Union at the expense of any solution of slavery, whether by total or half emancipation, or what not. The fact that he asked Herndon to bring him Clay's speeches to be read for the purpose of his First Inaugural, shows that he wanted to put style and oratorical form to his words; for the rest it was enough if he took a few postulates out of the Federalistic school of political criticism for the bone and sinew of his announcement. He was wont to utter all-hail to Jefferson when on the hustings of Illinois. But now that he was preparing his Inaugural he invited the inveterate enemies of Jefferson to his side. Lincoln was not Jefferson's son. He was Hamilton's.

The First Inaugural furnishes texts for a constitutional survey sufficiently complete by which to test Lincoln's theories and his acts as president. The subject as a whole would require a volume by itself, and therefore great condensation must be observed. Lincoln first adverted to the recent secession of seven Southern states, the first being South Carolina, which had seceded a little more than a month after the presidential election in the fall of 1860. Of this Lincoln said: "I hold that in the contemplation of universal law, the union of these states is perpetual." What "universal law" was, or had to do with the question, he did not stop to explain. "Perpetuity is implied," he went on, "if not expressed in the fundamental law of all national governments. It is safe to assert that no government proper ever had a provision in its organic law for its own termination." In other words he urged the fact that no government ever provided for its own termination as proof of the false conclusion that no government was terminable. Then he went on: "Continue to execute all the express provisions of our national constitution, and the Union will endure forever." That could have been said of the Union under the Articles of Confederation. "It being impossible to destroy it except by some action not provided for in the instrument itself." This was a truism, a platitude, which had no logical bearing upon the question of the right of states to get out of the Union, if they chose to do so.

All of this may be taken to constitute the first text of this examination; but the numeric order will not be observed, because the historical sketch to be given here begins with the formation of the Union, and not with the facts which show that it was dissolvable. Lincoln, therefore, after predicating the perpetuity of the Union, made this observation: "The Union is much older than the Constitution. It was formed in fact by the articles of association in

UNION OF THE CONSTITUTION 319

1774. It was matured and continued by the Declaration of Independence. It was further matured, and the faith of all the thirteen states expressly plighted and engaged that it should be perpetual by the Articles of the Confederation in 1778; and finally, in 1787, one of the declared objects for ordaining and establishing the Constitution was to 'form a more perfect Union.' " The lacunæ in this statement will be overlooked if one merely listen to the sound of these words. "The Union," he said, "is much older than the Constitution." He did not say "a Union." He wanted to convey the idea that the same union had passed from government to government under the various instruments which the fathers had adopted. The same mystical paraclete was always around ready to enter whatever new organic law the fathers established. But whether he said "the Union," or "a union" it was just as pertinent to his argument as if he had said that the union of England and Scotland was older than the Constitution of the United States. He then went on to this logical summation: "It follows from these views that no state, upon its own mere motion, can lawfully get out of the Union; that resolves and ordinances to that effect are legally void; and that acts of violence within any state or states against the authority of the United States are insurrectionary or revolutionary, according to circumstances." That is putting the case as emphatically as George III and his ministers formulated the law when dealing with the thirteen colonies. As to words, however, he did not regard their accepted meaning. There was no insurrection in the South then or at any time; there was no revolution unless the word be used in its generic sense. But we have seen that Lincoln in Congress had said, "Any people anywhere, being inclined, and having the power, have the right to rise up and shake off the existing government, and form a new one that suits them better. This is a most valuable, a sacred right." The seceding states had shown that they were inclined to shake off the existing government; and they had proven that they had the power to do so by resuming their sovereign powers, and by organizing a government perfect in every part and competent in every way to take its place among the family of nations. Moreover, this revolution was wholly peaceful. It was not a Latin, not a South American eruption of political forces in which property rights and international interests were imperilled; nor was anyone in the South asking for help against an unwished for revolt. All was tranquillity in the South, and all rejoicing that the Southern states had detached themselves from men like Phillips and Giddings, and Sumner and Seward, and the Congresses which they inflamed; and finally from Lincoln whose "house divided against itself" doctrine meant plainly enough that the South had to become all free. The South knew and had been saying for years that under the guise of freedom for the negro lurked centralization, with the bank, the tariff, and imperial economics as accompaniments more desired than negro emancipation. While we consider by reference to history whether the Union was older than the Constitution, we shall also see what the nature of the Union was before its character was destroyed by the War between the States.

Before the Revolution there were thirteen colonies, which later became the thirteen states. Some of these were known as Proprietary colonies, some as Provincial, and some as Charter colonies; but all were under Great Britain's sovereignty. These colonies were separate and distinct, and had no political relation to each other. As early as 1643 some of the New England colonies joined together for their mutual good and protection; but England ended this relationship by abrogating the charters of the colonies which formed it. In 1754 and in 1765 there was an attempt on the part of certain colonies to form a union for defense against the Indians, and to resist the growing aggressions of England. In 1774 something more definite was done toward a union, and this is the union to which Lincoln first referred in his Inaugural as being the beginning of the union idea. At this time the British Parliament passed the Boston Port Bill, and enacted still another law which changed the charter of Massachusetts. This state was from the first always doing something against someone or requiring something to be done for it. Now, because the charter had been taken from Massachusetts, all the colonies bristled with resentment. Virginia, where Jefferson and Washington lived, sent up the battle cry, and appealed to all the colonies to send delegates to a general convention or congress, in order that there might be joint consultation on the crisis. Twelve colonies responded to Virginia's call whose delegates met at Philadelphia on September 5, 1774. It was determined at the outset that the congress should be one of separate political organizations, that is

UNION OF THE CONSTITUTION 321

separate colonies, or geographical units; and every colony was allocated but one vote, with no reference to the number of delegates which it had sent. The object of this congress is shown by the powers which were conferred upon the delegates. Virginia empowered her representatives "To consider of the most proper and effectual manner of so operating on the commercial connection of the colonies with the mother country, as to procure redress for the much injured province of Massachusetts." Maryland and South Carolina similarly empowered their delegates.[1] All this congress did was to declare what the rights of the colonies were in the premises, and to make certain recommendations. Then the congress dissolved; recommending that the colonies send deputies again to meet in Congress on May 10, 1775.

Whatever union was created in 1774, was thus ended. However, delegates came again, and now what was called a permanent union was formed between the colonies. Words like permanent, perpetual, indissoluble are used by men who well know that time and circumstances make all things impermanent and transitory. They are the expressions of human nature trying to mold the future, they are bonds given to Fate while intending to avoid the bond if the consideration for it fails. This congress of May 10, 1775, was the one which, on July 4, 1776, adopted the Declaration of Independence.

With the adoption of the Declaration, the colonies became states. "We . . . solemnly publish and declare, that these United Colonies are and of right ought to be free and independent states . . . and that as free and independent states, they have full power to levy war, conclude peace, contract alliances, establish commerce, and to do all other things which independent states may of right do," are the words of the Declaration. By the treaty of peace between the states and Great Britain, at the close of the Revolution, the separate sovereignty of the states was acknowledged: "His Britannic Majesty acknowledges the said United States, viz: New Hampshire, Massachusetts-Bay, Rhode Island, and Providence Plantations, Connecticut, New York, New Jersey, Pennsylvania, Delaware, Maryland, Virginia, North Carolina, South Carolina and Georgia to be free, sovereign and independent states; that he treats with them as such; and for himself, his heirs, and successors, relinquishes

[1] Elliot's Debates, I, 42.

all claim to the government, and territorial rights of the same and every part thereof."

Meanwhile, after the Declaration in which the colonies had asserted their rights as sovereign states, this same congress formulated the Articles of Confederation. This was in 1777; and into this union eleven states entered in 1778; one in 1779 and one in 1781. These were articles of "confederation and perpetual union" between the states. Curtis, in his work on the Constitution, wrote: "The parties to this instrument were free, sovereign, political communities, each possessing within itself all the powers of legislation and government over its citizens which any political society can possess." Marshall, to whose school Lincoln belonged, held in deciding one of the landmark cases of American jurisprudence,[1] that the states before the adoption of the Constitution were sovereign. "It has been said," he declared, "that they [the states] were sovereign, were completely independent, and were connected with each other only by a league. This is true." These affirmations as to the sovereignty of the states, before the Articles of Confederation, could be multiplied out of the mouths of Webster, Calhoun and many others, but the point is not debatable enough to need further authority.

By the second article of this instrument which created the confederation, it was provided: "Each state retains its sovereignty, freedom and independence, and every power, jurisdiction and right which is not by this confederation expressly delegated to the United States, in congress assembled." In preserving the character of the confederation as a league of states, each state had one vote in Congress. And finally the XIIIth Article was written to read: "The Articles of this confederation shall be inviolably observed by every state, and the union shall be perpetual." Here to refer to Lincoln's Inaugural, the government formed by the Articles had no "provision in its organic law for its own termination;" but on the contrary had express words that it should be perpetual. And yet this union was dissolved and another one created under the Constitution.

Before we come to this, some notice must be taken of the movements which were made to amend the Articles of Confederation. On February 3, 1781, a resolution was adopted by Congress, looking to

[1] Gibbons vs. Ogden, 9 Wheat, I.

a tariff on imports, that power not having been given in the Articles. The resolution was rejected by the states. In April, 1783, the same movement was renewed; but the states would not accede to it. In 1784, Congress asked of the states power for fifteen years to regulate commerce with foreign nations. Not enough states agreed to this to make it effective. In 1785 Monroe, in Congress, moved that Congress be empowered to regulate trade. This proposal was ignored. Madison went to the legislature of his state, Virginia, and initiated there a program for investing Congress with the powers so previously rejected. This failed. But in January, 1786, the Virginia legislature passed a resolution, and by it appointed eight commissioners to meet like commissioners from the other states to consider a uniform system of commercial regulations for the states. This resolution was sent out; and New York, New Jersey, Pennsylvania, and Delaware responded, by appointing commissioners. These, from the several states mentioned, met at Annapolis in September, 1786. They accomplished nothing beyond recommending the holding of a general convention of all the states to meet at Philadelphia on the second Monday of May in 1787, there to take into consideration the situation of the United States, and to "devise such further provisions as shall appear to them necessary to render the Constitution of the federal Government adequate to the exigencies of the Union." Here it is to be noted, these men, such as Madison and Edmund Randolph, lawyers and scholars, spoke of the Articles as a Constitution. Yet later there were to be infinite dialetics by Webster to show, if he could, that the Articles were a compact, while the Constitution was only the result of a compact. This convention of May, 1787, was the one that formulated the Constitution, by which the inviolable and perpetual union of the Articles was dissolved, and a new government created.

It may be well to observe here the two theories respecting the origin of the government under the Constitution: whether it proceeded from the American people in mass, or whether from the states as sovereign bodies. The historian Motley wrote: "The Constitution was not drawn up by states, it was not promulgated in the name of states, it was not ratified by states. The states never acceded to it, and possess no power to secede from it. It was ordained and established over the states by a power superior to the states, by the people of the whole land, in their aggregate capacity, acting through conventions of delegates, etc."

This is the false historical doctrine which Lincoln imbibed, and upon which he waged war against the South. Even Marshall, who knew the whole course which led to the calling of the Constitutional Convention, and what was done in it, and what his own state did, both in sending delegates to it, and in ratifying the Constitution when it was submitted to Virginia, uttered strange words when passing upon the genesis of the government under the Constitution. In 1819, when holding that the charter of the United States Bank was constitutional, he said: "Counsel for the state of Maryland have deemed it of some importance, in the construction of the Constitution to consider the instrument not as emanating from the people, but as the act of sovereign and independent states, who alone are truly sovereign; and must be exercised in subordination to the states, which alone possess supreme dominion. It would be difficult to sustain this proposition. The convention which framed the Constitution was indeed elected by the state legislatures. But the instrument when it came from their hands was a mere proposal without obligation. . . . It was reported to the then existing congress of the United States, with a request that it might be submitted to a convention of delegates chosen in each state by the people thereof under recommendation of its legislature for their assent and ratification. This mode of proceeding was adopted, and by the Convention, by Congress, and by the state legislatures, the instrument was submitted to the people. They acted upon it in the only manner in which they can act safely, effectively and wisely, on such a subject, by assembling in convention. It is true they assembled in their several states—and where else should they assemble? No political dreamer was ever wild enough to think of breaking down the lines which separate states, and of compounding the American people into one common mass. Of consequence, when they act, they act in their states. The government of the Union is emphatically and truly a government of the people. In form and in substance it emanates from them. Its powers are granted by them, and are to be exercised directly on them, and for their benefit."[1]

By such sophistry was the Bank held constitutional, in the face

[1] McCullough vs. Maryland, 5 Wheat. 579.

of the fact well known to Marshall that the proposal in the Constitutional Convention to empower Congress to charter a bank of corporations had been considered several times and was finally voted down by eight states out of eleven, though his own state, Virginia, voted for it. He further disregarded the action of his own state, as well as the action of the states of New Hampshire, Massachusetts, South Carolina, Rhode Island, which expressly qualified their ratification of the Constitution by requesting amendments to the Constitution which should expressly reserve to the states all power not granted; and that Congress should be expressly prohibited from chartering corporations. Articles IX and X resulted from this, and these went into force in November, 1791. "It is true they assembled in their several states—and where else should they assemble?" They could have assembled in Philadelphia, if the American people were acting in mass. But on the other hand they could have gone to Bermuda without in the least changing their character as delegates of states and acting for such states. But there is no need to spend any more time on empty subtleties of this sort. The historical facts are too clear and too numerous for any such verbal follies as these are to prevail. An army of men who proclaim the falsity of these arguments may be killed and overcome by a superior army which asserts their truth; but otherwise they cannot prevail.

Before showing that the Constitution proceeded from the states, that it was made by states and ratified by states, each in their sovereign capacity, a subject requires brief attention, since it is one around which Webster exercised his thunderous rhetoric, in addition to being of the very character which would and did in fact intrigue the peculiar analysis of Lincoln and minds like his. If anyone will look at the Articles of Confederation, he will see that they are prefaced with the words: "To all to whom these presents shall come, we the undersigned delegates of the states affixed to our names did," and then follows the recital that they had formulated the Articles. The Articles then follow. Then at the last is the statement that the legislatures had approved of the Articles and had authorized the delegates to ratify and confirm them; and lastly are the signatures of the delegates signing on the part of and in behalf of the respective states serially set forth. When, however, we turn to the Constitution, we find that the preamble is: "We the people of the United States . . . do ordain and establish this constitution for the United States of America." So it was that Webster found in these words material for his arguments that the United States were a nation, above the states, and had a supreme sovereignty of their own as an entity standing upon its own feet. In like manner Motley justified his historical interpretation partly upon the basis of these words; and Story in his commentaries looked up to them as strong proof for his constitutional theories, while Lincoln, with his doctrine of the Union being older than the Constitution, and his mystical conception of the nature of the Union, could justify his dialectics upon these simple and easily explainable words.

When the preamble to the Constitution was first drawn, it read, "We, the people of the states of New Hampshire," and then followed the naming of all the states, "do ordain and declare, and establish the following Constitution, . . . for the government of ourselves and our posterity." The committee on revision, and on style too, changed these words to read: "We the people of the United States . . . do ordain and establish this constitution"—not "for the government of ourselves and our posterity"—but for "the United States of America." Instead, therefore, of the Constitution finally providing for a government of the people of the United States, it provided a Constitution for the States as United States, but of course in their relation to the people. It was thus made a Constitution for states, and to form a more perfect Union of states, already imperfectly operating under the Articles of Confederation. The whole history of the events leading up to the Constitutional Convention, from the time one was proposed, on through the selection of delegates, and in connection with the powers given by the states to their delegates, shows that the convention was called and sat not to change the character of the government as it was under the Articles, but to revise them with reference to matters of commerce and trade, revenue and taxation.

And how was the Constitution to be adopted? The instrument itself provided for that. "The ratification of the conventions of nine states shall be sufficient for the establishment of this Constitution between the states so ratifying." The states which ratified thus seceded from the perpetual union under the Articles, and in fact left out in the cold those four states which would not join the new

UNION OF THE CONSTITUTION   327

union, alike made perpetual and eternal. Finally, after the Constitution was drawn, and had been filed by the stylists, the delegates signing for their several states affixed their names to this postlude: "Done in convention, by the unanimous consent of the states present etc." That is done in Philadelphia, which answers Marshall's question, where should they have ratified it, except in their own states? Thus far it is incontrovertible that the Constitution was formulated by the delegates of states, and so drawn as to be for the government of states; its powers were granted to states, that is, to Congress, composed of senators, the direct ambassadors of states, and to members of the House, the representatives of the people of each state; it was to be binding between states. In all these particulars it differed in nothing from the Articles of Confederation, under which each state was sovereign. As no grant is ever implied against a sovereign, the states, by ratifying the Constitution, parted with no power except those expressed. No police power passed, no right of eminent domain; nothing in brief except what was specified. The Constitution having been drafted, it was signed by George Washington, president of the convention and deputy from Virginia, then by the deputies or delegates, not in mass, but in the name of the state for which each signed; and, being attested by the secretary of the convention, as its work, it was sent to Congress.

Was the Constitution then adopted by states, each for itself, or by the American people in mass? The Convention sent the Constitution to Congress with the suggestion that "it should afterward be submitted to a convention of delegates chosen in each state by the people thereof, under the recommendation of its legislature for their assent and ratification; and that each convention assenting to and ratifying the same should give notice thereof to the United States in Congress assembled." But no sooner was the Constitution by printed copies circulated through the states than a storm arose against it. The Convention had not been called into being to formulate a new instrument of government, but to revise an old one, to formulate amendments in certain specified particulars. "What they [the convention] actually did, stripped of all fiction and verbiage, was to assume constituent powers, ordain a constitution of government and of liberty, and demand a plebiscite thereon over the heads of all existing legally organized powers. Had Julius or Napoleon committed these acts they would have been pronounced *coups d'etat*." [1] In other words, the existing government, the existing congress was to have nothing to say about their own perpetuity; the Union under the Articles, declared to be permanent, was to be dissolved by a vote of the people, or by the legislatures of the states. For at first some of the sponsors of the new Constitution in the states wanted it ratified by the legislatures; but the more far sighted men insisted upon ratification by delegates in conventions, who had been elected by the people. In terms of legalism the constitution was ratified by the states not by the people in mass. A more realistic examination shows just how much the people had to say about the adoption of the Constitution, which formed Lincoln's Union, much older than the states, and Webster's Union, which, with liberty, should be one and inseparable "now and forever," and again Lincoln's Union with its "mystic chords of memory, stretching from every battlefield, and patriot grave," but not from the graves of disinherited and disfranchised men.

Many of the ablest men of the time fought the Constitution with all their power, and drew after them great followings against it, not only because the Convention had departed from its authorized power, but because it was an economic instrument intended to give the moneyed classes, the owners of securities, trade, shipping, banking, and manufactures, the control of the resources of the land. The result was that men divided into parties. Those favoring the Constitution called themselves Federalists, that is, friends and partisans of the federal system, embodied in the Constitution; the other party was the Anti-Federalists who saw consolidation and centralism in the new scheme. The politicians who demanded that the Constitution be ratified by a convention in each state, composed of delegates elected by the people of the state, had their way. Their secret fear was that if the Constitution was ratified by a legislature, a succeeding legislature would repeal the ratification. A convention, having ratified the Constitution or rejected it, as the case might be, was at an end. There was hurry to get the ratification effected, so much was at stake. The slavocracy, so-called, was as nothing in these anxious and clandestine celerities compared to the banks, the manufactures and the owners of securities, just as, later, the slavocracy

---

[1] "Political Science and Comparative Constitutional Law," Vol. I, 123, Burgess.

UNION OF THE CONSTITUTION 329

was without great power, save as it clung to the doctrine of state sovereignty in the name of Jefferson, against the mercantile interests of New England and the North, which wanted loose construction and more and more centralization in order to effect their privileges and monopolies. And in truth slavery was only the occasion of the War between the States; the cause was the conflict between these old forces of a confederated republic on the one hand, and an imperial nation on the other, which began as soon as the Constitution was printed and broadcasted over the states. The legal postulate that the Constitution was ratified by states is not impugned by a realistic examination of what actually occurred in that ratification, and it will show where sovereignty begins. For Lincoln, when speaking against territorial sovereignty or squatter sovereignty, whittled the question down to a point, as he was accustomed to whittling a stick with a penknife until he brought it to a point. How many does it take to start the principle of sovereignty? How and where is sovereignty bred? This history of the Constitution proves that sovereignty was not bred in the heart, but rather in the head and the enteric coils.

New Hampshire led off on December 14, 1787, when its legislature adopted a resolution calling upon the selectmen of the several towns to notify the duly qualified voters of the election to be held for the choosing of delegates to a convention which should pass upon the Constitution. The election was held about the middle of January, 1788, and many delegates were chosen who opposed the Constitution. A bitter contest ensued when the state convention met, so much so that the strong talent of the convention, Federalists all, adjourned the convention. A few months later the convention reassembled, and upon a vote the Constitution was ratified by a vote of 57 to 47.

Massachusetts' senate on October 20, 1787, passed a resolution, and secured soon the concurrence of the house. This resolution provided that the delegates to the convention should be elected by those inhabitants "qualified by law to vote in the election of representatives." The delegates being elected, they met in convention January 9, 1788. Here again was a bitter fight. The charge was freely made at the time that delegates were bought by New York money to vote for the Constitution. Charges such as this are nearly always impossible of proof. We do know that the Constitution was contested with all possible power in Massachusetts' convention, and that the Federalists won.

In Connecticut the election of delegates was held November 12, 1787, the convention met January 3, 1788, and ratified the Constitution by a vote of 128 to 40.

New York, by its legislature, issued a call for an election of delegates to be held the last Tuesday in April of 1788. When the convention met it was found that two thirds of the 64 delegates were against the Constitution. Finally, upon vote, the Constitution was carried by 30 to 27; but this was upon condition that a convention should be called to revise the Constitution.

On November 1, 1787, New Jersey's legislature called a convention, ordering the people to elect delegates to a convention, and providing that those might vote for delegates who were "entitled to vote for representatives in General Assembly." On December 18, 1787, the delegates met in convention, and unanimously ratified the Constitution.

Delaware's legislature adopted a resolution on November 10, 1787, calling for the election of delegates on November 26. On December 3, the delegates so elected met and after four days' argument ratified the Constitution by a unanimous vote.

Pennsylvania had the stormiest time of any of the states. Before the Constitution had been reported, before it was known officially what method was to be devised for the ratification of the Constitution, an attempt was made in the legislature then sitting to pass a resolution for the calling of an election for the choosing of delegates to a convention, the same to be chosen in the same manner as members of the general assembly. This resolution passed, but the time of the election and the date of the convention were not settled; and in this state of affairs the legislature adjourned from its morning to its afternoon session. The enemies of the Constitution determined, therefore, to prevent action by staying away from the session, so that there would not be a quorum. But the Federalists sent officers after the obstructing assemblymen, who were assisted by a Federalist mob; and these entered the rooms of the hiding members, and brought them to the legislative halls by force, with torn clothes, and in towering rages. Thereupon a resolution was passed fixing the

UNION OF THE CONSTITUTION   331

time of election for delegates and the time of the convention. On November 6, 1787, the convention met and ratified the Constitution by a vote of 46 to 23.

Maryland's legislature, in November, 1787, by a majority of one vote fixed the first Monday in April, 1788, for the holding of the election for delegates. The convention met on April 21, and after a week's session, in which such men as Luther Martin fought the Constitution with great legal ability, the convention ratified the Constitution by a vote of 63 to 11.

Virginia by her legislature called a convention to be elected in March, 1788. The delegates met in convention and debated the Constitution from June 2 to June 25. On the latter day the Constitution was ratified by the convention by a vote of 89 to 79. The cities voted for it; the country of the southern border counties and near Kentucky voted against it.

North Carolina by its legislature called a convention on December 6, 1787; the election of delegates was set for the last Friday and Saturday of March, 1788, the convention met July 21, 1788. They canvassed the Constitution until August 2, then they postponed ratification by a vote of 184 to 84, and adjourned sine die. The Constitution went into force without North Carolina's membership in the Union. Economic pressure brought that state in on November 21, 1789, after amendments to the Constitution were assured. The same thing would have happened with the seceding states of 1861. Economic pressure would have brought them back, without the shedding of a drop of blood.

South Carolina, on January 18, 1788, through its legislature, called a convention whose delegates were elected in April. The convention met in Charleston in May, where an acrimonious struggle ensued. However, on May 23 the Constitution was ratified by a vote of 149 to 73.

Georgia's legislature, on October 26, 1787, called a state convention to be elected "in the same manner as representatives are elected," at an election to be held on December 4, 1787. The delegates were thus elected; they met at Augusta on December 25, and after four days of discussion ratified the Constitution on January 2, 1788.

Rhode Island was stubborn to the last. She sent no delegates to the convention which framed the Constitution. She did not ratify the Constitution until May 29, 1790, and she did so then because the general government was about to coerce her, and the city of Providence threatened to join other powerful Rhode Island cities and bring about a secession from the state, and apply to the Federal Government for protection.

There is no answer to these facts. The Constitution was ratified by states, by sovereign states, not by the American people in mass. This is the history of the legalism of ratification. Going back of the legalism, another story emerges out of the records of those times. Beard in his work, *An Economic Interpretation of the Constitution of the United States,* made the following analysis: The movement for the Constitution was engineered by money, public securities, manufactures, trade and shipping. The initial steps in the forming of a new Constitution were taken by a small group of property interests. No popular vote was taken for the calling of the convention which drafted the Constitution. A very large class of persons without property had no representatives, and no voice in the convention. The delegates to the convention themselves had an economic interest in the formation of a new government. The Constitution drafted was an economic document. Three fourths of the adult males in the states failed to vote for delegates who ratified the Constitution, either positively abstaining from voting or else they were disfranchised by property qualifications. The Constitution was ratified by not to exceed one sixth of the adult males. The delegates in the state conventions represented the same economic groups which were represented in the Constitutional Convention. Beard showed that it is questionable whether the delegates in New York, Massachusetts, New Hampshire, Virginia, and South Carolina were chosen by voters who approved of the Constitution. The vote in New York has been preserved for us by the *Daily Advertiser,* and this vote in New York may be taken as an intrepretation of the general public will in many of the states. Albany, Ulster, Duchess, Orange, Columbia, Montgomery, Suffolk, and Washington Counties polled 11,230 Anti-Federalist votes; and 5496 Federal votes. The former thereby won 41 delegates to the state convention. New York County, Westchester, Queens, Kings, Richmond won but 25 delegates. With the

UNION OF THE CONSTITUTION   333

apportionment against them, the Anti-Federalists thus elected twice as many delegates as the Federalists.

Returning to the Union and government under the Constitution which Lincoln said he was sworn by an oath to defend and protect, while no one had an oath registered in heaven to destroy them, there is a popular supposition that in some way the states lost their sovereignty by the ratification of the Constitution; or if they did not suffer quite so serious a deprivation that there were clauses in the Constitution which made the government under it supreme, whereas the government under the Articles was limited. In this connection much has been said of the clause in the Constitution which reads: "This constitution, and the laws of the United States which shall be made in pursuance thereof; and all treaties made, or which shall be made, under the authority of the United States, shall be the supreme law of the land; and the judges in every state shall be bound thereby, anything in the Constitution or laws of any state to the contrary notwithstanding." But by Article XIII of the Articles of Confederation it was provided: "Every state shall abide by the determinations of the United States in Congress assembled, on all questions which by this confederation is submitted to them. And the Articles of this Confederation shall be inviolably observed by every state, and the union shall be perpetual." In truth all conventions and compacts between sovereigns are the supreme law of the land. A treaty between Great Britain and the United States would be the supreme law in both realms, and binding upon the sovereignties and upon the subjects and citizens of both governments without any clause to that effect in the organic law of either government. This must be so in the nature of things; and it is so by the express law of nations. The courts of both are bound to hold a treaty to be supreme, and no constitutional clause is necessary to empower them so to hold. And it is to be observed that only laws and treaties which are made in pursuance of the Constitution are the supreme law; whence it follows that the Federal government was in this clause expressed to be one of limited powers, and that obedience to it is due only to the circumscribed extent that it legislates and makes treaties consonant to the grant of powers from the states expressed in the Constitution.

This discussion of Lincoln's theories of the Union and the Constitution, naturally leads to a consideration of the right of secession which the Southern states asserted, and which Lincoln resisted by the waging of one of the most cruel and bloody wars of history. If the right or wrong of slavery was in his opinion not sufficiently clear to warrant him in denouncing those who had slaves, as he said, the right or wrong of secession was certainly not clear enough to justify the killing of thousands of men for the purpose of demonstrating by arms its wrong. The truth is Lincoln did not know the Constitution and its history sufficiently well to have a well based opinion on this subject. It is perhaps true that he was not aware of the fact that Webster, whom he followed, had modified his views on the nature of the Union, and the rights of states under it. As we have seen, Webster in 1830 had debated these vexed questions with Hayne, and in 1833 with Calhoun. In 1839 he expressed himself very differently from what he had done on those prior occasions. In January of the latter year he argued the case of The Bank of Augusta against Earle in the Supreme Court, when he used this language in addressing the Court: "But it is argued, that though this law of comity exists as between independent nations, it does not exist between the states of this Union. . . . In respect to this law of comity, it is said, states are not nations; a sort of residuum of sovereignty is all that remains to them. The National sovereignty, it is said, is conferred on this government, and part of the municipal sovereignty. . . . Suppose that this Constitution had said, in terms after the language of the court below—all national sovereignty shall belong to the United States; all municipal sovereignty to the several states. I will say, that however clear, however distinct, such a definition may appear to those who use it, the employment of it, in the Constitution, could only have led to utter confusion and uncertainty. I am not prepared to say that the states have no national sovereignty. The laws of some of the states, Maryland and Virginia, for instance, provide punishment for treason. The power thus exercised is certainly not municipal. . . . The term sovereignty does not occur in the Constitution at all. The Constitution treats states as states and the United States as the United States; and by a careful enumeration, declares all the powers that are granted to the United States, and all the rest are reserved to the states. . . . The states of this

UNION OF THE CONSTITUTION

Union, as states, are subject to all the voluntary and customary laws of nations." The Supreme Court, in passing on the case which Webster had thus argued, said: "It has, however, been supposed that the rules of comity between foreign nations do not apply to the states of this Union; that they extend to one another no other rights than those which are given by the Constitution . . . and that the courts are not at liberty to presume, in the absence of all legislation on the subject, that a state has adopted the comity of nations toward the other states. . . . The Court thinks otherwise. The intimate union of these states, as members of the same great political family; the deep and vital interests which bind them so closely together; should lead us, in the absence of proof to the contrary, to presume a greater degree of comity and friendship and kindness towards one another, than we should be authorized to presume between foreign nations. And when (as without doubt must occasionally happen) the interest or policy of any state requires it to restrict the rule, it has but to declare its will, and the legal presumption is at once at an end. But until this is done, upon what grounds could this court refuse to administer the law of international comity between these states? They are sovereign states. . . . We think it is well settled that by the law of comity among nations, a corporation created by one sovereignty is permitted to make contracts in another, and to sue in its courts; and that the same law of comity prevails among the several sovereignties of this Union."

Was Lincoln familiar with the letter which Webster wrote to the Barings in London in the year 1839? They had asked him for a legal opinion as to whether the legislature of one of the states had the legal and constitutional power to contract loans at home and abroad. "To this I answer," wrote Webster, "that the legislature of a state has such power; and how any doubt could have arisen on this point it is difficult for me to conceive. Every state is an independent, sovereign, political community, except in so far as certain powers, which it might otherwise have exercised, have been conferred on a General Government, established under a written Constitution, and exerting its authority over the people of all the states. This general government is a limited government. Its powers are specific and enumerated. All powers not conferred upon it still remain with the states and with the people. The state legislatures on the other hand, possess all usual and extraordinary powers of government, subject to any limitations which may be imposed by their own constitutions, and with the exception, as I have said, of the operation of those powers of the Constitution of the United States." If Lincoln had read this and absorbed its truth he never would have delivered the Cooper Institute Speech.

De Tocqueville's *Democratie en Amerique* is not on any list of books that Lincoln read. "However strong a government may be," De Tocqueville wrote, "it cannot easily escape from the consequences of a principle which it has once admitted as the foundation of its Constitution. The Union was formed by the voluntary agreement of the states; and these, in uniting together, have not forfeited their nationality, nor have they been reduced to the condition of one and the same people. If one of the states chose to withdraw its name from the contract, it would be difficult to disprove its right to do so, and the Federal Government would have no means of maintaining its claims directly, either by force or by right."

John Quincy Adams, an offshoot of Hamiltonian Federalism, and a bitter enemy of slavery as we have had occasion to see, delivered an address in 1839 before the Historical Society of New York, and committed himself as follows: "With these qualifications we may admit the same right in the people of every state in the Union, with reference to the general government, which was exercised by the people of the colonies with reference to the supreme head of the British Empire, of which they formed a part; and under these limitations have the people of each state of the Union a right to secede from the Confederated Union itself. Here stands the right. But the indissoluble Union between the several states of this confederated nation is, after all, not in the right, but in the heart. If the day should ever come (may heaven avert it), when the affections of the people of these states shall be alienated from each other; when the fraternal spirit shall give way to cold indifference, or collision of interest shall fester into hatred, the bands of political asseveration will not long hold together parties no longer attached by the magnetism of conciliated interests and kindly sympathies; and far better will it be for the people of the dis-United States, to part in friendship from each other, than to be held together by constraint; then will be the time for reverting to the precedents which occurred

UNION OF THE CONSTITUTION 337

at the formation and adoption of the Constitution, to form again a more perfect Union by dissolving that which could no longer bind, and to leave the separated parts to be reunited by the law of political gravitation."

There is a wealth of material and authority upon this matter in hand too great to be used in a study where Lincoln's mind is the main consideration. This much shows that Lincoln stood up in the delivery of his First Inaugural and opposed himself to the greatest thinkers that America had then produced on this matter of the nature of the Union and the right of states to get out of it if they chose, and that for a good or a bad reason. A bad reason would have proved the immorality of the step, not its lack of right. A good reason established the step both upon legality and morality. In this connection one can begin with Hamilton who feared secession if the state debts of the Revolution were not assumed by the Federal Government. He urged the funding of the debts to prevent secession, without even referring to the right of secession. He assumed without question that the right existed. One can refer to the words of Washington, Madison, Hamilton again, Jefferson, Rufus King, Ellsworth, Morris, Randolph—all fathers, so-called, and all of whom spoke of the United States Government as Federal in character, several of them calling the Constitution a compact. One can refer to Jackson's apologia in the South Carolina nullification matter as published in the *Washington Globe* shortly after his proclamation, and the argument upon the Force Bill of the time, in which he declared that the Constitution originated in a compact, and that it was one among the several states, and that it was not the work of the whole people in the aggregate. "The Constitution of the United States is founded in compact . . . this compact derives its obligation from the agreement, entered into by the people of each of the states, in their political capacity, with the people of the other states. . . . In the case of a violation of the Constitution of the United States, and the usurpation of powers not granted by it on the part of the functionaries of the general government, the state governments have the right to interpose and arrest the evil, upon the principles which were set forth in the Virginia resolutions of 1798 against the Alien and Sedition laws." In these words Jackson backed down from the coercion of South Carolina, while the difficulty with that state over the tariff bill was composed in compromise.

The Kentucky and Virginia resolutions, and Madison's report or state paper upon them must not miss something of reference. In 1798 Jefferson drew up Resolutions for the Kentucky legislature in which he laid down the doctrine that "the several states composing the United States of America, are not united on the principles of unlimited submission to their General Government; but that by compact under the style and title of a Constitution for the United States . . . they constituted a general government for special purposes, delegated to that government certain definite powers, reserving each state to itself, the residuary mass of right to their own self-government; and that whensoever the general government assumes undelegated powers, its acts are unauthoritative, void and of no force . . . that as in all cases of compact, among parties having no common judge, each party has an equal right to judge for itself, as well of infractions, as of the mode and manner of redress."

There were also the Virginia Resolutions, which passed the House of Delegates on December 21, 1798, which declared, the powers of the Federal Government resulted "from the compact to which the states are parties," and that its powers were "limited by the plain sense and intention of the instrument constituting that compact, as no further valid than they are authorized by the grants enumerated in that compact; and that in case of a deliberate, palpable and dangerous exercise of other powers, not granted by the said compact, the States, who are parties thereto, have the right, and are in duty bound, to interpose, for arresting the progress of the evil, and for maintaining, within their respective limits, the authorities, rights, and liberties, appertaining to them." These Virginia resolutions were sent out to the several states, and were by some of the states disapproved. Whereupon a committee was appointed in the 1799–1800 session of the Virginia House of Delegates, of which Madison, the so-called Father of the Constitution, was chairman, the business of the committee being to consider the communications of the several states which had noticed them, and to report upon them to the House. Madison made the report of the Committees. He first held that the position was clear that the powers of the

UNION OF THE CONSTITUTION 339

Federal Government resulted from a compact; and that in all the contemporaneous comment on the Constitution while it was depending for adoption it was said that all powers not granted were reserved; and that if any doubt could ever have existed on this subject it was removed by the Xth amendment. "The other position involved in this branch of the resolution, namely, that 'the states are parties to the Constitution or compact,' is in the judgment of the committee equally free from objection." Further, "it appears to your committee to be a plain principle, founded in common sense, illustrated by common practice, and essential to the nature of compacts that where resort can be had to no tribunal superior to the authority of the parties, the parties themselves must be the rightful judges in the last resort, whether the bargain has been pursued or violated. . . . The states, then, being the parties to the constitutional compact, and in their sovereign capacity, it follows of necessity, that there can be no tribunal above their authority, to decide in the last resort, whether the compact made by them be violated. . . . If the deliberate exercise of dangerous powers, palpably withheld by the Constitution itself, could not justify the parties to it, in interposing even so far as to arrest the progress of the evil, and thereby to preserve the Constitution itself, as well as to provide for the safety of the parties to it, there would be an end to all relief from usurped power."

Then Madison touched upon a subject which may be already in the reader's reflections. "But it is objected," he said, "that the judicial authority is to be regarded as the sole expositor of the Constitution in the last resort. . . . On this objection it might be observed: first, that there may be instances of usurped power, which the forms of the Constitution would never draw within the control of the judicial department." Parenthetically here Lincoln usurped power as president which even Chief Justice Taney tried to arrest and was overcome by Lincoln as head of the army. To go on with Madison: "Secondly that if the decision of the judiciary be raised above the authority of the sovereign parties to the Constitution, the decisions of the other departments, not carried by the forms of the Constitution before the judiciary, must be equally authoritative and final with the decision of that department. . . . The resolution supposes that dangerous powers not delegated, may not only be usurped and executed by the other departments, but that the judicial department also may exercise or sanction dangerous powers beyond the grant of the Constitution; and consequently that the ultimate right of the parties to the Constitution, to judge whether the compact has been dangerously violated, must extend to violations by one delegated authority, as well as by another; by the judiciary, as well as by the executive or the legislative." The judicial department was undoubtedly made the judge of questions submitted to it in relation to the "authority of the other departments of the government; not in relation to the rights of the parties to the constitutional compact, from which the judicial as well as the other departments hold their delegated trusts. . . . On any other hypothesis, the delegation of judicial power would annul the authority delegating it; and the concurrence of this department with the others in usurped powers, might subvert forever, and beyond the possible reach of any rightful remedy, the very Constitution, which all were instituted to preserve."

Strange now is it that these irrefragable protests should in the aftermath of the War between the States have brought down upon the head of Jefferson the hatred of every centralist historian and politician, with accusations against him violent enough to extend to a charge that it was he who originally counseled secession, and thus brought the war of the South against the North which Lincoln in noble obedience to the Constitution and the laws broke with the mighty force of a virtuous people in righteous arms and led by the God of Battles. It is stranger still that these arguments, made for the benefit of the people, for the liberty and peace and happiness of generations to come, should have been ignored or despised by the heedless throngs who have passed along the scene of life revering Hamilton, and making a demi-god of Lincoln. Yet before the heretical dogma of the supremacy of the Supreme Court arose and became sacred, it was not so with the people. Upon these Kentucky-Virginia resolutions, Jefferson was elected president in 1800 and again in 1804; Madison was elected upon them in 1808 and 1812; Monroe was elected upon them in 1816 and 1820. John Quincy Adams, who had repented of the principles of his father, who was responsible for the Alien and Sedition Laws to which the Kentucky-

Virginia resolutions were a protest, was elected upon them in 1824. Jackson twice came to the power of the presidency upon them. This was popular construction of the Constitution which lawyers and statesmen regard with respect, even as they pay heed to the legislative construction of the Constitution.

Whittier, in the calm of New England righteousness, fastened the name Ichabod on Webster, for his speech of March 7, without any leniency toward him, or consideration for the fact that Webster had been crowded out of his former logic by the giant strength of Calhoun, in whom he found no mere orator, as he had found in Hayne. Webster crossed swords with Calhoun in February of 1833. Calhoun referred to what Webster had said in 1830 in the Hayne debate: "But I am resolved not to submit in silence to accusations either against myself individually, or against the North, wholly unfounded and unjust—accusations which impute to us a disposition to evade the Constitutional compact." There, said Calhoun, he used the word compact, which he now has rejected. And he has flouted the word accede to the Constitution which Washington and Jefferson employed. Then he referred to what Webster had said in the instant debate: "The Constitution means a government, not a compact; not a constitutional compact, but a government. If compact, it rests on plighted faith, and the mode of redress would be to declare the whole void. States may secede if a league or a compact." "I thank the Senator for these admissions," said Calhoun. "It does not call itself a compact, but a constitution," said Webster. "The Constitution rests on a compact, but it is no longer a compact." Calhoun rejoined, "I would ask to what compact does the Senator refer, as that on which the Constitution rests? Before the adoption of the present Constitution, the states had formed but one compact, and that was the old Confederation; and certainly the gentleman does not intend to assert that the present Constitution rests upon that. What, then is his meaning? What can it be but that the Constitution itself is a compact? And how will his language read when fairly interpreted, but that the Constitution was a compact, but is no longer a compact? . . . He next states that 'a man is almost untrue to his country who calls the Constitution a compact.' I fear the Senator, in calling it a 'compact, a bargain,' has called down the heavy denunciation on his own head. He finally states that 'It is founded on compact, but not a compact.' 'It is the result of a compact.'"

Not only was it a compact, but it was an executory compact. The sovereign states had covenanted with each other that the general government should guarantee to every state a republican form of government; that full faith and credit should be given in each state to the public acts and records and judicial proceedings of every other state; that slaves and apprentices should be returned, when escaping, by the state into which they escaped, and without further detailment the Constitution required continual performance of its agreements. It was money and power on the one side which wanted what it called a sovereign nation; it was fear of money and power which wanted a confederated republic. This was the issue from the days of Hamilton on the one hand, with his bank report, and Jefferson, on the other, with his Kentucky Resolutions; and from the time when Chancellor Kent in 1826 published his *Commentaries*, and was the first man of note to deny that a state had the right to withdraw from the Union. It is not what Whittier wrote about Webster that has dimmed his reputation; it is that Webster, like Lincoln after him, had a divided mind, and that he clothed logical solecisms and false historical interpretations in sonorous rhetoric which became harsh when thoroughly digested. When debating with the watchful and remorseless Calhoun, Webster dared to deny the states sovereignty, because, he exclaimed, whoever heard of a sovereignty being suable as the states were made in the Constitution. How easy for Calhoun to reply that from time immemorial states were suable when they submitted themselves to be sued. What is an arbitration between France and England but a submission on the part of both to be sued, and to abide by the adjudication? In like manner Webster could spend his logic-chopping powers to the demonstration that the Constitution was not a compact; and yet at another time he spoke with such perspicacity as this: "Where sovereign communities are parties, there is no essential difference between a compact, a confederation and a league. They all equally rest on the plighted faith of the sovereign party. A league or confederacy, is but a subsisting or continuing treaty. If in the opinion of either party it be violated, such party may say that he will no longer ful-

UNION OF THE CONSTITUTION 343

fill its obligations on his part, but will consider the whole league or compact at an end, although it might be one of its stipulations that it should be perpetual." Reserved sovereignty includes the power to break the league whether the reason be good or bad, or none. The other party to the league can do nothing about it except to kill men for breaking it.

All confederated republics are both federal and national: federal with each other and national with the rest of the world. The Constitution was framed under the inspiration of Montesquieu more than any other authority. He had written of a government formed of several small republics bound together in such a way as to be a nation to the world, while each retained its own nationality and sovereignty. Montesquieu also treated of the division of powers in a government between the executive, the legislative and the judicial, each independent of the other. What the framers of the Constitution did was to federate the republics of the states so that the motto of the United States, *E Pluribus Unum*, would fittingly describe what was done; and then to divide the powers of the artificial nation into legislative, executive and judicial, making the general government their joint agent for the exercise of those powers.

A passing glance may be given to the charges flung by Southern statesmen against the North, that the North had on occasion advocated secession, and even taken steps toward it. There was Massachusetts, which in 1803 was reported to have resolved that the annexation of Louisiana was unconstitutional, and, as it created a new confederation, Massachusetts, as a party to the old compact, was absolved from adhering to the latter. There was the action of Massachusetts, whose legislature in 1844–45 resolved that the annexation of Texas would have no binding effect upon Massachusetts —another case of nullification. There was the Hartford convention of 1814, which resolved in the very language of the Kentucky resolutions of Jefferson, that a state, both in duty and in right, might interpose to protect its sovereignty, and that "states which have no common umpire must be their own judges, and execute their own decisions." Nathan Dane signed his name to this resolution, he who had drawn the Ordinance of 1787, for the government of the Northwest Territory.

If this were a work devoted only to this subject more time might be spent on the Resolutions of the Senate of December 28, 1837, the first of which was, that, "in the adoption of the Constitution, the states adopting the same acted, severally, as free, independent and sovereign states," which passed that body by a vote of 32 to 13, with 18 states voting for it and 6 against it. This was high legislative interpretation of the Constitution and by juridical rules must be respected. This review may end with the words of Montesquieu: "Several sovereign and independent states may unite themselves together by a perpetual confederacy, without ceasing to be, each, individually, a perfect state. They will together constitute a federal republic; their joint deliberations will not impair the sovereignty of each member, though they may, in certain respects, put some restraint on the exercise of it in virtue of voluntary engagements."

The recognition of these principles would have saved tens of thousands of lives and great treasure. That is desirable, if there be not something more desirable, like the triumph of God's truth as divined by fanatics and abetted by money and power. It was among the workable solutions of the strife between the North and the South for Lincoln to have accepted the Crittenden Compromise. He might have recognized the independence of the seceding states, as George III recognized the independence of the original thirteen states. If the South had won the war, he would have been compelled to have done so. What then would have become of his doctrine that "in contemplation of universal law and of the Constitution, the union of these states is perpetual"?

Chapter XIV   *Lincoln's Nomination and Election to the Presidency*

In October of 1859 Lincoln rushed in upon Herndon with the exciting news that he had been invited to deliver a lecture in New York City. He asked Herndon for advice as to the subject upon which he should lecture, and solicited the same counsel from other of his friends. Knowing that Lincoln had not succeeded in the lecture field, his friends advised him to deliver a political speech. Accordingly Lincoln accepted the invitation of the New York committee, but he said that he would deal with political questions in what he would say, and he fixed the time of appearance for a late day in February. About the time that Lincoln was digging industriously in the six volumes of Elliot's *Debates* in the preparation of his New York address, some of his friends met at the State House in Springfield, the faithful Judd among some others, who was then chairman of the Republican State Committee of Illinois, and there proposed Lincoln's name for the presidency. They asked him if his name might be used in that connection. Herndon wrote: "With his characteristic modesty he doubted whether he could get the nomination if he wished it, and asked until the next morning to answer us whether his name might be announced. Late the next day he authorized us, if we thought proper to do so, to place him in the field." He was asked by one of those present at the State House conference if he would take the nomination for vice president, if he could not be nominated to the presidency, and Lincoln answered that he would not. The state Republican convention was to meet at Decatur on May 9, but in the meantime Lincoln journeyed to New York.

One of the cardinal and primary instructions touching the American system of states on the one hand and the Federal Government on the other, has been that a state legislature is practically a constituent assembly, and may pass any law not prohibited by the state or the Federal Constitution; whereas Congress is not a constitutent assembly, and can pass only such laws as are warranted by the Constitutional grant of power by the states to Congress. Lincoln, agreeable to his usual disregard of principles of law in the interest of his originality, constructed his Cooper Institute speech on the postulate as to whether any "line dividing local from Federal authority," or "anything else properly forbade the Federal Government to control as to slavery in a territory." He stated the same thing in his address in a slightly different way, namely, whether there was "any line dividing local from Federal authority, or anything in the Constitution, properly forbade the Federal Government to control as to slavery in the territory." The constitutional question was whether there was anything in the Constitution which empowered Congress to control slavery in the territories, not whether silence in the Constitution on the subject gave Congress power to control it. In a word Lincoln turned the question upside down and then proceeded to make a speech in which he employed his peculiar powers of analysis with eloquence and interest. We have already dealt with the Ordinance of 1787, which Lincoln historically examined in this speech. Truly did he begin by saying that the facts with which he meant to deal were old and familiar. "If there shall be novelty, it will be in the mode of presenting the facts, and the references and observations following that presentation," he also said in beginning. And there was novelty enough. The fact that this speech stirred no discussion on the part of the able men in the Senate and elsewhere, to dissect and demolish Lincoln's thesis, shows that it was not regarded as important. At this time, too, he was best known as a defeated candidate for the Illinois senatorship. Remembering that Lincoln on August 2, 1848, had by his vote in Congress refused to extend the Northwest Ordinance over the territory of Oregon, another query is raised as to his process of thinking now in February, 1860, by which he arrived at the conclusion that there was nothing in the Constitution to prohibit Congress from excluding slavery from Nebraska, and that in consequence it had the right to do so, and was under duty to do so. In other words he was arguing in February for a right and a duty in Congress which he had thwarted by his vote in 1848 as to Oregon. Vainly shall we expect Lincoln to be consistent intellectually at any time; he remained the same divided mind to the last day of his life, who in the same speech, and sometimes in the same letter presented the antinomy of his nature.

On February 18, the *Evening Post* contained the announcement of a meeting to be held at Cooper Institute on the evening of February 21, in celebration of Washington's Birthday, which was to be addressed by Humphrey Marshall of Kentucky and others. All who favored the upholding of the Union, the rights of the several states, who stood for resisting all attempts to interfere with the respective institutions of the states, who opposed all sectional parties, and who wanted men elevated to office who would administer the government in the spirit of its founders, were invited to come to the meeting and listen to speeches of noted men, and to hear the singing of The Star-Spangled Banner by a famous singer. The Cooper Institute meeting at which Lincoln spoke was held in the evening of February 27. An admission fee of twenty-five cents was charged, which was for the benefit of the Plymouth Church. The *New York Herald* observed that the fee did not deter an attendance, and that the hall was about three-fourths filled.

Soon David Dudley Field appeared, accompanied by William Cullen Bryant then toward seventy. Bryant as a young poet had brutally satirized the great Jefferson. It was fitting enough that he was made the presiding officer of this meeting. Lincoln took a seat on the platform and awaited his introduction. The *Herald* gave this description of Lincoln: "Mr. Lincoln is a tall, thin man, dark complexioned, and apparently quick in his perceptions. He is rather unsteady in his gait, and there is an involuntary comical awkwardness which marks his movements while speaking. His voice, though sharp and powerful at times, has a frequent tendency to dwindle into a shrill and unpleasant sound. His enunciation is slow and emphatic, and a peculiar characteristic of his delivery was a remarkable mobility of his features, the frequent contortions of which excited the merriment which his words alone could not have well produced." As usual Lincoln was ludicrously dressed. His trousers hitched between his ankles and his knees; his large feet, loosely shod, spread themselves over the platform floor. And then David Dudley Field nominated Bryant for chairman of the meeting, which was followed by his unanimous election at the hands of the assemblage. After this, according to the *New York Times* of February 28, Bryant said that it was a grateful office to introduce an eminent citizen of the West, known to New York by fame only, but now here in person to address an audience of the city. The great West was a potent auxiliary in the battle being fought for freedom against slavery, and in behalf of civilization against barbarism. The movement was concerned, he said, with preserving for free settlers some of the fairest territory of the continent, where indeed free men were now building their cabins. He could see a higher and wiser agency than that of man in the causes that had filled with hardy people the vast fertile regions which formed the northern part of the valley of the Mississippi, where men were not ashamed to till their acres with their own hands, men who would be ashamed to subsist on the labor of the slave. (They were willing to subsist on the labor of hired men, working for corn bread and bacon and a place to sleep in a sod house, or log cabin.) These children, Bryant continued, formed a living bulwark against the advance of slavery, and from them was recruited the vanguard of the armies of liberty. "One of them will appear before you this evening in person—a gallant soldier of the political campaign of 1856—(Applause.)—who then rendered good service to the Republican cause, and who has been since the great champion of that cause in the struggle which took place two years later, for the supremacy of the Republicans in the legislature of Illinois; who took the field against Senator Douglas, and would have won in the conflict but for the unjust provisions of the law of the state, which allowed a minority of the people to elect a majority of the legislature. I have only, my friends, to pronounce the name of Abraham Lincoln of Illinois. (Cheers.) I have only to pronounce his name to secure your profound attention." Then, according to the *Times*, "Mr. Lincoln advanced to the desk, and, smiling graciously upon his audience, complacently awaited the termination of the cheering, and then proceeded with his address." "Mr. Cheerman," he began, for he still called a chair a "cheer," in the vernacular of central Illinois.

So much of this address has already been noticed that repetition is forbidden. Attention will be given to those parts of it which have not yet been discussed. Lincoln again criticised the Supreme Court for the Dred Scott decision. His tenacity was peculiarly evident as to something which he had fixed in his mind by repetition, as if he was understanding the subject and himself, too, better and better as he recapitulated more than twice-told arguments. He commented on the fact that the Supreme Court had founded its decision upon the Fifth Amendment to the Constitution, while Douglas planted his arguments upon the Tenth Amendment, "the powers not delegated to the United States by the Constitution . . . are reserved to the states respectively or the people." Then he made the irrelevant observation that these amendments were framed by the first Congress under the Constitution, which passed "the act already mentioned, enforcing the prohibition of slavery in the Northwest Territory." We have seen that Congress passed no such act. He admitted that the slavery question was more prominent than formerly; but denied that Republicans had made it so. It was not Republicans but Democrats who had opened up the question again. This was a thrust at Douglas's Kansas-Nebraska. "You charge that we stir up insurrections among your slaves. We deny it; and what is your proof? Harper's Ferry! John Brown was no Republican; and you have failed to implicate a single Republican in his Harper's Ferry enterprise. . . . You need not be told that persisting in a charge which one does not know to be true, is simply malicious slander." He went on with more special pleading. "Republican doctrines and declarations are accompanied with a continual protest against any interference whatever with your slaves." This could be proven by denying that anyone was a Republican who did interfere with the slaves; not otherwise. "In the present state of things in the United States, I do not think a general, or even a very extensive slave insurrection is possible. . . . The explosive materials are everywhere in parcels; but there neither are, nor can be supplied, the indispensable connecting trains. . . . Much is said by Southern people about the affection of slaves for their masters and mistresses; and a part of it, at least, is true. . . . Mr. Jefferson did not mean to say, nor do I, that the power of emancipation is in the Federal Government. . . . John Brown's effort was peculiar. It was not a slave insurrection. It was an attempt by white men to get up a revolt among slaves, in which the slaves refused to participate. That affair in its philosophy corresponds with the many attempts related in history at the assassination of kings and emperors. An enthusiast broods over the oppression of a people till he fancies himself commissioned by heaven to liberate them. . . . Orsini's attempt on Louis Napoleon, and John Brown's attempt at Harper's Ferry were in their philosophy precisely the same."

Then, as to Dred Scott again: "Perhaps you will say that the Supreme Court has decided the disputed Constitutional question in your favor. Not quite so. . . . The Court have substantially said it is your Constitutional right to take slaves into the Federal Territories, and to hold them there as property. When I say the decision was made in a sort of way, I mean it was made in a divided court, by a bare majority of the judges, and they not quite agreeing with one another in the reasons for making it. An inspection of the Constitution will show that the right of property in a slave is not distinctly and expressly affirmed in it. Bear in mind that the judges do not pledge their judicial opinion that such right is implicitly affirmed in the Constitution; but they pledge their veracity that it is distinctly and expressly affirmed there. . . . If they had only pledged their judicial opinion, that such right is affirmed in the instrument by implication, it would have been open to others to show that neither the word 'slave' nor 'slavery' is to be found in the Constitution." Even as it does not contain the word "apprentice." The lack of what might be called critical alertness, intellectual energy and enterprise in the American mind of the time, especially in journals, prevented such loose logic as this from being laughed away, taking Lincoln with it. But he wanted peace. "It is exceedingly desirable that all parts of this great confederacy shall be at peace, and in harmony with one another." A confederacy! That is a government of a league, a contract, Latin *fœdus*, *federatus*, that is leagued, joined in a confederacy. But we shall never see Lincoln convicted on a word, however used; nor held to the same use of one. Then he closed with these words: "Let us have faith that right makes might; and in that faith let us dare to do our duty as we understand it." Nothing could have been more pleasing than these words to Beecher and the members of Plymouth Church. Yet right does not make might; but might is always sufficient to itself, and is most wrong when pretending to be right, and is wrong. What might was to be conjured out of the right? Was it the continued attacks upon the South; was it an army? Lincoln, having passed through so much intellectual vacilation, now felt elation that he was anchored; and thus he was glad to counsel others to dare to do their duty as they understood it.

According to the *New York Herald*, the conclusion of Lincoln's address was met with cheers for Seward, and a call for more speeches. Whereupon Greeley addressed the assemblage in Zionistic rhetoric. He referred to Lincoln as a man who was born in a slave state, but who had become a proper example of what labor may be; and how effort and honest aspirations may bring a man from the humblest ranks of society and place him in connection with the highest. "It may be that we may be beaten one year, perhaps another and another, but in the great tide of time we are sure that the last wave will be higher than the first, and thus we shall go on from victory to victory. When I heard our friend say what he said so well about insurrections, I rejoiced to think that, where our policy prevails, though there may be differences, though there may be strikes, or temporary alienations, no man stands in fear of an insurrection. A free and educated laboring class is the certain bulwark of society, and where they exist there can be no insurrections." Greeley had evidently been reading Marx on the general economic question of capital and labor; but without seeing the question to its depth. Nor did he forecast the labor-injunction, nor the peace that is of despotism, to use Calhoun's words. Speaking of Kansas, Greeley said: "True a few men sacrificed their lives there—and noblemen they were too—but it was in a struggle which the thousands of years of peace that are to follow shall richly repay." These words were sweet to the ears of Hebraic-Puritanism, to the Bible culture that judges other men in the name of God, and then proceeds even with arms to carry out the judgment.

We may make brief references to the comments of the press on Lincoln's speech in order to show how it affected the editorial mind, if not the public at large as well. The *New York Herald*, in its issue of February 29, expressed itself editorially in dispraise of Lincoln's performance. "The first half of the orator's speech was an attempt to show that the Fathers of the Republic were all anti-slavery men, including Washington and Jefferson. In reply to this it is sufficient to say that they took a curious way of showing it, by holding slaves themselves, and by drawing up a pro-slavery Constitution, which provides for the perpetuation of the institution as long as any state thinks proper to retain it. Washington, in a letter to Lafayette, complained bitterly that the English in a raid carried off a number of his slaves from his estate; and it appears from his will that he held slaves to the day of his death, that he bought in slaves at an execution, and that he did not emancipate them even at his death, but bequeathed them to his wife and his sister-in-law for their lives, and after their decease he directed them to be manumitted—a disposition of the property which, it is scarcely necessary to say, he would not have made if he had had any children to inherit it. At the time of the Declaration of Independence, drawn up by Jefferson, every one of the thirteen colonies was slaveholding, and Jefferson inserted a clause in it against slavery, which was voted out, showing that the general sense of the country was in favor of the institution, though Mr. Lincoln says a majority of the signers of the Declaration were against it. And the other clause, therefore, retained, which speaks of all men as being 'born equal' and entitled to life and liberty, cannot have any reference to negroes, as has been shown in the decision of the Supreme Court of the United States. When the Constitution was adopted every state but one held slaves, and even that one ratified it with the promise to restore fugitives. It is idle, therefore, to quote the Fathers, including Washington and Jefferson, in favor of the present Republican crusade against slavery. It is true Jefferson for a time became tainted with the French Revolutionary leveling notions about negro slavery, and other things; but he afterwards changed those opinions, and no man denounced the Missouri Compromise line in 1820 more eloquently than he did, or inveighed more forcibly against that Northern aggression, and against all attempts of Congress to interfere with the slave labor of the South."

The *New York Tribune* made editorial comment on Lincoln's speech in its issue of February 28. "Since the days of Clay and Webster," it said, "no man has spoken to a larger assemblage of the intellect and mental culture of our city. Mr. Lincoln is one of nature's orators, using his rare powers solely to elucidate and to convince, though their inevitable effect is to delight and electrify as well." The *Evening Post* ended an editorial as follows: "There is to be no peace with the South, till the slave holders shall have forced us to say that slavery is right, not merely to admit it by silence, but to shout the accursed doctrine with all the strength of our lungs.

With the renunciation of the creed of liberty must come the reconsideration and rejection of our free constitution." The philosophy of the *Iliad* and the *Odyssey* had not entered Bryant's mind to the exclusion of Cotton Mather and Jonathan Edwards. Other press comments referred to the incendiary agitation of the *Boston Liberator* commenced thirty years before; and observed that it was only the strong arm of the Federal Government that prevented insurrections and local rebellions; and that when the bond of the Union was snapped, as it would be by abolitionism, the same proletarian mass in its fanaticism would bring revolution in New England or anywhere in the country, even as then it was ready to wage war against the South, and thus subvert the rights of property all over the North too, and reduce all distinctions to one common level. Property, whether slave or otherwise, has always had dreadful fears of consequences like these. It has happened, however, that the leveling has uniformly operated upon the toilers; while the drones have elevated themselves into secure places, as they did through negro emancipation. The monopolists never lose. That is something that never entered Lincoln's head, or Greeley's; not to mention radicals like Giddings, and Codding, and their like, including the temperance lecturers who were reciting the Declaration on street corners, and working in committees, wherever they could get in, for the tariff and the bank. That which the best human reason sees as the logical right, justice, cause, is always lost.

Lincoln was now en route to see his son Robert, who was in school at Philips-Exeter. On March 5 he made a speech at Hartford of which we have only an abstract. There he said that the slaves were worth $2,000,000,000, and commented on the influence which so much wealth had upon the religious and political convictions of the South. "Public opinion is founded to a great extent on a property basis," he said, thereby planting himself upon a genuine realism. He admitted that human nature was the same everywhere; therefore "what lessens the value of property is opposed; what enhances its value is favored." As public opinion at the South regarded slaves as property, and the North regarded them as human beings and entitled to freedom, the issue was drawn on this basis of property between the two sections. Besides slavery was morally wrong—and wrong especially "in its effect upon white free labor." So was raging, he said, the "irrepressible conflict." "The love of property, and a consciousness of right and wrong have conflict in places in our organization." But there was no struggle between the white man and the negro; "if there was I should be for the white man." He accused the Democracy of bushwhacking, of making false charges about John Brown, and he then repeated some of the arguments on this subject which he had made at Cooper Institute. There had been, or was recently a shoemakers' strike in Massachusetts; and he was glad America had a labor system in the North where men could strike. "All portions of this Confederacy should act in harmony and with careful deliberation." The South had not yet "demanded of us to yield the guards of liberty in our state constitutions, but it will naturally come to that after a while." This was the inciting doctrine which a northwesterner was preaching in New England.

On March 6 Lincoln spoke at considerable length at New Haven. On the whole it was a better performance than that of Cooper Institute. It was easier, more fluent, less mathematical, and it had some of the raciness of illustration of which he was notably capable, when his creativeness was in natural possession of itself. There was a happy blending of the colloquial, and of forensic analysis in this speech, and it was infused with a finer culture, as if he was in an atmosphere more refined than that of Illinois. Here he recapitulated the sequence of events since 1854; and then he claimed that nothing had ever endangered the Union save slavery—not that nothing had ever disturbed it, as he had previously phrased this subject. It might be a matter of opinion whether the Alien and Sedition laws of Adams endangered the Union in 1798; or the Hartford Convention, in its opposition to the embargo, endangered the Union in 1814–15; or the tariff endangered the Union in 1832; or the Mexican war in 1846–48. These were old subjects to Illinois, where Lincoln had been tripped upon them by Douglas; but here they may have had novelty. Then he advanced the argument that slavery was wrong, but he repudiated the idea that "we ought to attack it where it exists." "To me it seems that if we were to form a government anew, in view of the actual presence of slavery, we should find it necessary to frame just such a government as our fathers did. From the necessities of the case we should be compelled to form just such a government as our blessed fathers gave us; and surely, if they have so made it, that adds another reason why we should let slavery alone where it exists." He was not now saying that the fathers had found slavery and had made a government merely of the materials at hand, but he was saying, in effect, that they made it slave and free, as Douglas said in the debates. With great confidence he challenged anyone to produce a single Democrat who, before the Missouri Compromise, had said that the negro was excluded from the generalization of men when announcing that all men were created equal. This Connecticut audience probably had some historical opinions of their own on this subject. Some of them may have read that Dred Scott case; some may have known about Douglas's reply to this historical misstatement. He urged with great seriousness that slavery was morally wrong; but he claimed no right to touch this immorality where it existed. Nothing could be done but to keep it away from where it was not. They were dull minds who could not see that a belief in its immorality could not stop with keeping slavery from the territories, but must go on to its eradication from the states.

In this Connecticut audience there was undoubtedly intelligence which Lincoln felt constrained to respect. There were unquestionably men here who knew the history of their country, who, to be particular, were informed upon the genesis of the clause in the Constitution which forbade any restraint upon negro importation until 1808, and who had studied the progress of that clause through the Philadelphia Convention until it was voted upon by the delegates, when New Hampshire, Massachusetts, Maryland, North Carolina, South Carolina and Georgia, and their own state of Connecticut, voted for the clause; while New Jersey, Pennsylvania, Virginia and Delaware voted against it. There was no slavocracy here. Nor was there any with respect to the Fugitive Slave clause, since, at the time of the framing and the adoption of the Constitution, every state but Massachusetts had slavery. It was not a clause to favor the slavocracy of the cotton fields, of the raising of indigo. When Lincoln talked to audiences like these, he was more likely to face men who knew about the Ordinance of the Northwest Territory, and that as it was first drawn it would have covered with its exclusion of slavery the land that afterward became Georgia, Mississippi and Alabama; but when it passed in 1787 it related to territory where slavery could not exist. Here in New Haven, where Yale College spread its influence, the moral right or wrong of slavery might be interpreted in the light of those portions of the Bible which made it a right; for not far away was Andover, where the professor of theology, Dr. Moses Stuart, had written in support of slavery in a brochure entitled *Conscience and the Constitution;* and at Wesleyan University, nearer still, and in Connecticut, the Rev. Wilbur Fisk was preaching against abolitionism; while the Rev. Nathan Lord, D.D., the president of Dartmouth, had but recently published a pamphlet against the doctrines which Lincoln was advancing when he was perfectly free to speak his whole mind. These considerations may have operated to put finish and restraint into Lincoln's speech at New Haven. There are other things besides the rebirth of the mind to infuse utterance with gentleness and circumspection and the quality of newly discovered nobility.

According to Herndon, Lincoln returned from New York and his New England tour with great honors, while his Springfield friends received him with pride and congratulations. "I know the idea prevails that Lincoln sat still in his chair in Springfield, and that one of those unlooked-for tides in human affairs came along and cast the nomination into his lap; but any man who has had experience in such things knows that great political prizes are not obtained in that way. The truth is Lincoln was as vigilant as he was ambitious." [1]

At the beginning of this study we referred to the autobiographical sketch which Lincoln furnished Fell on December 20, 1859. Fell was corresponding secretary of the Republican State Central Committee, and had been, in his interviews with men, over Illinois gathering proof that there was sentiment in the state which favored Lincoln for the presidential nomination. Hence his desire to get a sketch from Lincoln for the purposes of publicity in his behalf. At the beginning of December, 1859, Joseph Medill, of the *Chicago Tribune*, went to Washington under cover of a pretended political correspondence for his newspaper, but in fact to work for the nomination of Lincoln. On February 16, 1860, the *Tribune* announced itself editorially as favoring Lincoln's nomination. In a few days Medill sent a letter from Washington, which was published in the *Tribune*, in which

[1] Herndon, II, 167.

NOMINATION TO PRESIDENCY 357

he reported that Lincoln's name was mentioned "ten times as often as it was a month ago," as a candidate upon whom radicals and conservatives could unite. All this Medill wrote in his *Reminiscences*. Truly a man who had stated both sides of so many questions as Lincoln had now done for years, and as he still did to a degree in New England in March of this year, was a man who could be pointed to as giving some encouragement and comfort to any political faith, except the right to let slavery go into the territories. Popularly this is true; fundamentally conservatives and radicals can never be united; they can only be fooled into an alliance. For you can fool all the people part of the time, and that is enough. The vote in the fall of 1860 showed plainly enough that the populace understood what Lincoln was in essence, and except for the needless rupture of the Democratic Party Lincoln would have been overwhelmingly repudiated at the polls.

The idea that Lincoln struggled on through poverty and adversity, holding to ideals, and without luck anywhere along the way, and that it was only a great moral impulse of God's truth marching on which chose him to do God's work, is one of the entrancing myths with which people love to bewitch themselves after first having created it. From the New Salem days onward, Lincoln was fortuned as much as any man who ever lived, who sprang from equal obscurity. He returned from his legislative experience at twenty-eight years of age crowned with honors, and welcomed in Springfield with generous gratitude, and with a card of admission handed to him to the aristocratic circles of the frontier capital. He had not cultivated his chances with prudence. His reticence, and his solitary withdrawals had kept him out of many local friendships. His secretiveness and his craft had made him suspect with many. His satire and his intellectual arrogance had brought him many enemies. His course in Congress had all but ruined him. His divided mind, expressing itself this way one time, and the other way another time, had undermined confidence in his capacity for steady principles. Profitable law business came to him, even such as a practitioner in Illinois at the present time would be glad to have; but he did not with study and professional interest make himself a lodestone for more. He might have been a prosperous lawyer, and he was anything but that. In a word, he had luck all the way, which was not turned aside by his high morality, but was neglected in his lack of vision, his failure to adhere to some settled ambition, in a kind of torpor and in a definite melancholy, and world weariness, and in troubled speculations upon the scene of life, which was the very soil which produced the moral preachments which at last distinguished his career. Herndon, though saying that Lincoln was physically lazy, insisted that Lincoln was mentally industrious. This is not true, for intellectual activity must depend largely upon bodily dispatch. One must be willing on a hot day to walk from the law office to the state library and gather the books together on some subject, just as Lincoln walked some miles when he was young to borrow a grammar. Lincoln could have been well versed in history; he knew little about the annals of his own country. He could have been read in philosophy; he was ignorant of the subject. He could have known economics; he was almost unversed in this branch of learning. All the while luck was standing near with all the books that one could wish for within a few steps of his office. But at last a great good fortune was his. No politician ever had more devoted friends. Judd, Palmer, Browning, Fell, Medill, Davis, all able men, and friends along the years, stood by him, and worked for him with untiring zeal as the convention of 1860 was approaching. This was the final luck which despite his previous coldness to its calls, returned to him unaffronted and made him president.

One way in which vigilance and ambition in his own behalf were exercised may be shown by a letter which he wrote to a political follower on March 16, 1860. This man had written to Lincoln for $100 with which to defray his expenses to Chicago while attending the national convention of the Republican Party there. Herndon, when writing about this, said, "for obvious reasons I withhold the friend's name." In truth it was the unscrupulous Mark W. Delahay, who had married into the Hanks family, as we have seen. We have scarcely noticed an utterance of Lincoln's yet which did not have in it a curious incongruity, as though he were two persons, and one self spoke, and then a contradictory self spoke. This occurred in answering Delahay's letter. "As to your kind wishes for myself," Lincoln wrote, "allow me to say I cannot enter the ring on the money basis—first because in the main it is wrong; and secondly I have not and cannot get the money." Was there anything more to say? Yes, there was the characteristic Lincoln qualification. "I say in the main,

NOMINATION TO PRESIDENCY   359

the use of money is wrong," he went on, "but for certain objects in a political contest, the use of some is both right and indispensable. . . . I now distinctly say this—if you shall be appointed a delegate to Chicago, I will furnish one hundred dollars to bear the expense of the trip." Then Lincoln sent Delahay the money. The same principle applied by a millionaire would make him invincible against a candidate like Webster or Clay, or Lincoln himself. Since Lincoln's day, with the monopolist in control of the politics of America, we have grown used to such tactics. Lincoln had done similar things before this time. When he was running against Douglas for the Senate, and was saying that from his poor, lean, lank face "no cabbages were sprouting," while Douglas, with his evil genius, presented the appearance of worldly luck and prosperity, Lincoln was enjoying the benefit of the support of the Springfield *Staats Anzeiger*, which he had bought up from its editor, Theodore Canisius, to support the Republican Party so long as Lincoln had an interest in the newspaper. With this organ he appealed to the Germans, and opposed the rising tide of Seward, who was being supported by the Chicago *Staats Zeitung*. Lincoln afterward rewarded Canisius by appointing him to the Consular service.[1] "Thou preparest a table before me in the presence of mine enemies: thou anointest my head with oil; my cup runneth over." The King of Glory does this; the Lord mighty in battle!

On April 14, Lincoln wrote again to Delahay. In the edition of Lincoln's Works published in 1894, the name of Delahay as Lincoln's correspondent is not given. A long dash hides the identity of the man Lincoln was thus writing to. Lincoln's Works were prepared by Nicolay and Hay at the request of Robert Lincoln, to whom their *Life of Lincoln* had been dedicated. Robert Lincoln was egregiously ashamed of his father's origin, and it may be inferred that he did not want Lincoln's letter to Delahay to be identified, both because of the character of Delahay, and because of the nature of the stipulations into which Lincoln was entering with such a man. In this last letter Lincoln wrote about his recent trip to New England. Then he mentioned the recent elections in Connecticut and Rhode Island, saying that they were a drawback "upon the prospects of Governor Seward." "Do not mention this as coming from me. I see by the

[1] Barton's "Life of Lincoln," Vol., I, 422.

dispatches that, since you wrote, Kansas has appointed delegates and instructed them for Seward. Do not stir them up to anger, but come along to the convention, and I will do as I said about the expenses." One wonders what the Seward men would have done if they could have brought to light this correspondence with Delahay.

The State Republican convention of Illinois was held at Decatur on May 9 and 10, 1860. Lincoln was present as a spectator; and thus, after thirty years, he was making a symbolical return; for Decatur was near the spot where Thomas Lincoln and the Hankses had settled after their trek from Indiana, on which Lincoln drove the oxen. Now instead of reading Webster's reply to Hayne, he was to hear himself endorsed by the convention for the presidency. Lincoln had another devoted friend, a little-great man in a little place, as the others were. This was Richard Oglesby, who was in the state convention, and rose dramatically to ask the chairman that an old Democrat from the county might be permitted to make a contribution to the campaign fund. Whereupon entered John Hanks, bearing two rails forming standards which were decorated with flags and streamers and with this device: "Abraham Lincoln, the rail candidate for president in 1860. Two rails from a lot of 3000 made in 1830 by Thos. Hanks and Abe Lincoln—whose father was the first pioneer of Macon County." A storm of applause arose, and calls were made upon Lincoln for a speech. Lincoln then said: "I cannot say whether I made those rails or not, but I am quite sure I have made a great many just as good."

In the convention was George Schneider, who was for Seward. Seeing the rails and the demonstration over them, he whispered to a delegate near him that Seward had lost Illinois. He had; for soon John M. Palmer, the renegade from Douglas, offered a resolution that "Abraham Lincoln is the choice of the Republican Party of Illinois for the presidency, and the delegates from this state are instructed to use all honorable means to secure his nomination by the Chicago convention, and to vote as a unit for him." This was tumultuously adopted.

Four days before the meeting of the National Republican convention at Chicago, curiosity arose as to Lincoln's stand on the tariff; and this had to be allayed. No one knew in these changed days of Lincoln's speech at Pappsville, near New Salem, in 1832, in which the half dressed, raw youth of twenty-three declared himself in favor of a high protective tariff. Now on May 12, 1860, Lincoln wrote to Dr. Edward Wallace: "Your brother, Dr. W. S. Wallace, shows me a letter of yours in which you request him to inquire if you may use a letter of mine to you in which something is said upon the tariff question. . . . In the days of Henry Clay, I was a Henry Clay tariff man, and my views have undergone no material change upon that subject. I now think the tariff question ought not to be agitated in the Chicago convention, but that all should be satisfied upon that point with a presidential candidate whose antecedents give assurance that he would neither seek to force a tariff law by executive influence, nor yet to arrest a reasonable one by veto or otherwise." Thus, whatever was wanted, Lincoln would answer the purpose. The monopolists should be satisfied with his record upon the tariff; on the other hand, Democrats who had joined the Republican Party need not be alarmed that he would force a tariff upon them; nor should tariff partisans be afraid that he would veto a tariff bill— if it was reasonable. "I really have no objection to these views being publicly known, but I do wish to thrust no letter before the public now upon any subject. Save me from the appearance of obtrusion, and I do not care who sees this or my former letter." Thus the secret word could be passed around. Pennsylvania wanted a tariff; and Thaddeus Stevens was a delegate to the Convention at Chicago, and he was personally interested in iron, as well as in slavery prohibition.

Thus Lincoln was coming as an entrant to the convention both as a rail splitter and a tariff man, and as the son of a carpenter. The rails were the symbol of honesty. Americans had by this time started the cultus of honesty. The honest man must bear tokens of his quality by which he might at once be received and dealt with as such. To quiet all fears and doubts, there was nothing better than common or shabby clothes, free and rustic manners, a preference for hard cider instead of champagne; being born in a log cabin was proof almost as strong as Holy Writ that the man was honest, for Jesus was born in a stable. Other proofs were espousals of the causes of the common people, where it could be done without trenching actually upon the rights of privilege. The Declaration of Independence never meant that banks and tariffs should not sit at the receipt of custom. The American heart has gushed with self-gratulation when it spoke of a judge, a senator, even a prize fight referee or a gambler, as an honest man; and so it hailed William Henry Harrison, and then Lincoln, and then Garfield, the latter rather by the indirection of calling him the canal boy. Honesty is a prerequisite in a referee or judge where the game is likely to be crooked and where the betters or the players are unskilled, and need some fair watcher or arbitrator to see to it that their honest earnings are not taken away from them. Honesty in a president is a something expressly called for, and when demanded in a loud voice must seem unfitting to older cultures than America's, where men understand that the brown stone mansion or the sidewalks of the city may send forth statesmen as honest as the prairies and the villages can produce. Professing honesty and protesting it is one of the sure symptoms of the Hebraic-Puritan infection, just because its adherents must prove what they know in their hearts they do not possess, in order to advance their conspiracies against their foes. This is the assuring murmur of the innocuous dove.

It seems clear that the visionary Seward and his advisers did not realize the brutality and the cunning that they were advancing to meet in coming to Chicago. It is true they sent bands of music and hordes of shouters, "rooters," so-called; and possibly in placing at the head of their strong men the prize fighter, Tom Hyer, they meant to prepare themselves for trouble. But one concludes that they did not know Chicago, which, as a city then of some 109,000, was in the fourteen-year-old stage of its barbarism and its vitality. The Lincoln supporters had gathered up the loudest voices obtainable, who were ready to confuse and shake the walls of resistance to their assault by a vast pandemonium at the psychological moment, so that fear would be thrown into the assembly and delegates would turn like startled geese all in one direction without knowing exactly why, and without a particle of parliamentary reason for it.

We have mentioned before the name of George Lunt. He was six years older than Lincoln, having been born in Massachusetts in 1803. He was a graduate of Harvard, an able lawyer, a man of profound principle and of great philanthropies. He was an orator, a poet of several creditable volumes. He had been a staunch Whig, and helped to nominate Zachary Taylor; but when the Whig Party was abolitionized he left it, and became a Democrat; and there in his home in Boston he watched the passing American scene with keen eyes and disapproving voice and pen, for he saw war to be inevitable from the Republican movement. He wrote a book of great historical and critical value called *The Origin of the Late War.* In this book he reported that the Chicago Convention was made up of Free Soil Whigs and Democrats, native Americans, foreign adventurers, abolitionists and their opponents, those for saving the Union, and those who wanted the Union dissolved, conservatives, radicals, sentimentalists, ideologists, economists and calculators—and Greeley, the truculent and unprincipled editor of the *New York Tribune.* Lunt lived until 1885, by which time the Lincoln myth making was under speed; and of Lincoln he said that he was "loosely constituted," whose "indecisive character cannot be compared with the firm texture which distinguished the calm and moderate, yet high toned and sagacious mind of Washington."

In this Armageddon at Chicago, this mountain of the gospel, of fruits and apples, were such men as William M. Evarts, Carl Schurz, David Wilmot, Joshua Giddings, George William Curtis, afterward the famous Mugwump of the spurious reform days of Cleveland. The type of mind is easily recognized, and perhaps to be found nowhere but in America, at least nowhere in such numbers and in such influence. It is the mind which notes Zionistic movements, indeed is on the lookout for them, and which changes its politics without regard to those fundamental convictions which hold men steady even in times of change and confusion. For of fundamental convictions they have none, but only nebulous moralities which have been oriented out of their external notions of God and what God wants. Because of this objective notion of God and morality, such men ally themselves with political causes and support them out of Holy Writ.

As we have said, Thaddeus Stevens was in this convention, a powerful man, though at the time sixty-eight years of age. He had a cruel face of an Indian or Aztec type. His eyes were dark and burned with the fires of human sacrifice. His nose was aquiline and large; his mouth turned down at the corners with almost savage severity; the lips were thin and set. He wore a black wig, having not a hair to his head. His mind was full of obsessions; his heart turned like the undying worm with terrible hatred. He had fought Jackson in Pennsylvania in behalf of Biddle and the Bank. At one time he was an Anti-Masonic, preaching that Masons should be deracinated from the American soil. He had effected a coalition between the Anti-Masonics and the Whigs, and had brought about the election of a governor of Pennsylvania upon that absurd alignment. In 1848 he was sent to Congress as a Free Soil Whig. All along he had lived at Lancaster, where his bachelor quarters were kept by Lydia Smith, a negro woman, whom he took into his house from the hut on the lawn when her husband died; and for years thereafter Lydia Smith went everywhere with him. In Lancaster it was common talk that Lydia Smith was his mistress. Stevens did not deny that she was; he did not change his manner of life to give disproof to the appearance that she was his mistress; yet nothing is known about it save that she lived in such a way with him that she might have been his mistress, and that he took no pains to quiet the scandal about himself. One cannot resist the emphasis that he began the practice of law at Gettysburg. This powerful, bitter man became the American Robespierre. He lived long, first to prod Lincoln because Lincoln did not go fast enough to suit him in the war upon the Southern states, then to make a speech in Congress in favor of the Alaskan purchase, a scheme of the lofty minded Sumner by which America embarked upon the acquisition of territory unfitted to be made into states; and he was the leader of that diabolism which looted the fallen commonwealths of the South. He advocated confiscation of plantations for the benefit of negroes. He was the genius of malevolent plots, and of wicked reprisals during so-called reconstruction.

Such was the Chicago Convention, which met in a building called the Wigwam, which accommodated ten thousand persons, while outside was a great crowd in key with the psychology growing rapidly more favorable to Lincoln. Large allegorical paintings of Liberty and Justice adorned the walls. The chairman's chair had been sent by Michigan. It was a huge rocker with its seat dug out of a log. The gavel for the chairman had been carved from a piece of wood taken from Commodore Perry's ship the *Lawrence*. "We have met the enemy and they are ours," was the implication. David Wilmot was made temporary chairman and George Ashmun the permanent chairman of the convention. Besides the delegates from the free states, there

NOMINATION TO PRESIDENCY

were delegates from Delaware, Maryland, Virginia, Kentucky, Missouri and Texas, and from the territories of Kansas, Nebraska, and the District of Columbia. There was suspicion that the delegates from the Southern states were present for no good purpose; but at last they were allowed to take their seats as delegates. Then arose the question, since so many states were not represented, whether nominations should be made by a majority of the number of delegates which would have been present if all the states were taking part in the convention, or by a majority of the delegates actually present. The latter method prevailed by a vote of 331 to 130. Then the platform was reported. The second resolution set forth the Declaration of Independence, quoting not only its words that all men are created equal, but that to secure liberty, life and happiness, "governments are instituted among men, deriving their just powers from the consent of the governed." This resolution also declared that the Federal Constitution, the rights of the states, and the union of the states "must and shall be preserved."

The fourth resolution might have been drawn by Douglas: "That the maintenance inviolate of the rights of the States, and especially the right of each state to order and control its own domestic institutions, according to its own judgment exclusively, is essential to that balance of power on which the perfection and endurance of our political fabric depends." The rest of this resolution would have stayed Lincoln from invading Virginia. It read: "We denounce the lawless invasion by armed force of the soil of any state or territory, no matter under what pretext, as among the gravest of crimes." The platform denounced the Supreme Court, by words plainly applicable to the Dred Scott decision. The twelfth resolution declared, "That while providing revenue for the support of the general government by duties upon imports, sound policy requires such an adjustment of these imposts as to encourage the development of the industrial interests of the whole country." The sixteenth resolution commended the Pacific Railroad, which, as we have seen, received an initial championship from Douglas, that had been distracted into influences responsible for this very gathering in the Wigwam. As originally reported, the platform did not contain the passage from the Declaration of Independence. Joshua Giddings moved to insert it, and the convention voted the proposal down.

Then George William Curtis rose with an amendment which contained the passage from the Declaration already mentioned; and the convention sustained him. Thus the new party, many of whose adherents had all their lives done all they could to degrade Thomas Jefferson, sought the votes of America upon one of his pronouncements.

On the third day the balloting for president began. The whole number of votes in the convention was 465, requiring 233 votes to nominate. Lincoln and his supporters faced the gravest danger in the movement well on foot to give Lincoln the nomination for the vice-presidency. Seward was concededly the leading man, and few outside of the Illinois delegation expected Lincoln to capture the nomination for the presidency. To prevent Lincoln from receiving the lesser honor, Palmer, Judd and Davis were now using all their efforts. Davis took Palmer over to the New Jersey delegation to drive them out of their obstinate stand to nominate Lincoln for the vice presidency. Palmer declared to them that he was a Democrat, not a Whig, and that as a Democrat he would never consent to put both Seward and Lincoln on the ticket, both Whigs. Then the question was asked whether the forty thousand Democrats in Illinois who would support a ticket made up of one Democrat and one Whig could be won to that support by Palmer; and they assured him that Palmer could perform this miracle. So the Lincoln men, without sleep and without rest went about from delegation to delegation arguing, pleading, and explaining. There was Pennsylvania to be won, too. A Chicago man went to see Thaddeus Stevens in Lincoln's behalf and spent hours telling the notorious Robespierre-to-be what Lincoln was in truth, and what Lincoln believed and did not believe. Pennsylvania wanted a tariff. How strong was Lincoln for the tariff? Meanwhile a committee of twelve men, made up from the delegations of Pennsylvania, New York, Ohio, Indiana, Illinois and Iowa, had agreed that if Lincoln's vote rose to a certain number, the votes of those states, so far as the committee could effect it, would be given to Lincoln. The record seems to be clear that Lincoln authorized no one to make any promises of patronage or of positions to anyone. At the same time Judge David Davis was Lincoln's manager at the convention, and, according to Herndon, he negotiated with the Indiana and Pennsylvania delegations that in case of Lin-

NOMINATION TO PRESIDENCY

coln's nomination and election Caleb Smith of Indiana and Simon Cameron of Pennsylvania should have places in Lincoln's cabinet.

Despite all this, if the balloting had been begun on Thursday, Seward would have been nominated, according to the best caculations that can be made. But an adjournment was taken until ten o'clock of Friday morning; and again the excited delegates, surrounded by thousands of nervous and expectant men, came together in the Wigwam. The great Evarts put Seward in nomination. Judd made the nominating speech for Lincoln. This was seconded by Caleb B. Smith, who had been promised a place in Lincoln's cabinet, by Davis. When Evarts concluded for Seward, the New York crowd, led by the bellowing voice of Tom Hyer, the prizefighter, tried to sweep the convention off its feet. But Chicago was not to be outdone in a rôle so peculiarly her own. When Judd and Smith had finished their orations, five thousand men leaped to their feet, yelling to the full power of their lungs. Outside ten thousand steam whistles blew, gongs were beaten, and drums, and thousands of people unable to get in the Wigwam set up the wild pandemonium. A voice cried out, when the din had subsided sufficiently for any single man to be heard: "Abe Lincoln has it by the sound—let us ballot." This was the kind of remark which fires the psychology of a crowd. At this juncture Judge Logan of Springfield arose crying out, "Mr. President, in order or out of order, I propose this convention and audience give three cheers for the man who is evidently their nominee." The New Yorkers were thus outmatched at the game of carrying a crowd, though they had prepared to do so. Fourteen-year-old Chicago had out-hooted and out-shouted the cultivated middle age of New York.

The balloting began. On the first ballot, Seward had $173\frac{1}{2}$ votes, Lincoln 102, Cameron of Pennsylvania $50\frac{1}{2}$, Chase of Ohio 49. The rest were given to men little remembered now. On the second ballot, Seward had $184\frac{1}{2}$, Lincoln 181, Cameron 2, Chase $42\frac{1}{2}$. On the third ballot, Seward had 180, Lincoln $231\frac{1}{2}$, Cameron none, Chase $24\frac{1}{2}$. The convention sat in silence, completely stunned. Coming out of their speechless astonishment, delegates began to whisper, "Two and one half more votes will give Lincoln the nomination." Instantly the chairman of the Ohio delegation arose and threw four votes to Lincoln. That nominated him; that put an end to the presidential hopes of firebrand Chase. Greeley, who held a proxy from an Oregon delegate, smiled with faint maliciousness to see the New York delegation suddenly knocked senseless near the prostrate body of Seward, whom Greeley had hated so long. If some hundreds or thousands of men pick a candidate, it is among the probabilities that the more numerous electorate will approve the choice. None knows better what the vast commonwealth wants than a convention made up from it, and sufficiently large to be its exponent.

The nomination of Lincoln was a case of perfect judgment on the part of a convention. He was as good a tariff and bank man as Seward, but he was not distinguished, cultivated, high toned. He was a rail splitter, a man of the people, as it is said. But in truth he had more common sense than Seward, more judgment and of a better fiber. He had never, like Seward, shown visionary tendencies, wandering about from the Whigs to the Anti-Masonics, and back to the Whigs. Moreover, he had not offended the South with acts as a Senator, as Seward had; nor set people by the ears with orations on irrepressible conflicts. Not everyone knew, and few cared, that Lincoln had preached the "house divided against itself" doctrine. In any case, that was taken from the Bible, and this campaign was to be one of religion applied to politics. Lincoln and his party were getting ready to do worse things against slavery than slavery had ever done, either to the slave or the country, and to do it in the name of Jehovah. Soon theocratic arguments and policies were to be advanced until the divisional line which Liberty draws between what the state may or may not do was to be lost to the understanding of the country.

All the while, Lincoln, down in Springfield, was controlling his nerves by playing ball, and hiding his anxiety under the gayety of physical sport. When the news came that he was nominated, he went to his residence to tell Mrs. Lincoln. Yet the convention at Chicago had to nominate a vice president. The choice fell upon Hannibal Hamlin, a Maine lawyer, born in the same year that Lincoln was. He had entered politics as an Anti-Slavery Democrat. He had been in Congress from 1843 to 1847. He had been in the Senate from 1846 to 1856, where he supported the Wilmot Proviso, and where he spoke against the Compromises of 1850. Because of the Kansas-

Nebraska Act he had left the Democrats and joined the Republicans. He had been governor of Maine, which office he resigned to enter the Senate again in 1857. Thus he, too, was from the North; and as a former Democrat he satisfied men like Palmer. He was in the Senate until he took his office as vice president, and as such, and otherwise, he became one of Lincoln's chief advisers, urging both the Emancipation Proclamation, and the arming of the negroes against the South. So it was that the Republican ticket was sectional, running upon a sectional platform; and the predictions of Douglas and others, respecting the consequences of slavery agitation, came to fruit in the Chicago convention.

A different tone now came into Lincoln's communications and into his personal intercourse. A grave dignity settled upon him. Soon a committee from the convention came to Springfield to notify Lincoln of his nomination. They greeted him in his humble, but respectable, house where he responded to the notification in serious and fitting words: "I tender to you, and through you to the Republican National Convention, and all the people represented in it, my profoundest thanks for the high honor done me. . . . Deeply and even painfully sensible of the great responsibility which is inseparable from this high honor—a responsiblity which I could almost wish had fallen upon some one of the far more eminent men and experienced statesmen whose distinguished names were before the convention—I shall by your leave consider more fully the resolutions of the convention, denominated the platform, and without any unnecessary or unreasonable delay respond to you, Mr. Chairman, in writing, not doubting that the platform will be found satisfactory." This was on May 19. On May 23 he addressed his acceptance of the nomination to George Ashmun, the permanent chairman of the convention. "The declaration of principles and sentiments which accompanies your letter meets my approval; and it shall be my care not to violate or disregard it in any part. Imploring the assistance of Divine Providence, and with due regard to the views and feelings of all who are represented in the convention—to the rights of the States and territories and people of the nation; to the inviolability of the Constitution; and the perpetual union, harmony, and prosperity of all—I am most happy to coöperate for the practical success of the principles declared by the convention."

At last he was a famous man. He had many callers now day by day. Artists came to paint his portrait, sculptors to make masks of his face. His correspondence became very heavy, so much so that John G. Nicolay was employed by Lincoln as a secretary, who thus placed himself in an exceptional position to become Lincoln's biographer. Letters came from Bryant, Hamlin, Thurlow Weed, Seward, Cameron, and many others which required appropriate attention. Nicolay took care of some of this correspondence. Also Lincoln prepared another autobiographical sketch, in which he went over the years of his life. In this he stressed his attitude during the war with Mexico, saying that that war was unconstitutional, "because the power of levying war is vested in Congress, and not in the president." In less than a year from the date of this sketch he was to inaugurate a war by power wholly usurped, a war compared to which the Mexican war was but a street brawl.

In September he was questioned by a correspondent whether he was in favor of a protective tariff, and replied: "The convention which nominated me, by the twelfth plank of their platform, selected their position on this question; and I have declared my approval of the platform and accepted the nomination. Now, if I were publicly to shift the position by adding or subtracting anything, the convention would have the right, and probably would be inclined to displace me as their candidate. And I feel confident that you on reflection would not wish me to give private assurances to be seen by some and kept secret from others." Lincoln had already resolved to make no speeches during the campaign. His debates with Douglas, his Cooper Institute address, his speeches as a whole, the platform and his acceptance of it, must answer to the public for a revelation of his convictions respecting the issues, and they must also be taken as adequate for a report of what he was as a whole. Douglas toured the country, but it was a vain quest, with his party done to death by Jefferson Davis. We have before referred to the Resolutions which Davis introduced in the Senate in February, 1860. Only one thing more need be said about them: the first one read: "That in the adoption of the Federal Constitution, the states adopting the same acted severally as free and independent sovereignties, delegating a portion of their powers to be exercised by the Federal government." This resolution passed the Senate by a vote of 36 to

NOMINATION TO PRESIDENCY

19, Andrew Johnson voting for it. All the Southern senators voted for it, as the senators of California did, and those of Minnesota, Oregon and Pennsylvania. Delaware and Illinois did not vote. No more was this interpretation of the Constitution to have legislative confirmation in the Senate; and Andrew Johnson in five years as the president was to repudiate his vote by imperial acts.

In late October, G. D. Prentice, the editor of the *Louisville Journal*, wrote to Lincoln asking him to set forth his views and intentions with respect to the political problems plainly arising. Lincoln composed an answer referring Prentice to the platform. Lincoln also intimated that he was afraid to be explicit; though in his usual argumentation with himself, he had not decided definitely to remain silent; but on the other hand bad men in the South might seize upon any letter he would write, as an "awful coming down," provided he varied ever so little from the platform. Then Lincoln laid the letter away with these words written on the back of it: "The within letter was written on the day of its date, and on reflection withheld till now." Whether Lincoln ever sent this letter or not cannot be determined from Lincoln's Works.

Election day fell on November 6. In every state, then, but South Carolina, the presidential electors were voted for by the people. In that state the legislature chose them. On the fifth of November, Governor Gist of South Carolina addressed a message to the legislature, in which he said that in ordinary times it would be the duty of the legislature to choose presidential electors; but there was a probability of the election of a sectional president by a sectional party, and that, if that party carried out the policy to which it was committed, the Southern states would become mere provinces of a consolidated despotism. He therefore asked the legislature to remain in session, and if Lincoln were elected to call a state convention to consider the method and measure of redress.

In North Carolina, Georgia, Florida, Alabama, Mississippi, Louisiana, Texas, Arkansas and Tennessee, Lincoln did not receive a single vote. In Virginia he polled 1929 votes to Douglas's 16,290, and Breckenridge's 74,323, and Bell's 74,681. Breckenridge, running on a platform which stood for the principle of slavery going into a territory by Constitutional force, the doctrine of the Davis resolutions referred to; and Bell running with Edward Everett on a platform of the Constitution and nothing but the Constitution, thus divided Douglas's vote in all the states, save those which gave no vote to Lincoln. In California Lincoln had but 657 more votes than Douglas; if he had received the vote that was drawn away to Breckenridge and Bell, Douglas would have carried California by 36,494 majority. In New Jersey, Douglas defeated Lincoln at the polls by 4577 votes in a total of 111,125 votes. Douglas would have carried Delaware and Maryland, except for the split in the vote occasioned by the Breckenridge and Bell tickets. Douglas received a very respectable vote in states like Maine, and New Hampshire; but in Pennsylvania the vote for the Breckenridge ticket was very heavy, though, when added to the Bell vote, did not equal Lincoln's. Douglas's vote in Wisconsin was not contemptible.

The vote in Illinois is an interesting study. Lincoln had 172,161 votes, and Douglas 160,215, Bell 4913 and Breckenridge 2404. Douglas carried 51 of the 102 counties of the state. Lincoln lost his home county, Sangamon, to Douglas, and the county of Menard, just north, where New Salem Hill is located. Lincoln carried northern counties, like Cook, where Chicago is located, and other counties in its neighborhood where the Germans and New Englanders were numerous. Douglas carried the counties of the Anglo-Saxons, the stocks from Virginia and Kentucky. The Democrats elected five out of the nine Congressmen from Illinois. On the congressional vote, Sangamon County was Democratic by 3845 to 2583, while in the Sangamon district, as a whole, the Democrats polled 12,808 votes and the Republicans 11,443. In the State legislature the Democrats had 12 senators to the Republicans' 13; and 35 members of the house to the Republicans' 40. Out of all this maze of cross purposes, Douglas received in the Electoral College but 12 votes, 9 from Missouri and 3 from New Jersey; Breckenridge had 72 votes, Bell 39; and Lincoln and Hamlin 180. But in the country at large Douglas had 1,375,157 popular votes to Lincoln's 1,866,452; while Breckenridge had 847,953, and Bell 590,631. If Douglas had received the whole Democratic vote he would have been triumphantly elected, by which is meant not the Democratic vote which Lincoln gathered in out of the Anti-Nebraska bolt, but the vote that was drawn away from him by the needless issue created by Davis with the foolish hope of overcoming the sectional Republican Party. These considerations

NOMINATION TO PRESIDENCY

are persuasive on the subject that the Republican Party and its candidate were not favored by the American people. There are other things besides unjust apportionment which thwart the popular will, and, as we shall see, lead it and keep it harnessed to war when men do not believe in the objective of the war and want peace.

On December 20, 1860, South Carolina seceded from the Union. In school histories the youth of America are indoctrinated with the idea that the political chiefs of the South spurred the people there to form the Confederate States of America; while Lincoln's unconstitutional acts are glossed over with the remark that what he did before Congress met on July 4, 1861, was validated by that Congress and made lawful for his great purpose of saving the Union. The ordinances of secession passed by the seceding states were strictly regular and in perfect conformity to the American system which had come down from the days of the Revolution. No state legislature assumed to pass any of these ordinances, just because the principle which was observed held that sovereignty did not reside in a legislature for such a purpose but in a convention of the people, to which delegates were elected, as they had been in the states when the Constitution was ratified. To give a typical ordinance, that of Georgia may be quoted: "We do declare and ordain, that the Union now subsisting between the state of Georgia, and other states, under the name of the United States of America, is hereby dissolved, and that the state of Georgia is in full possession and exercise of all those rights of sovereignty which belong and appertain to a free and independent state." What the seceding states did was to put themselves where they had been at the adoption of the Declaration of Independence, and before they united under the Constitution of 1787. The Georgia resolution carried in the convention by a vote of 208 yeas to 89 nays.

Before Lincoln took the oath of office, in March, 1861, seven states in all had seceded: Mississippi on January 9; Florida on January 10; Alabama, January 11; Georgia, January 19; Louisiana, January 26; and Texas, February 1. Buchanan did not know what to do, indeed he disbelieved in coercion; and moreover to do anything required great resources, and he had but a few months of official life. But there in Springfield was Lincoln seeing these states go out one by one, and utterly without power to prevent them, and with no plan conceived as to what should be done. He had to wait all of November, December, January, and February, day by day, all the while in a troubled mind and doubtful position, and with intervals of time on his hands which he could put to no use. In early January, an old friend called to see Lincoln; and Lincoln told him that he would give two years of his life if the two months which intervened between then and his inauguration were over. Lincoln was developing an anxiety neurosis, his nerves were being exhausted by a mind which was racing and was not moving anywhere. Lincoln told this friend that he had read upon his knees the story of Gethsemane, where the Son of God prayed in vain that the cup of bitterness might pass from him; and that he was in the garden of Gethsemane, with a cup overflowing with bitterness. Lincoln's friend then remarked that Christ's prayer was not answered, but that his death had redeemed the world from paganism, and that Lincoln's sacrifice might be as terrible and as significant. The friend in question was Judge Gillespie, and he related this interview. There is no way to disprove that it happened, or to prove it either, except by consideration of other things that Lincoln indisputably said at about this time, which show that his mind was agonized beyond endurance, and that his task was too much. The long dream of the presidency was turning into a nightmare of frightful proportions.

Then the winning of the Pennsylvania delegation in the convention, by the promises of David Davis that that state should have a place in the cabinet, made serious trouble for Lincoln. Soon after the election, Joseph Medill wrote to Herndon that Cameron was a corrupt and debased man; and this letter Herndon took to Lincoln, who protested that he had authorized no promise to be made of patronage. At this time he wanted to give the South some representation in the cabinet; but that was difficult to do. He spoke of Botts of Virginia, Stephens of Georgia, and Maynard of Tennessee. But by March 4, these men were swept away by the action of their states. However, there was the matter of Cameron to settle. In the latter part of December, Cameron came to Springfield, and, after a conference, departed with a letter from Lincoln appointing him to the secretaryship of war. The letter was dated December 31. On January 3, Lincoln wrote Cameron withdrawing the appointment. On January 13, Lincoln wrote Cameron saying that he had heard that

Cameron's feelings were wounded by the letter of the third. "I wrote that letter under great anxiety, and perhaps I was not so guarded in its terms as I should have been; but I beg you to be assured I intended no offense," were Lincoln's words.[1] In this letter he enclosed another dated back to January 3, and as a substitute of the offensive letter of that date. "When you were here, about the last of December, I handed you a letter saying I should at the proper time nominate you to the Senate for a place in the cabinet. It is due to you and to the truth for me to say you were here by my invitation, and not upon any suggestion of your own. You have not as yet signified to me whether you would accept the appointment, and with much pain I now say to you that you will relieve me of great embarrassment by allowing me to recall the offer. This springs from an unexpected complication, and not from any change of my view as to the ability and faithfulness with which you would discharge the duties of the place." After all this change of mind, and indecision Cameron won the war department at Lincoln's hands.

The days dragged by. More and more the air was pregnant with menace of Lincoln's life. Finally Lincoln sent Nicolay on to Washington to see General Scott in order that there might be military protection for Lincoln when he arrived in Washington, and during the inaugural ceremony. Old friends came in to see Lincoln and bid him good-by, fear was written in their faces. Hannah Armstrong, of New Salem days, told him in parting that she never expected to see him alive again; to which inept remark Lincoln turned a humorous word. Then he saw the double apparition of himself in the mirror. Herndon and Lincoln had an evening's talk and for the last. "I am sick of holding office already," Lincoln said. "I shudder when I think of the task ahead."

But there was no Tazewell now to which to run, no window out of which to slip. The time comes to everyone when the escapes are closed. Back of him was a new party hungry for offices, looking to him to seize the reins of government for the interests of a new regime; in front of him were the seceded states, and problems like huge bulks in the darkness, which he could not define or clearly see, although his mind worked incessantly to know what they were, while he raced to live the day before its dawn. The days dragged by. He

[1] Lincoln's Works, I, 665.

went to Coles County to say farewell to his stepmother; and there he put up a stone to the long neglected grave of his father, Thomas Lincoln, whom he could not go to see when the aged man was dying. This was penitence, which is wrung out of the heart when Fate corners the soul. There was still the unmarked grave in Kentucky in which Nancy Hanks had lain for forty years. His troubled and baffled heart must have turned to that; but a great stone had been rolled against the place where she lay. He had few friends in Kentucky. Out of a total vote of 145,000, he had received something like 1400 in that state, and he could go there on no missions however tender and personal. It might be there, while he was at his mother's grave, that the assassin, whom he dreaded, would reach him.

Finally, on February 11, the long tension of waiting was relieved. It was a stormy day with dark clouds hanging over Springfield when Lincoln, with Mrs. Lincoln and their boys, accompanied by Davis, Judd, and the governor of Illinois, Yates, and two secretaries, boarded the train at the Great Western Railway station. He had ridden into the village of Springfield twenty-five years before on a borrowed horse; now the place was a small city, and he was leaving, guarded by military officers, on the railroad which had come into the West since 1837. The Republic had changed, too, and was changing now with incredible speed. The clank of sabres and the rumble of caissons would be heard on Pennsylvania Avenue in a few days now, not to symbol the power of a confederated republic, and the respect its people pay to the chief man who administers the laws, but to protect a new president from hate and revenge among the people themselves. The Republic was vanished not only in administrative forms, but out of the hearts and the understanding of men, which alone make republics possible. Never again would a Thomas Jefferson walk in simplicity to the Capitol to assume the chief magistracy. Hamiltonianism, the tariff and the bank, had done their work at last.

There were a few moments left before the train started, and Lincoln stood looking over the crowd and into the serious faces turned toward him. The springs of his emotions hidden down under tough clay, and stayed by protective rock, burst forth. These people whom he had seen every day for years! This town of Springfield of thousands of lost, half used, wasted days; and that remoter past of New

Salem Hill! Ann Rutledge perhaps came into his mind. What was life, which could bring her into being for a few years, and then, now for so long, could hide her dust in Concord Cemetery; while he had gone so far from the days of the Rutledge Tavern, and was now leaving not "knowing when or whether ever I shall return"? This speech of farewell by Lincoln is in more than one version. Herndon gave it as it was printed in the Springfield press; Hay and Nicolay reported it from Lincoln's manuscript. It was true then that Lincoln had prepared these words. But they came out of these terrible days of suspense and fear and wonder which intervened between his election and the day of his departure for Washington. Lincoln knew the great wisdom of getting hold of the hearts of people. They are few who will study his debates and political speeches compared to the thousands who will melt with tenderness when reading his Farewell Address and the Gettysburg Address, while the history of America remains. The historical mystery is that Lincoln should not have been a Caligula, so that no enchantment cast by the beauty of his words should distract and cloud the judgment respecting his political life and his measures and acts in the War. May the free thinkers claim Lincoln? Was he a Christian? These words which he spoke just before he was borne away from Springfield will be the answer: "Trusting in Him who can go with me, and be with you, and be everywhere for good, let us confidently hope that all will yet be well." Patriarchal clergymen, like William Goodpasture, who preached for years at Concord Church, never uttered words more deeply penetrated with gospel faith. They may have emanated largely from Lincoln's talent for histrionics. Yet they are written endurably on the page of American history. His skepticism, his deism, his political posings must, on the other hand, be deduced by analysis from less memorable records.

Chapter XV   Lincoln as President, and the War

THE Northern people giggled when the report came that Jefferson Davis, in making his escape at Irwinville when the place fell into the hands of the Federal troops, disguised himself in his wife's sunbonnet, skirt and shawl, and hurried away. This did not happen. But Lincoln came to Washington so strangely dressed that no one would have known him. It was natural that he should have protected his life; but sometimes men would rather die than shrink before danger. Lincoln was badly frightened, however, and he had something more to think of than his own preservation. As the train sped on, the strain on Lincoln became almost more than he could endure. He could not help but reflect that he was a minority president, that his party was made up of fanatics and radicals, and that he had to depend on Seward the visionary, and Sumner the pedant, and others as worthless as they. There was not in Lincoln that spirit of Jackson, which said "I'll take the responsibility"; not that he did not take it finally after a long delay, that is, take it after the fashion that we shall see. But Jackson would have gone to Washington like a warrior to battle, provided he had entertained the theories of the Union, and the wrong of secession which Lincoln, in spite of all history and discussion, still hugged so close to his heart.

Lincoln made several speeches on the way to Washington, many of which we shall notice for the specific value they have to this study. He spoke of himself on one occasion as just one frail human being of fifty-two years of age, who was burdened with tasks and responsibilities beyond computation. He confessed to fatigue to audiences here and there; in fact at one time he was nearly ill. There was a tone of anxiety and fear in nearly everything he said. He was protesting the sincerity of his heart, something that one is likely to do when the wisdom of the mind gives out, and its convictions are blown about by vasty winds of an unreckoning infinity. With a sad frankness he intimated doubt of the wisdom of his head. All his life he had gone about and about every problem that came into his head or heart, and with respect to them had expressed himself in varying, if not contradictory, words, with something of that dramatic disposition which Browning manifested in his monologues of many hues and many faiths. The reader will recall what Lincoln wrote to Speed in 1842: "I must gain my confidence in my own ability to keep my resolves when they are made. In that ability you know I once prided myself as the only or chief gem of my character." At fifty-two years of age he was still trying to accomplish this spiritual task, and all these speeches on the way to Washington prove this. There was never a time when he did not see the external world with an unimaginative realism, as Herndon averred, but on the other hand the strange composition of his mind made his vision sometimes near-sighted, at others farsighted. His adjustment was defective, which prevented him from realizing the will likely to come to a man of his age, to see things not half-truly but truly altogether, because the uselessness of holding to unrealities is perceived to be futile. With such feelings and self-resolves he was struggling against intellectual convictions which had fastened themselves in his logic, and had clothed themselves in mysticism and religion. It was impossible for him, therefore, to rise to the strength of a new comprehension of the Union and the Constitution freed from old argumentations.

On February 12 he spoke to the legislature at Indianapolis. "What is invasion?" he asked. "Would the marching of an army into South Carolina without the consent of her people and with hostile intent toward them be invasion? I certainly think it would; and it would be coercion also, if the South Carolinians were forced to submit. But if the United States should merely hold and retake its own forts and other property, and collect the duties on foreign importations, or even withhold the mails from the places where they were habitually violated, would any or all of these things be invasion or coercion?" The Lincoln mind was working here as of old, and could not see that the two things he stated were exactly the same. He was deceiving himself, and concealing his purpose from the people. He then went on to compare a state in the Union to a county in a state, without perceiving that the States held no such relation to the Union as provinces do to an empire or counties to a state. Lincoln never uttered anything more puerile than this. Every state was a sovereign body; and a county was never anything but a political subdivision of the state whose residents were citizens of the state and not of the county, and owed allegiance to the state alone.

At Pittsburgh, on February 15, he gave the audience to understand what his principles were on the tariff: "It is often said that the tariff is the specialty of Pennsylvania. Assuming that direct taxation is not to be adopted, the tariff question must be as durable as the government itself . . . it is to the government what replenishing the meal-tub is to the family . . . it is as to whether, and how far, duties on imports shall be adjusted to favor home production in the home market, that controversy begins." Then Lincoln had his secretary read to the audience the twelfth resolution of the Chicago platform. In conclusion he said: "I have not strength, fellow citizens, to address you at great length, and I pray that you will excuse me."

At Buffalo, February 16, Lincoln, in replying to the hope expressed by the mayor that Lincoln would have strength for the task ahead of him, used these words: "I am sure I bring a heart true to the work. For the ability to perform it, I must trust in that Supreme Being who has never yet forsaken this favored land." When the train reached Albany Lincoln was all but ill. "I have neither the voice nor the strength to address you at any greater length." He had spoken but three or four minutes.

At Trenton, New Jersey, on February 21, he seemed to be in stronger physique. "The man does not live," he said when addressing the New Jersey assembly, "who is more devoted to peace than I am, none who would do more to preserve it, but it may be necessary to put the foot down firmly." Here the audience broke into loud and prolonged cheers. "And if I do my duty and do right you will sustain me, will you not?" There were loud cheers again, and cries of "Yes." Lincoln had felt his way along with encouraging results.

He made two addresses at Philadelphia. In reply to the mayor and the citizens, he said: "May my right hand forget its cunning, and my tongue cleave to the roof of my mouth if I ever prove false to those teachings" [the Declaration of Independence]. In Independence Hall he spoke again. There he said: "I have never had a feeling, politically, that did not spring from the sentiments embodied in the Declaration of Independence. . . . It was not the mere matter of separation of the colonies from the mother land, but that sentiment in the Declaration of Independence which gave liberty not alone to the people of this country, but hope to all the world, for all future time."

At Harrisburg, on February 22, Lincoln witnessed the "finest military array, I think I have ever seen," which tariff Pennsylvania turned out by way of suggestion to the seceded states of the might of the North. "They give hope," Lincoln observed, "of what may be done when war is inevitable." Did the seceded states have reason to believe that they might be invaded and coerced?

At Philadelphia on the night of the 21st, Lincoln had been notified of a plot to assassinate him at Baltimore, and naturally he recalled that Maryland had not invited him to speak on the way to Washington. Should he go on to Harrisburg, or follow the advice of his entourage and the detectives, and go straight to Washington? Lincoln was in a state of great nervousness; nevertheless he kept to his schedule, and spoke at Harrisburg as already detailed. But that night at Harrisburg, after all the greetings and speeches were over, Judd and the others proposed that Lincoln go directly to Washington now, secretly and in disguise. The military men saw the humiliating aspect of such a course and denounced it as cowardly. Lincoln, after the exhaustion of the long wait in Springfield and of this trip with its fatiguing hand shaking and making speeches, was prepared to believe that he was in danger. But in fact the dreadful passion of fear had seized upon his friends, though the only danger probably was from the attack of a lunatic, to which a president is always exposed. No soldier, no politician of the South, no responsible person of the South with all their hatred of Lincoln would have laid a hand on him. They had plans of their own quite different from anything of this kind. Nevertheless the detectives and Judd had their way. Lincoln and a friend were bundled into a carriage and driven in secret through the darkness to a deserted railroad crossing outside of Harrisburg, where an engine and one coach awaited them. They entered the coach and at ten o'clock the train was at West Philadelphia. There Lincoln and his companion got out, and entered another carriage. All the while Lincoln did not know exactly where he was going, or whether for that matter the driver was not taking him to a secret spot to be done to death.

Now followed a drive of about an hour, when the carriage came to the depot in Philadelphia where Lincoln took the train to Washington. The man with Lincoln all this while was Lamon, afterward one of his biographers. Lamon told the conductor that his companion was sick. He gave the tickets to the conductor while Lincoln lay secreted in the berth of the sleeper. At three in the morning the train reached Baltimore, and Lincoln was tossing sleeplessly in his berth. Lincoln looked out of the window. There was no enemy in sight. At six o'clock the dome of the capitol greeted Lincoln's grateful eyes—an unfinished dome it was, as unfinished as Lincoln's character. Lincoln was frightfully fatigued, he was ill; and with his face bundled in a shawl he left the train and walked through the crowd unknown and unobserved, and in a kind of trance. Seward was outside the station waiting for him; and the two drove to Willard's Hotel where Lincoln asked for a room. Entering it he flung himself on the bed exhausted.

In a few days he went to the Capitol, and in the president's room solicited the advice of Senator Harlan as to the cabinet. He mentioned that he had intended to appoint Cameron to be secretary of war. When the day of the inaugural came he drove with Buchanan to the Capitol. No one molested him, or in any way manifested any hostility toward him. The whole apprehension was founded in fear, which works such havoc with individuals and with nations, particularly in times of war or threatened war. Lincoln appeared to make his Inaugural carefully dressed for the occasion. He carried a gold headed cane, and wore a new silk hat. He was very pale, but mastered himself for the occasion. We need now to examine this Inaugural, which has already been considered in another place, in further exploration of the Lincoln mind.

He announced that he would take care that the laws of the Union should be faithfully executed in all the states. How was that to be done in the seceded states? There was no Federal officer to execute any law. Every one of them had resigned: Federal judges, collectors, postmasters, marshals—there was not one left in office in all the seceded states. This was not nullification where a state was still in the Union, but resisting its laws; but it was secession where there were no laws to execute, and no officers to execute them. What could he do therefore to execute the laws there except to do it himself? And how could he do it himself save as an emperor, a czar? There was no other way. As his words could mean nothing else but this,

LINCOLN AS PRESIDENT 383

they constituted a declaration of war. It was advice to the South to get ready for battle, just as the fulminations of the war ministers of George III were notice to the Thirteen States to prepare for invasion. Lincoln then declared that he would so observe his oath until "my rightful masters, the American people, shall withhold the requisite means." Did that mean that he would do nothing until Congress acted? The American people can act no other way save by their Congress. No, he did not mean that. For in six weeks he was to inaugurate a war without the American people having anything to say about it. He was to call for and send troops into the South, and thus stir that psychology of hate and fear from which a people cannot extricate themselves, though knowing and saying that the war was started by usurpation. Did he mean that he would bow to the American people when the law was laid down by their courts, through which alone can the law be interpreted as the Constitutional voice of the people? No, he did not mean that; because when Taney decided that Lincoln had no power to suspend the writ of habeas corpus, Lincoln flouted and trampled the decision of the court. Did he mean that there could be a plebiscite on his acts, whereby his rightful masters might approve or reject and forbid what he did? That could not be in the nature of things. There was no provision in the Constitution for any such process. There was only provision for the voice of the American people to speak through Congress and the Courts—and through Lincoln, in obedience, always, both in peace and war, to the Constitution.

In truth Lincoln's words in this particular had no meaning whatever. There need to be no bloodshed, he said; yet "the power confided to me will be used to hold, occupy and possess the property and places belonging to the Government, and to collect the duties and imposts." Could that be done without invasion? He had said at Indianapolis that marching an army into South Carolina would be invasion, which he would not do. But if to hold Fort Sumter or to collect duties at Charleston required an army, then there was invasion; and thus his words were contradictory here. Moreover he would appoint no Federal officers to take the place of those resigned in the seceded states. Then how could duties be collected in New Orleans, Savannah, Charleston, except by sending men there to do so, who would not be Collectors under the law, but representatives of Lincoln? And these would have to be supported by an army. For Lincoln knew that the seceded states were preparing for invasion, and that such processes would be considered invasion. He would deliver the mails, unless they were repelled; if they were repelled he did not say what he would do.

This was the Lincoln program. Yet all this quibbling and sophistry was clarified by war, was enforced by imperial arms, and what is remembered most now are the words with which he closed. When his feelings were moved, and, by consequence, when he wanted to move the feelings of his audience, he had a singular mastery of words. "Intelligence, patriotism, Christianity, and a firm reliance on Him who has never yet forsaken this favored land, are still competent to adjust in the best way all present difficulties." And yet he would have nothing to do with the Crittenden Compromise; he would not receive or recognize the Commissioners of the Confederate States who came to Washington to negotiate about the forts and places of the late United States, and to pay for them in full; he would not treat with his old friend Stephens at Hampton Roads in 1865 when the South was exhausted and wanted peace if they could be assured that their capitulation did not mean dishonorable and cruel vanquishment, as it turned out to be when they battled on to Lee's surrender. "In your hands, my dissatisfied fellow countrymen, and not in mine, is the momentous issue of civil war. The government will not assail you." So, as of old, in the debates with Douglas and in his speeches, was Lincoln putting himself on the defensive, and fastening the wrong of aggression upon the other side. But he was not speaking the truth. He meant to "put the foot down," to assail and coerce the South. Lincoln took no oath to protect the Constitution against the sovereignties which had rejected it. As originally written Lincoln had closed with the words concerning his oath to protect the government and the lack of an oath on the part of the South to destroy it, which was pure sophistry also. When Seward saw the draft of the Inaugural, he wrote these words for a conclusion: "I close. We are not, we must not be, aliens, enemies, but fellow countrymen and brethren. Although passion has strained our bonds of affection too hardly, they must not, I am sure they will not be broken. The mystic chords of memory which, proceeding from so many battlefields, and so many patriotic graves, pass through all the hearts and all the hearths in this broad continent of ours, will yet again harmonize in their ancient music when breathed upon by the guardian angel of the nation."

Then Lincoln took this paragraph, which Coolidge, or Garfield might have written, and made this prose poem of it: "I am loath to close. We are not enemies but friends. We must not be enemies. Though passion may have strained, it must not break our bonds of affection. The mystic chords of memory, stretching from every battlefield and patriot grave to every living heart and hearthstone all over this broad land, will yet swell the chorus of the Union, when again touched, as they surely will be by the better angels of our nature." Upon these moving words, and others of similar beauty, the fame of Lincoln rests; his blunders, his thinking power which was small, his lawyer-like honesty of mind and his many lacks of intellectual honesty, his mouth-tributes to liberty and his liberticides, his weaknesses and his strength, his sophistry and his cruel prosecution of the War—all these pass from memory. These words remain. They will not be dislodged from American thinking, even among men who have studied his life sufficiently to know how and where to put blame upon him.

So with the administration of the oath to Lincoln by Taney, whom Lincoln had denounced so unjustly, Lincoln drove to the White House. The long wait in Springfield was over.

Now the office seekers tortured him night and day. He had some trouble with the Senate too, respecting the confirmation of his cabinet appointments. The border states fought Montgomery Blair, who was nominated to the postmaster-generalship, and Edward Bates, nominated to be attorney general. At last they were confirmed. And Lincoln was now to sit in consultation with firebrand Chase, with visionary Seward, with the so-called corrupt Cameron from tariff Pennsylvania, with Caleb B. Smith from Indiana, who had helped Lincoln in the Chicago Convention, and with Gideon Welles, who, day by day, was to record in a diary what was happening, and what was being said; a diary which has proved a rich source book for writers on those times.

The background against which Lincoln's reflections were cast must now be drawn. On February 9, Jefferson Davis was elected provisional president of the Confederate States of America, and a

Constitution was proposed which was afterward adopted. It is worthy of note that while this Constitution legalized slavery, it outlawed the protective tariff, which had crept into the system of the United States and had made serious trouble from the days of Hamilton. On March 11, Jefferson Davis was inaugurated as president; and Alexander H. Stephens as vice president; and thus, at the south of the United States, stood another nation, perfect in all its parts, with an executive, legislative and judicial departments, with congressmen and senators, and judges, with a treasury, and an army, and something of a navy. It was the government of some 11,000,000 people, when all the states joined it which did join, coupled with the people of those states which affiliated themselves with it. But on March 11 when Davis took the administration of this new nation, Virginia still hung in the balance. Even after South Carolina seceded, Virginia had hopes that the disruption of the Union might be averted. An extra session of the Virginia legislature was convened on the 7th of January, 1861; and on the 19th, resolutions were passed asking all the states to send delegates to meet in Washington on February 4, there to consider plans of harmony and pacification. Thus was a peace congress created by the act of Virginia, to which Maine, New Hampshire, Vermont, Massachusetts, Rhode Island, Connecticut, New York, New Jersey, Pennsylvania, Ohio, Indiana, Illinois, Iowa, Delaware, Maryland, Virginia, North Carolina, Kentucky, Tennessee, and Missouri sent delegates. To this Congress came Chase from Ohio; and on the 6th of February he made a speech in which he said that Lincoln had been elected as a candidate of the people on a platform which denounced the extension of slavery, and that the North did not intend to throw the fruits of the victory away. He further said that the North would not enforce the Fugitive Slave Law; but on the other hand it would not disturb slavery within the states which had it. As to territories, the North would not respect the Dred Scott decision was his implied utterance, in discussing the restriction of slavery to the states where it already existed. These were the good tidings of golden rule Chase, the anarchical manifesto of a law enforcer.

The Peace Congress went to pieces like other pacificatory bodies and measures of the time. In January of 1861 several plans were submitted in Congress as a preventive of the impending clash of arms. Toombs had a plan, as did Davis, and Crittenden, and Douglas, and Seward. There was one by Bigler, and one by Rice. These events, looked at now, raise the wonder if men had not lost their minds, and could no longer comprehend the issues of the hour, so grave and so menacing. But certainly there were no intellects anywhere now like Clay's and Webster's, using that word to mean capacity to sway and to soothe and to devise something to be done. Douglas had been tripped and tied by the Lilliputians. Lincoln had no plan. As always, he was on the defensive, waiting to see what was proposed. At no time did he come forward, with power and authority and genius, saying that the Union might be saved on some given basis. He worked nothing out in this regard. What he said in 1837 he said now: no extension of slavery into the territories. And what he said in his Inaugural about holding the forts he still adhered to.

To return to Virginia; its legislature on January 7 passed an act calling a state convention for the purpose of expressing the sovereign will of the people of Virginia touching their relations to the Union; the election of delegates was to be held on February 4, and the convention was to meet on the 13th. The delegates were elected and met on the day appointed. They could have passed an ordinance of secession; but it was not done. They were watching the Peace Congress, which Virginia, which had raced to the assistance of Massachusetts in 1774, Virginia the state of Washington and Jefferson and Madison, had called to compose the distracted condition of affairs in the land. However, on the 28th of February a delegate in the Virginia convention urged immediate secession. Men are sometimes charged with criminal intent when only acting out of real prescience; and so Virginia and her leading men of this time have been accused of conspiracy and of harboring disunion purposes from the first, which they concealed under the leaves of the false olive, when in truth they were doing all in their power as high-minded men, who really loved the Union of the Constitution, to save it. Hay and Nicolay's work is particularly severe in its comment on the course of Virginia, perhaps because she was so clear in her great office of trying to avert the war which was descending upon the country. This resolution, offered on the 28th, was referred and not acted upon. Then Lincoln's Inaugural alarmed the convention like a thunderbolt. The convention then appointed a committee to see

Lincoln and ascertain what line of policy he intended to pursue. The question was asked by Virginia; and Virginia was worth holding to the Union, because it was across the Potomac from Washington, and because of the prestige of its place and history in America. The committee saw Lincoln on April 13, and he said to them: "If, as now appears to be true, in pursuit of a purpose to drive the United States from these places, an unprovoked assault has been made upon Fort Sumter, I shall hold myself at liberty to repossess, if I can, like places which have been seized before the Government was devolved on me. And in every event I shall, to the extent of my ability, repel force by force. . . . I scarcely need to say that I consider the military posts and property within the states which claim to have seceded as yet belonging to the Government of the United States as much as they did before the supposed secession. Whatever else I may do for the purpose, I shall not attempt to collect the duties and imposts by an armed invasion of any part of the country; not meaning by this, however, that I may not land a force deemed necessary to relieve a fort upon a border of the country." [1]

One would think that imposts and duties, money in a word, would be worth more to the United States than forts, such as those actually involved at the time. But the subtlety of Lincoln's position consisted in the recognition of what the country would say if he sent troops to Charleston to collect duties, and there was bloodshed in the attempt; and what the country would say if he sent food to starving men in Fort Sumter. For the rest, it is clear that Lincoln's reply to the Virginia Committees stuck in the bark with all the tenacity of his singleness of will. Men differed in their estimate of Lincoln as to whether he was weak or strong. Sumner said he resembled Louis XVI. Herndon saw Lincoln as Holland summed him after canvassing the estimates of many men who knew Lincoln in Illinois: as a man of great will, as a man of weak will, as a man of candor and as one of stratagems, as a man of cold heart and distant attachments, and as one of warm feelings and close intimacies.

This generation, which never saw him and must depend upon the words of those who did, may well conclude from the diverse opinions passed upon Lincoln that he was a strong man as weak men are strong, who, having taken one position, will not take another, out of

[1] Lincoln's Works, II, 33.

remembrance of the difficulty it was to take the first, and who are deterred by fears, also called cautions, of the future and its consequences, if a new ground be occupied. Lincoln moved slowly, because his mind worked slowly. He was not gifted with that celerity of thinking which distinguished Douglas, and geniuses like Napoleon. In all these negotiations and movements to avert war, Lincoln abided by the one policy that he had announced in his Inaugural. "In your hands, my dissatisfied fellow countrymen, and not in mine, is the momentous issue of civil war." Who was to drive his mind from that stronghold, when Douglas had brayed him as in a mortar on the "house divided against itself doctrine," and on the charge of conspiracy which Lincoln made against Taney and Buchanan? Douglas had convinced everyone but Lincoln himself that he was wrong. Lincoln went on with his utterances on these subjects to the last. This is what Herndon meant when he said that nothing could shake Lincoln when he had made up his mind. That is the quality of a weak man.

So now, amid the office seekers, and the consultations with his cabinet, Lincoln went about the White House with undulatory tread, with no method of business, answering but few letters, sometimes shutting himself away from everyone, sleeping badly, eating frugally at breakfast, partaking of a biscuit and a glass of milk for luncheon, reading nothing. His small gray eyes were sunk back in his head in steady thoughtfulness. His mind, neither versatile nor quick, as Herndon said, was working; for he was in touch with the so-called war governors of the free states, who controlled the militia of their states, which Lincoln knew he was going to need.

How was he going to get an army to send against the South? The Constitution made him depend upon Congress for that, as the only power that could declare war. But if he could get the violent, patriotic mediocrities who were the governors of the free states to send him troops he would not need to go to Congress for the means of war. He had sworn to support the Constitution, but while all the past years he had contemned Seward's dogma that there was a law higher than the Constitution, he was now approaching the time when he would embrace it. The lives of tens of thousands of men, the preservation or the waste of billions of wealth wrung by labor from the soil and the mines, the woe or the happiness and peace of women, of children, of generations of human beings, lay in the slow pulse of Lincoln's heart, who had placed the blame for war-to-be upon the South, and meant to have the blame fall that way.

April first came and Seward wrote his famous note in which he said to Lincoln: "We are at the end of a month's administration, and yet without a policy either domestic or foreign." The visionary secretary thought that it would be a good policy to demand an explanation from Great Britain and Russia and send agents into Canada, Mexico, and Central America to stir the spirit of independence on the continent against European intervention. If they did not explain their late maneuvers, then declare war against them. That was the best thing that Seward could think of to do in the posture of affairs. He believed that a foreign war would cement the South and the North with blood shed in such a common cause. Lincoln had much more common sense than Seward, and it asserted its power now. Lincoln referred Seward to the Inaugural, with particular reference to the matter of holding the forts, saying that Seward had approved that part of the Inaugural. He added that on March 9 he had ordered Gen. Scott to hold the military places of the country, and to call upon all departments for the necessary means to do so. Was that not a policy? It was, indeed a policy, and one which the Southern leaders divined at once; hence their preparations, not to strike the first blow but to resist the first blow about to be struck by the North. Herndon wrote that Lincoln's judgment was in some particulars childish. He confined this characteristic to the capacity to decide upon the fitness, the propriety, the harmony, the beauty of things. But this childishness took a more serious turn in the management of affairs out of which the War sprang.

As early as March 15, Lincoln required of his cabinet their opinions as to the wisdom of attempting to provision Fort Sumter. And we shall return to that in some detail. But there was also Fort Pickens that occupied the serious deliberations of these eight men, Lincoln and his cabinet, whom the people had put in power. Fort Pickens was on Santa Rosa Island in Pensacola Bay, an inlet of the Gulf of Mexico in the northwest part of Florida. Fort Sumter was on a drift of sand three miles in the Charleston harbor from the old and beautiful city of that name, which honored Hayne and Calhoun and treasured their graves in the churchyards of its beautiful churches, one of which was designed by Sir Christopher Wren. Whether South Carolina and Florida were out of the Union by fair legality had nothing to do with their fears of a hostile administration made up of the Chases and the Sewards and Sumners, and Lincoln, who might use these forts to shell Charleston, or in which to prepare expeditions against New Orleans. Seward thought that the reinforcement of Fort Sumter was but an assertion of power on the slavery question; while to reinforce Fort Pickens was a national or Union measure, and he wanted the Union and not slavery stressed in these days. Lincoln could not see the difference between the two forts; and no one else can. The casuistry of Seward shows that the fate of the American people was then in weak and inept hands. So far as this work goes, Fort Pickens quickly passes out of notice. On April 6 a naval expedition, under Lincoln's orders, started for Fort Pickens by way of Key West, which was reached on the 13th. On the 17th, Fort Pickens was invested by the Federal Government; and over it the United States flag flew thenceforward. Still Virginia, knowing all about this, did not secede.

As to Fort Sumter it was not worth a dollar to the Federal Government in actual, as distinguished from symbolical, value. Lincoln was not interested in it as a means to collect imposts. He had said in his Inaugural that he would possess the places of the Government. Fort Sumter was therefore a point where the government could assert its authority. As some ten million men lost their lives in the Thirty Years' War, which was waged to determine whether bread was flesh or only bread; and as Troy went down with woe unutterable over the elopement of Helen, so under Lincoln the War started over a fort located on a drift of sand something like the extent of a city block in size. Boys stand facing each other on either side of a chalk line on the walk and quarrel. Finally one steps over the line and the other strikes a blow. The Fort Sumter matter was as puerile as that. The maneuvering that Lincoln resorted to to provoke South Carolina to fire the first shot was copied by our army, which plotted the killing of Filipino sentries, by American sentries, and then when Filipino sentries retaliated raised the hypocritical cry that Aguinaldo had fired on the United States flag.

The night before Lincoln was inaugurated Commissioners appointed by the Confederate Goverment arrived in Washington on the mission of paying the Federal Government for Fort Sumter, and the other places which they claimed to be entitled to in virtue of secession, and their right to condemn them by the power of eminent domain, a sovereign power never delegated to the Federal Government by the states, and therefore reserved. Lincoln and Seward took the arrogant position from the start that the seceded states were not out of the Union. Hence there could be no commissioners, because there was no Confederate Government. The Commissioners could not be officially received without recognizing the Confederate Government. Therefore Seward would not see them. He held communication with them, as we shall see, but as persons only. As long as he could, Lincoln clove to the position that there was no Confederate Government; that what was called such was just a conspiracy, and, though of many millions, was still a conspiracy. More or less he had to step down from this lofty stand.

In response to Lincoln's request to his cabinet for opinions as to the wisdom of trying to provision Fort Sumter every member of the cabinet laid before Lincoln his several views. Seward's note to Lincoln contained these words: "Suppose the expedition successful, we have then a garrison in Fort Sumter that can defy assault for six months. What is it to do then? Is it to make war by opening its batteries and attempting to demolish the defenses of the Carolinians? . . . I may be asked whether I would in no case, and at no time advise force—whether I propose to give up everything? I reply no. I would not initiate war to regain a useless and unnecessary position on the soil of the seceding States." He would not initiate war!

Chase wrote to Lincoln: "If the attempt will so inflame civil war as to involve an immediate necessity for the enlistment of armies and the expenditure of millions, I cannot advise it in the existing circumstances of the country and in the present condition of the national finances."

Cameron, the secretary of war, advised against the step. "Whatever might have been done as late as a month ago, it is too sadly evident that it cannot now be done without the sacrifice of life

LINCOLN AS PRESIDENT

and treasure not at all commensurate with the object to be attained; and as the abandonment of the fort in a few weeks, sooner or later, appears to be an inevitable necessity, it seems to me that the sooner it is done the better."

Welles, the secretary of the navy, opposed the provisioning of the fort. "By sending, or attempting to send provisions into Sumter, will not war be precipitated? It may be impossible to escape it under any course of policy that may be pursued, but I am not prepared to advise a course that would provoke hostilities. It does not appear to me that the dignity, strength, or character of the government will be promoted by an attempt to provision Sumter in the manner proposed, even should it succeed, while a failure would be attended with untold disaster." Welles had been a Democrat until the Kansas-Nebraska trouble; and he spoke now like a disciple of Jefferson. It is to be noted that he regarded the attempt to provision the fort as the precipitation of war.

Smith, the secretary of the interior, submitted this opinion: "I therefore respectfully answer the inquiry of the President by saying that in my opinion it would not be wise under all the circumstances to attempt to provision Fort Sumter."

Attorney General Bates in his opinion said: "The possession of the fort, as we now hold it, does not enable us to collect the revenue or enforce the laws of commercial navigation. It may indeed involve a point of honor or a point of pride, but I do not see any great national interest involved in the bare fact of holding the fort as we now hold it. . . . It seems to me that we may, in humanity and patriotism, safely waive the point of pride in the consciousness that we have the power, and lack nothing but the will to hold Fort Sumter in such condition as to command the harbor of Charleston, cut off all its commerce, and even lay the city in ashes."

This opinion went to the moral point. It showed that magnanimity which Lincoln might have observed as the head of a great and powerful North, ready, as it seems he knew, to respond to his call of troops when he made it. That Christian spirit which he had frequently invoked might have made him mindful of the God he preached who had always favored "this blessed land." But perhaps God was to be served by putting down treason, by killing men who were conspiring to destroy the Union. Lincoln at last did not reckon wrongly of the Hebraic-Puritanism which his long village experience in the Middle West had acquainted him with.

In the meantime the Confederate Commissioners were assiduously addressing themselves to Seward to learn what was going to be done about Fort Sumter; and Seward kept assuring them in unofficial meetings that Fort Sumter would be evacuated. The Commissioners, when they went away from Washington, finally, empty handed, complained bitterly that they had been tricked. Much has been written to save Lincoln from being jointly accused with Seward in the Fabian tactics which were used in dealing with the Commissioners. But the first thing to settle is whether Seward was telling Lincoln what the Commissioners said to him, and what he said to them. And the second question is did Lincoln say nothing to Seward, or did he tell him to go ahead with his false promises until the land military strength was in readiness? If Seward was a secretive and cunning man, so was Lincoln. Above all, the course pursued by Seward with the Commissioners was written all over with the characters of Lincoln's nature: his caution, his reticence and the maturing of plans without his confidence being given to anyone; and his skill in leading an adversary along until he was ready to drive the knife into him, to "feed him to the eels."

General Scott was in favor of evacuating Fort Pickens; and this judgment was communicated to the cabinet at the first state dinner held at the White House on March 28. The next day there was a cabinet meeting, and another vote was taken upon the matter of attempting to provision Fort Sumter. Seward's memorandum declared that the dispatch of an expedition would provoke an attack and so involve a war at this point. He was in favor of the fort being abandoned. Chase could see no difference between Fort Sumter and Fort Pickens. War would result as well from provisioning one as the other. He was now in favor of provisioning both forts. Welles joined in this judgment. Smith wanted Fort Sumter abandoned. Blair was unwilling to share in the responsibility of provisioning Fort Sumter. Bates thought that Fort Pickens should be possessed. As to Fort Sumter, the time had come when it should be evacuated or relieved. At the end of this cabinet meeting Lincoln issued this order to the Secretary of War: "Sir: I desire that an

LINCOLN AS PRESIDENT

expedition, to move by sea, be got ready to sail as early as the 6th of April next, the whole according to memorandum attached, and that you coöperate with the Secretary of the Navy for that object."

On the 7th of April the "Relief Squadron," pharisaically called, started for Fort Sumter. It consisted of 11 ships, 285 guns, 2400 men, under orders to reënforce the Fort peaceably, "but forcibly if necessary." Justice Campbell had been acting as an intermediary between the Commissioners and Seward. On April 7, he addressed a note to Seward and asked, "if the assurances he had given, were well or ill founded." Seward replied, "Faith as to Sumter fully kept—wait and see." At that moment the Relief Squadron was on its way, and at sea. On the 8th of April the Commissioners learned the true state of affairs. Thereupon, on the 9th, they addressed a letter to Seward, a portion of which may be quoted. "Your government," they said, "has not chosen to meet the undersigned in the conciliatory and peaceful spirit in which they are commissioned. . . . Whatever may be the result, impartial history will record the innocence of the Government of the Confederate States, and place the responsibility of the blood and mourning that may ensue upon those who have denied the great fundamental doctrine of American Liberty, that 'Governments derive their just powers from the consent of the governed,' and who have set naval and land armaments in motion to subject the people of one portion of the land to the will of another."

The forces of the Confederate States were ready for the arrival of the "Relief Squadron." On the 12th of April the guns of the South opened fire on Fort Sumter; and on the 14th it was reduced and evacuated. Not a man was killed, but it was a glorious assertion of state sovereignty. Infinite nonsense has been written to the effect that the South commenced the hostilities, because it fired the first gun. Lincoln indulged in this sophistry too. But all the writers on international law hold that hostilities are begun by him who causes the first gun to be fired. Common sense proves that this must be true. If the United States sent a relief squadron to Southampton, England, carrying food to Americans there, whom England did not want to be succored, for state reasons of her own, the question could never be raised that England began hostilities by repelling the relief squadron with her guns. The situation is not altered at all by the Lincoln sophistry that the Southern states were lawlessly out of the Union, and that they were in an atrocious conspiracy to resist the law. That is but a begging of the question. We shall see how the Christian spirit in Lincoln turned to Jehoviac wormwood in his message to Congress of July 4, 1861, on this and other subjects. But what Lincoln could not deny, nor any of the insane men who soon came to the front when war madness took the North, was that the Southern states were a *de facto* government. How much more they could have been a *de jure* government than they actually were will puzzle the best mind to say.

The military display which Lincoln saw at Harrisburg in February was not for mere official ceremony. It was to show what tariff Pennsylvania could do with the already seceded South Carolina. While Lincoln was playing a dilatory game with Fort Sumter, he was seeing Governor Curtin of Pennsylvania, Governor Morton of Indiana and Governor Washburne of Maine, who were assuring him that those states would send him state troops for the subjugation of the South, and that the people of their states would support such a course. The United States army at this time consisted of 17,113 men and officers, with 3894 soldiers in the Department of the East, 3584 in the Department of the West, 2258 in Texas, 2624 in New Mexico, and 3382 in the Department of the Pacific. In anticipation of the collision about to take place at Fort Sumter, Gen. Scott was reporting to Lincoln from April 5 onward concerning the military situation, and the arrival of companies of armed men. On April 5 he informed Lincoln that the military machinations of the South were not formidable, or likely to come to a head. Virginia had not yet seceded, and Washington was in no danger. Lincoln in his state of nerves may have feared that some company of soldiers might get into Washington and kidnap him, as even such a course was afterward advised in the North with respect to Jefferson Davis; but the whole attitude of the Southern military plans proves that no violent hand would have been laid upon the city which George Washington of Virginia had founded. On April 8, Scott reported, however, that more troops were needed; on the 9th he advised the calling of ten companies of militia. On the 13th two companies of dismounted cavalry arrived in Washington, and the Secretary of War called for four more companies of volunteers

LINCOLN AS PRESIDENT

from the District of Columbia, so to make fifteen companies in all for the capital. There were nearly six companies of marines in the Navy Yard. Also on the 13th Sherman's battery from Minnesota arrived in Washington together with companies of foot artillery, and some troops from Texas. Washington was not defenseless.

On the 15th of April Lincoln issued a proclamation calling 75,000 militia into service, and convening Congress in extra session for July 4, the anniversary of the Declaration that all governments derive their just power from the consent of the governed! A quotation from the Constitution made at this point will throw light upon his lack of power to do this extraordinary act. Section 4 of Article IV reads: "The United States . . . shall protect . . . on application of the legislature, or the executive [of any state] (when the legislature cannot be convened) [such state] against domestic violence." As previously noted this clause was inserted in the Constitution out of the influence which Shays' Rebellion in Massachusetts exercised in the convention; and as a protective provision against slave uprisings. Madison in the XLIIIrd number of the *Federalist* made this observation: "Should it be asked, what is to be the redress for an insurrection pervading all the states, and comprising a superiority of the entire force, though not a constitutional right? The answer must be that such a case, as it would be without the compass of human remedies, so it is not within the compass of human probability; and that it is sufficient recommendation of the Federal Constitution, that it diminishes the risk of a calamity for which no possible constitution can provide a cure."

There was no insurrection in the South, unless the American people were one mass, without state sovereignties. There was no civil war begun or ever waged by the South, because such a war is one between different forces of the same political organization, as it was between the Parliamentarians and the Royalists in England in 1642. The war was between the states of the North and the states of the South. It was a war between states, not between groups of the same states. Lincoln called on states to furnish troops to subdue the states of the South. With so much said, a consideration of Lincoln's proclamation will be better understood, and the reader will be prepared for the further discussion of it.

"Whereas," it reads, "the laws of the United States have been for sometime past and now are opposed, and the execution thereof obstructed in the states of South Carolina, Georgia, Alabama, Florida, Mississippi, Louisiana and Texas by combinations too powerful to be suppressed by the ordinary course of judicial proceedings, or by the powers vested in the marshals by law." He said this, though there was not a Federal Court in the States named, nor the judge of such a court, nor a marshal, nor any judicial order that was resisted. Then he proceeded to call forth the militia of the several states to "suppress said combinations, and to cause the laws to be duly executed." Then he read what is known as the riot act to millions of people, that ancient act which officers were wont to read to mobs. It may be said that if the South had won the war, and the North had passed into decay or even into decline, all the history which would have been written would have made Lincoln ridiculous, and dishonored. Such is truth in this world and such the forces which write histories and moralities. For this proclamation brought about the secession of Virginia on April 17, with the loss to the Federal Army of Lee, who recognized that his allegiance was due to sovereignty, and not to delegated authority. North Carolina seceded on May 20, on the anniversary of the Mecklenberg Declaration of Independence. Tennessee called a special session of its legislature for April 25, and allied itself with the Confederacy on May 7. On June 24, at an election, its ordinance of secession was carried at the polls by a vote of 57,675 majority. Arkansas seceded on May 6. Missouri tried to remain neutral, but was soon plunged into civil war. Kentucky's governor refused to furnish Lincoln any troops, and the legislature sustained the governor's course. Some of the governors appealed to denounced Lincoln in unmeasured terms.

Lincoln gave his rightful masters, the American people, no chance to say whether they wanted these troops called out. He could have evacuated Fort Sumter, and called Congress in immediate special session to consider what should be done. Congress alone under the Constitution has the power to declare war. The president has nothing to say about it. Lincoln had inaugurated war and had usurped the power to do so. He had gone infinitely beyond what Polk did in the case of Mexico, and for which Lincoln had denounced Polk during the whole of his political life, to the time that he did this worse unconstitutional act himself. But if he had called Congress at once and let that body pass upon the course to be pursued, the whole difficulty might have been composed, or better ordered. As it was, the North being once plunged into war, no matter by what usurpation, took on the momentum of the mob and went forward to the end. Lincoln in this proceeding was at last dominated by the radicals and the war governors, by Chase and Seward, who were determined to settle the irrepressible conflict their own way, be the bloodshed what it might. The momentuous issues of "civil war" were in Lincoln's hands, and he directed them. Between the time of this proclamation and the first of July, Lincoln, by his own fiat, increased the army to 186,000 men. On the third of May Lincoln called for 42,034 volunteers to serve for a period of three years. He increased the regular army by the addition of eight regiments, including one regiment of cavalry, and one regiment of artillery; he increased the navy force by the addition of 18,000 seamen. In these acts he did what the sovereign of England could not do, and what only the Russian czar at that time could do. He did this in the name of law and to enforce the law, while he himself was violating the law and his oath of office. It was to preserve the Union, to be sure; but the Constitution had made all the provisions for the saving of the Union which the executive was authorized to use; and outside of these he was not to go, neither in the name of a higher law, nor through plebiscites, if any ever could have been taken in confirmation of what he did. In addition to these usurpations, he suspended the writ of habeas corpus as early as April 27, without the shadow of authority for doing so. On May 10 he suspended the writ generally over the country. On the 19th of April he issued a proclamation of blockade in all the ports of the seceded states. And thus when Congress convened he had an army at his back; he had public discussion, free speech and a free press strangled, and he was master of the lives of men under the laws of piracy for trying to run the blockade. He was thus an emperor with full despotic power and his rightful masters had had no word to say about it.

What was Congress to do with him? There was no Congress left except that of the Northern states. Between March 4, 1861, and July 4, he was in the exact position of Charles I, who ruled England without Parliament for eleven years. It happened with Lincoln that during these four months he levied war without the consent of Congress, as Charles did. Like Charles, too, he needed money to pay the soldiers. But when Congress met there was nothing to do but vote the money. By that time the mob spirit had America in its grip. There were enough, too, to justify Lincoln both in Congress and out. How did they dare to do otherwise? The radicals had taken over the government sufficiently even at this time to fill thinking men with fear. Chase and Seward were in the cabinet. Thaddeus Stevens and Sumner were in Congress. As for the press, Greeley first counseled the course of letting the Southern states depart in peace; then his journalistic instability fell easy prey to the rising madness. Within a short time of his advice to do nothing about secession, he was calling for ropes with which to hang Jefferson Davis for treason. In states like Missouri and Illinois, the local opposition to Lincoln and his course soon felt the arm of the military. For under the rule of a suspended habeas corpus, a man could be arrested for speaking unfavorably of Lincoln's measures, and, being thrown into prison, could not get out. The *Chicago Times* was suspended by mere military order. By Lincoln's fiat its presses were unlocked to continued publication. The civil courts were prostrated wherever a military officer wanted to dragoon public sentiment against the war already begun by Lincoln. The governors of the Northern states could not well be attacked on legal grounds for calling out their state militias to preserve the local peace. And who was to stay them from sending their militia beyond state lines, from Illinois to Missouri, from Massachusetts to Washington, anywhere in the land? There was no one to interfere with this sudden and powerful movement in the North. Who knows, the unknown father of Nancy Hanks may have had the blood of Charles I in him? Thus by a strange circuit from England to Virginia, thence to Kentucky and to Illinois, may have come from arbitrary royalty, this rail splitting man, who was not modest and not humble, but was self-confident and self-assertive.

According to John Hay, Lincoln frequently said, when talking of questions at issue or under discussion between himself and his advisers, "I know more about it than any of them." "It is absurd," wrote Hay, "to call him a modest man. It was his intellectual arrogance and unconscious assumption of superiority that men like Chase and Sumner never could forgive." [1] Yet by his prose poems, by his melancholy, by his sad and weary face, he was preparing the American culture which would take him for a god. For two hundred years the English prayer book contained a service appointed for remembering the cruel death of the martyred Charles I. In America we have had already more than sixty years of similar pious reverence for Lincoln.

Before July 4, 1861, arrived, there was something of the old vigor and clear seeing left in the Senate. Douglas was still there. On March 15 he offered a resolution for the withdrawal of United States troops from all the Southern forts except those at Key West and Tortugas. Speaking upon this resolution, he said: "I take it for granted no man will deny the proposition that whoever permanently holds Charleston and South Carolina is entitled to the possession of Fort Sumter. Whoever holds Pensacola and Florida is entitled to the possession of Fort Pickens." He went on to say that there were only three courses ahead: the restoration of the Union by amendments to the Constitution, which would ensure tranquillity; a peaceful dissolution of the Union; or war directed to the subjugation of the Southern states. "We cannot deny," he said "that there is a Southern Confederacy, *de facto*, in existence, with its capital at Montgomery. We may regret it. I regret it most profoundly; but I cannot deny the truth of the fact, painful and mortifying as it is. . . . I proclaim boldly the policy of those with whom I act. We are for peace." Douglas's resolutions were laid on the table by a vote of 23 to 11. The Senate was in possession of the Sumners, by the withdrawal of the Southern senators. And now it was that the Northern governors, already mentioned, hastened to Washington and offered their state troops to Lincoln. We have seen that Lincoln did not lack for a policy so much as Seward seemed to think. But he could carry it out only by arms. If the states would not help him, what could he do with the almost insignificant regular army? Yet it was in the air, somehow, as something suspected or whispered, that Lincoln would resort to the clauses of the Constitution already referred to, which empowered him to assist a state against domestic violence when requested to do

[1] Herndon, II, 226.

so in the manner pointed out in the Constitution. Hence on this March 15, Douglas discussed that possibility. "But we are told," he said, "that the President is going to enforce the laws in the seceded states. How? By calling out the militia and using the army and navy. These terms are used as freely and flippantly as if we were in a military government where martial law was the only rule of action, and the will of the monarch was the only law of the subject. Sir, the President cannot use the army, or the navy, or the militia, for any purpose not authorized by law; and then he must do it in the manner prescribed by law. What is that? If there be an insurrection in any state, against the laws and authorities thereof, the president can use the military to put it down only when called upon by the state legislature, if it be in session, or, if it cannot be convened, by the governor. He cannot interfere except where requested. If, on the contrary, the insurrection be against the laws of the United States, instead of a state, then the president can use the military only as a *posse comitatus* in aid of the marshal in such cases as are so extreme that judicial authority and the powers of the marshal cannot put down the obstruction. The military cannot be used in any case whatever, except in aid of civil process, to assist the marshal to execute a writ. I shall not quote the laws upon this subject; but if gentlemen will refer to the Acts of 1795 and 1807, they will find that under the act of 1795 the militia only could be called out to aid in the enforcement of the law when resisted to such an extent that the marshal could not overcome the obstruction. By the act of 1807 the president is authorized to use the army and navy to aid in enforcing the laws in all cases where it was before lawful to use the militia. Hence the military power, no matter whether navy, regulars, volunteers, or militia, can be used only in aid of the civil authorities. Now, sir, how are you going to create a case in one of these seceded states, where the president would be authorized to call out the military? You must first procure a writ from the judge describing the crime; you must place that in the hands of a marshal, and he must meet such obstructions as render it impossible for him to execute it; and then, and not till then can you call upon the military. You have no civil authorities there, and the President, in his Inaugural, tells you he does not intend to appoint any. . . . You are told, therefore, in his Inaugural that he is going to appoint no judges, no marshals, no civil officers in the seceded states that can execute the law; and hence we are told that he does not intend to send the army, the navy, or the militia for any such purpose. Then, sir, what cause is there for apprehension that the President of the United States is going to pursue a war policy, unless he shall call Congress for the purpose of conferring the power and providing the means? . . . But it may be said that the President of the United States ought to have the power to collect the revenue on shipboard, to blockade the ports, to use the military to enforce the law. . . . Be that as it may, the President of the United States has not asked for that power. He knew that he did not possess it under the existing laws— for we are bound to presume that he is familiar with the laws which he took an oath to execute. We are bound to presume that he knew, when he spoke of collecting the revenue, that he had no power to collect it on shipboard, or elsewhere than at the ports. We are bound to presume that when he said he would hold and possess the forts and other property of the United States, he knew he could not call out the militia for any such purpose, under the existing laws. We are bound to presume that he knew his total absence of power on all these questions."

But to no avail were unanswerably historical and legal arguments of this kind with men like Sumner and Stevens, and the men now left in possession of the United States Congress. Douglas would as well have demonstrated a proposition in Euclid to an Apache chief. There sat Sumner with his conceited face, his arrogant eyes, in his English spats as usual, smiling contempt upon the Douglas who had routed him so often in debate. It was not necessary now for Sumner to attempt a reply. Douglas was down, his party was destroyed; and Sumner need but sit quite calmly and smile with cool patronization. At the other end of Pennsylvania avenue was Lincoln who had nurtured his mind on loose construction, on the sophistries of an American people in mass, of a Union older than the states, upon the twisted reasoning which through fifty years had been used by Hamiltonians and Whigs that there was not any such thing as state sovereignty. By July 4, Lincoln was to have ready his message to Congress, in which his oft repeated doctrines were to be newly netted and knotted, in some particulars, and in such a way that pages of careful logic smoking him out of his holes would be necessary to show that he was wrong on history and wrong on the Constitution. More than ever, Lincoln, by July 4, took on the character of a Merlin, a wizard whose words captured men without a sound basis in law, as well as those who had none; while the vast crowd could not see the swift legerdermain with which he shifted terms and propositions, amid the bewildering charm of the pious talk he kept up while working his tricks.

The matter of blockading the ports was full of self-contradiction. If the Southern states were not out of the Union, if secession was utterly void, as Lincoln contended, then by what authority was Lincoln giving preference to other ports, by the blockading of the Southern ports? The Constitution reads: "No preference shall be given by any regulation of commerce or revenue to the ports of one state over those of another." Yet Lincoln claimed in his blockade proclamation that he was blockading the ports in pursuance of law, and in obedience to his oath of office. Nothing can be done with a mind that denies the plainest principles. Afterward Lincoln developed one of his characteristic sophisms. It was that the Southern states were not out of the Union—but out of their practical relation to it. But upon the supposition that the Seceded States were legally out of the Union, then they were a foreign nation, and his proclamation was an act of war; and thus he had usurped power, for the war power is vested in Congress, not in the president. But Lincoln's Merlin arts of reasoning caught him in their own web, and brought him discomfiture. By blockading the ports he made a legal acknowledgment that he was at public war with the Confederate States, and that they were neither in insurrection nor rebellion. This stultification was not all. By his proclamation he visited the punishment for piracy, that is hanging, on anyone who violated it under letters of marque. Thus he made pirates of privateers, against the basic principles of international law. The conclusion is that Lincoln was wrestling, and any hold that he could get, or any tactics that he could adopt to throw his adversary was a part of the game of winning—and saving the Union, supporting the Constitution! That meant the Jackson doctrine to the full: supporting the Constitution as he claimed to understand it, not as it read or had been construed by authority.

This was by no means a new question. In the days of Nullification, in 1832, it was feared that Jackson would blockade the port of Charleston. A political convention was held in Massachusetts, which was addressed by Webster. Among other things Webster said: "Sir, for one I protest in advance against such remedies as I have heard hinted. The administration itself keeps a profound silence, but its friends have spoken for it. We are told, sir, that the President will immediately employ the military force, and at once blockade Charleston. A military remedy, a remedy by direct military operation, has been thus suggested, as the intended means of preserving the Union. Sir, there is little reason to think that this suggestion is true. We cannot be altogether unmindful of the past, and, therefore, we cannot be altogether unapprehensive of the future. For one, sir, I raise my voice beforehand against the unauthorized employment of military power, and against superseding the authority of the law by an armed force, under pretence of putting down Nullification. The President has no authority to blockade Charleston; the President has no authority to employ military force, till he shall be required to do so by the civil authorities. His duty is to cause the laws to be executed. His duty is to support the civil authority. His duty is, if the laws be resisted, to employ the military force of the country if necessary, for their support and execution; but to do all this in compliance only with law, and with the decisions of the tribunals."

Lincoln, having declared this illegal blockade and fixed the penalty of piracy to its violation, encountered other objection than that the Confederate States could bring against it either by argument or by force. There were France and England, and any other foreign nation which wished to protest against it, to be won over to a policy whose observance to the legal end would have shocked the civilized world. On May 19, a little more than a month after Lincoln had promulgated his new doctrine of piracy, Earl Derby in the House of Lords, spoke as follows to the question: "He apprehended that if one thing was clearer than another, it was that privateering was not piracy, and that no law could make that piracy, as regarded the subject of one nation, which was not piracy by the law of nations. Consequently, the United States must not be allowed to entertain this doctrine, and to call upon her Majesty's

Government not to interfere. He knew it was said that the United States treated the Confederate States of the South as mere rebels, and that as rebels these expeditions were liable to the penalties of high treason. That was not the doctrine of this country, because we have declared that they are entitled to all the rights of belligerents. The Northern States could not claim the rights of belligerents for themselves, and on the other hand deal with other parties not as belligerents, but as rebels." Lord Brougham held that privateering was not piracy by the law of nations. And thus the debate proceeded.

This matter of the blockade ran into intricate negotiations of the past, even treaties, as well as matters of history, and it is difficult to simplify the subject and abbreviate its course and its end. However, in 1854 the United States, with regard to the impending Crimean war, submitted to the principal maritime nations these propositions: first, that free ships should make free goods; second, that neutral property on board an enemy vessel should not be subject to confiscation, unless it was contraband, like munitions and the like. In 1856 France and England gave assent to these propositions, with the abolition of privateering prefixed, and a clause added that a blockade to be binding must be effective, not merely one of manifesto, but actually enforcible. The United States was then asked to join in these stipulations, which the United States agreed to do, provided England and France would accept another proposition, which was that the goods of private persons, non-combatants, should be exempt from confiscation in maritime war. Great Britain and France refused so to agree. And when Lincoln became president the suspended negotiations were taken up by Seward. What England and France had agreed to was called the "Paris Agreement of 1856," and this the Confederate States adopted; and while negotiations were going on between the United States and England respecting the Paris Agreement of 1856, the British government was holding communication with the consul at Charleston, through the British Legation at Washington; and the French government was also in official touch with the Confederate Government. President Davis, seeing that this was recognition of the Confederate States as belligerents, announced that his government would adhere to the Paris Agreement of 1856; but insisted that the right of privateering be added. The consul at Charleston communicated this decision to the British Legation, saying that the wishes of Her Majesty's government had thus been complied with by the Confederate Government, and "it could not be expected that they [the Confederate States] should abolish privateering of their own accord," "particularly as it is the arm upon which they most rely for the injury of the extended commerce of the enemy." For this Lincoln revoked the exequatur of the British Consul; and about this controversy Seward wrote one of his ill-advised notes, which, but for Lincoln's mild modifications, might have brought war with England.

In November of 1861, James M. Mason and John Slidell, who were on their way to England on the British Mail Steamer *Trent*, were seized by Captain Wilkes of the United States Navy and carried to Fort Warren in Boston Harbor. The most intense excitement arose in England over this affair. Troops were sent to Canada. A formal demand was made upon Washington for the surrender of the prisoners, and for an apology for this outrage upon neutral rights. Seward complied with both requests, though Lincoln's House of Representatives had voted its thanks to Captain Wilkes. The result was that Mason and Slidell proceeded to England. Thus, with this assertion of international law, coupled with Lincoln's change of policy with respect to the exchange of naval prisoners, the deadly sting of the blockade, making privateers into pirates, was drawn. The United States were left to do what they could by the process of actual blockade, which turned out at last to be sufficent with their superior power and their increasing navy.

Lincoln's acts with regard to the habeas corpus came close indeed to the lives of the people, and aroused on the part of men learned in Constitutional law and liberty the gravest concern and the bitterest protest. In Maryland, which had not seceded, there was no less great sympathy with the South, and much popular sentiment against Lincoln's inauguration of the war. Lincoln, according to his usual way, proceeded cautiously with Maryland. He did not, until he had his plans matured, move in a way to disclose what grip he would take upon that state. As early as April 20, he wrote to the governor of Maryland a letter of pacific tone, in which he said that he made no point of bringing troops through Maryland to Washington; at the same time he summoned the governor by telegram to come to Washington for a conference with him. On the 25th of April, Lincoln wrote to Scott: "The Maryland legislature assembles tomorrow at Annapolis, and not improbably will take action to arm the people of that state against the United States. The question has been submitted to and considered by me whether it would not be justifiable, upon the ground of necessary defense, for you, as general in chief of the United States Army, to arrest or disperse the members of that body. I think it would not be justifiable nor efficient for the desired object. First, they have a clearly legal right to assemble. . . . Secondly, we cannot permanently prevent their action . . . I therefore conclude that it is only left to the commanding general to watch, and await their action, which if it shall be to arm their people against the United States, he is to adopt the most prompt and efficient means to counteract, even, if necessary, to the bombardment of their cities, and, in the extremest necessity, the suspension of the writ of habeas corpus."

On April 27 Scott was authorized to suspend the writ on the military line between Washington and Philadelphia. On May 25, John Merryman, a resident of Baltimore, while peaceably in his house at two o'clock in the morning, was arrested by a military officer, taken from bed, and conveyed to prison in Fort McHenry, without any warrant for his arrest from any court, or any other basis for it except the arbitrary will of the officer. At this time, though Lincoln had called out the militia, there were no military operations on land as yet, and Maryland was in the Union. A petition of habeas corpus was presented by Merryman to Taney, as Chief Justice of the Supreme Court, who awarded the writ. When it was served on the officer who had Merryman in custody, the officer refused to obey the order of the Chief Justice to bring the body of the prisoner before him; and as excuse of disobeying the writ, the officer alleged that Merryman had been arrested for general treason and rebellion, without specifying what the crime was, if any. The essence of the return was that the writ of habeas corpus had been suspended by the officer, and that it was done by the authority of Lincoln. Taney observed in his opinion, which he passed upon the case, that "the conspiracy of which Aaron Burr was the head became so formidable and was so extensively ramified as to justify, in Mr. Jefferson's opinion, the suspension of the writ. He claimed on his part no power to suspend it, but communicated his opinion to Congress, with all the proofs in his possession, in order that Congress might exercise its discretion upon the subject, and determine whether the public safety required it. And in the debate which took place upon the subject no one suggested that Mr. Jefferson might exercise the power himself."

The Chief Justice then showed that the power to suspend the writ was in the clause, among others, which specified the powers of Congress. "If the high power over the liberty of the citizens now claimed was intended to be conferred on the president, it would undoubtedly be found in plain words . . . but there is not a word in it [the Constitution] that can furnish the slightest ground to justify the exercise of the power." "He is not empowered to arrest anyone charged with an offense against the United States, and whom he may, from the evidence before him believe to be guilty; nor can he authorize any officer, civil or military, to exercise this power; for the 5th article of the Amendments expressly provides that no person 'shall be deprived of life, liberty or property, without due process of law'—that is judicial process." Taney then traced the history of the writ and said: "Accordingly, no power in England, short of that of Parliament, can suspend or authorize the suspension of the writ of habeas corpus." He quoted from Blackstone's *Commentaries on the Laws of England:* "But the happiness of our Constitution is that it is not left to the executive power to determine when the danger of the state is so great as to render this measure expedient. It is the Parliament only or legislative power that, whenever it sees proper, can authorize the crown, by suspending the habeas corpus, for a short and limited time, to imprison suspected persons without giving any reason for so doing." Taney then observed: "And if the president of the United States may suspend the writ, then the Constitution of the United States has conferred upon him more regal and absolute power over the liberty of the citizen than the people of England have thought it safe to entrust to the crown—a power which the Queen of England cannot exercise at this day, and which could not have been lawfully exercised by the sovereign even in the reign of Charles the First."

But there was American authority, and one with which Lincoln was familiar from the days of his studies in Springfield, when writing out his political speeches. This was Story's *Commentaries on the Constitution.* Story wrote: "Hitherto no suspension of the writ has ever been authorized by Congress since the establishment of the Constitution. It would seem, as the power is given to Congress to suspend the writ of habeas corpus in cases of rebellion or invasion, that the right to judge whether the exigency had arisen must exclusively belong to that body." There was more American authority. Chief Justice Marshall when deciding the case of ex parte Bollman and Swartwout, which may be read in full in the fourth volume of Cranch's *Reports,* had said: "If at any time the public safety should require the suspension of the powers vested by this act in the Courts of the United States, it is for the legislature to say so. That question depends upon political considerations, on which the legislature is to decide. Until the legislative will be expressed this court can only see its duty and obey the law." To this decision Taney referred. Then Taney used these words: "If the authority which the Constitution has confided to the judiciary department and judicial officers may thus upon any pretext or under any circumstances be usurped by the military power at its discretion, the people of the United States are no longer living under a government of laws, but every citizen holds his life, liberty and property at the will and pleasure of the army officer in whose military district he may happen to be found." Taney then ordered a copy of all the papers to be certified to Lincoln. "It will then remain for that high officer in fulfillment of his constitutional obligation to 'take care that the laws be faithfully executed' to determine what measures he will take to cause the civil process of the United States to be respected and enforced."

Thus fell the writ of habeas corpus when Lincoln put his foot down, as he suggested he might do when addressing the New Jersey senate on February 21. As a result, there was a reign of terror in the United States. Hundreds of men were thrown into prison by military officers and kept there without relief. They were men who had done nothing but express their opinions about the despotic course of affairs, or who were suspected of entertaining convictions hostile to Lincoln's acts. Such things were, in the wild state of the war spirit, flippantly and ignorantly denounced as treasonable; whereas there was but one treason, and that one clearly expressed in the Constitution.

The framers of the Constitution took into full view both war and peace, and provided for both fully. They were men learned in law and in history; and they were not unmindful that days of stress and extraordinary perils might be. They were what Lincoln called his "masters" who ratified the Constitution in the states; and what they wanted to be done and to be left undone in the so-called saving of the Union, they had mapped out. Taney in this decision had spoken for the American people, to the effect that Lincoln could not suspend the writ of habeas corpus, much less devolve the power to do so upon military commanders. No power but the court, no higher power than the chief justice could lay its command upon Lincoln. And when that command was given to him he disobeyed it. All his life he had preached law observance. When he was accused of attacking the judiciary during the Dred Scott excitement, Lincoln delivered himself epigrammatically to the effect that what he advocated was not the overthrow of the courts or the Constitution, but the overthrow of those who would pervert the Constitution. Now he contemned and perverted both the court and the Constitution. The abolitionists and radicals were exceedingly glad of what Lincoln had done. And Lincoln, who never forgot what he considered a wrong done him, and who had accused Taney of criminal conspiracy in the rendition of the Dred Scott decision, now stood in giant strength with his foot upon Taney's neck, and with more than 180,000 soldiers, summoned by his own word from the states, to back his defiance of the judiciary. It was at this time that Seward told Lord Lyons: "I can touch a bell on my right hand and order the arrest of a citizen of Ohio. I can touch the bell again and order the arrest of a citizen of New York. Can Queen Victoria do as much?" In New York mobs hovered about the offices of newspapers demanding that they display the American flag. It was a time when any hypocrite, any scoundrel could walk to the best men in the country and demand proof of patriotism from them. Franklin Pierce was challenged in his own state with respect to his loyalty, and he gave the soldierly reply that he did not have to wear the flag on his coat in order to demonstrate his loyalty to the Constitution as it had been made. Thus the summoning of this vast army, and the suspension of the writ of habeas corpus laid all the rights of constitutional government in the dust. Hate, old grudges, self-interests of all kinds flocked forth out of human nature to take advantage of the lawless days. By doing so they swelled the vast chorus of "the Union." In this vast motley of a land gone insane, where all the vilest passions were suddenly released, the rapacity of business reared its python head. Prospective war contractors ran out of the jungles of private frauds intent upon devouring the substance of the people.

On the 29th of April, President Davis, in a message to the Confederate congress, declared that Lincoln's acts were a declaration of war, and he asked them to devise means to protect the Southern states. "All we ask is to be let alone; that those who never held power over us shall not now attempt our subjugation by arms. This we will, this we must resist to the direst extremity." He also asked for troops. Meanwhile the popular election for the ratification of Virginia's ordinance of secession was to take place on May 23; and on that day it was ratified by the people of Virginia by a great majority. Those who voted against it mostly lived in the western part of the state. It was these men who afterwards set up the so-called state of West Virginia. With a view to crushing Virginia, Lincoln prepared to move troops against her. To this end General McDowell was to set out from Washington, General McClellan from Wheeling, General Butler from Fortress Monroe. In consequence the Confederates were preparing for this invasion. Of this vast army under Lincoln, thousands had tendered their services for the purpose of defending and protecting the capital. They were soon to see the devious and bloody path that Fate would lead them into, far away from the object for which old attachments and reverences had induced them to offer their services.

The history of the War between the States has not been yet as a whole written; and in this book its purpose will be subserved by studying Lincoln, not with reference to battles and campaigns, though his indecision and want of military science must be noted; but once the war is shown to be on, the Lincoln mind can be analyzed on the basis of Lincoln's messages and his acts with reference to various problems that arose, and as they were handled by him, down to the last message he ever sent to Congress. This is one of the most puzzling utterances of all the baffling strangeness that came from his unequal and contradictory mind. We are approaching the time now when something of that unbalance of reasoning took Lincoln which he had suffered from during his broken engagement with Mary Todd. Thin partitions do indeed divide genius and forms of genius from madness. Where the psychical forces are too energetic for the mental organization, a dizzy state of ideation comes to pass. When compared to calm and powerful intellects like Goethe's and Emerson's and Darwin's, Lincoln was now clearly unsphered. He had imbibed the historical falseness and the logical unsoundness of Story on the Constitution. He was in no state of strength, with war madness about him, to correct his reflections and his reasonings. His mental equipment, as nature had given it to him, and his own mind, as he had schooled and nurtured it, were now to possess him. Whether it was celestial or demoniac possession, everyone may fitly decide for himself after considering the record of his deeds.

Chapter XVI   Lincoln's War Message and The War

ON the eighty-fifth anniversary of the Declaration of Independence, July 4, 1861, Congress assembled in pursuance of Lincoln's call. Lincoln was not now the man who had come into Washington four months before, with his face muffled in a shawl to hide his identity. He was not the man who, all the way from Springfield to Washington, had been weak from anxiety, and half ill from fear. The slow process of his body had at last poured powerful hormones into his heart. He was in a towering rage, in a giant courage. With nearly two hundred thousand soldiers at his beck and call, with all the forces of government in his hands, he had nothing now to fear. He knew that Congress, the voice of his "masters," the American people of the North, would echo whatever he said. They dared not do otherwise. He could appeal over their heads to the people, as he had done with Taney. A people already plunged into war can do nothing, with human nature as it is, but go forward. This has been proven over and over again. As bad as the Philippine conquest was, and in spite of the objection of the best men in America to that imperial plot, the people found themselves caught between antitheses where there seemed nothing to do but to go on to the tragic end. Thus now, with Fort Sumter bombarded, with an army gathered, with warlike movements already on foot, with a great popular cry going up of "On to Richmond," with the general mind crazed with shouts of "treason," "rebellion," "slavocracy," and drugged with the poisonous stimulants of the press, Congress was to sit to carry out these irregular calls for righteous vengeance.

Lincoln knew all this. If he was slow to read a human face, he had a keen power of divining popular feeling. He had an unusual skill in moving and playing with events as a checker player moves the checkers on the board. Lincoln in his message first recounted the events which had occurred since he took office, giving his version of Fort Sumter. He claimed that the reduction of that fort was not in self-defense, because he had sent ships with the express notification to the Confederates that he meant only to give "bread to the few brave and hungry men of the garrison." He then referred to his inaugural words, "You can have no conflict without being yourselves the aggressors," and he had tried to keep this declaration good, and also free from ingenious sophistry, so that the whole world could clearly see it. He then asserted that the issue presented was whether a constitutional republic can maintain its territorial integrity against domestic foes. Thus seeing the issue, there was no alternative for him except to call out the war power of the government. The response had been gratifying. He then passed to the comment that the border states had not been uniform in their action, and that in some the Union sentiment had been repressed. He had repressed and was soon to silence the Confederate sentiment in Maryland; but once the position is taken that one is on the right side, every step becomes lawful and good. He questioned the action of Virginia, seeking to impugn its vote to secede, without remembering that the Revolution was not carried on in 1776 by the consent of everyone; but rather that a very powerful party of Tories did what they could to obstruct and defeat the American cause in their zealous adherence to the British crown. He canvassed what he had done in calling troops, saying that these "measures, whether strictly legal or not were ventured upon, under what appeared to be a popular demand and a public necessity." There had been no popular demand except that worked up by those who wanted war. He trusted "that Congress would readily ratify" what he had done. He had as well have said that if the Chief Justice had walked into the White House and assumed the executive powers Congress could ratify such a usurpation, and keep him in possession of the executive authority. After this he passed to the matter of the habeas corpus, saying that the legality and propriety of the suspension had been questioned, and that the attention of the country had been called to the proposition that one who has sworn to "take care that the laws be faithfully executed," should not violate them himself. There were two answers to this criticism, he insisted. One was "whether all the laws but one should go unexecuted, and that one be observed, though the Union go to pieces in consequence of the observance."

No such contingency was presented; this was just that logic of Lincoln's which could spread out all the links of a dialectic chain until he found a weak spot, however inapplicable to the facts. He dodged the Constitutional question by this sophistry: the Constitution does read that the writ may be suspended in cases of rebellion or invasion, and it is to be done for the public safety. There was rebellion, the public safety did require it; therefore it was properly suspended. More than that, the words of the Constitution were equivalent to saying that the prerequisites for the suspension were rebellion and the conservation of the public safety. Who was to judge of these things, and who was to suspend it were not written in the Constitution! "But the Constitution itself is silent." "It cannot be believed the framers of the instrument intended that in every case the danger should run its course until Congress could be called together, the very assembling of which might be prevented, as was intended by this case, by the rebellion." One may look in vain for any movement on the part of any responsible group in the Confederate states which plotted and planned and meant to prevent the Federal Congress from assembling. But, he went on, the attorney general would furnish a legal opinion on the legality of the suspension of the writ, and Congress could take such action as it saw fit. Lincoln should have consulted Story's *Commentaries* on this subject, sparing thereby the time he was to give again to Story's theories of the States and the Union. For the Union's preservation he wanted $400,000,000, and 400,000 men. He then passed to his favorite theme of the Union being older than the states, for which idea he was indebted to Story, who was not a historian, able lawyer that he was.

Lincoln in treating of this subject showed that he was in a consuming wrath. Speaking of secession, he said: "With rebellion thus sugar coated, they have been drugging the public mind of their section for more than thirty years, and until at length they have brought many good men to a willingness to take up arms against the government the day after some assemblage of men have enacted the farcical pretense of taking their State out of the Union, who could have been brought to no such thing the day before." The reader will now recall Lincoln's speech in Congress on the right of revolution; and his words in Connecticut only a few months before this when he called the government under the Constitution, a confederacy. He then went into the history of the states, saying that not one of them had been sovereign except Texas, and even Texas, in its temporary independence, was not known as a state. He overlooked the fact that it was the Republic of Texas. Lincoln undertook to define Sovereignty, saying that it was "a political community without a superior." Nothing could have been more puerile, more profoundly ridiculous. He said that the states were never severally sovereign, in the very face of the fact that the second article of the Articles of Confederation reads: "Each state retains its sovereignty." He observed that the word sovereignty was not in the Constitution; but he passed over the fact that the words "state" and "states" were written all through it; that it was made for states, and to be binding "between states." He was oblivious to the principle that there cannot be a state without state sovereignty; that the word state, like the words nation, kingdom, empire, imports sovereignty, that is, self-determination, complete political power over its own affairs to the exclusion of any other power. When Lincoln called sovereignty a "political community without a political superior," he substituted an attribute of sovereignty for the thing itself. The United States were politically superior in their aggregate powers to any state; but that did not affect state sovereignty, nor in any wise impugn the reserved sovereign powers of the states, or the right to withdraw what sovereign powers they had delegated to the general government. Such an attack on state sovereignty is without force. The attack must be made another way, the test being, as it proved, to overcome it with guns. The states were sovereign in that they were self-determining, they were existing by their own social forces, they were distinct political bodies, they could act as they chose in all matters without restraint from any other state, and without hindrance from Congress or the Federal courts or the Federal executive, except where they had pledged each other in the Constitution that the Congress, the Federal courts, the president could for the good of all the states so bound together, act with reference to specified subjects.

Lincoln had the opportunity of his whole life to publish a state paper that would have been authority, even if not invulnerable. It is only by the fact that the power of war massed the American people into one body and obliterated state lines that Lincoln's destruction of state sovereignty has met with the approval of writers on Constitutional law. Not one of respectability would dare to quote the reasoning of Lincoln in that message to Congress as the rightful basis of what he did to suppress the Confederate Government. Much violent rhetoric has been poured upon secession, until state sovereignty has long since grown to be suspected and despised, but that the states became sovereign by the Declaration of Independence, that they retained their sovereignty by the Articles of Confederation and by the Constitution, is impossible of denial. Those documents stand written and clear and never as documents to be expunged. Whether there is a higher law which will bless the saving of the Union as it is called, at some far time, though its salvation by war has cursed the land to this day, remains for some future generation to see. Lincoln's fame thus far rests upon what he did to restore the Union as it was before 1861. He did not do that. He only brought recalcitrant states back into the control of the Federal Government. When he did that, the Union of the Constitution was by the very nature of things extinguished; while the evil forces which the war loosed took possession of the land and men's lives, and they are still in that possession. Lincoln ended his message with these words: "And having thus chosen our course without guile and with pure purpose, let us renew our trust in God, and go forward without fear and with manly hearts." "Forward with God," as the German emperor expressed it in the World War.

On the 10th of July, six days after Lincoln's message, a joint resolution was offered in the Senate, which after reciting what Lincoln had done in calling 75,000 of the militia into service, in ordering the blockade of the Southern ports, in suspending the habeas corpus, in calling for 42,034 volunteers, in adding 22,714 men to the navy, contained this language, "that all of the extraordinary acts, proclamations, and orders, hereinbefore mentioned, be and the same are hereby approved and declared to be in all respects legal and valid, to the same intent, and with the same effect, as if they had been issued and done under the previous express authority and direction of the Congress of the United States." By failing to censure Lincoln, and by voting him what money and men he asked for to crush the Confederacy, these resolutions were impliedly passed. But they were never directly acted upon.

At this same special session of Congress, Andrew Johnson, still a senator from Tennessee, offered a resolution declaring the purposes of the war. It read as follows: "Resolved, that the present deplorable civil war has been forced upon the country by the Dis-Unionists of the Southern States now in revolt against the Constitutional Government and in arms around the Capital; that in this National emergency Congress, banishing all feeling of mere passion or resentment, will recollect only its duty to the whole country; that this war is not prosecuted upon our part in any spirit of oppression, nor for any purpose of conquest, or subjugation, nor for the purpose of overthrowing or interfering with the rights or established institutions of those states, but to defend and maintain the supremacy of the Constitution and all laws made in pursuance thereof, and to preserve the Union, with all the dignity, equality and rights of the several states unimpaired; that as soon as these objects are acknowledged the war ought to cease." This resolution was adopted. But how far it fell short of warranting the war as it was prosecuted, for justifying the Emancipation Proclamation, the XIIIth amendment, and the XIVth and the XVth, is at once perceived.

Men cannot be called honest and honorable in themselves when they are dishonest and dishonorable in politics, or for others; and especially in war do the recreant and faithless passions of men dominate their actions. This resolution did not warrant the erection of the tariff system in the government which had before the war been trimmed down to its lowest terms and was in the way of passing out, in the interests of free trade. Nor did it look to the reëstablishment of the national bank system. Moreover, there were few minds penetrating enough to see that the war was furnishing the occasion and the cause for Capitalism to take over the wealth of the land, and subdue the liberties of the people; and that the churches and churchmen would be laying eager hands on the new era for the supremacy of Hebraic-Puritanism. These consequences were beyond the prophetical powers of Andrew Johnson, just as he could not foresee that Thaddeus Stevens and Sumner, when they could not fully use him, would subject him to the humiliation of impeachment proceedings. It will be remembered that in May of 1860 Johnson had voted for Davis's resolution in the Senate which declared that "in the adoption of the Federal Constitution, the states adopting the same acted severally as free and independent sovereignties," and that that resolution passed the Senate by a vote of 36 to 19. The human mind is not constituted to be responsible; it is folly to expect it to be consistent;

nevertheless it is interesting as showing how Johnson changed, and as reflecting the insanity of the hour to consider a few of his words when speaking upon his war resolution. "Yes, we must triumph," he exclaimed. "I say let the battle go on—it is freedom's cause—until the Stars and Stripes (God bless them) shall again be unfurled upon every cross-road, and from every house top throughout the Confederacy, North and South. Let the Union be reinstated; let the law be enforced; let the Constitution be supreme."

Douglas had now for a month been in his grave—utterly unmourned of Lincoln, though Douglas, subordinating every feeling of pride, and every resentment of Lincoln's lifelong hatred of him, had gone to Lincoln and tendered his services on the Union side. Lincoln had sent him to Illinois to make speeches, so to hold the Union sentiment in line there. For in Sangamon County, in Menard, there was fierce revolt against Lincoln's usurpations. Douglas went and wore himself out in the cause, dying suddenly in June. But there was a senator left who spoke against what Lincoln had done. It was John C. Breckenridge who had really defeated Douglas for the presidency by needlessly thrusting forward Davis's view that the Constitution carried slavery into the territories against the will of their people. Breckenridge, speaking on the Johnson resolution, denied vehemently the doctrine of necessity, by which a president can do what he wills. "I deny that the president of the United States may violate the Constitution upon the ground of necessity. The doctrine is utterly subversive of the Constitution; it is utterly subversive of all written limitations of Government." Breckenridge had just as well have raised his voice against a cyclone. The storm now blowing whirled the strongest men about; and this storm was out of the conjuration of Breckenridge as much as any one man in the land.

While Congress was thus acting, Lincoln was being besieged to do something with the army. The blood cry went up "On to Richmond!" where the Capital of the Confederacy now was; and Lincoln, trying to resist the pulling of the radicals and the insane shouts of the vast mob which had been created by all these measures, resolutions, and summoning of armies, at last yielded. He too was the sport of the storm which he had caused the Fates to loose upon the country. Now the military chiefs differed about the wisdom of invading Virginia and forcing a battle upon its soil. Perhaps Lincoln remembered that he had promised not to invade any state, but on the contrary had declared that he would only hold the forts and places of the United States. General Scott held that the army was in no condition to fight a battle in Virginia; but Lincoln at last was ready to force Scott's hand at the bidding of the war crowd and the radicals. McDowell proposed to move upon the Confederate Beauregard, who had a force of 21,000 men behind the stream called Bull Run. He would do this if the Confederate Joseph E. Johnston, with his 9000 men, could be prevented from coming from the Shenandoah Valley and joining Beauregard. Lincoln observed that if Johnston tried to join Beauregard he would have the Federal Patterson with 18,000 to 22,000 men after him. So it was that on the afternoon of July 16, 1861, McDowell, with 30,000 men, composed mostly of three months' volunteers, supported by 1600 regulars, marched from the Virginia side of the Potomac and by the 18th were at Centreville. It constituted the largest American army that ever had been commanded by one general. The Confederate Congress was to meet on the 20th of July; and perhaps it could be broken up, its members arrested and Jefferson Davis put in chains. On the 18th, the outposts of the Confederate forces under Beauregard were encountered by McDowell at Bull Run, a small stream a few miles from the village of Manassas. An engagement followed which stopped McDowell for two days. It must be remembered that McDowell's force greatly outnumbered Beauregard's, therefore the situation was now critical for the latter. But Johnston, by a movement not surpassed for genius, hurried from the Shenandoah, and joined Beauregard. Patterson was not on his heels to prevent him, as Lincoln thought he would be.

Descriptions of this battle, which was fought to a finish on the 21st, are plentiful enough. It is beyond the scope of this book to go into its details. It suffices to say that thousands of the Federal troops had tendered their services to protect Washington, without dreaming that they would be sent into a campaign of this sort; while on the other hand the Confederates, under Beauregard and Johnston and Stonewall Jackson, fought with the desperation of men whose land is invaded. They fought as their ancestors had fought at Bunker Hill and at Trenton; and, with shouts against Lincoln of "Despot" and "Usurper," they swept the army of McDowell off the field. The victory was so complete that the Confederate soldiers, according to Johnston, believed the war was over, and left the army of the South in crowds to return to their homes. The Union troops, seized with panic, broke and ran and became a mass of confused disorganization, a terrified mob. The Union loss was 2984, the Confederate 1981. The Confederates captured 28 pieces of artillery, 5000 muskets, 500,000 cartridges, 64 artillery horses, 26 wagons and other property which had been abandoned in the headlong flight of the Union army. The word was flashed to Washington that the day was lost, and to save the city. The Confederates pursued the Union troops but a short distance. They could have gone on and taken Washington, perhaps, if they had tried to do so. Lincoln was bitterly disappointed, but he was of a nature to become more resolute under defeat. Men had been induced to enlist to save the Capital; the chief cry now was to save the Union. On this battlefield of Bull Run or Manassas two soldiers lay dying. One was a soldier under Lincoln. He exclaimed, "My God what is all this for?" The other was a Confederate soldier, who said, "Boys they have killed me, but never give it up." Nothing could better sum up the respective positions of these two forces of armed men, whose leaders on both sides were to attribute victory to God, and defeat to Inscrutable Providence. Tragedy never to be told was compressed in the brief words of these dying soldiers.

The arrest of supposedly disaffected men went on now faster and faster; and the habeas corpus was suspended by Lincoln's fiat in various parts of the country. As late as July 5, 1864, Lincoln was suspending the writ, on which date he deprived the people of Kentucky of their constitutional liberties and their access to the civil courts. On the 17th of September, 1861, the legislature of Maryland was scheduled to assemble at Frederick. General Banks was instructed by Lincoln's secretary of war, Cameron, to arrest all the members suspected of disloyalty; and they were arrested, some in Baltimore and some at Frederick. To show how such despotism was regarded in England, the words of the *Saturday Review* of London may be quoted. "It was as perfect an act of despotism as can be conceived. It was a *coup d'état* in every essential feature." By the end of September, Fort Lafayette was crowded with prisoners made such by Lincoln's mere word. Another prison had to be prepared for the hundreds gathered in for uttering so-called disloyal sentiments, for criticising Lincoln, for displaying a Confederate flag, for anything that displeased an upstart military officer. And so the overplus was sent to Fort Warren in Boston Harbor. Hundreds of men seized on these pretexts were crowded into the Old Capital Prison at Washington, at Camp Chase in Ohio, at Cairo in Illinois, at St. Louis and at Alton. In some of these prisons men were packed almost to suffocation, some in irons and without beds, and without sufficient ventilation. Thus the republic of Washington and Jefferson vanished.

The most conspicuous of these arrests was that of Vallandigham in the so-called military district of the Ohio, the headquarters of which were at Cincinnati under the command of General Burnside. There were no military operations in Ohio, but there was great objection to Lincoln's acts. The American spirit there had not been crushed. Vallandigham was an able lawyer, and was a member of Congress when the war opened. He became a sort of leader of the vast thousands in Indiana, Illinois and Ohio, who believed the war unnecessary and its prosecution despotic; and he was put forward as a candidate for governor of Ohio. In crises of this kind only one side of the subject is lawful to be discussed in the opinion of the war party, and that side is theirs. In that way can public opinion against the war be stifled, and the acts of the war party be made the acts of the people, and the will of God. When, therefore, Vallandigham in a speech at Mount Vernon, Ohio, declared that the war was unnecessary, that it was waged for the purpose of crushing out liberty and erecting a despotism, that the war could have been honorably terminated before this time of the Spring of 1863, Burnside, under his own order, numbered 38, proceeded to arrest Vallandigham. He was taken before a military commission, though all the courts, state and Federal, were open, where he could have had a jury trial according to the fundamental law. There he was tried, found guilty, and sentenced to confinement during the continuance of the war. In consequence it made no difference if the people of Ohio were against the war and wanted a governor who would help them to effectuate their actions peaceful and political against it; they were denied their clear legal privilege to do so by Lincoln's extraordinary course. Here Lincoln, with a sort of buffoon gesture, intervened. He sent Vallandigham beyond the Federal lines, where he passed to Bermuda, then to Halifax and finally, he settled down in Canada. It was considered a wonderful piece of humor by those who cared nothing for the Constitution, but who were fighting, as they claimed, for the restoration of the Union under the Constitution. The War between the States, on the Northern side, furnished one of the best possible records for studying the process carried on by a few men for creating the war spirit and then for suppressing any objection to the war; and finally of investing all they did with the divine will of the Almighty Ruler of the Universe.

The Confederates, too, were not backward in gathering in military prisoners to offset those taken from their ranks by the North. As early as July 6, 1861, President Davis addressed to Lincoln a note for an exchange of prisoners according to the usages of war. It came about in this way: the Confederate crew of the Confederate Privateer *Savannah* had been captured by the United States Brig *Perry*, and its crew sent in irons to New York to be tried for piracy. Davis in his note proposed to Lincoln that prisoners held by the Confederate government, according to number and rank, be exchanged for the crew of the *Savannah*. The note was delivered to Lincoln, but no audience with Lincoln was permitted. Lincoln utterly ignored the note. To recognize it and answer it was, in his opinion, to recognize the existence of a Confederate Government. As the crew of the *Savannah* was likely to be convicted and hanged for piracy, Davis took firm steps with Lincoln. He selected Colonels Corcoran, Lee, Cogswell, Wilcox and some others, as subjects of exact retaliation, in case the crew of the *Savannah* was dealt with as pirates. Lincoln drew back from this consequence of his lawless blockade. Finally the prisoners were exchanged. Lincoln and the Federal war party had England and Europe to consider; for England was already denouncing the blockade as utterly illegal; and to execute men as pirates who were in the war service of a government of *de facto* existence, to say the least of it, would have revolted civilized mankind.

When the Federals had more prisoners out of the Confederate ranks than the Confederates had out of the Federal ranks, the Lincoln policy was to exchange prisoners; when the proportions were the other way, the Federals diminished the usage of exchange. The Confederate Congress went so far as to pass a law that prisoners of war should have the same rations as the Confederate sol-

LINCOLN'S WAR MESSAGE

diers in the field. This was not always of the best; but the Confederate resources were soon taxed to their utmost. The Southern leaders challenged anyone to bring proof that the Confederate authorities ever sanctioned the crowding of prisoners into close dungeons like that of Fort Lafayette. Andersonville, in southwestern Georgia, has been a subject of fierce denunciation by Northern writers in making the charge that the Confederates resorted to atrocious brutality in the treatment of Northern prisoners. It is impossible here to go into that issue fully. It may be said that Andersonville was located in a healthful part of Georgia, where food was most abundant; and its stockade was directed to be built where there was pure running water. Unquestionably there was horrible suffering there; but it could have been relieved by an exchange of prisoners. Lincoln preferred to let his soldiers die there, rather than yield on the subject of an exchange of prisoners, and by doing so give recognition to the Confederates as belligerents. In this way he was a strong man. But Camp Douglas, Camp Rock Island and Camp Johnson were in northern country where the cold was intense, and where Confederate prisoners froze to death protected only by the thinnest clothing. On July 19, 1866, Stanton, Secretary of War, published a report on the subject of prisoners during the war. From this it appeared that the Confederates captured and held in prison from first to last 270,000 men; while the Federal score was 220,000 men; and that of the Federal prisoners in Confederate hands 22,576 died; while of the Confederate prisoners in Federal hands 26,576 died. Thus the Confederates, with 50,000 more prisoners, had 4,000 less deaths. All of this desperate suffering and mortality could have been avoided by an exchange of prisoners. In sentiment and its expression the deaths of the Federal prisoners were for the preservation of the Union, under the divine visitation of God. One wonders, therefore, why Henry Wirz, the keeper of the Andersonville prison, was brutally hanged when the North got full control of the South. He may have been brutal, but there was nothing but brutality about the whole war from beginning to end.

Lincoln's indecision, his weakness even, is written all over the first two years of the War. The various war moves and councils, and plans and change of plans, of terror and discouragement after defeat, of prayers and hopefulness after slightest victory, of great rejoicing after Antietam, of all the cardiographic ups and downs of public feeling and martial purpose—all these belong to a book on the war. So far as Lincoln the man is concerned it must suffice here to say that at the outset of the War he found General Scott in command of what army the United States then had. Scott was aging and incapable. Lincoln appointed in his stead McClellan, who distinguished himself at Antietam. Yet Lincoln lost faith in him. He was a Democrat and therefore subject to attack by the fanatical Republicans. Lincoln blunderingly interfered in McClellan's plans. Lincoln had war boards on his hands, of his own creation, with ill defined and conflicting powers; and he was pulled this way and that by members of Congress, and by his cabinet. Some wanted him to proceed so that the Republican party would be the beneficiary of martial victories. Others talked of emancipating the slaves, and making the war a battle for negro freedom. Seward had given him the issue of the Union at the beginning, and that really fitted into Lincoln's mystical thinking. In some particulars Lincoln's mental operations had a kind of clarity and steadiness all through this confusion; but he did not take hold of the war for a time with vigor and with definite vision. The South rolled up victories against all the armies that the North could send against them. And in these circumstances Lincoln removed Burnside for Hooker, and then Hooker for Meade. Then in the West a new man arose. It was Grant, and Grant supplanted Meade, leaving the latter with the glory of Gettysburg and a broken heart.

Writers on Lincoln through these vacillations have seen a moral and intellectual purpose constantly clarifying and growing more masterful in him. This opinion overlooks, or at least needs the support of, the always ignored fact that no man can do anything or be anything without people. All fames, all successes rest on people. Lincoln therefore grew in stature just as the people supported him, just as the new party grew strong under the accumulated processes of war propaganda. He merged into a better mastery of himself and the situation as a subdued people fed his being with the nutriment of will and service out of their own hearts. His strength was the strength of the people, the power of the army growing more and more efficient. His triumph was through the inevitable exhaustion of the South and the remorseless will of Grant. As a war president Lincoln was negligible enough. Jackson, even Cleveland, would have surpassed him at every point; saving only that Cleveland, especially, would not have proceeded with that crafty and patient psychology with which the war spirit was conjured and fostered to ultimate victory.

Passing from this subject to Lincoln's heart and mind, the open records of Lincoln's acts furnish matter for analysis at every step. So much has been written of Lincoln's tenderness, that his fame for that endearing quality is established, if not for good, then for all those who cannot weigh all the facts. Herndon and many other witnesses do not testify to his tenderness, but to his coldness. Nothing however could stir the imagination more than a story of a war president with imperial power stooping to save the life of a poor sentry who was under sentence of death for falling asleep on duty. Lincoln many times exercised clemency in behalf of such unfortunates. In the case of Vallandigham he asked the question if he should have a deserter shot, and let go the orator or politician who had persuaded the deserter to forsake his country's need. As usual with Lincoln, this catch question involved a mixed logic. But what were a few sentries more or less compared to the thousands who died in prison when they might have been exchanged and saved, but for Lincoln's indurate stubbornness? What is there sacred about the maintenance of any government, or any Union, which justifies the most revolting cruelties and killings? What is any government for except to give security and happiness to its people? But for Lincoln's acts, and his measures to maintain the so-called Union, there would not have been the great slaughter of the War, the incalculable ruin, the unspeakable revenge which glutted itself with torches and with rapine. That mind has refused to think which lets its field of contemplation be occupied with Lincoln's compassion for animals, and for children, and for sentries; and refuses, or fails, to look at the war thief, the butcher, the murderer and the ensanguined hypocrite whom Lincoln evoked from the reptilian neighborhoods of life. The Parisian massacres have blotted out that side of Robespierre which compelled him to resign his judgeship in the diocese of Arras rather than impose the sentence of death. Lincoln's tenderness toward sentries, by contrast, has induced forgetfulness of the cruelty with which he conquered the South. Closely analyzed, there is much in common between the characters of Robespierre and Lincoln. It is a similarity which was observed by Alexander H. Stephens who knew Lincoln, and understood him as well as any contemporary. With both Robespierre and Lincoln, there is affinityship in Seward, Sumner, Chase and Thaddeus Stevens. They all lacked that richness of sexuality which spreads the glow of good will and magnanimity, of easy generosities and understandings, of liberal reasonablenesses over the whole troubled human scene, and forgives and lets live out of the comprehension that most so-called moral principles are illusions.

In November of 1861 one Nathanial Gordon was convicted of being engaged in the slave trade and sentenced by the Circuit Court of the United States for the Southern District of New York to be put to death by hanging on the 7th of February, 1862. The judge who pronounced such a sentence was a malefactor of infinitely deeper dye than the slave trader. Realizing this, or at any rate believing that the sentence was inhuman, a large number of respectable citizens of New York besought Lincoln by petition to commute Gordon's sentence to one of imprisonment for life. There was nothing to be lost by Lincoln doing this, except possibly the approval of fanatical abolitionists. Mercy in a situation of this kind would have bred mercy in the hearts of other men. And where do the rules of Christianity cease to have influence with those who are always preaching them? In this case they ceased where they could have been effectually practiced. Lincoln refused to commute Gordon's sentence; he gave him a respite of 13 days. "In granting this respite," wrote Lincoln, "it becomes my painful duty to admonish the prisoner that relinquishing all expectation of pardon by human authority, he refer himself alone to the mercy of the common God and Father of all men." If he could not have mercy from God through men, the kind of mercy which he would have from God directly was poor consolation for this wretched man whose offense was nothing to that of arming negroes to shoot down their former masters in the South.

Soon Lincoln was to issue a proclamation of thanksgiving for victories in the field. "It has pleased Almighty God to vouchsafe signal victories to the land and naval forces engaged in suppressing an internal rebellion. . . . It is therefore recommended to the people of the United States that at their next weekly assemblages in their accustomed places of public worship, which shall occur after notice of this proclamation shall have been received, they especially acknowledge and render thanks to our Heavenly Father for these inestimable blessings." [1] It is impossible that a civilization based upon such barbaric superstition as this can ever produce a culture worth anything to the spirit of man. It is a civilization that must be destroyed in order that America can rise out of the hypocrisy and the materialism into which it was sunk by the War.

On September 30, 1862, Lincoln set down privately his meditations on the Divine will. "The will of God prevails," he wrote. "In great contests each party claims to act in accordance with the will of God. God cannot be for and against the same thing." It was evident then, however, that God was on both sides. "In the present civil war it is quite possible that God's purpose is something different from the purpose of either party; and yet the human instrumentalities, working just as they do, are of the best adaption to effect his purpose. I am almost ready to say that this is probably true; that God wills this contest, and wills that it shall not end yet. By his mere great power on the minds of the now contestants, he could have either saved or destroyed the Union without a human contest. Yet the contest began. And having begun, he could give the final victory to either side any day. Yet the contest proceeds." [2] This Calvinistic fatalism is the poisonous doctrine which justifies human cruelty. There was such a thing as pagan cruelty. It was honest. This is Christian cruelty, which is dishonest and irresponsible. It does what it would and then throws the burden upon an anthropomorphic deity.

Lincoln was gradually working toward the Jehoviac diabolism of his Second Inaugural. On March 30, 1863, he issued another proclamation, appointing a national fast day in which he called upon the people "to recognize the sublime truth, announced in the Holy Scriptures and proven by all history, that those nations only are blessed whose God is the Lord." The culture that produced the highest philosophy, poetry, art statesmanship that the world has

[1] Lincoln's Works, II, 143.
[2] Id., 243.

known knew nothing about the "God who is Lord," and if they had heard of him they would have laughed. Hebraic-Puritanism overcame this culture as a rising tide of filth might submerge a Greek temple. On July 15, 1863, after the terrible battle of Gettysburg, Lincoln issued a proclamation of thanksgiving in which he said: "It has pleased Almighty God to hearken to the supplications and prayers of an afflicted people, and to vouchsafe to the army and navy of the United States victories on land and on sea so signal and effective as to furnish reasonable grounds for augmented confidence that the Union of these states will be maintained. ... Now therefore be it known that I do set apart Thursday, the 6th of August next, to be observed as a day for national thanksgiving, praise and prayer; and I invite the people of the United States to assemble on that occasion in their customary places of worship and, in the forms approved by their own consciences, render homage to the Divine Majesty for the wonderful things he has done in the nation's behalf, and invoke the influence of his Holy Spirit to subdue the anger which has produced and so long sustained a needless and cruel rebellion ... finally to lead the whole nation through the paths of repentance and submission to the Divine Will back to the perfect enjoyment of union and fraternal peace." [1] With what pious sighs this message must have been received in Massachusetts! For there was to be greater bloodshed than ever to give unctuous satisfaction to righteous sadism. There is still another proclamation, the one of July 7, 1864; but it was of the same religious tenor and need not be specially noted.

Lincoln's troubled mind, his baffled speculations, expressed themselves in meditations, proclamations and letters throughout the war. He was plunged in doubt and in melancholy; he was unsure of himself and his own course. His pardoning of sentries is partly explainable upon grounds of self-doubt. It was a way of throwing something into the scale of mercy where nothing would be lost, and where possible treasure might be laid up in heaven. On one occasion he went to Fort Monroe with Chase and Stanton, and while there asked a colonel to bring him a Bible and a copy of Shakespeare. He invited the colonel to rest and to listen to passages from "Lear," "Macbeth" and from "King John" which Lincoln read with trem-

[1] Lincoln's Works, II, 370.

bling voice and with visible tears. He asked the Colonel, "Did you ever dream of a lost friend and feel that you were having a sweet communion with that friend, and yet a consciousness that it was not a reality?" The colonel replied that he had had such dreams. Lincoln rejoined, "So do I. I dream of my dead boy Willie again and again." In the South and in the North there were tens of thousands of mothers and fathers who were dreaming of their dead boys, who fell in battle for Lincoln's mystical notions of the Union. Did Lincoln believe that the war was necessary, that it was inevitable under God? During one of the many calls of Lincoln for troops Joseph Medill of the *Chicago Tribune* went to Washington to urge Lincoln to reduce the quota of troops of Cook County. Lincoln was very bitter toward Medill and the committee that accompanied him. Lincoln said: "Gentlemen, after Boston, Chicago has been the chief instrument in bringing this war on the country. The Northwest has opposed the South as New England has opposed the South. It is you who are largely responsible for making blood flow as it has. You called for war until we had it. You called for Emancipation and I have given it to you. Whatever you have asked you have had. Now you come here to be let off from the call for men which I have made to carry out the war you have demanded. You ought to be ashamed of yourselves. Go home and raise your 6000 men. And you, Medill, you are acting like a coward. You and your *Tribune* have had more influence than any paper in the Northwest in making this war." [1] Here Lincoln spoke the bitter truth. Except for men of the Medill type, there would have been no war. If so what was there Divine about the war?

At this point the various drafts may be noted, as bearing upon the response of Lincoln's American masters to the call for troops. As the regular army was nothing when Lincoln decided to subdue the South, he resorted to the expedients already detailed to get troops. Except for the governors of the Northern states, the violent, mediocre men who controlled the various state militias, Lincoln could have moved no hand against the South. He would have been as devoid of soldiers as he was in fact wanting in legal power to call out the soldiers which he at first summoned to put down "Insurrection." It was not long, however, before these first troops

[1] Tarbell's "Life of Lincoln," II, 149.

had to be supplemented. The South's resistance was beyond the expectation of many. And as the North saw what it was getting into, and the common man realized that he was not shouldering a musket to defend Washington, and to protect the person of Lincoln, but that there was war, indeed, in which he would be sent south to face the fierce soldiers under Jackson, and Lee, and Johnston, the prospect was anything but alluring.

In May of 1862 McClellan was trying to take Richmond. "On to Richmond!" had been the battle cry since Bull Run; and now McClellan after the bloody battles of the Seven Days in which his losses were 15,859, sent up a call for more troops. To furnish them it was necessary to resort to a piece of cunning. Stanton, the Secretary of War, Governor Curtin of Pennsylvania, and Governor Morgan of New York stipulated that the two governors should get the so-called loyal governors of the North to join with them in a request to Lincoln to call for more troops. Lincoln was thus concealed as wanting any more soldiers. It was the people of the loyal states who wanted them! But Lincoln approved this plan. Curtin and Morgan telegraphed to the various Northern governors, and got their permission to sign their names to the offer to Lincoln. And so on July 2, 1862, the newspapers announced that the governors were tendering to Lincoln more troops; and that Lincoln had accepted the patriotic tribute. Accordingly then, the governors called for volunteers; and there was no response of moment to the call. Consequently, on August 4, Stanton resorted to the draft. He sought 300,000 men for nine months' service. The American masters now rebelled and stampeded. Thousands prepared to file exemptions; other thousands began to leave the country. It was well enough to say to Hans, Baptiste and Patrick that the Declaration was meant for them; it was a different thing to be asked to die for it, because it was meant for them. The boats and the trains were jammed with escaping natives and foreigners. Policemen and soldiers stopped ships in the harbor, and trains in the towns and cities, and took from them hundreds of evaders. It was during this terror that Lincoln suspended the habeas corpus on one of the occasions already mentioned.

The draft of 1862 was a failure. The masters did not want the war. In March of 1863 Congress passed a conscription act which took in all men from 20 to 45. Now there was greater resistance. The law was mocked and opposed with all possible hatred in Indiana, Iowa, Illinois, Pennsylvania, New Jersey, and even in New Hampshire and Vermont. Enrollers were attacked in Ohio and forced to resign. In New York City there was riotous violence, as there was in Troy, New York, and over New Jersey. Newspaper offices were sacked, and the windows of the Provost-marshals' houses broken. In Philadelphia five regiments of soldiers were required in order to put down the frenzied populace. In Milwaukee, where two thirds of the people were Germans, there was bitter opposition to the war and Lincoln's policies. Had they not left Germany to be done with Prussianism forever? The whole result was that there were 292,441 names drawn, of which 39,887 failed to respond, leaving 252,554 for examination. Of these, 164,394 were exempted from service, leaving for duty 88,160 of which 52,288 bought exemptions, so that the net result of the conscription was 35,882 men. Then a test case was made up in Pennsylvania and the Supreme Court of that state held the Conscription act unconstitutional. In May of 1864 drafting was resorted to again in states that had not hitherto furnished their quotas. Again the American masters bought off, ran away, evaded by every device. This was not in places like Central Illinois, where the war was hated from the first; but in states like Ohio, Wisconsin, Minnesota. In New York City there were riots again; and Stanton was warned that the enforcement of the draft would bring down violence upon the Provost-marshals. In the early winter of 1865 Lincoln called for 300,000 more men; and fixed the draft for February 15. Yet in one way or another a vast Union army was in a state of fine discipline when Lee surrendered at Appomatox.

Meanwhile the long days of the war dragged by. Lincoln sometimes relieved his mind by reading Artemus Ward, much to the disgust of Stanton. On one occasion when Lincoln's sister-in-law was visiting the White House, Lincoln walked with her through the conservatory, saying that he had not been there before, and that flowers never interested him. In the cool Platonic and pine clad hills of Concord, Emerson calmly watched the war. He wished heartily that Lincoln had better manners. Hawthorne called upon Lincoln and found him a village philosopher. Bancroft saw little in Lincoln. Stanton called him a fool, for Dennis Hanks came on to Washington about some men who were in difficulty in Coles County, and Lincoln sent Hanks to see Stanton, who, though once a passionate believer in the Kentucky Resolutions of Jefferson, was now full of slaughters and obsessions, staring with fixed brilliant eyes, as he hurried about on missions of military efficiencies. He had no time for Hanks.

Many of the now persecutors of the South had believed in and had academically spoken of the right of secession. And in their heart of hearts they recognized its rightfulness, for the American character was born in secession. There is no one so truculent as the renegade to a principle. The country was seething with the hatred of men who had been Democrats. In Illinois there was John A. Logan, who had been a violent pro-slavery and pro-Southern politician. He turned to the other side and served in the Union army. Later he wrote an ignorant book, entitled *The Great Conspiracy*, that being his designation of the Southern secession. In Illinois, too, was Ingersoll, who ran for Congress on the Democratic ticket in 1860. Later he went about America praising the unspeakable James G. Blaine as one who had "torn the tongue of slander from the throat of treason." It was the same John A. Logan who ran for vice president on the ticket with Blaine in 1884. America was sorely in need of brave, stable, honest, thinking minds; and it did not have them. As to Lincoln, he was half way toward secession when he took the stand against the Dred Scott decision. He was a nullifier when he condemned the decision of Taney in the Merryman case. The very thing was in his blood for which he was willing to kill other people. He glozed it over by insistences, plain and intricate, that he was in the right, and the South was in the wrong; and by appeals to God, the sincerity of which is anything but clear.

After Lincoln's death, Herndon went about gathering the opinions of men as to Lincoln's character and mind. One man, of whom Herndon speaks as being of unquestioned ability and free both from partiality and prejudice, wrote to Herndon that "Mr. Lincoln's perceptions were slow, a little perverted, if not somewhat distorted and diseased." Herndon admitted that this judgment of Lincoln was unobjectionable, provided the language be toned down to mean that Lincoln saw everything from a peculiar angle, and, so seeing, was susceptible to nature's impulses. Upon the supposition that Lincoln was in deep moral sympathy with the emancipation of the negro, and with the abolition of slavery, he could not have taken the stands he did, and said the things he did, through the years, that we have already studied. There were many men in America and in England, and elsewhere, who could not look with patience upon slavery. Not so with Lincoln. Herndon wrote that Lincoln issued the Emancipation Proclamation through a sense of duty, and love of principle, and in obedience to his oath of office. The first two reasons assigned for his action are as untrue as the last is legally erroneous. He was not required by his oath of office to emancipate the negroes. It was even a questionable war measure, because, while it is true that in war the property of the enemy may be seized as a measure to weaken him, yet emancipation was not seizing the negro as property. It was rather in the direction of inspiring negroes to rise and kill the white people, under all the circumstances. And that was not civilized warfare. Whatever its effect, it was a war measure, just as Lincoln called it, and as such needed no constitutional warrant. It was another case where Lincoln contradicted his own theory that the South was not a belligerent. Herndon asked himself the question whether Lincoln emancipated the negro through love; and then answered himself by quoting Lincoln's words: "I would not free the slaves if I could preserve the Union without it." This was not true either. The freeing of the slaves was not an indispensable move for the saving of the Union. He could have gone steadily ahead with the army and saved the Union. The freeing of the negroes, from a military standpoint, was a negligible act; and Lincoln knew as early as July of 1862 that it would prove futile. But suppose he followed the issue as laid down in the War Resolutions of Johnson, which passed the Senate, and in doing so won the war, with slavery left remaining in the Southern states just as it was when the war commenced? Was not slavery the occasion of the War? Was it not slavery that tariff Massachusetts and the abolitionists had attacked the South upon for thirty years? Men can play the idiot and still retain the good will of history provided some particular idiotic course be not so extreme as to divert the main stream of life into some inlet, from which it recoils after all to sweep on through the logical channel. The time came when Lincoln was balancing the question of his own place in history. Even if he lost the war, and yet had tried to emancipate the slaves, he could see himself lifted up for the gaze of the centuries. Anyone could previse that slavery was a doomed institution everywhere in the world. It was hard to defend the institution in America against the charge that in a republic it was an anachronism. Lincoln gradually grew to see that emancipation would be a historic monument to himself; and after he had issued the Proclamation he declared that it was the central act of his administration, and the great event of the Nineteenth Century. In its essence it was no greater than England's peaceful abolition of slavery many years before the War between the South and the North. But the act had dramatic settings which made it more memorable, and Lincoln more preëminently famous than Wilberforce.

With these observations, Lincoln's mind may now be traced in its workings toward emancipation. On July 22, 1862, Lincoln submitted to his cabinet the first draft of an Emancipation Proclamation. In the suppression of the so-called insurrection in the Southern states, he proposed that at the next session of Congress he would recommend the adoption of a practical measure for giving pecuniary aid to those states which should then be practically sustaining the authority of the United States, and which should then have adopted, or should thereafter adopt the gradual abolition of slavery. In other words, in states where there was disaffection, but in which the Federal Government was largely in control, if they would abolish slavery, pecuniary aid would be given such states. The object was to restore relations between such states and the Federal Government, where partially suspended or disturbed. This was compensated emancipation; and it was to strengthen the Union. Finally, in the states in so-called rebellion on January 1, 1863, he would, as commander in chief of the army and navy, and as a war measure, emancipate the slaves. Thus this plan contemplated the winning over by money of the border states, and the subjection of the powerful seceded states by freeing in their midst the negroes, who might, in the intoxication of shackles suddenly stricken from them, turn upon their masters, and thus, with a negro insurrection and the horrors of massacre, break the military cap-

LINCOLN'S WAR MESSAGE   437

tains of the South. It is interesting here to see how Lincoln at this stage of his development regarded the negro as a human being.

On August 14, 1862, a committee of colored men called upon Lincoln at the White House, seeking to learn what was to be the fate of the negro people in America. Lincoln addressed them, first saying that a sum of money had been appropriated by Congress for the purpose of aiding the colonization of the negroes in Africa. Why should there be colonization? Lincoln asked. Why should the negroes leave this country? Lincoln answered his own questions by saying that there was a broader difference between negroes and white people than between any other two races. He thought the physical disparity between the races worked to great disadvantage to both. He believed the presence of the negroes in America had an evil effect on the whites; for now the whites were cutting each other's throats on account of the negroes. There would be no war except for the negroes in America. Therefore it would be better if the two races were separated. For when the negro ceased to be a slave he would be far removed from being on an equality with the white man. He urged the free negroes, such as were before him on this committee, to lead the way toward colonization, and thus to carry with them the negroes whose minds had been clouded by slavery; and to do this though they would prefer to remain in America. He said that the colony of Liberia had long been in existence, and was a success; but he was thinking about some place in Central America, which, being closer to the old homes of the negroes in the United States, would satisfy their feelings better. In South America, too, there was chance that the negroes could be put on an equality with the best people there. In the meantime, if the negroes wanted to work in the coal mines, Lincoln would see that they were not wronged in that service. But if they would start a colony he would help them to do so. He wanted the committee to think carefully upon these suggestions, not only in their own interest and that of the negroes as a whole, but for the good of mankind in general. There was no failure here on Lincoln's part to realize the problem that the unfortunate Southern people had had on their hands for years; but as New England had relieved herself of the presence of negroes by sending them South; so now would Lincoln free

America of the evil of race antagonism by shipping the negroes to Central America or Liberia.

On September 13, 1862, a committee from the religious denominations from Chicago waited upon Lincoln, presenting him with a memorial for negro emancipation. "I am approached," Lincoln said with evident spirit, "with the most opposite opinions and advice, and that by religious men who are equally certain that they represent the divine will. . . . I hope it will not be irreverent for me to say that if it is probable that God would reveal his will to others on a point so connected with my duty, it might be supposed that he would reveal it directly to me. . . . Why, the rebel soldiers are praying with a great deal more earnestness, I fear, than our own troops, and expecting God to favor their side; for one of our soldiers who had been taken prisoner told Senator Wilson a few days since that he met with nothing so discouraging as the evident sincerity of those he was among in their prayers."

Then Lincoln came directly to the subject. "What good would a proclamation of emancipation do, especially as we are now situated? I do not want to issue a document that the world will see must necessarily be inoperative, like the Pope's bull against the comet. Would my word free the slaves, when I cannot even enforce the Constitution in the rebel states? Is there a single court or magistrate, or individual that would be influenced by it there? And what reason is there to think it would have any greater effect upon the slaves than the late law of Congress, which I approved, and which offers protection and freedom to slaves of rebel masters who come within our lines? Yet I cannot learn that that law has caused a single slave to come over to us. And suppose they could be induced by a proclamation of freedom to throw themselves upon us, what should we do with them? How can we feed and care for such a multitude? General Butler wrote me a few days since that he was issuing more rations to the slaves who have rushed to him than to all the white troops under his command. They eat and that is all. . . . Now, then, tell me, if you please, what possible result of good would follow the issuing of such a proclamation as you desire?" [1]

Four days after this speech the battle of Antietam was fought,

[1] Lincoln's Works, II, 234–5.

in which Lee was outnumbered two to one. No less the Union loss was 12,000 and the Confederate 10,000. It was a drawn battle for Lee, and the losses were more than he could afford to incur; but on the other hand McClellan, according to military authorities, threw away the chance he had by reason of his superior numbers. And now the Congressional elections were approaching; and Lincoln in the circumstances needed political support. On the 22nd of September he issued a preliminary Emancipation Proclamation, intended to free slaves in states or portions of states in which the so-called rebellion existed. At that the situation had not changed from what it was when he addressed the Chicago clergymen. He could not enforce emancipation in the South as he could gather the fruits of the suspension of the habeas corpus in Ohio.

By now the country was stirred by the horrible actions of Northern commanders. The infamous General Butler had taken possession of New Orleans in May of 1862; and lifted himself up to a shocking despotism. He shackled the press completely. He proceeded to regulate the markets and the food supply, the currency and the social life of the people. He issued order Number 28 in which he ruled that any woman who treated a Federal officer with disrespect should be dealt with as a prostitute. Some of the women had shown their hatred of the loathsome autocracy by lifting their skirts when they passed a Federal soldier or officer.

Copies of this order 28 reached London, and Lord Palmerston wrote to Adams, the American Minister to England: "I cannot refrain from taking the liberty of saying to you that it is difficult, if not impossible, to express adequately the disgust which must be excited in the mind of every honorable man by the general order of General Butler. Even when a town is taken by assault it is the practice of the commander of the conquering army to protect to the utmost the inhabitants, and especially the female part of them." Lincoln, who had revoked the emancipation of negroes at the hands of General Frémont in Missouri, did nothing to expunge order 28 of Butler, and to reprimand him. One can imagine what General Washington would have done in such circumstances. On the contrary, Lincoln sent a special message to Congress on December 12, 1862, in which he mentioned that he had in his possession three valuable swords which had been taken by Butler from a Confederate commander, and which Butler had sent to him. If they were to be bestowed upon anyone, Lincoln recommended that they should be given to Butler, in compliment of Butler's military services. Lincoln was also writing to Butler suggesting that the ordinance of secession of Louisiana might now be rescinded under Butler's power—though possibly after all the ordinance was void from the beginning! Whole volumes would not contain the story of Northern atrocities and horrors; and the country was growing nauseated with the report of them. The question then troubling Lincoln was, how would his rightful masters vote in the fall elections of 1862?

In September, Maine elected a Republican governor, but his majority was about half what it had been in 1860. Maine also elected two Democratic congressmen. In October, Pennsylvania, Ohio, and Indiana elected members of Congress. All of these states were carried by Lincoln in 1860. They now turned against him. Ohio elected 14 Democratic congressmen out of a total representation of 19. Indiana elected 8 Democratic congressmen out of a total representation of 11. New Jersey elected 4 Democratic congressmen out of a total representation of 5; New York elected 14 Democrats out of a total representation of 31. Nebraska went Republican by only 153 votes out of a total of 4513. Delaware was Democratic. Michigan elected one Democratic congressman out of a total representation of 6. Wisconsin elected 3 Democratic congressmen out of a total representation of 6. Minnesota, with two Congressmen, was Republican, but very close. New Hampshire barely elected a Republican governor.

In Lincoln's home state the vote was significant. Illinois was then entitled to 13 congressmen, and 8 Democrats were elected. In the Congressional District in which Sangamon County was located, the Democrats were victorious by a vote of 12,808 to 11,443; and Sangamon County went Democratic by 3845 to 2583. Menard County, of New Salem Hill, was in a Congressional District of seven other counties. The Republicans were in such disfavor that they did not nominate a candidate for Congress. Menard County, at the time having a population of something over 9000, was carried by the Democrats for the state ticket by a majority of 974 votes. The Democrats elected a state treasurer by a majority of 6546 in a total vote of 256,778 votes. This Democratic strength and popular protest was in the face of the most lawless and unprincipled tactics on the part of Lincoln's party. In 1858, in Illinois, in order to defeat Douglas, the Republicans resorted to the colonization of voters; and in the plot to do this were Trumbull, Medill, and Lincoln's particular friend Judd. In this election of 1862, the soldiers were voted by the Republicans. In Iowa there were 18,989 soldiers voting; in Wisconsin 10,414. Nothing was spared to carry the election in order to justify the war and uphold Lincoln. God needed help also.

Thus Lincoln's masters spoke. Did it mean that the war should cease, or that the people did not like the way the war was prosecuted, or that they wanted it more successfully and ably waged? They spoke on all these questions. Thousands disapproved his suspension of the habeas corpus and the arbitrary arrests. Other thousands disliked the Emancipation Proclamation. Nearly everyone detested the vile despotism of General Butler. Many hated the war in every way, and believed it wicked and unnecessary. The land was in mourning; the graveyards were filling up. And what was it all about? The people had no chance to express themselves on any direct issue. The election was not a plebiscite of direction that the war should cease. And so it went on to terrible carnage. In December of 1862 Burnside attacked Lee at Fredericksburg, losing 13,000 men to Lee's loss of 4000. On April 30, 1863, Hooker, who had superseded Burnside, as we have seen, was defeated by Lee at Chancellorsville, though Lee had 61,000 men and Hooker had 105,000 men. The slaughter was incredible. But here one night the Sublime Malice which stood at the elbow of the South compassed the death of Stonewall Jackson at the hands of his own men, who did not recognize that it was Jackson and fired at him. He was not instantly killed, but being mortally wounded he was carried away to a field hospital where he passed away murmuring commands of war out of a spirit winged to death in its flight, and wondering to the last what dispensation it was that had selected him for removal from his ardent devotion to the South, and his passionate hatred of the North. If he had lived, the South would likely have won the battle of Gettysburg, which was fought in July of 1863. Here again the North in history was aided by some favorable Imagination playing with symbols. It was only an accident that the battle was not fought at Cashtown. The Cashtown address would not have suited the Muses of Memory as the Gettysburg Address has. The luck of the North was beginning now, and these were the esoteric signs.

In the Southern army was Basil Lanneau Gildersleeve, perhaps the most learned and eloquent Hellenist that America has produced, who saw in the struggle between the North and the South the disastrous contest of Sparta and Athens repeated. Indeed Virginia poured the flower of her youth from her colleges and academies into the cause of the Declaration of Independence: governments derive their just powers from the consent of the governed. They fought with a courage, a manliness, and a devotion never perhaps equaled since the days when Athens inspired the noblest men to give their lives for their city. One can see some of the faces of these youths in pictorial histories of the war. They have been preserved for us to look into their eyes and to appraise their beautiful brows, while we read that they carried Thucydides and Homer with them as they marched, and pored over annals and poems when they camped. Perhaps the most perfect face of all these young men was that of Pelham, the cannoneer, who stood by his guns with the fiery spirit of the archangel Michael; and who was killed in battle at Kellysville. He was not then twenty years old. These were the men who composed the army of the South and whom Lincoln denounced as traitors, as rebels, and as criminals. They were led by Lee, a collateral relative by marriage of Washington. While Butler was stealing silver spoons, and heaping degradation upon the women of New Orleans; and while Sherman carried war with Hunnish frightfulness through Georgia to the sea, Lee fought with ever decreasing forces against the greatest armies that the North could send against him, and without a stain upon his honor as a gentleman and as a captain of civilized soldiers.

The contest between the North and the South was far more fundamental than the matter of slavery. Lincoln knew this; but he understood the issue to be drawn between the Union on the one hand and the rights of the states on the other hand. It was that in one aspect. Lincoln was unread in history and in Constitutional law, and his theories and preachments were frequently erroneous and even puerile. But there was something deeper than this collision between the two theories of the nature of the Union which separated the North and the South in sympathy; that was the difference in blood between the two peoples. It was fundamentally an ethnological struggle which the South and the North fought to the finish.

Calhoun, the most powerful statesman intellectually in America from the 1830s to his death in 1850, and who could have driven Lincoln to fast cover on his statement that the Union was older than the States, very early pointed out that a centralized national government could not be erected save upon the ruins of liberty. The very essence of liberty, he said, consisted in the division of power; while consolidation of power could be nothing but despotism. This had been pointed out by Patrick Henry in the Virginia Convention called to consider the Constitution of 1787. Old magazines and old books have to be searched in order to see how the scholarly men of the South, at a very early time in the abolition movement, in the discussions of the bank and the tariff, predicted that consolidation would work legislative plunder, and that, in consequence, American character would be debased; while the mob would be led by designing hypocrites. They foretold that the time would come when there would be no more Washingtons and Jeffersons in America, because despotism meant the death of genius. To prevent these catastrophes, which Walt Whitman catalogued in his "Democratic Vistas of 1870," they implored the people to foster and cherish state institutions which alone could preserve liberty and nurture real greatness. They foresaw that, though a centralized government was called a democratic republic, it would be that in name only; and that it would be the most corrupt and oppressive government which greedy and unscrupulous men could devise. In 1837, Calhoun declared that the contest had been on for years between the sponsors of a national consolidated government, in which the constituent parts were the American people in mass, and the government of a federal republic, such as it was made by the Constitution. The Southern thinkers saw patriotism at its best in a devotion to a small unit, with a nation as the distant and lesser attachment. And they declared that, once this state patriotism was destroyed, all the individual spirituality of a people would be destroyed. With all the rest of what they believed and preached, the South was conservative. It hated socialism as the twin brother of abolitionism. It regarded the North as filled with noisy numbers where every species of fanaticism found a fertile soil. The North was filling up with foreigners, with Germans and with Swedes, who did not understand the American system; and these stocks the Northern politicians were cultivating. As we have seen, Lincoln appealed to them in his campaign against Douglas; and at last the South was to face these aliens under Schurz, and other commanders, dealing the death blow to the only real American culture, as the South regarded itself. In 1839 Michael Chevalier published at Boston his book entitled *Society, Manners and Politics in the United States*. In this work he declared that the people of the South were a different stock entirely from those of the North. "They are the same men who cut each other's throats in England under the name of Roundheads and Cavaliers." The Southern writer fostered the idea that they were better bred than the Northern men; that they were the descendants of the Normans, while the Northern people sprang from the quarrelsome Briton who had produced at last the Puritan. They insisted that the North was made up of disaffected religionists, grumblers, busy-bodies and fanatics; while the Southern breeds came from men who understood government and order and had been the builders of rational states over the earth. We have seen that Lincoln came from blood which fled to Hingham and there established Puritanism. He was the very opposite in temperament and in mind from Lee, who could look back to a cavalier and warrior ancestry of the best blood in England. Lincoln, whether we call him an atheist, a deist, a free thinker, was in truth a Hebraic-Puritan product.

While Lincoln was writing moving letters, such as the one he addressed to Mrs. Bixby, and while Northern clergymen and their congregations prayed to the God of Battles for the success of the Northern Armies; and while the armies marched to the tune of "John Brown's Body," and Mrs. Howe gave the same cadence and prosodical tone to the beauty of the lilies in which Christ was born, speeding men to die to make men free as Christ died to make men holy—while all this carnival fared onward of sentiment and mysticism, idiocy and hypocrisy compounded of hate and Zionistic dreams out of the Hebrew Scriptures, a very different vision was seen by the capitalists who realized the chance had come to seize the wealth and the sources of wealth in the land. During the war the North was riotously prosperous. Luxuries abounded in New York and the cities. Wine, laces, silks, jewels, expensive living and aristocratic fashion fed themselves on the blood of the young men of the land, who did not know what the fight was about at first, and at last went on just to kill and to subdue. War contractors stole the country blind; the corporations began to multiply; and the monopolist behind the smoke of battle laid his plans unseen, to appropriate the laws and the courts to his special use.

As we have seen, the tariff had been a source of discord between the states. The South was an agricultural country and for the most part was opposed to the tariff. But the tariff principle is in its nature a corrupting agency, and it was possible to make rents in the resistance of the South. A rapid survey will tell the story. The first tariff, that of 1789, was the work of Hamilton. Under it, however, the duties were very moderate and so remained until 1816. After the war of 1812, demand arose for closely connected measures: protection to American manufacturers, and internal improvement. The Democrats, or Jeffersonians, were against both, on principle based upon Constitutional construction, and upon economic grounds. Greater changes followed in 1824, 1828 and 1832. Those of 1828 were affected by political manipulation, trading and selling and bargaining, which caused the tariff act of that year to be called the Tariff of Abominations. These abominations were renewed in 1832. The opposition from the South had grown so strong that concession had to be made to it. The nullification of 1833 brought about compromise, by which the rates of duty established by the act of 1832 were to be gradually reduced, to reach in 1842 a general level of 20%. In 1842, when the final rate of 20% was to have gone into effect, the protectionists had the control of Congress, and after a brief period of two months, during which this 20% schedule was in force, a tariff act was passed which once more established the protective system, and enacted a scale as high as that of 1832. Four years later the South compelled a change. The Democratic Party was now in control of Congress. In the act of 1846, a system of duties was fixed, purely ad valorem, and very moderate. Protected articles were taxed at a rate of 30%, in some cases 25%, or even 20%. In 1857 the duties were further reduced, the rate of most protected goods going down as low as 20%. So the tariff remained until the War, when, by reason of the desertion of the Southern members from Congress, to make laws in the Congress of the Confederate States, or to lead the troops of the South, the protectionist was once more in absolute control of the Congress of the United States; while its president, Lincoln, had been a protectionist since the days of his Pappsville speech in 1832. Hence came about in 1861 the Morrill tariff bill. And the principle passed into the McKinley bill of unsavory memory. Nothing has done more to imperialize the United States than the tariff. It is with us today more powerful than ever. Its beneficiaries contribute the money by which presidents are elected and senators and congressmen are given power to pay back with more privileges the bribe of campaign contributions. It is one of the chief engines which has made American plutocracy.

There was another thing to be settled, and the battle of Gettysburg furnished the spirit and the power with which to do it. The principle of the national bank had been fought with conscientious vigor by the Democrats. Yet Lincoln had implied that Jackson violated his oath of office by vetoing the bank bill during his second term. The time was now ripe to expunge that lawlessness. Plundering monopolists wanted a bank which would be above the states, and under the control of central authority at Washington. Bureaucracy was already lifting its hundred heads. The war furnished the excuse for the resuscitation of the bank idea, for so long dead. The American masters were fighting on the field, others were traveling in Europe, or dancing or dining, or wooing, or singing, or praying; others were attending to business and wanted the bank. The Democrats were impotent, divided and discredited. There could be no better time to reëstablish the bank. Indeed the war was being waged to prove that the American people were one mass, that the Constitution was full of implied powers, that Congress had a sovereignty which was ambulatory and could go where it pleased, or stay where it would. Besides Marshall had held a national bank to be a constitutional agency for the general welfare, and to carry into effect express delegations of power in the Constitution. Above everything, Lincoln had always believed in the bank, and fought for the bank when he was a raw youth in the Illinois legislature. Then the bonds which firebrand Chase had been issuing, to get money from the money changers with which to pay army contractors and the soldiers from the prairies and the hills, could not be marketed at profitable rates. For the capitalist who has money can always make further exactions as condition upon which he will buy bonds or anything else. And while it was right to shoot deserters, to imprison evaders, one can never expect a capitalist to part with his money save he get the full return for it in good measure heaped up. In these circumstances Chase, who had preached the golden rule as an abolitionist lawyer, could see no way of selling the bonds for the purposes of saving the Union except by creating a compulsory market for them. That could be done, it occurred to him, by offering special privileges to banks organized under Federal charters. The special privilege was to give the banks the power to issue money, based upon a deposit of government bonds. The result of all this was that such banks drew the interest on the bonds, and whatever usury they could exact when they loaned their paper money so based on the bonds. It was a handsome gift to the bankers. But the Union had to be saved. It might be that out of this Chase plan a vast money power would spring. Even so, government of the people, for the people, and by the people must not perish from the earth! On February 25, 1863, the bank act was passed. It was supplemented by the act of June 3, 1864. Some advantage was overlooked in the first law. There were hosts of state banks, all prosperous; and with all that had been given the national banks they could not dominate the money market, they could not overcome the state banks. These state banks were issuing paper money, too; but all the interest they made was on the loan of such money. They had no bonds to swell the account with. The act of June 3, 1864, drove the state banks out of the note issuing business by taxing their issues 10% after July 1, 1866. An illustration will show the working of a national bank under the Chase law. Incorporators bought $100,000 in bonds, for which they paid the market price, 10% or 15% under par, whatever it happened to be. They deposited these bonds with the United States Government. They then issued $90,000 in paper money, that being the amount permitted upon a deposit of $100,000 in bonds. The $90,000 could be loaned at whatever the interest rate was, or could be manipulated to be. It was possible, therefore, for the national banks to make 14% or more on their investment. They drew interest on the bonds at par, not on what they paid for the bonds; and they exacted interest on their note issues according to the chances.

The presidential year of 1864 came, and there was opposition to Lincoln having a second term. This arose in his party, if it can be said that he had a party. A convention was called for May 31, 1864, to be held at Cleveland. The call was signed by Rev. Dr. Cheever of New York, B. Gratz Brown of Missouri, Lucius Robinson of New York. Wendell Philipps associated himself with this faction; and so did the negro Frederick Douglass. They were done with Lincoln. They adopted a platform which, among other things, announced that the rights of free speech, free press and the habeas corpus should be held inviolate—except in districts where martial law had been proclaimed. They demanded an amendment to the Constitution abolishing slavery; they called for economy in the prosecution of the war. They held that "the one term policy for the presidency adopted by the people is strengthened by the force of the existing crisis." They declared that reconstruction belonged to the people in Congress, and not to the executive. They asked that the lands of the rebels be confiscated for distribution among the soldiers. They nominated Frémont for president, and General Cochrane for vice president. This was a measure of justice, they announced. Lincoln was nominated by the Union National Convention at Baltimore. The name Republican was carefully omitted. Lincoln received the votes of all the states represented in the convention, except those of Missouri, which were cast for Grant. Hannibal Hamlin was shelved for Andrew Johnson, the Democrat. The platform lauded Lincoln. It praised the soldiers and sailors of the North, and declared that the nation owed them some permanent recognition for their services; and ample permanent provision for their widows and orphans. Thus pensions and bounties began to sprout in the fat lineaments of the North, which had drawn sustenance from the lean face of Lincoln, where no cabbages had once sprouted. McClellan won the empty honor of the Democratic nomination. The war had been a failure; and Lincoln, during the summer of the campaign, expected to be defeated and made some plans accordingly. But meanwhile the North rolled up victories, and when the election came off Lincoln carried such states as Tennessee, Louisiana, Arkansas, where in 1860 he had not polled a single vote. The Lincoln soldiers carried him to victory. On September 19, 1864, Lincoln wrote to General Sherman saying that the Indiana state election would occur on October 11, and to lose Indiana would have a bad effect on the presidential election. "The draft proceeds not withstanding its strong tendency to lose us the state. Indiana is the only important state voting in October whose soldiers cannot vote in the field.[1] Anything you can safely do to let her soldiers go home and vote at the state election will be greatly in point." [2] In this wise were the American masters given their voice. Lincoln as a stump orator had said that the Declaration would prove a hard nut to crack by those who tried to do away with it. It was now troubling his own teeth in politics and in the field. At Springfield in 1857, when taking Douglas to task, he had proclaimed that the authors of the Declaration "meant it to be, thank God it now is proving itself a stumbling block to all those who, in after times, might seek to turn a free people back into the hateful paths of despotism." And now he was about to trip on the same block. But he did not; and no one ever will in this land, if they ever did. In 1900 it was mocked and derided by the Republicans. It was called a self-evident lie, as Pettit had denominated it when the Nebraska Bill was pending, and which aroused Lincoln to such righteous indignation in his speech at Peoria on October 16, 1854. The Republican Convention was held in 1900 on June, 19, and at Philadelphia, where the Filipinos were told to stand back, because "our authority could not be less than our responsibility," since the currents of Destiny, and the will of God had placed the fate of that people in the hands of a "sovereign nation." All the Republican orators that year declared that putting down insurrection in the Philippines was exactly what Lincoln did when dealing with the Southern states. They told the truth. They meant to say that both the Filipinos and the Southerners were in the same and in equal wrong. That is something else, as it is something else as to the right of both the South and the Filipinos to have resisted. There was some false pre-

[1] That this was not true, see Opinion of Judges, 30 Conn., 591.
[2] Lincoln's Works, II, 577.

tense in the inauguration of the Mexican war; but it was of an open and simple sort, and of a quality so uncouth that it did not affect the general morale of the country, and the liberties of Americans. It was as crude in its ill-concealed aggression as Lowell's satire was rustic and vernacular. The Lincoln attitude, however, toward the South, and the political-religious sentiments with which he invested it, was of hidden and deep malignancy. It had poisoned fibres and tentacles which had the tendency to become fissiparous, and to create a pathology of national hypocrisy; and this was equally true, though on a smaller scale, of the Philippine conquest of McKinley. Out of these two contests, with their half truths uttered for causes speciously good, and with their criminal objects veneered with religious pharasaism, arose the American spirit of this day, with prohibition and other social tyrannies on the one hand, and with the putrefying rulerships of trusts and money on the other hand. These things put together make the America of today the spectacular thing that it is in point of great cities and material conquests, and the empty and wearisome land that it is in point of æsthetic living conditions. From 1865 to 1900 there were fast and systematic policies of overthrowing liberty in America, and the forms through which it could be expressed, for the benefit of money oligarchies and Hebraic-Puritanism. Taking him for what he really was, there is no irony in the rôle that Lincoln played in the revolution which Calhoun foresaw, but only foresaw along political lines. Calhoun did not prognosticate, as no man could, the paralysis that was to come to the spiritual life of America as the result of the combined efforts of imperialists and fanatics. It is only by considering Lincoln superficially, by mistakenly accepting him as the rail splitter and the democrat, that any surprise can be felt that he played the part of the destroyer of the American system which had been created by men who tried to make a land all free out of the fresh conditions of a new world.

Chapter XVII   *Last Days of Lincoln*

WITH Lincoln elected to a second term as president, and with the cause of the Confederacy visibly crumbling, Lincoln's thoughts were turning to the future problems which were already taking form out of the swiftly moving events. He was a much worn man, as the photographs taken of him at this time fully show. A last photograph for which he sat a few days before his death is almost startling in its curious strangeness, with the contour of his head and face edged and notched as of a leaf which has been wind-rifted and sent whirling in some bewitched way, half emptied of its vitality, if not sere with frost. But by this time the fears which he had of assassination, and which on his way to Washington had enervated his powerful body, had nearly passed away. He had been in Washington now for nearly four years, meeting office seekers, and persons on missions of clemency, and politicians, some of them disgruntled, and nothing had happened. No one had offered him anything like unmannerly offense. He had been about the War Office, and back and forth to his summer place on the Potomac, and on no occasion had anything happened to suggest that violence would be done him. There would be four years more of office, and the war would surely end before that time. Herndon was back in Springfield waiting for him, and Lincoln had money enough saved to live comfortably while adding to his income in the resumed practice of law. He was soon to be fifty-six years old; but he might well have reflected that for one of his physique and careful habits he had twenty years yet to live. Should they not be crowned with peace and honor, especially with slavery abolished, and the Southern states restored to their "practical relation" to the Union? The South could not last much longer. Her army was dwindling under fire and through desertions; and the economic resources of the South were running to exhaustion. No adequate life of Jefferson Davis has yet been written. Few have had a word to say about his stability of purpose, his courage in disaster, his devotion to the cause for which he was giving his disciplined powers, his training and experience as a soldier, and the wisdom and enlightenment of a long service as a senator and a cabinet officer of the United States before he assumed the herculean tasks of the presidency of the Confederacy. The magnifying glass of awe and reverence have been used on Lincoln, with which to bring out virtues and abilities not visible to the naked eye of realistic examination. Thus in all comparison between Davis and Lincoln, Davis has been made to look inferior, sometimes inept, lacking in judgment, understanding, or even petty and mean. Perhaps for the forces of history, and the mythmaking of favorable economics, Davis said nothing so available for treasurable memory as Lincoln; but neither did Cromwell, neither, perhaps, did Washington. But in massiveness of character, in strength of mind Lincoln does not match with these; nor was he equal to Davis as an executive, a statesman mind. A man's own generation may not know him—that is a frequent remark. The only sense in which that is true is that a man's own generation may not and cannot know him for what historic forces will use him, and where they will place him. But it is from a man's contemporaries and these alone that succeeding generations know what the man was face to face, and how he acted when he spoke or wrote, as his letters or his orations report him. History might have taken Davis's speeches and inaugurals and poured into them the strength of millions for whom favorable currents made them the expression and the life. A man is in bad historic plight when there is no single sentence with which to manifest the best of him; but on the other hand whose case must be argued. There are so many times and places where only a word can be given to a contrasting character whose life, no less, was interwoven with the life of another. If when considering in chief the life of the latter it would be fortunate for the fame of the former if there were some easily accessible judgment to be taken for the modeling of the general scene. However erroneous the impressions of Davis may be, or however wrongly created in the North, and by New England writers, those impressions cannot be corrected here. The wise reader may reflect, however, upon the sufferings of Davis during the War; it is not difficult to know how he struggled with inadequate finances, and with every problem of state which Lincoln had, and how through engrossing difficulties he bore himself with a high rectitude, and with a soldierly patience.

Lincoln often observed that both North and South prayed to the same God, which was another way of saying that the South and the North were equally conscientious on the issue of the war. If Davis's moral principles are to be impugned for standing with the South, Lincoln's may as well be for standing with the North; for both must face the bar of reason, and be tested not only by what they knew, but by what they should have known, when heading enterprises of such grave importance to millions of men. At the time that we have now reached in this study, Davis was facing a Northern army of more than a million men, while the Southern army was reduced below 200,000 men. And when the final defeat came, what was to be his fate, what the punishment to be meted to his beloved South at the hands of fanatics and partisans and the violent patriotism of the Northern governors, those men of muscular beef-fed minds, and Hebraic-Puritan principles? Davis understood these men thoroughly. He knew they would not scruple to do anything to him that they could do without incurring the intolerable indignation of the civilized world. Would they hang him, would they imprison him? Lincoln never had such prospects to face. He dreaded nothing but assassination. Yet Davis with all such dread possibilities to contemplate went on to the end without flinching. Happily for everyone now torn and tortured by the wounds and deaths and hunger of war, the end was soon to come. And after that days more terrible than those of the war.

All through this study we have seen Lincoln adhering with pertinacity to any opinion once formed, to any decision once taken. This is so where he did not translate them into action. When he did that he often saw himself on the other side of where he stood when he was merely thinking, and perhaps he wondered sometimes how he got to a position so different from that where he stood when dreaming or reasoning. Herndon wrote that Lincoln could not be moved after he had once made up his mind. This record shows that that is not true; and in any case it is not subtle enough as a judgment to reach the Lincoln nature. But taking a concrete illustration of Lincoln's fixity of purpose, the matter of compensation to slave owners for their slaves freed by law, we find that Lincoln, as early as 1837, though conceding the full power of Congress to abolish slavery in the District of Columbia advocated compensation to the slave owners; and in 1865, when he knew that the South could scarcely last long, he drafted a message to Congress, but did not send it, in which he asked for leave to pay $400,000,000 to the states of Alabama, Arkansas, Delaware, Florida, Georgia, Kentucky, Louisiana, Maryland, Mississippi, Missouri, North Carolina, South Carolina, Tennessee, Texas, Virginia, and West Virginia. This money was to be paid them on condition that they ceased resisting the North by April 1, 1865, and upon their adopting the amendment then pending which abolished slavery. Under these circumstances all political offenses were to be forgiven, and liberality would be recommended to Congress in the treatment of the South as a whole, on subjects not lying within executive control.[1] This was February 5, 1865, after Sherman's march to the sea, and while Lee was hardly pressed by Grant in Virginia. In thinking out this plan and in setting it down in writing, was Lincoln actuated entirely by generous impulses, or partly by considerations of expediency, and to some extent by that intellectual desire for self-consistency, which he realized that he did not fully possess? These questions can be answered by considering what happened before February 5, and what happened after, and by going to the heart of Lincoln's Second Inaugural, with its triple distilled Hebrew curses, its myrrh mixed with honey and gall. On October 1, 1864, Sherman wrote to Grant that he wanted to leave Tennessee with his army, march to Atlanta and destroy it, cross Georgia and devastate it, wrecking the railroads along the way to Savannah and Charleston. The purpose was to shake the hearts of the soldiers still fighting under Lee and Johnston, and to make them fly home to succor their wives and children. Anything is fair in war, save a few things like rape, needless mutilations, burnings at the stake. So it was fair to starve the women and children, to burn cities, and to spread terror, in order to fill the Southern soldiers with intolerable agony for the safety of their homes and their families. One of Sherman's expressions was "War is hell." St. Gaudens has put this man in speaking bronze astride a war steed, which is eagerly stretching forward its feet in obedience to the fierce spirit of its rider. So Sherman, who never said anything of moment, or contributed anything to the culture of America, saving always that

[1] Lincoln's Works, II, 635-6

he was devoted to the Union, and did the most terrible deeds to preserve it, has received more honor in bronze and in verse than Thomas Jefferson, or Emerson or Whitman. This is to be noted, because it is one of the items which prove that the American civilization is in the hands of merchants and monopolists, who must have armies and captains to protect their privileges. Sherman was just another Attila; but he met no rebuff as Attila did, nor was there any Pope Leo to meet him on the way of his march of terror and turn him back in the name of ancient wisdom and culture.

On October 9, Sherman wrote again to Grant, saying that he could make Georgia howl. On the 13th Lincoln wrote to the muscular minded Governor Morton that the soldiers from Sherman's army, sent home to Indiana to vote, need not remain for the presidential election. They could vote for him in the field. On this same day Lincoln gave his consent to Sherman's march from Atlanta to the sea, and to the howling of Georgia on the way. On the 16th of November Sherman set forth with 62,000 men and vast train bands and provisions. It was a frolic. The soldiers were feasting and singing, and marauding and foraging. Sometimes the soldiers as they swung along chanted the runic hymn of "John Brown's body lies a-moldering in the grave," for that horse thief and murderer had become one of the gods of the Republican Party in the new Hebrew hierarchy. Other soldiers, more aware of the identification of bloodshed with piety, sang "In the beauty of the lilies Christ was born across the sea," which Julia Ward Howe had published in 1862 in the *Atlantic Monthly* under the editorship of James Russell Lowell, who later was to see Lincoln as the first American, since Lincoln, though born in Kentucky, and nurtured in Indiana and Illinois, was Massachusetts in spirit and in truth. When the soldiers came to the lines, "Glory, glory, hallelujah, his soul is marching on," they put their full voices into the sacrificial chant. There was no enemy, no army to block Sherman's way. The Southern men were in the North for the most part. And thus it was a vast picnic. Sherman had issued a special field order in which he authorized liberal foraging. In consequence the soldiers went forth here and there, bringing in hams and turkeys, smoked bacon, corn meal, family carriages loaded with loot, cattle and mules confiscated and driven into camp. "They did some things they ought not to have done," said Sherman speaking of his soldiers. At the same time the soldiers were so devoted to him and so thirsting with insatiable desire to wreak vengeance upon South Carolina that Sherman could not go beyond a mild censure of the atrocious deeds of his army of plunder and devastation.

Sherman and his army reached Atlanta; and the city was burned. But not by Sherman's order, Northern historians say. In pagan days there would have been a fully authenticated command from the general, "Burn this city." But these were Christian days. A Federal soldier could steal up an alley with cotton waste and oil and fire one building; another could do the same thing in another part of the city. So the city would burn. But not by order of Sherman. Yet confessedly, by Sherman's order, bridges were burned, warehouses were burned, cotton storages destroyed, railroads torn up. At Milledgeville, the capital at the time of Georgia, magazines, arsenals, factories, warehouses were given to the torch. And thus at last Sherman reached Savannah. There Sherman sent a report of what he had done: "We have consumed the corn and fodder in the region of the country thirty miles on either side of a line from Atlanta to Savannah, as also the sweet potatoes, cattle, hogs, sheep and poultry, and have carried away more than 10,000 horses and mules, as well as a countless number of their slaves. I estimate the damage done to the state of Georgia and its military resources at $100,000,000; at least $20,000,000 of which has enured to our advantage, and the remainder is simple waste and destruction. This may seem a hard species of warfare, but it brings the sad realities of war home to those who have been directly and indirectly instrumental in involving us in its attendant calamities." This is pure hypocrisy and falsehood. Honorable captains with 1,000,000 men under their command, and with less than 200,000 men to oppose them, should have taken defeat rather than stoop to such barbarism as was this march of Sherman to the sea. And in point of fact, everyone knew that Lee was the chief arm of strength of the South, and that he was already doomed by superior and ever increasing numbers under Grant. Was it wonderful that Grote abhorred the conduct of the North, and that Carlyle said, "no war ever raging in my time was to me more foolish looking?" When asked to write something at length about the War, he reduced it all to this: "Peter of the North to Paul of the South: Paul, you unaccountable scoundrel, I find you hire your servants for life, not by the month or year, as I do. You are going straight to hell. Paul: Good words, Peter. The risk is my own. I am willing to take the risk. Hire your servants by the month or the day and get straight to heaven; leave me to my own method."

On the night of December 20, Sherman having reached Savannah, the Confederates evacuated it, and Sherman took possession of the city, and sent to Lincoln a message which the latter received on the evening of Christmas day. "I beg to present you," Sherman said, "as a Christmas gift, the city of Savannah with 150 heavy guns and plenty of ammunition and also 25,000 bales of cotton." On the next day Lincoln wrote to Sherman, "Many, many thanks for your Christmas gift, the capture of Savannah. When you were about leaving Atlanta for the Atlantic coast, I was anxious, if not fearful; but feeling that you were the better judge, and remembering, that 'nothing risked, nothing gained,' I did not interfere. Now the undertaking being a success, the honor is all yours; for I believe none of us went further than to acquiesce." Two days later Lincoln issued a pass to F. P. Blair to go South to see Jefferson Davis. But before telling about that remarkable adventure and what came of it, we must finish with Sherman's depredations in South Carolina.

The firing of a helpless city, which is unconditionally surrendered, is too terrible to be condoned even in the mixed morality of a Sherman, who could see nothing not justified by civilized warfare in what he confessed to doing, but who shrank from the stigma of having burned Columbia, the capital of South Carolina; and who upon his oath testified that in the whole course of his march he heard of but two cases of rape which were committed by his soldiers. By the code of war wanton destruction of property, robbery, even killing in cases of this sort are right enough. Rape is proscribed. Hence we find that in some histories written with obvious Northern bias, and in others whose authors felt indebted to the financial aid of the tariff, or to monopoly for the leisure in which to set down their researches, Sherman is handled with scrupulous delicacy on the subject of the burning of Columbia. Rhodes in his history of the War wrote that Columbia was fired neither by Sherman, nor Wade Hampton, "nor any other Federal or

Confederate Officer." He does not say that Sherman forbade the city being fired; or that, to use Lincoln's words, "I did not interfere," or that he went no "further than to acquiesce." He does not say that Sherman interfered, or in any way acquiesced. Nor did Lincoln caution Sherman to deal with the fallen foe in generosity, and with full regard to the laws of civilization. All the way along the soldiers had been burning and destroying. Why not in Columbia, which they had longed to reach to sate their insatiable desire to punish South Carolina? It is not a tenable position that Sherman did not know all the possibilities of a drunken and revengeful army suddenly turned loose upon the capital of the most bitterly hated state of all the states which the North was at last vanquishing.

William Gilmore Simms, a creditable poet, an author of a celebrity which has passed in the fortunes of literature, but a man of honor and high character, was living in South Carolina at the time of Sherman's reaching Savannah and Columbia. He wrote a pamphlet on the destruction of Columbia, from which some extracts may be taken. They are as credible as anything Sherman said, even though Northern historians have ignored this voice of the Southern poet, as well as the books in the libraries of Charleston and Columbia in which Sherman is charged with the destruction of the Southern capital. "The march of the Federals into our state," said Simms, "was characterized by such scenes of license, plunder and general conflagration, as very soon showed that the threats of the Northern press, and of their soldiery, were not to be regarded as mere *brutum fulmen*. Day by day brought to the people of Columbia tidings of atrocities committed, and more extended progress. Daily did long trains of fugitives line the roads, with wives and children, and horses and stock and cattle, seeking refuge from the pursuers. Long lines of wagons covered the highways. Half naked people cowered from the winter under bush-tents in the thickets, under the eaves of houses, under the railroad sheds, and in old cars left them along the route. All these repeated the same story of suffering, violence and poverty and nakedness. Habitation after habitation, village after village—one sending up its signal flames to the other, presaging for it the same fate—lighted the winter and midnight sky with crimson horrors. No language can describe, nor can any catalogue furnish an adequate detail of the wide-spread destruction of homes and property. Granaries were emptied, and where the grain was not carried off, it was strewn to waste under the feet of the cavalry, or consigned to the fire which consumed the dwelling. The negroes were robbed equally with the whites of food and clothing. The roads were covered with butchered cattle, hogs, mules and the costliest furniture. Valuable cabinets, rich pianos were not only hewn to pieces, but bottles of ink, turpentine, oil whatever could efface or destroy, was employed to defile and ruin. Horses were ridden into the houses. People were forced from their beds to permit the search after hidden treasure. The beautiful homesteads of the Parish country, with their wonderful tropical gardens, were ruined; ancient dwellings of black cypress, one hundred years old, which had been reared by the fathers of the Republic—men whose names were famous in Revolutionary history—were given to the flames as recklessly as were the rude hovels; choice pictures and works of art from Europe, select and numerous libraries, objects of peace wholly, were all destroyed. The inhabitants, black no less than white, were left to starve, compelled to feed only upon the garbage to be found in the abandoned camps of the soldiers. The corn scraped up from the spots where the horses fed, has been the only means of life left to thousands but lately in affluence."

With malice toward none!

Coming to the city of Columbia, Simms thus described what happened: "Hardly had the troops reached the head of Main street, when the work of pillage began. Stores were broken open within the first hour after their arrival, and gold, silver, jewels and liquors, eagerly sought. . . . And woe to him who carried a watch with a gold chain pendant, or who wore a choice hat, or overcoat, or boots or shoes. He was stripped in the twinkling of an eye. It is computed that from first to last twelve hundred watches were transferred from the pockets of their owners to those of the soldiers. Purses shared the same fate. . . . Among the first fires at evening was one about dark, which broke out in a filthy purlieu of low houses of wood on Gervais street, occupied mostly as brothels. Almost at the same time a body of the soldiers scattered over the eastern outskirts of the city fired severally the dwellings of Mr. Secretary Trenholm, General Wade Hampton, Dr. John Wallace, J. U. Adams, Mrs.

Starke, Mr. Latta, Mrs. English, and many others. There were then some twenty fires in full blast, in as many different quarters . . . thus enveloping in flames almost every section of the devoted city. . . . The men engaged in this were well prepared with all the appliances essential to their work. They did not need the torch. They carried with them, from house to house, pots and vessels containing combustible liquids, composed probably of phosphorus, and other similar agents, turpentine, etc., and with balls of cotton saturated in this liquid, with which they also overspread floors and walls, they conveyed the flames with wonderful rapidity from dwelling to dwelling. Each had ready a box of lucifer matches, and, with a scrape upon the walls, the flames began to rage. . . . The work begun thus vigorously, went on without impediment, and with hourly increase throughout the night. Engines and hose were brought out by the firemen; but these were soon driven from their labors—which were indeed idle against such a storm of fire—by the pertinacious hostility of the soldiers; the hose was hewn to pieces, and the firemen, dreading worse usage to themselves, left the field in despair. . . . By midnight, Main street, from its northern to its southern extremity, was a solid wall of fire . . . throughout the whole of this terrible scene the soldiers continued their search for spoil. The houses were severally and soon gutted of their contents. Hundreds of iron safes warranted impenetrable to fire and burglar, it was soon satisfactorily demonstrated, were not Yankee proof."

In the beauty of the lilies Christ was born across the sea!

"In one vault on Main Street," Simms went on, "seventeen casks of wine were stored away, which an eye witness tell us barely sufficed, once broken into, for the draughts of a single hour—such were the appetites at work and the numbers in possession of them. Rye, corn, claret and Madeira, all found their way into the same channels, and we are not to wonder, when told that no less than one hundred and fifty of the drunken creatures perished miserably among the flames kindled by their own comrades, and from which they were unable to escape. . . . And while these scenes were at their worst—while the flames were at their highest and most extensively raging—groups might be seen at the several corners of the streets, drinking, roaring, reveling—while the fiddle and accordion were playing their popular airs among them."

John Brown's body lies a-moldering in the grave! The canonized horse thief was now fully avenged. "Ladies were hustled from their chambers—their ornaments plucked from their persons. . . . It was in vain that the mother appealed for the garments of her children. They were torn from her grasp and hurled into the flames. . . . The pistol to the bosom or head of woman, the patient mother, the trembling daughter was the ordinary introduction to the demand: 'Your gold, silver, watches, jewels.' . . . Nor were these acts those of common soldiers. Commissioned officers, of rank so high as that of Colonel, were frequently among the most active in spoliation, and not always the most tender or considerate in the manner and acting of their crimes.' . . . 'And what do you think of the Yankees now?' was a frequent question. 'Do you not fear us now?' 'What do you think of secession?' 'We mean to wipe you out.' 'We'll burn the very stones of South Carolina.' Even General Howard, who is said to have been once a pious parson, is reported to have made this reply to a citizen who expostulated with him on the monstrous crime of which his army had been guilty: 'It is only what the country deserves. It is her fit punishment; and if this does not quiet rebellion, and we have to return, we'll do this work thoroughly. We will not leave woman or child.' . . . In several cases, newly made graves were opened, the coffins taken out, broken open, in search of buried treasure, and the corpses left exposed."

Was Sherman responsible for these horrors, for the burning of Columbia? Many people will take the responsibility of laying them all right at his door, no matter what he denied, or how historians have tried to save his name by glossing over the facts. It is first to be noted that these wanton acts of destruction were in many particulars the very ones which he had authorized on the march. Next he came into a city knowing and boasting that his men were thirsting insatiably for revenge upon South Carolina. To this must be added his knowledge of the soldier character when in drink, and in an abandoned discipline such as prevailed when the army entered the city; and that he had been authorizing the use of the torch along the way through Georgia. If Sherman had been at the head of marauders, merely, who had marched through a country wasting and burning and looting and brutally despoiling a people, and then had entered a city where the same course was pursued, and he had been called to account in a criminal court, the whole circumstances would have convicted him of complicity for everything that happened in Columbia, for every robbery and for every death. The time being one of war, and the South being so greatly in the wrong, the rules of evidence are suspended by historians, where the rationale of judicial proof would keep all deductive processes and all analysis active and aware of every detail which showed acquiescence or complicity. Lincoln who knew what the purpose of Sherman's march was, and what might well happen in its course, must stand at the bar of history to be tested by whoever wants to discover what was in his mind when, with all this horror to background the days and to fill the thoughts of everyone with tragic grief, he could say: With charity for all, as he did on March 4, 1865, a few months after the burning of Columbia.

To recur now to the Blair mission to see Jefferson Davis. His name was Francis Preston Blair, and before the War he had been on friendly relations with President Davis. Blair was known as a sort of Warwick of the Lincoln administration; and evidently he conceived the wonderful idea that he could bring about peace, now that Sherman had cut the South in two. According to Lincoln, Blair set forth for Richmond, without any authority of representation, without any power of negotiation. There was a good deal of correspondence between military men and between Lincoln and Seward and others touching this visit, of Blair to Richmond, and the Hampton Roads conference which resulted from it. All of this Lincoln submitted to the Senate on February 10, 1865, in response to a resolution of that body of the 8th requesting information of the conference at Hampton Roads. It is not necessary to go into this, save in a few particulars. Richmond in general and President Davis in particular were astonished to see Blair. Blair and Davis went into secret conference, and evidently the first person to know what the interview was about was the vice president, Stephens. Blair's visit to Richmond was in early January, 1865; and the next day after he saw President Davis, Stephens was called into secret conference by Davis and told in strictest state confidence what Blair had said. Blair had proposed that there be a suspension of military hostilities, which was to be effected by a military convention, seeming to embrace another object than the end of the War, namely, the enforcement of the Monroe Doctrine against France. By this time Ferdinand Joseph Maximilian, Archduke of Austria, had been set up by the arms of France as the emperor of Mexico. The idea was that the North and the South could heartily join together in the suppression of the monarchic principle thus sought to be grafted upon the New World. Blair very plausibly represented to Davis that a joint movement and discussion of the Mexican question might lead to the restoration of the Union, and without the further effusion of blood. This in brief was what Davis told Stephens that the conference with Blair was about. On January 12, 1865, Davis wrote a letter to Blair in which he said: "I have deemed it proper, and probably desirable to you, to give you, in this form, the substance of remarks made by me to be repeated by you to President Lincoln . . . I have no disposition to find obstacles in forms, and am willing now, as heretofore, to enter into negotiations for the restoration of peace; am ready to send a commission whenever I have reason to suppose it will be received, or to receive a commission, if the United States Government shall choose to send one." This letter was shown by Blair to Lincoln, who wrote to Blair: "You having shown me Mr. Davis's letter to you of the 12th instant, you may say to him that I have constantly been, am now, and shall continue ready to receive any legal agent whom he or any other influential person now resisting the national authority may informally send to me, with the view of securing peace to the people of our common country." It will be noted that Lincoln, as usual, did not speak of Davis as a president or recognize the existence of the Confederate States of America; and all through the correspondence he maintained this attitude and manner of designation. Yet why did Blair come to Richmond, and for whom? His presence there was in no wise solicited by President Davis, or anyone in the administration of the Confederacy. It was natural for Davis to suppose that Blair was acting for Lincoln, and with some sort of authority to open negotiations of some character, and indeed why not of the very description which he did lay before Davis in the interview of early January? Without further detail then, Lincoln, on January 31, deputed Seward to go to Fortress Monroe, there to confer with Stephens, Hunter and Campbell, who had been appointed a commission by President Davis to confer with whomsoever Lincoln sent to meet them in making some accommodation about the end of the war. By this time Stephens and his associates had left Richmond, and, proceeding by permission of Grant, had passed the Federal lines, and were being received and entertained by Grant, with all marks of respect and with cordial hospitality. Stephens later wrote his impressions of Grant, which were highly complimentary, and he generously acknowledged the courtesies which Grant bestowed upon him and upon Hunter and Campbell. These men had reason to believe that Lincoln was in a mood to discuss generous terms for the end of the War. But they did not know that the next day after Lincoln appointed Seward to confer with them in a discussion of peace, Lincoln sent a telegram to Grant, who was at City Point, Virginia, in which he said: "Let nothing which is transpiring change, hinder or delay your military movements or plans." To this Grant replied on February 1: "Your dispatch received. There will be no armistice in consequence of the presence of Mr. Stephens and others within our lines. The troops are kept in readiness to move at the shortest notice, if occasion should justify it." So that, while these men might be consulting on peace, Grant might be moving his troops, if he saw a chance to win a victory. All this; and in addition Lincoln decided at the last minute to be present himself at the conference; and on the night of February 2, he reached Hampton Roads, where he found Seward, who had already arrived there. New letters from Davis had come and Lincoln saw "for the first time the answer of the Richmond gentleman [President Davis] in which the latter authorized Stephens and his associates to proceed to Washington for "informal conference with him [Lincoln] upon the issues involved in the existing war." Lincoln had come to Hampton Roads because Grant wanted him to do so. According to Stephens, Grant was exceedingly anxious that the war should end, and was doing all he could to prosper the conference between Stephens and his associates on the one hand, and Seward on the other; but with Lincoln, too, as it turned out. Despite, therefore, the austere and formal attitude of Lincoln, and his persistent refusal to recognize Davis's official position, or to speak of him in other terms than that of Mr. Davis, or the "Richmond gentleman," Lincoln, the president of the United States, was in Hampton Roads in person to enter into conference with the vice president of the Confederacy, and the other men appointed by Davis as the result of Blair's unsolicited mission to Richmond. This is one of the most dramatic moments of the great tragedy of the War. It is most moving when all the circumstances are considered, and all the persons who participated in the conference are taken into account in their pasts, their actions for four years past, and their thoughts and feelings as the talk proceeded. We need only look at Lincoln and at Stephens, with a side glance now and then at Seward, when he interpellates with lawyerlike sagacity, as though he would prevent Lincoln from committing himself too much.

Stephens was a small man now of about fifty-three years of age. He never weighed quite one hundred pounds. He was frail and needed to bundle up more than ordinary men do to keep warm. When he and Lincoln were in Congress together in 1847-8, Lincoln, seeing Stephens one day in the House wrapped in many coats, remarked that he was the smallest nubbin' in the greatest amount of shucks that he had ever seen. Now all these many years had passed. Lincoln was president of the United States as the result of the sectional strife which Stephens had all along protested against with eloquence and wisdom; and Stephens was vice president of the government which had been set up to get away from centralization, from despotism, as Calhoun called it. But though Stephens was delicate of body, he had a hero's heart and a great mind. His eyes burned with a bright ethereal fire under a forehead of square fullness, with no Clay retreat in it, and without the overloaded oppressiveness of the Webster forehead. His face was thin, his hair was combed rather flatly, yet loosely, a little way down his brow, and it upcurled into longer locks around his neck. His mouth was firm. His whole countenance bespoke benignity, high intelligence, and a penetration not easily baffled. This was the man who had made Lincoln weep when speaking in Congress in the long ago, and of whom Lincoln wrote to Herndon, saying that he had just heard the finest speech of his whole life. Perhaps Lincoln was thinking of this on this night on the boat, which lay at anchor off Fortress Monroe, as the waters lapped around the hull, and the sounds of the sea drifted about under the mystery of the indifferent stars. Was he possibly thinking that in the event of final triumph of the arms of the North Stephens and Davis would be indicted for treason, and would be kept in prison in this very fort near by? For if there was no Confederate government, there could be no vice president and no president of a Confederate Government. The Constitution of the United States, as made by the fathers, reads: "Treason against the United States shall consist only in levying war against them." Stephens and Davis had levied war, provided there were no Confederate States of America. Whether there was or not depended upon the affirmation that there was not, coupled with an army which could make it good.

The hour arrived for the conference. Stephens and his associates were conducted into the saloon of the steamer, like school boys soon to meet the master on some matter of discipline. Very soon Lincoln and Seward entered. Lincoln looked passive, but dark, pensive but resolute. He had become a giant. Not far away was Grant with a great army of irresistible power. Lincoln was commander in chief of this army. Back of the army was a prosperous North, ready and willing now to pour out untold millions to conquer the South. Lincoln as a president newly returned to power was more master of the country than ever. His black hair and beard added to the seriousness of his countenance, to the depressing and discouraging atmosphere of his presence. His little gray eyes were far sunk in his head, in watchful and wary meditation. He was no longer afraid of assassination; he was free of anxiety that the American masters would support him. By usurpations and by the trapped acquiescence of the American people he held all earthly power in his hands. This little man before him, this representative of the Richmond gentleman, this so-called vice president of a government that never existed—what was he going to say, when his eager eyes began to burn, and the clear reasoning of his mind began to flow from his lips?

At first Lincoln and Stephens inquired about each other's friends, mutually known in the past, and now separated by the War. Lincoln asked especially about Mr. Toombs; and Stephens about Truman Smith of Connecticut. Also they spoke of the part they had played together in the election of Zachary Taylor in 1848. Lincoln on the whole was agreeable, and brightened with a certain cheerfulness at the recollection of old days. These greetings having been exchanged Stephens said: "Well, Mr. President, is there no way of putting an end to the present trouble, and bringing about a restoration of the general good feeling and harmony" of the "different states and sections of the country?" Whether Lincoln looked at Seward, or Seward indicated to Lincoln that he must not yet speak, no less Seward broke in: "It is understood, gentlemen, that this is to be an informal conference. There is to be no clerk or secretary—no writing of record of anything that is said. All is to be verbal." So it was, and we rely here upon the report of the conference made by Stephens.[1] Thereupon Lincoln, adhering to his old ideas, replied that there was but one way that he knew of to end the war and bring about harmony, and that was for those who were resisting the laws of the Union to cease that resistance, since all the trouble came from an armed resistance against the national authority. Stephens then alluded to the Maximilian usurpation, and inquired if the North and South could not unite in a defense of the Monroe Doctrine, since, war or no war, North and South, or a nation of North and South made no difference as to the equal interest in keeping the monarchic principle from America. Lincoln then came out with his usual wrestling tactics. He said: "I suppose you refer to something that Mr. Blair has said. Now it is proper to state at the beginning that whatever he said was of his own accord, and without the least authority from me. When he applied for a passport to go to Richmond, with certain ideas which he wished to make known to me, I told him flatly that I did not wish to hear them. If he desired to go to Richmond of his own accord I would give him a passport; but he had no authority to speak for me in any way whatever. When he returned and brought me Mr. Davis's letter, I gave him the one to which you alluded in your application for leave to cross the lines. I was always willing to hear propositions for peace on the conditions of this letter and on no other. The restoration of the Union is a *sine qua non* with me, and hence my instructions that no conference was to be held except upon that basis."

[1] Stephens, "Constitutional View of the War," II, 599, et seq.

It is to be observed that Blair had gone to Richmond with Lincoln's consent; and that on January 18, Lincoln had written Blair that he was and had always been "willing to receive any agent whom he [Davis] or any other influential person now resisting the national authority may informally send to me with the view of securing peace to the people of our common country." Making full allowance for the use of the term "our common country," yet if Blair had no authority to speak for Lincoln, what was Lincoln here now to speak about in a conference which had resulted from Blair's interposition? Lincoln knew that Blair had advanced the plan of a pacification by a common defense of the Monroe Doctrine, and that no other plan of ceasing hostilities had been suggested by anyone. If there was nothing to the conference except this reassertion of Lincoln's stubborn terms of peace, why was Lincoln here? Why was not Seward a sufficient representation of the United States to convey a message and a decision as stale as that? Naturally this revealed purpose of Lincoln's expressed in the emphatic way in which he delivered it to Stephens fell with numbing force upon the hopes of Stephens. He proceeded no less to elaborate the idea of joining hands to drive France from Mexico, and in that way to unite the North and South during a cessation of hostilities. After France was disposed of, the North and the South, who had thus allied themselves to assert the Monroe Doctrine, would be in a better frame of mind to adjust their internecine differences.

The psychology of this proceeding was not amiss. The difficulty was that a right psychology at the start in the complexity of the future becomes a tangle and a failure. Such far-sighted programs are not for men; the gods sometimes order their success, as in the World War, which the South thought did much to harmonize it more fully with the North, just because soldiers from both sections, with equal patriotism, made war upon Germany. Stephens' suggestion indicated that the war and his anxieties and exhaustions had unsettled his customary clarity of mind. For while Seward's plan when war was imminent, contemplating a war on France to divert America from its domestic division, was visionary to the last degree, so was the plan of Stephens now. It had originated in the poor brain of Blair, and was caught at by Davis and Stephens as though it came from Lincoln. They had the right to believe it was workable if

Lincoln would join in it. Seward ventured to say that Stephens' ideas were specious. The Union could never be restored on the basis of defending the Monroe Doctrine. Stephens argued that matter with Seward. Lincoln and Seward both said then that the feeling in the North was very strong for the Monroe Doctrine. Then Lincoln repeated what he had said before, namely that there could be no armistice while the matter of the Union was undisposed of. Stephens then suggested a military convention called by Lincoln as commander in chief of the armies of the North, and to be called by Davis for the South, which should consider the problems pending. Lincoln replied that thereby he would be recognizing the South as a separate power, which he would never do.

Judge Campbell, one of the Davis commissioners, spoke up at this juncture, and asked how restoration was to take place, supposing that the South were consenting to it. "By disbanding their armies, and permitting the national authorities to resume their functions," Lincoln curtly replied. Stephens inquired what would be the status of that portion of the slave population in the South which had not been freed by the Emancipation Proclamation. Lincoln replied that that was a judicial question for the Courts. His own opinion was that the Proclamation was a mere war measure. What would become of the states of the South, would they be admitted to representation in Congress if they abandoned the war, asked Stephens. Lincoln, though saying that they should be so admitted, refused to enter into any stipulation upon the subject. Stephens argued that the South should know what was ahead of it in a matter as serious as this; but Lincoln stuck to the position that he could not make any agreement upon this question while the South was in arms. Stephens rejoined that if Lincoln could issue the Emancipation Proclamation as a war measure, he could give the South some assurance on this subject, likewise as a war measure. Lincoln here grew argumentative and explained what the Emancipation Proclamation was, and how he came to issue it.

Stephens and his associates, being unable to elicit anything definite from Lincoln on any subject, the observation was made that nothing else could be made of Lincoln and Seward than that they demanded unconditional submission of the South. Seward now grew spirited and retorted that the words "unconditional submission," had not been used. Then Hunter, one of the Davis deputies, said: "What else could be made of it? No treaty, no stipulation, no agreement, either with the Confederate States jointly, or with them separately, as to their future position or security. What was this but unconditional submission to the mercy of conquerors?" To this the disingenuous Seward replied with a sophism: "They were not conquerors further than that they required obedience to the laws." Moreover the South would be again under the Constitution with all its protections and guarantees, and its courts; and, that being so, it was not unconditional surrender for the South to come back without stipulation. The Constitution was the all sufficient stipulation. Stephens and his associates were not deceived by that casuistry. They already prevised the horrors and despotisms of Reconstruction under the leadership of the Sumners and the Thaddeus Stevenses.

Lincoln spoke at some length now about compensated emancipation. That idea still hung in his never changing mind. He said that he believed the North would approve an appropriation of $400,-000,000 to pay the South for her slaves. Was that bribe to be despised? The South needed money badly enough. The course of the conference was diverted to the subject of an exchange of prisoners. Stephens in his humanity brought this up. Lincoln well knew about the horrible suffering in the military prisons. Lincoln then and there had the power to say that the prisoners should be exchanged at once. But he merely promised to confer with General Grant about it. However, Stephens made a proposition to Lincoln for some immediate exchanges; and to these Lincoln agreed. No exchanges meant further prison horrors. The conference, which was now prolonged to four hours, began to trickle, and to distract further memory of things to say by ominous drippings of watery monosyllables. Stephens then urged Lincoln to reconsider the subject of an armistice. Lincoln rose to leave, saying that he would reconsider it; but that he did not think that he would change his mind. Lincoln, with his undulatory, cautious and cunning step, planting his feet down side by side as he walked, left the saloon, his height of six feet four inches weaving under the door. Seward followed. Stephens and his fellows sat there, looking at the backs of the rail splitter and the abolitionist.

With the background of Sherman's march to the sea, with all its horrors, and with the pathetic futility of the conference in Hampton Roads still fresh in Lincoln's memory, he stood up on March 4, 1865, and delivered his Second Inaugural. When he said, "With malice toward none, with charity for all, with firmness in the right as God gives us to see the right," he was too saturated with the hypocrisy of Hebraic-Puritanism to realize the enormity of such blasphemy against human nature and human reason. The gigantic inconsistency of such words was totally unperceived by his mind, now fed by war, and by imperial power, by intellectual arrogance completely reared out of old humilities often professed, until his dual nature no longer knew its divided self, if indeed what was insensitive and egocentric, and triple-hardened resolution, in it was not in complete possession of a manner of thinking that had been double-faced all along, many colored, but which hid its change of hue by a genius for mimesis. Was it not fixed now in the black of sternest Puritanism?

Long years before Herndon had read to Lincoln one of Theodore Parker's sermons, and after doing so made this shallow revivalistic observation: "I have always noticed that ill-gotten wealth does no man any good. This is as true of nations as of individuals. I believe that all the ill-gotten gain wrenched by us from the negro through his enslavement will eventually be taken from us, and we will be set back where we began. Lincoln thought my prophecy rather direful."[1] This Hebraic-Puritan idea took root in Lincoln's mind; and so in his Second Inaugural he developed it into these demonical words: "The Almighty has his own purposes. 'Woe unto the world because of offenses! for it must needs be that offenses come; but woe to that man by whom the offense cometh.' If we shall suppose that American slavery is one of those offenses which, in the providence of God, must needs come, but which having continued through his appointed time, he now wills to remove, and that he gives to both North and South this terrible war, as the woe due to those by whom the offense came, shall we discern therein any departure from those divine attributes which the believers in a living God always ascribe to him?" Not Jonathan Edwards in his maddest Calvinism ever uttered words to equal these of Lincoln. They

[1] Herndon, II, 33.

mean that slavery, which the New World did not want, had to pay for it in agony and blood, but that the debt had to be paid by those who did not contract the debt. They mean that a just God willed this, and effected his will by a war which cost the country from 750,000 to 1,000,000 lives and $22,000,000,000 of money. If God was now willing the removal of slavery it was through men like Lincoln, who had given the North and the South this war, without any need for it at all, and who within a few weeks of the day of this Inaugural willed that the war should go on, and that the peace proposals of Stephens should come to nothing save upon terms of ignominious capitulation, without promises or assurances of any sort as to the fate of the South. There are only two ways of interpreting these words of Lincoln: either one interprets them as a Christian and accepts what he said as true and just, because it is taken from the Bible; or else one has retained his reasoning faculties, and abhors them as the incredible outpouring of a mind at last completely fanaticized.

Just preceding these words Lincoln said in his Inaugural: "It may seem strange that any men should dare to ask a just God's assistance in wringing their bread from the sweat of other men's faces; but let us judge not, that we be not judged." Let us not judge, but let us put our judgment into the obscene mouth of the Jewish Jehovah. Let us utter the monstrous curse, but have no responsibility in it. Let us not judge; but let us prosecute with utter remorselessness the war, just as if we had passed a judgment upon the South. Killing, and burning, and conquering can be as effectually done without words of condemnation as with them. In truth, to look daggers, and to use them, but not to speak them may be a way of keeping the victim ignorant of what the strife is about. By not judging in express words, however, we shall not be judged. Let us be careful therefore what we say, lest we take the wrong stand for God's work. Do God's work and keep a shut mouth. Who at the time of war exhaustion had time to disentangle so many irrelevant ideas double criss-crossed with so many irrelevant conclusions, and sealed together with Hebraic-Puritan poetry? Today a whole volume could be written to separate and lay out for view the complexed strands of this sophistry and superstition. Consider by way of one wholly revealing glance how such moral hypocrisy as this would have fallen upon an audience of Pericles' Athens. If it be strength to utter words that only great analysis can blow to nothing, and since great analysis cannot exist in vacuo, but must have an audience, then Lincoln had strength of mind. Here he was to the very last, when thousands were dropping with fatigue, and many who could have put him to flight were either dead or silenced by war madness, still uttering the puerilities of his young manhood and of his first message to Congress. He was thus a strong man; and indeed a stubborn man. To a correspondent who wrote Lincoln in compliment upon his inaugural address he replied that he expected it to wear as well as anything that he had produced. But "men are not flattered by being shown that there has been a difference of purpose between the Almighty and them." That is, there has been no judgment, but just a showing that God condemned the South!

On March 18, Lincoln annulled the sentence of two men of the name of Smith who had been convicted of fraud in war contracts. On the second of April the Confederates evacuated Richmond. On the fifth, Lincoln went to Richmond to take symbolical possession of the city which his armies had won. He walked to the White House of the Confederacy, entered and sat in the chair but lately occupied by President Davis. He had but a few soldiers with him for guard; the city was half burned, and in the disorder of drunken men, and the confusion of capitulated streets; yet no one affronted Lincoln. The Sublime Malice was not ready. A few days after this, April 9, Lee surrendered to Grant at Appomatox. Grant forbade his troops to cheer. A gallant foe lay exhausted. It was unmanly, it was brutal to send up huzzas over the bowed heads of brave men. But Lincoln walked the streets of Richmond and teetered in the chair of the head executive of the Confederacy. All fears of assassination had fully fled from his mind now. Otherwise he must have considered the free exposure that he was making of himself to any watchful Aristogiton. Let us apply Lincoln's favorite formula of excluded middle to this symbolical resumption of executive authority over the South. The chair was either lawfully or unlawfully occupied by Davis. If lawfully, why jest thus at the wounds of the South? If unlawfully, why thus symbolically assert an authority over the seat that Davis had never had any title to?

When Lee surrendered, the Boards of Trade and the Stock Exchanges broke into song. The favorite hymn was "Praise God from Whom all blessings flow." "Gloria in Excelsis" was sung in the churches. The streets of Northern cities resounded with the words of "Rally round the flag," and "John Brown's Body." It was time to resuscitate the song that Hamilton sang with such effect at dinners in New York, and which he delighted a company with the night before Burr killed him. It was called "The Bible and the Drum." Massachusetts Whittier and Lowell wept and summoned the Hebraic Muse of triumph over enemies. Lowell felt a "strange and tender exaltation. I wanted to laugh and I wanted to cry. . . . There is something magnificent in having a country to love." To him there was no goodness in having two republics instead of none.

On the 6th of April Lincoln wrote to Grant. He referred to the conference with Stephens and others in February, and added that in Richmond, on April 6, he had seen Judge Campbell, into whose hands he had placed an "informal paper" in which he warned the South through Campbell that if "the war be now further persisted in by the rebels, confiscated property shall at the least bear the additional cost, and that confiscation shall be remitted to the people of any State which will now promptly and in good faith withdraw its troops and other support from resistance to the government." Though Lee had surrendered, the war was not quite over. Johnston had not handed his sword to Sherman. Not until April 18, did these two generals come to agreement for a military convention and a settlement.

On the 11th of April Lincoln issued another famous proclamation by which he closed five ports in Virginia, seven in North Carolina, three in South Carolina, three in Georgia, three in Mississippi, four in Florida, one in Louisiana and four in Texas. The wrestler was now closing in on the winded South.

On the evening of the 11th of April Lincoln made his last public address. "We meet," he began, "this evening not in sorrow, but in gladness of heart. The evacuation of Petersburg and Richmond, and the surrender of the principal insurgent army give hope of a righteous and speedy peace, whose joyous expression cannot be restrained. In the midst of this, however, He from whom all blessings flow must not be forgotten." He then passed to the subject of reconstruction, with particular reference to Louisiana and its new Constitution. "We all agree that the seceded states, so called, are out of their practical relation with the Union, and that the sole object of the government, civil and military, in regard to those states is to again get them into that proper practical relation." He turned to the colored man: "The colored man, too, in seeing all united for him, is inspired with vigilance and energy, and daring to the same end. Grant that he desires the elective franchise, will he not attain it sooner by saving the already advanced steps toward it than by running backward over them?"

These last words fell upon ears that thrilled with horror and hatred. John Wilkes Booth was listening.[1] Before his vision rose the South that he loved with a lover's madness, ruled by negro votes, deployed by the North to that end. According to one report, Booth at that moment vowed to kill Lincoln. His brain, like Lincoln's, was made up of atoms internally whirling with electrons around protons. This was the mechanism of his thinking, as it was of Lincoln's. These several sets of electrons and protons were soon to collide with each other, indeed had now impinged, to the wreck of the two planetary systems of the two individuals; and such microcosmic disaster was to adumbrate itself to the larger world of electrons and protons called the Union, the United States of America, and their people, in woe beyond calculation. For no strength of human thinking can discover that Lincoln's death did any good and the history of the country might have been fairer and better if Lincoln had lived his term out and gone back to Springfield, as Johnson returned to Tennessee, a rejected and discredited man. As in the case of the French Revolution, the radicals in Congress were soon to turn on each other, and on the men who tried to preserve some sanity in the affairs of the nation. Revolution, such as the destruction of state sovereignty was, was to breed counter revolution, and further radicalism. And Lincoln, now aging and worn, and never quick to adjust himself to new conditions, might have fallen disastrously into the clutch of the Stevenses and others, who were bent now on the utmost measures of punishment and humiliation for the South. Lincoln had at the time of his death no great hold on the people, no position of authority with his own cabinet—no pre-

[1] Herndon, II, 289.

eminent sway with Congress, though that body had denied him nothing for the prosecution of the War.

"If we shall suppose," that the atoms of Booth's brain were but apparently following the same laws of motion as those of the external world, which he contemplated, with Lincoln in the foreground, it was impossible for him to know whether he saw objects by a course which paralleled the whirling of external atoms, or whether the external atoms were conspiring with the Sublime Malice to make him believe that he was following truly in his thinking the whirling of the external atoms; when in point of fact his inner world and the outer world were moving in opposite directions. So with Lincoln, too. His vision of the Union was a matter of internal orbiting, and whether it harmonized by going in a sphere which tracked the outer world he could not know. He sought to will the outer world, and to aggrandize his will by moral appeals to the "judgments of the Lord," which are "true and righteous altogether." "Fondly do we hope—fervently do we pray that this mighty scourge of war may speedily pass away. Yet, if God wills that it continue until all the wealth piled by the bondsman's two hundred and fifty years of unrequited toil shall be sunk, and until every drop of blood drawn with the lash shall be repaid by another drawn with the sword, as was said three thousand years ago, so still must it be said, 'The judgments of the Lord are true and righteous altogether.'" This was the man whom Booth heard, on the night of April 11, suggest the possibilities of negro suffrage.

The unexpected is most likely to happen. The brave man is likely to turn coward. The fearful man may become suddenly reckless. In times of little danger men are cautious; in times of peril they are hazardous. Lincoln, one would think, took great chances in walking through the streets of Richmond. He had entered Washington in 1861 disguised. Why now in Washington go about unguarded? Perhaps Lincoln in his superstitious thinking had come to believe that he was the special care of God; that nothing could happen to him.

He was not of the Cæsar mold, who saw the things that threatened him as looking but on his back, afraid to face him. That was not the character of his egotism. He may have visioned himself, however, as a Colossus, which he had indeed become, who bestrode the country, above criticism, and above danger and under the care of God. His imagination was scarcely of the kind which could see himself further lifted up by death, while the Lincoln that men then knew would be dead and forgotten; though he may have reflected that time would justify all his acts. However, the night he went to Ford's Theatre, he might well have protected himself with soldiers. When hate has been wounded and has crawled away, it is not safe to sit on the stone under which it may have dragged its angry length. So the passage to the presidential box in which he sat might have been so securely guarded that Booth could not have sneaked up to the door and pointed his pistol through a hole already bored through its panel. There, with acclaim pouring into his ears, with the actors and actresses departing from their lines to paraphrase words of honor for him, with laughter and happy words murmuring over the audience, sudden blackness fell on the mind of Abraham Lincoln. Or was it a shower of spiritual sparks from a soul crashing against the atoms of the bullet, projected by the atoms of the Booth brain? Then was there the thousandth part of a second in which the soul of Abraham Lincoln, struggling not to be disrupted, made a last great flame of light in which all the past came before his inner eyes, from the days of Pigeon Creek and New Salem to the very moment of the curtain rising upon the mimic stage of the theater? Or did he hear a voice which said, "What is it all about?" Or did an infinite peace enter his whole being with the soothing warmth of an altar's flame? Or did he note in some subconscious way through the hours of life that remained the persistent beat of his powerful heart, not afraid that it would cease, but in wonder and in calm pride that it continued to pulse? In any case the end had come; while Booth's bullet was the last one fired for States' Rights.

Chapter XVIII   The One Cause Which Was Lost

THE Gettysburg Address is Lincoln's most famous utterance. In a measure it parallels the oration of Pericles over the dead who had first fallen in the war between Athens and Sparta. Where Lincoln said, "Fourscore and seven years ago our fathers brought forth on this continent a new nation conceived in liberty," Pericles had said, "I shall begin first with our ancestors: it is both just and proper that they should have the honor of the first mention on an occasion like this." But while Pericles clung closely to the historic truth in referring to the past as the background of what he said, Lincoln carefully avoided one half of the American story, just because Gettysburg could not be lauded if he had said that "governments derive their just powers from the consent of the governed." When our fathers brought forth this government it was by the assertion of this truth. Lincoln at Gettysburg could not celebrate such a philosophy, for with all his original, if not perverted, view of things, he knew that it was on this field where the right to set up a new government had received its first deadly blow. The Gettysburg oration, therefore, remains a prose poem, but in the inferior sense that one must not inquire into its truth. One must read it apart from the facts; for it has become a fact itself above the facts and in contradiction of them. In the long perspective of things how is a battle a fact, and a poem not a fact? The poem may be the fact at last and the battle a fiction. It was untrue that our fathers in 1776 had brought forth a new nation; for in that year our fathers brought forth thirteen new nations, each of which was a sovereign state. Therefore the war was not testing whether that nation, or any nation so conceived and so dedicated, could long endure. The war was testing whether sovereign states which had ratified a Constitution and formed a Union, could repeal their ratification and set up another Union; and whether 11,000,000 people might exercise their right "to alter or abolish," that Union, so far as they themselves were concerned, and "to institute new government, laying its foundation on such principles, and organizing its powers in such

THE ONE CAUSE WHICH WAS LOST 479

form, as to them shall seem most likely to effect their safety and happiness." Lincoln dared not face the facts at Gettysburg. He had so long duped his own mind with the falsely formed judgments of his early and inadequate thinking and reading that he was unable to deal realistically with the history of his country, even if the occasion had been one when the truth was acceptable to the audience. Thus we have in the Gettysburg Address that refusal of the truth which is written all over the American character and its expressions. The war then being waged was not glorious, it was brutal and hateful and mean minded. It had been initiated by radicals and fanatics, by Boston and by Chicago, by men like Garrison and Medill. What therefore could Lincoln say of the North comparable to what Pericles said of Athens? "The freedom which we enjoy in our government extends also to our ordinary life. There far from exercising a jealous surveillance over each other, we do not feel called upon to be angry with our neighbor for doing what he likes, or even to indulge those injurious looks which cannot fail to be offensive, although they inflict no positive penalty." Lincoln was debarred giving utterance to anything like this; for the war had come from intermeddling and jealous surveillance, and from anger, and from the Hebraic-Puritan principle of assuming to act as one's brother's keeper, when the real motive was to become one's brother's jailer. Nor could Lincoln say of the North: "We cultivate refinement without extravagance, and knowledge without effeminacy; wealth we employ more for use than for show, and place the real disgrace of poverty not in owning to the fact, but in declining the struggle against it. . . . And it is only the Athenians who, fearless of consequences, confer their benefits not from calculations of expediency, but in the confidence of liberality. . . . Such is the Athens for which these men, in the assertion of their resolve not to lose her nobly fought and died; and well may every one of their survivors be ready to suffer in her cause." The soldiers at Gettysburg on neither side died for any such culture as this. The army of Athens had sacrificed itself for Homer, for Æschylus and Sophocles; while Whittier and Lowell had no ideas that could better a nation, in fact none that were not at strife with the more or less classical thinking of the fathers, and especially with that of Jefferson. Though Lincoln had cursed the South in his second Inaugural, by placing one of Jehovah's maledictions in his mouth, to be shouted by ventriloquism against a people that he had treated as traitors and not as belligerents, he did not have the intellectual courage then nor at Gettysburg to say openly as Pericles did: "No, holding that vengeance upon their enemies was more to be desired than any personal blessings, and reckoning this to be the most glorious of hazards, they joyfully determined to accept the risk, to make sure of their vengeance and to let their wishes wait. . . . Thus choosing to die rather than to live submitting, they fled only from dishonor, but met danger face to face, and after one brief moment, while at the summit of their fortune, escaped, not from their fear, but from their glory." In Lincoln's case the subjugation of the South had to be smeared over with religion, it had to be made at one with the creed of Methodists and Baptists, with the whole rank and file of Calvinism, with the nauseating piety and the sadistic righteousness of America as a Christian nation, in order to conceal its purpose, in order to satisfy those who fought for the Lord, if they fought at all, that such was their battle at Gettysburg. All the while the only oration which could have been spoken beautifully and truly to the last word was one which might have been pronounced on the army of Lee, upon the men of Pickett who fell in the pasture between Seminary and Cemetery ridge, and who died in swarms at the little wall behind which the armies of centralism had taken their stand. "For it is only the love of honor that never grows old; and honor it is, not gain, as some would have it, that rejoices the heart of age and helplessness," said Pericles. That was the trouble with Gettysburg; consciously or otherwise the Northern soldiers who died there died for gain, not honor, not liberty; and all the aftermath of Reconstruction, all that America is today in hypocrisy and greed and materialism is the proof of this assertion. The Jehovah and the God that Lincoln appealed to was not that seemingly infinite influence which dominates the order of man's life and keeps natural law at work in the spiritual world. With whatever poetry a war be glossed, its effects come out of the lethal purpose with which it was waged, and from the character of the deeds with which it was prosecuted. How could "this nation under God . . . have a new birth of freedom," out of Gettysburg? It was as impossible as that America should grow great and noble and free from the blood of the three thousand Filipinos who perished at the hands of William McKinley near Manila's wall. The Republicans of 1900 asserted that the resistance of the Filipinos was the same thing as the so-called rebellion of the Southern people. This is answered by saying that the subjugation of the two was precisely the same thing. The consequences were, therefore, ignominious. God is not mocked, may be said by the atheist even, provided he understand that cause and effect are inevitable in human life.

When Herndon went to New York and Boston in 1858 to see Philipps, Parker, Sumner, Seward, Garrison, Beecher and Greeley on the mission of advancing Lincoln's political fortunes, he returned to Springfield with some of Parker's sermons. One of these was "The effect of Slavery on the American people," in which Parker had said, "Democracy is direct self-government, over all the people for all the people, by all the people." This was the source of Lincoln's words at Gettysburg, "that government of the people, by the people, and for the people, shall not perish from the earth."

Lincoln's mind was not profound enough, it was not sufficiently penetrating and realistic to see that government of the people had perished in America as the result of the War. He did not understand the immediate and the remote consequences of his war measures, though impliedly admitting that he had exceeded his authority as president. If he was to throttle free speech, and a free press, if he was to suspend the habeas corpus, and blockade ports, and refuse to exchange prisoners, and to deny belligerent rights in the stubborn assertion that the states were still in the Union and to vote soldiers in his own behalf; if he was to twist and to turn upon his own reasoning and positions, and to refuse terms of peace, and to order men to be killed, and to be obdurate in the name of religion, why might not others do the same thing? Why might not his successors in office wage similar wars, and use his words as authority for doing so; and in waging such wars do all that he had done? Jefferson had seen that the Missouri Compromise was the death knell of the Union. So it was. How was Lincoln's war, which started in sectionalism, to do aught but exacerbate that sectionalism? Any other result was impossible. One wonders altogether what was in Lincoln's mind respecting the future out of such a past. Perhaps he really accepted everything as the punishment of a just God, who had been offended by sins which must needs have been committed. This is probable only, for whether Lincoln invoked God because he believed in a God, or whether his histrionic gift befooled him into invoking God, must remain a question. At this point it is open to see by those who have eyes what corruption of thinking the Bible has been to the World, and what woe it has caused wherever it has had sway. How can America profit herself by worship of Lincoln? In looking at his image to make ourselves according to its nature how shall America be made? The Union that he mystically adored, the Union under the Constitution of 1787, perished with the War. That object of his concern cannot be ours. With consolidation came imperial America; and Lincoln's prayers and works for the Union cannot be our ritual and our endeavors. On the night of April 11, when his speech was listened to by Booth, Lincoln was feeling his way with reference to the restoration of the seceded states. He was claiming that they had been away on a visit, but that they never had separated themselves from their home. Soon Thaddeus Stevens and his associates were to hold that they were out of a practical relationship to the Union, and that they should stay out until they had swallowed the last drop of the cup of poison, until they had yielded to bureaucracy and centralism their police power, their ancient freedoms. And thus Lincoln, trifling with a metaphor, devised no real program for reconstruction. There were vast questions to be solved without doubt. But Lincoln required much time in which to think anything out; and besides there was Congress where the radicals were aching to get at the throat of the South, and Lincoln knew that he would not have everything his own way. If he had been a Napoleon with desire to reconstitute the Union as it was, or a Jefferson who would have had that desire at heart in the circumstances, he would have set down with swift hands and clear thinking some definite plan. As it was he bequeathed to the mad age about to dominate the country a few metaphors, and a few suggestions for reconstruction.

When Lincoln and Seward saw Stephens at Hampton Roads the Thirteenth Amendment had just been submitted to Congress by resolution. Southern leaders well understood that in the posture of affairs slavery could not last. Indeed before the Thirteenth Amend-

THE ONE CAUSE WHICH WAS LOST 483

ment was adopted Tennessee and Missouri had abolished slavery; and wherever the Northern Army was supreme the Emancipation Proclamation had been effectual. If the war then was about slavery, did not the Thirteenth Amendment, acquiesced in by the conquered states, settle everything? If the North meant to keep faith on the Andrew Johnson resolutions in the Senate of July, 1861, as to the purpose of the War, and as to its ceasing when the seceded states were brought back into the Union, why did not all controversy cease when the states were brought back? The reason is that the master minds of the Republican Party, the offshoots of Hamiltonism, had further purposes, seeing the capitalistic advantages that now revealed themselves. They cared nothing for the Union compared to what they cared for money and power. They turned out to be the only disunionists, inasmuch as they were willing to fight and to destroy the federal system and principle.

Lincoln was not an economist, but he saw dimly a new labor situation with the negro turned into the labor market. He had said that he believed in placing the man above the dollar; and so it was that the rising corporations were not sure of Lincoln, while Lincoln was afraid of them. When death removed him from the path of these plunderers they had no one to reckon with but a vice president, a former Democrat, raised to be the executive chief. What they did to Johnson has been told in a recent book.[1] It is a chapter that scarcely another civilized country can parallel.

The first thing that had to be done, and was done, was to stir and to keep stirred the hate that had motivated the War, and to perpetuate the sectionalism in which it was begun. This was to be done in order to plunder the South. To this infernal program the Hebraic-Puritan abolitionist lent a willing hand. He had cursed the slave holder, he had lauded the oppressor of the laborers in the mills, and the mines of the North, who paid wages, and was therefore a holy man; but now he flocked south for loot, to despoil the enemies of Zion and the ever living Jehovah. There was wealth left in the South. That industry which is pathetic in the circumstance that neither flood, nor fire, nor war can wholly stay it, was not dead in the South. Though the farms had gone to waste there, and the fields were covered with weeds, and the tools and the implements

[1] Bowers' "The Tragic Era."

were mostly gone; though banks had closed, and the railways were in ruins, and the negroes were wandering about, such of them as did not still seek food and roof with their old masters—though all this, cotton was about to be raised. Piety and plunder in the person of the new capitalist, by the use of sectional hatred took over the control of Congress. The army had said that the states were back in the Union; the Johnson war resolution said that they were back in the Union; the courts, some of them at least, held that the states were back in the Union. Thaddeus Stevens and his conspirators declared that the states were out of the Union. When the former Confederate States, in acceptance of the defeat elected representatives to Congress, and the men so elected presented their credentials to the House, the Clerk, under the instruction of Stevens, refused to recognize them by omitting to read their names from the roll. They were, therefore, out of the Union, knocking to get in; and as Lee said, the North had thus turned secessionist. Then came the law of March 2, 1867, by which the Southern states were divided into five military districts, and placed under military officers who had all power over life, liberty, and property, leaving only to Johnson to pass finally upon death sentences. Before this, on December 18, 1865, with Lincoln a little more than six months in the tomb at Springfield, Stevens rose in the House and said that the Southern states should not be recognized as capable of acting in the Union until the Constitution was amended so as to make it what the framers intended. He was hinting at the XIVth Amendment which not one of the original framers of the Constitution would have looked upon except with horror, if not for itself, then for its effect upon the people at that time, who would have repudiated emphatically any interference with the police power of the states, or any central control of the matter of citizenship. For under the original Constitution there was no national citizenship, except as it was derived from state citizenship. Stevens argued that the states were to be kept out for the benefit of the Union party, by which he declared he meant the radical wing of the Republican Party.

With the division of the seceded states into military districts, treasury agents of the North swooped upon the South looking for property to confiscate. They made common cause with local thieves

THE ONE CAUSE WHICH WAS LOST 485

and stole everything they could find in the way of cotton, tobacco and corn. The troops of the North did what the politicians at Washington wanted them to do. They intimidated the Southern voters, they stuffed the ballot boxes, and when such criminal methods did not suffice to choke the voice of the South, they deliberately threw out elected candidates that defeated candidates of the Centralists might be given the offices. They established state militias composed of negroes and disreputable whites, and put their support upon the impoverished people. There were ninety-six thousand of such troops in South Carolina at one time. They lived on the public treasury, and spent their time chiefly in dominating the elections of the Republicans. Was all this not enough? No, there were some other things to be done. Regard for the Declaration of Independence, and duty to God required that the negro be given the ballot. Hence the negro was enfranchised, and, in order to make that more effectual, the whites were disfranchised. The negro did not know enough to use the ballot for his own interests; but he could be told how to use it for the Republicans and the corporations. And he was told. All this sounds like the cracking of the neck and the coiling and uncoiling of a python swallowing its prey; and in fact there was nothing left in America but the reptilian perspective.

At the very time that negro suffrage was thus forced upon the South, some Northern states under the rule of the Republicans refused the ballot to the negro. In Illinois, not until its Constitution of 1870, was the negro given equality and the vote. Of what use was the franchise to the negro? Indeed he could do nothing with his freedom. As under the Emancipation Proclamation few negroes left their masters, so now as soon as the negro saw that freedom relieved him no whit from work to earn his bread, he returned, after wandering, to the old plantation. Still all this was not enough. The Freedmen's Bureau was established, taking over the lives of the negroes to the smallest details. For this work hundreds of Federal agents were appointed who had the power to withhold from the negroes bread and roofs if they did not vote as Stevens and his associates wanted them to. Then came oath bound secret societies, so-called Union Leagues, which, by terrorism and corruption finally dominated the negroes, charging fees for their services in that behalf. The peace of despotism was on the South. Every drop of blood drawn with the lash was made to be repaid by a thousand drawn by the sword, and sucked forth by the tax-gatherer, the parasite and the thief.

These insatiable despots voted enormous bond issues, and stole the money. They planned public improvements, and voted state debts until the people staggered under fabulous burdens. The money was pocketed; the improvements were not made. Had the North become wholly maniacal? Was there no civilization left? There was neither sanity nor anything but barbarism anywhere. These desperate scoundrels and impostors, these Hebraic-Puritans and capitalists stopped at nothing. They even enacted a law in 1868 forbidding the Supreme Court from holding any of the laws passed by them to be unconstitutional; and the Supreme Court laid down. They had to do so or go to prison under the rule of the radical Republicans in Congress. It should be remembered that the Supreme Court still had members who had come over from the old days of states' rights. The system was still in its beginning, and had not been perfected, by which Federal judges were selected by the banks and the railroads. At the same time Congress was bestowing millions of dollars and millions of acres of land upon the railroads; and soon there was the feculence of the Credit Mobilier, and the cloacas of the political rings in the cities. The Union had become disintegration. There was no new birth of freedom. It was all the spawn of lowest hell. At last the Stevenses, the corporations, ceased to care for the Negro. The nausea of satiety took the country.

A greater achievement was at hand than the enforcement of the doctrine that all men are created equal. The XIVth Amendment was rammed down the throats of the South. In 1866–67, despite the horrors that they were enduring, Texas, Georgia, Florida, Alabama, North Carolina, Arkansas, Virginia, Mississippi and Louisiana refused to ratify this imperializing article; some of these states by unanimous votes. Alabama gave it only ten favorable votes; Arkansas but three, Virginia but one. But at last they had to submit. Two years later judicial slyness slipped a new enfranchisement into the capitalistic conquest. Lincoln made firebrand Chase Chief Justice of the Supreme Court in 1864, about the time that Sherman started on his march of devastation through Georgia. Later he appointed Field, of California, to the Supreme Bench.

THE ONE CAUSE WHICH WAS LOST 487

Field was originally from Connecticut, and had taken up with the Republican programs long before his elevation. In 1809 Chief Justice Marshall held that a corporation was not a citizen. In 1869 Field, with Chase as Chief Justice, held that a corporation was a citizen. Thus with the XIVth Amendment passed, the corporations had the Federal Courts for their cities of refuge; and the states became what Lincoln called them in his Indianapolis speech, nothing but counties.

Thus monopolists had the tariff and the bank, both Lincoln institutions; and the corporations, creatures of the states, rose up to despise their paternities, and to pick the pockets of their creators. So it is that today a street railway, or any public service corporation, after getting its franchise from a city in consideration of furnishing service, and at a fixed rate, may repudiate the contract in the Federal Court under the clause of the XIVth Amendment which provides that no state shall deprive any person of property without due process of law. The Supreme Court, recently, in a case where the corporation was earning more than 6% on its investment, held that it was confiscatory not to allow it to earn more; and in addition to that allowed what had been given to the corporation by the city to be added into its property upon which it should earn a dividend. This is another way of saying that it is confiscatory to make anyone pay his obligations, if he cannot conveniently afford to do so.

The Republican Party from the first was chiefly concerned with letting in a new set of thieves to the public treasury, as Douglas said in effect in the debates; but they came in under the guise of piety and humanitarianism. Reconstruction was a smoking chimney which drove rats and bats and snakes into the room of American life. And where before there had been decisions like Dred Scott, which preserved the principles of liberty and democratic government in the large, though they were tainted with the maintenance of slavery, decisions came to be thinly tinted with liberty, but fleshed with tyrannous plutocracy. It was Ironic Malice which caused the South to assert a great principle of liberty for the control of their own domestic institutions, the specific matter being the negro. It was the same Malice which let the North assert humanitarianism and liberty, but for the benefit of privilege and centralism. Life is irrational at best; but such antitheses make it next to idiotic. American jurisprudence since the War has grown as financial oligarchs would have it grow; and the churches which could invoke the wrath of God against Taney, see nothing to object to in a tariff Democrat like Chief Justice White, in a Taft satrap mind fat and well fed by privilege, or in Hughes who all his professional career helped the corporations to overreach the people. Yet none of these men is comparable in intellect and in morality to Taney, who has been written down for seventy years by the Puritan and the political impostor.

There has been a steady and increasing deterioration in the quality of the men who have filled the state and the Federal offices since the War. The United States has had no president in seven decades past who was the equal of James Monroe, and not one who for courage and ability was up to the knees of Andrew Jackson. If for this office there has been no falling off of natural talent available for service, as probably there has not been, the schemes of privileged business will not allow such men to speak and to act. If there are still men of sound principles who would be glad to lead their country, the times have been such since the War that men of American fundamental thinking could not emerge to lead and to raise their voice for a definite American culture. It takes both vision and opportunity to express it to make a great president, or a great writer. After Johnson there was Grant, who became the associate of Jay Gould, and whose administration ended in a smudge. After him was the prohibitionist Hayes, who was the beneficiary of a stolen election, and entered the White House to assert the trifling morality of banishing wine from the table. Then came Garfield and Arthur, both mediocrities of the Gilded Age. Then Cleveland whose strength was not popularly understood. His secret friends were the banks. He was the unsuspected pioneer of the gold standard at a time when the Republicans had not aroused to the immense advantage of discarding the gold and silver currency of the Constitution. McKinley, oleaginous and pious, came along with his high tariff; and after him was the picturesque Roosevelt who made a hurrah for a time with the "big stick," and the "square deal," while abandoning his free trade convictions. He had helped to maneuver McKinley into the "large policy," of colonialism; and while prosecuting the conquest of the Philippines with patriotic energy he was preaching against so-called sexual immorality. He with Hay, Page and Lodge were the Anglophiles who denounced secession with patriotic curses, but who were traitors to and betrayers of the republican principle. At the time that Roosevelt was making a menacing gesture toward the monopolists he was holding to friendly intercourse with the master corruptionists who dominated the country, and on the other hand he was denouncing Gorky for living with a woman who was not his wife. Soon came Taft, a complete failure, educated in the spurious wisdom of centralism. By this time the Constitutional doctrine of admitting a state with such a constitution as it chose to adopt had been thrown aside. Utah had to give up polygamy before being received into the holy family of the states. Arizona could not enter without discarding her provision for the recall of judges, an expedient which had been conceived out of the vast tyranny and corruption of the American judiciary. This was the Taft conception of republican government. There was Wilson, compounded of Calvinistic Toryism and Bagehot liberalism, and whose mind split into ruins. At last commercialism has had its long cry gratified. A business man is president, graduated out of trade experiences and engineering. This is what the tariff, the bank, and privilege have done to America. In the Senate there has been no man to equal Douglas either in morality or ability since he passed from the scene. His state, Illinois, for long years sent to the upper House a professional cultivator of patronage, who traded post offices for delegates, and borrowed money from appointees as payment for offices bestowed. He relied upon his facial resemblance to Abraham Lincoln to win the populace. It would be an offense to history to name him or the others. Many of them got office because they had helped to put down the "rebellion." Some of them bought their way to the Senate. Two who were elected were denied admission because of vast corruption which they resorted to in the election. In Illinois alone within thirty years two Federal judges had to resign or be impeached. The Illinois governors since the War have been men of no strength of character, no ideals, Altgeld alone excepted. A story as bad as this may be told of Indiana, of Michigan, of Pennsylvania. Since January 1, 1929, two Federal judges and five state judges of New York have faced charges of malfesance in office. All of this sounds like the pages of Thucydides who described the disintegration that came upon Greece after the Peloponnesian War. America is just as rotten at the top as it is at the bottom. The corrupt judge and senator, the monopolist in big-business are brothers in arms of the racketeer and the gunman.

Whitman, writing of America in 1870, said: "I say we had best look our times and lands searchingly in the face, like a physician diagnosing some deep disease. Never perhaps was there more hollowness at heart than at present, and here in the United States. The depravity of the business classes of our country is not less than has been supposed, but infinitely greater. The official services of America, national, state, and municipal, in all their branches and departments, except the judiciary, are saturated in corruption, bribery, falsehood, maladministration; and the judiciary is tainted." He also said, "A lot of churches, sects, etc., the most dismal of phantasms I know, usurp the name of religion." All this is true today; but there is something more now. Piety and hypocrisy have become religion and legalism. America has evolved the Baptist and the Methodist. Either is perfectly correct in his own life; he does nothing crooked in his own dealings, but in office he serves the system which despoils the land, and does it within the law which has been built up by the Ben Butlers the Jay Goulds and the Mark Hannas. Today we have a Christian republic; no slavery, no polygamy, no saloons; only monopolists, bureaucrats, corrupt courts, imbecile Senates obeying Wall street, fanatics, clergymen who thrive on the crumbs that fall from Dives' table. Under these are the helpless millions who cannot make their votes effectual, and who are compelled to surrender the fruits of their toil to drones and exploiters.

Whitman saw great cities about him; but what were the cities of those days compared to the cities of this? When he was writing *Democratic Vistas*, the South was in ruins. Today the skyscraper towers in Atlanta, in New Orleans, in the cities of Texas, and in Oklahoma. Such cities for size and wealth and buildings were never seen before in the world. Some may think when looking at them that America has survived every calamity and waste of the War. Indeed these buildings and ostentatious prosperities are the result of the War, just as fat mushrooms may spring up after a storm.

THE ONE CAUSE WHICH WAS LOST 491

A marble stable might be built to house donkeys and swine. The question is, therefore, what is inside these towers, and these palaces built even in places like Austin, and along the Pacific shore near Carmel? There is little or nothing in them. They are owned, for the most part, by men who made their money out of patents, war contracts, the stock market, real estate, the tariff and what not. There they sit amid their splendors dull and damned, and plotting to perpetuate the regimes by which they came to prosperity. This might possibly be called a civilization; it is not a culture. What true and beautiful thing can grow in such a soil? It takes truths to make men, even men of gifts. In a mass of lies and falsities, good men cannot arise, they cannot think or act. The ruling voters and leaders of today carry the Bible in one hand and the drum in the other; they measure with the golden rule, and meet judgment with the sword. Lincoln was the first president to invest the government with Christianity, and to put its poisonous inoculation deep down in the flesh of the Republic. The Mexican war was half pagan, and therefore had the quality of honesty. We wanted land and we took it. The War between the states was for God, and Lincoln made it so. But there was nothing in Lincoln's philosophy which forbade riches and privileges; rather the contrary. Hence he laid the foundation for a state where carpenters and rail splitters have nothing to say now in America.

Phillips and his kind, finding themselves balked by the laws and the Constitution, hooted at them, and, like unmannerly boors, tramped with their muddy boots the tapestry of the halls of the republic, on missions of irreverence and plunder. Lincoln himself, thwarted by the authority of Congress and the Courts, hawked at them, as he had accused men of subverting the Declaration; or he twisted them out of form, and their original meaning by the artifice of his sophistry. What can the common man do against an economic despotism? He must live, and he cannot live without submitting himself to those who own the courts and the Congresses, and the president, as well as the officers of the state governments. A sordid and vulgar spirit has taken possession of the masses far beyond what Whitman saw in them in his day. What are they to do, when they see money everywhere magnified, and the power which money gives dominating every department of American life? If the people cannot save themselves, as seems to be the case, who is there to save them in the present condition of economic and spiritual life in America? If they cannot be saved what shall save America from slipping down heavy and dull into the depths where all aborted hopes are lost? All this condition of affairs was foreseen by men seventy years ago; we were warned against it all through the Gilded Age, all through the days when the Grand Army of the Republic carried the elections for men like Benjamin Harrison, and almost carried it for spurious characters like James G. Blaine. Now we have crime commissions to deal with the bank robber, the bandit, the bootlegger, and the gunman. These depraved men are the natural offspring of the criminal classes at the top of American life. Who is so unreflecting that he does not know that these desperate malefactors of the alleys and the purlieus are well aware of the corruption of American life, and that what they do is in imitation of the great men of finance and business? It is little to say that the so-called criminal classes read the newspapers and the magazines, as well as some books, and that they know America as well as anyone, so far as their own angle of vision is concerned. They are not ignorant of the fact that McKinley stole the Philippine Islands, that the Boxer rebellion was stirred up by thieves extorting extra territoriality. They can see that piety and the pocketbook have been made allies and inseparable comrades in arms. Why be industrious and honest in such a civilization? is the question that they have answered for themselves with the bomb and the gun. They know too that they are hunted by officers whom the best thought of the country denounces as barbarians and murderers.

Aside from the monopolist, who now rules the country, if indeed there be anyone who is not both a monopolist and a churchman? Plainly the churches rule the country. The prohibitionist of today was the abolitionist of 1860. In 1851 Neal Dow brought about prohibition in Maine. Douglas in the debates half forecast the possibility of centralization with reference to a social and domestic question like this, when debating with Lincoln, who was unconsciously laying the foundation for a demoralizing tyranny such as national prohibition has become. When the infamous Butler went on his New Orleans expedition, Neal Dow was with him as a brigadier-general. Later, in 1876, Dow ran for president on the prohibition ticket, polling some 10,000 votes in the United States. His

THE ONE CAUSE WHICH WAS LOST 493

platform was the national observance of the Sabbath, the use of the Bible in the public schools, as a "text book of the purest morality." But on the other hand the public schools must be kept "from the control of every religious sect." Such was the thinking of Neal Dow. Indoctrinate the children with the Bible, but save them from imbibing minor tenets like forms of baptism, transubstantiation, and election! Just make them Christians! Neal Dow and his kind were the fathers of the present crafty imbeciles who run the Anti-Saloon League and the Federal Council of the Churches of Christ drawing sustenance from Hebraic-Puritanism and the Bible. These two organizations are interlocking in their officers and committeemen. Corporation lawyers, bishops and clergymen run these organizations with their lobbies at Washington, and with their terrorisms directed against senators and congressmen. Not only are these bodies and their policies supported by Moravians, Primitive Methodists, Seventh Day Baptists, Campbellites and by Lutherans, by all the weird cohorts of diseased imaginations and corrupted logics, but by the Presbyterians and the Methodists. No one of the religious sects stands apart from them except the Catholics and the Episcopalians. Like the abolitionists of old, these madmen care nothing, as they know nothing, about liberty, about constitutional government. They set prohibition enforcers to shoot down men; and then they have so far terrorized the courts that these murderers are exonerated. Or else, as recently happened, a Federal Circuit Court of Appeals, when passing upon the murderer of a duck-hunter, held that the pneumonia which followed the gunshot wound may have killed the man, and not the bullet. These churchmen have struck down the right of trial by jury; they have helped to wipe out the rule that a man is entitled to be tried in the district where the crime is alleged to have been committed; with the monopolist, they have numbed the freedom of the press and of speech. They are coadjutors in the intricate censorships over America by which literary expression is denied that liberty out of which only great work can come. And they advocate the calling out of the Federal Army to enforce a law that millions of people despise and mean to violate. The words of Washington mean nothing to them, who said in his Farewell Address: "The spirit of encroachment tends to consolidate the powers of all the departments of the government in one, and thus to create, whatever the form of the government, a real despotism." Lincoln is one of their patron saints. For not only was Lincoln a temperance lecturer, but he was for the evangelical Bible, and for the use of the army in a holy cause. Yet with all this power of fanaticism built up against the day to be, the colleges of America are pouring forth thousands of good minds every year, who have read the history of America, and of liberty; and who know the notable American characters, not as they have been made by the mythologist, but as they actually were in life in their time and place. The Lincoln which emerged out of the devoted suppressions of Hay and Nicolay, clothed in the partisan eulogiums, and mystical acclaims of men bent upon giving to Lincoln and to what he did the sacred legitimacy of God-designed and God-created events, has ceased to convince these minds which are coming into the work of ordering America. They know Lincoln as he was; and they have studied what he did, and why he did it, and what the American civilization was which for the most part rejected him at first, then fell victim to his usurpations, though trying to repel them, then was overcome by the forces of business and religion, until the unspeakable sordidness and hypocrisy of Reconstruction fouled the whole blood of the land. The War between the States demonstrated that salvation is not of the Jews, but of the Greeks. The World War added to this proof; for Wilson did many things that Lincoln did, and with Lincoln as authority for doing them. Perhaps it will happen again that a few men, deciding what is a cause of war, and what is necessary to its successful prosecution, may, as Lincoln and Wilson did, seal the lips of discussion and shackle the press; but no less the ideal of a just state, which has founded itself in reason and in free speech, will remain. Negro slavery is a small evil compared to that in which, to paraphrase Euripides, men cannot speak their thoughts.

Our greatest Americans are Jefferson, Whitman and Emerson; and the praise that has been bestowed on Lincoln is a robbery of these, his superiors. Armed with the theology of a rural Methodist, Lincoln crushed the principles of free government. Though not a church member, nor a credal convert, he evolved out of the superstition of Pigeon Creek into a career in which he dramatized Jehovah as a celebrant of the horrible doctrines of sin and atonement.

THE ONE CAUSE WHICH WAS LOST 495

Tragic pity and comprehensiveness did not belong to his mind; and thus his thinking went no farther than to say, "Thus saith the Lord." He saw Jehovah ruling the insane scene because he rules it. And if it could be said that his nature gave him a choice of action between compassion on the one hand and Jehoviac sternness on the other he elected the latter as his rôle.

No great literature has come out of the War between the States. There are two reasons for this: the preëminent theme which the war suggests is that liberty was dishonored and destroyed. That cannot be chosen for poetry or drama because the civilization that has risen out of the war does not believe this, and could not understand its exposition if it were given. The second reason is that a literary culture like that of Lowell, and Longfellow, founded chiefly on the Bible, glimpses but superficially, and only in instances of particular injustice and suffering, the infinite and profound currents of life in societies and in nations, which, largely comprehended, show the fateful tragedy of this world of men flowing everywhere mysteriously. The profound pity and understanding necessary to portray the War has not yet come to the American mind; and thus the life of the nation which may be seen in the mirror of its national poetry has had no reflect better than derivative performances like Lowell's Ode which is evangelical and insipid. Appomatox was as tragic to the South as Salamis was glorious to Athens; but with Salamis the victory was on the side of men of incomparable genius. With Appomatox the victory was on the side of business and hypocrisy; and thus there was no better god than Jehovah to whom Whittier could raise his hymns. Added to what the War did to American institutions must be set down what all the sacrifice and heroism of the War on both sides did not do for the arts, for literature, for the vision of the American mind. Not only could no great poem like the *Persians* be written in celebration of the victory of the North; but no literature of a lesser order worthy to be called literature came from it, or could conceivably come from it, so far as the North was concerned. The South was too spent to record her woes, even if writers had lived there equal to the task. Glory and inspiration came to England with the defeat of the Spanish Armada, refreshing and thrilling the national genius like a fresh breeze from the sea. America had only the songs of Wall Street, and the prayers of Beecher, though the War was waged on a scale more gigantic than any before it. The creative mind drooped and sickened contemplating the monstrous revenges and thievings of the sons of God who ravished the South during reconstruction.

> What spring of good hath seercraft ever made
> Up from the dark to flow?
> 'Tis but a weaving of words, a craft of woe
> To make mankind afraid,[1]

sang Æschylus in the *Agamemnon*. America has been afraid ever since the war, and has been more and more ruled by seercraft. Out of this the exploiter has grown fat, for his best accomplice is the religious impostor, the church, in a word. The epic grandeur of the American story lies in this: that a few free spirits conceived a new state, making it hereditary to the tested idealism of the ages; and set it to follow a career of justice to the common man upon a fresh soil, where the poisonous growths of the troubled lands of the old times had not come. After this, and as if in sublime malice, the choking weeds of Hebraic-Puritanism were sown; and thus the evils of empire and ancient privileges began to thrive, scarcely before the new wheat was started. Ages may be required for creative vision to stand externally to this field and its epos, and to see the work of Lincoln, whose only literacy was out of the Bible, and who developed an oratory from it, inspired by its artifice of emotional reiteration, and equipped with its sacred curses and its dreadful prophecies, its appeals to moralities where there was no thought, no real integrity. With this manner of molding a people events of a materialistic basis have coöperated to hypnotize an America which was intended to see clearly and without deception or self-deception. Lincoln's fame rests upon this unreal mood, this insubstantial structure; and the question is can it last? If the final aspect of the tragedy prove to be that he became the symbol of America, though he was the ruin of its character and its primal hope, will it avail that he was the influential pattern of its spiritual creation? It will avail only in the sense that he was fated to make world

[1] Gilbert Murray's translation.

THE ONE CAUSE WHICH WAS LOST 497

tragedy for the contemplation of some recurring Æschylus, with genius great enough to sing the heights and the depths of the insoluble ways of Time. There was first the chance that Machiavelli and John Wesley would not be the predominant influence in the New World; but that the wise and true spirits of the ages which have overlooked the fate of men would, out of their wisdom and compassion, guide the life of the New Atlantis. From Jeffereson onward, for more than fifty years, republican principles, guarded and nourished by state sovereignty, by government of the people in the hands of the people, kept the too violent winds of descending conspiracies from blowing out the altar fires of liberty. This was true, though there were two Whig victories during that time. But all the while a patient, secret, self-conscious influence was gathering power, appropriating it from the people and from the states, and storing it in a central government for the purposes of business and money, and under the guise of law and order, of religion, and even of liberty. The election of Harrison first and then of Taylor were but gestures toward centralization; for Tyler, who quickly succeeded to the presidency, was a Democrat, and stood for Democratic policies. What happened to many minds of democratic quality was that the sentimentalism of a disproportioned and distorted morality lowered the strength of the level-headedness which belonged to them as guardians of the principles of a confederated republic. This was true, for instance, of the Democrat, Andrew Johnson, from whom, indeed, little else could be expected, considering his intellectual equipment. But with Lincoln all was different. From the first he was a centralist, a privilegist, an adherent of the non-principled Whig Party, which laid the foundation of the Republican Party of 1854, and which has grown into the reckless, ignorant and unscrupulous imperial organization of the present time. It has followed the line of its inheritance. It started with no theory of the government, with no principles for its administration, save to tax and to use the people, to absorb the vitality of the states in order to have all powers in the hands of central groups, courts and bureaus; and it is triumphant now with its armies and its navies, with its amalgamation of wealth and government. The history of America since the day of Lincoln has been nothing but a filling in of the outlines of implied powers, which Lincoln did more than even Hamilton and Webster to vitalize; it has been nothing but further marches into the paths which he surveyed toward empire and privilege.

THE END

REVIEWS

H. L. Mencken
New York Herald Tribune
February 8, 1931

Andrew Nelson Lytle
Virginia Quarterly Review
October, 1931

From the *New York Herald Tribune* "Books," February 8, 1931.
©Copyright 1931 by The New York Times Company. Reprinted with permission.

The Birth of Order
by H. L. Mencken

Mr. Masters, it appears, has his doubts about Lincoln. He is ready to admit the romantic glamour of the martyr, but he is unable to find much dignity in the man. The Lincoln that he sets before us indeed lived and died a second-rater—a sublime one, perhaps, but still a second-rater. There is no evidence that he brought anything more noble to either the law or politics than an urgent yearning to get on. He was never really a leader, even of the causes that fate made him lead. The war upon slavery was conceived, planned and executed by other men, and not a few of them were clearly better men. Lincoln, to the last moment, hung back. But destiny concentrated all the spotlights upon him at the instant of victory, and if he had no other talent he had at least a great capacity for dramatizing such situations. No other American, in fact, ever surpassed him there—not Jackson, or Jefferson, or Washington. So the schoolbooks are now full of Abe, and viewing him realistically becomes a grave indecorum, and he seems likely to outlast all of them, including even Washington.

Mr. Masters does not concern himself specifically with the origins and growth of the Lincoln Legend: that business, he is aware, has been very effectively attended to by Mr. Lloyd Lewis. What interests him mainly is the concatenation of events which made Lincoln possible, and the accidents whereby so obscure and irresolute a man came to play a heroic role. On form, he should have been something quite different from what he came to be. The natural tendency of a poor young man in the '40s was to follow Jackson, for Jackson had been poor himself and was the prophet and paladin of equality. But Lincoln, after his trip down the Mississippi in 1828, seems to have got some doubts about equality. What he began to want was superiority—in public place, in popularity and renown, above all in social dignity—and to the getting of it he devoted the rest of his life. He became, in brief, both a social pusher and a chronic job-seeker. In the first character he made a preposterous and almost intolerable marriage but still one that helped him on. In the second he turned his back on the Jacksonian tradition and allowed himself to be carried out by the tide that was eventually to wash away the old Republic altogether and leave in its place a plutocratic oligarchy hard to distinguish from the Roman.

The best part of Mr. Masters's book is devoted to the way in which this change was effected, under Lincoln's hand and largely with his aid. His most memorable feat, perhaps, was his appointment of the Lord God Jehovah to the honorary chairmanship of the Republican National Committee. Lincoln himself was anything but a good Christian. In his youth he had been celebrated in his circle as a scoffer and we have the authority of Mrs. Lincoln for believing that he retained his doubts to the end of his life. But with the beginning of the war he began to use pious phrases, and by the time he wrote the Emancipation Proclamation he had taken God into full partnership, and was writing like an Old Testament prophet. It was soon manifest that this was a device of tremendous effectiveness, and all the other American Presidents have employed it ever since.

Mr. Masters considers this curious *volte face* at some length, but can come to no conclusion as to its causes. It may be that Lincoln, facing the dreadful burdens of the war, found his agnosticism insufficient to sustain him, and so turned back transiently to the simple faith of his people. This is possible, but somehow it seems improbable, for agnostics usually find their unbelief ample for their needs. It seems to me more likely that Lincoln was simply swept along emotionally by the Christian fervors of the time. Certainly he was not the first to speak of the war as a holy crusade. The whole North, in fact, rang with hosannas and hallelujahs, and the clergy took an even bolder hand in public affairs than they do today. My guess is that Lincoln, like many another skeptic, succumbed to the circumambient poetry without noticing that it was also theology, and hence by his principles unsound. He was, in truth, always carried away by poetry, and in the Gettysburg Address, he took millions along with him.

Of more importance, perhaps, was his assault upon the Constitution, and especially upon the Bill of Rights. Since the overflow of the alien and sedition acts in the first years of the century the Constitution had been in full force and effect, in time of war as well as in time of peace. It had survived unscathed the War of 1812 and the War with Mexico. But Lincoln was scarcely in office before he began to subordinate it to military measures, and by the end of the Civil War it was in such a state of decay that it has never recovered. Every guaranty of the Bill of Rights was heaved overboard. The American people, North and South, went into the war as citizens of their respective states, they came out subjects of the United States. And what they thus lost they have never got back. No President since, not even Grover Cleveland, has ever followed Jefferson. They have all tried to be Lincolns.

Mr. Masters believes that this double transformation—of the old American liberties into a series of oppressions mitigated by privileges and of the old American distrust of theology into the hard dogmatism of a national religion—may be traced directly to Lincoln's door. It is true, of course, that he was not the prime mover, for he was seldom the prime mover in anything; he preferred to drift along amiably, gathering principles as he proceeded. But he was at least the chief instrument of the change, and surely he made no effort to oppose it. Thus Mr. Masters, as an incorrigible Democrat and a lifelong worshiper of Jefferson, is constrained to put him considerably lower than the schoolbooks. He had some fine qualities, and he probably served his troubled hour as well as any other could have served it, but if history is to be anything save a puerile kind of poetry, then the historians must remember also his gross and lamentable weaknesses and the evil that he did.

Lincoln the Man reveals a scholarship that many of Mr. Masters's admirers, I suppose, have never suspected. There is little new in it in the way of facts, but many of the interpretations of what is generally known are novel and arresting. The chapters devoted to the complicated politics in the period between the Missouri Compromise and the Civil War are especially illuminating, for in this dark field, it turns out, Mr. Masters is something of an expert, so his elucidations have much value. He is thoroughly at home, too, in discussing the Lincoln-Douglas debates, and his leaning toward Douglas is supported by very plausible argument. But the best part of the book, I think, comes at the end, after Lincoln has gone to martyrdom. Seldom have I read so brilliant a picture of the decay of the old American spirit; with its horrible consequences in politics, business and daily life. The writing here is so eloquent as to be genuinely moving. And under it there is visible the fine earnestness of an American who really loves his country. It is not orthodox doctrine that Mr. Masters preaches, as orthodoxy runs among us today, but I can find no article in it that Jefferson would have questioned.

The style is adequate to the subject—in the main quite simple, but with sufficient resources of rhetoric when they are needed . . . . Altogether, the work has many merits, and deserves to be read. There is no trace in it of the facile iconoclasm that is now so popular among amateur biographers and historians. When it comes to Lincoln Mr. Masters is surely no amateur. He has been soaked in the subject since his schooldays, and he brings to it the rich stores of an alert and highly independent mind . . . .

From *The Virginia Quarterly Review*, October, 1931.

The Lincoln Myth
By Andrew Nelson Lytle

It was a long time before the four years of battling between the North and the South could be regarded through other than romantic eyes. Only recently has certain historical research demanded a reinterpretation of the struggle in the terms of modern industrial

America. The reasons for this are very strong. The victors, as they were constructing the myths which would sustain their power, managed to withdraw all the virtue into their camp. The seceding states, as a very important part of these myths, were painted in the most uncomplimentary colors. They were rebels, slave-drivers, stubborn, ambitious, bent on destroying a great nation for a purely selfish reason. In the face of this the Southern people kept silent and went about their business of binding together the fragments of their wrecked establishment. They did not argue; they made no defense when they were charged as the criminals responsible for the catastrophe; for, having failed in the final argument of battle, they appreciated the futility of saying anything further. But at last many of the generals and lawyer statesmen deserted their plantations and moved to town to become bank presidents or to sit on directors' boards of railroads. The next generation also, lacking the memory which had sustained their fathers' aloofness, made overtures to the industrially-growing North. In this way the strongest myth of all, the myth that pretends the Union is preserved, slowly spread South. So, North and South, it was impossible to discuss the issues of the war realistically, to discover in its wearisome marches and bitter engagements the distress and confusion of our commercial empire. It remained a thing fixed, apart, a tragic interlude, a skeleton in the closet hanging in a museum.

And it is this myth which Mr. Masters, in his *Lincoln the Man*, so thoroughly destroys. His method of destruction is indirect, but it is indirection with a purpose. By showing the true character of the Northern war president, he automatically demolishes the omniscient, great-hearted, simple, democratic, Jeffersonian rail-splitter who from his earliest days swore to do away with slavery and who loved the Union above all things.

If Lincoln loved the Union, he was responsible, more than any man, for its destruction, for he consciously violated the constitution in calling out armies for the reduction of the cotton States. The war was not a war of slavery versus freedom; it was a war between those who preferred a federated nation to those who preferred a confederation of sovereign states. Slavery was the ink thrown into the pool to confuse the issue. Lincoln, who had always been a Hamiltonian, saw that Hamilton's principles finally triumphed. As the great body of people, particularly in the Northwest, believed in the Jeffersonian state, it was necessary to make the Lincoln myth in order to cover the growing centralization which would make it possible for the trusts and corporations to gobble up the substance and liberties of the people.

Mr. Masters has made this unusually clear, and his biography has the strength and order of a good lawyer's brief. Its unity is unusual for a work of this kind, spreading to the minutest details. Indeed, at times he follows the central thesis too closely, more closely than one can believe nature ever did. But in the end the facts are believed and the interpretation accepted. One feels that no high court of opinion would deny them; only the jury that believes the myth could render a negative judgment.

The Lincoln that gradually appears from Mr. Masters' pen is the antithesis of all that we have been taught to believe he was. He was secretive, cold, and humorous as the wilderness understood humor. Without any creative ability, he possessed a strong poetic sense which allowed him to take other men's thoughts and improve them. This quality was one of the secrets of his power over audiences. His immediate family was not strong or gifted enough to grow out of its pioneering habits. Apparently young Lincoln was strongly affected by this. He was ashamed of his background and, years later, refused to be with his father on his death bed. This desire to live away from his family stirred an ambition to distinguish himself. He lacked, however, the physical and mental vigor which ambition requires, and the author makes it clear that his long years of poverty were due to this cause and not to a lack of opportunity. From the beginning, out of this desire to rise in the world, he attached himself to the Whig Party, the moneyed political wing. He could not, therefore, have been a friend of the people. He lacked the character or the philosophical clarity to understand the connotation of the American theory of the Union between sovereign states. He was an opportunist in the purest sense, that the end justifies the means. This, added to his native gifts, made him the masterly politician he was, and the author makes much of his reliance on *Chitty on Pleading*, a book full of intellectual cunning and one which advises the defensive, thereby placing the burden of proof on the opponent. Lincoln's tactics with the Fort Sumter affair show how well he learned the rules. Indeed, the influence of this book can be traced through all his public life. "His mind worked better," writes Mr. Masters, "when he was exposing what he considered a fallacy than when he was constructing an original thesis."

There can never be any question as to this political acumen. He refused to commit himself definitely on any principle, but always left some loophole through which he could crawl. He did this so successfully that it was almost impossible for Douglas to convince the Black Republican audiences that Lincoln had refused to accept their platform while running for senator on it. A man who would like to advance himself in public life should know the tricks, but if he is a noble man or a great statesman, he also orders his life according to some underlying principle or philosophy of life. This Lincoln did not do. It is fascinating to follow the change in his speeches as he approached Washington and a declaration of war on the Southern country. If there was any underlying impetus to his actions, it was only this desire to distinguish himself. From this it follows that his conception of the American Union was, since he was too lazy to study its beginnings, a geographical one, that is, one in which he and others like him could rise to power. But a Union is not geography. It is a political concept.

A people lives by myths, religious and social. And it is always a dangerous thing to tamper with them. But the Lincoln myth is definitely a bad myth, and Mr. Masters deserves great credit for shattering it, for it helps to sustain the industrial imperialism which was made possible by Lincoln's successful prosecution of the war. "From 1865 to 1900," says Mr. Masters, "there were fast and systematic policies of overthrowing the liberty of America, and the forms through which it could be expressed, for the benefit of money oligarchies and Hebraic-Puritanism. Taking him for what he really was, there is no irony in the role that Lincoln played in the revolution which Calhoun foresaw along political lines. Calhoun did not prognosticate, as no man could, the paralysis that was to come to the spiritual life of America as the result of the combined efforts of imperialists and fanatics. It is only by considering Lincoln superficially, by mistakenly accepting him as the rail-splitter and the democrat, that any surprise can be felt that he played the part of the destroyer of the American system which had been created by men who tried to make a land all free out of the fresh conditions of a new world."

Index

Abell, Mrs. Bennett, 49, 59
Abolition. *See* Slavery
Abolition Party, 101
Abolitionist Republicans. *See* Republican Party
Abolitionists, activities, 40, 175; condemn Compromise of 1850, 195; attack upon Douglas, 208, 209; reply of Douglas, 210; handle Dred Scott case, 253, 292; after-war plunder of the South, 483. *See also* Hebraic-Puritan spirit
Adams, John, quoted, 158
Adams, John Quincy, 25, 215, 340; advocated purchase of Texas, 93; amendment to Arkansas Bill, 175; quoted on right of secession, 336
Æschylus, quoted, 496
Alamo, battle of the, 94
Alaskan purchase, 364
Alien and Sedition Laws, Adams responsible for, 340
Allen, Charles, in Armstrong case, 133, 134
Altgeld, John P., 489
Almanac case, Armstrong trial, 132, 135
Amendments to Constitution. *See* Constitution
American colonies, history: beginning of Union, 320
American life, corruption in, 489; rule by monopolists, 490; by churches, 492
American Party, 200, 216
American pharisaism, 288. *See also* Hebraic-Puritan spirit
Andersonville military prison, 425
Angle, Paul M., *new Letters and Papers of Lincoln,* 75
Antietam, battle of, 438
Anti-Federalists, 328; delegates won in New York, 332
Anti-Masonic Party, 215
Anti-Nebraska partisans, 238, 248; convention of, 236
Anti-Saloon League, 493
Anti-slavery activities. *See* Slavery
"Appeal of the Independent Democrats in Congress to the People of the United States," 203, 230; excerpts, 209
Arizona, lost to the South, 176
Arkansas, bill for admission into Union, 175; secession of, 398
Armstrong, Duff, trial of, 129-135
Armstrong, Hannah, 129, 375; kindness to Lincoln, 131, 135; asks him to defend son, 131
Armstrong, Jack, 32, 129, 135
Armstrong, John, 129; story of Duff Armstrong trial, 130, 134
Army, Confederate, devotion of, 438, 442
Army, Federal, Lincoln's plans for raising, 389, 396; standing army, statistics, 396; call for 75,000 militia, 397; further increases: call for 42,034 volunteers, 399; governors offer state troops to Lincoln, 401; legal use of, 402; governors aid in raising militia, 431; call for volunteers resisted: draft conscription, 432; riots and evasions, 433; despotism of Northern commanders, 439
Arnold family of Rhode Island, 36
Arrests, military. *See* Habeas corpus, suspension of writ of: military prisoners
Arthur, Chester A., 488
Articles of Confederation, provision for taxation, 223; formulated: movements to amend, 322; whether a constitution or a compact, 323; preamble, 325
Articles of Union and Confederation, principle of levying taxes, 222
Ashmore, Gideon M., 90
Ashmun, George, 369; at Chicago convention, 364
Athenians, slavery, 157
Atlanta, burning of, 456
Atlantic Monthly, 455; spurious Ann Rutledge letters, 48
Atlas, 106

INDEX

Bailey's *Etymological Dictionary,* 21
Baker, Edward D., Lincoln's attempt to take delegation from, 48, 72, 74, 82; Mexican War, 84
Bancroft, George, 433
Bank at Springfield, 37, 38
Bank of Augusta against Earle, 334
Bank of the United States, 81, 245, 248, 252, 324; Lincoln's support of, 31, 34, 446
Banks, Nathaniel P., 422
Banks. *See also* National banks
Banks, state, injured by national bank acts of 1863 and 1864, 447
Barings of London, Webster's reply to, 335
Barn Burners, 101, 103, 216
Bateman, Newton, Lincoln's talk with, 152
Bates, Edward, appointed to cabinet, 385; on provisioning Fort Sumter, 393, 394
Beard, Charles A., *Economic Interpretation of the Constitution,* quoted, 160; cited, 332
Beauregard, Pierre G. T., 421
Beecher, Henry Ward, quoted on Union, 195
Beecher Bibles, 229
Bell, John I., votes polled, 371
"Benedict Arnold" Douglas, 197, 211. *See also* Douglas, Stephen A.
Benton, Thomas Hart, 187; aids Pacific railroad, 199; campaign for Senate, 200
Berry, William F., 30
Berry and Lincoln, 30
Beveridge, Albert J., *Abraham Lincoln,* cited, 1, 7, 11, 64, 88, 104, 193, 317; quoted, 203
Bible, Lincoln's reading of, 21, 116, 149, 496; a cause of Civil War, 173; and slavery, 271, 272, 310; a cause of corruption of thinking, 482
"Bible and the Drum, The," 474
Bigler, William, 387
Bixby letter, 153, 444
Black Hawk War, Lincoln in, 29, 31, 43, 60
Blackstone, *Commentaries on the Laws of England,* quoted, 409
Blaine, James G., 434, 492
Blair, Francis Preston, mission to see Jefferson Davis, 462, 467
Blair, Montgomery, as counsel for Dred Scott, 255; appointed to cabinet, 385; on provisioning Fort Sumter, 394
Blockade of ports, Lincoln's proclamation, 399; legal questions involved, 404; Webster and Earl Derby quoted on, 405; international complications, 406; Lincoln draws back from, 407, 424
"Bloody shirt," 192
Bloomington state convention, 237
Blow, Taylor, buys Dred Scott family, 262
Bollman and Swartout case, cited, 410
Booth, John Wilkes, hears Lincoln's last speech: analysis of madness of, 475; kills Lincoln, 477
Boston Liberator, 353
Botts, John Minor, 374
Brayman, Mason, 124
Breckenridge, John Cabell, votes polled, 371; denies doctrine of necessity, 420
Breese, Sidney, 178
Brooks, Preston Smith (Bully), attacks Sumner, 228, 241
Brougham, Lord, on privateering, 406
Brown, B. Gratz, calls convention to oppose Lincoln, 448
Brown, John, 2, 455; raids and crimes, 230; Harper's Ferry enterprise, 349; false charges against, 354
Browning, Orville Hickman, 108, 237, 238, 358; Republican platform, 239
Browning, Mrs. Orville Hickman, Lincoln's letter about Mary Owens, 50; excerpts, 53
Bryant, Anthony, 90
Bryant, Jane, 90
Bryant, William Cullen, 88; at Cooper Institute meeting: introduces Lincoln, 35, 311, 347
Buchanan, James, 136, 295, 373; accused of conspiracy in Dred Scott case, 261, 290; quoted, 262; warfare upon Douglas, 277, 312; Douglas's reply to, 279
Bull Run, battle of, 421
"Bully Brooks," 228
Burnside, Ambrose E., 154, 426, 441; arrest of Vallandigham, 423
Burr, Aaron, 77, 408
Burt, A., amendment to Oregon bill, 176
Business. *See* Corporations: Economic factors
Butler, Benjamin F., 412, 438; capture

INDEX

of New Orleans: despotism, 439; Lincoln's reaction toward, 440
Butler, Mrs. and Mrs. William, 67
Butterfield, Justin, 117
Byron, George Noel Gordon Byron, Lord, 73

Cabin life, 15
Calhoun, John, 34; at Lecompton convention, 277
Calhoun, John Caldwell, 28, 162, 170, 179, 181, 184, 311, 317, 341, 351, 450; resolutions on slavery issues, text, 177; on the Union and slavery, quoted, 183; on the Constitution as a compact, quoted, 341; maintains states are suable, 342; most intellectual statesman: sees ruin in consolidation of power, 443
California, slavery, 176; constitution: admission to the Union, 181, 187; a free state, 189
Cameron, John, 47
Cameron, Simon, promised place in cabinet: votes received at Chicago convention, 367; difficulties over appointment of, 374; appointed to cabinet, 382, 385; on provisioning Fort Sumter, 392; orders arrests in Maryland, 422
Camp meeting orgy described by Helm, 13
Campbell, John A., acts for Confederate commissioners, 395; at Hampton Roads conference, 464, 469; receives warning to South against farther hostilities, 474
Canisius, Theodore, 359
Capitalism, an outcome of the Civil War, 419; profits by war, 445
Carlyle, Thomas, quoted, 456
Cartwright, Peter, 85, 86
Cass, Lewis, 101, 102, 178, 187
Catron, John, Dred Scott case, 258
Centralization, Lincoln a centralist and privilegist, 3, 497; as motive back of negro freedom, 320; the Constitution an instrument of, 159, 328, 332; Southern statesmen see danger in consolidation of power, 443
Chaffee, Calvin Clifford, 253, 292; sells Dred Scott family, 262
Chaffee, Mrs. Calvin Clifford, makes bill of sale of Dred Scott, 254; sells Scott family, 262

Chancellorsville, battle of, 441
Charles I, Lincoln in position of, 399, 400
Charleston, Webster on blockading the port of, 405
Chase, Salmon P., 123, 204, 211, 399; on slavery, quoted, 195; "Appeal of the Independent Democrats in Congress . . ." 203, 209, 230; career: attack upon Douglas, 208; votes received at Chicago convention, 367; appointed to cabinet, 385; speech at Peace Congress, 386; on provisioning Fort Sumter, 392, 394; plan for raising money: bank acts of 1863 and 1864, 447; made Chief Justice, 486; holds a corporation a citizen, 487
Cheever, George B., calls convention to oppose Lincoln, 448
Chevalier, Michael, *Society, Manners and Politics in the United States,* cited, 444
Chicago, attitude toward Douglas and Fugitive Slave Law, 191; as terminal for Pacific railroad, 200; mob treatment of Douglas, 211
Chicago convention. See Republican Party
Chicago Historical Society, 88
Chicago Times, suspended, 400
Chicago Tribune, 240, 261, 266, 288, 312; supports Lincoln for president, 356; influence in making the war, 431
Chicago University, founded by Douglas, 117, 314
Chitty on Pleading, 33
Choate, Rufus, 105, 192, 234; quoted, 232
Christ. See Jesus
Christian republic, America a, 490, 491
Churches, opposition to Lincoln, 43, 74, 152; and slavery, 152, 261, 272; rule America, 492; support prohibition, 493; accomplices of the exploiter, 496
Civil War, causes, 173, 179, 203, 207, 329, 479; forecasts of, 229, 234; Lincoln's usurpations of power, 383, 389, 398, 399, 407, 414; efforts to prevent, 386, 420; South wrongly blamed for commencing, 395; nature of, 397; contest more fundamental than slavery, 442; an ethnological struggle, 443; wealth and tariff as result of, 445; plans to

INDEX

end, discussed by Blair and Davis, 462, 467; Hampton Roads conference, 464-470; end of, 473; rejoicing in North, 474; no great literature as result of, 495. *See also* Army: Navy

Clay, Henry, 25, 26, 32, 94, 95, 101, 113, 184, 229, 311; Lincoln a follower of, 24, 26, 31; quoted, 162; compromise measures, 174, 181, 187; position on slavery, 181; Lincoln's eulogy on, excerpt, 194; Lincoln's admiration of, 310

Clay, James B., 232

Clay Bill. *See* Compromises of 1820 and 1850

Cleveland, Grover, 427, 488

Cobb, Howell, elected speaker, 181

Cochrane, General, nominated for vice-presidency, 448

Codding, Ichabod, 247, 266; organizes Republicans in Illinois, 215; attempts to place Lincoln on committee, 216

Codding platform, 268. *See also* Republican party

Cogsdale, Isaac, 45

Colonies, slavery in, 38, 158; history of: beginning of Union, 320

Colonization of voters, 441

Colorado, Missouri Compromise line through, 180

Columbia, South Carolina, burning of, 457

Commercial regulations for the states, early attempts to secure, 323, 326

Compensated emancipation, 436, 453, 470

Compromises of 1820 and 1850. *See* Missouri Compromise

Confederate Army, devotion of, 438, 442

Confederate States of America; Lincoln's refusal to recognize, 384, 392, 424, 463, 469; elects Davis, 385; Constitution: officers: hesitation of Virginia, 386; Commissioners offer to pay for Fort Sumter and other places, 392; tricked by Seward, 394, 395; letter to Seward, quoted, 395; fire on Fort Sumter: not guilty of commencing hostilities, 395; called a conspiracy to resist the law, 396; negotiations over Paris Agreement of 1856, 406; treatment of prisoners of war, 424, 425; restoration of, discussed at Hampton Roads conference, 467-470. *See also* Southern States

Confederated republics, 343

Congress, legislation of 1774 covering slavery in the territories, 167, 168; question of territorial control of slavery, 170, 240, 243, 257, 259; of 1774: object and powers, 320; adopts Declaration of Independence, 321; formulates Articles of Confederation, 322; power to regulate commerce denied to, 323; Lincoln acts without authority of, 383; 400; Lincoln's first message to, 414; Senate resolution approving war measures, 418; power to declare war, 398

Conkling, James C., 151

Connecticut, ratification of Constitution, 330

Conscription act held un-constitutional, 433

Consolidation of power. *See* Centralization

Constable, Charles H., 91

Constitution, implied powers, 81; principle of direct taxation and of representation, 159, 221; provision on which Fugitive Slave Laws were based, quoted: use of word "person" in, 160; slaves affirmed property under, 161; provisions for regulation and division of territory, 169; territorial powers granted to Congress, 259; interpretation of Jefferson Davis in Resolutions of February, 1860, 294, 370, 419; doctrine of the Union being older than the Constitution, 318, 326; formulated: theories respecting origin of government under, 323; preamble, 325, 326; ratification, 326, 328; opposition to, 327; an economic instrument, 328, 332; history of legalism of ratification, 332; question of state sovereignty under, 323, 333; founded in compact, 337, 341; framed under inspiration of Montesquieu, 343; legislative interpretation of, 344; clause forbidding restraint upon negro importation, 355; called a self-evident lie, 449; Thirteenth Amendment, 482; Fourteenth Amendment, 484, 486

INDEX

Constitutional Convention, 323; influence of economic factors, 159
Cooper Institute Speech, 314, 345-351
Corporations not sure of Lincoln, 483; Supreme Court on citizenship of, 487
Corruption in American life, 489
Courts and law practice in Illinois, 117
Cowper, William, quoted, 299
Criminal classes, 492
Crittenden, John J., 387
Crittenden Compromise, 344, 384
Curran, John Philpot, quoted, 91
Curtin, Andrew G., 396; raises troops, 432
Curtis, Benjamin Robbins, Dred Scott case, 256
Curtis, George Ticknor, affirms constitutionality of Missouri Compromise, 257, 258; quoted, 322
Curtis, George William, at Chicago convention, 363, 366

Daily Advertiser, 332
Dane, Nathan, 343
Davis, David, 82, 87, 108, 149, 376; quoted, 138; aids Lincoln's nomination for president, 358, 366
Davis, Jefferson, 3, 85, 387, 396; disapproves Compromise of 1850, 197; aids Pacific railroad, 202; drawing away from Douglas, 279; constitutional interpretation in resolutions of February 1860, 294, 370, 419; did not escape in disguise, 378; elected provisional president, 385; inaugurated, 386; Greeley calls for hanging of, 400; insists upon right of privateering, 406; message to Confederate Congress: request for troops, 412; negotiations with Lincoln for exchange of prisoners, 424; mind and character, 451; compared with Lincoln, 452; Blair mission to, 462, 467; appoints commission to Hampton Roads conference, 464; Lincoln occupies chair of, 473
Dayton, William L., 136
Declaration of Independence, Jefferson's effort to exclude slavery by, 157; equality clause, 305, 307, 309; adoption of, 321; passage from, in Republican platform, 365
Delahay, Mark W., 228, 278; Lincoln's relations with, 358, 359

Delaware, ratification of Constitution, 330
Democratic Party, 2, 24, 207; nominates Lincoln for Illinois Legislature, 34; platform, 1844, 94; radicals form Free Soil party, 103; ballots in 1856 convention, 136; loses election of 1848, 181; platform of 1852 comfirms Compromise of 1850, resolution, text, 191; split in 1860, 197; nominates Douglas, 198; members join forces with Republicans, 238; convention, 1856: platform, 245; victory, 251; adopts article admitting slavery in territories, 295; injured by Jefferson Davis's resolutions, 370; votes polled in 1860 election, 371; men who served the Union side, 434; results of 1862 elections, 440; attitude toward the tariff, 445; opposition to national bank, 446; nominates McClellan for president, 448
Derby, Earl, on Lincoln's blockade proclamation, quoted, 405
Dickerson, Edward M., in McCormick's reaper litigation, 125, 127
Dickey, T. Lyle, quoted, 274
Direct taxation. *See* Taxation
District of Columbia, slavery in, 100, 189, 284
Disunionists, 311
Division of power necessary to liberty, 443
Dixon, Archibald, amendment to Nebraska bill, 206, 207
Dodge, Augustus C., 201; bills for organization of Nebraska, 202
Dorsey, Azel W., 16
Dougherty, John, 278
Douglas, Stephen Arnold, 2, 80, 172, 174, 182, 243, 359, 369, 387, 389, 487; ancestry, 36; early life, 36, 38; character and ability, 37, 265, 489; attentions to Mary Todd, 63, 64; marriages, 63; Lincoln's hatred of, 64, 274; early political career, 80; influence upon Lincoln: debates subtreasury question with Lincoln, 81; in Senate: marriage to Martha Martin, 92; more honest of mind than Lincoln, 117, 198; Chicago University founded by, 117, 314; ballots received in 1856 convention, 136; attitude toward slavery in Northwest Territory, 167; adheres

INDEX

to Compromise of 1820, 177, 178; attacked for Kansas-Nebraska Act, 179, 190, 191, 197, 203, 210, 211, 226 (defended, 203; quoted in defense, 205); offers amendment to Oregon bill, 180; stand on Compromise of 1850, 187, 189, 197, 204; Lincoln's envy of, 191; treatment of, by Chicago, 191, 211; campaigning for Pierce, 193; trailed by Lincoln, 193, 219, 281; nominated for president, 197; candor: not a statesman of the slavocracy, 198, 203; public services, 198; statesmanship employed with railroads and territories, 198, 201; aids Pacific railroad, 199; Nebraska bill, 202-207, 209; attack of abolitionists upon, 208, excerpts, 209; reply, 210; Kansas-Nebraska Act, 210, 211; answered by Lincoln in Peoria speech, 219; greatness of, at 43, 234; alliances against, 238, 311; loses nomination at 1856 convention, 245; draws Illinois crowds with speeches, 250; charged with conspiracy in Dred Scott decision, 264, 289, 305 (answer to charge, 290); Springfield speech dealing with Kansas-Nebraska Act and Dred Scott decision, 265; as quarry of Lincoln and Republicans, 265, 286; views on negro equality, 266, 309; Lincoln's reply to Springfield speech, 267; questions Lincoln's adherence to Republican platform, 269, 279, 281; attacks "house divided against itself" doctrine, 273, 300, 302; nominated for third term as senator, 275; challenged to debate with Lincoln, 275; political setting, 277; the debates, 280-313 (mentioned, 29, 142, 178, 179, 217, 240); opposition to Lecompton Constitution, 277, 293; break with Buchanan, 277, 311; shows courage and principle, 277, 279; deceived as to Lincoln's participation in Republican platform, 285, 286; denounced, 288; on admission of Kansas, 292: English bill, 293; on exclusion of slavery prior to formation of a state constitution, 294; shows up Lincoln's inconsistencies and evasions, 307; plurality of, 311; campaign financially disastrous, 312; death, 313, 420; nobility, 314; loses in presidential campaign, 370; votes polled, 371; offers resolution for withdrawal of troops from South, 401; on the president's use of the military power, quoted, 402; offers services to Lincoln: speeches in Illinois, 420; efforts to defeat, in 1862 elections, 441; forecasts possibility of centralization, 492;

Douglas, Mrs. Stephen Arnold, 92

Douglass, Frederick, 281, 288; opposes reëlection of Lincoln, 448

Dow, Neal, 492

Doyle murder, 230

Draft. *See* Army

Dred Scott decision, 161, 169, 251; attacked by Lincoln, 251, 252, 262, 263, 288; the case, 252, 292, 348, 350; charges of conspiracy, 252, 253, 261, 263, 288; opinion of the court, 258; excerpt, 259; denunciations of radicals, 261; legal repugnance between Kansas-Nebraska Act and, 266, 294

Dresser, Charles N., officiates at Lincoln's wedding, 72

Drummond, Thomas, 125, 126

Duelling, 77

Durley, Williamson, 96

Economic factors, influence upon Constitution, 159, 328, 332; upon struggle for free and slave territory, 175. *See also* Monopoly

Edwards, Cyrus, 117

Edwards, Ninian W., 43, 60, 61; quoted, 65

Edwards, Mrs. Ninian W., 43, 61; on Lincoln's courtship of Mary Todd, 63

Effie Afton, 128

Elections. *See* Democratic Party: Republican Party

Elliot's *Debates*, 345

Ellis, A. Y., 32

Emancipation. *See* Slavery

Emancipation Proclamation 82, reasons for issuing, 435-438; Lincoln doubts efficacy of, 438; preliminary, 439; a war measure, 469; effect upon slavery, 483, 485

Emerson, cited, 127, 128

Emerson, John, owner of Dred Scott, 252

INDEX

Emerson, Mrs. John, 253. *See also* Chaffee, Mrs. Calvin Clifford
Emerson, Ralph Waldo, 234, 433, 494
Emigrant Aid Society, 229
England, slave trade, 157, 158; abolition of slavery, 436
English bill, 293, 294
Equality clause, Declaration of Independence, 305, 307, 309
Ethnological difference between North and South, 443, 444
Evarts, William, M., at Chicago convention, 363, 367
Evening Post, 347, 352
Everett, Edward, 371
Ewing, William L. D., quoted, 38

Fanatics. *See* Abolitionists
Federal Army. *See* Army, Federal
Federal Council of the Churches of Christ, 493
Federal Navy. *See* Navy
Federalist, 160, 397
Federalists, 328; plot to centralize the government, 172, 173; aid ratification of Constitution, 329, 330; delegates won in New York, 332
Fell, J. W., autobiographical letter to, cited, 4, 6, 7; works for nomination of Lincoln, 356, 358
Female suffrage, 35
Ficklin, Orlando B., 90, 91
Field, David Dudley, 347; appointed to Supreme Court, 486; holds a corporation a citizen, 487
Field, Roswell M., as counsel for Dred Scott, 254, 255
Fillmore, Millard, 248
Fisk, Wilbur, 163, 356
Florida, slavery in, 169; mileage, 176
Ford, Thomas, cited, 38
Forsyth against Reynolds, 123
Fort Pickens, 390, 391, 394
Fort Sumter, 390; Lincoln's action in regard to, 388, 390, 391; Confederacy offers to pay for, 392; cabinet opinions on provisioning of, 392, 394; evacuation of, promised by Seward, 394; "Relief Squadron" to: fired on, 395
Fourteenth Amendment, 484, 486
France, negotiations over Paris Agreement of 1856, 406; plan to unite North and South against, 463, 468
Francis, Simeon, 68, 77

Francis, Mrs. Simeon, 68
Franklin, Benjamin, 169
Fredericksburg, battle of, 441
Free Masonry, opposition to, 215
Free Soil Party, 101, 103, 193, 207, 208, 214, 216; Lincoln's efforts to undermine, 104
Freedmen's Bureau, 485
Freedom of speech and of press strangled, 399, 400, 410, 422
Frémont, John Charles, 136, 248, 439; nominated for presidency, 248, 448
Fugitive Slave Law. *See* Slavery
Fullerton, Hugh, 108

Galton, *Inquiries into the Human Faculty,* cited, 16
Garfield, James A., 488
Garland, Hugh A., as counsel in Dred Scott case, 254, 255
Garrison, William Lloyd, 39, 229; antislavery activities, 40; denounces Constitution, 311
Genius of Universal Emancipation, 94
Gentry, Allen, 24
Gentry, James, hires Lincoln, 23
Gentry, Matthew, Lincoln's poem on, text, 19
Gentryville store, Lincoln at, 23
Georgia, slavery, 158; pro-slavery covenant in deed of western lands, 168; ratification of Constitution, 331; ordinance of secession, text, 373; Sherman's march through, 455;
Germans, Republican appeals for support of, 239, 269, 312; Lincoln's appeals, 200, 249, 300, 359; opposition to the war, 433
Gettysburg Address, 478
Giddings, Joshua R., 100, 247; "Appeal of the Independent Democrats in Congress," excerpts, 209; at Chicago convention, 363, 365
Gildersleeve, Basil Lanneau, 442
Gillespie, Joseph, 236, 374
Gist, William H., message to South Carolina Legislature, 371
Globe Tavern, Springfield, 73, 74
God, Lincoln's Jehovah, 70, 150, 480, 482, 494; Lincoln on the will of, quoted, 429, 438
Goethe, quoted, 56
Goodpasture, William, 377
Gordon, Nathaniel, Lincoln refuses to pardon, 428

INDEX

Goudy, W. C., 108
Graham, Mentor, 33, 49
Graham, William Alexander, resolution to extend Missouri Compromise, 178
Grant, Ulysses S., 85, 238, 448, 488; supplants Meade, 426; Stephens's impression of: furthers Hampton Roads conference, 464; forbids troops to cheer victory, 473
Great Britain, negotiations over Paris Agreement of 1856, 406; action in *Trent* affair, 407
Greeley, Horace, 249, 363, 368; influence of, 231; denounces Dred Scott decision, 261; at Cooper Institute meeting, quoted, 351; policy toward South, 400
Green, Bowling, 46
Grigsby, Aaron, 12, 17
Grigsby, Nathaniel, 12; quoted, 20
Grote, George, cited, 456

Habeas corpus, suspension of writ of, 383, 399, 400, 407, 408-412, 422, 432
Hale, Edward Everett, *Kansas and Nebraska*, 229
Hale, John P., 101, 193; disunion petition, 311
Hamilton, Alexander, 27, 169, 337, 340; duel with Burr, 77; first tariff the work of, 445; song given before duel, 474
Hamiltonians, 25, 27; Lincoln's principles those of, 81, 82
Hamlin, Hannibal, nominated for vice president: career, 368; shelved for Andrew Johnson, 448
Hampton, Wade, 457
Hampton Roads conference, 462, 464-470
Hanks family, 5, 9, 11, 13; all Democrats, 24
Hanks, Dennis, 8, 9, 10, 12, 21, 23; quoted, 12; visit to Washington, 434
Hanks, Harriet, 140
Hanks, John, carries rails into state convention, 360
Hanks, Joseph, 9
Hanks, Lucy, 11, 12
Hanks, Nancy, 5; marriage to Thomas Lincoln: death, 9; Lincoln's reticence about, 11, 66; ancestry: appearance, 11; mind and character: burial, 12; probably figured in religious orgy, 13; grave unmarked, 13, 376; sickness, 16

Hanks, Thomas, 360
Hardin, John J., 85
Harding, George, in McCormick reaper litigation, 125, 126, 127
Harlan, Senator, 382
Harper's Weekly, 261
Harris, Thomas L., 286
Hartford convention, resolution on state rights, 343
Harvester machine, litigation over patents, 125-128
Hawkins, Sir John, 158
Hawthorne, Nathaniel, 433
Hay, John, 489; quoted, 400
Hayes, Rutherford B., 488
Hayne, Robert Y., 341
Hebraic-Puritan spirit, 179, 211, 216, 234, 244, 246, 272, 275, 291, 303, 419, 429, 444, 471, 496
Helm, J. B., cited, 13
Helper, *Impending Crisis of the South*, 39
Henning, Fanny, 69
Henry, Patrick, 443
Herndon, William Henry, 1, 82, 243, 249, 374; cited, 11, 12, 21, 22, 33, 42, 46, 56, 64, 75, 80, 116, 138, 148, 149, 154, 184, 278, 311, 358, 366, 375, 377, 388, 390, 434, 435, 453, 481; quoted, 30, 61, 138, 139, 140, 146, 345, 356, 471; Mary Owens' story given to, 57; on Mary Todd, quoted, 62; partnership with Lincoln: influence and help of, 84; concern about Lincoln's Mexican War speech, 97; steers Lincoln from Republican convention, 216; joins party, 218; mayor of Springfield, 228; at Anti-Nebraska convention, 236; activities in behalf of new party: commits Lincoln to it, 237
Hill, Samuel, 46, 47
Hillis, Lois E., 46
Hingham, ancestral home of Lincolns, 5
Hodder, Frank Heywood, "Genesis of the Kansas-Nebraska Act," 203
Holland, J. G., 388; *Life of Abraham Lincoln*, 152
Holmes, John, report on Maine Bill, 171
Holst, Hermann Eduard von, 197
"Honest Abe," 274
Hooker, Joseph, 426, 441
Howard, General, 461
Howard, William Alanson, Committee on Kansas, 230

INDEX

Howe, Julia Ward, 444, 455
Hunkers, 101, 216
Hunter, R. M. T., at Hampton Roads conference, 464, 470
Hyer, Tom, leads Seward rooters, 362, 367

"Ichabod," 184, 185
Illinois, Lincoln's activities in legislature, 34, 37, 38, 40-44; Lincoln's opposition to reapportionment of, 35; constitutional provision against duelling, 77; civil rights denied to negroes, 88, 89, 148, 267, 485; statute providing for sale of negroes, 90; courts and law practice, 117; effect of apportionment of, upon Lincoln's plurality, 311; after-war politicians, 489; Illinois Central Railroad, 198; tax case; 119, 123; Lincoln attorney for, 228
Illinois Daily Journal, 193, 249
Imperialism a result of the War, 482
Inaugural Address, first, 311, 318, 337, 382; influence of Webster upon, 28, 184; material used when preparing, 184
Inaugural Address, Second, 454
Indiana, soldier vote, 449
Indians, slavery, 157, 166
Ingersoll, R. G., 434
Insurrections, negro. *See* Slavery
Intelligencer, 33, 111, 182, 195, 282
Iowa, demands organization of Nebraska and aid for railroad, 201, 202; Supreme Court ruling on shipment of liquor, 266
Isthmus and steamship railroad interests, 199
Iturbide, Augustin de, 93

Jackson, Andrew, 4, 34, 61, 76, 184, 215, 305, 341, 378, 404, 405, 427, 488; elected president, 25, 32; popularity, 26; opposition to Bank of United States, 34, 446; on the Constitution as a compact, quoted, 337
Jackson, Thomas J. (Stonewall), 421; death, 441
Jefferson, Thomas, 4, 25, 81, 82, 289, 309, 310, 340, 347, 352, 366, 494; stand against slavery, 157; quoted, 158; plan for new states: names, 169;

disapproval of Missouri Compromise of 1820, 172; on relation of states to the Constitution, 338; accused of counseling secession, 340; on suspension of writ of habeas corpus, 409
Jehovah. *See* God
Jesus, Lincoln's belief concerning, 149, 152; sophism: Lincoln's attempt to identify his cause with, 270, 273; evil done by, 271
Johnson, Andrew, 371, 483, 484, 497; war resolution in Senate, quoted, 418, 420; impeachment, 419, 483; nominated for vice president, 448
Johnson, Reverdy, McCormick reaper case, 126; as counsel in Dred Scott case, 256
Johnston, John D., 10
Johnston, Joseph E., 421, 474
Johnston, Sarah Bush, marriage to Thomas Lincoln, 9; books of, 20; cited, 21
Joliet Signal, 215
Jones, Senator, 201, Bill for organization of Nebraska, 202
Judd, Norman Buel, 108, 128, 345, 376, 381, 441; aids Lincoln's nomination for president, 358, 366; nominating speech, 367
Judiciary, present powers, 118; honesty, 121; Madison on powers of, 339; corrupted by money power, 488. *See aslo* Supreme Court
Jury and judiciary, 118

Kansas, slavery war in, 228; emigrants sent to, 229; arms and ammunition for, 229, 242; struggle over Lecompton Constitution, 277, 293; admission of, 292; English bill, 293
Kansas-Nebraska Act, 179, 187, 190; Douglas attacked for, 179, 190, 191, 197; opinions about Douglas's management of, 203; speech of Douglas in support of bill, 210; bill passed: repeal of Missouri Compromise, 211; Lincoln's Peoria speech on, quoted, 219; legal repugnance between Dred Scott decision and, 266, 294
Kelso, Jack, 32
Kent, James, denies right of secession, 342
Kentucky, refuses to furnish troops, 398

INDEX

Kentucky Resolutions, 338, 340; excerpt, 338
King, Rufus, 223
Know-nothing Party, 216, 228, 231, 236, 239, 247, 269
Koerner, Gustave, 236

Lafayette, Marquis de, 166
Lamon, Ward Hill, cited, 56; accompanies Lincoln to Washington, 382
Lanphier, Charles Henry, 285
Law practice in Illinois, 117
Lecompton Constitution, struggle over, 277, 293
Lee, Robert E., 85, 154, 439, 441, 442, 444, 456; why lost to the Union, 398; surrender, 473; quoted, 484
Lewis, William, against Thomas Lewis, 123
Liberator, 40
Liberty Party, 101, 216
Lieb, Charles, coöperates with Republicans against Douglas, 278
Lincoln family, 5, 8, 11
Lincoln, Abraham, grandfather of the President, 6, 8; wounded by Indian: death, 6, 7
Lincoln, Abraham
  Private Life: Appearance: Education
  ancestry, 4, 5, 9, 10, 11; birth, 4, 16; autobiographical sketches, 4, 6, 7, 29, 33, 356; boyhood and youth, 9, 10, 15-28; unkindness of father to: sends money to father, 10, 140; mortified about his mother 11, 66; value of estate at time of death, 13, 451; failure to erect stone over mother's grave, 13, 376; education: scholarship, literary efforts, 16, 17, 20, 21, 33; poems, *with text*, 17-19; taste in poetry, 18, 116; first speech, 20; essay on government, 22; books read by, 20, 21, 22, 33, 114, 317; reading habits, 20, 21, 32, 33, 84, 113, 114, 116; habits and activities of youth, 20, 23, 32; attitude toward women, 20, 34, 74, 76; lack of self-culture, 21, 84, 113, 115, 119, 358, 442, 496; appearance, 21, 88, 347; appearance before his death, 451; phenomenal strength, 23, 29; popularity and friendships, 23, 29, 32, 34, 80, 83, 142, 358; desire to rise in life, 24; flatboat trips to New Orleans, 24, 28; early contacts with slavery, 24, 68, 147; feeling toward his father, 24, 140; influence of Webster upon, 28; life in New Salem, 28, 29-38; in rôle of rail splitter, 29; poverty: inability to make money, 29, 32, 44, 60, 81, 108, 121, 312; mercantile ventures, 29; with Berry, 30; dress, 31, 44, 142, 347, 378, 382; influence of wrestling upon mind of, 32; constant reading of newspapers, 33, 111, 115, 228; romantic adventures: Ann Rutledge, 34, 45-49, 70, 76; friendship of Mrs. Hillis, 46; Mary Owens, 49-59; letters to Mary Owens, 50; to Mrs. O. H. Browning, 53; reasons for marriage to Mary Todd: resulting unhappiness, 61, 76; disparities in disposition, 62; courtship: friendship of Joshua Speed, 63; dread of marriage, 64; failure to appear on wedding night: resulting wretchedness, 65; nature of mental malady, 66; proposal of marriage to Sarah Rickard, 67; correspondence with Speed about their romances, 67, 69-72, 74; courtship of Mary Todd renewed: visit to Speed in Kentucky, 68; letter to Mary Speed, 69; wedding, 72; takes wife to Globe Tavern, 73, 74; first written reference to his wife, 73; letters and telegrams to her, excerpts, 74; relations with his boys, 75; size of hat, 88; voice, 103, 347; reasons for being poor, 109; studies Euclid, 115; reading of Shakespeare, 116, 430; home in Springfield, 125, 143; does not go to father's deathbed: message to father, quoted, 141; bids farewell to friends, 375; marks grave of father, 376

As Lawyer
licensed to practice law, 38, 44; as lawyer, 83, 115-137, 228; severs relationship with Stuart: partnership with Stephen T. Logan, 83; partnership dissolved: takes Herndon as partner: influence of Herndon, 84; riding the circuit, 86, 115; handles litigation for slave owner Matson, 90, 297; not over scrupulous about cases handled, 91, 108, 119, 124; back in Springfield, 108;

INDEX

Illinois Central tax case, 119, 123; an honest lawyer, 120; gives free service, 120, 131; lack of order and method, 121; as jury lawyer, 122; law cases tabulated, Illinois courts, 122; United States Supreme Court, 123; McCormick reaper case, 125; effect of case upon: renewed determination to study law; Rock Island Bridge case, 128; Duff Armstrong case, 129; assists in divorce case, 131; attorney for Illinois Central Railroad, 228

Public Life
as an aid to monopoly and privilege, 3, 497; political influences during youth: Henry Clay, 24, 26; denied grocery experience, 29; Black Hawk War, 29, 31; early interest in politics, 29, 33; Whig candidate for legislature: platform, 30; first political speech, quoted, 31; in favor of protective tariff, 31, 82, 100; defeated, 32; political offices in New Salem: Democratic candidate for legislature: record, 34; advocates enlargement of suffrage, 35; attitude toward civil rights of negroes, 35, 89, 148, 221, 475; candidate for reëlection: platform, 35; record during second term: aids location of capital at Springfield, 37; later terms in legislature, 38, 40-44; position on slavery, in Illinois legislature, 38, 40, 86; Stone-Lincoln resolutions, 42, 96; removal to Springfield, 38, 43; aristocratic friendships, 43, 60, 74; opposition of churches to, 43, 74, 152; attempt to take delegation from Baker, 48, 72, 74, 82; melancholy over defeat and obscurity, 55; hatred of Douglas, 64, 274; career aided by *Sangamon* Journal, 68, 82; literary attacks on James Shields, 68, 71, 77; encounter with Shields, 77; an apostle of the implied powers of the Constitution; influence of Douglas; debates subtreasury question, 81; a Hamiltonian in principle, 81, 82; nominated for Congress, 84; position on Mexican War, 85, 92, 97; elected to Congress, 86; life in Washington, 92; record in Congress, 92, 96-103; on the question of Texas and slavery, quoted, 96; votes for Wilmot Proviso, 96, 101, 178, 231; attitude on slavery at time of Mexican War: speeches in Congress, 97; excerpts, 99, 102; views on right of president to invade, quoted, 97; on right of a people to form new government, quoted, 99; control of slavery in District of Columbia, 100; at Whig Conventions of 1848, 101, 105; on Zachary Taylor, 102, 103, 105; New England trip: speeches, 104; devotion to Whigs: return to Illinois, 107; melancholy over his prospects, 107, 112; unsuccessful attempts to secure office, 116; Springfield Whigs file protest against; refuses governorship of Oregon, 117; ballots received in 1856 convention, 136; inability to suggest remedy for slavery, 147, 220, 303; opposition of clergymen: talk with Newton Bateman, 152; views on slavery, 152, 231, 235, 241, 284, 287, 435; religious utterances, 154, 377, 384, 418, 428, 429, 430, 471, 476, 480, 482; consideration of word "person" in Constitution, 160; denies right of property in a slave under the Constitution, 161; Cooper Institute speech, 161, 167, 184; position on power of Congress to exclude slavery from a territory, 170; stand on Missouri Compromises, 178, 193, 195, 249; praised for stand against slavery, 179; political eclipse, 190; envy of Douglas, 191; Whig committeeman for Illinois: letters and writings lost, 193; speech before Scott Club, Springfield, quoted, 193, 195; trails Douglas, 193, 219, 281; attitude toward Whig platform of 1852, 193, 213; eulogy on Henry Clay, excerpt, 194; appeals for German support, 200, 249, 300, 359; gradual awakening: activities after Kansas-Nebraska Act, 213; leading Whig in Illinois, 216; holds aloof from Republican party, 216, 219, 233, 236; Peoria speech: elected to legislature on Whig ticket, 219; resigns from legislature, 225; seeks nomination for Senate, 226; depressed

INDEX

after failure, 227; political inactivity, 228; association with Delahay, 228, 278; letter to Speed defining his politics, 231; manner and spirit of political change: at Anti-Nebraska convention, 236; joins Republicans at Bloomington convention, 237; helps to draw up platform, 239; the "Lost Speech," excerpts, 240, 243; at Republican National convention, 1856, 248; during presidential campaign: campaigns for Frémont, 249; attacks Dred Scott decision, 251, 252, 262, 263, 288, 348, 350; on rulings of Supreme Court, 251, 252; nominated for Illinois senatorship, 262, 269; "house divided against itself" speech, 262, 270, 273; accuses Douglas of conspiracy in Dred Scott decision, 264, 289, 305; answers Douglas on Dred Scott decision, 267; views on negro equality, 267, 307, 309; questioned on adherence to platform, 269, 279, 281-288; takes moral ground to identify his course with religion, 270, 273, 299, 302; during campaign for senatorship, 274; "house divided against itself" doctrine, 274, 301, 302; challenges Douglas to debate, 275; political setting, 277; the debates, 280-313 (mentioned, 29, 142, 178, 179, 217, 240); attitude toward Buchanan's campaign against Douglas, 278; questions Douglas on admission of Kansas, 292; on exclusion of slavery prior to formation of a state constitution, 294; slavery as a moral issue, 299; inconsistencies and evasions held up by Douglas, 307; Illinois apportionment causes defeat of, 311; First Inaugural, 311, 318, 337, 382 (influence of Webster upon, 28, 184; material used when preparing, 184); campaign financially disastrous, 312; fails as lecturer: invitation to speak at Cooper Institute, 314; mentioned for presidency, 314, 345; sentiment for the Union, 316; limited understanding of the Constitution and the Union, 317, 334; on perpetuity of the Union, 318, 322; doctrine of the Union being older than the Constitution, 318, 326; on secession and insurrection, 319; usurpation of power, 339, 383, 398, 399, 400, 404, 481; prepares for Cooper Institute speech, 345; subject matter, 346; Bryant's introduction, 347; the speech: the Dred Scott decision, 348, 350; John Brown's raid, 349; press comments on speech, 351; Hartford speech, 353; New Haven speech, 354; supporters work for nomination of, 356; vigilant in his own behalf, 356, 358; success due to luck: election due to break in Democratic Party, 357; and devotion of friends: relations with Delahay: defrays campaign expense, 358, 359; "rail candidate" at state convention: nominated for president, 360; stand on the tariff, 360, 370, 380; enters campaign under symbol of honesty, 361; the Chicago convention, 362; nomination for vice presidency averted: refuses to make campaign promises, 366; ballots for, 367; receives news of nomination, 368; acceptance of nomination, quoted, 369; becomes famous: visitors and publicity, 370; decides to remain silent during campaign, 370, 371; votes received, 371; anxiety during period before inauguration, 374; cabinet appointments, 374, 382, 385; sees double apparition in mirror, 375; farewell to Springfield, 375, 376; precautions against assassination, 375, 381; trip to Washington: speeches, 378; fatigue, 378, 382; ideas about invasion, 379, 383; reaches Washington in disguise: program outlined in inauguration speech, 382; close of speech, quoted, 384; acts without authority of Congress, 383; policy of possessing places of the Government, 383, 388, 390, 392; suspends writ of habeas corpus, 383, 399, 400, 407, 408-412, 422, 432; refuses to recognize Confederate States, 384, 392, 424, 463, 469; takes oath of office, 385; interview with Virginia Committee, 388; Fort Sumter, 388, 390, 391, 392, 394; plans for raising

INDEX

army, 389, 396; as a war president: assumption of power, 389, 398, 399, 407, 414; overrides Seward's foreign policy, 390; Fort Pickens, 390, 391; efforts to provoke South Carolina to fire first shot, 391; accused of Fabian tactics in dealing with Confederate Commissioners, 394; calls confederacy a conspiracy to resist the law, 396; convenes Congress in extra session: proclamation calling for 75,000 militia, 397; causes secession of Virginia, 398; orders blockade of Southern ports: increases army and navy: calls for volunteers; usurpation of power, 399; strangles free speech and free press, 399, 400, 410, 422; contradictions in blockade proclamation, 404; change of policy, 407, 424; proceeds cautiously with Maryland, 407; defies the judiciary, 411; prepares for move against Virginia, 412, 421; first message to Congress, 414; in towering wrath over secession, 414, 416; destruction of state sovereignty, 417; yields to clamor for war, 420; intervenes in behalf of Vallandigham, 423; obdurate about exchange of prisoners, 424, 425, 470; vacillations at beginning of war, 425, 430; army appointments, 426; reputed tenderness: cruelty in his war measures, 427; compared with Robespierre, 428; thanksgiving proclamations, 428, 430; proclamation appointing national fast day, 429 (text, 154, 155); meditations on the will of God, quoted, 429, 438; reads Shakespeare, 430; dreams of dead son: methods used in raising troops: interview with Medill about call for troops, 431; Emancipation Proclamation, 435, 438, 439, 469; reasons for issuing the Emancipation Proclamation, 435-438; plans for compensated emancipation and gradual abolition of slavery, 436, 453, 470; sees committee of negroes: advises colonization and promises aid, 437; reply to Chicago delegation urging emancipation, 438; fails to reprimand General Butler: issues preliminary Emancipation Proclamation, 439; reëlection opposed: nominated, 448; elected: asks to have Indiana soldiers returned to vote, 449; enters second term: a much worn man, 451; Second Inaugural, 454; consents to Sherman's march to the sea, 455; thanks Sherman for Savannah, 457; Blair mission to see Jefferson Davis, 457, 461, 467; correspondence with Blair, 463; Hampton Roads conference, 462, 464-470; Second Inaugural, 471, 479; quoted, 471; in Richmond: occupies Davis's chair, 473; warns South against farther hostilities: proclamation closing Southern ports: last speech, quoted, 474; assassination, 477; Gettysburg Address, quoted, 478; implies that he had exceeded his power as president, 481; feeling his way toward restoration: no real program for reconstruction, 482; appointments to Supreme Court, 486; invests government with Christianity, 491; coming to be known as he really was, 494

Mind: Character: Habits

Character, habits and mind, 2, 20, 21, 32, 56, 59, 80, 83, 84, 120, 138-156, 357, 363, 388, 394, 400, 413, 414, 434, 481; apotheosis, 1, 3, 401, 494; fame and its basis, 2; contradictions and inconsistencies, 2, 3, 56, 59, 82, 103, 138, 317, 363, 388; appeal of his eloquent utterances, 2, 3, 377, 384, 385; a sophist, 3, 276, 297, 316; ashamed of early life and poverty, 10, 141; mental gifts, inheritance of, 11; religious views, 14, 21, 34, 149-156, 272 (about God, 70, 150, 429, 438, 480, 482, 494; about Jesus, 149, 152); inactivity: laziness, 20, 29, 32, 115, 116, 119, 358; an advocate of temperance, 20, 30, 43, 228; and the Bible, 21, 116, 149, 496; style in speeches, 22, 128; storytelling gift, 23, 32, 87, 142; tenderness for animals, 23, 76; division in his thinking, 25, 92, 97, 235, 264, 307; "humble Abraham Lincoln," 31, 219, 274; intellectual cunning: twisting dialectic, 33, 52, 86, 122, 252, 384, 404; love of children, 34, 75, 76; equivocation and duplicity,

INDEX

42, 116, 404; presentiment of his death, 45, 145, 149, 375; a superstitious man, 45, 148; melancholy: mental malady, 46, 55, 65, 66, 107, 143, 227, 413; ambition to marry for position and money, 59, 60; a sensitive man, 66, 225; feels need of ability to keep his own resolves, 71, 128, 379; coldness, 74, 76, 139, 142; remarkable memory, 116, 143; use of censurable methods, 116, 228, 278; reticence and secretiveness, 132, 137, 138, 198; power of mimicry, 138, 139, 142; sense of humor, 142; deficient in æsthetic gifts, 142; lacks love of the beautiful, 143; an under-sexed man, 145; ruled by judgment and conscience, 146, 435; belief in his destiny, 148; fear of assassination, 154, 375, 378, 381, 382, 451; ambition, political, 225, 228, 356; compared with Douglas, 234; originated nothing: used what others had said, 250, 270, 481; a convert to fanatical Zionism, 272; a demagogue, 273; his touch of poetry and genius, 275, 276, 404, 413; Stephens's opinion of, 316; compared with Seward, 368; whether weak or strong, 388; not a modest man, 400; reputed tenderness: cruelty, 427; compared with Robespierre, 428; opinions of eminent men about, 433, 434; a Hebraic-Puritan product, 444, 471; compared with Jefferson Davis, 452; fixity of purpose, 453

Biography

  Works, 359. See also Angle, Paul M., Beveridge, Albert J., Holland, J. G., Herndon, William Henry, Nicolay, John G., and Hay, John

Lincoln, Enoch, 5
Lincoln, John, 6
Lincoln, Levi, 5
Lincoln, Mary (Todd), 57, 111, 125, 143, 227; goes to Globe Tavern after wedding, 73, 74; Lincoln's first written reference to, 73; Lincoln's lack of tenderness: his letters and telegrams to, quoted, 74; refuses to go to Oregon, 117; on Lincoln's religion, 150; on Lincoln's presentiment, 154. *See also* Todd, Mary

Lincoln, Mordecai, I and II, 6
Lincoln, Mordecai, III, 6, 7, 8, 21
Lincoln, Robert, 75, 353; ashamed of his father's origin, 359; a millionaire, 60
Lincoln, Samuel, 5, 6
Lincoln, Sarah, 9, 12, 16; Lincoln's verses in honor of marriage of, 17
Lincoln, Thomas, 6; date of birth, 7; character, 8; wanderings: marriages: children, 9; death: politics: religion, 10; treatment of Abraham: Abraham sends money to, 10, 140; burial of wife, 12; probably figured in religious orgy, 13; poverty and shiftlessness, 16; move to Decatur, 28; relations with his son: last illness, 140; gravestone erected, 376
Lincoln, Mrs. Thomas. *See* Hanks, Nancy: Johnston, Sarah Bush
Lincoln, Willie, Lincoln dreams of, 431
Lincoln Museum, Springfield, 125
Liquor shipment into Iowa, Supreme Court ruling, 266
Literature, Civil War no inspiration for, 495
Locofocos, 216
Lodge, Henry Cabot, 489
Log cabin life, 15
Logan, John A., 434
Logan, Stephen T., partnership with Lincoln, 83; rivalry: end of partnership, 84; defeated for Congress, 107; quoted, 367
London *Times*, 229
Longfellow, Henry Wadsworth, 235, 495
Longworth, Thomas, 123
Lord, Nathan, 356
Louis XVI, Lincoln said to resemble, 388
Louisiana Purchase, 170, 180, 190, 259
Louisiana Territory, slavery, 168, 171
Louisville Journal, 27, 33, 371
Lovejoy, Owen, 281, 282
Lowell, James Russell, 85, 455, 479, 495; quoted, 178, 179, 474
Lowndes, William, 171
Lundy, Benjamin, 94
Lunt, George, 106; on Lincoln and Chicago convention, 362

Madison, James, 25, 160, 169, 223, 323, 340; report upon Kentucky and Virginia Resolutions, 338; ex-

INDEX

cerpts, 339; on redress for insurrection, 397
Maine, bill for admission into Union: joined to Missouri bill, 171
Manny, John H., McCormick reaper litigation, 125
Marbury against Madison, 256
Maritime war problems: blockade of ports, 404
Marryat, Frederick, quoted, 194
Marshall, Humphrey, 347
Marshall, John, 81, 252, 256, 289, 325, 446; quoted, 322, 324; on suspension of writ of habeas corpus, quoted, 410; holds a corporation not a citizen, 487
Martin, Luther, 331
Martin, Martha, 92
Martineau, Harriet, cited, 161
Marx, Karl, 306
Maryland, ratification of Constitution, 331; sympathy with South: Lincoln proceeds cautiously with, 407; Cameron's despotism in, 422
Mason, James M., seized on the *Trent*, 407
Masonry, opposition to, 215
Massachusetts, abolition of slavery, 158; aided by colonies when charter taken from, 320; ratification of Constitution, 329; nullification, 343
Match-lighters, 216
Matheny, James Harvey, 305; as best man at Lincoln's wedding, 72
Matson, Robert, case of, 90, 297
Matteson, Joel Aldrich, 226, 227
Maximilian, 463, 467
Maynard, Horace, 374
McClellan, George B., 412, 426, 439; call for more troops, 432; nominated for president, 448
McClernand, John A., 40, 182
McCormick reaper litigation, 125
McDougall, William, quoted, 144
McDowell, Irvin, 412, 421
McKinley, William, 4, 391, 481, 488
McKinley tariff bill, 446
McLean, John, 123, 126, 127, 248; Dred Scott case, 256, 258
McNamar, John, 32; engagement to Ann Rutledge, 46, 47
Meade, George G., 426
Medill, Joseph, 240, 356, 374, 441; works for nomination of Lincoln, 356, 358; *Reminiscences,* 357; interview with Lincoln about call for troops, 431
Melancholia, causes of, 144
Merryman, Elias H., 78
Merryman, John, arrest of, 408
Methodist Episcopal Church, division of, 272
Metzger, James Preston, murder of, 129, 134
Mexican War, 84, 450, 491; opposition to, 85, 179; Lincoln's position on, 85, 92, 97; causes of, 92; a cause of the Civil War, 179
Mexico, history, 92; question of slavery in territory acquired from, 176; appropriation bill for settlement with, 178
Military power, legal use of, Douglas on, 402; Webster on, 405
Military prisoners, in Maryland, 422; Vallandigham of Ohio, 423; exchange of, 424, 470; treatment, 424; sufferings: statistics, 425. See also Habeas Corpus, suspension of writ of
Military prisons, 425
Militia. *See* Army
Mill, John Stuart, cited, 40
Milton, John, 147
Missouri, slavery, 169; bill for admission into Union: joined to Maine bill: amendments, 171; struggle for representation, 173; admitted to Union, 174; action on Compromise of 1850, 200; tries to remain neutral, 398
Missouri Compromise of 1820, 96, 170; slavery restricted south of 36° 30': Jefferson's disapproval, 172; a cause of the war, 173; vote testing adherence to, 177; principle of, repudiated: attempts to extend line to Pacific, 178, 180; abandoned by the North, 181; replaced by Compromise of 1850, 190; in Kansas-Nebraska struggle, 206, 207
The Compromise of 1850, proposed by Clay, 181; struggle over, 182-189; replaces Compromise of 1820, 190; confirmed in Whig and Democratic platforms, 191; Lincoln's attitude toward, 193, 195, 249; effect upon Fugitive Slave Law: condemned by abolitionists, 195; disapproved by Southern extremists,

INDEX

197; Douglas's position on, 197, 204; action of Missouri legislature, 200; in Kansas-Nebraska struggle, 204, 206, 207; repeal of, 211; repeal excoriated by Republican platform, 239; by Lincoln, 241; constitutionality tested by Dred Scott case, 257, 258

Mitch Miller, 130

Monopoly and privilege in America, 490; abetted by churches, 492, 496; Lincoln an aid to, 3, 497

Monroe, James, 25, 323, 340, 488

Monroe Doctrine, plan for pacification by a common defense of, 463, 468, 469

Montesquieu, C. de S. de, on confederated republics, 343; quoted, 344

Morgan, Edwin D., 432

Morgan, William, 215

Morrill tariff bill, 446

Morris, Martin, Lincoln's letter to, 48, 72; quoted, 48, 73

Morton, Oliver P., 396, 455

Motley, John Lothrop, 326; quoted, 323

National banks, opposed by Democrats, 446; Chase's plan: acts creating, 447. *See also* Bank of the United States

National Intelligencer. See Intelligencer

National Republicans, 215

Native Americans, 101

Navy, increased by 18,000 seamen, 399; legal use of, 402

Nebraska, demand for organization, 200, 201; bills, 202; Douglas's report on bill, 203; quoted, 204; amendments, 206; slavery, 346. *See also* Kansas-Nebraska Act

Negroes, Lincoln's views on civil rights of, 35, 89, 148, 221, 475; denied civil rights in Illinois, 88, 89, 148, 267, 485; Illinois statute providing for sale of, 90; population, 1808, 158; treatment of, in North, 165; social equality, 306; views of Douglas, 266, 309; of Lincoln, 267, 307, 309; Lincoln advises colonization in Latin America: promises aid, 437; given suffrage: results, 485. *See also* Slavery

Nelson, Samuel, Dred Scott case, 257

New England Emigrant Aid Company, 229

New Hampshire, ratification of Constitution, 329

New Jersey, ratification of Constitution, 330

New Mexico, lost to the South, 176; territory, 179, 182, 184, 187, 189, 190

New Orleans, capture of: despotism of Butler, 439

New Salem Museum, letters in, 120

New York, ratification of Constitution, 330

New York Express, 231

New York Herald, 347, 351

New York Times, 209, 347, 348

New York Tribune, 111, 231, 242, 249, 256, 261, 306, 352, 363

Newhall Singers, 46

Nicolay, John G., cited, 150; becomes Lincoln's secretary, 370; sent to ask military protection for Lincoln, 375

Nicolay, John G., and Hay, John, 75, 494; cited, 377; Lincoln's works prepared by: *Life of Lincoln,* 359; severe on course of Virginia, 387

Norris, James H., convicted of murder, 129, 134

North Carolina, pro-slavery clause in deed of Western lands, 168; ratification of Constitution, 331; secession of, 398

Northwest Territory, 157, 258, 355; Ordinance of 1787, 157, 166, 167, 259, 343, 346, 355; restriction of slavery, 157, 165, 166, 168; slaves in, 166; government, 167; constitutional provisions for regulation and division of, 169

Nullification, South Carolina, 305, 337; Massachusetts, 343

Offut, Denton, employs Lincoln, 28, 29

Oglesby, Richard, 360

"Oh, Why Should the Spirit of Mortal Be Proud?", 18

Old Northwest. *See* Northwest Territory

Ordinance of 1787, Northwest Territory, 157, 166, 167, 259, 343, 346, 355; adopted: provisions, 167

Oregon, 94; slavery, 96, 180; Lincoln refuses governorship of, 117; mileage: territorial government bill, 176, 179; amendments, 177, 180; admission of, 292, 293; territorial question, 346

INDEX

Ottawa, Illinois, during Lincoln-Douglas debate, 280
Owens, Mary, 49; Lincoln's romance with, 49; married to Jesse Vineyard, 50; letters of Lincoln to, excerpts, 50-52; letters to Herndon, excerpts, 57

Pacific railroad, 198, 202, 365
Pacific Steamship Company, 199
Page, Walter H., 489
Paine, John, 243
Palmer, John McA., 238; aids Lincoln's candidacy for president, 358, 366; nominates Lincoln for president, 360
Palmerston, Lord, on Butler's order, 28, 439
Paris Agreement of 1856, 406
Parker, Charles E., testimony in Armstrong trial, 134
Parker, Theodore, 195, 288, 471, 481
Parrish, John, quoted, 270
Parties, political, 25, 101, 200, 207, 208, 215, 328. *See also parties by name*
Patterson, 421
Paxson, F. L., 203
Peace Congress called by Virginia, 386
Pelham, bravery at Kellysville, 442
Pence, L. S., 7
Pennsylvania, ratification of Constitution, 330
People's Party, 246. *See also* Republican Party
Pericles, oration compared with Gettysburg Address, 478; quoted, 478, 479, 480
"Person," use of, in Constitution, 160
Péttit, John, slur on Declaration, 449
Philippine Islands, conquest, 3, 4, 260, 391, 449, 450, 481, 489
Phillips, Wendell, 42, 229, 243, 248, 491; quoted on Fugitive Slave Law, 195; a disunionist, 311; opposes reëlection of Lincoln, 448
Pierce, Franklin, 193, 207, 290; challenged with respect to his loyalty, 411
Pigeon Creek Baptist Church, 10
Pinckney, Charles Cotesworth, 169
Pioneers, callousness, 13; life of, 15
Piracy as penalty of violating blockade, 404, 405
Pitcher, John, 23
Plymouth Church, 347
Political parties, 25, 101, 200, 207, 208, 215, 328. *See also parties by name*
Politicians, corruption of, 489
Politics during Lincoln's youth, 24
Polk, James K., 94, 398; most notable act: elected president, 95; attacked by Lincoln for invasion of Mexico, 97
Pollard's *The Lost Cause,* 3
Population as basis for taxation, 222, 293
Ports, closing of, 474. *See also* Blockade of ports
Portugal, slave trade, 158
Posey, Francis, 9
Post Office department used to defeat Douglas, 278
Prentice, G. D., 371
Presidential campaigns, 1824, 25; 1836, 36; 1844, 94; 1848, 101; 1856, 136, 248; 1860, 371; 1864, 448
President, right of, to invade, Lincoln quoted on, 97; use of military power by, 402, 405; on power of, to suspend writ of habeas corpus, 409
Presidents, deterioration in quality of: enumerated, 488
Price, Edward L., 105
Prisoners. *See* Military prisoners
Privateers made pirates, 404
Prohibition, 492
Property interests. *See* Economic factors
Puritanism. *See* Hebraic-Puritan spirit
Purple, N. H., 123

Railroad to the Pacific, 198, 202, 365
Railroads, Illinois, 198; Iowa, 202
Randolph, Edmund, 323
Randolph, John, 27
Reconstruction period. *See* Southern States
Representation and direct taxation, Constitutional provisions for, 159, 221
Republican Party, ballots in 1856 convention, 136; organization of, 214; Lincoln holds aloof from, 216, 219; Springfield convention, 217; resolutions, 218; organized on national basis: attitude of Whigs toward, 232; Bloomington state convention, 1856, 237; Lincoln joins party, 238; platform, 239; National convention, 246; platform, 247; campaign, 249; Codding platform, Springfield convention, 268; nominates Lincoln for Senate: platform

INDEX

of 1858, 269; Codding platform adopted in northern Illinois, 279; Rockford resolutions, 285; desire for offices: a sectional party, 303; Illinois state convention, 1860: nominates Lincoln, 360; Chicago convention, 362; platform, 365; balloting, 366, 367; nominates Lincoln, 367; and Hannibal Hamlin, 368; votes polled in 1860 election, 371; results of 1862 election, 440; opposition to second term for Lincoln within, 448; responsible for reconstruction evils, 484, 485

Republics, confederated, 343

Revolution, Lincoln's views on, 319

Rhode Island, ratification of Constitution, 331

Rhodes, James F., 197; cited, 457

Rice, peace plan, 387

Richards, John T., tabulation of Lincoln's law cases, 122

Richardson, William A., bill for organization of Nebraska, 202

Richmond, Lincoln takes possession of, 473

Rickard, Sarah, Lincoln's proposal of marriage to, 67

Riley, General, calls constitutional convention in California, 181

Robespierre, 427; similarity to Lincoln and his cabinet, 428

Robinson, Lucius, calls convention to oppose Lincoln, 448

Rock Island Bridge Company case, 128

Roosevelt, Theodore, 95, 488

Ross, Lewis W., 108

Rutherford, Hiram, Matson case against, 90

Rutledge family, 46, 47

Rutledge, Ann, engagement to John McNamar, 32, 46, 47; Lincoln's romance with, 34, 45, 70, 76; ancestry, 46; grave, 49

Rutledge, David, 49

Rutledge, James, 46, 169

St. Gaudens, Augustus, Sherman statue, 454

St. Louis, as terminal for Pacific railroad, 200, 201

Sanford, John F. A., 253, 254

Sangamon Journal, 33, 35, 85; a useful adjunct to Lincoln's career, 68; publishes satire against James Shields, 68, 77; keeps Lincoln's name before the people, 82, 84

Santa-Anna, 93

Saturday Review of London, 422

Savannah, capture of, 457

Savannah, imprisonment of crew, 424

Schneider, George, 236, 360

Schurz, Carl, 363, 444

Scott, Dred, 251, 253, 262, 292, 297. *See also* Dred Scott decision

Scott, Winfield, 192, 193, 421; ordered to hold military places, 390; in favor of evacuating Fort Pickens, 394; begins reporting to Lincoln: calls for more troops, 396; superseded by McClellan, 426

Scripps, J. L., 10

Secession of Southern states, 318, 373, 398, 412; right of, 319, 334, 434; advocated by Northern states, 343

Secret societies in the South, 485

Seward, William Henry, 27, 136, 160, 193, 195, 208, 211, 249, 351, 387, 389, 399; quoted, 81, 411; anti-slavery speech in Boston, 106; political alliances, 215; charges conspiracy in Dred Scott case, 261; "irrepressible conflict" doctrine, 270; enmity of Taney, 288; as candidate for president, 359, 360, 362, 366, 368; result of ballot for, 367; compared with Lincoln, 368; drafts conclusion of First Inaugural, 384; appointed to cabinet, 385; complains of lack of policy: his foreign policy, 390; on repossessing forts, 391, 392, 394; refuses to recognize Confederate States, 392; reassures Confederate Commissioners, 394, 395; charged with tricking them, 394; negotiations over Paris Agreement of 1856, 406, 407; *Trent* affair, 407; at Hampton Roads conference, 464-470

Shaw, J. Henry, 135

Shays' Rebellion, 160, 397

Shelley, Percy Bysshe, 24, 140

Sherman, John, Committee on Kansas, 230

Sherman, William Tecumseh, 397, 454, 474; march to the sea, 455; denies burning Columbia, 457

Shields, James, 79, 193; literary attacks on, 68, 71, 77; encounter with Lincoln, 68, 77; public service, 80;

INDEX

sent to Senate, 107; candidate for Senate, 218, 226, 227; quoted, 226

Short, James, 48, 72

Simms, William Gilmore, on Sherman's depredations, quoted, 458

Sixth Massachusetts Regiment, 229

Slidell, John, seized on the *Trent*, 407

Slavery, Lincoln's views on, 2, 152, 231, 235, 241, 284, 287, 435; Lincoln's early contacts with, 24, 68, 147; in the American colonies, 38, 158; Lincoln's position on, in Illinois legislature, 38, 40, 86; Stone-Lincoln resolutions, 42, 96; activities of abolitionists, 40; abolished in Mexico, 93; Wilmot Proviso to exclude slavery from territory acquired from Mexico, 96; Lincoln's attitude at time of Mexican War, 97; in the District of Columbia, 100, 189, 284; Lincoln's inability to suggest remedy for, 147, 220, 303; position of the churches on, 152, 261, 272; Jefferson's stand against, 157; restriction of, in Northwest Territory, 157, 165; survey of, 157; in the United States, 159; Constitutional provision for suppression of insurrections, 160; protected by the Constitution, 160, 161; conditions in the South: opinions of travelers and writers, 161-166; in the territories, 166, 168-190, 197, 202, 213, 220, 240, 243, 257, 259, 294, 304, 346; Missouri Compromise of 1820, 170, 172; in the public domain acquired from Mexico, 176; Calhoun's resolutions, text, 177; not mentioned in Nebraska bill, 202; Republican party formed to resist extension of, 214; resolutions of Springfield convention, 218; struggle over, in Kansas, 228; doctrine of local control of, 266; as a moral issue, 270, 299; and the Bible, 271, 272, 310; struggle over Lecompton Constitution of Kansas, 277, 293; "house divided against itself doctrine," 301, 302; Constitutional clause forbidding restraint upon negro importation, 355; as a cause of war, 435; Lincoln's reasons for emancipation of, 435-438; abolition of, in England, 436; plan for compensated emancipation and gradual abolition, 436, 453, 470; Thirteenth Amendment, 482; when abolished, 483; Fourteenth Amendment, 484, 486. *See also* Dred Scott decision: Negroes: Slaves

Fugitive Slave Law, 241, 261, 297, 298; Lincoln's stand on, 147, 242, 284, 287, 289; Constitutional basis of, 160; Webster's stand on, 185; action of Chicago, 191; under the Compromise of 1850, 195, 213; flouting of, 239

Slaves, Virginia's plan for emancipation of, 40; Indian, 157, 166; as factor in provision for taxation and representation, 222; money value, 353; effect of Emancipation Proclamation upon, 483, 485

"Sly Jerry." *See* Stuart, John T.

Smith, Caleb B., promised place in cabinet, 367; appointed, 385; on provisioning Fort Sumter, 393, 394

Smith, Lydia, 364

Smith, Truman, 466

Soldier vote, 441, 449

Soulé, Pierre, amendment to Clay Compromise Bill, 188

South Carolina, slavery, 158; nullification, 305, 337; secedes from Union, 318, 373; ratification of Constitution, 331; legislature remains in session during 1860 campaign, 371; Lincoln's efforts to provoke, 391

Southern states, secession of, 318, 373, 398, 412; delegates at Republican convention, 1860, 365; ordinances of secession, 373; no insurrection in or civil war waged by, 397; secession, Lincoln quoted on, 416; statesmen see danger in consolidation of power, 443; conservatism: superior culture and ancestry of people, 444; Lincoln's last utterance on reconstruction, 475; Lincoln's lack of program for reconstruction of: delay in restoration of, 482; sectionalism continued by North, 483; representatives refused recognition in Congress: reconstruction period: military rule: plunder of, 484. *See also* Confederate States of America

Spain, slavery under, 157

INDEX

Spanish Treaty of 1819, 171
Sparrow, Henry, 11, 12
Speed, Joshua F., 61; takes Lincoln to call on Mary Todd, 63; his contemplated marriage: Lincoln as confidential friend, 63; quoted, 64, 69; moves to Kentucky, 67; correspondence with Lincoln, excerpts, 67, 69-72, 74, 147, 231; Lincoln's visit, 68
Speed, Mary, Lincoln's letter to, excerpt, 69
Springfield, Illinois, location of capital at, 37; cost of moving capital, 38; Lincoln aids bank, 37, 38; in Lincoln's day, 61, 72, 108, 109
Staats Anzeiger, bought by Linocln to support Republican Party, 359
Staats Zeitung, supports Seward, 359
Stanton, Benjamin, on the Dred Scott case, 257
Stanton, Edwin McMasters, in McCormick reaper litigation, 126, 127; quoted: logic fascinates Lincoln, 127; report on prisoners of war, 425; raises troops through aid of governors, 432; called Lincoln a fool, 434
State Register, 285, 287
States, provisions for admission to Union, 169, 188; question of sovereignty of, under the Constitution, 294, 323, 333, 370, 417, 419; creation of: sovereignty acknowledged, 321, 322; whether Constitution proceeded from, 323; ratification of Constitution by, 326, 328, 329; sovereignty of, as seen by Southern statesmen, 443. *See also* Southern States: Union
Stephens, Alexander H., 92, 162, 182, 374; *Constitutional View of the War,* 2; cited, 192; opinion of Lincoln, 316; inaugurated as vice president of the Confederacy, 386; told object of Blair mission, 462; at Hampton Roads conference: impression of Grant, 464-470; appearance: mentality, 465; proposes exchange of prisoners, 470
Stevens, Thaddeus, 419; at Chicago convention, 361, 366; appearance, 363; career, 364; reconstruction ideas, 482; refuses to recognize Southern states, 484

Stone, Daniel, 40, 41; Stone-Lincoln resolutions on slavery, 42, 96
Story, Joseph, *Commentaries on the Constitution,* 113, 317, 326, 416; quoted, 410
Stowe, Harriet Beecher, *Uncle Tom's Cabin,* 162, 166
Stuart, John T., 43, 149, 237; Lincoln's confession of unhappiness, quoted, 65; defeats Douglas for Congress, 81; Lincoln severs relationship with, 83
Stuart, Moses, *Conscience and the Constitution,* 356
Stuart-Wortley, Lady Emmeline, cited, 161
Sub-treasury question debated by Lincoln and Douglas, 81
Suffrage, enlargement of, advocated by Lincoln, 35
Sumner, Charles, 204, 211, 260, 364, 388, 403, 419; becomes Free Soiler: denounces war, 103; quoted, 154; memorial against slavery: amendment to Nebraska bill, 206; psychology of, 206, 207; attack upon Douglas, 208, 209; reply of Douglas, quoted, 210; assaulted by Brooks, 228, 241
Supreme Court, power to decide upon constitutionality of laws, 81; bias of judges, 121, 244; Lincoln on rulings of, 251, 252; Dred Scott decision, 252, 253, 255-260, 261, 263, 289, 348, 350; power to annul a law of Congress, 256; on sovereignty of states, quoted, 335; question of supremacy of, 339, 340; denounced by Republican platform, 365; forbidden from holding laws unconstitutional, 486; on citizenship of corporations, 487. *See also* Judiciary
Supreme Court of Pennsylvania holds Conscription act unconstitutional, 433
Swett, Leonard, 122; quoted, 150

Taft, William Howard, 489
Taney, Roger Brooke, 123, 258, 339; Dred Scott decision, 161; quoted, 169; opinion of court, 258, excerpt, 259; abuse of, 261; cited, 266, 267; feeling against Seward, 288; charged with conspiracy, 289, 290; decision

INDEX

on suspension of writ of habeas corpus, 383, 408, 410, 411; administers oath to Lincoln, 385

Tariff, protective, 25, 99, 185, 245, 248, 419; Lincoln's stand on, 31, 82, 100, 360, 370, 380; disturbance of 1832, 305; imports, early attempts to secure, 323; outlawed by Confederate Constitution, 386; history of, 445; regains ground during war: influence of, 446

Taxation and representation, Constitutional provisions for, 159, 221

Taylor, Dick, 43

Taylor, John W., amendment to Missouri Bill, 171

Taylor, Zachary, 113, 181; Lincoln on principles of, 102, 103, 105

Tennessee, provision for slavery in, 168; secession of, 398

Territorial Register, 228

Territories, slavery in, 166, 168-190, 197, 202, 213, 220, 240, 243, 257, 259, 294, 304, 346; slavery restricted north of 36° 30': public domain given to North and South, 172; economic reasons for slavery struggle, 175; Douglas's services in organization of, 198, 201. *See also* Dred Scott decision: Northwest Territory

Texas, history, 92; attempt to join United States, 94; annexation, 95; struggle to exclude slavery from: Lincoln quoted on the question of, 96; admitted as a slave state, 176

Thayer, Eli, organizes emigrant aid societies, 229

Thirteenth Amendment, 482

Thomas, Jesse B., mimicked by Lincoln, 138; amendment to Missouri Bill, 171, 172

Thompson, Lorenzo D., 32

Tocqueville, C. A. H. C. de, *Democratie en Amerique,* excerpt, 336

Todd, Mary, 62, 66; reasons for Lincoln's marriage to: arrival in Springfield: age, 61; attentions of Douglas, 63, 64; courtship of Lincoln, 63; literary attacks on James Shields, 68, 71, 77; renewal of Lincoln's courtship, 68; wedding, 72. *See also* Lincoln, Mary (Todd)

Todd, Robert S., 62

Toombs, Robert, 179, 188, 189, 387; speech in Boston, quoted, 163; speeches on slavery, quoted, 182, 187

Townsend, William Henry, *Litigant,* 124

Trent affair, 407

Tribune. *See New York Tribune*

Trumbull, Lyman, 441; against Douglas, 225; candidate for Senate, 226, 227; in Illinois campaign, 278, 280, 281, 286, 288, 305; against admission of Oregon, 292

Turner, Thomas J., 285

Uncle Tom's Cabin, 162, 166

Union, disunionists, 311; Lincoln's sentiment for, 316; perpetuity of, 318, 322; formation of, 318, 320; doctrine of the Union being older than the Constitution, 318, 326; right of secession from, 319, 334; sovereignty of states before adoption of Constitution, 321, 322; theories respecting origin of, 323; question of state sovereignty, under the Constitution, 323, 333; supremacy under the Constitution, 333; Virginia's efforts to avoid disruption of, 386. *See also* States

Union Leagues, 485

Union National Convention nominates Lincoln and Johnson, 448

United States. *See* States: Union

United States Bank. *See* Bank of the United States

United States Circuit Court of Appeals formed, 198

Upham, William, moves insertion of Wilmot Proviso in Appropriation bill, 178

Utah, territory, 179, 182, 187, 189, 190

Vallandigham, Clement L., arrest and banishment, 423

Van Buren, Martin, 36, 101, 102, 103

Vineyard, Jesse, 50

Vineyard, Mrs. Jesse, 57. *See also* Owens, Mary

Virginia, plan for emancipation of negroes, 40; interest in Northwest Territory, 167; calls convention to aid Massachusetts, 320; calls first congress, 320; efforts to secure commercial regulations for the states, 323; ratification of Constitution, 331; efforts to avoid disruption of the Union, 386, 387;

INDEX

calls Peace Congress, 386; accused of conspiracy, 387; Committee interviews Lincoln, 388; secedes from Union, 398; ordinance of secession ratified, 412; movement of troops against, 412, 420
Virginia Resolutions, 338, 340; excerpt, 338
Von Holst, Hermann Eduard. *See* Holst
Voters, colonization of, 441

Wallace, Edward, 361
Wallace, W. S., 361
Ward, Artemus, 433
Ward, James, removed from office, 278
Washburne, E. B., 226, 227, 288
Washburne, Governor, 396
Washington, arrival of troops in, 396
Washington, George, 169, 352; quoted, 493
Washington Globe, 337
Watson, P. H., retains Lincoln in McCormick reaper case, 125
Wealth as a result of the war, 445
Webster, Daniel, 36, 101, 113, 170, 181, 234, 243, 316, 317, 323, 325, 326, 341; reply to Hayne, 28; on Compromise of 1850, 184; "Ichabod," 184, 185; on Soulé amendment, 189; approves Whig platform: loses nomination, 192; quoted, 334, 335, 342; quoted, 272; debate with Calhoun, 341, 342; excerpts, 342; on blockade of Charleston and use of the military power, quoted, 405
Webster, Fletcher, 232
Welles, Gideon, appointed to cabinet: diary, 385; on provisioning Fort Sumter, 393, 394
West Indies, slavery, 157
Whig Party, 27, 175, 207; Lincoln's candidacy for Illinois Legislature, 30; Lincoln as leader in Illinois, 43, 216; nominates Lincoln for Congress, 84; in 1844, 94; conventions of 1848, 101, 105; Lincoln's devotion to, 101, 107; Springfield members file protest against Lincoln, 117; wins election of 1848, 181; platform of 1852 confirms Compromise of 1850, 191, 213; resolution, text, 192; Lincoln's attitude: committeeman for Illinois, 193; fuses with Republican party, 214; attitude of Whigs toward Republican party, 232; death of, 238; convention, 1856: platform, 246; defeat, 251
White, Hugh L., 36
Whiteside, John Davis, Lincoln-Shields affair, 78
Whitman, Walt, "Democratic Vistas of 1870," 443; quoted, 490; one of greatest Americans, 494
Whitney, Asa, 198
Whitney, Henry Clay, 46, 121, 227; quoted, 88, 138; Lincoln's Lost Speech, 240
Whittier, John Greenleaf, 184, 185, 235, 474, 479, 495
Wigwam, Chicago, 364
Wilkes, Captain, seizes Mason and Slidell, 407
Wilmot, David, 92, 178; presents proviso, 96; at Republican convention, 248; at Chicago convention, 363, 364
Wilmot Proviso, 96, 176, 178, 184, 187, 189, 204, 231; Lincoln's support of, 96, 101, 178, 231
Wilson, James, 169, 223
Wilson, Woodrow, 489, 494
Winthrop, Robert C., 92, 104, 105
Wirt, William, nominated for president, 215
Wirz, Henry, hanged, 425
Woman suffrage, 35
Women, first participation in political campaign, 250
Wyandot Indians, 201

Yates, Richard, 376
"Young Hickory." *See* Polk, James K.